INCENTIVES FOR GLOBAL PUBLIC HEALTH

This portrait of the global debate over patent law and access to essential medicines focuses on public health concerns about HIV/AIDS, malaria, tuberculosis, the SARS virus, influenza and diseases of poverty. The essays explore the diplomatic negotiations and disputes in key international forums, such as the World Trade Organization, the World Health Organization and the World Intellectual Property Organization.

Drawing upon international trade law, innovation policy, intellectual property law, health law, human rights and philosophy, the authors seek to canvass policy solutions that encourage and reward worthwhile pharmaceutical innovation while ensuring affordable access to advanced medicines. A number of creative policy options are critically assessed, including the development of a Health Impact Fund, prizes for medical innovation, the use of patent pools, Open Source drug development and forms of 'creative capitalism'.

THOMAS POGGE is Leitner Professor of Philosophy and International Affairs at Yale University, Professorial Fellow at the ANU Centre for Applied Philosophy and Public Ethics (CAPPE), Research Director at the Oslo University Centre for the Study of Mind in Nature (CSMN) and Adjunct Professor at the University of Central Lancashire.

MATTHEW RIMMER is a senior lecturer and Associate Director of Research at the ANU College of Law, and Associate Director of the Australian Centre for Intellectual Property in Agriculture.

KIM RUBENSTEIN is Professor and Director of the Centre for International and Public Law (CIPL) at the ANU College of Law, Australian National University.

CONNECTING INTERNATIONAL LAW WITH PUBLIC LAW

This series of books flows from workshops bringing public and international lawyers and public and international policy makers together for interdisciplinary discussion on selected topics and themes. It aims to broaden both public and international laws' understanding of how these two areas intersect. Until now, international and public law have mainly overlapped in discussions on how international law is implemented domestically. This series is unique in consciously bringing together public and international lawyers to consider and engage in each other's scholarship.

Series Editors

Professor Kim Rubenstein, Australian National University
Professor Thomas Pogge, Yale University

Books in the series

Incentives for Global Public Health: Patent Law and Access to Essential Medicines
Edited by Thomas Pogge, Matthew Rimmer and Kim Rubenstein

Sanctions, Accountability and Governance in a Globalised World
Edited by Jeremy Farrall and Kim Rubenstein

INCENTIVES FOR GLOBAL PUBLIC HEALTH

Patent Law and Access to Essential Medicines

Edited by

THOMAS POGGE,

MATTHEW RIMMER

and

KIM RUBENSTEIN

CAMBRIDGE
UNIVERSITY PRESS

CAMBRIDGE UNIVERSITY PRESS
Cambridge, New York, Melbourne, Madrid, Cape Town, Singapore,
São Paulo, Delhi, Dubai, Tokyo

Cambridge University Press
The Edinburgh Building, Cambridge CB2 8RU, UK

Published in the United States of America by Cambridge University Press, New York

www.cambridge.org
Information on this title: www.cambridge.org/9780521116565

First published 2010

Printed in the United Kingdom at the University Press, Cambridge

A catalogue record for this publication is available from the British Library

Library of Congress Cataloguing in Publication data
Incentives for global public health : patent law and access to essential medicines / edited by
Thomas Pogge, Matthew Rimmer, and Kim Rubenstein.
p. cm. – (Connecting international law with public law)
Includes bibliographical references.
ISBN 978-0-521-11656-5 (hardback)
1. Pharmaceutical policy. 2. Patent laws and legislation 3. Drugs – Patents. 4. Patents
(International law) I. Pogge, Thomas Winfried Menko. II. Rimmer,
Matthew. III. Rubenstein, Kim. IV. Title. V. Series:
Connecting international law with public law.
[DNLM: 1. Legislation, Drug – organization & administration. 2. Drugs, Essential – supply
& distribution. 3. Health Services Accessibility – legislation & jurisprudence. 4. Human
Rights. 5. International Cooperation. 6. Patents as Topic – legislation & jurisprudence.
QV 33.1 I36 2010]
RA401.A1I43 2010
362.17′82–dc22
2010010211

ISBN 978-0-521-11656-5 Hardback

CONTENTS

CONTRIBUTORS

Editors

Having received his PhD in philosophy from Harvard University, PROFESSOR THOMAS POGGE is Leitner Professor of Philosophy and International Affairs at Yale University, Professorial Fellow at the ANU Centre for Applied Philosophy and Public Ethics (CAPPE), Research Director at the Oslo University Centre for the Study of Mind in Nature (CSMN) and Adjunct Professor at the University of Central Lancashire. He is Editor for Social and Political Philosophy for the *Stanford Encyclopedia of Philosophy* and a member of the Norwegian Academy of Science. With support from the Australian Research Council, the BUPA Foundation and the European Commission, he currently heads a team effort towards developing a complement to the pharmaceutical patent regime that would improve access to advanced medicines for the poor worldwide. His recent publications include *World Poverty and Human Rights*, 2nd edn. 2008; *Global Justice* and *Global Ethics*, both 2008; and *John Rawls: His Life and Theory of Justice* and *Freedom from Poverty as a Human Right*, both 2007.

DR MATTHEW RIMMER is a senior lecturer and Associate Director of Research at the ANU College of Law, and Associate Director of the Australian Centre for Intellectual Property in Agriculture. He holds a BA (Hons) and a University Medal in literature, and an LLB (Hons) from the Australian National University. Dr Rimmer received a PhD in law from the University of New South Wales for his dissertation on *The Pirate Bazaar: The Social Life of Copyright Law*. He is a member of the ANU Climate Change Institute and a director of the Australian Digital Allliance. Dr Rimmer is the author of *Digital Copyright and the Consumer Revolution: Hands off my iPod* (2007) and *Intellectual Property and Biotechnology: Biological Inventions* (2008). He edited the collection *Patent Law and Biological Inventions* (2006). Dr Rimmer was a chief investigator in an ARC Discovery Project, 'Gene Patents in Australia: Options for Reform' (2003–5), and an ARC Linkage Grant, 'The Protection of Botanical Inventions' (2003). He has published widely on copyright law and information technology, patent law and biotechnology, access to medicines, clean technologies and traditional knowledge.

PROFESSOR KIM RUBENSTEIN is Professor and Director of the Centre for International and Public Law (CIPL) at the ANU College of Law, Australian National University. A graduate of the University of Melbourne and Harvard University, Professor Rubenstein's current research projects are at the cutting edge of the intersection between public and international law. Her public law work spans constitutional and administrative law, and also includes her expertise in citizenship law. Her international law work focuses on the status of nationality. Her book, *Australian Citizenship Law in Context* (2002) represents the foundation of her continued scholarly work, looking at the disjuncture between the exclusive legal notion and the more inclusive normative understanding of citizenship.

Other Contributors

JONATHAN BURTON-MACLEOD holds a BSc from Harvard University, a law degree from Queen's University, Canada, and a Masters in Law from Harvard Law School. Burton-MacLeod's initial focus was biochemistry and he worked at the Centers for Disease Control, Atlanta. In law school, his focus remained on international health, with study conducted at the University of Cape Town Faculty of Law. His graduate law degree focused on theories of law and society in the globalization of law, viewed through the lens of public health. Since finishing, much of Burton-MacLeod's research has focused on American and comparative Constitutional law. He was a lecturer at the ANU College of Law. Burton-MacLeod is currently an Assistant Professor and Assistant Dean (Research) at Jindal Global Law School and Assistant Director at the Centre for Global Governance and Policy.

RAJSHREE CHANDRA is a Senior Lecturer at Janki Devi Memorial College, Delhi University with fifteen years' teaching experience in the

Department of Political Science. She has completed a Masters and MPhil from the Centre for Political Studies, Jawaharlal Nehru University (JNU) (New Delhi), and her Doctorate is from the Centre for the Study of Law and Governance (JNU). Her doctoral dissertation is an inquiry into the moral premises of intellectual property rights, as encompassed by the TRIPS regime. Her research interests concern the impact of patent rights on healthcare.

PROFESSOR ROCHELLE C. DREYFUSS is the Pauline Newman Professor of Law at New York University School of Law. She holds BA (Wellesley College) and MS (University of California) degrees in Chemistry and a law degree (Columbia Law School), and she clerked for Chief Judge Wilfred Feinberg of the US Court of Appeals for the Second Circuit and Chief Justice Warren E. Burger of the US Supreme Court. She is a member of the National Academy of Sciences (NAS) Committee on Science, Technology and the Law and the National Institute of Health's Advisory Committee on Genetics, Health and Society, as well as the American Law Institute, where she was Co-reporter for its Project on Intellectual Property: Principles Governing Jurisdiction, Choice of Law, and Judgments in Transnational Disputes. She is a past consultant to the Federal Courts Study Committee, the Presidential Commission on Catastrophic Nuclear Accidents and the Federal Trade Commission. She was also a member of NAS Committees on Intellectual Property in Genomic and Protein Research and Innovation and Intellectual Property Rights in the Knowledge-Based Economy.

ASSOCIATE PROFESSOR THOMAS FAUNCE (BA/LLB (Hons), BMed, PhD) has a joint position in the ANU College of Law and Medical School at ANU. He has directed two three-year ARC research projects on (1) the impact of international trade agreements on Australian medicines policy and (2) regulation of nanomedicine in Australia. He has been a consultant for UNESCO on its global ethics and health law database and published widely in this field. His latest book is *Who Owns our Health? Medical Professionalism, Law and Leadership beyond the Age of the Market State* (2007).

PROFESSOR WILLIAM FISHER received his undergraduate degree (in American Studies) from Amherst College and his graduate degrees (JD and PhD in the History of American Civilization) from Harvard

University. Between 1982 and 1984, he served as a law clerk to Judge Harry T. Edwards of the US Court of Appeals for the DC Circuit and then to Justice Thurgood Marshall of the US Supreme Court. Since 1984, he has taught at Harvard Law School, where he is currently the Hale and Dorr Professor of Intellectual Property Law and the Director of the Berkman Center for Internet and Society. His academic honours include a Danforth postbaccalaureate fellowship (1978–82) and a postdoctoral fellowship at the Center for Advanced Study in the Behavioral Sciences in Stanford, California (1992–3).

ASSOCIATE PROFESSOR BARBARA ANN HOCKING is an academic at QUT Faculty of Law. She has been a visitor at the Faculty of Law at the University of Tasmania for two years. She is the editor of *Towards a Nexus of Law and Biology: New Ethical Challenges* (2009) and was recently awarded an Australian Linkage International Fellowship (ARCIF) to work on intersections between avian influenza planning and human rights. She is currently preparing a second edition of her book *Liability for Negligent Words* (1999) with Scott Guy.

DR CHARLES LAWSON is a senior research fellow with ACIPA and an associate professor at the Griffith Law School at Griffith University. Dr Lawson's research interests include some aspects of intellectual property, competition, trade, access, taxation, public and administrative law and risk assessment and management.

DR KATHLEEN LIDDELL (DPhil (Oxon), LLB (Hons), BSc (Melb), MBioethics (Monash)) is the Herchel Smith Lecturer in Intellectual Property Law at Cambridge University and a fellow of Downing College. Her research focuses on the legal and ethical frameworks surrounding medical research, biotechnology and bioinformation. Her research benefits from funding provided by the Wellcome Trust, the Cambridge Genetics Knowledge Park and the Sasakawa Peace Foundation. It forms part of a programme of investigations organized by the Centre for Intellectual Property and Information Law and the Cambridge Centre for Medical Genetics and Policy.

DR ANDREW MITCHELL is an Associate Professor at Melbourne Law School. He has studied law at the University of Melbourne, Harvard Law School and Cambridge University. In addition to his Melbourne teaching, Dr Mitchell has taught WTO law to undergraduate and postgraduate students at Bond University, Monash University and the University of Western Ontario, and to Australian and overseas government officials at the Australian Department of Foreign Affairs and Trade and the International Development Law Organization respectively. His monograph *Legal Principles in WTO Disputes* was published in 2008.

DR HITOSHI NASU joined the ANU College of Law in December 2006. Prior to his appointment to the ANU, he was a part-time lecturer at the University of Sydney, teaching international law. He completed a PhD in 2006 by submitting a doctoral thesis entitled *Precautionary Approach to International Security Law: A Study of Article 40 of the UN Charter*.

ASSOCIATE PROFESSOR ELIZABETH SIEW-KUAN NG has been teaching intellectual property law at the Faculty of Law, National University of Singapore since 1986. She is the author of several books and has published widely and delivered papers at numerous international conferences on intellectual property law. She was a consultant to the World Intellectual Property Organization ('WIPO'), Switzerland; a visiting scholar to the US Court of Appeal for the Federal Circuit, Washington DC; and tutor in IP law of the WIPO Worldwide Academy, Switzerland. She served on many national and international projects to advise on intellectual property laws. Professor Ng regularly gives opinions on intellectual property law to clients in the public and private sectors. She holds an LLB (Hons) from the University of London and an LLM (First Class) from the University of Cambridge. She was awarded the Sweet & Maxwell Law Prize (1981) and the Faculty of Law prize (1983) from the University of London and the Clough prize (1984) from the University of Cambridge. She is also a barrister-at-law of the Middle Temple, England, an advocate and solicitor of the Supreme Court of Singapore, a fellow of the Cambridge Commonwealth Society, University of Cambridge and Team Leader (Information Communication Technology section) of the East Asian International Economic Law and Policy ICT Research Network of the University of Hong Kong.

PROFESSOR DIANNE NICOL is a professor in the Law Faculty at the University of Tasmania and a deputy director of the Centre for Law and Genetics (CLG), a cross-institutional research group based at the

University of Tasmania and Melbourne University. She teaches in the areas of intellectual property law, equity, media law, IT law and biotechnology and the law. She is Associate Dean for Research in the Law Faculty and Graduate Research Co-ordinator. She is also Chair of the University Animal Ethics Committee. Her research focuses on intellectual property issues in health and biotechnology, particularly on use of patented inventions.

DR JANE NIELSEN is a lecturer in law at the Law Faculty, University of Tasmania. Dr Nielsen's primary research interests concern the intersection of intellectual property and competition law, particularly as these issues pertain to the medical biotechnology industry. Dr Nielsen completed her PhD thesis in this area and has published a number of related papers. She also has an interest in the issue of compulsory licensing and its role in ensuring access to technologies. Her current project is to consider the role of patent pooling in facilitating access to, and distribution of, key biotechnology research tools and technologies.

PROFESSOR NOAH NOVOGRODSKY is an associate professor at the University of Wyoming law school and the former head of the International Human Rights Program at the University of Toronto Faculty of Law. Professor Novogrodsky has been a visiting professor at Georgetown University Law Center and a Schell fellow at Yale Law School. Professor Novogrodsky holds a BA degree from Swarthmore College (Political Science and English Literature), an MPhil Degree in International Relations from Cambridge University and a Juris Doctor from Yale Law School. Professor Novogrodsky's current research agenda focuses on the impact of AIDS treatment on the field of human rights law.

DR KRISHNA RAVI SRINIVAS is an associate fellow with RIS researching intellectual property rights and trade and environment issues. He holds a PhD from National Law School University, Bangalore. He has been a visiting scholar on a Fulbright Fellowship at the Law School, University of Pennsylvania, a visiting scholar at the Law School, Indiana University, Bloomington, a post-doc fellow at the South Centre, Geneva and a member of Visiting Faculty at IIM-Bangalore. His articles have been published in, *inter alia*,

Economic & Political Weekly, *EOLSS Encyclopaedia*, *Environmental Politics*, *International Social Science Journal* and *Asian Journal of WTO & International Health Law and Policy*. His research interests include use of Open Source models in biodiversity, drug discovery/development, biodiversity/biocommons and intellectual property rights.

TALHA SYED is an Assistant Professor at the University of California, Berkeley Law School, where he teaches and researches on intellectual property (with a focus on patents), torts, health law and legal theory. He has a BA (Hons) from the University of Western Ontario, an LLB (gold medallist) from the University of Victoria and is an SJD (doctoral) candidate at Harvard University. His academic honours include an Academic Fellowship from the Petrie-Flom Center for Health Law Policy, Biotechnology and Bioethics at Harvard Law School, research awards from the Weatherhead Center for Justice, Welfare and Economics at Harvard University and the Social Science and Humanities Research Council of Canada, and several Certificates for Distinction in Teaching from Harvard College.

DR TANIA VOON is an associate professor at Melbourne Law School and a former legal officer of the Appellate Body Secretariat of the World Trade Organization ('WTO'). She has previously practised law with Mallesons Stephen Jaques and the Australian Government Solicitor and taught law at Monash University, Bond University and the University of Western Ontario. She completed her PhD at the University of Cambridge and her LLM at Harvard Law School. Her book, *Cultural Products and the World Trade Organization*, was published in 2007.

KATHARINE YOUNG is a research fellow at the Regulatory Institutions Network at ANU. She earned her BA and LLB (Hons) from the University of Melbourne and an LLM at Harvard Law School. She was an SJD candidate at Harvard Law School where she held a graduate fellowship at the Edmond J. Safra Foundation Center for Ethics. She has served as Consultant Scholar at the NYU School of Law's Center for Human Rights and Global Justice, as Assistant to the Project Director of Health Rights and Ghana's Poor for Harvard Law School and the Fulbright Foundation, and as a graduate fellow at Harvard University's Project on Justice, Welfare and Economics. In 2001, she was Associate to Justice Michael Kirby in the High Court of Australia. Her current fields of research include comparative constitutional law, law and development, law and economics, and international human rights. Her scholarly publications include 'The Minimum Core of Economic and Social Rights: A Concept in Search of Content' in the *Yale Journal of International Law* (2008).

SERIES EDITORS' PREFACE

The idea for this series began in June 2005 when Kim Rubenstein applied for the position of Professor and Director of the Centre for International and Public Law at the ANU College of Law. The Centre is recognized as the leading Australian academic centre bringing together public lawyers (constitutional and administrative law broadly, but also specific areas of government regulation) and international lawyers from around the world. Established in 1990 with its inaugural director Professor Philip Alston, the impact of the Centre and its work can be seen further at law.anu.edu.au/cipl/.

In discussing with the law faculty ideas for the Centre's direction, Kim raised the concept that underpins this series. Each volume flows from workshops bringing public and international lawyers and public and international policy makers together for interdisciplinary discussion on selected topics and themes. The workshops attract both established scholars and outstanding early scholars. At each of the workshops participants address specific questions and issues, developing each other's understandings and knowledge about public and international law and policy and the links between the disciplines as they intersect with the chosen subject. These papers are discussed and reviewed at the workshop collaboratively. After the workshop the papers are finalized for the editing phase for the overall manuscript.

The series seeks to broaden both public law and international laws' understanding of how these two areas intersect. Until now, international and public law have mainly overlapped in discussions on how international law is implemented domestically. While there is scholarship developing in the area of global administrative law, and some scholars have touched upon the principles relevant to both disciplines, the publications to date contain only a subset of the concept underpinning this series. This series is unique in consciously bringing together public and international lawyers to consider and engage in each other's scholarship.

Beyond the first topic of sanctions, the other four topics in the series (including this second volume on health), draw from the research themes underpinning the International Alliance of Research Universities ('IARU') which is made up of the ANU, Berkeley, University of Cambridge, University of Copenhagen, ETH Zurich, National University of Singapore, Oxford University, Peking University, the University of Tokyo and Yale. The remaining three topics and volumes will be around environment, movement of people and security.

The Alliance has also supported the funding of participants from the IARU in some instances so that they can attend in person at the ANU. This does not preclude non-IARU academics from participating, as will be seen in the rich array of participants in the first two volumes.

After the first successful workshop was complete, Professor Rubenstein contacted Professor Thomas Pogge to co-host the second workshop and, in addition to doing that, he has enthusiastically joined with Professor Rubenstein as a joint series editor. His contributions to each volume are an expression of his cosmopolitan outlook, which is a theme engaged with throughout the series.

Kim Rubenstein
and
Thomas Pogge
June 2009

EDITORS' PREFACE

As explained in the Series Editors' Preface, this series is a result of workshops bringing together public and international lawyers. From this second volume onwards, the topics revolve around the International Alliance of Research Universities' ('IARU') thematic research topics.

When Kim Rubenstein began thinking about organizing the second workshop around the theme of health, she was encouraged to contact her ANU colleague Thomas Pogge in the Centre for Applied Philosophy and Public Ethics. Thomas responded enthusiastically and work began to brainstorm the call for papers.

This second workshop was entitled: 'Incentives for Global Public Health: Patent Law and Access to Essential Medicines.' This title is inspired by Professor Pogge's research programme, which explores institutional mechanisms that would create additional incentives to develop essential medicines while also ensuring real access to the resulting new products even for the world's poorest populations.

This topic provides excellent material for the themes the series is meant to explore. A majority of human beings are endangered by serious diseases for which advanced medicines are either not being developed at all or are inaccessible to them. To explain this huge healthcare deficit, we must study the relevant parts of international and public law together and examine their interplay. To judge these national and international rules – and those who formulate, promulgate and enforce them – we need to relate these rules to internationally recognized human rights and ask, for example, whether it is not a violation of human rights legally to prevent generic manufacturers from supplying essential medicines cheaply to poor patients. To lift, through institutional reforms, the great disease burden from the world's poor, we need to take a broadly holistic approach that takes advantage of the fact that innovation is cost-free at the margin: the cost of pharmaceutical R&D is the same regardless of whether access to its products is confined to the affluent or extended to all. The existing regime of national and international intellectual property rules can then be criticized not merely as immoral, but also as irrational insofar as there are great collective benefits to be unlocked through a more efficient system of rules governing pharmaceutical innovation.

Our workshop took place on 26–28 May 2008 at the Australian National University. The twenty paper presenters and a further eleven participants, who had read all the papers, enjoyed vigorous discussion, engaging fully with each other and the material. We thank Professor Simon Bronitt, former Director of ANU's National Europe Centre, for providing us with a dynamic venue. We thank Chikosa Banda, Clancy Kelly, Dr Luigi Palombi and Antony Taubman for presenting stimulating papers at the workshop even though they were unable to contribute to the resulting book. Dr Kieran Donaghue, Professor Peter Drahos, Associate Professor Anna George, Dr Ian Heath, Dr Janet Hope, Professor Sarah Joseph, Teresa Lawler, Hafiz Aziz ur Rehman, Dr Michael Selgelid, Professor Judy Whitworth and Renata Zanetti either participated in discussions or chaired various sessions and we thank them for their valuable contributions to the workshop. The event was ably organized by the redoubtable Kavitha Robinson.

The call for abstracts was sent out to the Law Deans of the IARU and we thank the respective universities for their support to their participants (in particular Cambridge University for supporting Chikosa Banda's travel and the National University of Singapore for supporting Elizabeth Siew-Kuan Ng's travel), and to the ANU, IARU secretariat for its support in covering the IARU participants' costs at the ANU. This was in addition to other financial support from the ANU, including the Vice Chancellor's travel fund in supporting Professor Dreyfuss and Professor Novogrodsky's participation and the remaining expenses which were split evenly between the Centre for International and Public Law and the Centre for Applied Philosophy and Public Ethics.

We are also grateful to Teresa Lawler, who was a CIPL intern at the time of the workshop and continued to help us develop the resulting papers. Special thanks are due to Trevor Moses for the effort he has put in for both volumes in the series, providing outstanding support, particularly in the final stages of bringing the entire volume together. We thank him immensely! We also thank Jennifer Braid from the ANU College of Law for her assistance in the early stages of putting this volume together, before she moved from the ANU to work at the High Court of Australia. Matthew Peterson also provided sterling research assistance. Kim and

Thomas thank their co-editor Matthew for doing the lion's share of the day-to-day managing of the project.

And all three of us thank the staff at Cambridge University Press, and especially Finola O'Sullivan for her enthusiasm in getting this volume and series off the ground. We are grateful for Kate Ollerenshaw's impeccable copy-editing.

Finally, we would like to thank our colleagues at the ANU College of Law and the Centre for Applied Philosophy and Public Ethics and our respective families and friends for their support and inspiration in all that we do.

Thomas Pogge,
Matthew Rimmer
and
Kim Rubenstein
June 2009

Introduction

Access to essential medicines: public health and international law

THOMAS POGGE, MATTHEW RIMMER AND KIM RUBENSTEIN

1. Prologue

Historically, there have been intense conflicts over the ownership and exploitation of pharmaceutical drugs and diagnostic tests dealing with infectious diseases.

Throughout the 1980s, there was much scientific, legal and ethical debate about which scientific group should be credited with the discovery of the human immunodeficiency virus and the invention of the blood test devised to detect antibodies to the virus.[1] In May 1983, Luc Montagnier, Françoise Barré-Sinoussi and other French scientists from the Institut Pasteur in Paris published a paper in *Science*, detailing the discovery of a virus called lymphadenopathy ('LAV').[2] A scientific rival, Robert Gallo of the National Cancer Institute, identified the AIDS virus and published his findings in the May 1984 issue of *Science*.[3] In May 1985, the United States Patent and Trademark Office awarded the American patent for the AIDS blood test to Gallo and the Department of Health and Human Services. In December 1985, the Institut Pasteur sued the Department of Health and Human Services, contending that the French were the first to

[1] Hal Hellman, 'Chapter 10, Gallo versus Montagnier, the AIDS War', *Great Feuds in Medicine: Ten of the Liveliest Disputes Ever* (2001), 165–84.

[2] Françoise Barré-Sinoussi, 'Isolation of a T-lymphotropic Retrovirus from a Patient at Risk for Acquired Immune Deficiency Syndrome (AIDS)' (1983) 220 *Science* 868–71.

[3] Robert Gallo *et al.* 'Frequent Detection and Isolation of Cytopathic Retroviruses (HTLV-III) from Patients with AIDS and at Risk for AIDS' (1984) 224 *Science* 500–3; J. Schupbach *et al.* 'Serological Analysis of a Subgroup of Human T-lymphotropic Retroviruses (HTLV-III) associated with AIDS' (1984) 224 *Science* 503–5; and Mangalasseril G. Sarngadharan *et al.* 'Antibodies Reactive with Human T-lymphotropic Retroviruses (HTLV-III) in the Serum of Patients with AIDS' (1984) 224 *Science* 506–8.

identify the AIDS virus and to invent the antibody test, and that the American test was dependent upon the French research.

In March 1987, an agreement was brokered by President Ronald Reagan and French Prime Minister Jacques Chirac, which resulted in the Department of Health and Human Services and the Institut Pasteur sharing the patent rights to the blood test for AIDS.[4] In 1992, the Federal Office of Research Integrity found that Gallo had committed scientific misconduct, by falsely reporting facts in his 1984 scientific paper.[5] A subsequent investigation by the National Institutes of Health, the US Congress and the US Attorney-General cleared Gallo of any wrongdoing.

In 1994, the US Government and the French Government renegotiated their agreement regarding the AIDS blood test patent, in order to make the distribution of royalties more equitable.[6] Under the agreement, the US and French research institutions would keep 20 per cent of royalties made from testing kits that each team has developed from its own laboratories. The remaining 80 per cent would be pooled. A quarter of the pool was allocated to the World AIDS Foundation. Under the new agreement, the French received two thirds of the remainder and the Americans one third. In a written statement, Gallo observed he had 'consistently acknowledged the significant contributions of the Pasteur scientists' and that 'it is now time for this episode to be permanently closed'.[7] By 2002, Gallo and Montagnier were sufficiently reconciled to write a joint paper for *Science*, expressing the common belief that 'a global coordinated response is required to fight the scourge of AIDS'.[8]

As a coda to the dispute, Montagnier and his compatriot Françoise Barré-Sinoussi were awarded a Nobel Prize in Physiology or Medicine in 2008 for the discovery of the human immunodeficiency virus. The Nobel Assembly noted in a press release: 'never before has science and medicine been so quick to discover, identify the origin and provide treatment for a new disease entity'.[9]

4 Luc Montagnier *et al.* 'Human Immunodeficiency Viruses Associated with Acquired Immune Deficiency Syndrome (AIDS), a Diagnostic Method for AIDS and pre-AIDS, and a Kit Therefore', United States Patent No: 4,708,818. See also Luc Montagnier, *Virus: The Co-Discoverer of the Virus Tracks its Rampage and Charts its Future* (1999).

5 Philip Hilts, 'Federal Inquiry Finds Misconduct by a Discoverer of the AIDS Virus', *The New York Times*, 31 December 1992.

6 Philip Hilts, 'Key Patent on AIDS to Favor the French', *The New York Times* (12 July 1994).

7 Ibid.

8 Robert Gallo and Luc Montagnier, 'Prospects for the Future' (2002) 298 *Science* 1730–1.

9 The Nobel Assembly at Karolinska Institute, 'The Nobel Prize in Physiology or Medicine in 2008', 6 October 2008, nobelprize.org/nobel_prizes/medicine/laureates/2008/press.html.

Although Gallo was not included in the Nobel Prize citation, Montagnier did acknowledge the contribution of his sometime colleague and sometime rival. In return, Gallo released a statement, observing: 'I am pleased my long-time friend and colleague Dr Luc Montagnier, as well as his colleague Françoise Barré-Sinoussi, have received this honor.'[10] He added: 'I was gratified to read Dr Montagnier's kind statement this morning expressing that I was equally deserving'.[11]

The dispute between Luc Montagnier and Robert Gallo was not an isolated case of scientific rivalry and patent races. It foreshadowed further patent conflicts over research in respect of HIV/AIDS.[12] Michael Kirby, former Justice of the High Court of Australia, diagnosed a clash between two distinct schools of philosophy – 'scientists of the old school … working by serendipity with free sharing of knowledge and research', and 'those of the new school who saw the hope of progress as lying in huge investments in scientific experimentation'.[13] Indeed, the patent race between Robert Gallo and Luc Montagnier has been a precursor to broader trade disputes over access to essential medicines in the 1990s and 2000s.[14] The dispute between Robert Gallo and Luc Montagnier captures in microcosm a number of themes of this book: the fierce competition for intellectual property rights; the clash between sovereign states over access to medicines; the pressing need to defend human rights, particularly the right to health; and the need for new incentives for research and development to combat infectious diseases as both an international and domestic issue.

2. Connecting public and international law

This volume is the second in a new series bringing public and international lawyers and public and international policy-makers together to examine key issues in the twenty-first century. This series broadens both

[10] Robert Gallo, 'Statement', *New Scientist* (7 October 2008), www.newscientist.com/commenting/thread?id=dn14881-4.

[11] Ibid.

[12] See for instance the dispute in the Supreme Court of Canada over the patent ownership of AZT in *Apotex Inc.* v. *Wellcome Foundation Ltd*, [2002] 4 S.C.R. 153.

[13] Justice Michael Kirby, 'Foreword' in Matthew Rimmer, *Intellectual Property and Biotechnology: Biological Inventions* (2008), vi. See also Ian Freckleton and Hugh Selby (eds.) *Appealing to the Future: Michael Kirby and his Legacy* (2009).

[14] Patricia Thomas, *Big Shot: Passion, Politics and the Struggle for an AIDS Vaccine* (2001); Anne-Christine D'Adesky, *Moving Mountains: The Race to Treat Global AIDS* (2004); and Lawrence Gostin, *The AIDS Pandemic: Complacency, Injustice, and Unfulfilled Expectations* (2006).

public and international laws' understanding of how these two areas intersect and is unique in consciously bringing together public and international lawyers to consider and engage in each other's scholarship. What can public lawyers bring to international law and what can international lawyers bring to public law? What are the common interests? What tensions become apparent when we consider public and international law together?

This second volume focuses on these questions in the context of the contemporary debate over access to essential medicines.

This debate takes place against the background of staggering health discrepancies: both between affluent and less-developed countries and also, within the latter, between rich and poor households. Among the world's poor, some 18 million die annually from Group I causes – communicable diseases, maternal and perinatal conditions and nutritional deficits – which cause only minimal harm among the affluent. Eighteen million is equivalent to just over 30 per cent of all human deaths.[15] And this percentage is considerably larger when, taking age at death into account, one estimates how many years of human life are lost due to Group I causes.[16] Life expectancy is 79.4 in the high-income countries and 49.2 in the African region.[17] Similarly dramatic health inequalities exist within the less-developed countries. In Peru, under-five mortality is 11 per 1,000 among the richest 20 per cent of the population versus 63 among the poorest 20 per cent, for example, and in Nigeria the corresponding figures are 79 versus 257.[18]

These huge health discrepancies stem in part from the fact that poor people are at greater risk of disease, due to lack of food, shelter, uncontaminated water, clothing and physical security. Another crucial factor is that the world's poor have little access to medical care and, in particular, to the medicines that could help them cope with their debilitating and often life-threatening conditions.

This lack of access to essential medicines has three components. First, medicines for diseases concentrated among the poor are neglected by pharmaceutical research. This phenomenon has come to be known as the 10/90 gap, alluding to the claim that 'only 10 per cent of global health research is devoted to conditions that account for 90 per cent of the

[15] World Health Organization, *The Global Burden of Disease: 2004 Update* (2004), 10, 17–18.

[16] Ibid., 23. [17] Ibid., 5.

[18] United Nations Development Programme, *Human Development Report 2007/2008* (2007), Table 8, 255–6.

global disease burden'.[19] Pneumonia, diarrhoea, tuberculosis and malaria, which account for over 20 per cent of the global burden of disease, receive less than 1 per cent of all public and private funds devoted to health research.[20] And diseases confined to the tropics tend to be the most neglected: of the 1556 new drugs approved between 1975 and 2004, only 18 were for tropical diseases and 3 for tuberculosis.[21]

The second component of the access problem of the poor is that existing medicines are, during their initial years on the market, typically priced vastly higher than their cost of production.[22] Such high prices are facilitated by patents, which grant the patentee the exclusive right to produce and distribute the medicine. Patents are conferred in nearly all national jurisdictions for the purpose of incentivizing and rewarding innovation. A firm enjoying such market exclusivity will price its product to maximize profit, which is (simplifying slightly) its mark-up multiplied by its sales volume. In view of the prevailing huge inequalities in income and wealth, the optimal price tends to be high. If a medicine is important, sales to, or for, the people in affluent countries and the affluent individuals in the poor countries will not be spoiled by a high price. And reaching some of the remaining 80 per cent of humankind is simply not worthwhile because the patentee would lose more from the necessary price reduction than it would gain through an increased sales volume. Interestingly, this holds even *within* many poor countries, where the profit-maximizing price often excludes a majority of the national population.[23]

[19] Drugs for Neglected Diseases Working Group, *Fatal Imbalance: The Crisis in Research and Development for Drugs for Neglected Diseases* (2001) also at www.msf.org/source/access/2001/fatal/fatal.pdf, 10. See also Louis Currat, Andres de Francisco, Sameera Al-Tuwaijri, Abdul Ghaffar and Susan Jupp, *Global Forum Health 10/90 Report 2003–2004* (2004).

[20] Ibid., 122.

[21] Pierre Chirac and Els Toreele, 'Global Framework on Essential Health R&D' (2006) 367 *The Lancet* 1560; Drugs for Neglected Diseases Working Group, *Fatal Imbalance*, see above n. 19, 10. See also Patrice Trouiller, Piero Olliaro, Els Torreele, James Orbinski, Richard Laing and Nathan Ford, 'Drug Development for Neglected Diseases: A Deficient Market and a Public-Health Policy Failure' (2002) 359 (9324) *The Lancet* 2188, 2189.

[22] See Oxfam International, 'Investing for Life: Meeting Poor People's Needs for Access to Medicines through Responsible Business Practices' (Briefing Paper No 109, Oxfam, November 2007), 20, giving examples of high prices with mark-ups of up to sixty times what a generic supplier would charge.

[23] Sean Flynn, Aidan Hollis and Mike Palmedo, 'An Economic Justification for Open Access to Essential Medicine Patents in Developing Countries' (2009) 37 *Journal of Law, Medicine & Ethics* 184.

The third component of poor people's lack of access to essential medicines is the dearth of even minimally adequate local health infrastructure. In most of the less-developed countries, there is great scarcity of clinics and hospitals, of diagnostic equipment, as well as of doctors and nurses who are often very actively recruited to move to more affluent countries. In the year 2000, some 65,000 physicians and 70,000 nurses born – and mostly also trained – in Africa were working overseas,[24] leaving behind huge gaps in their home countries' healthcare coverage as well as in their education budgets. The effect of poor health infrastructure is that poor patients get no competent diagnosis and then end up with no medicine at all, with the wrong medicine, with fake or diluted medicine (often sold by street vendors), or without instruction about how to take the medicine for optimal effect. Medicine that is diluted or not taken properly can contribute to the emergence of drug-specific resistance as patients are not exposed to enough of the active ingredient for a sufficiently long period to kill off the more resilient pathogenic agents. The emergence of drug-resistant strains of communicable diseases (such as multi-drug-resistant and extensively drug-resistant tuberculosis) can greatly aggravate the damage done by a disease – especially among the poor who are unable to afford the more advanced second-line and third-line therapies which are typically still under patent.

This thumbnail sketch of the access to medicines problem brings out the interplay of national and international dimensions and, in particular, the great challenges the national health systems of poorer countries confront on account of an international environment they can do very little to influence. To be sure, poor countries agreed to adopt a US-style pharmaceutical patent regime when they signed the Trade-Related Aspects of Intellectual Property Agreement ('TRIPS Agreement') – but they had little choice as refusing to sign would have meant exclusion from the World Trade Organization ('WTO').[25] Moreover, many poor countries lack pharmaceutical manufacturing capacity and therefore were much more severely affected by India's accession to the TRIPS

[24] Michael Clemens, and Gunilla Pettersson, 'New Data on African Health Professionals Abroad' (2008) 6(1) *Human Resources for Health*, www.human-resources-health.com/content/6/1/1.

[25] Marrakesh Agreement Establishing the World Trade Organization, opened for signature 15 April 1994, 1867 UNTS 3, annex 1C (Agreement on Trade-Related Aspects of Intellectual Property Rights) (entered into force 1 January 1995) ('TRIPS Agreement').

Agreement than by their own.[26] Poor countries also have little control over the doctors and nurses they train – they cannot force them to stay, nor pay them anything like the salary they are being offered by foreign recruiters. Recipient countries might implement legislation that would constrain the importation of medical professionals from poor countries or would at least require employers to cover the antecedent expenses of training these professionals. But a recipient country is unlikely to pass such legislation on its own, as it would only disadvantage itself in the competition with other rich countries over the gains from recruiting doctors and nurses from the developing world.

Given the enormous magnitude of the access to medicines problem, it is fairly obvious that this problem cannot be overcome through the various global health initiatives of recent years, even though these have indeed been impressive. As stated in the recent *WHO Global Strategy*:

> Member States, the pharmaceutical industry, charitable foundations and nongovernmental organizations have taken initiatives in recent years to develop new products against diseases affecting developing countries and to increase access to existing health products and medical devices. However, these initiatives are not sufficient to surmount the challenges of meeting the goal of ensuring access and innovation for needed health products and medical devices.[27]

In addition to these initiatives, substantial progress calls for an integrated solution that combines public law and international law elements to form an effective reform package: 'Proposals should be developed for health-needs driven research and development that include exploring a range of incentive mechanisms, including where appropriate, addressing the de-linkage of the costs of research and development and the price of

[26] India is home to some of the largest pharmaceutical manufacturing firms, which used to supply the less-developed countries with cheap generic versions of medicines that were still under patent in the affluent states. An editorial for *The New York Times* has observed: 'But when India signed the World Trade Organization's agreement on intellectual property in 1994, it was required to institute patents on products by Jan. 1, 2005. These rules have little to do with free trade and more to do with the lobbying power of the American and European pharmaceutical industries. India's government has issued rules that will effectively end the copycat industry for newer drugs. For the world's poor, this will be a double hit – cutting off the supply of affordable medicines and removing the generic competition that drives down the cost of brand-name drugs.' (Editorial, 'India's Choice', *The New York Times*, 18 January 2005).

[27] *Global Strategy and Plan of Action on Public Health, Innovation and Intellectual Property*, World Health Assembly 61st mtg, Res WHA61.21 (2008) ('*WHO Global Strategy*').

health products and methods for tailoring the optimal mix of incentives to a particular condition or product with the objective of addressing diseases that disproportionately affect developing countries'.[28]

This volume considers the design and assessment of national and international law governing the discovery, development and delivery of advanced medicines. It seeks to advance creative solutions to the long-standing problems in respect of intellectual property and access to essential medicines. Drawing upon international trade law, innovation policy, intellectual property law, health law, human rights and philosophy, this volume encourages interdisciplinary collaboration in regard to two important objectives: encouraging and rewarding worthwhile pharmaceutical innovation and ensuring affordable access to advanced medicines, even for the poor. These objectives can stand in some tension with each other: affordable access for the poor is likely to reduce the profitability of patent monopolies and hence also the incentives for conducting pharmaceutical research.

In bringing together public and international lawyers as well as experts in public health, economics and moral philosophy, this volume facilitates dialogue among academics, governments, industry and civil society over access to essential medicines and enlarges our understanding of the intersections at play. We hope this dialogue will not merely enrich the various academic disciplines, but also stimulate new reform ideas and implementation efforts that will improve access to important medicines worldwide.

3. The international institutions

On the international level, trade, intellectual property rights and health have been governed by several international institutions, including the World Trade Organization, the World Intellectual Property Organization and the World Health Organization. This section of the introduction sets out basic information about these key international institutions, and the treaties and declarations they administer, as background to the chapters that follow.

3.1 The World Trade Organization

The World Trade Organization[29] has been a key actor in the debate over patent law and access to essential medicines. The TRIPS Agreement

[28] Ibid., article 4 [29] World Trade Organization, www.wto.org/.

requires WTO members to establish minimum standards for protecting and enforcing intellectual property rights.[30] In particular, members of the WTO are required to provide patent protection for pharmaceutical drugs for at least twenty years. Nonetheless, the treaty does recognize the countervailing need of member states to protect public health. Article 8 of the TRIPS Agreement declares: 'Members may, in formulating or amending their laws and regulations, adopt measures necessary to protect public health and nutrition, and to promote the public interest in sectors of vital importance to their socio-economic and technological development, provided that such measures are consistent with the provisions of this Agreement.' The TRIPS Agreement contains a number of provisions designed to promote the public interest in the field of public health. It allows governments to provide for exceptions, exclusions and limitations to rights in order to address national emergencies, to facilitate public non-commercial use or to remedy anti-competitive practices.[31] This can be done, for example, in the form of compulsory licensing,[32] exhaustion regimes[33] and other types of exceptions, such as the defence of experimental use[34] and the 'Bolar' exemption for pharmaceutical drugs, provided certain conditions are fulfilled.[35]

[30] TRIPS Agreement, above n. 25; Daniel Gervais, *The TRIPS Agreement: Drafting History and Analysis* (2nd edn, 2003); and Nuno Pires de Carvalho, *The TRIPS Regime of Patent Rights* (2003).

[31] Article 30 of the TRIPS Agreement deals with exceptions to rights conferred; and article 31 of the TRIPS Agreement considers other uses of patented inventions, which do not require the authorization of the rights holder.

[32] By issuing a compulsory licence, a state allows for the use of a patented invention in return for reasonable compensation. Gervais, *The TRIPS Agreement*, above n. 30, 244–53.

[33] Under the system of international exhaustion, once a patented invention has been placed onto the market with authorization, the patent holder loses control over the actions performed on it by the buyer. Gervais, *The TRIPS Agreement*, above n. 30, 111–15.

[34] The defence of experimental use allows users to experiment on a patented invention, without seeking permission or paying royalties to the patent holder. The US common law defence of experimental use is limited to amusement, idle curiousity and strictly philosophical inquiry; whereas the European Union directive in respect of experimental use covers potentially both commercial and non-commercial use. See Matthew Rimmer, *Intellectual Property and Biotechnology: Biological Inventions* (2008), 162–73.

[35] A 'Bolar exemption' is named after a legislative response to the decision in *Roche Products, Inc.* v. *Bolar Pharmaceuticals Co., Inc.*, 733 F 2d 858 (Fed Cir, 1984). It is a safe harbour exemption that allows generic companies to conduct research and tests in preparation for regulatory approval of a generic version of a pharmaceutical drug that is still under patent. There has been legal debate over the scope of the safe harbour provided by the Drug Price Competition and Patent Term Restoration Act 1984 ('the Hatch-Waxman' Act) (United States): *Merck KGAA* v. *Integra Lifesciences I, Inc.*, 545 US 193 (2005). Some jurisdictions have equivalent 'springboarding' provisions: section 119A of the Patents Act 1990 (Cth)

There have been dramatic battles over patent law and access to medicines under the shadow of the TRIPS Agreement. These conflicts have involved international law, constitutional law, intellectual property law, competition law and trade law. While patent law had been around for centuries, the TRIPS Agreement marked the first time patent protection for pharmaceutical products was available and, more significantly, enforceable on a global scale. The repercussions were significant. The fact that intellectual property rights were now tied to the international trading regime meant that mechanisms for the enforcement of these rights were far more effective than previously. Countries, such as Canada, accustomed to issuing compulsory licences for the generic manufacturing of medicines began to face challenges from other states and from pharmaceutical companies.[36]

After a number of high-profile conflicts over access to essential medicines in South Africa[37] and Brazil,[38] and a panic over bioterrorism in North America,[39] the WTO issued the Declaration on the TRIPS Agreement and Public Health ('Doha Declaration') at the fourth WTO Ministerial Conference in Doha in 2001.[40] Susan Sell and John Odell have suggested that the Doha Declaration was made possible by a

allows springboarding as an exception to patent infringement on any pharmaceutical patent at any time for purposes solely in connection with gaining regulatory approval of a pharmaceutical product in Australia or another territory. See Rimmer, *Intellectual Property and Biotechnology*, above n. 34, 173–81.

36 WTO Panel Decision on *Canada: Patent Protection of Pharmaceutical Products: Complaint by the European Communities and their Member States*, 17 March 2000, WT/DS114/R.

37 *The Pharmaceutical Manufacturers' Association of South Africa* v. *Government of South Africa*, Notice of Motion, Case Number 4183/98, in the High Court of South Africa (Transvaal Provincial Division).

38 *Brazil – Measures Affecting Patent Protection*, WT/DS199/4, G/L/454, IP/D/23/Add.1, 19 July 2001, (01–3506). For an archive of documents on the WTO challenge by the United States against Brazil, see: www.cptech.org/ip/health/c/brazil/. Paul Champ and Amir Attaran, 'Patent Rights and Local Working under the WTO TRIPS Agreement: An Analysis of the U.S.–Brazil Patent Dispute' (2002) 27(2) *The Yale Journal of International Law* 365–93.

39 Ciproflocaxin dispute over compulsory licences during the 2001 anthrax scare, www.cptech.org/ip/health/cl/cipro/; Project Bioshield Act 2004 (United States); and David Resnik and Kenneth De Ville, 'Bioterrorism and Patent Rights: "Compulsory Licensure" and the case of Cipro' (2002) 2(3) *The American Journal of Bioethics* 29–39.

40 Declaration on the TRIPS Agreement and Public Health: Adopted on 14 November 2001, WTO Doc WT/MIN(01)/DEC/2 (2001) ('the Doha Declaration'); and Frederick Abbott, 'The Doha Declaration on the TRIPS Agreement and Public Health: Lighting a Dark Corner at the WTO' (2002) 5 *Journal of International Economic Law* 469–505.

common and united front from a coalition of civil society organizations, developing countries and mid-tier nations, such as Thailand, India and Brazil.[41] Devi Sridhar notes: 'While perhaps imperfect from an ideal moral perspective, compromise was arguably necessary to achieve agreement on the Declaration, which was highly preferable to no Declaration at all.'[42]

The Doha Declaration recognized 'the gravity of the public health problems afflicting many developing and least-developed countries, especially those resulting from HIV/AIDS, tuberculosis, malaria and other epidemics'.[43] The statement affirmed that 'the TRIPS Agreement does not and should not prevent Members from taking measures to protect public health'.[44] Article 6 of the Doha Declaration recognized that WTO members with insufficient or no manufacturing capacities in the pharmaceutical sector could face difficulties in making effective use of compulsory licensing under the TRIPS Agreement. It noted the need to find an expeditious solution to this problem. Ellen 't Hoen has remarked that the Doha Declaration has had a galvanizing impact upon nation states: 'Between 2001 and end 2007, 52 developing and least-developed countries have issued post-Doha compulsory licences for production or import of generic versions of patented medicines, given effect to government use provisions, and/or implemented the non-enforcement of patents'.[45]

In August 2003, the World Trade Organization developed a decision on the export of pharmaceutical drugs to address the need for the export of pharmaceutical drugs to countries lacking local manufacturing capacity ('WTO General Council Decision of 30 August 2003').[46] The decision emphasized that a WTO member country could export pharmaceutical

[41] Susan Sell, *Private Power, Public Law: The Globalization of Intellectual Property Rights* (2003); and John Odell and Susan Sell, 'Reframing the Issue: The WTO Coalition on Intellectual Property and Public Health, 2001', in John Odell (ed.), *Negotiating Trade: Developing Countries in the WTO and NAFTA* (2006).

[42] Devi Sridhar, 'Improving Access to Essential Medicines: How Health Concerns can be Prioritised in the Global Governance System' (2008) 1 *Public Health Ethics* 83–8.

[43] Article 1 of the Doha Declaration, above n. 40.

[44] Article 4 of the Doha Declaration, above n. 40.

[45] Ellen 't Hoen, *The Global Politics of Pharmaceutical Monopoly Power: Drug Patents, Access, Innovation and the Application of the WTO Doha Declaration on TRIPS and Public Health* (2009), xvi.

[46] Implementation of Paragraph 6 of the Doha Declaration on the TRIPS Agreement and Public Health, WTO Doc WT/L/540 (2003) (WTO General Council Decision of 30 August 2003).

products made under compulsory licences, subject to a number of substantive and procedural terms. In 2005, at the Hong Kong meeting, the WTO proposed that the WTO General Council Decision of 30 August 2003 should be incorporated into the formal text of the TRIPS Agreement 1994 ('TRIPS Waiver').[47] As of February 2009, only twenty countries and the members of the European Union have supported the TRIPS Waiver. Adoption of the measure requires support from two-thirds of the members of the WTO. The deadline to accept the TRIPS Waiver was extended till December 2009.

The international regime for the export of pharmaceutical drugs under compulsory licence has been criticized as ineffectual – which may explain the lack of enthusiasm for the TRIPS Waiver.[48] Only a select number of countries have implemented domestic legislation to allow for such exports. Significant manufacturers of pharmaceutical drugs – such as the US, Japan, Switzerland and Australia[49] – have not established schemes. Thus far, the export mechanism has been underutilized. As of 2009, Rwanda is the first and only country to utilize the WTO General Council Decision of 30 August 2003 by applying to import cheap generic drugs from Canada.[50] Furthermore, there have also been concerns that the United States Trade Representative has negotiated TRIPS-Plus bilateral and regional trade agreements that undermine the intent and impact of the Doha Declaration and the WTO General Council Decision of the 30 August 2003.[51]

[47] Amendment of the TRIPS Agreement, WTO Doc WT/L/641 (2005) (Decision of 6 December 2005 of the General Council) ('TRIPS Waiver').

[48] Brook Baker, 'Arthritic Flexibilities for Accessing Medicines: Analysis of WTO Action Regarding Paragraph 6 of the Doha Declaration on the TRIPS Agreement and Public Health' (2004) 14 *Indiana International and Comparative Law Review* 613.

[49] Australia has ratified the WTO General Council Decision of 30 August 2003; but still has not implemented the treaty in domestic legislation: Joint Standing Committee on Treaties, *Protocol Amending the TRIPS Agreement* (2007).

[50] Matthew Rimmer, 'The Jean Chrétien Pledge to Africa Act: Patent Law and Humanitarian Aid' (2005) 15(7) *Expert Opinion on Therapeutic Patents* 889–909; and Matthew Rimmer, 'Race against Time: The Export of Essential Medicines to Rwanda' (2008) 1(2) *Public Health Ethics* 89–103.

[51] See Peter Drahos, 'BITS and BIPS: Bilateralism in Intellectual Property' (2001) 4 *Journal of World Intellectual Property* 791–808; Michael Westerhaus and Arachu Castro, 'How Do Intellectual Property Law and International Trade Agreements Affect Access to Antiretroviral Therapy' (2006) 3(8) *The Public Library of Science Medicine* 1230–6; Peter Drahos, 'Weaving Webs of Influence: The United States, Free Trade Agreements and Dispute Resolution' (2007) 41(1) *Journal of World Trade* 191–210, and Thomas Faunce, *Who Owns our Health?: Medical Professionalism, Law and Leadership beyond the Age of the Market State* (2007).

The Doha Declaration and the WTO General Council Decision of 30 August 2003 have not ended the acrimonious disputes over patent law and access to essential medicines. Antony Taubman has observed that compulsory licences remain contentious: 'Bilateral trade representations continue over compulsory licensing, even though TRIPS itself, the Doha Declaration and the subsequent waiver and amendment marked significant progress in articulating and clarifying multilateral standards in this domain.'[52] In 2007, Novartis was unsuccessful in its arguments to the High Court of Judicature at Madras that Indian patent laws were invalid under the TRIPS Agreement and contrary to the Indian Constitution.[53] In Thailand, the government issuance of a number of compulsory licences earned the ire of brand-name pharmaceutical companies, especially Abbott Laboratories, which threatened to stop registering drugs in that country.[54] There has been controversy over the willingness of the Government of Brazil to engage in compulsory licensing.[55] The outbreak of avian influenza led to concerns over access to patents in respect of Tamiflu and Relenza.[56] Furthermore, the Indonesian Government objected to the filing of patents in respect of viral samples taken from avian influenza.[57]

As Peter Yu has observed, mid-tier nations such as Brazil, Russia, India, China and South Africa (the BRICS alliance) have pushed a new compact in respect of intellectual property, development and access to essential medicines.[58]

In spite of such diplomatic skirmishes and trade disputes, the Director-General of the WTO, Pascal Lamy, has been hopeful of greater

52 Antony Taubman, 'Rethinking TRIPS: "Adequate Remuneration" for Non-Voluntary Patent Licensing' (2008) 11(4) *Journal of International Economic Law* 927–70.

53 *Novartis AG and another* v. *Union of India and others* (6 August 2007, High Court of Judicature at Madras for W.P. Nos. 24759 and 24760 of 2006), judis.nic.in/chennai/qrydisp.asp?tfnm=11121.

54 Ministry of Public Health and National Health Security Office, Thailand, *Facts and Evidences on the 10 Burning Issues Related to the Government Use of Patents on Three Patented Essential Drugs in Thailand*, February 2007.

55 Brazil disputes over compulsory licensing of essential medicines: www.cptech.org/ip/health/c/brazil; and Lawrence A. Kogan, 'Brazil's IP Opportunism Threatens U.S. Private Property Rights' (2007) 38 *University of Miami Inter-American Law Review* 1.

56 Dispute over compulsory licences in respect of Tamiflu during the 2005 and 2006 controversy over avian influenza: www.cptech.org/ip/health/tamiflu/index.html.

57 Pandemic Influenza Preparedness: Sharing of Influenza Viruses and Access to Vaccines and Other Benefits, World Health Assembly 60th mtg Res WHA60.28 (2007).

58 Peter Yu, 'Access to Medicines, BRICS Alliances, and Collective Action' (2008) 34 *American Journal of Law and Medicine* 345.

harmony between trade-related intellectual property rights and public health concerns. In December 2008, Lamy maintained that 'international trade helps improve the health conditions of many people both indirectly – through increase in incomes – and directly, through imports of health-related products or through health-related services'.[59] He recognized 'the issue of TRIPS and public health is certainly one of the most emotive and, consequently, frequently debated issues'.[60] The Director-General identified a number of important steps taken in the WTO since the adoption of the Doha Declaration – such as the 'major reduction of prices, enhanced international funding, a greater recognition of the need to find a balance within the intellectual property system, as well as the use of some of the TRIPS flexibilities by certain WTO members'.[61] Lamy stated that 'the continuous and constructive engagement of all relevant stakeholders would still be required' in order to achieve 'further improvements in access to medicines for patients around the world'.[62]

3.2 *World Intellectual Property Organization*

The World Intellectual Property Organization ('WIPO') was established in 1967 to 'promote the protection of intellectual property throughout the world through cooperation among States and, where appropriate, in collaboration with any other international organization'.[63] The international institution has for some time escaped critical scrutiny. Christopher May has observed: 'the relative inattention to the WIPO may reveal a tacit acceptance of its own public depiction of itself as merely a technical agency'.[64] He comments that the 'WIPO is a highly politicized organization whose role in the contemporary global political economy requires more thorough analytical attention'.[65]

WIPO has been criticized for promoting high standards of patent protection in respect of pharmaceutical drugs. Frederick Abbott observes

[59] Pascal Lamy, 'Access to Medicines Has Been Improved' (Geneva: The World Trade Organization), 9 December 2008, www.wto.org/english/news_e/sppl_e/sppl111_e.htm.

[60] Ibid. [61] Ibid. [62] Ibid.

[63] World Intellectual Property Organization, www.wipo.int/portal/index.html.en; and article 3 of the Convention Establishing the World Intellectual Property Organization, opened for signature 14 July 1967, 848 UNTS 3 (entered into force 26 April 1970).

[64] Christopher May, *The World Intellectual Property Organization: Resurgence and the Development Agenda* (2007), 1.

[65] Ibid., 1.

that, 'WIPO representatives routinely encourage developing countries to adopt and maintain strict standards of IP protection and to avoid implementing or using the flexibilities recognized in the TRIPS Agreement'.[66] He despairs: 'two directly conflicting sets of advice can be given by WHO and WIPO to patent authorities and to trade and public health officials at the same meeting'.[67] Abbott concludes: 'given the divergent perspectives of the various multilateral institutions, it perhaps is not surprising that their activities in respect of public health and medicine are not co-ordinated'.[68]

There has been a long-standing debate over the relationship between intellectual property rights, access to knowledge and development.[69] The UK Government commissioned a special report on the integration of intellectual property rights and development concerns.[70] Chapter 2 of the report focused on the question of public health and access to essential medicines, noting: 'for developing countries, a major concern was how the adoption of intellectual property regimes would affect their efforts to improve public health, and economic and technological development more generally, particularly if the effect of introducing patent protection was to increase the price and decrease the choice of sources of pharmaceuticals'.[71] The report recommended that developing countries should reconfigure their domestic patent laws and policies to limit the extent of patenting of pharmaceutical drugs and facilitate the introduction of generic competition. The report advocated the adoption of such measures as compulsory licensing, government or 'Crown' use, the 'Bolar exemption' and patent exhaustion, as well as the exclusion of methods of human treatment from the scope of patentable subject matter.

The 2004 Geneva Declaration on the Future of the World Intellectual Property Organization called for a fundamental reform of this UN agency to address 'a global crisis in the governance of knowledge,

[66] Frederick Abbott, 'Managing the Hydra: The Herculean Task of Ensuring Access to Essential Medicines' in Keith Maskus and Jerome Reichman (eds.), *International Public Goods and Transfer of Technology under a Globalized Intellectual Property Regime* (2005), 393–424 at 401.

[67] Ibid., 401. [68] Ibid., 402.

[69] Peter Drahos and Ruth Mayne (eds.), *Global Intellectual Property Rights: Knowledge, Access and Development* (2002).

[70] Commission on Intellectual Property Rights, *Integrating Intellectual Property Rights and Development Policy* (2002), www.iprcommission.org at 5 February 2009.

[71] Ibid., 29.

technology and culture'.[72] Of particular concern was that 'without access to essential medicines, millions suffer and die'.[73] The Geneva Declaration emphasized that there was a need for the WIPO to 'promote access to medicines for all', declaring: 'Humanity stands at a crossroads – a fork in our moral code and a test of our ability to adapt and grow.'[74] James Boyle has identified charters and declarations as having an important symbolic effect: 'the level of public and media attention paid to them indicates that intellectual property policy is now of interest beyond a narrow group of affected industries'.[75]

Various key mid-tier and developing countries, including Brazil, Argentina and India, have pushed for WIPO to adopt a Development Agenda.[76] The so-called 'Friends of Development' argued: 'The proposal that WIPO should be guided by the broader goals of the UN system is a response to and reflects recent developments in many different international forums, where it has been recognized that intellectual property protection has serious crosscutting implications for several different areas of public policy, including education, public health, nutrition, the environment, cultural diversity and the promotion of science and technological development more generally.'[77] The group noted: 'in this regard, the adoption of the Doha Declaration on the TRIPS Agreement and Public Health at the 4th Ministerial Conference of the World Trade Organization represented a crucial milestone, whereupon the international community recognized that TRIPS, as an international

72 The Geneva Declaration on the Future of the World Intellectual Property Organization 2004, www.cptech.org/ip/wipo/genevadeclaration.html at 5 February 2009. See also James Boyle, 'A Manifesto on WIPO and the Future of Intellectual Property' (2004) 9 *Duke Law and Technology Review* 1–12, www.law.duke.edu/journals/dltr/articles/pdf/2004 DLTR0009.pdf; May, *The World Intellectual Property Organization*, above n. 64; Amy Kapczynski, 'The Access to Knowledge Mobilization and the New Politics of Intellectual Property' (2008) 117 *Yale Law Journal* 804–85; Neil Weinstock Netanel (ed.) *The Development Agenda: Global Intellectual Property and Developing Countries* (2008); Daniel Gervais, (ed.), *Intellectual Property, Trade and Development: Strategies to Optimize Economic Development in a TRIPS-Plus Era* (2007); and Jeremy de Beer, (ed.) *Implementing the World Intellectual Property Organization's Development Agenda* (2009).

73 The Geneva Declaration on the Future of the World Intellectual Property Organization, above n. 72.

74 Ibid.

75 James Boyle, *The Public Domain: Enclosing the Commons of the Mind* (2008), 244.

76 The Friends of Development, 'Proposal to Establish a Development Agenda for WIPO: An Elaboration of Issues Raised in Document WO/GA/31/11', Inter-Sessional Intergovernmental Meeting on a Development Agenda for WIPO, IIM/1/4, 6 April 2005.

77 Ibid., 5.

instrument for the protection of intellectual property, should always operate in a manner supportive of the public health objectives of all countries'.[78]

In October 2007, the WIPO General Assembly adopted a series of forty-five recommendations to enhance the organization's development activities.[79] The recommendations are organized into six clusters. The first cluster relates to technical assistance and capacity building. The second cluster looks at norm-setting, flexibilities, public policy and public domain. The third cluster concerns technology transfer, information and communication technologies ('ICT') and access to knowledge. The fourth cluster concerns assessment, evaluation and impact studies. The fifth cluster concerns institutional matters including mandate and governance. The final cluster focuses upon enforcement, emphasizing the need 'to approach intellectual property enforcement in the context of broader societal interests and especially development-oriented concerns ... in accordance with Article 7 of the TRIPS Agreement'.[80]

In 2008, the Australian academic, bureaucrat and diplomat, Francis Gurry, was elected Director-General of WIPO, winning out over the Brazilian Graça Aranha in a close election. In his acceptance speech, Gurry emphasized the need to effectively implement the Development Agenda, and 'translate the political consensus into concrete and effective projects'.[81] The effective implementation of the Development Agenda – especially as it relates to concerns about public health and access to essential medicines – will be a critical test of Gurry's leadership at WIPO.

3.3 *The World Health Organization*

The World Health Organization ('WHO') aspires to realize 'the attainment by all peoples of the highest possible level of health'.[82] The organization has a mandate 'to stimulate and advance work to eradicate epidemic, endemic and other diseases', and to 'furnish appropriate

[78] Ibid., 5.

[79] World Intellectual Property Organization, *Development Agenda*, www.wipo.int/ip-development/en/agenda/.

[80] Ibid.

[81] Francis Gurry, 'WIPO's New Director General Outlines Challenges and Priorities', Geneva: World Intellectual Property Organization, 22 September 2008, www.wipo.int/about-wipo/en/dgo/dg_gurry_acceptance_speech_2008.html.

[82] The World Health Organization, www.who.int/en/; and article 1 of the World Health Organization Constitution 1946.

technical assistance and, in emergencies, necessary aid upon the request or acceptance of Governments'.[83]

The WHO has been criticized for not living up to its mandate: for being diffident and ineffectual in the debates over patent law and access to medicines.[84] In 2001, Dr Bernard Pecoul of Médecins Sans Frontières lamented: 'As the world's leading health agency, and armed with the clear mandate of recent World Health Assembly [('WHA')] resolutions, the World Health Organization can and should do much more'.[85]

Responding to concerns of the WHA in 2003,[86] the Director-General of the WHO established the Commission on Intellectual Property Rights, Innovation and Public Health in 2004. After a number of meetings, workshops and classifications, the Commission released its report on *Public Health, Innovation, and Intellectual Property Rights* in 2006.[87] The report sought to classify infectious diseases into three distinct categories. Type I diseases are 'incident in both rich and poor countries, with large numbers of vulnerable populations in each'.[88] Examples of Type I diseases are measles, hepatitis B, diabetes, cardiovascular diseases and tobacco-related illnesses.[89] Type II diseases – sometimes called 'neglected diseases' – are 'incident in both rich and poor countries, but with a substantial proportion of the cases in poor countries'.[90] The report noted: 'HIV/AIDS and tuberculosis are examples: both diseases are present in both rich and poor countries, but more than 90 per cent of cases are in the poor countries'.[91] Type III diseases – often described as 'very neglected diseases' – are those that are 'overwhelmingly or exclusively incident in developing countries, such as African sleeping sickness (trypanosomiasis) and African river blindness (onchocerciasis)'.[92] The Commission offered a number of recommendations to improve access to

[83] Article 2 of the World Health Organization Constitution 1946.

[84] Matthew Rimmer, 'The Race to Patent the SARS Virus: The TRIPS Agreement and Access to Essential Medicines' (2004) 5(2) *Melbourne Journal of International Law* 335.

[85] Médecins Sans Frontières, 'Access to Essential Medicines: Can the World Health Organization Do More?', 15 May 2001.

[86] The World Health Organization, www.who.int/intellectualproperty/en/.

[87] Commission on Intellectual Property Rights, Innovation, and Public Health, *Public Health, Innovation, and Intellectual Property Rights* (2006). For further analysis, see Kevin Outterson, 'Should Access to Medicines and TRIPS Flexibilities Be Limited to Particular Diseases?' (2008) 34 *American Journal of Law and Medicine* 279.

[88] Commission on Intellectual Property Rights, Innovation, and Public Health, above n. 87, 13.

[89] Ibid. [90] Ibid. [91] Ibid. [92] Ibid.

essential medicines (particularly focusing upon Type II and Type III diseases).

In May 2008 the WHO's Intergovernmental Working Group on Public Health, Innovation and Intellectual Property (IGWG) agreed upon a global strategy and plan of action to promote incentives for the promotion of research and development of neglected diseases.[93] Director-General of the WHO, Dr Margaret Chan, observed of the initiative:

> I am fully committed to this process and have noted your desire to move forward faster. We must make a tremendous effort. We know our incentive: the prevention of large numbers of needless deaths and suffering.[94]

The resolution summarizes the aims of the strategy thus:

> The global strategy on public health, innovation and intellectual property aims to promote new thinking on innovation and access to medicines, as well as, based on the recommendations of the CIPIH report, provide a medium-term framework for securing an enhanced and sustainable basis for needs driven essential health research and development relevant to diseases which disproportionately affect developing countries, proposing clear objectives and priorities for R&D, and estimating funding needs in this area.[95]

The *WHO Global Strategy* is animated by a number of guiding principles. First, the 'WHO shall play a strategic and central role in the relationship between public health and innovation and intellectual property within its mandates (including those contained in relevant WHA resolutions), capacities and constitutional objectives, bearing in mind those of other relevant intergovernmental organizations'.[96] Second, the *WHO Global Strategy* noted the importance of human rights: 'the enjoyment of the highest attainable standard of health is one of the fundamental rights of every human being without distinction of race, religion, political belief, economic or social condition'.[97] Third, 'the promotion of technological innovation and the transfer of technology should be pursued by all states and supported by intellectual property rights'.[98] Fourth, 'intellectual property rights do not and should not prevent Member

[93] *WHO Global Strategy*, above n. 27.
[94] World Health Organization, 'World Health Assembly Closes: Agreement Reached on Influenza Virus Sharing, Intellectual Property' (23 May 2007).
[95] Article 13 of the *WHO Global Strategy*, above n. 27.
[96] Article 15, ibid. [97] Article 16, ibid. [98] Article 19, ibid.

States from taking measures to protect public health'.[99] Fifth, 'international negotiations on issues related to intellectual property rights and health should be coherent in their approaches to the promotion of public health'.[100] Sixth, 'the strengthening of the innovative capacity of developing countries is essential to respond to the needs of public health'.[101] Seventh, 'research and development of developed countries should better reflect the health needs of developing countries'.[102] Eighth, 'intellectual property rights are an important incentive in the development of new health care products'.[103] However, it was recognized that 'this incentive alone does not meet the need for the development of new products to fight diseases where the potential paying market is small or uncertain'.[104] Ninth, 'countries should monitor carefully supply and distribution chains and procurement practices to minimize costs that could adversely influence the price of these products and devices'.[105] However, a number of principles were deleted from the draft strategy, because of a lack of consensus among the member states.[106]

The *WHO Global Strategy* has eight key elements. First, WHO seeks to 'provide an assessment of the public health needs of developing countries with respect to diseases that disproportionately affect developing countries and identify their R&D priorities at the national, regional and international levels'.[107] Second, WHO aims to 'promote R&D focusing on Type II and Type III diseases and the specific R&D needs of developing countries in relation to Type I diseases'.[108] Third, WHO seeks to 'build and improve innovative capacity for research and development, particularly in developing countries'.[109] Fourth, WHO will strive to

[99] Article 20, ibid. [100] Article 21, ibid. [101] Article 22, ibid. [102] Article 23, ibid.
[103] Article 25, ibid. [104] Article 25, ibid. [105] Article 26, ibid.
[106] There was a consensus to delete article 17, which provided that '[The right of everyone to the enjoyment of the highest attainable standard of physical and mental health is recognized [as a fundamental human right] in the international Human Rights [commitments]/[instruments], [and as a fundamental human right as recognized]/ [in particular,] in the International Covenant on Economic, Social and Cultural Rights]'. Proposed article 18 had two variations – one that 'the objectives of public health and the interests of trade should be appropriately [coordinated and mutually supportive]' or, more strongly, '[The right to health takes precedence over commercial interests.]' In the end it was deleted. The World Health Organization, *Draft Global Strategy and Plan of Action on Public Health, Innovation and Intellectual Property*, Intergovernmental Working Group on Public Health, Innovation, and Intellectual Property (3 May 2008), www.who.int/phi/documents/IGWG_Outcome_document03Maypm.pdf ('*Draft Global Strategy*').
[107] Articles 27–8 of the *WHO Global Strategy*, above n. 27. [108] Articles 29–30, ibid.
[109] Articles 31–2, ibid.

'improve, promote and accelerate transfer of technology between developed and developing countries as well as among developing countries'.[110] Fifth, WHO will 'encourage and support the application and management of intellectual property in a manner that maximizes health-related innovation, especially to meet the R&D needs of developing countries, protects public health and promotes access to medicines for all, as well as explore and implement, where appropriate, possible incentive schemes for R&D'.[111] Sixth, WHO will seek to 'improve delivery of and access to all health products and medical devices by effectively overcoming barriers to access'.[112] Seventh, WHO will aim to 'secure and enhance sustainable financing mechanisms for R&D and to develop and deliver health products and medical devices to address the health needs of developing countries'.[113] Finally, WHO will strive to 'develop mechanisms to monitor and evaluate the implementation of the strategy and plan of action, including reporting systems'.[114]

The *WHO Global Strategy* recognizes that 'the price of medicines is one of the factors that can impede access to treatment'.[115] This suggests that the aim of reducing the price of pharmaceutical drugs should be included in the global strategy. But the US Government expressed reservations on this point.[116] The question of differential pricing for pharmaceutical drugs remains a sensitive and fraught subject for commercial companies.[117]

The *WHO Global Strategy* encouraged all parties to 'explore and, where appropriate, promote a range of incentive schemes for research and development including addressing, where appropriate, the de-linkage of the costs of research and development and the price of health products, for example through the award of prizes, with the objective of addressing diseases which disproportionately affect developing countries'.[118] As part of the process of developing a global strategy, the WHO held public hearings and consultations 'to contribute to developing a solution to a major public health challenge – how to enhance innovation, research and development to address diseases predominantly

110 Articles 33–4, ibid. 111 Articles 35–6, ibid. 112 Articles 37–9, ibid.
113 Articles 40–2, ibid. 114 Articles 43–4, ibid. 115 Article 11, ibid.
116 *Draft Global Strategy*, above n. 106.
117 Patricia Danzon and Adrian Towse, 'Theory and Implementation of Differential Pricing for Pharmaceuticals', in Keith Maskus and Jerome Reichman (eds.), *International Public Goods and Transfer of Technology under a Globalized Intellectual Property Regime* (2005), 425–56.
118 Article 36(5.3) of the *WHO Global Strategy*, above n. 27.

affecting poor populations'.[119] There was extensive discussion about such possibilities as medical innovation prizes, a Health Impact Fund, patent pools, Open Source drug discovery and priority review mechanisms.[120] Some have explored the option of university licensing and technology transfer.[121] There have also been an array of comments and submissions from member states, including Bolivia, Brazil, Chile, Columbia, Costa Rica, Nicaragua, Paraguay and Cuba; as well as China, India, Malaysia, the Philippines, Qatar, Uzbekistan and Japan; Morocco; the United States and Canada.[122]

The *WHO Global Strategy* has been the target of criticism, especially from members of civil society and development organizations.[123] Tido von Schoen-Angerer, Director of Médecins Sans Frontières' Access to Essential Medicines Campaign, was disappointed by the failure of the WHO to take concrete action towards reforming the medical innovation system. He lamented that the 2008 meeting failed to agree on any tangible proposals in regard to access to medicines: 'Concrete proposals to ensure urgently needed drugs and diagnostics are developed for developing country diseases have not received support.'[124] Schoen-Angerer demanded: 'What we need to see is a wider, more ambitious framework for R&D and political leadership, in particular from WHO.'[125]

119 World Health Organization, *Report on Developments since the First Session of the Intergovernmental Working Group on Public Health, Innovation and Intellectual Property*, Summary of the Second Hearing, A/PHI/IGWG/2/INF.DOC./4 (2 November 2007), www.who.int/gb/phi/pdf/igwg2/PHI_IGWG2_ID4-en.pdf.

120 David Ridley, Henry Grabowski and Jeffrey Moe, 'Developing Drugs for Developing Countries' (2006) 25(2) *Health Affairs* 313–24; Duke University, 'Duke Faculty Propose Incentives for Developing Drugs for Neglected Diseases', Duke University, 7 March 2006; and Food and Drug Administration Amendments Act 2007 (United States).

121 Gail Evans, 'Strategic Patent Licensing for Public Research Organizations: Deploying Restriction and Reservation Clauses to Promote Medical R&D in Developing Countries' (2008) 34(2–3) *American Journal of Law and Medicine* 175–223.

122 World Health Organization, 'Member States' Comments and Inputs to the IGWG 2 Conference Paper', A/PHI/IGWG/2/Conf.Paper1/Rev.1 (Geneva: World Health Organization, January 2008), www.who.int/phi/submissions/submissions_confpaper/en/index.html.

123 Knowledge Ecology International, 'Statement of James Love, Director of Knowledge Ecology International on end of IGWG II bis' 3 May 2008, www.keionline.org/index.php?option=com_content&task=view&id=177&Itemid=1.

124 Tido von Schoen-Angerer, 'MSF Intervention at IGWG 2.2', 2008, www.accessmed-msf.org/msf-intervention-at-igwg-22/.

125 Ibid.

It is doubtful whether the WHO has the political power or will to implement any such strategies – particularly those of a more radical bent.[126] The US and the EU have thus far been successful in frustrating and 'stonewalling' attempts in the WHO to develop meaningful incentives for research and development of essential medicines.

4. Structure of the volume

This collection is divided into four sections: international trade; innovation; intellectual property; and healthcare. These sections draw upon and from international law and public law in a variety of ways, highlighting the gains from bringing together international and public law academics and policy-makers. The first section considers the debate over intellectual property and public health within international trade law. This is followed by an assessment of alternative forms of innovation, both within and without the current framework, and of whether these might provide more equitable outcomes for those suffering from diseases neglected by current research and development. The third section then considers a number of creative developments in intellectual property law and the potential that schemes such as patent pools and Open Source drug development have for addressing this crisis. The fourth section focuses more broadly on the human right to health and its correlative national and international duties to ensure all human beings have access to basic healthcare insofar as this is reasonably possible. The chapters of this final section reflect upon how international institutions, state and non-state actors have collaborated, and might further collaborate, in the context of the flexibilities and limitations present in the current system, towards realizing the human right to health.

4.1 International trade

The first four chapters consider the debate over access to essential medicines from the perspective of international trade infused with public law principles.

Rochelle C. Dreyfuss considers the establishment of the WTO and the significance of the TRIPS Agreement. She charts the requirements

126 Knowledge Ecology International, 'KEI Statement to Resumed IGWG II bis', 1 May 2008.

that the TRIPS Agreement imposes regarding patent law and pharmaceutical drugs. Focusing on the example of India, Dreyfuss considers the flexibilities and the limitations of the current regime. She suggests that the TRIPS Agreement is inhospitable to the dynamic nature of intellectual property and the demands for development and technology transfer. Dreyfuss argues that the TRIPS Council could better utilize the expertise of WIPO, WHO and other international institutions. Such collaborations could help make the international system much more responsive to the healthcare needs of human beings worldwide. Dreyfuss contends that, unless norms for global governance are established and implemented, this comparative disadvantage will continue to grow.

Andrew Mitchell and Tania Voon consider the debate over whether there should a formal amendment to the TRIPS Agreement to facilitate the export of pharmaceutical drugs for the benefit of least-developed and developing countries. The authors reflect upon the steps taken within the WTO to resolve the tension between patent law and public health concerns. They explain why WTO members sought to reform the TRIPS Agreement through the implementation of the Doha Declaration and the WTO General Council Decision of the 30 August 2003 and consider whether the TRIPS Waiver will receive sufficient support from WTO members. Mitchell and Voon contend that WTO members need to re-evaluate their commitment to affordable medicines and test the efficacy of the TRIPS Waiver before making it permanent. The authors also consider the interaction between the TRIPS Waiver, bilateral free trade agreements and regional patent systems emphasizing the international and domestic overlay.

Hitoshi Nasu considers the impact of a number of US bilateral free trade agreements – so-called TRIPS-Plus agreements – upon access to essential medicines. Drawing creatively from public law theory, he argues that such bilateral free trade agreements ultimately result in democratic deficit, normative fragmentation and regulatory failure.

Finally, Elizabeth Siew-Kuan Ng considers the debate over access to essential medicines in light of the broader development concerns by WIPO. She highlights the need to persevere with the quest to strike a delicate balance between protecting inventions to encourage innovation and investment, and ensuring that such protection does not stifle further innovation and access to medicine for public health. Ng argues that selected avenues of reform, especially compulsory licensing, may in fact play a bigger role in addressing these issues.

4.2 Innovation

The second part of this collection evaluates some of the key initiatives and proposals towards improving access to essential medicines – such as a Health Impact Fund, medical innovation prizes and a health technology safety and effectiveness treaty, which have both international and domestic consequences.

Thomas Pogge contends that by pricing advanced medicines beyond the reach of the poor and encouraging neglect of diseases concentrated among them, the TRIPS Agreement is responsible for avoidable death and disease on a massive scale.[127] Pharmaceutical patents as globalized through the TRIPS Agreement cannot be defended by appeal to natural rights. Nor can they be justified in terms of mutual benefit or usefulness, because the global poor are deprived of their freedom to buy medicines at competitive prices yet often cannot benefit from the enhanced arsenal of advanced medicines. One way of mitigating the injustice involves the creation of a Health Impact Fund ('HIF'), an international agency that would provide a standing option to register any new medicine for health impact rewards. By registering, a firm would agree to sell its product globally at a price fixed by the HIF at the lowest feasible cost of production and distribution. In exchange, the firm would receive for a fixed time payments based on this product's assessed global health impact. If adequately funded, the HIF would serve as a complement to the patent regime by alleviating its deficiencies. In particular, the HIF would generate a stream of pharmaceutical innovations that would be cheaply available to all and would end the systemic research neglect of diseases concentrated among the poor.

Kathleen Liddell takes Pogge's proposed HIF and examines it in light of the current patent system and past lessons from international patent law.[128] In the spirit of constructive criticism, she expresses a number of reservations about the system. Liddell suggests there are unresolved tensions in the relationship between the HIF and patent law. She expresses fears that the HIF could be co-opted or captured by pharmaceutical drug companies. Liddell wonders whether there is sufficient empirical evidence to justify a reform of this magnitude. She hopes,

[127] For a broader discussion of the Health Impact Fund model, see Aidan Hollis and Thomas Pogge, *The Health Impact Fund: Making New Medicines Available for All* (2008), www.yale.edu/macmillan/igh/hif_book.pdf.

[128] Cf. also Aidan Hollis, 'The Health Impact Fund: A Useful Supplement to the Patent System?' (2008) 1 *Public Health Ethics* 124–33.

though, that the architects of the HIF will be able to address and resolve such concerns in future iterations of the model.

William W. Fisher and Talha Syed from Harvard Law School provide a critical evaluation of an alternative model of research and development – prizes for medical innovation.[129] The authors suggest that a prize system has several virtues: it could avoid the drawbacks of the patent system, provide superior information to governments on the social benefits of particular innovations and reduce socially wasteful expenditure by pharmaceutical firms. Fisher and Syed recognize that prize systems have potential disadvantages as well. In particular, such schemes could result in an inefficient diminution in labour, lead to opportunistic 'rent-seeking' behaviour, discourage sequential innovation and increase government costs. Fisher and Syed have sought to devise an optimal prize system, which capitalizes on the potential advantages and minimizes the potential hazards of such a scheme.[130]

Thomas Faunce explores the value, in the context of current global policy debates about health technology innovation, of a WTO–WHO Agreement on Health Technology Safety and Cost-Effectiveness Evaluation ('HTSCEE Agreement'). Building on the models provided by the Australian Pharmaceutical Benefits Scheme ('PBS') and the scientific evidence-based exceptions to the Agreement on the Application of Sanitary and Phytosanitary Measures ('the SPS Agreement'), he discusses how the HTSCEE Agreement would interact with the operation of WTO Dispute Settlement Organs ('DSOs') to demonstrate that the WTO focus on reducing barriers to trade is compatible with support for regulatory regimes designed to ensure that trade in health technologies does not unreasonably harm the public interest. Faunce explores the strengths and weaknesses of a WTO–WHO HTSCEE Agreement against the UN treaty approach, which he had previously advocated in this area.[131]

[129] This chapter is part of a larger research project. See also William W. Fisher and Talha Syed, 'Global Justice in Health Care: Developing Drugs for the Developing World' (2007) 40 *University of California Davis Law Review* 581; and William W. Fisher and Talha Syed, *Drugs, Law, and the Health Crisis in the Developing World* (2010, forthcoming).

[130] For other models of medical innovation prizes, see Joseph Stiglitz, 'Scrooge and Intellectual Property Rights: A Medical Prize Fund Could Improve the Financing of Drug Innovations' (2006) 333 *British Medical Journal* 1279–80; James Love and Tim Hubbard, 'The Big Idea: Prizes to Stimulate R&D for New Medicines' (2007) 82(3) *Chicago-Kent Law Review* 1519–54; and Knowledge Ecology International, 'Selected Innovation Prizes and Reward Programs', *KEI Research Note 1*, 7 March 2008, www.keionline.org/misc-docs/research_notes/kei_rn_2008_1.pdf at 10 March 2009.

[131] See also Faunce, *Who Owns our Health?*, above n. 51.

4.3 *Intellectual property*

There has also been much interest in debates over whether intellectual property law can offer creative solutions to the problems posed by access to essential medicines.

Dianne Nicol and Jane Nielsen consider the use of industry-based mechanisms, such as patent pools,[132] in three stages of the public health innovation cycle: discovery, development and delivery. The benefit of these mechanisms is that they may engender greater commitment on the part of industry than involuntary, 'top down' regulation. Nonetheless, the authors recognize that patent pools also have certain risks – such as failing to provide a return on investment and exacerbating competition problems. Nicol and Nielsen conclude that patent pools focusing upon the delivery phase – such as a pool for HIV/AIDS combination medicines – have the greatest promise. The authors are doubtful that a broader international framework for managing multiple patent pools, dealing with a variety of infectious diseases, could easily be established.

The chapter by Nicol and Nielsen is particularly topical, given that Andrew Witty, the Chief Executive Officer of GlaxoSmithKline, has proposed a Least Developed Country Patent Pool for medicines for neglected tropical diseases.[133] Some argue that such a proposal does not go far enough. Brook Baker of Health GAP contends: 'The Glaxo announcement is illusory largely because its publicity, at least with respect to access to existing medicines, far outweighs its effect.'[134] He stresses: 'Although Glaxo remains in discussions with the UNITAID patent pool on the idea of donating its HIV/AIDS medicines, it has not yet committed to allowing follow-on innovation for these life-saving medicines.'[135]

[132] UNITAID, 'Eighth Board Meeting: UNITAID Moves toward a Patent Pool for Medicines' (2–3 July 2008), www.unitaid.eu/en/Eighth-Board-Meeting-Geneva-2-3-July-2008.html at 10 March 2009; and Knowledge Ecology International, 'Cost Benefit Analysis of UNITAID Patent Pool', 20 June 2008, www.keionline.org/misc-docs/1/cost_benefit_UNITAID_patent_pool.pdf.

[133] Andrew Witty, 'Big Pharma as a Catalyst for Change', Harvard Medical School, 13 February 2009, www.gsk.com/media/Witty-Harvard-Speech-Summary.pdf.

[134] Brook Baker, 'GSK Access to Medicines: The Good, the Bad, and the Illusory', *Intellectual Property Health List*, 15 February 2009.

[135] Ibid. See also Christian Barry and Matt Peterson, 'Shallow Cuts: GSK's Voluntary Price Reductions and Patent Pooling Are Not Enough', *Policy Innovations* (4 March 2009), www.policyinnovations.org/ideas/commentary/data/000113.

Krishna Ravi Srinivas considers whether Open Source drug discovery has the potential to address the twin problems of innovation and access. Using India's experience in implementing the Open Source Drug Discovery Project as a starting point he examines the potential benefits and problems of such a scheme. He contends that, although it may make sense for the WHO to talk in terms of Type I, II and III diseases, the time has come to go beyond these categories: to address the cross-cutting problems of innovation and access on a global scale and to examine alternatives to the patent system. While the patent system may yet have a place in providing incentives for innovation there needs to be an examination of alternative mechanisms and ideas for the stimulation of creative solutions.[136]

Charles Lawson and Barbara Hocking address the development of the WHO's arrangements for accessing viruses and the development of vaccines to respond to potential pandemics (and other lesser outbreaks) following Indonesia's challenge to the existing access and benefit sharing arrangements for 'its' H5N1 viruses. Their chapter examines the ongoing 'conflict' between the United Nations' Convention on Biological Diversity (CBD) and the WTO's TRIPS Agreement in the context of debates about the paramountcy of intellectual property and the potential for other policy imperatives to override respect for intellectual property and the TRIPS Agreement.

Matthew Rimmer examines the use of trademarks and celebrity endorsements to promote greater access to essential medicines. He focuses upon the role played by charities, philanthropists and foundations – notably the (RED) Campaign, the Gates Foundation and the Clinton Foundation. Rimmer is particularly interested in the credos of 'creative capitalism', a term that has been promoted and popularized by Bill Gates.[137] This

[136] For further literature on Open Source drug discovery, see Yochai Benkler, *The Wealth of Networks: How Social Production Transforms Markets and Freedom* (2006), 344–6; Amy Kapczynski, Samantha Chaifetz, Zachary Katz and Yochai Benkler, 'Addressing Global Health Inequities: An Open Licensing Approach for University Innovations' (2005) 20 *Berkeley Technology Law Journal* 1031; Stephen Maurer, Arti Rai and Andrej Sali, 'Finding Cures for Tropical Diseases: Is Open Source an Answer?' (2004) 1(3) *Public Library of Science, Medicine* 183; Stephen Maurer, 'Open Source Drug Discovery: Finding a Niche (or Maybe Several)' (2007) 76(2) *University of Missouri at Kansas City Law Review* 405–34; Don Tapscott and Anthony Williams, *Wikinomics: How Mass Collaboration Changes Everything* (2006); and Janet Hope, *BioBazaar: Biotechnology and the Open Source Revolution* (2008).

[137] Michael Kinsley (ed.), *Creative Capitalism: A Conversation with Bill Gates, Warren Buffett and Other Economic Leaders* (2008).

ideology encourages corporations to engage in commercial activities, which may help solve global inequities, especially in healthcare. The (RED) Campaign, the Gates Foundation and the Clinton Foundation are exemplars of 'creative capitalism'. Rimmer notes the influence and power of such marketing campaigns. He questions, though, the transparency, accountability and sustainability (common concerns of public lawyers) of such philanthropic campaigns. He suggests that, notwithstanding the development of such alternative models, there remains a need for substantive reform of the existing patent system.

4.4 *Healthcare*

The final section of the volume considers how the debate over access to essential medicines has been framed in terms of international human rights discourse about the right to health. In several case studies, it considers the clash between patent rights and the right to health, as understood both in constitutional law, a key foundation of public law, and in international law. Heinz Klug suggests that asserting a human rights perspective is helpful to understanding the debate over access to essential medicines: 'Instead of relying on thin strands of legal flexibility, NGOs, international organizations, countries and governments attempting to address the global HIV/AIDS pandemic should promote a human rights-based interpretation that places public health ahead of economic claims.'[138]

Noah Novogrodsky begins the section with an analysis of the role of non-state actors in the struggle for access to essential medicines.[139] While previous chapters discuss the regulations and actions of international and state institutions, Novogrodsky explores the role of NGOs in the debate over access to essential medicines in the context of HIV/AIDS. He suggests that, in the future, the influence of NGOs will be defined by direct action and the development of new ideas rather than by the quality of advice provided to country delegations.

Katharine Young explores how the human rights discourse on the right to health can challenge a 'user fee' system of healthcare, when

[138] Heinz Klug, 'Access to Essential Medicines – Promoting Human Rights Over Free Trade and Intellectual Property Claims', in Keith Maskus and Jerome Reichman (eds.), *International Public Goods and Transfer of Technology under a Globalized Intellectual Property Regime* (2005), 481–92, 492.

[139] See also Stephen Lewis, *Race against Time* (2005); and AIDS-Free World, www.aids-freeworld.org/.

embedded in a concrete and critical legal praxis. First, Young considers, in particular, the exceptional role played by the Treatment Action Campaign.[140] In South Africa, thirty-nine pharmaceutical drug companies complained that government regulations violated the TRIPS Agreement and constitutional protections for the right of property.[141] In response, the South African Government argued that the legislation complied with relevant international treaties and adequately protected the constitutionally enshrined right to health. Led by the brilliant activist, Zachie Achmat, the Treatment Action Campaign intervened in the dispute as an *amicus curiae*, and led a spirited media campaign against the actions of the pharmaceutical drug companies. Second, Young examines the *Zakari* case in Ghana, in which a patient was detained in a hospital until he had paid the fees associated with his care. In response to the case, the Legal Resources Centre brought a habeas corpus action, based on the constitutional protection of personal liberty from arbitrary incarceration at the hands of the state. The non-governmental organization also sought additional remedies flowing from the state's infringement of Mr Zakari's right to health. Young suggests that the two cases provide lessons for health rights movements elsewhere, by focusing attention on the aspects of praxis that force an encounter between 'aspirational' norms and other legal rights.

Rajshree Chandra looks at another country with constitutional protection for the right to health – India – and a 2006 patent claim over Glivec, a drug used for leukaemia. Novartis had been granted exclusive marketing rights in 2003, which curbed the production of generics and effectively meant that, both in India and abroad, treatment had to be withdrawn from patients unable to afford the drug. When the patent claim was made three years later, the Chennai Patent Office rejected Novartis's claim on the basis that the application failed to meet the requirements of patentability under section 3(d) of the Patents Act 1970 (India), as amended by the Patents (Amendment) Act 2005

[140] See also Helen Watchirs, *Measuring Legal Implementation of International Human Rights Norms in the Context of HIV/AIDS* (2001).

[141] *The Pharmaceutical Manufacturers' Association of South Africa* v. *Government of South Africa*, Notice of Motion, above n. 37. See also Kara Bombach, 'Can South Africa Fight AIDS? Reconciling the South African Medicines and Related Substances Act with the TRIPS Agreement' (2001) 19(2) *Boston University International Law Journal* 273; and Mark Heywood, 'Debunking "Conglomo-talk": A Case Study of the Amicus Curiae as an Instrument for Advocacy, Investigation and Mobilisation' (2001) 5(2) *Law, Democracy and Development* 133.

(India). This was upheld in the High Court of Judicature at Madras. This decision means that generic manufacturers may manufacture and sell the drug at a dramatically reduced price. This precedent has implications not only for Indian citizens, but also for the rest of the world, given its reliance on India for the supply of generic medicines.

Finally, Jonathon Burton-MacLeod considers the recent controversies in Thailand over compulsory licensing of patented pharmaceutical drugs. The Government of Thailand invoked the flexibilities under article 31 of the TRIPS Agreement to provide access to the HIV/AIDS drugs, Efavirenz and Kaletra, and the heart-disease drug, Plavix. Burton-MacLeod suggests that the dispute raised important questions about the subtleties of article 31 of the TRIPS Agreement. The author explores the diverse responses to the actions of the Government of Thailand. He notes that Brazil emulated the example of Thailand by engaging in compulsory licensing in respect of Efavirenz, that the European Commission and the European Parliament equivocated over the dispute, and that the United States Trade Representative and Abbott Laboratories responded with aggressive threats of sanctions and boycotts. As Burton-MacLeod shows, the dispute over Thailand's compulsory licensing represents new territory for both international trade law and intellectual property law.

5. Conclusion

The failure of international and domestic regimes to provide adequate medicines and healthcare, especially in developing countries, is currently a high-profile issue, with serious and far-reaching implications.

This collection on patent law and access to essential medicines is particularly timely given the concern about a pandemic in respect of influenza A (H1N1) – colloquially known as 'swine flu'.[142] Michelle Childs, the Director of Policy and Advocacy at Médecins Sans Frontières' Campaign for Access to Essential Medicines, has warned:

> If a pandemic were to occur, the test of global solidarity will be whether there is a focus on developing countries who would likely be hit worst, since they would be the least prepared. The production of generic

[142] World Health Organization, 'Influenza A (H1N1)', www.who.int/csr/disease/swineflu/en/index.html at 18 June 2009; and Médecins Sans Frontières, 'Generics and Access to Influenza Treatment' (7 May 2009), www.msfaccess.org/main/access-patents/generics-and-access-to-influenza-treatment/.

> versions of influenza medicines will be crucial to ensure these countries can not only get hold of these drugs but also at an affordable price. Rich countries cannot just buy their way out at the expense of developing countries.[143]

In this context, our volume offers a range of creative ideas for overcoming the impediments to access to essential medicines so as better to address public health concerns, including influenza A (H1N1). In examining how the international regime has worked in interaction with national healthcare regimes, by bringing public and international lawyers together, the volume addresses how the system might be reformed into a more effective global framework in which no human beings – whatever their financial situation or geographic location – must suffer or die from preventable disease.

[143] Ibid.

PART I

International trade

1

TRIPS and essential medicines: must one size fit all? Making the WTO responsive to the global health crisis

ROCHELLE C. DREYFUSS*

1. Introduction

The establishment of the World Trade Organization ('WTO') marked an important new chapter in the administration of patent law, especially regarding inventions in the medical arena. Although intellectual property protection has long been governed by international norms,[1] the principal international instrument on patents – the Paris Convention for the Protection of Industrial Property – largely focused on procedural issues.[2] It required each state to accord national treatment to the citizens of other signatories, but it left most details on the scope and the substance of patent rights to the domestic law of each of its members.[3] While many countries provided plenary protection to pharmaceutical products in order to stimulate their discovery, others took the position that medicines were too important to their citizens' welfare to privatize.

In 1994, that regime was significantly modified. Intellectual property, now conceptualized as a trade issue, became the subject of a new international instrument, the Agreement on Trade-Related Aspects of

* I would like to thank Thomas Pogge, Matthew Rimmer and Kim Rubenstein for focusing me on this issue; Graeme Dinwoodie, Andreas Lowenfeld and Louise Teitz for their helpful comments on a precursor to this article; and the Filomen D'Agostino and Max E. Greenberg Research Fund for its financial support.

[1] See, e.g., Berne Convention for the Protection of Literary and Artistic Works, opened for signature 9 September 1886, 1161 UNTS 3 (entered into force 29 January 1970).

[2] Paris Convention for the Protection of Industrial Property, opened for signature 20 March 1883, 21 UST 1583 (entered into force 26 April 1970) ('Paris Convention').

[3] Paris Convention, above n. 2, article 2. One exception is article 5, which restricts the ability of member states to order compulsory licensing for failure to work the patent.

Intellectual Property Rights ('TRIPS Agreement' or 'TRIPS').[4] Under the WTO framework, adherence to TRIPS is not only required of every WTO member,[5] it is also enforceable through the WTO's elaborate Understanding on Dispute Settlement ('DSU'), an essentially adjudicative mechanism, administered by the Dispute Settlement Board ('DSB'), complete with an Appellate Body to entertain appeals from Panel decisions and sanctions for non-compliance.[6] Because TRIPS imposes substantive patent law standards, including a requirement that protection be accorded 'in all fields of technology',[7] it is no longer possible for a WTO member to exclude medicines from the purview of protection.

While the WTO is certainly a boon to any country seeking large foreign markets for its products, observers have been extremely concerned about TRIPS' 'one size fits all' aspect, which ignores the heterogeneity of the world's population and especially the problems that confront developing nations.[8] Because these countries generally do not innovate at world levels, patents have highly adverse distributive consequences for them.[9] Specifically, while the patents mandated by TRIPS may enhance incentives to engage in medical research, they shift wealth from developing nations to the developed economies that are the source of most pharmacological advances. In effect, patents act as a tax, putting treatment beyond the reach of all but the richest of the world's populace.

The key question, however, is whether the TRIPS Agreement is *necessarily* a one size fits all system. As a formal matter, the Agreement is a

[4] Marrakesh Agreement Establishing the World Trade Organization, opened for signature 15 April 1994, 1867 UNTS 3, annex 1C (Agreement on Trade-Related Aspects of Intellectual Property Rights) (entered into force 1 January 1995) ('TRIPS Agreement').

[5] Marrakesh Agreement Establishing the World Trade Organization, opened for signature 15 April 1994, 1867 UNTS3 (entered into force 1 January 1995), article II(2) ('Marrakesh Agreement').

[6] Marrakesh Agreement Establishing the World Trade Organization, opened for signature 15 April 1994, 1867 UNTS 3, annex 2 (Understanding on Rules and Procedures Governing the Settlement of Disputes) (entered into force on 1 January 1995) ('DSU').

[7] TRIPS Agreement, above n. 4, article 27(1).

[8] See, e.g., Elizabeth Siew-Kuan Ng, 'Global Health and Development: Patents and Public Interest', in Thomas Pogge, Matthew Rimmer and Kim Rubenstein (eds.), *Incentives for Global Public Health: Patent Law and Access to Essential Medicines* (2010), 101.

[9] See generally Jerome Reichman and Rochelle C. Dreyfuss, 'Harmonization without Consensus: Critical Reflections on Drafting a Substantive Patent Law Treaty' (2007) 57 *Duke Law Journal* 85; cf. Margaret Chon, 'Intellectual Property and the Development Divide' (2006) 27 *Cardozo Law Review* 2821 (discussing the education problem posed by copyrighted materials).

minimum standards regime, which (in theory) gives members freedom to tailor their laws to their individual circumstances.[10] Furthermore, TRIPS' statement of Principles and Objectives acknowledges the importance of balancing interests, promoting social welfare and protecting public health.[11] While it is true that to date, outcomes in the DSB have tended to straitjacket member states and create fodder for the 'one size fits all' critique,[12] adjudicators currently lack judicially manageable standards for converting the aspirations articulated in TRIPS' Principles and Objectives provisions into concrete legislative safeguards for public interest concerns.[13]

But there are reasons to believe that the situation is susceptible to change. Emerging economies, such as India, South Africa and Brazil, are becoming far more sophisticated about their intellectual property needs. In the latest series of trade negotiations (the Doha Round), a coalition among these countries, less-developed economies, and an increasingly proactive set of non-governmental organizations ('NGOs'),[14] provoked the adoption of the Doha Declaration, which made a significant change to the TRIPS Agreement as it pertains to healthcare.[15] And more can be expected. Countries in the developed world are now confronting novel technologies, such as synthetic biology, genomics and bioinformatics. As they cope with the problem of applying a legal regime developed during the Industrial Age to the advances of the Knowledge Economy, they too

[10] See, e.g., TRIPS Agreement, above n. 4, articles 30, 31, 41(5).

[11] Ibid., articles 7, 8.

[12] See, e.g., Graeme Dinwoodie and Rochelle C. Dreyfuss, 'Intellectual Property Law and the Public Domain of Science' (2004) 7 *Journal of International Economic Law* 431; Graeme Dinwoodie and Rochelle C. Dreyfuss, 'TRIPS and the Dynamics of International Property Lawmaking' (2004) 36 *Case Western Reserve Journal of International Law* 95.

[13] Rochelle C. Dreyfuss and Andreas Lowenfeld, 'Two Achievements of the Uruguay Round: Putting TRIPS and Dispute Settlement Together' (1997) 37 *Virginia Journal of International Law* 275; Rochelle C. Dreyfuss, 'Regulating Dynamic Innovation in a Complex Political Economy: Administering Intellectual Property on the International Stage' (New Delhi, 5–6 January 2008).

[14] See, e.g., Noah Novogrodsky, 'Beyond TRIPS: The Role of Non-State Actors and Access to Essential Medicines', in Thomas Pogge, Matthew Rimmer and Kim Rubenstein (eds.), *Incentives for Global Public Health: Patent Law and Access to Essential Medicines* (2010), 343. Examples of such organizations include Intellectual Property Watch, ip-watch.org/index.php?res= 1024&print= 0; Médecins Sans Frontiéres ('MSF'), Campaign for Access to Essential Medicines, www.accessmed-msf.org/index.asp; and Knowledge Ecology International ('KEI') www.keionline.org/index.php?option=com_frontpage&Itemid=1.

[15] See Ministerial Declaration: Adopted on 14 November 2001, WTO Doc WT/MIN(01)/DEC/1 (2001); Declaration on the TRIPS Agreement and Public Health: Adopted on 14 November 2001, WTO Doc WT/MIN(01)/DEC/2 (2001) ('the Doha Declaration').

are beginning to feel TRIPS' pinch.[16] As important, observers have become concerned about the legitimacy of WTO law-making more generally.[17] With new approaches for making the WTO accountable, transparent and democratic, it should become easier to correct the shortcomings in the TRIPS Agreement.

Section 2 of this chapter describes the requirements the TRIPS Agreement imposes regarding patent protection. Using an example drawn from India's new patent law,[18] it demonstrates the Agreement's capacity to accommodate diverse interests as well as the weaknesses in the current regime. Section 3 takes up the question of how to make that international system more responsive to the healthcare needs of the global community. It suggests that the the TRIPS Council, which was created to administer the TRIPS Agreement,[19] could better utilize the expertise of the World Intellectual Property Organization ('WIPO'), the World Health Organization ('WHO') and other institutions that deal with issues of intellectual property, development, health and human rights.

Even if fully effectuated, the suggestions in section 3 will not completely alleviate the global health crisis. TRIPS can certainly be altered to improve access to *existing* medicines. However, patent law relies in a fundamental way on the market to fuel innovation. Thus, it cannot create incentives to meet the needs of populations too poor to provide the level of profits that technological entrepreneurs seek. For neglected diseases, like malaria and dengue fever, it is necessary to devise an entirely new incentive structure, such as the one advanced by Thomas Pogge in this

[16] See, e.g., James Bessen and Michael Meurer, *Patent Failure: How Judges, Bureaucrats and Lawyers Put Innovators at Risk* (2008); Ségolène Aymé, Gert Matthijs and Sirpa Sioni, 'Patenting and Licensing in Genetic Testing' (2008) 16 *European Journal of Human Genetics* 53; Reichman and Dreyfuss, 'Harmonization Without Consensus', above n. 9.

[17] See, e.g., Daniel C. Esty, 'Good Governance at the Supranational Scale: Globalizing Administrative Law' (2006) 115 *Yale Law Journal* 1490. See also Claude Barfield, *Free Trade, Sovereignty, Democracy: The Future of the World Trade Organization* (2001); Tomer Broude, *International Governance in the WTO: Judicial Boundaries and Political Capitulation* (2004).

[18] Patents Act 1970 (India) s. 3(d). This provision is set out and its application more fully explored in Rajshree Chandra, 'The Role of National laws in Reconciling Constitutional Right to Health with TRIPS Obligations: An Examination of the Glivec Patent Case in India', in Thomas Pogge, Matthew Rimmer and Kim Rubenstein (eds.), *Incentives for Global Public Health: Patent Law and Access to Essential Medicines* (2010), 381.

[19] TRIPS Agreement, above n.4, article 68 (charging the Council with the duty to monitor the operation of the Agreement, provide a forum for consultations regarding compliance, and to 'carry out such other responsibilities as assigned to it by the Members' of the WTO).

volume.[20] This chapter also comments on the compatibility of some of these proposals with TRIPS.

2. TRIPS: substantive standards and their interpretation

As noted in the introduction to this chapter, adherence to TRIPS is now required of all WTO members. As a result, any country that wants the benefit of large markets for its output is obliged to protect creative products, even if it is a net importer of intellectual materials. These obligations are enforceable: any member claiming to be affected by another state's failure to abide by TRIPS can file a complaint with the DSB. Although the process begins with consultations aimed at finding a diplomatic solution, a dissatisfied complainant can move to a more adjudicatory procedure, including a hearing before an ad hoc Panel with the possibility of review by the Appellate Body. Reports (be they of a Panel or the Appellate Body) can be blocked only by a consensus of the WTO membership. If the respondent loses, then it must comply by changing its law or by paying compensation. Otherwise, the complainant can retaliate with trade sanctions, either in the intellectual property sector or in another area covered by the WTO Agreement.[21]

At first blush, the requirements regarding technological protection appear quite stringent. With some exceptions, a patent must be available for advances that are 'new', involve 'an inventive step' and are 'capable of industrial application'.[22] States are not permitted to discriminate by field of technology or by place of invention.[23] Patents must subsist for at least twenty years,[24] and they must confer the exclusive right to prevent others from making, using, selling, offering to sell or importing the claimed invention.[25] In addition, the Agreement requires members to protect secret information

[20] Thomas Pogge, 'The Health Impact Fund: Better Pharmaceutical Innovations at Much Lower Prices', in Thomas Pogge, Matthew Rimmer and Kim Rubenstein (eds.), *Incentives for Global Public Health: Patent Law and Access to Essential Medicines* (2010), 135. See also Matthew Rimmer, 'The Lazarus Effect: The (RED) Campaign and Creative Capitalism', in Thomas Pogge, Matthew Rimmer and Kim Rubenstein (eds.), *Incentives for Global Public Health: Patent Law and Access to Essential Medicines* (2010), 313; and Krishna Ravi Srinivas, 'Open Source Drug Discovery: A Revolutionary Paradigm or a Utopian Model?', in Thomas Pogge, Matthew Rimmer and Kim Rubenstein (eds.), *Incentives for Global Public Health: Patent Law and Access to Essential Medicines* (2010), 263.

[21] For a complete discussion of dispute settlement, see Andreas Lowenfeld, *International Economic Law* (2nd edn, 2008) 161.

[22] TRIPS Agreement, above n. 4, article 27(1).

[23] Ibid., article 27(1). [24] Ibid., article 33. [25] Ibid., article 28.

from disclosure 'in a manner contrary to honest commercial practices'[26] and to protect data about drugs submitted to obtain pre-market clearance 'against unfair commercial use'.[27]

On closer inspection, however, it is possible to discern why TRIPS is denominated a minimum standards regime. For patents, the Agreement does not define how high the inventive step must be, what comprises an industrial application or what constitutes making, using, selling, offering to sell or importing. Most important, the patent provisions contain two general exceptions, along with several more focused provisions.[28] The first of these exemptions allows members to award compulsory licences if they comply with a series of requirements designed to balance the interest in use against the rights of the patent holder.[29] (Most troubling at the inception of TRIPS, this included the requirement that any government authorized use must be 'predominantly for the supply of [its own] domestic market';[30] it was that provision which was altered by the Doha Declaration). The second exemption consists of a three-part test allowing members to make 'exceptions to the rights conferred' so long as they are (1) 'limited', (2) 'do not unreasonably conflict with normal exploitation of the patent' and (3) do not 'unreasonably prejudice the legitimate interests of the patent holder, taking account of the legitimate interests of third parties'.[31] As to data, the Agreement does not include general exceptions – but it also does not define the kinds of commercial uses that are unfair or the types of business practices that are not considered honest.[32]

In theory, these lacunae leave ample room for members to craft laws suited to their own situations. An innovative provision in India's new patent law furnishes an example of the sort of latitude that members arguably enjoy. Section 3(d) of the Patents Act 1970 (India) uses the freedom to define 'invention' and 'inventive step', to render unpatentable

[26] Ibid., article 39(2). [27] Ibid., article 39(3).

[28] The specific exceptions include inventions needed to protect public order, morality, health and the environment, article 27(2); diagnostic, therapeutic and surgical methods, article 27(3)(a); as well as plants and animals, article 27(3)(b).

[29] TRIPS Agreement, above n. 4, article 31. [30] Ibid., article 31(f). [31] Ibid., article 30.

[32] In addition, the Agreement gave less-developed countries more time in which to comply with the requirements: TRIPS Agreement, above n. 4, articles 65–6. These time periods have been extended, see Extension of the Transition Period under Article 66.1 of the TRIPS Agreement for Least-Developed Country Members for Certain Obligations with Respect to Pharmaceutical Products, WTO Doc IP/C/25 (2005) (Decision by the Council for TRIPS of 27 June 2002); Extension of the Transition Period under Article 66.1 for Least-Developed Country Members, WTO Doc IP/C/40 (2005) (Decision of the Council for TRIPS of 29 November 2005).

any 'new form of a known substance which does not result in the enhancement of the known efficacy' as well as any 'new use for a known substance'.[33] The statute includes an explanation which provides, in part, that 'salts, ... metabolites, ... combinations and other derivatives of known substances shall be considered to be the same substance, unless they differ significantly in properties with regard to efficacy'.

This provision has many salutary benefits for India. Most obviously, it prevents evergreening: a drug company cannot extend patent protection on a drug beyond an initial twenty-year term by simply patenting a new form of the identical substance. For pharmaceuticals, it also means that if a known medicine is found, after its patent expires, to treat another disease – for example, to treat a neglected disease – the new treatment might remain in the public domain, where it can be freely advertised for its new application and distributed to patients suffering from that disease. The provision may also enable formulations that improve public access to be released into the public domain. Depending on how the Indian courts interpret 'efficacy', it may not be possible to patent formulations that do no more than reduce the need for refrigeration, offer easier methods of administration or are better targeted to the genetic make-up of the Indian population.[34]

Admittedly, if new uses and formulations are, indeed, unpatentable, the major players in the pharmaceutical sector will lack incentives to discover them. But even here, the provision could work to India's advantage. With lower operating costs and expectations for profit, Indian pharmaceutical companies are uniquely positioned to conduct the required research.[35] India would thus benefit from what Jerry Riechman calls 'fair following' – the ability to push its workforce to the technological frontier by giving it the opportunity to engage in significant incremental innovation.[36] Along those lines, India could go even further. It could define 'using' the patented invention to include only commercial uses, which would allow research scientists to look for new

[33] Patents Act 1970 (India) s. 3(d).

[34] See Shamnad Basheer and Prashant Reddy, 'The "Efficacy" of Indian Patent Law: Ironing Out the Creases in Section 3(d)' (2008) 5 *Script-ed* 232, www.law.ed.ac.uk/ahrc/script-ed/vol5-2/basheer.asp at 15 January 2009.

[35] See David Opderbeck, 'Patents, Essential Medicines, and the Innovation Game' (2005) 58 *Vanderbilt Law Review* 501 (noting that Indian drug companies have not institutionalized the 'blockbuster model' of working on drugs only if there is the potential for considerable return).

[36] See generally Jerome Reichman, 'From Free Riders to Fair Followers: Global Competition Under the TRIPS Agreement' (1997) 29 *New York University Journal of International Law and Politics* 11.

applications of a patented medicine during its term of protection. Similarly, it could decide that it is not 'unfair commercial use' to permit researchers to examine pre-market clearance data for clues to new uses and formulations. The benefits of a robust research programme in India would, of course, extend well beyond India's borders, to all countries suffering from diseases that are neglected by the companies that focus on 'blockbusters'.

But despite India's apparent freedom to structure patent law to meet its needs, it is clear why TRIPS is perceived as a one size fits all system. Indeed, the pharmaceutical company Novartis is already claiming that India's law violates the Agreement and there is reason to believe that DSB adjudicators will be sympathetic to its claim.[37] Thus, in a study that Graeme Dinwoodie and I conducted in 2005–7, we found that, in the cases decided up to that time,[38] adjudicators tended to approach decisions from an almost purely trade perspective. They looked at patent law as a method for commodifying information (for, essentially, creating new trading chips), rather than through the prism of intellectual property theory, where the dynamic nature of intellectual production would focus more attention on the balance between user and producer interests. Wary of any measure that permits 'leakage' – that lets opportunities seep out of the control of the rights holder – decision-makers significantly limited the flexibilities allegedly built into the Agreement.[39]

[37] *Novartis* v. *Union of India* (2007) (6 August 2007, High Court of Judicature at Madras for W.P. Nos. 24759 and 24760 of 2006), judis.nic.in/chennai/qrydisp.asp?tfnm= 11121.

[38] The six TRIPS cases are: *India – Patent Protection for Pharmaceutical and Agricultural Chemical Products*, WTO Doc WT/DS50/AB/R, AB-1997–5 (1997) (Report of the Appellate Body) ('*India – Pharmaceuticals*'); *Canada – Term of Patent Protection*, WTO Doc WT/DS170/AB/R, AB-2000–7 (2000) (Report of the Appellate Body); *Canada – Patent Protection of Pharmaceutical Products: Arbitration under Article 21.3(c) of the Understanding on Rules and Procedures Governing the Settlement of Disputes*, WTO Doc WT/DS114/R (2000) (Award of the Arbitrator James Bacchus) ('*Canada – Pharmaceuticals*'); *United States – Section 110(5) of US Copyright Act: Request for the Establishment of a Panel by the European Communities and their Member States*, WTO Doc WT/DS160/R, 70 (2000) ('*US – 110(5)*'); *United States – Omnibus Appropriations Act of 1998*, WTO Doc WT/DS176/AB/R, AB-2001–7 (2001) (Report of the Appellate Body); *European Communities – Protection of Trademarks and Geographic Indications for Agricultural Products and Foodstuffs*, WTO Doc WT/DS174/R (2005) (Report of the Panel) ('*EC – GI*'). Technically, there were seven disputes as both the United States and the European Communities brought an *India – Pharmaceuticals* challenge.

[39] See Dinwoodie and Dreyfuss, 'Intellectual Property Law and the Public Domain of Science', above n. 12; Graeme Dinwoodie and Rochelle C. Dreyfuss, 'Diversifying without Discriminating: Complying with the Mandates of the TRIPS Agreement' (2007) 13 *Michigan Telecommunication and Technology Law Review* 445. Since that study, one

The cases involving the three-part exceptions tests are good examples of the current approach. WTO panellists have now had three opportunities to interpret these tests. In *Canada – Pharmaceuticals*,[40] they examined the three-part exceptions test described above to decide whether Canada could allow generic drug makers to conduct bioequivalence testing during the patent period and to stockpile drugs during the last six months prior to patent expiration. In *US – 110(5)*, they looked at the closely related copyright exceptions test[41] to determine whether the US could permit small establishments to play broadcast music without authorization. And in the *EC – GI* case, which involved a somewhat differently worded trademark exceptions test,[42] the issue was the relationship between geographic indications and trademarks using geographic terms. In each of these cases, certain exceptions were permitted. But others were rejected and the reasoning of all three cases casts considerable doubt on the leeway that countries have to tailor their laws.

First, the parts of the tests were construed as cumulative. Since each subtest was interpreted as distinct from the others, a measure that runs foul of any one of them will be rejected, even if it fares well under the others. For instance, once the Panel decided that Canada's stockpiling exception was not *limited*, it never reached the *interests of third parties*, such as patients eager for low-cost medicines. As a result, no matter how compelling a state's interest is, it cannot compensate for intruding on right-holder prerogatives. Second, the Panels largely ignored the Agreement's Principles and Objectives, on the theory that taking them into account would amount to a renegotiation of the Agreement. Third, although the tests use language like 'normal exploitation', 'legitimate interests' and 'unreasonably prejudice', which appears to invite normative interpretation, the adjudicators looked at the terms mechanically – they counted the number of rights and ignored their value to right holders. The adjudicators' views were also heavily influenced by domestic

new case was decided: *China – Measures Affecting the Protection and Enforcement of Intellectual Property Rights*, WT/DS362/R (26 January 2009). It was somewhat more deferential to national autonomy interests. However, the TRIPS Agreement clearly requires more deference regarding obligations on enforcement, see, e.g., article 41.5 (providing that the enforcement part of the TRIPS Agreement 'does not create any obligation to put in place a judicial system for the enforcement of intellectual property rights distinct from that for the enforcement of law in general ...'). Thus, the case does not clearly suggest a change in the DSB's perspective.

40 *Canada – Pharmaceuticals*, above n. 38.

41 TRIPS Agreement, above n. 4, article 13.

42 Ibid., article 17.

legislation that existed when TRIPS was negotiated. While that permitted the *Canada – Pharmaceuticals* Panel to approve the exception for bioequivalence testing, which is found in other countries' laws, the approach privileges long-standing exceptions built into the laws of developed countries, while making new exceptions, uniquely tailored to the needs of developing countries, appear suspicious.

In *Canada – Pharmaceuticals*, the complainant also argued that bioequivalence testing violated the bar on technological discrimination. Although, in the end, the Panel rejected the complaint, it did so only because it thought that Canada was not targeting pharmaceuticals and would handle any product that required pre-market testing in the same way. In fact, the adjudicators treated the provision as structural, as the equivalent of the National Treatment and Most Favoured Nation obligations, which require nations to treat the nationals of all members of the WTO equivalently and constitute the core of any free trade regime. They therefore held that even de facto discrimination is actionable and refused to allow Canada to use the three-part exceptions test to excuse it. Because there are not many actions that can be classified as both 'limited' enough to qualify as an allowable exception and even-handed enough to be considered non-discriminatory, it is difficult to imagine any significant approach to healthcare delivery that would survive this scrutiny.

The methodology employed by these Panels – mechanistic interpretation drawing on laws pre-dating TRIPS – could put into jeopardy many of the proposed strategies for dealing with the global health crisis. India's new provision is a case in point. True, it relies on raising the inventive step, which TRIPS does not define. However, adjudicators might look at *existing* patent laws to inform their decision on what a member is required to classify as 'inventive'. Since many developed countries do award patents on second uses,[43] the DSB could decide that India is not fully meeting its obligation to offer patents on 'inventions'. Furthermore, although the text of the Indian measure is carefully drafted to apply to all substances, the accompanying explanation mentions salts, derivatives, and – crucially – metabolites, which suggests that India meant to single out pharmaceuticals for special (i.e. discriminatory) treatment.

[43] See *Actavis UK Ltd* v. *Merck & Co. Inc.*, [2008] EWCA Civ 444; Susy Frankel, 'A Patentable Invention: Will Current Proposed Law Reform Clarify Patentable Subject Matter?' (2005) *New Zealand Business Law Quarterly* 350 (discussing recognition of so-called 'Swiss claims'). See also Richard Castellano 'Patent Law for New Medical Uses of Known Compounds and Pfizer's Viagra Patent' (2006) 46 *IDEA* 283.

Adjudicators might also be suspicious of the extensions proposed above regarding the utilization of patented substances and pre-clearance data for research purposes. The DSB may be unwilling to accept an interpretation of 'using' that leads to an experimental use exception broader than the exceptions found in developed countries. Furthermore, the ban on making normative judgments would probably constrain the evaluation of terms like '*unfair* commercial use' or '*honest* business practices'.

Proposals for dealing with the neglected disease problem, such as the ideas suggested by Yochai Benkler and his collaborators,[44] Geertrui Van Overwalle,[45] David Opderbeck[46] or Jenny Lanjouw,[47] are equally vulnerable. Because these approaches tap the patent profits earned in the lucrative drug markets of the developed world to provide funding for research on the diseases that plague less-developed countries, they arguably interfere with patent holders' legitimate interests in WTO-wide protection. Of course, these exceptions to patent rights would help patients, but the last prong of the exceptions test would never be reached under the cumulative analysis used by the Panels. Thomas Pogge's approach is more defensible because it gives innovators the option of utilizing the current market-based patent system or forgoing monopoly pricing and earning returns through a newly created Health Impact Fund. However, even this approach could be challenged. Once one firm opts for Health Impact Fund returns, its discoveries will be available at marginal cost. For advances that treat the same disease, that availability could depress the profits that can be earned under the patent system.

There are other ways in which the TRIPS Agreement is inhospitable to the dynamic nature of intellectual property values and the problems of development. The transition periods afforded to the least-developed countries are far too short; the promises made for technology transfer are proving to be illusory.[48] As the circumstances leading to the Doha Declaration demonstrated, the trade hands who drafted the Agreement

[44] Amy Kapczynski *et al.*, 'Addressing Global Health Inequities: An Open Licensing Approach for University Innovations' (2005) 20 *Berkeley Technology Law Journal* 1031.

[45] Geertrui Van Overwalle, 'Reconciling Patent Policies and University Mission' (2006) 13 *Ethical Perspectives* 234.

[46] Opderbeck, 'Patents, Essential Medicines, and Innovation Game', above n. 35.

[47] Jean Lanjouw, 'A New Global Patent Regime for Diseases: U.S. and International Legal Issues' (2002) 16 *Harvard Journal of Law and Technology* 85.

[48] See Commission on Intellectual Property Rights, *Integrating Intellectual Property Rights and Development Policy* (2002) 28–30, www.iprcommission.org at 5 February 2009; Frederick M. Abbott, 'Intellectual Property Rights in a Global Trade Framework: IP Trends in Developing Countries' (2004) 98 *American Society of International Law and*

displayed a poor understanding of the impact that TRIPS requirements would have on countries that have little capacity to produce technology or to craft laws that support the growth of a technology sector.

3. Reconceptualizing TRIPS

Arguably, patience is the best strategy for making TRIPS more responsive to public access interests. Although the DSU takes an adjudicative approach to dispute resolution, as a formal matter, decisions do not have *stare decisis* effect.[49] Accordingly, the trade dominated, mechanical outcomes described in section 2 may not endure; they may not even be used were section 3(d) of the Patents Act (India) challenged. For one, the disputes that are most meaningful in terms of healthcare issues – the cases on the exceptions tests and in particular, *Canada – Pharmaceuticals* – were decided by ad hoc Panels and were not reviewed by the Appellate Body. Since the Appellate Body is a permanent institution, with members appointed for specified terms, it can be expected to be more sympathetic to overarching policy matters, to pay greater attention to issues of continuity and to be more wary of the adverse consequences that might flow from overly strict, and distributively unjust, interpretations of the Agreement.

Furthermore, most of the cases decided so far have involved developed nations as both complainants and respondents. In these disputes, neither side had a strong interest in pressing the public interest-regarding aspects of the Agreement. For example, none of the cases involving the exceptions tests were appealed – perhaps because even the losing parties wanted to avoid an overly generous interpretation of TRIPS' flexibilities. Significantly, the two cases that did not involve developed countries – first, a case

Procedure 95; Gregory Shaffer, *Defending Interests: Public Private Partnerships in W.T.O. Litigation* (2003). In addition, the US continues to put countries it believes to be violating its intellectual property interests on watch lists and uses bilateral agreements to achieve 'TRIPS-Plus' concessions. See Andrew Mitchell and Tania Voon, 'The TRIPS Waiver as a Recognition of Public Health Concerns in the WTO', in Thomas Pogge, Matthew Rimmer and Kim Rubenstein (eds.), *Incentives for Global Public Health: Patent Law and Access to Essential Medicines* (2010), 56; and Hitoshi Nasu, 'Public Law Challenges to the Regulation of Pharmaceutical Patents in the US Bilateral Free Trade Agreements', in Thomas Pogge, Matthew Rimmer and Kim Rubenstein (eds.), *Incentives for Global Public Health: Patent Law and Access to Essential Medicines* (2010), 77.

49 Cf. DSU, above n. 6, article 3(2); Marrakesh Agreement, above n. 5, noting that the DSU cannot change the obligations of the parties and only a Ministerial Conference or the General Council can render authoritative interpretations of the agreements.

involving India and more recently, a case involving China,[50] challenge the actions of emerging economies at the cusp of development. It may be that developed countries understand that it is too early to challenge what developing countries are doing. Or perhaps they are concerned that adjudicators will interpret TRIPS quite differently if a developing country, whose long-term goal is to instantiate a more flexible view, were to make a strong case for tempering trade values with interests grounded in intellectual property law or human rights concerns.[51]

It is also important to consider the broader political context in which WTO adjudicators are operating. Aside from the changes made in the compulsory licensing provision, the Doha Round has failed.[52] The members' inability to reach consensus on any of the issues raised means that adjudicators face a legitimacy problem: if they reach the wrong result on a given question, there is little hope that the decision will be corrected by the membership as a whole.[53] Without a functioning 'legislature' (that is, the General Council of the WTO), adjudicators may think that the best course is to adhere to literal, formalistic constructions and to eschew normative visions. Were the WTO law-making system functioning properly, adjudicators might be more adventurous.

Of course, if the WTO were functioning properly, patience would not necessarily be the best strategy. Now that the shortcomings of TRIPS are well-recognized, the better approach may be to change the Agreement or its interpretation. In that way, countries that wish to experiment with new ways to encourage innovation in the medical sector could do so

[50] See above nn. 38 and 39. India was the subject of a complaint concerning adherence to transition rules; China was challenged on its adherence to TRIPS' enforcement obligations.

[51] For examples of arguments grounded in human rights: see Katharine Young, 'Securing Health through Rights', in Thomas Pogge, Matthew Rimmer and Kim Rubenstein (eds.), *Incentives for Global Public Health: Patent Law and Access to Essential Medicines* (2010), 357.

[52] Robert Wolfe, 'Decision-Making and Transparency in the "Medieval" WTO: Does the Sutherland Report Have the Right Prescription?' (2005) 8 *Journal of International Economic Law* 631.

[53] See, e.g., Richard Steinberg, 'Judicial Lawmaking at the WTO: Discursive Constitutional and Political Constraints' (2004) 98 *American Journal of International Law* 247, 254; Claus-Dieter Ehlerman and Lothar Ehring, 'The Authoritative Interpretation Under Article IX:2 of the Agreement Establishing the World Trade Organization: Current Law, Practice and Possible Improvements' (2005) 8 *Journal of International Economic Law* 803 ('Authoritative Interpretation'); Claus-Dieter Ehlerman and Lothar Ehring, 'Decision-Making in the World Trade Organization' (2005) 8 *Journal of International Economic Law* 51. See also above n. 17.

without worrying that their actions would be challenged in the WTO. In fact, the WTO framework can be viewed as accommodating this approach. As noted earlier, the WTO Agreement created the TRIPS Council to administer the Agreement – to monitor compliance, conduct negotiations on issues left open when the WTO was established and carry out assignments made to it by WTO members.[54] Taken as a whole, these activities effectively create a forum for reconciling divergent views of TRIPS obligations, formulating norms and devising judicially manageable standards.[55]

There are, however, problems with relying on the Council to elucidate the meaning of the TRIPS Agreement. The line between 'interpretation' and 'modification' is illusive; under current procedures, any construction that makes an actual change in the Agreement would require a vote of the TRIPS Council, followed by a vote of the General Council. Since, under current procedures, both Councils operate by consensus, states interested in maximum protection could veto proposals to relax the standards.[56] At the same time, however, dissatisfaction with the current stalemate is producing a growing interest in the other voting options set out in the WTO Agreement. The 'authoritative interpretation' approach, which would permit the General Council to adopt by a three quarters vote, an interpretation recommendation by the TRIPS Council,[57] would be particularly helpful in the context of TRIPS. It could be used to impart meaning to terms like 'legitimate', 'unreasonable' and 'normal' and to clarify the relationships among provisions, such as among the subparts of the exceptions tests and between the exceptions tests and the provision barring technological discrimination.

As important is the question whether the TRIPS Council can manage to relinquish the trade perspective that has animated both the drafting and interpretation of the Agreement and begin, instead, to grapple with the complex problems presented by the confluence of strengthened

[54] Marrakesh Agreement, above n. 5; TRIPS Agreement, above n. 4, article 68. For example, the Council was called upon to implement the Doha Declaration. For further discussion, see Dreyfuss, 'Regulating Dynamic Innovation', above n. 13.

[55] See generally Kal Raustiala, 'Compliance and Effectiveness in International Regulatory Cooperation' (2000) 32 *Case Western Reserve Journal of International Law* 387, 434–8.

[56] Daniel Gervais, *The TRIPS Agreement: Drafting History and Analysis* (2nd edn, 2003), 359 (noting that although the Council has the power to set its own internal rules, it generally operates by consensus); Marrakesh Agreement, above n. 5, article IX setting out decision-making rules of the General Council.

[57] Ibid., article IX, especially IX(2); Ehlermann and Ehring, 'Authoritative Interpretation', above n. 53.

intellectual property rights, development needs and the global health crisis. An early draft of TRIPS contemplated the creation of an Expert Group to advise what was then called the 'Committee on TRIPS' on the non-trade issues that it would be likely to encounter. Although that proposal was rejected,[58] the Agreement permits the Council to 'consult with and seek information from any source it deems appropriate' to carry out its obligations.[59] The Council has not, however, made particularly good use of this power. Its meetings are held in secret and it gives only observer status to other intergovernmental organizations;[60] NGOs are not permitted to attend.[61] The WTO Agreement does, however, require the TRIPS Council to work with WIPO and in 1995, the two agreed 'to establish a mutually supportive relationship'.[62]

In many ways, WIPO, a specialized agency of the UN, is a perfect partner for the Council. WIPO was established in 1970 as the successor of the United International Bureaux for the Protection of Intellectual Property ('BIRPI'), which was founded in 1893 to administer the major multilateral intellectual property instruments.[63] Currently, WIPO administers upwards of twenty multilateral intellectual property conventions. Not only does it have extensive experience in the field, its governance structure is highly conducive to experimentation. It uses a voting procedure that requires less than unanimity, and does its work through small standing committees, which routinely monitor the creative environment, identify emerging

[58] Negotiating Group on Trade-Related Aspects of Intellectual Property Rights, Including Trade in Counterfeit Goods, *Status of Work in the Negotiating Group: Chairman's Report to the GNG*, GATT Doc MTN.GNG/NG11/W/76 (23 July 1990); Gervais, *The TRIPS Agreement*, above n. 56, 358.

[59] TRIPS Agreement, above n. 4, article 68.

[60] Cf Esty, 'Good Governance at the Supranational Scale', above n. 17, 1544.

[61] A sense of Council meetings can be gleaned from its annual reports, meeting minutes, working documents and decisions, available at www.wto.org/english/tratop_e/trips_e/intel6_e.htm. For example, the 2006 Annual Report indicates that the Council has granted regular observer status to the OECD, UNCTAD and WIPO: World Trade Organization *Annual Report (2006) of the Council for TRIPS*, WTO Doc IP/C/44 (2006).

[62] TRIPS Agreement, above n. 4, articles 63, 68; Agreement between the World Intellectual Property Organization and the World Trade Organization, WIPO Doc WO030 (22 December 1995) preamble, www.wipo.int/treaties/en/agreement/pdf/trtdocs_wo030.pdf at 16 January 2009.

[63] Convention Establishing the World Intellectual Property Organization, opened for signature 14 July 1967, 848 UNTS 3 (entered into force 26 April 1970) ('WIPO Convention'). For further discussion, see Dreyfuss, 'Regulating Dynamic Innovation', above n. 13.

issues and make concrete proposals.[64] For example, the Standing Committee on the Law of Patents recently issued a report on the state of international patent law. Significantly, the report outlined many of the issues explored in this volume, including the need for flexibility in dealing with developing countries, the use of prize funds and other alternatives for encouraging research on neglected diseases, and the possibility of developing a new instrument on medical research and development.[65] Since its inception, WIPO has been immersed in development issues.[66] Currently, it is engaged in an ambitious 'Development Agenda', designed to consider the relationship between intellectual property protection and the UN Millennium Development Goals and to help implement the development-oriented provisions of the TRIPS Agreement, including operationalizing TRIPS' Principles and Objectives.[67]

Admittedly, using WIPO as the TRIPS Council's expert adviser is not without its problems. The Convention establishing WIPO states that the organization's primary goal is to 'promote the protection of intellectual property throughout the world', and many of its actions suggest that it is endeavouring to increase – rather than decrease – patent obligations.[68] Furthermore, much of its earlier work on development was largely regarded as a failure.[69] Still, there is reason to think that WIPO's

[64] That said, the preference (at least among some members) is for consensus, cf. Peter Drahos, 'An Alternative Framework for the Global Regulation of Intellectual Property Rights' (2005) 21(4) *Journal Für Entwicklungspolitik* 44.

[65] Standing Committee on the Law of Patents, *Report on the International Patent System*, 12th sess, WIPO Doc SCP/12/3 (2008), 127, 172, 286 www.wipo.int/edocs/mdocs/scp/en/scp_12/scp_12_3.pdf at 19 January 2008.

[66] See Debora Halbert, 'The World Intellectual Property Organization: Past, Present and Future' (2007) 54 *Journal Copyright Society USA* 253, 262.

[67] See, e.g., Argentina and Brazil, *Proposal by Argentina and Brazil for the Establishment of a Development Agenda for WIPO*, 31st (15th extraordinary) sess, WIPO Doc WO/GA/31/11 Add (27 August 2004); World Intellectual Property Organization, *Draft Agenda, Provisional Committee on Proposals Related to a WIPO Development Agenda*, 4th sess, WIPO Doc PCDA/4/1 Prov. (2007) ('*PCDA*').

[68] WIPO Convention, above n. 63, especially the preamble and articles 3–4. See also Halbert, 'The World Intellectual Property Organization', above n. 66, 263–4, 270 (noting that WIPO persists in suggesting to developing countries that they adopt developed nations' approaches to intellectual property). WIPO is also working on a substantive patent law treaty that would further limit flexibilities and exacerbate distributive injustices, see Reichman and Dreyfuss, 'Harmonization without Consensus' above n. 9. It also hopes to commodify even more information, including folklore and traditional knowledge, see *PCDA*, above n. 67, annex, 11, 18.

[69] See, e.g., Ruth Okediji, 'The International Relations of Intellectual Property: Narratives of Developing Country Participation in the Global Intellectual Property System' (2003) 7

involvement could be highly beneficial. Now that the WTO has taken the lead in international intellectual property law-making, WIPO has been left somewhat bereft of purpose; its embrace of the Development Agenda can be understood as a search for a new role. More important, the stark dichotomy within WIPO's membership is dissolving. Earlier negotiations were characterized by tense debate between the developed and developing world. But that polarization has abated now that there are emerging economies – composed of nations such as India, China, South Africa and Brazil – that are reaping benefits from protecting intellectual property, yet continue to struggle with many of the problems strong protection poses to development.[70] Indeed, it is already clear that outcomes are changing as coalitions form among emerging economies, developing countries, the many new NGOs that have entered the fray and the various sectors in the developed world that find strong protection incompatible with their interests.[71]

But there are other significant problems. First, because the membership of WIPO and the WTO are not coextensive, there is no straightforward way to incorporate WIPO's insights into the administration of TRIPS. One idea is to use a procedure found in some of the other WTO agreements, which permits DSB adjudicators to utilize principles set out by expert international bodies, such as the Codex Alimentarius Commission or the International Standards Organization.[72] If a similar approach were taken with intellectual property, WIPO could, for example, set out best practices for nations to utilize when they wish to adopt exceptions or award compulsory licences; these practices could then be used as a defence to a WTO challenge.

Singapore Journal of International and Comparative Law 315, 327; Chon, 'Intellectual Property and the Development Divide', above n. 9.

70 See, e.g., Debra Steger, 'The Culture of the WTO: Why it Needs to Change' (2007) 10 *Journal of International Economic Law* 483, 483 (describing China, Brazil and India as converting the bi-polar North/South trading system into one that is multi-polar).

71 See, e.g., Jerome Reichman and Pamela Samuelson, 'Intellectual Property Rights in Data' (1997) 50 *Vanderbuilt Law Review* 51, 99–100, 100 fn 214. The Doha Declaration is also an example of the power of such coalitions.

72 See Joel Trachtman, 'The Constitutions of the WTO' (2006) 17 *European Journal of International Law* 623, 638–9 (citing the *European Communities – Trade Description of Sardines*, WTO Doc WT/DS231/AB/R, AB-2002-3 (2002) (Report of the Appellate Body), adopting Codex Alimentarius rules in a case involving the Marrakesh Agreement Establishing the World Trade Organization, opened for signature 15 April 1994, 1867 UNTS 3, annex 1A (Agreement on Technical Barriers to Trade) (entered into force 1 January 1995) ('TBT').

Unfortunately, however, TRIPS' references to WIPO are not on the same footing as references to non-WTO intergovernmental organizations found in other framework agreements. The Technical Barriers to Trade Agreement, for example, explicitly envisions the development of international standards by non-WTO bodies and even directs members to use them.[73] In contrast, the TRIPS Agreement is highly specific about which parts of the WIPO instruments are incorporated into the Agreement and which are subject to the DSU.[74] Similarly, the agreement between WIPO and the WTO is largely confined to securing transparency and providing technical assistance to WTO members. Although there may be instances in which procedures approved by WIPO would be considered illustrative of the terms of the TRIPS Agreement,[75] wholesale adoption of WIPO interpretations could be thought to 'diminish the rights and obligations provided in the covered agreements', in violation of the DSU.[76]

Nonetheless, there are several ways that WIPO developments could be incorporated into TRIPS. WIPO's identification of TRIPS flexibilities could be regarded as guidance on what laws WTO members can permissibly enact.[77] Once members move on these recommendations, the legislation would arguably qualify as 'a subsequent practice' that establishes the meaning of the Agreement.[78] Alternatively, a formal procedure for importing WIPO guidance could be developed. For example, TRIPS could be amended to expand WIPO's role in interpretation. The system as a whole would then retain its basic structure, but so long as WIPO continues to operate by majority vote, there would be more flexibility to respond to changing circumstances. If, however, nations are reluctant to

[73] TBT, above n. 72, article 2(4)

[74] See, e.g., TRIPS Agreement, above n. 4, arts 9, 14, 16, 22, 39.

[75] See, e.g., *US – 110(5)*, above n. 38, 6.69 ('[S]ubsequent developments [such as the WIPO Copyright Treaty ('WCT')] may be of rather limited relevance in the light of the general rules of interpretation as embodied in the Vienna Convention [on the Law of Treaties]. However, in our view, the wording of the WCT … nonetheless supports … that the Berne Union members are permitted to provide minor exceptions to the rights provided …').

[76] DSU, above n. 6, article 3(2).

[77] See, e.g., World Intellectual Property Organization, *Advice on Flexibilities Under the TRIPS Agreement*, www.wipo.int/ip-development/en/legislative_assistance/advice_trips.html at 16 January 2009.

[78] Vienna Convention on the Law of Treaties, opened for signature 23 May 1969, 1155 UNTS 331 (entered into force 27 January 1980), article 31(3)(b). *Canada – Pharmaceuticals*, above n. 38, may, however, cast doubt on this approach because the Panel rejected Canada's claim that other members' exemptions for regulatory review drug testing constituted a subsequent practice for interpretive purposes: 7.42.

bet on the direction in which WIPO will move, a less formal relationship may be preferred. If so, the WTO could alter the agreement between WIPO and the TRIPS Council to expand the range of issues they consider jointly. The TRIPS Council could then be given the task of bringing desirable modifications to the attention of the General Council.[79]

A second problem with WIPO is that it does not have particular expertise in health issues or human rights. If the WTO were to find a way of bringing WIPO's input to bear on the interpretation and administration of the TRIPS Agreement, the WTO should consider adopting similar arrangements with other organizations. As noted earlier, the WTO already relies on the Codex Alimentarius, which was developed by the WHO (in co-operation with the Food and Agriculture Organization ('FAO')).[80] Further collaboration with WHO would have many advantages. Also a specialized agency of the UN, WHO was created in 1948 'to promote and protect the health of all peoples'.[81] In addition to its work on sanitary conditions, it has authority to adopt regulations on a variety of other matters, including public health practices and standards for international diagnostic procedures.[82] Like WIPO, it operates with a flexible voting procedure. It also regularly works with other international organizations, including the UN's Committee on Economic, Social and Cultural Rights ('CESCR'), with overlapping interests in healthcare.[83] As Thomas Faunce's chapter in this volume suggests, there are many open questions in TRIPS to which WHO could make valuable contributions.[84] Similarly, there is burgeoning case law and commentary on the relationship between intellectual

[79] A similar suggestion was proposed by Ernst-Ulrich Petersmann, 'Challenges to the Legitimacy and Efficiency of the World Trading System: Democratic Governance and Competition Culture in the WTO' (2004) 7 *Journal of International Economic Law* 585, 601.

[80] See Codex Alimentarius, available at www.codexalimentarius.net/web/index_en.jsp.

[81] World Health Organization Constitution, preamble. [82] Ibid., article 21.

[83] Ibid., articles 18, 19. See generally Wolfgang Hein and Lars Kohlmorgan, 'Global Health Governance: Conflicts on Global Social Rights' (2008) 8 *Global Health Policy* 80.

[84] Thomas Faunce, 'Innovation and Insufficient Evidence: The Case for a WTO – WHO Agreement on Health Technology Safety and Cost-Effectiveness Evaluation', in Thomas Pogge, Matthew Rimmer and Kim Rubenstein (eds.), *Incentives for Global Public Health: Patent Law and Access to Essential Medicines* (2010), 209. WHO has also studied questions regarding data exclusivity and other problems at the intersection of TRIPS and health, see *Global Strategy and Plan of Action on Public Health, Innovation and Intellectual Property*, World Health Assembly 61st mtg, Res WHA61.21 (2008) ('*WHO Global Strategy*').

property rights and human rights,[85] as well as other human rights organizations that could offer valuable input. Formalizing a role for institutions with related jurisdiction and capacities would address another problem with which the international community is struggling, namely the propensity of nations and interest groups to play international organizations off against each other through 'regime shifting'.[86]

There are other developments afoot that may also help reverse the adverse effects that the TRIPS Agreement has had on the global health crisis. There are now several organizations that are trying to turn TRIPS into less of a one size fits all regime. In the professoriate, there is increasing discussion of countering the minimum standards in TRIPS with maximum limits on the enforcement of intellectual property rights.[87] On the copyright side, the Open Society Institute is proposing limitations and exceptions to TRIPS' rights that are drawn from intellectual property, human rights, competition and consumer law;[88] an analogous effort is underway at the Max Planck and Queen Mary Institutes.[89] Although private parties and NGOs may have trouble attracting the attention of the WTO or the TRIPS Council, some of the emerging economies – particularly Chile on behalf of Asian Pacific Economic Cooperation members ('APEC') – appear to be taking a leading role.[90]

[85] See, e.g., *Anheuser-Busch Inc.* v. *Portugal* (10 October 2005) App No 73049/01 Eur Court HR. See generally, Laurence Helfer, 'Toward a Human Rights Framework for Intellectual Property' (2007) 40 *University of California Davis Law Review* 971.

[86] See Eyal Benvenisti and George Downs, 'The Empire's New Clothes: Political Economy and the Fragmentation of International Law' (2007) 60 *Stanford Law Review* 595; Laurence Helfer, 'Regime Shifting: The TRIPS Agreement and New Dynamics of International Intellectual Property Lawmaking' (2004) 29 *Yale Journal of International Law* 1.

[87] See, e.g., Graeme Dinwoodie, 'The International Intellectual Property Law System: New Actors, New Institutions, New Sources' (2004) 8 *Proceedings of the 98th Annual Meeting of the American Society of International Law* 213, 219; Rochelle C. Dreyfuss, 'TRIPS – Round II: Should Users Strike Back?' (2004) 71 *University of Chicago Law Review* 21; Marianne Levin and Annette Kur, *Towards More Balanced, User-Friendly Paradigms in IP Law: A Project Reform of TRIPS* (Special Session at the Annual Meeting of the International Association for the Advancement of Teaching and Research in Intellectual Property, 5 September 2006).

[88] P. Bernt Hugenholtz and Ruth L. Okediji, *Conceiving an International Instrument on Limitations and Exceptions to Copyright: Final Report* (2008), www.ivir.nl/publications/hugenholtz/limitations_exceptions_copyright.pdf at 16 January 2009.

[89] See Christophe Geiger, Jonathan Griffiths and Reto Hilty, 'Towards a Balanced Interpretation of the "Three-Step Test" in Copyright Law' (2008) 30(12) *European Intellectual Property Review* 489.

[90] *Chile – IPEG Survey on Copyright Limitations and Exceptions: Preliminary Report on Copyright Limitations and Exceptions*, APEC Doc 2008/SOM1/IPEG/007 (2008).

Furthermore, growing interest in global administrative law has made intergovernmental organizations more aware of their transparency and accountability obligations.[91] As this regulatory movement grows, so too will the opportunity to incorporate concerns about global health and human rights values into TRIPS law-making.

4. Conclusion

The decision to conceptualize intellectual property as a trade issue has complicated the problem of keeping the world's population healthy. While patent obligations may enhance the potential profits available to innovators and thus encourage medical research, TRIPS raises prices in developing countries and puts the benefits of this research out of the reach of many. Furthermore, by focusing attention on patents as the sole incentive system, TRIPS virtually assures that diseases uniquely afflicting the poor will be neglected.

TRIPS need not, however, be construed as a one size fits all regime. In fact, considerable 'wiggle room' was built into its fabric. For member states, the trick is to find ways to implement these flexibilities and tailor the law to local needs. For the WTO, the goal should be greater sensitivity to human rights and, specifically, to the public-access values that are embedded in traditional intellectual property law. As countries like India start developing novel approaches to patent law, as WIPO and the WTO embark on their development agendas, as WHO's influence becomes more salient and NGOs find ways to influence the international law-making process, the trade perspective is likely to recede.

[91] See, e.g., Benedict Kingsbury, Nico Krisch and Richard Stewart, 'The Emergence of Global Administrative Law' (2005) 68 *Law and Contemporary Problems* 15.

2

The TRIPS Waiver as a recognition of public health concerns in the WTO*

ANDREW D. MITCHELL AND TANIA VOON

1. Introduction

Patent protection for pharmaceutical products as mandated in the Agreement on Trade-Related Aspects of Intellectual Property Rights ('TRIPS Agreement' or 'TRIPS')[1] of the World Trade Organization ('WTO') represents a potentially significant obstacle to public health measures, particularly for developing countries seeking to import medicines to deal with serious public health concerns, such as the HIV/AIDS crisis. Since 2001, WTO members have acknowledged this tension while working slowly towards a formal amendment of WTO rules that would facilitate compulsory licensing of pharmaceuticals for the benefit of least-developed country ('LDC') members, as well as other members lacking sufficient manufacturing capacity to use the existing flexibilities in the TRIPS Agreement in respect of public health. As the first shipment of drugs from Canada to Rwanda under the new arrangements has recently taken place (in September 2008),[2] we take the opportunity to reflect on the steps taken to date within the WTO to resolve the patent/public health tension.

In section 2, we explain why WTO members needed to reform the TRIPS Agreement in order to improve access to medicines for public health reasons, before turning in section 3 to the temporary solution

* This chapter is derived from a larger work appearing as Andrew D. Mitchell and Tania Voon, 'Patents and Public Health in the WTO, FTAs and Beyond: Tension and Conflict in International Law' (2009) 43(3) *Journal of World Trade* 571. The authors thank Elizabeth Sheargold for her expert research and editorial assistance. Any errors and the opinions expressed here are ours.

[1] Marrakesh Agreement Establishing the World Trade Organization, opened for signature 15 April 1994, 1867 UNTS 3, annex 1C (Agreement on Trade-Related Aspects of Intellectual Property Rights) (entered into force 1 January 1995) ('TRIPS Agreement').

[2] Staff Writer, 'First Generic Drugs En Route to Africa under 5-Year-Old WTO Deal' (2008) 12(31) *Bridges Weekly Trade News Digest* 5.

reached in the form of a waiver of certain TRIPS obligations. In section 4 we then consider the more permanent solution of a formal amendment that is envisaged for the future. This chapter then turns in section 5 to consider how the waiver has been used in practice. This section demonstrates that the waiver remains underutilized, suggesting that members need to re-evaluate their commitment to affordable medicines and test the workability of the waiver before making it permanent. Finally, in section 6 we examine the additional limited exceptions to patent protection granted in the waiver for bilateral free trade agreements and regional patent systems.[3] However, we conclude that the potential of this use of the waiver is also not being realized.

2. The need for reform of the TRIPS Agreement

In this section, we examine why the TRIPS Agreement as originally drafted made it difficult for some developing countries to gain access to affordable medicines to deal with public health emergencies.

2.1 Objectives and principles of the TRIPS Agreement

The preamble to the TRIPS Agreement recognizes 'the underlying public policy objectives of national systems for the protection of intellectual property, including developmental and technological objectives'. At the same time, a number of other public policy objectives may need to be reconciled with the rights and obligations contained in the TRIPS Agreement, and public health is one of these. The TRIPS Agreement expressly acknowledges these competing interests, highlighting in article 7 the need to protect and enforce intellectual property rights 'in a manner conducive to social and economic welfare'. Specifically as regards public health, article 8.1 sets out the following principle:

> Members may, in formulating or amending their laws and regulations, adopt measures necessary to protect *public health and nutrition* ... provided that such measures are consistent with the provisions of this Agreement.[4]

[3] The related issue of how some preferential trade agreements, particularly those involving the United States, are being used to extend patent protections and diminish the flexibilities of the TRIPS Agreement is considered in Hitoshi Nasu, 'Public Law Challenges to the Regulation of Pharmaceutical Patents in the US Bilateral Free Trade Agreements', in Thomas Pogge, Matthew Rimmer and Kim Rubenstein (eds.), *Incentives for Global Public Health: Patent Law and Access to Essential Medicines* (2010), 77.

[4] Emphasis added.

Articles 7 and 8 of the TRIPS Agreement could represent both 'context' and 'purpose' in interpreting other TRIPS provisions pursuant to article 31(1) of the Vienna Convention on the Law of Treaties ('VCLT')[5] and thereby temper the strong rights granted to intellectual property holders by the TRIPS Agreement. However, they are fairly vague and aspirational provisions and therefore would be unlikely to resolve difficulties where the drafting is unambiguous and the 'ordinary meaning' of given treaty terms is clear, as is arguably the case for compulsory licensing in connection with patented pharmaceuticals.

2.2 Transitional access to generic medicines for developing countries

WTO members must generally make patents available for pharmaceutical products,[6] and patent owners have the 'exclusive rights ... to prevent third parties not having the owner's consent from ... making, using, offering for sale, selling, or importing ... that product'.[7] Typically, the granting of these rights through the patent system means that patented medicines are more expensive than 'generic' or 'off-patent' medicines.[8]

The higher prices associated with patented medicines create particular difficulties for developing countries seeking to manufacture or import them to deal with serious public health concerns, such as the HIV/AIDS crisis. However, developing country members benefited from a longer transition period than developed country members to implement the

[5] Opened for signature 22 May 1969, 1155 UNTS 331 (entered into force 27 January 1980). Articles 31 and 32 of the VCLT are widely recognized as reflecting both customary international law and 'customary rules of interpretation of public international law', which therefore apply in interpreting the WTO agreements pursuant to the Marrakesh Agreement Establishing the World Trade Organization, opened for signature 15 April 1994, 1867 UNTS 3, annex 2 (Understanding on Rules and Procedures Governing the Settlement of Disputes), article 3(2) (entered into force 1 January 1995) ('DSU'): see, e.g., *United States – Standards for Reformulated and Conventional Gasoline*, WTO Doc WT/DS2/AB/R, AB-1996–1 (20 May 1996) 16–17 (Report of the Appellate Body).

[6] TRIPS Agreement, above n. 1, article 27(1). [7] Ibid., article 28(1)(a).

[8] Frederick M. Abbott, 'The Doha Declaration on the TRIPS Agreement and Public Health: Lighting a Dark Corner at the WTO' (2002) 5 *Journal of International Economic Law* 469, 472; Declaration on the TRIPS Agreement and Public Health: Adopted on 14 November 2001, WTO Doc WT/MIN(01)/DEC/2 [3] (2001) ('the Doha Declaration'); Jillian Cohen-Kohler, Lisa Forman and Nathaniel Lipkus, 'Addressing Legal and Political Barriers to Global Pharmaceutical Access: Options for Remedying the Impact of the Agreement on Trade-Related Aspects of Intellectual Property Rights (TRIPS) and the Imposition of TRIPS-Plus Standards' (2008) 3 *Health Economics, Policy and Law* 229, 231–2.

TRIPS Agreement, many having had until 1 January 2005 to establish patent systems covering pharmaceutical products in accordance with section 5 of part II of the TRIPS Agreement.[9] For LDC members, the transition period ended on 1 January 2006 (unless extended by the Council for TRIPS).[10] Until those dates, the relevant members could take advantage of cheaper generic versions of patented drugs[11] (whether manufactured domestically or imported) to attend to public health crises without violating their obligations under the TRIPS Agreement to grant and enforce exclusive patent rights. Accordingly, these grace periods relieved financial pressure on developing country and LDC members for the first decade of the WTO and the TRIPS Agreement. However, they did not provide a longer-term solution to the problem of affordable access to medicines for all WTO members.

2.3 Ongoing exceptions for all members: articles 30 and 31

The transition periods for implementing the TRIPS Agreement as a whole did not provide the only legal basis for developing country and LDC members to obtain generic medicines. For some, the exceptions regarding patents under articles 30 and 31 offered a viable alternative avenue. Article 30 allows members to

> provide limited exceptions to the exclusive rights conferred by a patent, provided that such exceptions do not unreasonably conflict with a normal exploitation of the patent and do not unreasonably prejudice the legitimate interests of the patent owner, taking account of the legitimate interests of third parties.[12]

Although reading article 30 in the light of articles 7 and 8 (as suggested above) could assist developing country members who, for public health reasons, wish to manufacture or import generic versions of patented medicines without the patent owner's consent, the likely outcome in the case of a challenge to such a practice in the WTO dispute settlement system is uncertain. Articles 30 and 31 of the TRIPS Agreement appear to

[9] TRIPS Agreement, above n. 1, articles 65(1), 65(2), 65(4).

[10] Ibid., article 66(1). The Council for TRIPS is open to all WTO members and is responsible for overseeing the functioning of the TRIPS Agreement and for conducting negotiations concerning the TRIPS Agreement under the Doha Development Agenda.

[11] Commission on Intellectual Property Rights, Innovation and Public Health, *Public Health, Innovation and Intellectual Property Rights* (2006) 134–5.

[12] For an application of article 30, see: *Canada – Patent Protection of Pharmaceutical Products*, WTO Doc WT/DS114/R (2000) (Report of the Panel) ('*Canada – Pharmaceutical Patents*').

be mutually exclusive,[13] and since article 31 implicitly contemplates compulsory licences it is probably the preferable legal basis for this kind of conduct.

Article 31 allows members to authorize 'other use' of the subject matter of a patent without the patent owner's consent, 'including use by the government or third parties authorized by the government'. Thus, a member could grant a 'compulsory' licence (i.e., without the patent owner's consent) to a pharmaceutical company within its jurisdiction to manufacture or import a patented pharmaceutical product, provided that it complies with a number of stringent conditions set out in paragraphs (a) to (l) of article 31. These include:

- that the right holder 'be paid adequate remuneration in the circumstances of each case, taking into account the economic value of the authorization' (paragraph (h));[14] and
- that the use 'be authorized predominantly for the supply of the domestic market of the Member authorizing such use' (paragraph (f)).

In addition, paragraph (b) requires that the proposed user attempt to obtain from the patent owner a voluntary licence to make or import a patented pharmaceutical before they do so pursuant to a compulsory licence. This requirement may create problems when the pharmaceutical product is needed to deal urgently with a public health crisis. The drafters of the TRIPS Agreement recognized this by providing in article 31(b) that a member may waive this requirement 'in the case of a national emergency or other circumstances of extreme urgency or in cases of public non-commercial use'. Although disputes may arise as to the meaning of these terms and whether they are justiciable or to be determined unilaterally by the relevant member, these problems are common to treaties and may in fact embody 'constructive ambiguity',[15] allowing

[13] Article 31 applies '[w]here the law of a Member allows for other use of the subject matter of a patent without the authorization of the right holder', and footnote 7 to article 31 provides that 'other use' refers to 'use other than that allowed under Article 30'.

[14] Subject to article 31(k). On the 'adequate remuneration' requirement, see generally Frederic Scherer and Jayashree Watal, 'Post-TRIPS Options for Access to Patented Medicines in Developing Nations' (2002) 5 *Journal of International Economic Law* 913. See also Arvind Subramanian, 'The AIDS Crisis, Differential Pricing of Drugs, and the TRIPS Agreement' (2001) 4 *Journal of World Intellectual Property* 323, 332–5.

[15] See *Negotiations on Improvements and Clarifications of the Dispute Settlement Understanding: Further Contribution of the United States on Improving Flexibility and Member Control in WTO Dispute Settlement*, WTO Doc TN/DS/W/82/Add.1 (2005) 2 (Communication from the United States).

sufficient flexibility to cover a range of scenarios to be assessed on a case-by-case basis.

A greater problem with article 31 for some members is that they lack sufficient capacity to manufacture the requisite pharmaceuticals under compulsory licence. Although these members could issue a compulsory licence to import patented pharmaceuticals, this would be of benefit only if the pharmaceuticals were priced below market, most likely because they were made under compulsory licence in the exporting country.[16] Yet article 31(f) requires compulsory licences to be predominantly for the supply of the domestic market. The word 'predominantly' is not defined, and it could encompass both quantitative and qualitative factors. For example, it might require that more than 50 per cent of the pharmaceuticals manufactured under the licence be sold on the domestic market (calculated by sales value or volume),[17] or that the purpose of a compulsory licence cannot be to supply a foreign country in need. In any case, this requirement means that only a relatively small portion of pharmaceuticals manufactured pursuant to compulsory licences worldwide may be legitimately exported to countries in need and lacking manufacturing capacity.

3. Transitional solution: the interim waiver

3.1 *Declaration on the TRIPS Agreement and public health*

The previous section explained why the TRIPS Agreement as originally drafted left a gap in members' ability to protect themselves in extreme public health situations. Members lacking appropriate manufacturing capacity in the pharmaceutical sector (particularly developing country and LDC members) could not take proper advantage of the flexibilities under article 31 for compulsory licensing. Growing recognition of this problem, *inter alia*, led the WTO members to issue the Declaration on

[16] A few other limited possibilities exist for sourcing lower-priced medicines, including in particular: the patent might have expired in the exporting country, the patent owner might have chosen not to patent them in the exporting country, the exporting country might be an LDC member still subject to an extended transition period pursuant to article 66(1) of the TRIPS Agreement, or the exporting country might be a non-WTO member or a recently acceded member still enjoying a transition period. See Abbott, 'The Doha Declaration on the TRIPS Agreement and Public Health', above n. 8, 497; Subramanian, 'The AIDS Crisis', above n. 14, 326.

[17] Carlos Correa, *Trade Related Aspects of Intellectual Property Rights: A Commentary on the TRIPS Agreement* (2007) 321.

the TRIPS Agreement and Public Health ('Doha Declaration') at the fourth WTO Ministerial Conference in Doha in 2001.[18]

As a statement of principle, the Doha Declaration was clear. It 'affirm[ed] that the TRIPS Agreement can and should be interpreted and implemented in a manner supportive of WTO members' right to protect public health and, in particular, to promote access to medicines for all'[19] and recognized that '[e]ach Member has the right to grant compulsory licences and the freedom to determine the grounds upon which such licences are granted'.[20] It also stated in paragraph 5(c) that:

> Each Member has the right to determine what constitutes a national emergency or other circumstances of extreme urgency, it being understood that public health crises, including those relating to HIV/AIDS, tuberculosis, malaria and other epidemics, can represent a national emergency or other circumstances of extreme urgency.

The Doha Declaration also had a number of more immediate and substantive effects. First, it provided LDC members with an additional transition period to implement the provisions of the TRIPS Agreement regarding patents for pharmaceutical products, ending on 1 January 2016.[21] Although this is merely a temporary solution for LDC members and one that does not address the problem of insufficient manufacturing capacity, it at least provides additional time for LDC members to bring their intellectual property systems into conformity.[22] Second, and more importantly, paragraph 6 of the Doha Declaration stated:

> We recognize that WTO Members with insufficient or no manufacturing capacities in the pharmaceutical sector could face difficulties in making effective use of compulsory licensing under the TRIPS Agreement. We instruct the Council for TRIPS to find an expeditious solution to this problem and to report to the General Council before the end of 2002.[23]

[18] The Doha Declaration, above n. 8. For discussion of the negotiations leading to this declaration, see ibid., 480–90.

[19] Ibid., [4]. [20] Ibid., [5(b)].

[21] Ibid., [7]; Extension of the Transition Period under Article 66.1 of the TRIPS Agreement for Least-Developed Country Members for Certain Obligations with Respect to Pharmaceutical Products, WTO Doc IP/C/25 (2002) [1] (Decision of the Council for TRIPS of 27 June 2002); Least-Developed Country Members – Obligations under Article 70.9 of the TRIPS Agreement with Respect to Pharmaceutical Products, WTO Doc WT/L/478 ((2002) [1] (Decision of the General Council of 8 July 2002).

[22] LDC members may nevertheless have to establish a 'mailbox' system for accepting patent applications: Abbott, 'The Doha Declaration on the TRIPS Agreement and Public Health', above n. 8, 502–3.

[23] The Doha Declaration, above n. 8, [6].

3.2 *Decision implementing paragraph 6 of the Doha Declaration*

Paragraph 6 of the Doha Declaration was implemented by a decision of the General Council in August 2003 ('WTO General Council Decision of 30 August 2003'),[24] whereby members agreed to waive article 31(f) of the TRIPS Agreement so that LDC members and other members lacking sufficient manufacturing capacity may now import pharmaceutical products created under compulsory licence, subject to certain conditions. Under the system established by the WTO General Council Decision of 30 August 2003, provided that these conditions are satisfied, any WTO member may issue a compulsory licence to manufacture and export 'pharmaceutical products' 'needed to address ... public health problems' by an 'eligible importing Member'.[25] All LDC members are *eligible importing members*, and any other WTO member may become an eligible importing member simply by notifying the Council for TRIPS of its intention to use the system as an importer (whether in general or, for example, only in the case of a national emergency or other circumstances of extreme urgency).[26]

The conditions for using the system include:

- the eligible importing member must notify the Council for TRIPS: of the names and expected quantities of the required pharmaceutical products; if not an LDC, that it 'has established that it has insufficient or no manufacturing capacities in the pharmaceutical sector for the product(s) in question'; and (if the product is patented in its territory) that it will grant a compulsory licence in accordance with article 31 for its import;[27]

[24] Implementation of Paragraph 6 of the Doha Declaration on the TRIPS Agreement and Public Health, WTO Doc WT/L/540 (2003) (WTO General Council Decision of 30 August 2003). See also: Duncan Matthews, 'WTO Decision on Implementation of Paragraph 6 of the Doha Declaration on the TRIPS Agreement and Public Health: A Solution to the Access to Essential Medicines Problem?' (2004) 7 *Journal of International Economic Law* 73, 83–98; Frederick M. Abbott, 'The WTO Medicines Decision: World Pharmaceutical Trade and the Protection of Public Health' (2005) 99 *American Journal of International Law* 317, 326–45.

[25] WTO General Council Decision of 30 August 2003, above n. 24, [1].

[26] Ibid., [1(b)]. Several members have indicated that they will not use the system as importers (see above n. 3), while others have indicated that they will only use the system as importers in situations of national emergency or other circumstances of extreme urgency: World Trade Organization, *Minutes of Meeting Held in the Centre William Rappard on 25, 26 and 30 August 2003*, WTO Doc WT/GC/M/82 (13 November (2003) [29].

[27] WTO General Council Decision of 30 August 2003, above n. 24, [2(a)].

- the compulsory licence issued by the exporting member must specify that: only the amount required by the importing member may be manufactured; the entirety of the production under the licence must be exported to that member; and products manufactured under the licence must be clearly identified as being made under the system set out in the WTO General Council Decision of 30 August 2003, for example, by specific labelling and distinctive colouring;[28]
- the exporting member must notify the Council for TRIPS of the grant of the licence and the attached conditions, including the quantity to be manufactured and the country of export;[29] and
- eligible importing members must 'take reasonable measures within their means, proportionate to their administrative capacities and to the risk of trade diversion to prevent re-exportation of the products that have actually been imported into their territories under the system'.[30]

The WTO General Council Decision of 30 August 2003 also includes a waiver of article 31(h) so that an importing member need not pay adequate remuneration where it has already been paid by the manufacturer in the exporting country.[31]

3.3 *Legal status of the Doha Declaration and the WTO General Council Decision of 30 August 2003*

Despite the apparent clarity of the WTO General Council Decision of 30 August 2003, several uncertainties surround it and the Doha Declaration. To begin with, what is their legal status when it comes to interpreting article 31 of the TRIPS Agreement? As regards the Doha Declaration, it is not framed as a 'decision', and it does not purport to amend the TRIPS Agreement. Accordingly, it might properly be regarded as an authoritative interpretation of the TRIPS Agreement[32] pursuant to article IX:2 of the Marrakesh Agreement Establishing the World Trade Organization ('Marrakesh Agreement').[33] In contrast, several aspects of the WTO

[28] Ibid., [2(b)(i)]–[(ii)]. [29] Ibid., [2(c)]. [30] Ibid., [4]. [31] Ibid., [3].

[32] For further discussion of the legal status of the declaration, see generally James Gathii, 'The Legal Status of the Doha Declaration on TRIPS and Public Health under the Vienna Convention on the Law of Treaties' (2002) 15 *Harvard Journal of Law and Technology* 291. See also Abbott, 'The Doha Declaration on the TRIPS Agreement and Public Health', above n. 8, 491–2.

[33] Marrakesh Agreement Establishing the World Trade Organization, opened for signature 15 April 1994, 1867 UNTS 3 (entered into force 1 January 1995) ('Marrakesh Agreement'). For detailed analysis reaching the same conclusion, see Holger

General Council Decision of 30 August 2003 indicate that the members conceived it as a 'waiver' of obligations imposed by paragraphs (f) and (h) of article 31 of the TRIPS Agreement pursuant to paragraphs 3 and 4 of article IX of the Marrakesh Agreement.[34] In particular, the preamble to the decision states that 'exceptional circumstances exist justifying waivers from the obligations set out in paragraphs (f) and (h) of article 31 of the TRIPS Agreement with respect to pharmaceutical products', calling to mind the language of article IX:3 of the Marrakesh Agreement, which begins: 'in exceptional circumstances, the Ministerial Conference may decide to waive an obligation imposed on a Member by this Agreement or any of the Multilateral Trade Agreements'. The rest of the WTO General Council Decision of 30 August 2003 explains the terms and conditions governing the application of the waiver and when it will terminate,[35] as required by article IX:4 of the Marrakesh Agreement.

In sum, the WTO General Council Decision of 30 August 2003 appears to be intended as a binding waiver of certain TRIPS obligations and to conform to the requirements of the Marrakesh Agreement in this regard, even though article IX appears to contemplate waivers of obligations for individual members. The Doha Declaration may also affect the interpretation of the decision (especially through the reference in paragraph 1) and the TRIPS Agreement. The end result is that members may rely on these documents in interpreting their rights and obligations under article 31 of the TRIPS Agreement, significantly enhancing the opportunities for access to generic medicines for countries facing grave public health problems. This is a major achievement, particularly given the difficulty in obtaining consensus among WTO members on any given matter.

3.4 *The Chairman's statement and article 31(b)*

Other ambiguities in interpreting and applying the Doha Declaration and the WTO General Council Decision of 30 August 2003 exist but should not be overstated. In particular, an asterisked footnote to the decision records that the General Council adopted it 'in the light of a statement read out by the Chairman', Mr Carlos Pérez del Castillo of

Hestermeyer, *Human Rights and the WTO: The Case of Patents and Access to Medicines* (2007) 279–82.

34 Ibid., 285.

35 Amendment of the TRIPS Agreement, WTO Doc WT/L/641 (2005) [11] (Decision of 6 December 2005 of the General Council) ('TRIPS Waiver').

Uruguay.[36] The statement could be seen as altering the meaning of certain parts of the WTO General Council Decision of 30 August 2003, including by strengthening the obligations on eligible importing members to take reasonable measures to protect re-exportation and to establish that they have insufficient manufacturing capacity for the pharmaceutical needs in question.

The legal effect of the Chairman's statement on the interpretation of the WTO General Council Decision of 30 August 2003 is unclear, given the words in the footnote just mentioned contrasted with the Philippines' insistence that the statement 'did not represent all the understandings shared by the membership'.[37] However, this ambiguity was largely resolved by a 'corrigendum' to the Decision, which added at the start of the asterisked footnote regarding the Chairman's statement: '*Secretariat note for information purposes only and without prejudice to Members' legal rights and obligations*'.[38] This suggests that the drafters intended that the Chairman's statement carry little interpretative force. Another possible difficulty with the system established by the Doha Declaration and the WTO General Council Decision of 30 August 2003 is that it may not allow eligible importing members to act quickly enough if article 31(b) of the TRIPS Agreement is read as allowing a waiver of the obligation to attempt to obtain a voluntary licence only where the 'national emergency or other circumstances of extreme urgency' exist in the member manufacturing the pharmaceutical. In that case, eligible importing members would still need to make efforts for a reasonable period of time to obtain a licence from the patent owner on reasonable commercial terms and conditions. This could significantly delay endeavours to curb or combat a public health crisis.

The ordinary meaning and context (including the other paragraphs of article 31 of the TRIPS Agreement) could support different readings of this provision. For instance, on one hand, article 31 originally envisaged compulsory licences for the predominant supply of the domestic market in accordance with article 31(f), which might mean that a 'national emergency' must indeed be in the manufacturing member. On the

[36] The statement is reproduced in World Trade Organization, *Minutes of Meeting Held in the Centre William Rappard* on 25, 26 and 30 August 2003, above n. 26, [29].

[37] World Trade Organization, *Minutes of Meeting Held in the Centre William Rappard on 28 August 2003*, WTO Doc IP/C/M/41 (7 November (2003) [4]–[8].

[38] Implementation of Paragraph 6 of the Doha Declaration on the TRIPS Agreement and Public Health, WTO Doc WT/L/540/Corr.1 (2005) (WTO Decision of the General Council of 30 August 2003) (emphasis in original).

other hand, one might argue that the clear words of article 31(f) regarding the 'domestic market' are absent from article 31(b), so that it is not possible to conclude that the national emergency must necessarily be in the domestic market of the manufacturing member. Paragraph 9 of the WTO General Council Decision of 30 August 2003 suggests that it does not affect the interpretation of article 31(b),[39] so that it may be inappropriate to use it to justify interpreting 'national emergency' to cover emergencies in the importing member. However, in our view, the terms of article 31(b) are sufficiently vague to encompass emergencies in the importing member, particularly when read in the light of the Doha Declaration[40] and articles 7 and 8 of the TRIPS Agreement.[41]

The above interpretation of the Chairman's statement and of article 31(b) of the TRIPS Agreement reduces the burden on eligible importing members in complying with the WTO General Council Decision of 30 August 2003 in order to benefit from the system it establishes. Nevertheless, the Decision is no more than an interim waiver from the obligations in paragraphs 31(f) and (h) of the TRIPS Agreement. It is not intended as a permanent solution. We turn now to the more ambitious project of amending the terms of the TRIPS Agreement itself.

4. Permanent solution: a formal amendment

The General Council eventually reached agreement on how to amend the TRIPS Agreement more than two years after the WTO General Council Decision of 30 August 2003. On 6 December 2005, the General Council submitted to members for their acceptance a protocol amending the TRIPS Agreement.[42] This would introduce a new article 31*bis* and an annex into the TRIPS Agreement and effectively render the waiver permanent.[43] Its terms are essentially the same as those in the Decision.[44]

In accordance with article X:3 of the Marrakesh Agreement, the Protocol will take effect[45] for those members that have accepted it

[39] Paragraph 9 of the WTO General Council Decision of 30 August 2003, above n. 24, states: 'This Decision is without prejudice to the rights, obligations and flexibilities that Members have under the provisions of the TRIPS Agreement other than paragraphs (f) and (h) of article 31, including those reaffirmed by the Declaration, and to their interpretation.'

[40] The Doha Declaration, above n. 8, [5(c)]. [41] See above section 2.1.

[42] TRIPS Waiver, above n. 35, [1]. [43] Ibid., protocol [1].

[44] The protocol does not refer to the Chairman's statement. See above section 3.4.

[45] TRIPS Waiver, above n. 35, [3], protocol [4].

'upon acceptance by two thirds of the Members and thereafter for each other Member upon acceptance by it'.[46] Two thirds of the current WTO membership of 153[47] is 101. At the end of 2007 the deadline for acceptance of the Protocol was extended from 1 December 2007 to 31 December 2009 'or such later date as may be decided by the Ministerial Conference' because acceptance was 'taking longer than initially foreseen'.[48] At the date of writing, twenty-one members had accepted the Protocol, including the European Communities.[49] The European Communities' instrument of acceptance confirms that the Protocol will be binding on the member states of the European Union, such that an additional twenty-seven WTO members may be taken to have accepted the Protocol.[50] Although this brings the total number of acceptances to forty-eight, it still leaves a significant gap between the existing number of acceptances and the threshold required to bring the Protocol into force, calling into question members' commitment to ensuring affordable access to medicines for developing countries.

Making the waiver permanent by formally amending the TRIPS Agreement would demonstrate the WTO's solidarity and concern about this issue. On the other hand, even if the amendment entered into force, members would have to avoid lauding this 'technical' achievement as an end in itself, thereby diminishing the need for further action. Moreover, if the waiver itself is not working, making it permanent would be pointless and potentially counter-productive.

Members' apparent lack of enthusiasm for amending the TRIPS Agreement may reveal apathy (given that the waiver will continue to operate anyway), wariness (given that this would be the first ever formal amendment to the core text of a WTO agreement),[51] or despair (if the

[46] Marrakesh Agreement, above n. 33, article X(3).

[47] WTO, *Members and Observers*, www.wto.org/english/thewto_e/whatis_e/tif_e/org6_e.htm at 23 April 2009.

[48] Amendment of the TRIPS Agreement – Extension of the Period for the Acceptance by Members of the Protocol Amending the TRIPS Agreement, WTO Doc WT/L/711 (2007) (Decision of the General Council of 18 December 2007). See also Amendment of the TRIPS Agreement: Proposal for a Decision on an Extension of the Period for the Acceptance by Members of the Protocol Amending the TRIPS Agreement, WTO Doc IP/C/45 (2007).

[49] WTO, *Members Accepting Amendment of the TRIPS Agreement*, www.wto.org/english/tratop_e/trips_e/amendment_e.htm at 23 April 2009.

[50] Council of the European Union, Instrument of Acceptance, SGS7/16652 (19 November 2007), www.wto.org/english/tratop_e/trips_e/popup_amendment_ec_e.htm.

[51] WTO members may modify their schedules, which form part of the WTO agreements, subject to certain conditions. Several members have done so.

Protocol is regarded as providing insufficient protection to developing country members or patent holders, given the realities of day-to-day access to medicines and pressures imposed by members' various constituencies).[52] The following sections are intended to shed light on some of these possible reasons by examining how the waiver to the TRIPS Agreement has operated in practice to date.

5. The waiver in practice

On 17 July 2007, Rwanda (an LDC) became the first member to notify the Council for TRIPS of its intention to import a pharmaceutical product under compulsory licence pursuant to the WTO General Council Decision of 30 August 2003. The notification concerned the HIV/AIDS drug TriAvir, manufactured in Canada by generic pharmaceutical company Apotex Inc.[53] In turn, Canada notified the Council for TRIPS in early October 2007 of its grant of a compulsory licence as an eligible exporting member to enable the manufacture and export of TriAvir to Rwanda.[54]

This example is the exception rather than the rule. No other member apart from Rwanda has to date notified the Council for TRIPS of its intention to import a product pursuant to the WTO General Council Decision of 30 August 2003.[55] No other member apart from Canada has to date notified the Council for TRIPS of its intention to grant a compulsory licence as an eligible exporting member.[56] No WTO member has notified the Council for TRIPS of its intention to use the system as an importer (as required under paragraph 1(b) of the Decision for all members other than LDCs).[57] Moreover, only a handful of members

[52] For notes on the reactions to the WTO General Council Decision of 30 August 2003, above n. 24, by member states, non-governmental organizations and pharmaceutical companies, see Abbott, 'The WTO Medicines Decision', above n. 24, 317–18.

[53] *Rwanda – Notification under Paragraph 2(A) of the Decision of 30 August 2003 on the Implementation of Paragraph 6 of the Doha Declaration on the TRIPS Agreement and Public Health*, WTO Doc IP/N/9/RWA/1 (2007).

[54] *Canada – Notification under Paragraph 2(C) of the Decision of 30 August 2003 on the Implementation of Paragraph 6 of the Doha Declaration on the TRIPS Agreement and Public Health*, WTO Doc IP/N/10/CAN/1 (2007). See also Matthew Rimmer, 'The Jean Chrétien Pledge to Africa Act: Patent Law and Humanitarian Aid' (2005) 15 *Expert Opinion on Therapeutic Patents* 889, 891–5.

[55] World Trade Organization, *Notifications by Importing WTO Members*, www.wto.org/english/tratop_e/trips_e/public_health_notif_import_e.htm at 23 April 2009.

[56] World Trade Organization, *Notifications by Exporting WTO Members*, www.wto.org/english/tratop_e/trips_e/public_health_notif_export_e.htm at 23 April 2009.

[57] World Trade Organization, *Notifications by Importing WTO Members*, above n. 55.

have implemented legislation to enable them to issue compulsory licences in accordance with the waiver.[58] The US, in particular, was first to accept the Protocol in 2005 but has still not implemented corresponding legislation.[59] The widespread failure to put the waiver into effect may indicate that the mechanism it establishes is too cumbersome to provide a workable solution.

The 2007 report of the Commission on Intellectual Property Rights, Innovation and Public Health of the World Health Organization ('WHO') called on developed and developing country members alike to take the necessary regulatory steps to allow them to use the system envisaged by the WTO General Council Decision of 30 August 2003 (as exporters and importers respectively).[60] It also explained reluctance to use the waiver by reference to the commercial interests of manufacturers of generic pharmaceutical products:

> Although their business models are different, generic companies share with the research-based industry the common motivation of serving the interests of their shareholders. The mechanism will not be used if the financial incentives for participation, taking account of the risks involved, are deemed inadequate.[61]

Commentators and non-governmental organizations ('NGOs') have argued that the commercial incentives are inadequate and the waiver is unworkable or problematic[62] because, *inter alia*:

[58] World Trade Organization, *Annual Review of the Decision on the Implementation of Paragraph 6 of the Doha Declaration on the TRIPS Agreement and Public Health*, WTO Doc IP/C/46 (2007) annex 1 [19] (Switzerland) (Report to the General Council); World Trade Organization, *Annual Review of the Decision on the Implementation of Paragraph 6 of the Doha Declaration on the TRIPS Agreement and Public Health*, WTO Doc IP/C/42 (2006) [5] (European Communities) (Report to the General Council); World Trade Organization, *Annual Review of the Decision on the Implementation of Paragraph 6 of the Doha Declaration on the TRIPS Agreement and Public Health*, WTO Doc IP/C/37 (2005) [5] (Canada), [6] (India), [7] (Korea) (Report to the General Council); World Trade Organization, *Annual Review of the Decision on the Implementation of Paragraph 6 of the Doha Declaration on the TRIPS Agreement and Public Health*, WTO Doc IP/C/33 (2004) [4] (Norway) (Report to the General Council). See also Rimmer, 'The Jean Chrétien Pledge to Africa Act', above n. 54, 891–905; Matthew Rimmer, 'Race against Time: The Export of Essential Medicines to Rwanda' (2008) 1 *Public Health Ethics* 89.

[59] See above n. 49 and corresponding text.

[60] Commission on Intellectual Property Rights, Innovation and Public Health, above n. 11, 139.

[61] Ibid., 136.

[62] See, e.g., Cohen-Kohler, Forman and Lipkus, 'Addressing Legal and Political Barriers to Global Pharmaceutical Access', above n. 8, 237, 240, 247; Correa, *Trade Related Aspects*

- The waiver does not affect article 31(b) of the TRIPS Agreement, which usually requires the proposed user to attempt to obtain an ordinary commercial licence from the right holder, potentially involving lengthy negotiations.
- The transparency and notification requirements are too burdensome and unrealistic. In particular, it is difficult to determine in advance precisely how much of a given product will be needed in a given country.
- The requirements imposed to prevent trade diversion (such as distinctive colouring and labelling of pharmaceuticals) are too onerous.
- Before a successful transaction can take place, implementing and amending legislation may be required not only in exporting countries but also in importing countries.

These points have some validity but should be tested and do not necessarily represent insurmountable obstacles. For example, attempts to negotiate a voluntary licence need continue only for a 'reasonable period of time', and members may waive the requirement to make such attempts in circumstances including national emergencies.[63] Similarly, importing and exporting members must indeed make detailed notifications but they do so in good faith, not necessarily with perfect foresight.[64] Finally, distinguishing products is required only if it 'is feasible and does not have a significant impact on price'.[65] Of course, members need not make use of these allowances under the article 31 of the TRIPS Agreement and the waiver. If members' implementing legislation imposes stricter conditions, this will reduce its utility in delivering medicines. This appears to have been a key problem with the Canadian legislation,[66] despite the fact that Canada has been a 'pioneer and pathfinder' in this area.[67]

of Intellectual Property Rights, above n. 17, 339–42; Hestermeyer, *Human Rights and the WTO*, above n. 33, 271–2, 275–6; Matthew Rimmer, *A Submission to the Joint Standing Committee on Treaties: The Hong Kong Amendment to the TRIPS Agreement* (Submission 2, 9 May 2007) cited in Joint Standing Committee on Treaties, Parliament of Australia, *Report 86: Treaties tabled on 27 March and 9 May 2007* (2007) ch. 9; Médecins Sans Frontières, *Neither Expeditious, Nor a Solution: The WTO August 30th Decision is Unworkable* (August 2006), www.accessmed-msf.org/fileadmin/user_upload/medinnov_accesspatents/WTOaugustreport.pdf at 23 April 2009.

[63] See above, section 3.3.

[64] See Correa, *Trade Related Aspects of Intellectual Property Rights*, above n. 17, 330, 334.

[65] WTO General Council Decision of 30 August 2003, above n. 24, [2(b)(ii)].

[66] Rimmer, 'Race against Time', above n. 58, 4–5, 9–10. [67] Ibid., 9.

The limited use of the waiver to date and the dearth of implementing legislation mirror the low rate of acceptance of the Protocol, suggesting that members are not discounting the need for the Protocol simply because they are relying on the waiver instead. However, are members refraining from implementing the waiver because it is unworkable, or is the waiver lying dormant because members have not passed the necessary legislation? Claims that the waiver cannot work seem premature in the absence of implementing legislation by many members, and they may unwittingly provide an excuse for members not to follow through in their support of the waiver and Protocol.

That is not to say that the waiver is easy to implement or perfectly drafted; it is obviously a compromise and the best that the members were able to agree on in the circumstances. However, in our view, attempting to operationalize it while working around its flaws is preferable to discarding it altogether and hoping for a better solution to emerge from the WTO in the near future. In the meantime, members may be wise to avoid rendering the waiver permanent, in case it does have to be declared a failure. Some commentators have already reached this conclusion. Matthew Rimmer, for example, describing the WTO General Council Decision of 30 August 2003 as an 'imperfect model' and the Protocol as 'inappropriate and undesirable', pronounces: 'The codification of such a flawed model would only exacerbate the public health crisis in developing countries caused by infectious diseases, such as HIV/AIDS, tuberculosis and malaria.'[68]

6. FTAs and regional patents promoted for developing countries

The WTO General Council Decision of 30 August 2003 and the Protocol provide an additional limited waiver of the requirement in article 31(f) of the TRIPS Agreement regarding predominant local supply in connection with certain free trade agreements ('FTAs'), including regional agreements. The Decision and the Protocol provide that a developing country or LDC member of such an FTA need not comply with the obligation under article 31(f) of the TRIPS Agreement 'to the extent necessary to enable a pharmaceutical product produced or imported under a compulsory licence in that Member to be exported to the markets of those other developing or [LDC] parties to the [FTA] that share the health

[68] Ibid., 12.

problem in question'.[69] In theory, this provides additional leeway for developing country members to avoid the article 31(f) obligation in addressing public health problems.

Although an FTA for this purpose is not precisely defined, we infer from the text that it must satisfy three criteria:

(i) the FTA must meet the definition of a 'free-trade area' or 'customs union' in article XXIV(8) and comply with the requirements in article XXIV(5) of the General Agreement on Tariffs and Trade 1994 ('GATT 1994');[70]
(ii) the FTA must constitute a '[r]egional or global arrangemen[t] entered into amongst developing country Members for the mutual reduction or elimination of tariffs and … for the mutual reduction or elimination of non-tariff measures, on products imported from one another', as described in paragraph 2(c) of the Enabling Clause, and comply with paragraph 3(a) of the Enabling Clause;[71] and
(iii) at least half the current members of the FTA must be on the United Nations list of LDCs.[72]

The third of these requirements is the most significant barrier to the use of this waiver. In addition to half of its members being LDCs, to be of benefit, the FTA would need to encompass a member with sufficient manufacturing capacity in the generic pharmaceutical field to respond to

[69] WTO General Council Decision of 30 August 2003, above n. 24, [6(i)]; TRIPS Waiver, above n. 35, article 31*bis*(3).

[70] The WTO General Council Decision of 30 August 2003 (paragraph 6(i)) and the protocol (paragraph 3 of article 31*bis*) refer to 'a regional trade agreement within the meaning of Article XXIV of the GATT 1994' without specifying any particular paragraphs of article XXIV or whether a regional trade agreement means a free-trade area, a customs union, or both. On the many uncertainties concerning articles XXIV(5), XXIV (8): see Nicolas Lockhart and Andrew Mitchell, 'Regional Trade Agreements Under GATT 1994: An Exception and its Limits', in Andrew Mitchell (ed.), *Challenges and Prospects for the WTO* (2005) 217. See also James Mathis, *Regional Trade Agreements in the GATT/WTO: Article XXIV and the Internal Trade Requirement* (2002); Joel P. Trachtman, 'International Trade: Regionalism', in Andrew Guzman and Alan Sykes (eds.), *Research Handbook in International Economic Law* (2007), 151.

[71] Decision on Differential and More Favourable Treatment, Reciprocity, and Fuller Participation of Developing Countries, GATT BISD 26S/203, GATT Doc L/4903 (28 November 1979) ('Enabling Clause'). The Enabling Clause forms part of the General Agreement on Tariffs and Trade 1994, www.wto.org/english/res_e/booksp_e/analytic_index_e/gatt1994_e.htm, ('GATT'), paragraph 1(b)(iv) of the language of annex 1A incorporating the GATT 1994 into the Marrakesh Agreement.

[72] WTO General Council Decision of 30 August 2003, above n. 24, [6(i)]; TRIPS Waiver, above n. 35, article 31*bis*(3).

its own needs as well as those of other members of the FTA. Identifying with certainty an FTA that meets these criteria is extremely difficult.

Some commentators point to the Economic Community of West African States ('ECOWAS') as a qualifying FTA.[73] Twelve of the fifteen member states of ECOWAS are LDCs,[74] so it certainly meets the third and perhaps hardest criterion. It has been notified to the WTO under the Enabling Clause,[75] but the Committee on Regional Trade Agreements ('CRTA') has not yet determined whether it complies with the Enabling Clause.[76] Apart from anything else, we wonder whether paragraph 2(c) of the Enabling Clause refers to FTAs among WTO members only, which it seems to on its face. In that case, ECOWAS would not qualify at present because Liberia (an LDC member state of ECOWAS) commenced the WTO accession process only in 2007[77] and is therefore unlikely to become a member for several years. As several LDCs are not yet WTO members it would be difficult to satisfy at once the second and the third criteria mentioned above.

Another possibility is the Protocol on Trade of the Southern African Development Community Free Trade Area ('SADC'), of which six of the twelve member states are LDCs, and all are WTO members.[78] The SADC Protocol has been notified to the WTO under article XXIV of the GATT 1994[79] but the CRTA has not yet determined whether it meets the requirements of article XXIV. Indeed, the CRTA has not yet determined the compliance of any FTA notified since the WTO was established, adding to the uncertainty of article XXIV of the GATT 1994, the Enabling Clause,

[73] We thank Professor Noah Benjamin Novogrodsky for his helpful comments on this issue at the Australian National University's workshop on *Incentives for Global Public Health: Patent Law and Access to Essential Medicines* (Canberra, 26–28 May 2008).

[74] Economic Community of West African States, *ECOWAS Member States*, www.ecowas.int/ at 23 April 2009.

[75] Economic Community of West African States, Revised Treaty, WTO Doc WT/COMTD/N/21 (2005) (Notification from the Parties to the Agreement).

[76] World Trade Organization, *Regional Trade Agreements Notified to the GATT/WTO and in Force: A–Z Table*, www.wto.org/english/tratop_e/region_e/a_z_e.xls at 23 April 2009.

[77] World Trade Organization, *Accessions: Republic of Liberia*, www.wto.org/english/thewto_e/acc_e/a1_liberia_e.htm at 23 April 2009.

[78] South African Development Community, *Background to the Free Trade Area*, www.sadc.int/fta/index/browse/page/57 at 23 April 2009; World Trade Organization, *Factual Presentation – Protocol on Trade in the Southern African Development Community (SADC): Report by the Secretariat*, WTO Doc WT/REG176/4 (2007) [1] (Report by the Secretariat).

[79] Protocol on Trade in the Southern African Development Community, WTO Doc WT/REG176/N/1/Rev.1 (2004) (Notification by Tanzania – Revision).

and the additional waiver from article 31(f) of the TRIPS Agreement. Even if the SADC Protocol complies with article XXIV, it must also comply with the Enabling Clause to benefit from that waiver.

If ECOWAS or SADC do qualify as FTAs under this waiver, they have the potential to provide a valuable alternative route for developing countries to access affordable medicines, while at the same time building the manufacturing capacity of non-LDC member states like Ghana[80] and South Africa. However, the brief review above of these two FTAs (perhaps the only potentially qualifying FTAs) demonstrates how difficult it is to meet the three criteria and to be sure that an FTA qualifies. The LDC requirement also means that a given FTA may move in and out of compliance according to changes in the United Nations list of LDCs, threatening interruption to a working scheme of drug production and distribution once established.

WTO members are unlikely to reopen negotiations on access to medicines under the TRIPS Agreement in the near future. Nevertheless, in order for the results of past negotiations to have a greater positive and practical impact on developing countries, the FTA waiver of article 31(f) of the TRIPS Agreement needs to be modified. First and most importantly, the requirement that at least half the members of the FTA must be LDCs should be removed. This will considerably expand the potential scope of the waiver.[81] Second, members should clarify that an FTA that includes non-members of the WTO may still qualify, perhaps as long as they are LDCs, developing countries engaged in the WTO accession process or WTO observers. Third, FTAs should not have to comply with both article XXIV of the GATT 1994 and the Enabling Clause, which contain different but related requirements. An FTA that satisfies the Enabling Clause or that is between developing countries and satisfies article XXIV should be sufficient.

7. Conclusion

Access to affordable medicines cannot be ensured through international trade alone. Other aspects of this problem include difficulties in

[80] Sarah Perkins and Melanie de Wit, 'The African Private Sector Steps in to Fill the Drug Gap' (2007) 370 *The Lancet* 722, 723.

[81] See Peter Yu, 'Access to Medicines, BRICS Alliances, and Collective Action' (2008) 34 *American Journal of Law and Medicine* 345, 346; Sisule Musungu, Susan Villanueva and Roxana Blasetti, *Utilizing TRIPS Flexibilities for Public Health Protection through South–South Regional Frameworks* (2004) 35–81.

delivering medicines, observing complicated drug regimes, and establishing effective medicines regulations. Thus, '[i]ncorporating the public health-related TRIPS flexibilities into national law and policy is necessary but not sufficient to deal with the patent-related obstacles to improving access to medicines'.[82] Yet enabling these health-related TRIPS flexibilities is still a necessary part of addressing the conflict between patents and public health. The WTO should be applauded for having reached an interim solution to this conflict, particularly for countries lacking sufficient manufacturing capacity in the pharmaceutical industry, in the form of the WTO General Council Decision of 30 August 2003.

However, the WTO General Council Decision of 30 August 2003 is neither perfect nor complete. Its flaws stem largely from its complexity, and they are reflected in how little the Decision has actually been used. Although given its restricted use in practice, it may be for the best that the waiver has not yet been made permanent. More members need to start acting on the waiver to test its workability. While the Decision and the Protocol have also recognized that FTAs and regional patents can also be used to assist countries with insufficient manufacturing capacity, the range of FTAs that qualify to benefit from this waiver is too restricted. Yet WTO members must not use the limitations of the existing TRIPS solution to avoid making good on their promise that the TRIPS Agreement 'can and should be interpreted and implemented in a manner supportive of WTO Members' right to protect public health and, in particular, to promote access to medicines for all'.[83] As long as the WTO General Council Decision of 30 August 2003 continues to be underutilized, the potential benefits of this TRIPS Waiver will remain unknown.

[82] Ibid., 23. [83] The Doha Declaration, above n. 8, [4].

3

Public law challenges to the regulation of pharmaceutical patents in the US bilateral free trade agreements

HITOSHI NASU*

1. Introduction

The international trade law regime has been flourishing with its institutionalization and judicialization under the auspices of the World Trade Organization ('WTO'). While some people applaud the development towards constitutionalization,[1] the intergovernmental nature of the legal regime, especially at the law-making phase, has remained at the penumbra. Illustrative is the barrier against access to essential medicines caused by pharmaceutical patent protection under the WTO regime. Pressures have been mounting to alleviate the problem in multinational forums,[2] and yet the initiative by the US to set a higher level of intellectual property protection over pharmaceutical products through bilateral trade agreements has impeded change.

This chapter examines the issue of access to essential medicine within the framework of public international law as one of the challenges posed to its legitimacy with particular focus on the US bilateral free trade agreements. As examined in the next section, the conclusion of such bilateral trade agreements represents an attempt to erode flexibilities permitted for developing countries under the WTO regime within the conventional international law framework. However, this conventional wisdom has been called into

* The author would like to express his gratitude to James McCombe for his research assistance.

1 See, e.g., Deborah Cass, *The Constitutionalization of the World Trade Organization: Legitimacy, Democracy, and Community in the International Trading System* (2005).

2 See Andrew D. Mitchell and Tania Voon, 'The TRIPS Waiver as a Recognition of Public Health Concerns in the WTO', in Thomas Pogge, Matthew Rimmer and Kim Rubenstein (eds.), *Incentives for Global Public Health: Patent Law and Access to Essential Medicines*, 56.

question. Section 3 will examine three challenges to international law as it applies to the US bilateral free trade agreements: democratic deficit; normative fragmentation; and regulatory failure. Section 4 will explore how public law values can help international trade regulation to overcome the limits of the traditional international law framework stemming from the private nature of treaty law.

2. The status of US bilateral trade agreements

The cycle of regulatory growth concerning the access to essential medicines reached a critical stage when the Uruguay Round of Multilateral Trade Negotiations produced the Agreement on Trade-Related Aspects of Intellectual Property Rights in 1994 ('TRIPS Agreement' or 'TRIPS'),[3] which extended the minimum standards of intellectual property rights protection for any inventions, whether products or processes, in all fields of technology without discrimination, provided they are new, involve an inventive step and are capable of industrial application.[4] The regulation of intellectual property rights remained unfinished business, however, for multinational companies have continued to exploit forum-shifting in their search for an even higher set of standards,[5] resulting in even more restricted access to essential medicines in developing countries. Despite the setback suffered from the 2001 Doha Declaration,[6] and the subsequent General Council Decision of 30 August 2003 on the Implementation of Paragraph 6 of the Declaration,[7] the US Government has since then pushed

[3] Marrakesh Agreement Establishing the World Trade Organization, opened for signature 15 April 1994, 1867 UNTS 3, annex 1C (Agreement on Trade-Related Aspects of Intellectual Property Rights) (entered into force 1 January 1995) ('TRIPS Agreement').

[4] Ibid., article 27(1).

[5] For details, see Peter Drahos, 'Expanding Intellectual Property's Empire: The Role of FTAs' (2003) *International Centre for Trade and Sustainable Development*, ictsd.neti/ip/24737 at 2 March 2009; Peter Drahos and John Braithwaite, *Information Feudalism: Who Owns the Knowledge Economy?* (2002), ch. 3.

[6] Declaration on the TRIPS Agreement and Public Health: Adopted on 14 November 2001, WT/MIN(01)/DEC/2 (2001) ('the Doha Declaration').

[7] Implementation of Paragraph 6 of the Doha Declaration on the TRIPS Agreement and Public Health, WTO Doc WT/L/540 (2003) (WTO General Council Decision of 30 August 2003). This decision led subsequently to agreement on a permanent amendment to the TRIPS Agreement on 6 December 2005. The original date by which WTO

forward with its agenda by initiating dozens of bilateral and regional free trade agreements,[8] which commonly require the stronger protection of intellectual property rights than what was internationally agreed upon in the TRIPS Agreement ('TRIPS-Plus agreements').[9]

The terms of the TRIPS-Plus agreements vary slightly between instruments. Table 3.1 shows the different pharmaceutical patent provisions in each agreement (see page 80 below). Typically included in relation to pharmaceutical products are:[10]

members had to accept this amendment by a two thirds majority was 1 December 2007. However, this did not take place, and the date has been extended until 31 December 2009. As of 8 May 2008, fifteen member states including the US have accepted the amendment: see WTO, *Members Accepting Amendment of the TRIPS Agreement*, www.wto.org/english/tratop_e/trips_e/amendment_e.htm at 23 January 2009.

[8] Peru–US Trade Promotion Agreement, signed 14 December 2007 (entered into force 1 February 2009); The Republic of Korea–US Free Trade Agreement (KORUSFTA), signed 30 June 2007 (pending US Congress approval); Panama–US Trade Promotion Agreement, signed 28 June 2007 (pending US Congress approval); Columbia–US Free Trade Agreement, signed 22 November 2006 (pending US Congress approval); Oman–US Free Trade Agreement, signed 19 January 2006 (entered into force 1 January 2009); Bahrain–US Free Trade Agreement, signed 14 September 2004 (entered into force 4 August 2006); Central American–Dominican Republic Free Trade Agreement (CAFTA), signed 5 August 2004 (entered into force between the United States and El Salvador on 1 March 2006, followed by Honduras and Nicaragua on 1 April 2006, Guatemala on 1 July 2006 and the Dominican Republic on 1 March 2007. The remaining partner country, Costa Rica, approved the agreement in a national public referendum on 7 October 2007, although entry into force is pending passage of necessary implementation legislation by the Costa Rican legislature); Morocco–US Free Trade Agreement, signed 15 June 2004 (entered into force 1 January 2006); Australia–US Free-Trade Agreement (AUSFTA), signed 18 May 2004 (entered into force 1 January 2005); Chile–US Free Trade Agreement, signed 6 June 2003 (entered into force 1 January 2004); Singapore–US Free Trade Agreement, signed 6 May 2003 (entered into force 1 January 2004). There are also FTAs implemented before the Doha Declaration: Jordan–US Free Trade Agreement, signed 24 October 2000 (entered into force 17 December 2001); NAFTA, signed 17 December 1992 (entered into force 1 January 1994); Israel–US Free Trade Agreement, signed 22 April 1985 (entered into force 1 September 1985).

[9] The concept of 'TRIPS-Plus agreements' is more fully explained in the Introduction to this volume.

[10] See also, Carlos Maria Correa, 'Implications of Bilateral Free Trade Agreements on Access to Medicines' (2006) 84 *Bulletin of the World Health Organization* 399, 400–1; Bryan Mercurio, 'TRIPS-Plus Provisions in FTAs; Recent Trends', in Lorand Bartels and Federico Ortino (eds.), *Regional Trade Agreements and the WTO Legal System* (2006) 215, 224–34; Carsten Fink and Patrick Reichenmiller, 'Tightening TRIPS: The Intellectual Property Provisions of Recent US Free Trade Agreements (2005) 20 *The World Bank Trade Note*, siteresources.worldbank.org/INTRANETTRADE/Resources/Pubs/TradeNote20.pdf at 23 January 2009.

Table 3.1 *Comparison of pharmaceutical patent provisions between TRIPS and US Domestic Law / US-Free Trade Agreements*

	Patent terms extension	Compulsory licences	Linkage	Test data protection	Parallel imports
US Domestic Law	When a delay exceeds 3 years, but subject to conditions and qualifications (35 USC 156)	— (28 USC 1498)	FDA required to consider patent status when reviewing generic applications (21 USC 355)	5 years for new chemical entities; 3 years for other pharmaceuticals (21 USC 355(c)(3)(E))	Right of patent owner to prevent (19 USC 1337)
Israel–US FTA, signed 22 April 1985 (entered into force 1 September 1985)	- - -	- - -	- - -	- - -	- - -
NAFTA, signed 17 December 1992 (entered into force 1 January 1994)	Party may extend patent term to compensate for delays caused by regulatory approval processes (1709.12)	— (1709.10)	- - -	- - -	- - -
Jordan–US FTA, signed 24 October 2000 (entered into force 17 December 2001)	Party shall make available an extension for unreasonable curtailment of the patent term as a result of marketing approval process (4.23(a))	Limited to anti-competitive remedy and public non-commercial use etc. (4.20)	- - -	— (4.22)	- - -

Singapore–US FTA, signed 6 May 2003 (entered into force 1 January 2004)	When a delay exceeds 4 years from the filing or 2 years after a request for examination (16.7.7)	Limited to anti-competitive remedy and public non-commercial use (16.7.6)	– – –	At least 5 years (16.8.1)	Right to assign or transfer a patent and to conclude licensing contracts (16.7.2)
Chile–US FTA, signed 6 June 2003 (entered into force 1 January 2004)	When a delay exceeds 5 years from the filing or 3 years after a request for examination (17.9.6)	– – –	Yes + notify the patent holder of the identity of the person requesting marketing approval (17.10.2)	At least 5 years (17.10.1)	– – –
Australia–US FTA, signed 18 May 2004 (entered into force 1 January 2005)	When a delay exceeds 4 years from the filing or 2 years after a request for examination (17.9.8)	Limited to national emergencies, as anti-trust remedy, and for public non-commercial use (17.9.7)	Yes + notify the patent holder of the identity of the person requesting marketing approval (17.10.4)	At least 5 years + 3 years for new clinical information (17.10.1&2)	Exclusive right of the patent owner to prevent (17.9.4)
Morocco–US FTA, signed 15 June 2004 (entered into force 1 January 2006)	When a delay exceeds 4 years from the filing or 2 years after a request for examination (15.9.7)	– – –	Yes + notify the patent holder of the identity of the person requesting marketing approval (15.10.4)	At least 5 years + 3 years for new clinical information (15.10.1)	Exclusive right of the patent owner to prevent (15.9.4)
CAFTA–DR FTA, signed 5 August 2004 (entered into force 2006–7)	When a delay exceeds 5 years from the filing or 3 years after a request for examination (10.9.6)	– – –	Yes + notify the patent holder of the identity of the person requesting marketing approval (15.10.2)	At least 5 years (15.10.1)	– – –

Table 3.1 (*cont.*)

	Patent terms extension	Compulsory licences	Linkage	Test data protection	Parallel imports
Bahrain–US FTA, signed 14 September 2004 (entered into force 4 August 2006)	When a delay exceeds 4 years from the filing or 2 years after a request for examination (14.8.6)	– – –	Yes + notify the patent holder of the identity of the person requesting marketing approval (14.9.4)	At least 5 years + 3 years for new clinical information (14.9.1)	– – –
Oman–US FTA, signed 19 January 2006 (entered into force 1 January 2009)	When a delay exceeds 4 years from the filing or 2 years after a request for examination (15.8.6(a))	– – –	Yes + notify the patent holder of the identity of the person requesting marketing approval (15.9.4)	At least 5 years + 3 years for new clinical information (15.9.2)	– – –
Colombia–US FTA, signed 22 November 2006 (pending US Congress approval)	When a delay exceeds 5 years from the filing or 3 years after a request for examination (16.9.6)	– – –	Discretionary, but must notify the patent holder of the identity of the person requesting marketing approval (16.10.3 & 4)	For a 'reasonable period of time' (normally 5 years) except for public health measures (16.10.2)	– – –
Panama–US TPA, signed 28 June 2007 (pending US Congress approval)	When a delay exceeds 5 years from the filing or 3 years after a request for examination (15.9.6)	– – –	Discretionary, but must notify the patent holder of the identity of the person requesting	For a 'reasonable period of time' (normally 5 years) except for public health measures (15.10.2)	– – –

					marketing approval (15.10.3 & 4)				
Korea–US FTA, signed 30 June 2007 (pending US Congress approval)	When a delay exceeds 4 years from the filing or 3 years after a request for examination (18.8.6)	–	–	–	Yes + notify the patent holder of the identity of the person requesting marketing approval (18.9.5)	At least 5 years + 3 years for new clinical information except for public health measures (18.9.1 & 2)	–	–	–
Peru–US TPA, signed 14 December 2007 (entered into force 1 February 2009)	When a delay exceeds 5 years from the filing or 3 years after a request for examination (16.9.6)	–	–	–	Discretionary, but must notify the patent holder of the identity of the person requesting marketing approval (16.10.3 & 4)	For a ‘reasonable period of time’ (normally 5 years) except for public health measures (16.10.2)	–	–	–

- the extension of the patent term to compensate for unreasonable delays that occur in granting the patent;[11]
- the restriction of the grounds for compulsory licences;[12]
- the prohibition of granting marketing approval to any third party during the patent term (linking marketing approval to patent status);
- the protection of undisclosed test data from being used by a third party to market the same or similar products;[13] and
- until recently the prevention of parallel importation of pharmaceutical products.[14]

Each new agreement sets precedents for other agreements that are negotiated later.[15] The terms of the provisions are also subject to alterations as a result of debates in the United States Congress, as was recently seen in the conclusion of the US–Peru Free Trade Agreement.[16]

The conclusion of such bilateral trade agreements represents an attempt to erode flexibilities permitted for developing countries under the TRIPS Agreement with regard to the protection and promotion of public health, and to remove or alter domestic public health policies that allegedly pose unnecessarily restrictive non-tariff barriers to trade.[17] It is evident that the acceptance of tighter regulation of pharmaceutical products is 'suicidal' for developing countries in that they are thereby

[11] The patent term under TRIPS is simply twenty years from the filing date: TRIPS Agreement, above n. 3, article 33.

[12] TRIPS allows states to grant a compulsory licence to a generic manufacturer after first attempting to obtain from the patent holder a voluntary licence for generic production on reasonable commercial terms except in the case of a national or other extreme emergency: TRIPS Agreement, above n. 3, article 31(b). The 2001 Doha Declaration affirms the freedom of states to determine the grounds upon which compulsory licences are granted: the Doha Declaration, above n. 6, [5(b)].

[13] Under TRIPS, the Parties are only required to protect such data against 'unfair commercial use': TRIPS Agreement, above n. 3, article 39(3).

[14] Parallel importation is not prohibited under TRIPS by states adopting the standard of international patent exhaustion: TRIPS Agreement, above n. 3, article 6. See also, Mitchell and Voon, 'The TRIPS Waiver as a Recognition of Public Health Concerns in the WTO', above n. 2.

[15] Maria Fabiana Jorge, 'Trade Agreements and Public Health: Are US Trade Negotiators Building an Intellectual Property Platform Against the Generic Industry? Are They Raising the Standards to Go Beyond the US Law?' (2007) 4 *Journal of Generic Medicines* 169, 172.

[16] See Martin Vaughan, *US–Peru Trade Deal: The First Test of Renegotiated IP Provisions* (5 November 2007) Intellectual Property Watch, www.ip-watch.org at 23 January 2009.

[17] Frederick Abbott, 'The WTO Medicines Decision: World Pharmaceutical Trade and the Protection of Public Health' (2005) 99 *American Journal of International Law* 317, 348–58; Ellen Shaffer *et al.*, 'Global Trade and Public Health' (2005) 95 *American Journal of Public Health* 23, 23–4.

agreeing to cut the supply of low-priced medicines to save people from endemic or pandemic diseases. Behind the conclusion of such bilateral trade agreements reportedly lies the fact that a threat of or an actual recourse to trade sanctions under section 301 of the Trade Act 1974 (US) has had significant influence upon less powerful states in trade negotiations. The tendency of this phenomenon has only grown following the TRIPS Agreement.[18] The coercive nature of the trade negotiations arguably casts doubt on the justificatory force of the bilateral trade agreements.[19]

Yet the traditional rules of public international law show little sympathy for such bilateral trade agreements. One could argue that the threat or the actual recourse to trade sanctions by the US Government amounts to the threat or use of force and that bilateral trade agreements concluded under such circumstances are deemed void *ab initio*.[20] Yet the drafting history of the Vienna Convention on the Law of Treaties appears to support the view that absolute nullity attaches only to those treaties procured by the threat or use of physical or armed force.[21] After great debate, the proposal to define the expression 'force' as including economic or political pressure could not win the support of the vast majority of Western states which considered that it would seriously prejudice the stability of treaty relations.

There is also a doubt whether the less powerful party to a bilateral trade agreement with the US would be willing to take issue with the validity of the treaty. Coercion as a ground for absolute nullity must apply with respect to the treaty in its entirety, not with respect to particular clauses in the treaty.[22] Therefore, as long as the less powerful party gains benefits from maintaining the trade agreement (generally greater access for agricultural products and raw materials to the large US market), there is little incentive for such a state to raise the issue of validity. There is no legal ground upon which a state is prohibited from

18 See, e.g., Peter Drahos, 'Negotiating Intellectual Property Rights: Between Coercion and Dialogue', in Peter Drahos and Ruth Mayne (eds.), *Global Intellectual Property Rights: Knowledge, Access and Development* (2002) 161, 172–4.

19 See Thomas Pogge, 'Human Rights and Global Health: A Research Program' (2005) 36 *Metaphilosophy* 182, 198–9.

20 Vienna Convention on the Law of Treaties, opened for signature 23 May 1969, 1155 UNTS 331, articles 51–2 (entered into force 27 January 1980) ('VCLT').

21 Ian Sinclair, *The Vienna Convention on the Law of Treaties* (2nd edn, 1984) 177–9. See also Lord McNair, *The Law of Treaties* (1961) 206–11.

22 VCLT, above n. 20. For the principle of separability of treaty provisions in the context of invalidity, see Donald Greig, *Invalidity and the Law of Treaties* (2006) 108–13.

entering into an agreement even if it involves significant public health or human rights ramifications.

Nevertheless, the actual or potential, adverse impact of TRIPS-Plus agreements for public health in developing countries has raised real concerns over the conclusion of such bilateral deals. There is a gulf between the ideals of international law and the realpolitik of bilateral trade negotiations. There are three challenges posed to international law in its application to the US bilateral free trade agreements: democratic deficit; normative fragmentation; and regulatory failure.

3. Three challenges of US bilateral trade agreements

3.1. Democratic deficit

The US negotiation of bilateral trade agreements has been driven by the initiative of the United States Trade Representative ('USTR'), a Cabinet-level trade official.[23] The USTR's initiative in concluding such bilateral trade agreements is mandated by the Trade Act 2002 (US), which sets out the principal negotiating objects to promote adequate and effective protection of intellectual property rights through, *inter alia*, ensuring that intellectual property rights provisions in trade agreements 'reflect a standard of protection similar to that found in United States law'.[24] Furthermore, the result of the amendment introduced by Senators Edward Kennedy and Diane Feinstein in 2006 added to the principal negotiating objectives a need to respect the 2001 Doha Declaration.[25] In accordance with those objectives, the US Government has been authorized to negotiate trade deals and have them approved under 'fast-track' rules, requiring the Congress either to approve or reject them, not to amend them, within a set timeframe.[26]

While these provisions may well be seen as the democratic endorsement of the US trade policy, some of the intellectual property rights rules in the trade agreements are reportedly more restrictive than the existing

[23] See Tom Faunce, 'Global Intellectual Property Protection for Innovative Pharmaceuticals: Challenges for Bioethics and Health Law', in Belinda Bennett and George Tomossy (eds.), *Globalisation and Health: Challenges for Bioethics and Health Law* (2006) 87; Frederick Abbott, 'Toward a New Era of Objective Assessment in the Field of TRIPS and Variable Geometry for the Preservation of Multilateralism' (2005) 8 *Journal of International Economic Law* 77.

[24] Trade Act, 19 USC § 2102(b)(4)(A)(i)(II) (1974).

[25] Ibid., § 2102(b)(4)(C) (1974).

[26] Trade Act, 19 USC § 2903 (2002).

US law.[27] The patent term extension is permitted under US law as well, and yet it is subject to conditions and qualifications to limit the length of extension.[28] The US Food and Drug Administration ('FDA') is required to consider patent status when reviewing generic applications, in a similar manner required under many of the bilateral trade agreements.[29] Despite the wealth of resources at its disposal, far in excess of that of its counterparts in developing countries, the FDA has been unable to prevent abuses of the system by patent holders, causing delays in the availability of generic drugs. As a result, generic manufacturers are now allowed under the US law to go to market under certain circumstances while a patent challenge is pending in court,[30] whereas no analogous measures are included in the bilateral trade agreements.[31]

Even if a tighter restriction makes sense for a wealthy nation like the US, the inadequate governmental or private healthcare system in developing countries will not be capable of absorbing the consequences of such a tighter restriction. For example, the five years of test data protection and marketing exclusivity as a result thereof, even after the expiry of the patent term, was approved by the Drug Price Competition and Patent Term Restoration Act 1984 ('the Hatch-Waxman' Act) (US) in exchange for measures that streamlined approval of generic drugs after the period of exclusivity expired.[32] The direct transplantation of this restriction into bilateral trade agreements has meant a longer period for developing countries to wait to obtain generic, lower cost drugs.[33]

The inclusion of substantive provisions to restrict the margin of appreciation given under the TRIPS Agreement appears at odds with another mandate under the Trade Act 1974 (US), that the 2001 Doha

[27] The comparison between the US law and TRIPS-Plus provisions in each bilateral trade agreement is shown in Table 3.1.

[28] The extension has two clear limitations: (1) it cannot exceed five years; and (2) the total life of a patent from the time of marketing approval cannot exceed fourteen years: 35 USC § 156 (2008). For details, see Jorge, 'Trade Agreements and Public Health', above n. 15, 173.

[29] Federal Food, Drug, and Cosmetic Act 21 USC § 355 (2008).

[30] Federal Food, Drug, and Cosmetic Act 21 USC § 355(j)(5)(B)(iii) (2008).

[31] Frederick Abbott, 'Intellectual Property Provisions of Bilateral and Regional Trade Agreements in Light of U.S. Federal Law' (2006) *United Nations Conference on Trade and Development – International Centre for Trade and Sustainable Development Issue Paper No 12*, www.ictsd.org/pubs/index.htm at 27 January 2009; United States House of Representatives Committee on Government Reform – Minority Staff Special Investigations Division, *Trade Agreements and Access to Medications under the Bush Administration* (June 2005), www.reform.house.gov/ at 27 January 2009.

[32] 35 USC 156 (2008) ('Hatch-Waxman Act').

[33] US House of Representatives Committee on Government Reform, above n. 31, 7–8.

Declaration should be respected.[34] The aggressive approach adopted by the US to bilateral trade agreements stands in sharp contrast to the EU's simple structure built upon its commitment to adhere to multilateral agreements.[35]

The deviation from what it is mandated to achieve under the US legislation by the USTR's bilateral trade negotiators indicates the weakness of democratic control over the drafting of an international agreement. In fact, a report released by congressional researchers found that the USTR had shown little flexibility, maintaining uniformly high demands for the patent protection of pharmaceutical drugs. The USTR was only willing to make concessions in respect of compulsory licensing and parallel importation, and provide dubious undertakings in side letters that intellectual property chapters did not affect the ability of countries to take necessary public health measures.[36] Concerns are not limited to the effect of those TRIPS-Plus agreements in developing countries, but are also about their impact on American consumers' access to affordable medicines as well as the business interests of the US generic industry,[37] which could jeopardize the balance achieved under the Hatch-Waxman Act 1984 (US) between innovation and access to medicines.

Even worse, and arguably responsible for the USTR's inflexible approach, were the 'fast-track' rules for congressional approval of a bilateral trade agreement. Since 2002, the USTR has used this procedure to push controversial trade agreements through Congress, including those with Chile, Singapore, Morocco, Australia, Bahrain and Oman. Trade negotiations have reportedly been accelerated to an alarming speed, denying legislators and the public the appropriate time to consider the serious ramifications of these agreements and, as a result, failing to hold trade negotiators accountable.[38]

34 Trade Act, 19 USC § 2101(4)(C) (1974).

35 See Maximiliano Santa Cruz, 'Intellectual Property Provisions in European Union Trade Agreements: Implications for Developing Countries' (2007) *United Nations Conference on Trade and Development – International Centre for Trade and Sustainable Development Issue Paper No 20*, www.ictsd.org/pubs/index.htm at 27 January 2009; Assafa Endeshaw, 'Free Trade Agreements as Surrogates for TRIPs-Plus' (2006) 28 *European Intellectual Property Review* 374, 376–7.

36 US Government Accountability Office, *International Trade – An Analysis of Free Trade Agreements and Congressional and Private Sector Consultations under Trade Promotion Authority* (November 2007), www.gao.gov/new.items/d0859.pdf at 27 January 2009.

37 Jorge, 'Trade Agreements and Public Health', above n. 15, 170.

38 For criticism against the fast-track procedure, see Todd Tucker and Lori Wallach, *The Rise and Fall of Fast Track Trade Authority* (2008) Public Citizens Global Trade Watch, 108–14 www.citizen.org/documents/riseandfall.pdf at 27 January 2009.

General criticism has been levelled that a long-term election cycle does not provide effective democratic control over international law-making at the initiative of executive governments.[39] When it comes to negotiating and implementing regulatory treaties, expedited procedures tend to reduce the involvement of the legislature and judiciary in the international regulatory process even more.[40] Globalization and the rise of multinational corporations have also spurred on the democratic deficit at the international level.[41] The democratic deficit in treaty-making and international relations more generally may not be perceived as a concern by virtue of their nature, requiring caution and secrecy rather than open democratic discourse.[42] Yet the very fact that the USTR's initiative departed from its legislative mandate indicates that the democratic foundation for the authority to conclude bilateral trade agreements may have been undermined at least to the extent that the level of regulation is more restrictive than the existing US law and does not respect the 2001 Doha Declaration.

The USTR's endeavour could well be perceived to retain democratic legitimacy to the extent that it has attempted to ensure that intellectual property rights provisions in trade agreements reflect US standards and respect the 2001 Doha Declaration. Yet trading partners with the United States may find that TRIPS-Plus agreements lack the same degree of legitimacy, democratic or otherwise. The Colombia–US FTA was particularly problematic partially due to Colombia's atrocious human rights record.[43]

3.2. *Normative fragmentation*

The legitimacy of the TRIPS-Plus bilateral trade agreements concluded on US initiative was challenged in many different multinational forums including the World Health Organization ('WHO') and United Nations (UN) human rights bodies. Despite the initial discontent with granting the WHO competence to review health-related intellectual property

[39] Louis Henkin, *Constitutionalism, Democracy and Foreign Affairs* (1990) 65.

[40] Anonymous, 'Discretion and Legitimacy in International Regulation' (1993–4) 107 *Harvard Law Review* 1099.

[41] Susan Strange, 'The Erosion of the State' (1997) 11 *Current History* 365, 366–7.

[42] For discussion, see Jack Goldsmith and Eric Posner, *The Limits of International Law* (2005) 195–205; Thomas M. Franck, 'Can the United States Delegate Aspects of Sovereignty to International Regimes?', in Thomas M. Franck (ed.), *Delegating State Powers: The Effect of Treaty Regimes on Democracy and Sovereignty* (2000) 1, 2–3.

[43] Gimena Sanchez and Vicki Gass, *WOLA's Human Rights Arguments against the Colombia FTA* (7 April 2008), www.wola.org/ at 27 January 2009.

issues, the WHO has taken the initiative in offering pragmatic suggestions for states to reconcile competing objectives. While showing some understanding of the rationale underlying the TRIPS Agreement with emphasis on its inherent flexibility, WHO's position against the TRIPS-Plus bilateral trade agreements has been more straightforward.[44] The position adopted by UN human rights bodies has generally been far more critical of intellectual property rights in this area,[45] likewise criticizing the adoption of TRIPS-Plus standards.[46]

Compliance with TRIPS-Plus agreements may lead states to fail to comply with rules of international law, such as that allowing the use of test data except for unfair commercial use under TRIPS and the right to health enshrined in article 12(2) of the International Covenant on Economic, Social and Cultural Rights.[47] Even if the treaty obligations do not conflict with each other,[48] compliance with one rule may well frustrate the goals of another rule. Concerned about the potential impact of such conflicts of rules, the International Law Commission took up the task of studying the fragmentation of international law, resulting in the 2006 Report of the Study Group chaired and finalized by Professor Martti Koskenniemi.[49] The Report examined practical, legal techniques that are already available to resolve such normative conflicts.

[44] World Health Organization, *Globalization, TRIPS and Access to Pharmaceuticals: WHO Policy Perspectives on Medicines*, No 3, WHO Doc WHO/EDM/2001.2 (March 2001) 6.

[45] See, e.g., Laurence Helfer, 'Regime Shifting: The TRIPs Agreement and New Dynamics of International Intellectual Property Lawmaking' (2004) 29 *Yale Journal of International Law* 1, 49–51; David Weissbrodt and Kell Schoff, 'A Human Rights Approach to Intellectual Property Protection: The Genesis and Application of Sub-Commission Resolution 2000/7' (2003) 5 *Minnesota Intellectual Property Review* 1.

[46] See, e.g., United Nations, *Report of the High Commissioner – The Impact of the Agreement on Trade-Related Aspects of Intellectual Property Rights on Human Rights*, [10]–[15], [27]–[58], UN Doc E/CN.4/Sub.2/2001/13 (2001); Stephen Marks, *Report of the High-Level Task Force on the Implementation of the Right to Development on its Second Meeting*, [67], UN Doc E/CN.4/2005/WG.18/TF/3 (2005); Julia-Antoanella Motoc, *Specific Human Rights Issues – Human Rights and the Human Genome: Interim Report Submitted by the Special Rapporteur*, [28], UN Doc E/CN.4/Sub.2/2005/38 (2005).

[47] International Covenant on Economic, Social and Cultural Rights, opened for signature 16 December 1966, 993 UNTS 3 (entered into force 3 January 1976).

[48] Article 1 of TRIPS provides that: 'Members may, but shall not be obliged to, implement in their law more extensive protection than is required by this Agreement, *provided that such protection does not contravene the provisions of this Agreement*' (emphasis added).

[49] United Nations, *Fragmentation of International Law: Difficulties Arising from the Diversification and Expansion of International Law*, UN Doc A/CN.4/L.682 (13 April 2006) ('Koskenniemi Report').

One of the techniques elaborated on in the Koskenniemi Report and relevant to the conflicts between TRIPS and TRIPS-Plus agreements is the rule on the modification of multilateral treaties. Article 41 of the Vienna Convention on the Law of Treaties allows two or more of the parties to a multilateral treaty to unilaterally modify the treaty between themselves if it is not prohibited by the treaty, only in circumstances where the modification would not affect the enjoyment by the other parties of their rights or the performance of their obligations under the treaty and the modification would not be incompatible with the effective execution of the object and purpose of the treaty as a whole. It is arguable that the terms of the TRIPS-Plus agreements potentially affect the enjoyment by other WTO members of their rights and benefits under the TRIPS Agreement, frustrating abilities to produce and market more affordable generic medicines after the expiry of the twenty-year patent term of a brand-name medicine or to take advantage of compulsory licences. Yet the practical significance of this legal technique to resolve normative conflicts is limited, for the *inter se* agreement concluded in deviation from the original treaty is not thereby invalidated.[50] Instead, it may provide a ground for suspension or termination of the original treaty or a cause for the operation of the rules of state responsibility.

Whether or not intended to alleviate such potential conflicts, some of the TRIPS-Plus agreements contain a 'side letter', which provides that nothing in the agreements impede a party's 'ability' to take necessary measures to protect public health.[51] However, the interpretive value of the letters is limited or even questionable, according to the position taken by the Bush administration that interpretation of the agreements will only be 'informed' by letters.[52] The uncertainty surrounding the significance of this letter does not help parties to the bilateral trade agreement in deciding the legality of the use of compulsory licensing, nor does it resolve the normative conflicts in any systematic way.

When there is a conflict between competing policies or rationalities of different international organizations, multinational forums often operate to reformulate the principles based on a different rationale and to allow for building responsive external linkages within the self-organization of

[50] Ibid., 164 [319].

[51] A side letter is incorporated into CAFTA and the agreements with Morocco, Bahrain and Peru.

[52] See Mercurio, 'TRIPS-Plus Provisions in FTAs', above n. 10, 234–5; Abbott, 'The WTO Medicines Decision', above n. 17, 353; US House of Representatives Committee on Government Reform, above n. 31, 11.

the regime.[53] Illustrative is the incorporation of public health rationales into the WTO regime through the adoption of the 2001 Doha Declaration and the WTO General Council Decision of 30 August 2003. This is in fact the strategy that less powerful states have taken advantage of: consciously creating legal inconsistencies and conflicts by way of forum-shifting.[54] Such soft law-making could have a normative effect in implementing the TRIPS Agreement. Yet it remains to be seen whether multinational, normative soft law-making sets the minimum standards of fairness and equity and to what extent such minimum standards can render TRIPS-Plus standards illegitimate. Those counter-regime norms will not easily be translated into effective prescriptions over national regulators without introducing new multilateral treaty-making efforts.[55]

3.3. *Regulatory failure*

International trade law traditionally imposed only a narrow set of limits on national autonomy confined to measures at the border such as tariffs and quotas. Even though it has become more intrusive in the post-Uruguay Round era, the role of the WTO has remained limited to the allocation of regulatory jurisdiction. Each member state retains the scope for exercising a margin of appreciation with regard to the way in which it complies with trade law to the extent that doing so does not impose 'excessive' costs on foreign states in trade terms.[56] In fact, the TRIPS Agreement is explicit in stating that '[m]embers shall be free to determine the appropriate method of implementing the provisions of this Agreement within their own legal system and practice'.[57] The US bilateral trade agreements limiting the margin of appreciation in exercising the regulatory authority over pharmaceutical patents extend well beyond such boundaries.

TRIPS is in essence an attempt to harmonize the regulatory framework for intellectual property rights, characterizing certain products or processes as private goods, rather than public goods, through the vehicle of

[53] Andreas Fischer-Lescano and Gunther Teubner (Michelle Everson trans.), 'Regime-Collisions: The Vain Search for Legal Unity in the Fragmentation of Global Law' (2004) 25 *Michigan Journal of International Law* 999, 1027–30.

[54] Helfer, 'Regime Shifting', above n. 45, 58–9. [55] Ibid., 60.

[56] Joel Trachtman, 'Regulatory Jurisdiction and the WTO' (2007) 10 *Journal of International Economic Law* 631, 647.

[57] TRIPS Agreement, above n. 3, article 1(1).

patent law. There is no legal definition of 'public goods'. In economic terms, public goods are characterized by their non-rivalrous and non-excludable nature. Knowledge is often labelled an 'impure public good' in that although consumption of knowledge does not exclude others from its benefits or diminish its availability, the character of the good can be changed by the use of legal norms to erect exclusionary barriers to the good.[58] For the purpose of international regulation of goods, it is up to states to decide collectively whether to confer legal protection as a public good or a private good.[59] The conclusion of the TRIPS Agreement can thus be seen as the move to enclose the knowledge of how to produce essential medicines in the private domain, as expressly stated in its preamble.[60]

Yet the TRIPS Agreement does not exclude the public use of private goods. It allows for limited exceptions to the exclusive rights conferred by a patent (article 30) and for other use of a patented product through compulsory licence (article 31). It was the collective decision that WTO member states made to create a system of collective regulation on the cross-border use of private goods. The collective decision characterized the legal nature of patented products in such a way as to allow for their public use under certain circumstances. The restriction of such public use of a private good by bilateral trade agreements as well as the extension of the patent term poses questions as to the legitimacy of such agreements.

The excessive influence by a powerful foreign state upon the behaviour of national regulators has arguably resulted in a regulatory failure, especially in developing countries where the introduction of tight regulation of intellectual property may have generated more costs than benefits. The situation may well be seen as comparable to where national regulators are 'captured' by the regulated industry.[61] When viewed in

[58] See, e.g., Joseph Stiglitz, 'Knowledge as a Global Public Good', in Inge Kaul, Isabelle Grunberg and Marc A. Stern (eds.), *Global Public Goods: International Cooperation in the 21st Century* (1999) 306. See also Peter Drahos, 'The Regulation of Public Goods' (2004) 7 *Journal of International Economic Law* 321.

[59] Sarah Heathcote, 'Les biens publics mondiaux et le droit international: quelques réflexions à propos de la gestion de l'intérêt commun' (2002) 13 *L'Observateur des Nations Unies* 137, 139–53.

[60] The preamble to the TRIPS Agreement '[r]ecogniz[es] that intellectual property rights are private rights'.

[61] For the concept of 'capture', see, e.g., Toni Makkai and John Braithwaite, 'In and Out of the Revolving Door: Making Sense of Regulatory Capture' (1992) 12 *Journal of Public Policy* 61; Michael Levine and Jennifer Forrence, 'Regulatory Capture, Public Interest and Public Agenda: Toward a Synthesis' (1990) 6 *Journal of Law, Economics and Organization* 167.

light of the resources relevant to the holding of regulatory power and the exercise of regulatory capacity, the USTR's initiative, combined with the informational and organizational capacities of multinational corporations, can be seen as an occupation of 'regulatory space'.[62] Yet, while offering a fruitful agenda for research on the behaviour of different actors, those analytical concepts do not assist in making normative decisions as to how regulation should interact with its environment or how to make it legitimate.[63] Can international law provide shared values by reference to which the regulatory failure caused by such bilateral trade agreements can be addressed in substantive terms?

4. Public law perspective to the bilateral trade regulation of essential medicines

4.1. *Legitimacy of TRIPS-Plus agreements*

The Commission on Intellectual Property, Innovation and Public Health examined the role of intellectual property in stimulating innovation for diseases that disproportionately affect developing countries. Its report published in 2006 urged that '[b]ilateral trade agreements should not seek to incorporate TRIPS-Plus protection in ways that may reduce access to medicines in developing countries'.[64] Sound as it may be as a public health policy, there is no rule of international law that would render TRIPS-Plus agreements unlawful or invalid within the traditional framework of public international law. However, the democratic deficit, the normative fragmentation, and the regulatory failure in the TRIPS-Plus agreements are serious enough to cast doubt on international law's legitimacy.[65]

[62] For the concept of 'regulatory space', see Colin Scott, 'Analysing Regulatory Space: Fragmented Resources and Institutional Design' (2001) *Public Law* 329; Leigh Hancher and Michael Moran, 'Organizing Regulatory Space', in Leigh Hancher and Michael Moran (eds.), *Capitalism, Culture, and Economic Regulation* (1989), 271.

[63] See Tony Prosser, 'Theorising Utility Regulation' (1999) 62 *Modern Law Review* 196, 205.

[64] Commission on Intellectual Property Rights, Innovation and Public Health, *Public Health, Innovation and Intellectual Property Rights* (2006) recommendation 4.21. See also, Ellen 't Hoen, 'Report of the Commission on Intellectual Property Rights, Innovation and Public Health: A Call to Governments' (2006) 84 *Bulletin of the World Health Organization* 421.

[65] The same question has been posed in legal theory as to the legitimacy of the law adopted in a procedurally democratic way without compliance with certain substantive values.

It may well be due to its rigidity and formalism, drawing largely on the private nature of international law, that the traditional international law on treaties faces its limits in examining the substantive aspects of contemporary treaty-making practice. This is particularly so when, as is the case with TRIPS-Plus agreements, a treaty has significant ramifications for or direct impact upon the regulation of domestic markets. Restriction of the grounds for compulsory licensing and the obligation to protect test data, for example, intervene in directing the way in which national regulators may regulate the use of pharmaceutical patents and test data.

The limits of international law arising from regulatory treaty-making are also observed in the development of supranational regulatory regimes, such as those in Europe. It could be said that distrust of the effectiveness of intergovernmental agreements to address the transnational market failure in Europe has led national authorities to delegate their regulatory powers to a supranational authority.[66] As the European Union, whose decisions are directly affecting European citizens, increasingly performs similar functions to a national state, calls have been expressed for appropriate legitimation of its authority. Some commentators rely on the application of the liberal–democratic criteria of legitimacy, whereas others stress the difference between national polity and a supranational entity directing attention to legitimacy by outcome.[67] Different ideas of legitimation can be categorized, using Scharpf's terminology, into 'input legitimacy' and 'output legitimacy'.[68] On the input side, legitimacy requires mechanisms or procedures to link political or administrative decisions to the preferences of citizens, whereas output legitimacy will be ensured by producing effective outcomes that achieve the goals that citizens collectively care about.

Legitimacy in international law is a jurisprudential construct that helps explain the general conformity of states to the international rule of law in the absence of a coercive power or other motivations. Franck thus examined the legitimacy in international law as:

See, e.g., Wojciech Sadurski, 'Law's Legitimacy and "Democracy-Plus"' (2006) 26 *Oxford Journal of Legal Studies* 377.

66 Giandomenico Majone, 'The Rise of the Regulatory State in Europe' (1994) 17 *West European Politics* 77, 89–90.

67 For different criteria of legitimacy, see, e.g., Piret Ehin, 'Competing Models of EU Legitimacy: The Test of Popular Expectations' (2008) 46 *Journal of Common Market Studies* 619.

68 See Fritz Scharpf, *Governing in Europe: Effective and Democratic?* (1999).

> A property of a rule or rule-making institution which itself exerts a pull toward compliance on those addressed normatively because those addressed believe that the rule or institution has come into being and operates in accordance with generally accepted principles of right process.[69]

The right process, according to Franck, not only includes the notion of valid sources but also encompasses literary, socio-anthropological and philosophical insights. The notion of legitimacy is also relevant to international regulatory agreements. Chayes and Chayes thus suggest in the context of international regulatory treaties that the legitimacy of a norm depends on the extent to which it emanates from a fair and accepted procedure, is applied without invidious discrimination and does not offend minimum standards of fairness and equity.[70] The question is whether TRIPS-Plus agreements are concluded in accordance with a right and fair process and to what extent they conform to minimum standards of fairness and equity.

The conclusion and implementation of a bilateral trade agreement do not involve delegation of regulatory powers to a supranational institution. Nevertheless, some provisions of the TRIPS-Plus agreements suffer the same legitimacy deficit due to the restriction of regulatory powers by external force. Both directions of transnational regulation are pursued in the interest of multinational, export-oriented industries. In both cases, the implementation of international treaties is intended to dictate the way in which national authorities regulate the domestic market. It appears reasonable therefore to make international law involving the restriction of regulatory powers of national authorities likewise subject to the test of input and output legitimacy. Two questions underlie this move: what mechanisms or processes should be put in place to link treaty-making to preferences of citizens? What collective values must be expressed and maintained in treaty-making processes?

4.2. *Input legitimacy*

As explained above, a democratic deficit is to an extent inherent in international law-making, especially in the case of regulatory treaties.[71] International law-making can still retain its traditional legitimacy

[69] Thomas M. Franck, *The Power of Legitimacy among Nations* (1990) 19.

[70] See Abram Chayes and Antonia H. Chayes, *The New Sovereignty: Compliance with International Regulatory Agreements* (1995) 127.

[71] See section 3.1.

without democratic pedigree when the tasks in question, especially those of a transnational or supranational nature, require an answer that goes beyond the purview of individual states.[72] Democratic decision-making at the national or local level is not enough to rectify the democratic deficit at the international level, as long as the interests of all the principal stakeholders are not represented. International law's legitimacy is thus called into question when the interests at stake are felt closer to each individual citizen. The lack of representation during the negotiations of TRIPS-Plus agreements, which have tended to be driven and dictated by the interests of big brand pharmaceutical companies, is well documented,[73] indicating the weakness of input legitimacy.

The input legitimacy of US bilateral trade agreements is further eroded by the fact that the negotiations tend to have been conducted in a non-transparent manner at the initiative of the USTR, leaving the public with no opportunity to access the texts or influence the outcome of negotiations.[74] The increased transparency may in fact have helped stall the negotiations for the Free Trade Area of the Americas ('FTAA'); an ongoing process since 1994. In positively responding to the increased calls for transparency during and after the North American Free Trade Agreement ('NAFTA') negotiations, US trade ministers decided in 2001 to release the draft negotiating texts to the public, thereby providing grounds for the business community and civil society to voice their interests and concerns. The negotiation process has reportedly failed to respond adequately to those external stakeholders.[75]

The lack of transparency and opportunity for wider community involvement stands in sharp contrast to the multilateral trade negotiations. It is reported that the multilateral trade negotiations over TRIPS were also profoundly affected by the use of trade sanctions by the US and

[72] See Andreas L. Paulus, 'Subsidiarity, Fragmentation and Democracy: Towards the Demise of General International Law?', in Tomer Broude and Yuval Shany (eds.), *The Shifting Allocation of Authority in International Law* (2008) 193, 204–6.

[73] See, e.g., Susan K. Sell, 'Industry Strategies for Intellectual Property and Trade: The Quest for TRIPS, and Post-TRIPS Strategies' (2002) 10 *Cardozo Journal of International and Comparative Law* 79.

[74] See Frederick Abbott, 'The Doha Declaration on the TRIPS Agreement and Public Health and the Contradictory Trend in Bilateral and Regional Free Trade Agreements' (Quaker United Nations Office Occasional Paper No 14, 2004) 3, www.quno.org at 28 January 2009.

[75] See Donald R. Mackay, 'Challenges Confronting the Free Trade Area of the Americas' (June 2002), Canadian Foundation for the Americas Policy Paper, www.focal.ca at 2 February 2009.

to a lesser extent the European Community ('EC').[76] Yet the multilateral forum helps diffuse the pressure applied by powerful developed states and also provides avenues for NGO groups to play an effective role in counterbalancing this pressure.[77] In fact, Brazil and Argentina refused to renew FTAA negotiations with the US in 2005 prior to the WTO meetings precisely because they could leverage the power they have built in alliance with other emerging economies such as India, China and African countries, giving them a far broader base to confront the US.[78]

4.3. *Output legitimacy*

The effectiveness of the outcome of trade negotiations necessarily depends on the priorities of the negotiating parties. There is no doubt that further restrictive regulation of access to essential medicines has immediate, negative impacts upon public health in developing countries. On the other hand, attention should also be focused on the need to devise an economically stable innovation system for long-term benefit to all countries.[79] The question comes down to whether there are shared values within the international community by reference to which a moral disagreement can be resolved. The core value expressed by the Hatch-Waxman Act 1984 (US) – achieving the right balance between innovation and access to medicines within the US – does not appear to be shared by the wider international community. It is even more difficult to maintain output legitimacy of regulatory provisions that are stricter than the existing US law, inasmuch as the former are pursued in the interests of a handful of multinational companies rather than to achieve the goals that even US citizens collectively care about.

A common feature of national regulators is the administrative and technical discretion given to them with decisional autonomy. The independent and yet influential status of national regulators not subject to the principle of the separation of powers has raised an issue of

[76] See, e.g., Susan K. Sell, 'Intellectual Property Protection and Antitrust in the Developing World: Crisis, Coercion, and Choice' (1995) 49 *International Organization* 315.

[77] See, e.g., Scott Lucyk, 'Patents, Politics and Public Health: Access to Essential Medicines under the TRIPS Agreement' (2006–7) 38 *Ottawa Law Review* 191, 214–15.

[78] Laura Carlsen, *Timely Demise for Free Trade Area of the Americas* (23 November 2005), Americas Program, Center for International Policy, americas.irc-online.org/am/2954 at 2 February 2009.

[79] See, e.g., Jerome Reichman, 'Nurturing a Transnational System of Innovation' (2007) 16 *Journal of Transnational Law and Policy* 143, 152.

accountability. The US literature on this issue has emphasized legislative and executive oversight, strict procedural requirements and substantive judicial review as ways of holding regulators accountable.[80] Yet when a regulatory treaty is involved to restrict the margin of appreciation given to national authorities, executive oversight and strict procedural requirements can play little role in enhancing the output legitimacy. Likewise, substantive judicial review would also be of little help unless the separation of domestic law from international law allows for a robust judicial intervention as is the case in the US.

There is an emerging view that a rights-based approach should be taken towards medicines programmes,[81] based on the right to health as enshrined in article 12(2) of the International Covenant on Economic, Social and Cultural Rights.[82] This right can strengthen national essential medicines programmes by requiring consultation with all beneficiaries of the medicine, setting up mechanisms for transparency and accountability, ensuring equality and non-discrimination in access to essential medicines and creating safeguards and redress mechanisms for human rights violations.[83] The rights-based approach may provide a justification for not implementing economic efficiency-based policies on the ground that people do not enter markets as equals and therefore such policies will defeat other social values such as access to essential medicines among worse-off members of the international community.[84] The development of institutional mechanisms based on the rights-based approach may contribute to a more objective assessment of the output legitimacy of the higher set of standards of intellectual property protection established in bilateral trade agreements compared to multilateral agreements.

5. Conclusion

Bilateral trade agreements have a strategic value rather than an immediate economic value for the US. It appears that the US Government's leverage is greater in bilateral negotiations than in larger forums where other major

80 See, e.g., Martin Shapiro, *Who Guards the Guardians?: Judicial Control of Administration* (1988).

81 See, e.g., Hans V. Hogerzeil, 'Essential Medicines and Human Rights: What Can They Learn from Each Other?' (2006) 84 *Bulletin of the World Health Organization* 371.

82 See above n. 47.

83 Hogerzeil, 'Essential Medicines and Human Rights', above n. 81, 373–4.

84 See Anna Coote, *The Welfare of Citizens: Developing New Social Rights* (1992).

and emerging economic powers are also present.[85] Developing countries have been responding to such tactics by taking advantage of forum-shifting in different multilateral arenas. Growing awareness within US politics of the wider effects of TRIPS-Plus agreements has resulted in some domestic impetus for change. For instance, modifications to the US–Peru TPA followed as a result of negotiation by congressional Democrats with the Bush administration.[86] Yet recourse to soft law-making and reliance on the shift in US domestic politics are too opportunistic to counter the hard law system supported by legalized dispute resolution mechanisms and unilateral trade sanctions.

The traditional framework of treaty law, drawing on the private nature of international law, does not adequately address its own legitimacy issues arising from the democratic deficit, normative fragmentation and regulatory failure that the US bilateral trade agreements have been causing and reinforcing in developing countries. The use of bilateral agreements in dictating the exercise of regulatory powers is irreconcilable with the public nature of regulation in both domestic and transnational contexts without the development of a public law framework. Multinational forums are more appropriate, if not perfect, venues for engaging in public law-making since they involve participation of a wider community of members and the self-adjustment techniques accommodate different policies and rationales. Given the public nature of transnational regulation, it is reasonable to argue that bilateral trade agreements dictating to national regulators on standard-settings are subject to public law scrutiny in light of input and output legitimacy, requiring wider community consultation and institutional rights-based development.

[85] Richard Feinberg, 'The Political Economy of United States' Free Trade Arrangements' (2003) 26 *World Economy* 1019, 1034–6.

[86] See Vaughan, *US–Peru Trade Deal*, above n. 16; Lori M. Wallach, 'Our Statements: Majority of House Democrats Stand Up for Constituents' (8 November 2007) *Public Citizens*, citizen.typepad.com/eyesontrade/2007/11/our-statement-m.html at 3 February 2009.

4

Global health and development: patents and public interest

ELIZABETH SIEW-KUAN NG*

1. Introduction

Rapid advancements in science and technology have posed immense challenges to the international patent system, which has created wealth for as many as it has sparked outrage in others. This technological revolution has triggered unprecedented global competition that is likely to accentuate the polarity and disparity between nations in intellectual property rights creation, exploitation and utilization.

Whilst some differences may never be equalized, global and open dialogues must prevail for further utilization of the inherent flexibility within the international patent system in order to forge shared values for a robust patent regime that meets common approval. The lack of homogeneity in industry, national economic and technological performance may compel more rigorous differentiation over time, space and subject-matter to accommodate overriding public interests, such as those relating to public health and development.

Due care must be taken to ensure greater flexibility in implementation and avert the risk of alienation of any member nation or alignment of national blocs along lines of mutual interest. Whilst the temptation may often be to argue for enhanced protection, an over-zealous protection of intellectual property may stifle further innovation. Whilst no one denies that the patent owner deserves returns from the investment of considerable resources and ought to be adequately protected, the trade-offs

* The author would like to thank all the participants of the Australian National University's workshop on *Incentives for Global Public Health: Patent Law and Access to Essential Medicines* (Canberra, 26–28 May 2008) for their very helpful comments on earlier drafts, particularly Professors Kim Rubenstein and Thomas Pogge and Dr Matthew Rimmer. The views expressed in this work are, of course, solely those of the author and the commentators do not necessarily agree with them.

cannot be ignored. We need to strike a better balance between public and private interests rather than assume that enhanced protection will continue to provide a panacea for innovation.

This chapter[1] will build on the work of eminent scholars in relation to patents and public health issues. It will seek to highlight the need to persevere with the quest to strike a delicate balance between, on the one hand, the protection of ideas to encourage innovation and investment therein and, on the other, ensuring that protection itself does not stifle further innovation and access to medicine for public health. It will provide some observations on selected avenues of reform. The chapter will also highlight development issues, particularly those relating to the recently adopted World Intellectual Property Organization ('WIPO') Development Agenda[2] which is clearly a step in the right direction towards ensuring that the development of an intellectual property protection regime does not proceed along a 'one size fits all' regime.

2. Role of the patent system

The traditional role of the patent system, which seeks to balance the competing objectives of encouraging innovation through appropriate incentives and providing reasonable access to, and use of, the knowledge and information therefrom, persists today. Whilst it is undeniable that legal protection for the fruits of innovation enables the patent owner to benefit from an 'exclusive market position' with the temporary ability to set prices above the marginal costs of production, there is also great societal benefit in the dissemination of, and access to, knowledge and information that may be derived therefrom.

The patent system needs to achieve an appropriate trade-off between protection and access. This is particularly so in the development of new technologies and medicines that entail considerable investment in research and development, which is fraught with significant risks and uncertainties. The pharmaceutical industry in developed countries is 'more strongly dependent on the patent system than most other

[1] This work is based on parts of an earlier report by the author that was commissioned by the Director-General of the World Intellectual Property Organization (WIPO) and submitted by the WIPO Secretariat to the WIPO 39th General Assembly of member states of WIPO, see Elizabeth Siew-Kuan Ng, *The Impact of the International Patent System on Developing Countries,* WIPO Doc A/39/13 Add.3 (2003) (Report presented to the WIPO under terms of a Special Service Agreement).

[2] The World Intellectual Property Organization Development Agenda, www.wipo.int/ip-development/en/agenda/.

industrial sectors to recoup its past R&D [research and development] costs, to generate profits, and to fund R&D for future products'.[3] Indeed, the Coalition for Intellectual Property Rights ('CIPR') noted that:

> Successive surveys have shown that the pharmaceutical companies, more than any other sector, think patent protection to be very important in maintaining their R&D expenditures and technological innovation. The industry understandably takes a close interest in the global application of IPRs, and generally resists the contention that they constitute a major barrier to access or a deterrent to development in developing countries.[4]

Whilst it may be easy to give in to the temptation for enhanced protection as a means of 'promoting the public good', some critics have cautioned against shifting 'control and ownership over technology from the public to the private, serving to commodify vital technological information that they argue should remain in the public domain'.[5] Its impact particularly in relation to access to medicine in developing countries needs to be carefully assessed, since if prices are raised this will 'fall especially hard upon poor people, particularly in the absence of widespread provision for public health as exists in most developed countries'.[6]

It is, therefore, important that in seeking to strike this delicate balance the international patent system averts the perception of prioritization of private rights over public welfare, particularly in the field of public health and development. In this regard, it may be timely to heed the call of the Friends of Development for the promotion of a 'fair balance between intellectual property protection and the public interest' taking into account the different levels of development of the stakeholders of the intellectual property system

3. TRIPS Agreement: a tilt in global intellectual property rules towards developed countries

While few would argue that intellectual property protection is needed in the developed world, some 'question whether it is appropriate to extend

[3] Commission on Intellectual Property Rights ('CIPR'), *Integrating Intellectual Property Rights and Development Policy* (2002) 29, www.iprcommission.org/ at 5 February 2009.

[4] Ibid.

[5] World Intellectual Property Organization, *Patent Agenda: Options for Development of the International Patent System*, WIPO Doc A/37/6 (2002) annex I, 3 (Memorandum of the Director-General) ('WIPO Patent Agenda').

[6] CIPR, above n. 3, 30.

its coverage to the developing world, which the TRIPS Agreement is gradually doing'.[7] The World Bank has observed that many of the developing countries agreed to the Agreement on Trade-Related Aspects of Intellectual Property Rights ('TRIPS Agreement' or 'TRIPS')[8] in order to gain concessions from rich ones in other areas of economic activity (or for greater aid).[9] However, the 'promise of long-term benefits seems uncertain and costly to achieve in many nations, especially the poorest countries'.[10] This is particularly so in countries which lack the requisite technological capability to benefit from domestic innovation and hence generate less intellectual property. It is therefore an open question as to whether these developing countries actually did gain concessions from the developed world in agreeing to the TRIPS Agreement. However, as with all international agreements, the benefits from participation are difficult to quantify, let alone equalize. The links between intellectual property rights, innovation, foreign direct investment and long-term economic growth are poorly understood and remain controversial. Although the theoretical literature emphasizes the importance of intellectual property regimes, the empirical evidence is ambiguous overall.[11] It appears to be non-linear and certainly seems to be dependent on other factors, such as the level

[7] Sir Richard Sykes, 'Presentation at the Royal Institute of International Affairs', London, 14 March 2002) cited in CIPR, above n. 3, 30.

[8] Marrakesh Agreement Establishing the World Trade Organization, opened for signature 15 April 1994, 1867 UNTS 3, annex 1C (Agreement on Trade-Related Aspects of Intellectual Property Rights) (entered into force 1 January 1995) ('TRIPS Agreement').

[9] See, e.g., Sanjaya Lall and Manuel Albaladejo, 'Indicators of the Relative Importance of IPRs in Developing Countries' (Working Paper No 85, Queen Elizabeth House Working Paper Series QEHWPS85, 2002); Carlos Alberto Primo Braga, Carsten Fink and Claudia Paz Sepulveda, *Intellectual Property Rights and Economic Development* (2000); Keith Maskus, *Intellectual Property Rights in the Global Economy* (2000).

[10] The World Bank, *Intellectual Property: Balancing Incentives with Competitive Access* (2001) 128, siteresources.worldbank.org/INTGEP2002/Resources/gep2002complete.pdf at 23 April 2009.

[11] Ibid., 146. Some studies find no relationship between the level of intellectual property rights protection and foreign direct investment ('FDI') or licensing: see, e.g., Braga, Fink and Sepulveda, *Intellectual Property Rights and Economic Development*, above n. 9. Other studies show a positive effect of strong intellectual property regimes on FDI both in influencing location decisions by multinational corporations and in inducing foreign firms to invest in production rather than in distribution activities: Beata S. Javorcik, 'Does Foreign Direct Investment Increase the Productivity of Domestic Firms? In Search of Spillovers through Backward Linkages' (2004) 94 *American Economic Review* 605; Jeong-Yeon Lee and Edwin Mansfield, 'Intellectual Property Protection and U.S. Foreign Direct Investment' (1996) 78 *The Review of Economics and Statistics* 181; Edwin Mansfield, 'Intellectual Property Protection, Foreign Direct Investment and

of economic development,[12] maturity of the legal system, political will to adopt appropriate initiatives, quality of the labour force, effective transfers of technology, effective functioning of state machinery and the nature of the sector.[13]

Be that as it may, the perception of a tilt in the global intellectual property rules in favour of the developed world and the uncertainty surrounding the nature of the long-term benefits to the less-developed world have made the underlying unhappiness of some less-developed countries more acute in recent years. This is particularly so when compared with the immediate costs and benefits of settling for a weaker

Technology Transfer' (Working Paper No 19, The World Bank, 1994); Keith Maskus, 'The International Regulation of Intellectual Property' (1998) 134 *Review of World Economics* 186. Some evidence suggests that while a stronger intellectual property rights regime is associated with a rise in flows of knowledge to affiliates and in inward FDI towards middle-income and large developing countries, this is not the case for poor countries: Carsten Fink and Keith Maskus (eds.), *Intellectual Property and Development: Lessons from Recent Economic Research* (2005); Bernard Hoekman, Keith Maskus and Kamal Saggi, 'Transfer of Technology to Developing Countries: Unilateral and Multilateral Policy Options' (2005) 33 *World Development* 1587; Pamela Smith, 'How Do Foreign Patent Rights Affect U.S. Exports, Affiliate Sales, and Licenses?' (2001) 55 *Journal of International Economics* 411. In addition to dismantling barriers to foreign investment, some middle-income countries have encouraged greater FDI flows by implementing stronger regimes governing intellectual property rights. A few countries have encouraged joint ventures rather than FDI to maximize technology transfers to local firms. However, this strategy seems to work only for countries with substantial market power. In particular, fear of losing control over cutting-edge technologies sometimes causes multinational firms forced into joint ventures to reserve their best technologies for the domestic market and transfer only older less-efficient ones: ibid., 121. Alternatively, they may only be willing to license out-of-date technologies: Maskus, *Intellectual Property Rights in the Global Economy*, above n. 9; see also International Intellectual Property Alliance, 'Initial Survey of the Contribution of the Copyright Industries to Economic Development' (April 2005), www.iipa.com/pdf/2005_Apr27_Economic_Development_Survey.pdf at 23 April 2009. Data on US multinationals show that the likelihood of entering into licensing agreements increases as developing countries increase their protection of intellectual property rights: Pol Antras, Mihir Desai and Fritz Foley, 'Multinational Firms, FDI Flows and Imperfect Capital Markets' (Working Paper No W12855, National Bureau of Economic Research, 2007).

12 See, e.g., Carsten Fink, 'Intellectual Property Rights and US and German International Transactions in Manufacturing Industries' (Manuscript, The World Bank, 1997).

13 Intellectual property appears to have little impact on investment in lower technology goods, such as textiles and apparel; services sectors, such as distribution and hotels; or in sectors where the sophistication of the technology itself or the cost of production already serves as an effective barrier to entry. Indeed, the increased ease with which some products such as pharmaceuticals, chemicals, food additives and software are reproduced may explain the rising interest in establishing intellectual property rights. See also The World Bank, *Intellectual Property*, above n. 10, 147; Keith Maskus, 'Intellectual Property Rights and Foreign Direct Investment' (Policy Discussion Paper No 22, Centre for International Economic Studies, University of Adelaide, 2000).

intellectual property regime. The controversy arising from the HIV/AIDS pandemic and global health crisis that has triggered and spurred the call for better access to medicines and treatments, as well as the recently adopted WIPO Development Agenda, are manifestations of increased tensions between the developed and developing worlds.

The intensity of these tensions has in no small part been exacerbated by the arguments of various interest and lobby groups. On the one hand, some deduce that 'there is no reason why a system that works for developed countries could not do the same in developing countries'.[14] On the other hand, others proceed on historical perspectives that in the early industrialization of today's developed world, weak patent protection was leveraged off to enable them to build up their scientific and technological capabilities through copying and reverse engineering. The call for a stronger patent regime grew over time as these countries progressed up the technological ladder to become leaders in their fields.[15]

Some will find these arguments neither persuasive nor entirely fallacious. Be that as it may, it is submitted that whilst the effects of the TRIPS Agreement on industry and technology will vary according to the countries' levels of economic and technological development, it has been noted that 'TRIPS decidedly shifted the global rules of the game in favour of [industrialized countries]' since the overwhelming majority of intellectual property is created there.[16] This has resulted in some less-developed countries being faced with immediate obstacles, such as 'administrative costs and higher prices for medicines and key technological inputs'.[17] There is little doubt that some developing countries have valid concerns that need to be addressed. However, the solution

[14] CIPR, above n. 3, 1.

[15] See Lall and Albaladejo, 'Indicators of the Relative Importance of IPRs in Developing Countries', above n. 9; see also Edmund Kitch, 'The Patent System: A Design for All Seasons?' (Paper presented at the WIPO Conference on the International Patent System, Geneva, 25–27 March 2002).

[16] The World Bank, *Intellectual Property*, above n. 10. See also The World Bank, *Global Economic Prospects: Technology Diffusion in the Developing World* (2008), siteresources.worldbank.org/INTGEP2008/Resources/complete-report.pdf at 5 February 2009.

[17] See The World Bank, *Intellectual Property*, above n. 10. For an interesting analysis of global governance and the international IP system, see Rochelle C. Dreyfuss, 'Regulating Dynamic Innovation in a Complex Political Economy: Administering Intellectual Property on the International Stage' (Paper presented at the CPR & NYU Workshop on Global Regulatory Governance: India, the South and the Shaping of Global Administrative Law, The Ambassador Hotel, New Delhi, 5–6 January 2008). See also Hitoshi Nasu, 'Public Law Challenges to the Regulation of Pharmaceutical Patents in the US Bilateral Free Trade Agreements', in Thomas Pogge, Matthew Rimmer and Kim

does not lie in recriminations of international obligations that have been duly adopted in the exercise of national sovereignty. Instead, consensual compromises that might mitigate the effects of unforeseen and unintended repercussions should be sought.

It is submitted that the key to averting undesirable escalations of tensions between nations is to further enhance the flexibility that could be built into the existing framework of the international patent system. The timely adoption of the WIPO Development Agenda and the World Trade Organization ('WTO') Doha Declaration on the TRIPS Agreement and Public Health ('Doha Declaration') are clearly desirable steps in our search for meaningful solutions.

4. Development issues: WIPO Development Agenda: a step towards rebalancing the system

It would be idle to pretend that any group of nations is homogeneous. The international patent system should strive to support differentiation of patent laws by degree, content and industry compatible with the economic, social, political and technological developments of a country.

As each nation evolves through various stages of technological, economic and social development, it is likely to derive different types and degrees of benefits from any system of rules. It is highly unlikely that the international patent system will succeed in moving in tandem with the subjective needs of any nation whether it is at its early stages of technological industrialization or is a technological leader in the world. There are clearly differing rates of participation and gains experienced by all participants from both the developing and developed worlds in the international patent system.

In this regard, a drive towards a 'one size fits all' patent regime should be avoided as it will only serve to exacerbate the existing gap between the developed nations (generally regarded as net exporters and owners of intellectual property rights) and developing nations (generally regarded as net importers and users of intellectual property rights). This call has been reiterated by the CIPR:

> [D]eveloping countries should not be deprived of the flexibility to design their IP systems that developed countries enjoyed in earlier stages of their own development, and higher IP standards should not be pressed on

Rubenstein (eds.), *Incentives for Global Public Health: Patent Law and Access to Essential Medicines* (2010), 77.

> them without a serious and objective assessment of their development impact ... We need to make sure that the IP system facilitates, rather than hinders, the application of the rapid advances in science and technology for the benefit of developing countries.[18]

The role of intellectual property and its impact on development must be carefully assessed. Intellectual property protection is a:

> policy instrument the operation of which may, in actual practice, produce benefits as well as costs, which may vary in accordance with a country's level of development. Action is therefore needed to ensure, in all countries, that the costs do not outweigh the benefits of IP protection.[19]

This has also been echoed in the Geneva Declaration on the Future of WIPO, which has called for a 'more balanced and realistic' assessment of the 'social benefits and costs of intellectual property rights as a tool, but not the only tool, for supporting creative intellectual activity'.[20] The Declaration also cautions that the adoption of the 'highest levels of intellectual property protection for everyone' may lead to 'unjust and burdensome outcomes for countries that are struggling to meet the most basic needs of their citizens'.

WIPO, as a global United Nations (UN) intellectual property standards-setting body, therefore, has a critical role to play in ensuring that an appropriate balance is struck between the 'public domain and competition' on the one hand and private property rights on the other. The newly launched WIPO Development Agenda is a step in the right direction towards seeking to redress any imbalances that may, or may be perceived to, exist.

4.1 WIPO Development Agenda

The WIPO Development Agenda was first proposed in 2004 by Argentina and Brazil to enhance and integrate the 'development dimension' into policy-making on intellectual property protection and to incorporate development fully into all WIPO activities. It called, *inter*

[18] CIPR, above n. 3, 8.

[19] Argentina and Brazil, *Proposal by Argentina and Brazil for the Establishment of a Development Agenda for WIPO*, 31st (15th extraordinary) sess, WIPO Doc WO/GA/31/11 (27 August 2004).

[20] Geneva Declaration on the Future of the World Intellectual Property Organization, www.cptech.org/ip/wipo/futureofwipodeclaration at 5 February 2009.

alia, for the development dimension to be incorporated into intellectual property norm-setting to safeguard public interest flexibilities, transfer of technology, enforcement of intellectual property rights, technical co-operation and assistance. The ongoing debates had pointed to the fact that the Agenda was not merely a technical assistance agenda, nor a compartmentalized one. Rather, development should be 'mainstreamed' into all WIPO activities which some claim will mean changing 'the culture of an organization'[21] that 'tended to see itself as basically the promoter of greater IP [intellectual property] protection for right-holders'[22] and bringing it 'more in line with the 21st Century'.[23]

Other proposals that have been put forward include, *inter alia*, those from:

- Mexico to develop a 'global partnership for development'[24] in support of the Millennium Development Goals as derived from the Millennium Declaration.
- Chile for an appraisal of the importance of the public domain 'for ensuring access to knowledge' and promotion of innovation and complementary systems in addition to, and within, the intellectual property system; and a study on what are the 'appropriate levels of intellectual property' protection taking into account the needs of each country, 'specifically its degree of development and institutional capacity'.[25]
- Colombia for the 'development of Agreements between WIPO and private enterprises' to allow 'national offices of developing countries access to specialised databases for patent searches'.[26]
- African Group calling, *inter alia*, for 'development-oriented' and 'demand-driven' technical assistance; access to and transfer of technology and knowledge; use of flexibilities under the TRIPS Agreement and the Doha Declaration to promote 'access to essential medicines',

21 Committee on Development and Intellectual Property *Revised Draft Report*, 2nd sess, WIPO Doc CDIP/2/4 Prov. 2 (2008).

22 Ibid., [14]. 23 Ibid.

24 UNDP, UNDP Millennium Development Goals: Goal 8, www.undp.org/mdg/goal8.shtml at 19 May 2009.

25 Chile – Provisional Committee on proposals related to a WIPO Development Agenda (1st sess, 20–24 February 2006): Proposal by Chile (PCDA/1/2), www.wipo.int/edocs/mdocs/mdocs/en/pcda_1/pcda_1_2.doc at 19 May 2009.

26 Colombia – Provisional Committee on proposals related to a WIPO Development Agenda (1st session, 20–24 February, 2006): Proposal by Colombia (PCDA/1/3), www.wipo.int/edocs/mdocs/mdocs/en/pcda_1/pcda_1_3.doc at 19 May 2009.

'food', 'information and knowledge for education and research'; 'norm setting for the protection of genetic resources, traditional knowledge and folklore'.[27]

The WIPO Development Agenda was finally pushed through after three years of negotiations with support from other Friends of Development.[28] Pursuant to the Agenda, a new Committee on Development and Intellectual Property ('CDIP') was created to implement the forty-five recommendations that were agreed in 2007 under the Agenda. Of these, nineteen could be implemented immediately without additional resources. The first meeting of the Committee in March 2008 explored ways to implement these recommendations, which can broadly be categorized into six clusters, namely:

Cluster A: Technical assistance and capacity building;
Cluster B: Norm-setting, flexibilities, public policy and public domain;
Cluster C: Technology transfer, information and communication technology ('ICT') and access to knowledge;
Cluster D: Assessment, evaluation and impact studies;
Cluster E: Institutional matters including mandate and governance;
Cluster F: Other issues.

This was followed up in the second session in July 2008, where the Committee continued to develop a programme for the appropriate implementation of the adopted recommendations. A strong signal has also been given by the Director-General, Mr Francis Gurry, on the importance of the Development Agenda when he pledged his personal supervision of the work of the organization in this matter.

The WIPO Development Agenda provides a major opportunity for the WIPO to address the role of intellectual property in development and seek to achieve a more equitable balance by ensuring that:

> protection and enforcement of intellectual property rights should contribute to the promotion of technological innovation and to the transfer and dissemination of technology, to the mutual advantage of producers

[27] Africa – The African Proposal for the establishment of a Development Agenda for WIPO (Inter-Sessional Intergovernmental Meeting on a Development Agenda for WIPO, 3rd sess, 20–22 July 2005) (IMM/3/2 Rev), www.wipo.int/edocs/mdocs/mdocs/en/iim_3/iim_3_2_rev.doc at 19 May 2009.

[28] The Friends of Development are Argentina, Brazil, Bolivia, Cuba, Dominican Republic, Ecuador, Egypt, Iran, Kenya, Peru, Sierra Leone, South Africa, Tanzania, Uruguay and Venezuela.

and users of technological knowledge and in a manner conducive to social and economic welfare, and to a balance of rights and obligations.[29]

In its search for equitable solutions, it is vital that the international patent system holds firmly to 'its core principles: principles that have the public interest at their center'.[30] It should encourage international co-operation that will enhance a flexible patent policy tool for public and private stakeholders in developed, developing and least-developed countries alike so that patent rights are managed as 'part of a nation's stock of intangible assets' to be exploited for the ultimate and widespread public benefit of all. This is particularly so in the field of public health and access to medicines, which has generated immense international concern and debate in recent years.

5. Public interests: public health and access to medicine

In recent years, major concerns have been expressed by some developing countries that the implementation of effective intellectual property regimes may 'affect their efforts to improve public health'[31] and that patents on pharmaceuticals 'may be hampering governments' attempts to deal with urgent policy issues'[32] by 'unacceptably imped[ing] access to affordable healthcare, thus frustrating public health programs'.[33]

Since one of the key objectives of the patent system is to reward innovation by allowing innovators to charge higher prices for protected products, it has been argued that a fully functional patent system would result in an inverse relationship between the cost of such products and affordability of access.[34] This has also been reiterated by the CIPR which regards the 'cost of pharmaceutical products as an important concern in developing countries' since most poor people in these countries:

29 TRIPS Agreement, above n. 8, article 7.

30 WIPO Patent Agenda, above n. 5, annex I, 3.

31 CIPR, above n. 3, 29.

32 WIPO Patent Agenda, above n. 5, 2.

33 Ibid., 28. See, e.g., the recent outcry by a consortium of non-governmental organizations in Kenya over the high cost of AIDS/HIV drugs. This has called for a consideration of the following: 'how does a mercilessly globalizing world balance the 3Ps – Pharmaceuticals, Patents and Profits – with the right of patients to access essential drugs?' See Odour Ong'wen, 'Crocodile Tears: How "TRIPS" Serves West's Monopoly', *The East African* (Nairobi), 12 March 2001.

34 See Lall and Albaladejo, 'Indicators of the Relative Importance of IPRs in Developing Countries', above n. 9, 2–3. See also CIPR, above n. 3, 30.

> pay for their own drugs and state provision is normally selective and resource-constrained. This is generally not the case in the developed world where costs are mainly met by the state or through insurance schemes.[35]

Some have gone further to suggest that the global intellectual property system is facing a crisis of public legitimacy as citizen groups around the world are raising questions, for example, on how patents may be blocking the access of ordinary people to medicines.[36] This can be contrasted with the views expressed by those in the pharmaceutical industry, such as Sir Richard Sykes, that 'IP protection is not the cause of the present lack of access to medicines in developing countries'.[37]

Be that as it may, it is submitted that access to affordable medicine involves a complex web of intricate issues, including 'non-patent-related' obstacles such as: poverty; corruption; civil strife, economic and societal problems, inadequate healthcare infrastructure, diagnostics and medical workforce; poor supply, distribution and delivery systems particularly to rural areas; sub-standard medicines; financial and administrative mismanagement, taxes and customs duties, complexity of medical therapy, etc. These have been discussed elsewhere and will not be repeated here.[38]

The need to alleviate suffering arising from the global health crisis, particularly among those in developing and least-developed countries that are facing a critical need for urgent access to pharmaceutical products to treat HIV/AIDS, malaria, tuberculosis and other

[35] Ibid.

[36] See, e.g., Martin Khor, 'Patents System Facing Legitimacy Crisis' (26 March 2001) Third World Network, www.twnside.org.sg/title/et0110.htm at 5 February 2009.

[37] Per Sir Richard Sykes (former Chairman of GSK) in March 2002 quoted in CIPR Report, above n. 3, 30.

[38] See, e.g., World Health Organization Commission on Macroeconomics and Health, *Macroeconomics and Health: Investing in Health for Economic Development* (2001); Alec van Gelder and Franklin Cudjoe, 'Patent-Busting: Punishing the Poor', *The Straits Times* (Singapore), 2 May 2008, 23; Richard Wilder, 'Market Segmentation: Techniques, Actors and Incentives – The Use of Intellectual Property Rights' (Paper presented at the Workshop on Differential Pricing and Financing of Essential Drugs, WHO and WTO Secretariats, Norway, 8–11 April 2001); Bryan Mercurio, 'Resolving the Public Health Crisis in the Developing World: Problems and Barriers of Access to Essential Medicines' (2007) 5 *Northwestern University Journal of International Human Rights* 1. See also CIPR, above n. 3.

diseases[39] merits serious attention. Together these three diseases have claimed 5.7 million lives in 2001.[40] Some have argued that:

> healthcare considerations must be the main objective in determining what IP regime should apply to healthcare products. IP rights are not conferred to deliver profits to industry except so that these can be used to deliver better healthcare in the long term. Such rights must therefore be closely monitored to ensure that they do actually promote healthcare objectives and, above all, are not responsible for preventing poor people in developing countries from obtaining healthcare.[41]

In this context, the CIPR has also succinctly noted the dilemma facing healthcare in developing countries as follows:

> How can the resources necessary to develop new drugs and vaccines for diseases that predominantly affect developing, rather than developed, countries be generated when the ability to pay for them is so limited? Even when there is a developed country market from which these resources can be recovered through high prices, how can the affordability of these drugs in developing countries be secured? How can conflicts between the two objectives – covering R&D costs and minimizing consumer costs – be resolved?[42]

5.1 *Some observations on selected avenues of reform*[43]

Article 8 of the TRIPS Agreement provides that: 'Members may … adopt measures necessary to protect public health … and to promote the public interest in sectors of vital importance to their socioeconomic and technological development.'

This has been affirmed by the Doha Declaration:

> We agree that the TRIPS Agreement does not and should not prevent Members from taking measures to protect public health. Accordingly,

39 For a discussion on access and benefit sharing in relation to infectious diseases and the emergence of a new international federalism, see also William Fisher and Talha Syed, 'A Prize System as a Partial Solution to the Health Crisis in the Developing World', in Thomas Pogge, Matthew Rimmer and Kim Rubenstein (eds.), *Incentives for Global Public Health: Patent Law and Access to Essential Medicines* (2010), 181.

40 See World Health Organization Commission on Macroeconomics and Health, *Scaling up the Response to Infectious Diseases – A Way out of Poverty* (2002).

41 See, e.g. CIPR, above n. 3, 30.

42 CIPR, above n. 3, 31.

43 Some of these proposals have been discussed in the author's earlier work, see Ng, *The Impact of the International Patent System on Developing Countries*, above n. 1.

> while reiterating our commitment to the TRIPS Agreement, we affirm that the Agreement can and should be interpreted and implemented in a manner supportive of WTO Members' right to protect public health and, in particular, to promote access to medicines for all.[44]

The ultimate goal in this discussion is to ensure that medicines can fulfil their central role in improving access to medicine for some and health for all. In this regard, it is important to note that adequate safeguards to ensure the safety of drug supply are imperative. Similarly, the recommendations proceed solely on the basis of improving access to and affordability of medicines. It does not purport to analyse other 'non-patent-related' factors contributing to problems relating to medical access and affordability, which have been mentioned above.

Numerous options proposed include the call to incorporate a general exception into the draft Substantive Patent Law Treaty that deals with the protection of public health and the environment.[45] Other policy avenues include compulsory licensing, parallel imports, limiting patentability, price control and differential pricing, patent pools, charity (drug donation), provision of aid, voluntary licensing and appealing for greater corporate responsibility to society. In conjunction with the other published studies on the laws and other related issues,[46] some observations on a few of the selected proposed options will be discussed.

[44] See Declaration on the TRIPS Agreement and Public Health: Adopted on 14 November 2001, WTO Doc WT/MIN(01)/DEC/2 (2001) ('the Doha Declaration'), [4]. Note also articles 8 and 73 of the TRIPS Agreement relating to the protection of public health and essential security interests. Indeed, it has been argued that the flexibility and safeguards allowed under the TRIPS Agreement, particularly those relating to the protection of public health, should be preserved: see Carlos Correa and Sisule Musungu, 'The WIPO Patent Agenda: The Risks for Developing Countries' (Working Paper No 12, Trade-Related Agenda, Development and Equity, South Centre, 2002) ('South Centre Report') 27. See also The Royal Society of the United Kingdom, *Keeping Science Open: The Effects of Intellectual Property Policy on the Conduct of Science* (2003) 15, where the Royal Society endorsed the importance of ensuring an adequate supply of medicines to developing countries at low prices.

[45] See South Centre Report, above n. 44, 20. See also F. M. Scherer and Jayashree Watal, 'Post-TRIPS Options for Access to Patented Medicines in Developing Countries' (2002) 5 *Journal of International Economic Law* 913, 916 on how many of today's developed countries also excluded pharmaceutical products from patent protection until quite recently.

[46] See, e.g., CIPR, above n. 3; see World Intellectual Property Organization, *Agenda for Development of the International Patent System*, WIPO Doc A/36/14 (6 August 2001); World Intellectual Property Organization, *Patent Agenda: Options for Development of the International Patent System*, WIPO Doc A/37/6 (19 August 2002); South Centre Report, above n. 44, 20; Scherer and Watal, 'Post-TRIPS Options for Access to Patented Medicines in Developing Countries', above n. 45; Keith Maskus, *Parallel Imports in*

5.2 *Off-patent drugs*

It has been noted that the vast majority of pharmaceutical products are off-patent and are therefore available for use in the public domain. A recent survey suggests that only about 20 per cent of antiretroviral drugs for treating HIV/AIDS remain patented.[47]

Developing countries have been urged to create a 'vigorously competitive supply' of these generics and to ensure that 'trade in generic drugs is not restricted and that vigorously competitive world markets emerge'.[48] However, it has been noted that many developing countries 'have hurt themselves by not taking full advantage of the opportunities for encouraging generic substitution'.[49] This has led to the argument that perhaps the impact of patents on public health may be 'moot for many in the developing countries where inadequate healthcare and health infrastructure poses a much more immediate and significant problem'.[50]

Table 4.1 below reveals further interesting information.

Notwithstanding this, issues concerning the affordability of patented drugs will continue to dominate the agenda. Indeed, the African,

Pharmaceuticals: Implications for Competition and Prices in Developing Countries (2001); International Intellectual Property Institute ('IIPI'), Patent Protection and Access to HIV/AIDS Pharmaceuticals in Sub-Saharan Africa (2000), www.iipi.org/reports/HIV_AIDS_Report.pdf at 5 February 2009; and Thomas Faunce, 'Innovation and Insufficient Evidence: The Case for a WTO Agreement on Health Technology Safety and Cost-Effectiveness Evaluation', in Thomas Pogge, Matthew Rimmer and Kim Rubenstein (eds.), *Incentives for Global Public Health: Patent Law and Access to Essential Medicines* (2010), 209.

47 See Michael Kirk, 'Competing Demands on Public Policy' (Paper presented at the WIPO Conference on the International Patent System, Geneva, 25–27 March 2002) quoting a recent study on fifty-three African countries published in the *Journal of the American Medical Association* that only three of fifteen antiretroviral drugs for treating HIV/AIDS remain patented.

48 Scherer and Watal, 'Post-TRIPS Options for Access to Patented Medicines in Developing Countries', above n. 45, 60. See also a recent survey by Frost & Sullivan Asia Pacific noting that the East Asian market is driven by generic pharmaceutical companies whose current strength lies in their dominance of local markets. A recent survey on the generic pharmaceutical markets in Malaysia, the Philippines, Singapore and Taiwan shows the following: the total generic pharmaceutical market in the four countries was estimated at more than US$500 million in 2001 and is expected to reach over US$1 billion by 2007: Frost & Sullivan Asia Pacific, *The Asian Generic Pharmaceutical Market* (2002), pharmalicensing.com at 5 February 2009. See also Frost & Sullivan Asia Pacific, *The Generic Invasion – An Inside Scoop to the Pot of Gold* (2003), pharmalicensing.com at 5 February 2009.

49 Scherer and Watal, 'Post-TRIPS Options for Access to Patented Medicines in Developing Countries', above n. 45.

50 Mercurio, 'Resolving the Public Health Crisis in the Developing World', above n. 38.

Table 4.1 *Expiry of patent protection in essential drugs*

Medicines	Patents and Related Information
Anti-tuberculosis/ Anti-malarial	Some 95 per cent of the pharmaceutical products on the World Health Organization's Essential Drugs List are now 'off patent'.[51] The 2007 WHO model list of essential medicines includes 10 anti-tuberculosis drugs and 14 anti-malarial drugs.[52]
Antiretroviral	Most antiretroviral drugs are not protected by patents in the majority of developing countries.[53] The WHO's Essential Drugs List includes some drugs used for the treatment and prevention of HIV/AIDS, which are now 'off patent'.[54] The 2007 WHO model list of essential medicines includes 20 antiretroviral medicines.[55]

Caribbean and Pacific Group of States have noted that, in view of the outbreak of new diseases such as severe acute respiratory syndrome (SARS), a solution that is straightforward, easy to implement and effectively workable needs to be found as a matter of urgency.[56] A further evaluation of some possible solutions is therefore timely.

5.3 *Patented drugs*

The call by some developing countries for better access to affordable medicine is an important and pertinent issue in relation to some patented drugs. While the price demanded by the owner of the patent is undoubtedly a major component, it may well be misleading to conclude that some drugs are exorbitant by virtue only of the fact that they

[51] World Intellectual Property Organization, *Striking a Balance: Patents and Access to Drugs and Health Care*, www.wipo.int/export/sites/www/freepublications/en/patents/491/wipo_pub_491.pdf at 5 February 2009.

[52] See World Health Organization, *Essential Medicines Model List* (15th list, March 2007), www.who.int/medicines/publications/08_ENGLISH_indexFINAL_EML15.pdf at 29 April 2009.

[53] IIPI, above n. 46, 36.

[54] World Intellectual Property Organization, *Striking a Balance*, above n. 51.

[55] *WHO Essential Medicines Model List*, above n. 52.

[56] See African, Caribbean and Pacific Group of States, *Paragraph 6 of the DOHA Declaration on the TRIPS Agreement and Public Health*, WTO Doc IP/C/W/401 (2003) (Communication from the African, Caribbean and Pacific Group of States).

are patented. It should be borne in mind that it is difficult to establish meaningful criteria to determine absolute or objective affordability. It is often relative and varies directly with the degree of poverty. The final price of a patented drug payable by the consumer is a function of many variables that incorporate the selling price of the manufacturer, availability of substitutes or alternative treatment, distribution costs and profit mark-ups, economies of scale, regulatory and structural impediments, subsidies, taxes and other custom tariffs.

Moreover, the argument that 'nations cannot simply free-ride on the research and development efforts of multinational pharmaceutical enterprises'[57] may be difficult to ignore. It is submitted that the options highlighted below may yield some relief to the tensions between these competing interests.

5.3.1 Competition from generics

It has been noted that 'pharmaceutical product prices fall sharply when generic entry occurs following the expiration of the patents'.[58] As such, developing countries that are not, or not yet, subject to the obligation of full implementation of the TRIPS Agreement may exploit the opportunity to take full advantage of generics. Resources permitting, some developing countries could improve their generic drug manufacturing capability to manufacture and export lower-cost generic versions of patented drugs to countries that permit or encourage the import and use of generic substitutes. By its nature, this may not be a long-term solution for some but it remains extremely attractive.

In addition, the invention and development of competing drugs and treatment for the same disease/condition may be another option to constrain the 'monopoly power of patented drugs'.[59] It is, therefore, mainly in the new 'break-through drugs that face little therapeutic competition in treating critical and widespread disease conditions'[60] that more serious pricing and access concerns arise.

57 Scherer and Watal, 'Post-TRIPS Options for Access to Patented Medicines in Developing Countries', above n. 45.

58 Ibid. 59 Ibid.

60 Ibid. It is noted that there are actually very few drugs of this kind. A survey found that of the 148 new drugs introduced into the United States market between 1978 and 1987, only thirteen (or about 8 per cent) had no close substitute in their therapeutic class: Z. John Lu and William S. Comanor, 'Strategic Pricing of New Pharmaceuticals' (1998) 80 *Review of Economic and Statistics* 108, quoted in Scherer and Watal, 'Post-TRIPS Options for Access to Patented Medicines in Developing Countries', above n. 45.

5.3.2 Parallel imports

Parallel imports in patented pharmaceutical products arise 'for a variety of factors associated with price differences across markets: price discrimination by manufacturers, vertical price setting within distribution systems and differential systems of price controls'.[61] Parallel imports therefore affect the maintenance of differential pricing and regulation thereof. It has been referred to as a 'form of arbitrage, tending to reduce differences in prices across diverse markets'.[62]

The TRIPS Agreement leaves each WTO member free to establish its own regime for the exhaustion of intellectual property rights, subject to the Most Favoured Nation and National Treatment provisions of articles 3 and 4.[63] The freedom to apply the doctrine of Exhaustion of Rights to limit the rights conferred by patents has led to a wide variety of national policies on parallel import or 'parallel trade'. A country may implement a 'national exhaustion' regime and prevent parallel imports; a 'regional exhaustion' system to limit exhaustion within a 'single economic market'; or 'international exhaustion' to legalize parallel imports.[64]

This is another area that developing countries may seek to explore in their search for access to affordable drugs. However, in order to encourage pharmaceutical companies to supply medicines at preferential prices, it is important to address their concerns that these may emerge in other markets through parallel exports. It has been noted that the parallel export of 'drugs sold at low prices in less-developed nations could undermine the willingness of the pharmaceutical manufacturers to sell at those low prices or even to supply low-income

[61] See Maskus, *Parallel Imports in Pharmaceuticals*, above n. 46, 41 and more generally for the potential benefits and costs of permitting parallel imports. See also Wilder, 'Market Segmentation', above n. 38; CIPR, above n. 3, 41.

[62] Scherer and Watal, 'Post-TRIPS Options for Access to Patented Medicines in Developing Countries', above n. 45.

[63] The Doha Declaration, above n. 44, [5(d)]. See also article 6 of the TRIPS Agreement that provides for exhaustion of rights as follows: 'For the purposes of dispute settlement under this Agreement, subject to the provisions of Articles 3 and 4 nothing in this Agreement shall be used to address the issue of the exhaustion of intellectual property rights.' For a discussion on compulsory licensing and parallel importation, particularly the softening of the US and EU response thereto, see IIPI, above n. 46, 14–19.

[64] The 'exhaustion' doctrine, also 'sometimes known as the "first sale" doctrine, allows a member state to limit application of a patent right once a product protected by the patent has been sold': see IIPI, above n. 46, 30. For a detailed discussion on parallel imports in pharmaceuticals, see Maskus, *Parallel Imports in Pharmaceuticals*, above n. 46. See also Wilder, 'Market Segmentation', above n. 38.

markets at all'.[65] Thus, it may be necessary for developing countries to implement satisfactory control measures to prevent subsequent parallel exports of drugs imported at reduced prices.[66] In this context, it has been emphasized that:

> there is an important rationale for restricting parallel exports of medicines from low-income countries to high-income countries, though the former group could remain open to [parallel import] ... This idea could be supplemented by regimes of regional exhaustion among poor countries in order to increase market size within which prices are integrated.[67]

Measures to prevent parallel exports are also important in ensuring that pharmaceutical products that are manufactured under compulsory licensing are not utilized or re-exported beyond the purposes for which the licences were granted.

5.3.3 Compulsory licensing

The use of compulsory licensing to enhance access to affordable patented drugs is controversial.[68] The threat of compulsory licensing was successfully used by Brazil in the pursuit of its National STD/AIDS programme

[65] See Scherer and Watal, 'Post-TRIPS Options for Access to Patented Medicines in Developing Countries', above n. 45.

[66] The EU Regulation of 26 May 2003 that aims to prevent pharmaceutical products sold to developing countries at reduced prices from being brought back into the European market underscores the need to insulate and track parallel imported drugs within regional blocs of developing countries and strictly enforce against re-exportation from their borders. This provides an extra mechanism for protection, which applies irrespective of whether these medicines are IP-protected, in order to encourage companies to supply medicines at reduced prices: see *The Implementation of the Doha Declaration on the TRIPS Agreement and Public Health*, WTO Doc IP/C/W/402 (2003) (Communication by the European Communities and their Member States). This is also echoed by the Royal Society that: 'Access to such medicines is critical if society is to fight the major pandemics affecting the third world. Poverty is the critical issue but IPRs must not be used to prevent availability of medicines at low prices. A corollary is that developed and developing countries should cooperate in ensuring legal and practical measures to prevent resale in developed countries of low-priced medicine destined for developing countries.' Royal Society, above n. 44, 15.

[67] See Maskus, *Parallel Imports in Pharmaceuticals*, above n. 46, 3. This was echoed by Scherer and Watal, 'Post-TRIPS Options for Access to Patented Medicines in Developing Countries', above n. 45.

[68] Take, for example, the fundamental problems that South Africa, Brazil and Thailand now face over the patent system – namely the problem of the multilateral trading system securing monopoly rights over, among other things, life-saving knowledge and technology, see Helene Bank, *Differential Pricing and Politics of Health Development* (25 April 2001) Third World Network, www.twnside.org.sg/title/politics.htm at 6 February 2009. See also IIPI, above n. 46.

in negotiations with pharmaceutical companies.[69] It has also garnered much worldwide attention recently. Take, for example, Thailand's use of compulsory licensing in relation to antiretroviral drugs for HIV/AIDS, cancer and heart disease.[70] This has precipitated similar calls from other developing countries, such as India and the Philippines, for the urgent need to lower the cost of medicines and make them more affordable to sufferers.[71]

Compulsory licensing has been said to 'introduce the dynamic effects of competition that can pressure prices lower over time'.[72] Indeed, the CIPR has opined that they 'do not regard compulsory licensing as a panacea, but rather as an essential insurance policy to prevent abuses of the IP system'.[73] This has been echoed by the call for governments, as

> custodian of the public interest, [to] closely monitor the activities of patent owners and be prepared to intervene actively with counter-measures where necessary. Compulsory licensing and ... competition laws are the obvious tools ... Governments [should] further facilitate compulsory licensing and application of competition law in situations where single or multiple patents, do on balance, unreasonably affect use and development of inventions.[74]

However, the TRIPS Agreement has narrowed the circumstances under which compulsory licensing may be deployed to remedy anti-competitive and other practices.[75] One of the restrictions under article 31(f) is that the use must be 'predominantly for the supply of the domestic market' of the authorizing state. While this condition may be waived, where the compulsory licence is granted to remedy anti-competitive practices,[76] its effect in curtailing the export of drugs

[69] CIPR, above n. 3, 42.

[70] See, e.g., Sinfah Tunsarawuth, 'Thailand: 20 More Drugs in Pipeline for Possible Compulsory Licences', *Intellectual Property Watch*, 2 November 2007, www.ip-watch.org/ at 11 February 2009.

[71] See, e.g., Tatum Anderson, 'India Cancer Patients Seek to Use Courts for Access to Patented Drugs', *Intellectual Property Watch*, 3 April 2003, www.ip-watch.org/weblog/2008/04/03/india-cancer-patients-seek-to-use-courts-for-access-to-patented-drugs/ at 11 February 2009; Peter Ollier, 'Philippines Plans to Follow India in Limiting Patentability', *Managing Intellectual Property Weekly News* (Hong Kong), 6 May 2008.

[72] See Consumer Project on Technology, 'Statement of Information to the Competition Commission of South Africa on Complaint against GlaxoSmithKline and Boehringer Ingelheim' (3 February 2003), www.cptech.org/ip/health/cl/cl-cases/rsa-tac/cptech-statement.doc.

[73] CIPR, above n. 3. [74] See Royal Society, above n. 44, 10.

[75] See article 31 of the TRIPS Agreement, above n. 8, and note also article 40 relating to control of anti-competitive practices in contractual licences.

[76] See TRIPS Agreement, above n. 8, article 31(f).

manufactured under such licences will greatly impact on some developing countries that rely on such imports. These are countries that are unable to make effective use of the compulsory licensing option available to them due to lack of infrastructure and technological capability to 'reverse engineer' and manufacture drugs themselves.

This concern was clearly noted in paragraph 6 of the Doha Declaration as follows: 'We recognize that WTO Members with insufficient or no manufacturing capacities in the pharmaceutical sector could face difficulties in making effective use of compulsory licensing under the TRIPS Agreement ...'[77]

The resulting 2003 temporary waiver of article 31(f) of the TRIPS Agreement was intended to pave the way for allowing WTO members to export drugs made under compulsory licensing to countries without domestic manufacturing capabilities.[78] In 2005, WTO members agreed on the first ever amendment to the TRIPS Agreement which will make the temporary waiver permanent.[79] This development has been hailed as a tremendous breakthrough that will make it easier for developing and least-developed countries to import cheaper drugs made under compulsory licensing.

Whilst it clearly went some way towards plugging the lacuna in the TRIPS Agreement, it may not be the 'miracle solution' that some had thought it would be. Indeed, both developing and developed countries appear to be slow in implementing the process. This may be due to several reasons including: the complexity of the procedural requirements for implementing the waiver which may make the process difficult to exploit; the need for special packaging, labelling and marking of these drugs which may erode the cost-effectiveness and efficiency of the system; and uncertainty relating to issues, such as the countries that are eligible to utilize the system, effective measures to prevent parallel export, adequacy of remuneration, etc. To date, only Canada and Rwanda have notified the TRIPS Council regarding the utilization of

[77] The Doha Declaration, above n. 44, [6].

[78] See Implementation of Paragraph 6 of the Doha Declaration on the TRIPS Agreement and Public Health, WTO Doc WT/L/540 (2003) (WTO General Council Decision of 30 August 2003). See also Duncan Matthews, 'From the August 30, 2003 WTO Decision to the December 6, 2005 Agreement on an Amendment to TRIPS: Improving Access to Medicines in Developing Countries' (2006) 2 *Intellectual Property Quarterly* 91; and Mercurio, 'Resolving the Public Health Crisis in the Developing World', above n. 38.

[79] Amendment of the TRIPS Agreement, WTO Doc WT/L/641 (2005) (Decision of 6 December 2005 of the General Council) ('TRIPS Waiver').

this procedure. It remains to be seen whether these waivers will be effective in ensuring that countries with insufficient or no pharmaceutical manufacturing capacities can participate fully in a compulsory licensing scheme of which they were clearly the intended beneficiaries. I will not deal further with these issues which are discussed comprehensively in other chapters of this volume.[80]

In utilizing any compulsory licensing scheme, it is important to seek an appropriate balance between the public interest and the legitimate private interests of patent holders. Whilst the Doha Declaration clearly recognizes that public health issues can override private property interests of patent holders and reinforces the right given to each WTO member state to 'grant compulsory licences and the freedom to determine the grounds upon which such licences are granted',[81] there are still outstanding issues that need to be addressed. These include determining the appropriate level of remuneration and finding a suitable body to make compulsory licensing determinations. In this regard, several established royalty guidelines may be considered, such as those discussed in the UN Development Programme Human Development Report 2001, Japan Patent Office 1998, Canadian proposed Royalty Guidelines 2004 and the Tiered Royalty method. These have already been discussed elsewhere[82] and will not be reiterated here.

It is beyond the scope of this work to propose a detailed guideline for implementing an appropriately balanced compulsory licensing scheme. However, it is submitted that adequacy of remuneration should not be based solely on what the general patient population can afford and the final arbiter on this issue should not lie with the government body that granted the compulsory licence.

This author submits that in determining the adequacy of remuneration for drugs manufactured under compulsory licensing, a 'quota system' based on a percentage of global turnover may be explored. Such a scheme could be based, for example, on a 'progressive computation' of entitlement

[80] See, e.g., Andrew Mitchell and Tania Voon, 'The TRIPS Waiver as a Recognition of Public Health Concerns in the WTO', in Thomas Pogge, Matthew Rimmer and Kim Rubenstein (eds.), *Incentives for Global Public Health: Patent Law and Access to Essential Medicines* (2010), 56; and Noah Novogradsky, 'Beyond TRIPS: The Role of Non-State Actors and Access to Essential Medicines', in Thomas Pogge, Matthew Rimmer and Kim Rubenstein (eds.), *Incentives for Global Public Health: Patent Law and Access to Essential Medicines* (2010), 343.

[81] The Doha Declaration, above n. 44, [5]; CIPR, above n. 3, 44–51.

[82] See James Love, 'Measures to Enhance Access to Medical Technologies, and New Methods of Stimulating Medical R&D' (2007) 40 *University of California, Davis Law Review* 679.

under a tiered system. Take, for example, Tier 1 (free drug supply based on corporate social responsibility ('CSR') or charity), Tier 2 (zero per cent royalty), Tier 3 (royalty plus *x* per cent royalty), etc. The availability of the tier for WTO member states could be based on factors, such as per capita income relative to other claimants. Under such a scheme, co-payment by government subsidy might be needs-based, for example, on a means testing of patients. An independent body would need to be established to monitor and ensure an equitable balancing of the needs of various competing interests. This would unfortunately require considerable funding and diversion of precious resources, which some might argue should be better spent subsidizing the cost of drugs.

Be that as it may, as the costs of drugs continue to escalate, particularly for those without cheaper equivalents, patients worldwide (from both developing and developed countries) will be compelled to pay 'hundreds and even thousands of dollars for prescription medications … or do without'.[83] The increasing pressure that is being exerted on insurance schemes, states and citizens to 'meet ever rising bills for patented drugs'[84] cannot be ignored. This will be exacerbated by an aging population and the emergence of new diseases which will have a profound impact on the social and economic systems of the world. It is, therefore, submitted that a compulsory licensing scheme that is properly calibrated and utilized within appropriate parameters can play an important role in ensuring an effective balance between the public interest and the legitimate private interest of patent holders.

While the threat of compulsory licensing may be a weapon that can 'enhance [a nation's] bargaining power',[85] it is certainly far from a 'magic wand' for obtaining affordable access to patented medicines in developing countries.[86] In fact it is noted that 'in practice … compulsory

[83] See, e.g., Gina Kolata, 'Co-Payments Go Way Up for Drugs with High Prices', *The New York Times*, 14 April 2008.

[84] CIPR, above n. 3, 29.

[85] Scherer and Watal, 'Post-TRIPS Options for Access to Patented Medicines in Developing Countries', above n. 45. Take, for example, Thailand's experience where it has been said that: 'Before we announced compulsory licensing, the companies always said the price they offered us was already a "no-profit" price. But after our enforcement, they cut their price further.' See statement of Sorachai quoted in Tunsarawuth, 'Thailand: 20 More Drugs in the Pipeline for Possible Compulsory Licences', above n. 70.

[86] Scherer and Watal, 'Post-TRIPS Options for Access to Patented Medicines in Developing Countries', above n. 45. Note also the view expressed by the IIPI that 'it is not at all clear whether the attempts to abrogate patent protection through compulsory

licensing is rarely imposed'.[87] The Nuffield Council further acknowledges that:

> Opposition to compulsory licensing is particularly strong in the pharmaceutical industry at a time when the costs of research and development are rising and the rate of production of new medicines is falling. Moreover, there is a view more generally that once compulsory licensing is deployed in one sector, the principle will be more readily applied elsewhere. We recognise the dilemma: in the case of medicines generally, there are those that are too expensive to be made available for all of the patients who need them; but the widespread imposition of compulsory licensing could seriously erode the capacity for research and development of the pharmaceutical industry. A careful balance would, therefore, need to be struck so that compulsory licensing is only invoked in those cases in which the existence of a monopoly is creating an unacceptable and unfair situation. The guiding principle here would be that the protection which was granted by the patent system should be commensurate with the contribution made by the inventor. In fact, extensive application of compulsory licensing … may not be required, as experience has shown that the mere threat of compulsory licensing has been sufficient to encourage industry to devise other solutions.[88]

The Nuffield Council concludes its observations by rejecting a 'wholesale and indiscriminate use of compulsory licensing'.[89] Instead, it supports further exploration of an Organisation for Economic Co-operation and Development ('OECD') suggestion to create a 'clearing house' to reduce transactions and obstacles to commercial laboratories seeking licences for 'genetic inventions'.[90] Pursuing other options, such as charity, has been said to be the 'only alternative to death or debility'.[91] In this regard, it may be useful for some nations or patent owners to consider

licensing and parallel importation will ultimately result in better access to medicines and healthcare': see IIPI, above n. 46, 20.

87 See Nuffield Council on Bioethics, *The Ethics of Patenting DNA: A Discussion Paper* (2002) 54–5.

88 Ibid., 55. Other solutions may include the use of differential pricing of antiretroviral medicines for the treatment of HIV/AIDS in several developing countries.

89 Further arguments against the use of compulsory licensing include the potential costs and complexity accompanied by a detrimental decrease in the incentive to invalidate or revoke patents as it would be easier to obtain a licence than to dispute the patent.

90 See Organisation for Economic Co-operation and Development, 'Short Summary Report of the Workshop on Genetic Inventions, Intellectual Property Rights and Licensing Practices' (Berlin, 24–25 January 2002), www.oecd.org/ at 9 February 2009.

91 Scherer and Watal, 'Post-TRIPS Options for Access to Patented Medicines in Developing Countries', above n. 45.

granting 'voluntary or consensual' licences in appropriate circumstances in the spirit of good CSR.[92]

5.3.4 Consensual licensing: good corporate citizenship

The pharmaceutical and biotechnology industries are major multi-billion dollar conglomerates of international players whose products profoundly affect public health and safety in both the developed and developing world. The licensing of the production and exploitation of drugs by the pharmaceutical industry solely for the promotion and safeguard of public health in appropriate circumstances other than under compulsion of law and single-minded pursuit of profits may ameliorate the lack of access to affordable medicine in some developing countries. This adoption of some degree of voluntary self-regulation will not only constitute another milestone by the stakeholders of patents that will ease some of the tensions that inevitably arise between them and society at large, but will also greatly enhance their public standing.

Today, multinational corporations disregard their social roles in the community at their own peril. It is no longer possible to operate a business globally while remaining totally aloof from social issues around it. CSR has gained increasing prominence and importance as can be seen in its exponential growth in the last decade, with more companies than ever engaged in serious efforts to define and integrate CSR into all aspects of their businesses.[93] The idea that business has obligations to society that go beyond, and yet are not inconsistent with, profit and shareholder value is gaining increasing appeal among global corporations. Measured by profit alone, some of the developing countries form such small markets that they have only a small effect on the profit margin of the pharmaceutical industry and so have little or no impact on the industries' R&D, manufacturing and marketing policies.

The adoption of good CSR may be an ideal response to the growing calls by leading institutional investors for pharmaceutical companies to take a more proactive stance towards the public health crisis, 'whether

[92] CSR has been defined by the World Business Council for Sustainable Development ('WBCSD') as 'the continuing commitment by business to behave ethically and contribute to economic development while improving the quality of life of the workforce and their families, as well as the local community and society at large'. See World Business Council for Sustainable Development, *Corporate Social Responsibility: Making Good Business Sense* (January 2000).

[93] See Global Ethics Monitor, *Corporate Responsibility News*, www.globalethicsmonitor.com at 9 February 2009.

from a reputation, market development or corporate citizenship perspective'.[94] Indeed, a group of Europe's largest institutional investors[95] has put forward a 'Statement of Good Practice' calling on companies – including AstraZeneca plc, GlaxoSmithKline plc and Novartis AG to:

(1) establish 'sustainable, differential pricing for relevant product ranges in relation to the disease burden'[96] based on capacity to pay in the various markets,
(2) enforce patents 'with sensitivity to local circumstances'[97] (e.g. 'not enforcing patents' in the poorest countries, such as 'LDC countries')[98] and
(3) take measures 'to protect and ... segment markets'[99] to prevent 're-importation' or diversion of 'differentially priced products'[100] back to the developed world.

The International Federation of Pharmaceutical Manufacturers Associations ('IFPMA') has highlighted the significant contributions of the pharmaceutical industry's programmes towards the improvement of public health in many countries, particularly developing countries.[101] However, there have been recent allegations of anti-competitive conduct by some pharmaceutical companies, which have been regarded by some as examples of 'bad corporate citizenship'. Yet, does labelling yield results? It remains an 'open' question as to what constitutes 'bad' conduct in a voluntary scheme.[102]

[94] See Pharmaceutical Shareowners Group ('PSG'), *Investor Statement and Framework on Pharmaceutical Companies and the Public Health Crisis in Emerging Markets* (March 2003), 2 also quoted in the United Kingdom Department for International Development ('DFID'), *Increasing People's Access to Essential Medicines in Developing Countries: A Framework for Good Practice in the Pharmaceutical Industry* (March 2005), www2.dfid.gov.uk/Pubs/files/pharm-framework.pdf at 18 May 2009.

[95] Representing £600 billion (US$940 billion) in assets. They include Henderson Global Investors, ISIS Asset Management, Morley Fund Management and Schroder Investment Management.

[96] See PSG, above n. 94, 3. [97] Ibid. [98] Ibid. [99] Ibid. [100] Ibid.

[101] The International Federation of Pharmaceutical Manufacturers Associations ('IFPMA') has noted that from 1998 to 2002, the ten largest pharmaceutical companies contributed US$2.2 billion for health-related programmes in the least-developed countries, see Harvey Bale, 'The Pharmaceutical Industry and Corporate Social Responsibility', *International Federation of Pharmaceutical Manufacturers Associations*, www.responsiblepractice.com/english/insight/ifpma/ at 18 May 2009.

[102] Is there such a concept as 'bad Samaritan'? Where there are violations of the law, legal avenues of redress already exist.

Moving forward, the industry would have to develop a framework to strike a delicate balance between the preservation of stakeholders' immediate economic interests through strict enforcement of patent rights and the provision of access to affordable life-saving drugs for the poor. That balance may be expressed in the form of consensual licensing, the actual form of which is a matter that requires further consideration.

5.3.5 Limiting patentability

Finally, developing countries may also utilize the flexibilities within the TRIPS Agreement to limit the patentability of inventions that may impact on public health. These include permissible specific exclusions, such as those relating to methods of medical treatment, namely, diagnostic, therapeutic and surgical methods for the treatment of humans or animals;[103] and general limited exceptions provided that 'such exceptions do not unreasonably conflict with a normal exploitation of the patent and do not unreasonably prejudice the legitimate interests of the patent owner, taking account of the legitimate interests of third parties'.[104] However, regard should be given to the basic requirement that 'patents … be available for any inventions, whether products or processes, in all fields of technology, provided that they are new, involve an inventive step and are capable of industrial application'.[105] The difficulty in balancing these various competing interests has generated controversy in recent years where some developing countries have sought to limit the patentability of new forms or derivatives of known substances.[106]

While it is submitted that the patent regime can rise to the challenge of improving the accessibility of some medicines and treatment, particularly to the poor, and possibly differential pricing for costly treatments that often accompany new medical breakthroughs,[107] there is also an urgent need to consider corresponding enhancements in incentivizing research and development in 'Third World/neglected' diseases.

[103] TRIPS Agreement, above n. 8, article 27(3).

[104] Ibid., article 30. [105] Ibid., article 27(1).

[106] See section 3(d) of the Patents Act 1970 (India). See also the Universally Accessible Cheaper and Quality Medicines Act 2008 (the Philippines) (discussed in Ollier, 'Philippines Plans to Follow India in Limiting Patentability', above n. 71).

[107] See also, The World Bank, *Intellectual Property*, above n. 10, 129–50.

6. Incentives for R&D: 'Third World/neglected' diseases

Some may argue that a stronger patent regime may provide the incentive[108] for pharmaceutical firms to discover new treatments for some 'Third World' diseases.[109] However, the public health crisis has focused international attention on its lack of ability to generate R&D into diseases where patients lack the financial ability to pay the price necessary to allow private sector recovery of R&D costs.[110] Indeed, the 'reality is that private companies will devote resources to areas where an optimal return can be made'.[111]

The dearth of investment into this much-needed area of research and development has generated international concerns that have prompted, *inter alia*, the WHO's involvement in discussions relating to intellectual property which some argue may more appropriately be within the domain of the WTO and WIPO.[112] Be that as it may, it is worth noting

[108] This has been noted by the World Bank to be 'marginal', see ibid.

[109] Such as Type III diseases. Type III diseases (e.g., Chagas disease, dengue and dengue haemorrhagic fever, leishmaniasis, leprosy, lymphatic filariasis, malaria, onchocerciasis, schistosomiasis and human African trypanosomiasis) are overwhelmingly or exclusively incident in developing countries. Compare with Type II diseases (e.g. HIV/AIDS and TB) which are incident in both rich and poor countries, but with a substantial proportion of the cases in poor countries; and Type I diseases (e.g. diabetes, cardiovascular disease and cancer) which are incident in both rich and poor countries, with large numbers of vulnerable populations in each. See definition by the WIPO in the Draft Global Strategy and Plan of Action on Public Health, Innovation and Intellectual Property, WIPO Doc A/PHI/IGWG/2/INF.DOC./6 (31 August 2007) (Intergovernmental Working Group on Public Health, Innovation and Intellectual Property – Provisional Agenda Item 3). See also Katharine Young, 'Securing Health through Rights', in Thomas Pogge, Matthew Rimmer and Kim Rubenstein (eds.), *Incentives for Global Public Health: Patent Law and Access to Essential Medicines* (2010), 357, where the author discusses issues relating to the 'right to health' and the political economy of health financing and delivery.

[110] See, e.g., Draft Global Strategy and Plan of Action on Public Health, Innovation and Intellectual Property, above n. 109; Margaret Chan, 'Opening Remarks at the Intergovernmental Working Group on Public Health, Innovation and Intellectual Property', World Health Organization (28 April 2008).

[111] See CIPR, above n. 3, 33. See also Chikosa Banda, 'The Transactional Role of Patents: The Case of Product Development Partnerships' (Paper presented at the Global Governance of HIV/AIDS: Intellectual Property and Access to Essential Medicines Conference, University of Liverpool, UK, 8 October 2008) where the author argued that in relation to diseases of the developing world, patents do not operate primarily as incentives due to the lack of availability of lucrative markets.

[112] See Kaitlin Mara and William New, *WHO Members Inch toward Consensus on IP, Innovation and Public Health* (2 May 2008) Intellectual Property Watch, www.ip-watch.org/weblog/index.php?p=1024 at 10 February 2009.

that WHO has embarked on a global strategy and plan of action on public health, innovation and intellectual property that is focused on the public health needs of developing countries, including the 'question of appropriate funding and incentive mechanisms for the creation of new medicines and other products against diseases that disproportionately affect developing countries'.[113] The WHO initiative seeks to examine whether the international patent system is providing adequate incentives for private sector investment into R&D into 'Third World/neglected' diseases.[114] The draft global strategy and action plan has been hailed by the WHO Director-General Margaret Chan as:

> a unique opportunity for public health. An agreed framework can make the cycle of product discovery, development and delivery more efficient and more sensitive to health needs in the developing world ... [T]he international community will have a common tool, and an agreed way to tackle some of the most pressing problems in public health ... forging ways to tackle the gaps in access to health care and, in so doing, to reduce the gaps in health outcomes ... making the benefits of advances in medicine and science more inclusive.[115]

The usage of prizes as a possible incentive for R&D was debated at the recently concluded WHO negotiations.[116] Other proposals that have been mooted elsewhere such as innovation grants,[117] Private and Public Partnerships ('PPPs') schemes (e.g., Bill & Melinda Gates Foundation sponsored projects),[118] advance market commitments

113 Draft Global Strategy and Plan of Action on Public Health, Innovation and Intellectual Property, above n. 109.

114 Ibid.; Chan, 'Opening Remarks', above n. 110. See also Mara and New, *WHO Members Inch toward Consensus on IP, Innovation and Public Health*, above n. 112.

115 See Chan, 'Opening Remarks', above n. 110.

116 See Kaitlin Mara and William New, *WHO IP and Health Group concludes with Progress; Tough Issues Remain for Assembly* (6 May 2008) Intellectual Property Watch, www.ip-watch.org/ at 10 February 2009.

117 Knowledge Ecology International, *Prizes to Stimulate Innovation*, www.keionline.org/index.php?option=com_content&task=view&id=4&Itemid=1 at 10 February 2009. See also Draft Global Strategy and Plan of Action on Public Health, Innovation and Intellectual Property, above n. 109, article 5(3)(a). Aidan Hollis, *Prize, Advanced Market Commitments and Pharmaceuticals for Developing Countries* (2007), www.iprsonline.org/ictsd/Dialogues/2007-10-22/7%20ThinkPiece_Hollis.pdf at 10 February 2009. See also Matthew Rimmer, 'The Lazarus Effect: The (RED) Campaign and Creative Capitalism', in Thomas Pogge, Matthew Rimmer and Kim Rubenstein (eds.), *Incentives for Global Public Health: Patent Law and Access to Essential Medicines* (2010), 313.

118 See, e.g., Draft Global Strategy and Plan of Action on Public Health, Innovation and Intellectual Property, above n. 109, article 7(2); and Mercurio, 'Resolving the Public Health Crisis in the Developing World', above n. 38.

('AMCs'),[119] patent buy-out, open sourcing,[120] patent pools,[121] stronger domestic initiatives and financial or fiscal incentives to encourage more effective participation by the pharmaceutical industry should also be considered to ameliorate this problem. A final initiative discussed by Thomas Pogge in his chapter in this volume is an option for pharmaceutical innovators to forgo patent exclusivity worldwide in exchange for a treaty-backed payment stream proportional to the actual global health impact of the inventions as an alternative (or perhaps complementary scheme) to the existing patent regime.[122]

Faced with these grave international concerns, it is vital that the international patent system adapts and evolves to meet the public health challenge by holding to its core principles that have the 'public interest at their centre'. Unless these are satisfactorily addressed and articulated, tensions and imbalances are likely to be exacerbated.

7. Conclusion

This work has proceeded on the basis of an urgent need to resolve some of the conflicts and disputes which have garnered much worldwide attention in the field of public health and development. There are many other challenging issues and solutions beyond those highlighted

[119] Note the report in Intellectual Property Watch that the WHO IGWG negotiations that were concluded in May 2008 have apparently removed advance market commitments; see Mara and New, *WHO Members Inch toward Consensus*, above n. 112. See also Owen Barder, Michael Kremer and Heidi Williams, 'Advance Market Commitments: A Policy to Stimulate Investment in Vaccines for Neglected Diseases' (2006) *The Economists' Voice*, www.bepress.com/ev at 10 February 2009; Hollis, *Prize, Advanced Market Commitments and Pharmaceuticals for Developing Countries*, above n. 117.

[120] See Rimmer, 'The Lazurus Effect', above n. 117; Krishna Ravi Srinivas, 'Open Source Drug Discovery: A Revolutionary Paradigm or a Utopian Model?', in Thomas Pogge, Matthew Rimmer and Kim Rubenstein (eds.), *Incentives for Global Public Health: Patent Law and Access to Essential Medicines* (2010), 263.

[121] See, e.g., Dianne Nicol and Jane Nielsen, 'Opening the Dam: Patent Pools, Innovation, and Access to Essential Medicines', in Thomas Pogge, Matthew Rimmer and Kim Rubenstein (eds.), *Incentives for Global Public Health: Patent Law and Access to Essential Medicines* (2010), 235.

[122] See Thomas Pogge, 'The Health Impact Fund: Better Pharmaceutical Innovations at Much Lower Prices', in Thomas Pogge, Matthew Rimmer and Kim Rubenstein (eds.), *Incentives for Global Public Health: Patent Law and Access to Essential Medicines* (2010), 135. See also Kathy Liddell, 'The Health Impact Fund: A Critique', in Thomas Pogge, Matthew Rimmer and Kim Rubenstein (eds.), *Incentives for Global Public Health: Patent Law and Access to Essential Medicines* (2010), 155, for a critical analysis of this initiative.

in this work. Some of these are discussed in other chapters in this volume. Moving forward, further dialogue and research will be fruitful in prioritizing key common concerns aimed at enhancing access to affordable medicine for some and health for all.

The public health issue involves a complex milieu of competing legal, political, economic and social interests. It is important to avoid abuse by both patent owners (e.g. through exorbitant pricing) and users (e.g. through freeriding). At the end of the day, it is also essential to encourage good governance and accountability, as well as reciprocity (e.g. through participation in clinical trials, sharing of disease information, etc.). A review of the entire matrix of developments to ensure coherence with existing schemes such as parallel imports, differential pricing, generics, compulsory licensing, drug donation, government and international aid and corporate social responsibility may also be timely.

There is, therefore, an urgent need to reconcile and effectively manage the competing policy interests to facilitate better access to drugs in certain circumstances. In searching for meaningful solutions to alleviate the suffering generated by the global health crisis, the scope of access to affordable medicine and medical treatment should be broadened to include preventive and defensive medicine and treatment, as well as better dissemination and sharing of new medical knowledge. We should accelerate preventative treatment issues to generate a more defensive disease management scheme. Take, for example, smallpox where access to vaccination globally, coupled with international resolve and efforts, led to the eradication of the disease. In recent years, there has also been increasing usage of emotive labels, such as 'charity' to appeal to sympathy and 'lifestyle medicine' to connote luxury to which the poor should not be entitled. The use of these labels does not advance any cause and obscures the serious issues that need to be addressed and effectively managed.

Last but not least, the link between intellectual property protection and trade between nations is increasingly being entrenched by bilateral, plurilateral and multilateral agreements. Since free trade may not be conducted among equals, any lack of equilibrium may precipitate hasty and exclusive developments in patent protection in some countries. This is particularly so in recent years as some nations seek to pursue economic synergies through Free Trade Agreements ('FTAs'). While it is undeniable that FTAs may provide an impetus for accelerating some aspects of patent reform, the risks of imbalances are not insignificant.

The importance of flexibility in creating an effective international patent system that would better optimize the benefits that may accrue to all nations at different stages of development is critical. One of the key objectives is to avert any risks of potential alienation of the stakeholders of the patent system (namely, inventors and industry, consumers and the general public, governments and policy-makers, national and international markets)[123] or alignment of parties along lines of mutual self-interest. I am aware that some of the issues raised in this article may be controversial and challenging to some quarters. Few initiatives possess universal appeal. Change is a process and in itself is unlikely to constitute an immediate panacea for the confluence of political, economic and social pressures constantly being exerted on the patent system. We can ill afford to be indifferent to differences. Courses may change but the final destination may prove to be worth the delicate journey.

[123] World Intellectual Property Organization, *Agenda for Development of the International Patent System*, WIPO Doc A/36/14 (6 August 2001) 1.

PART II

Innovation

5

The Health Impact Fund: better pharmaceutical innovations at much lower prices

THOMAS POGGE*

1. Introduction

The poverty endured by the bottom half of humankind poses serious dangers to their health and survival. The poor worldwide face greater environmental hazards than the rest of us: from contaminated water, filth, pollution, worms and insects. They are exposed to greater dangers from people around them: through traffic, crime, communicable disease and the cruelties of the more affluent. They lack means to protect themselves and their families against such hazards through clean water, nutritious food, good hygiene, ample rest, adequate clothing and safe shelter. They lack the means to enforce their legal rights or to press for political reform. They are often obliged by dire need or debt to incur additional health risks: by selling a kidney, for instance, or by accepting hazardous work in prostitution, mining, construction, domestic service, textile and carpet production. They lack financial reserves and access to public sources of medical knowledge and treatments, and therefore face worse odds of recovering from disease.

Mutually reinforcing, these factors ensure that the poor bear a hugely disproportionate burden of disease – especially of communicable, maternal, perinatal and nutritional conditions – and a hugely disproportionate share of premature deaths: 30 per cent of all deaths each year, 18 million, are from poverty-related causes. These much greater burdens of morbidity and premature mortality in turn entail large economic burdens that keep most of the poor trapped in lifelong poverty.

* This essay is part of a collective effort, funded by the Australian Research Council, the BUPA Foundation, and the European Commission to which Christian Barry, Laura Biron, Leila Chirayath, Kieran Donaghue, Jocelyn Finlay, Aidan Hollis, Miltos Ladikas, Matt Peterson, Michael Ravvin, Doris Schroeder, Michael Selgelid, Jie Tian, Ling Tong, Kit Wellman and Judith Whitworth have contributed substantially.

It is possible to make substantial progress against the global burden of disease ('GBD') directly. Existing huge mortality and morbidity rates can be dramatically lowered by reforming the way the development of new medical treatments is funded. I will sketch a concrete, feasible and politically realistic reform plan that would give medical innovators stable and reliable financial incentives to address the diseases of the poor. If adopted, this plan would not add much to the overall cost of global healthcare spending. In fact, on any plausible accounting, which would take note of the huge economic losses caused by the present GBD, the reform would actually pay for itself. Moreover, it would distribute the cost of global healthcare spending more fairly across countries, across generations and between those lucky enough to enjoy good health and the unlucky ones suffering from serious medical conditions.

2. The problem

With medicines, the fixed cost of developing a new product is extremely high for two reasons. It is very expensive to research and refine a new medicine and then to take it through elaborate clinical trials and national approval processes. Moreover, most promising research ideas fail somewhere along the way and thus never lead to a marketable product. Both reasons combine to raise the research and development ('R&D') cost per new marketable medicine to somewhere around half a billion dollars or more. Commencing manufacture of a new medicine once it has been invented and approved is cheap by comparison. Because of this fixed-cost imbalance, pharmaceutical innovation is not sustainable in a free market system: competition among manufacturers would quickly drive down the price of a new medicine to near its long-term marginal cost of production, and the innovator would get nowhere near to recovering its R&D investment.

The conventional way of correcting this market failure of undersupply is to reward innovators with patents that entitle them to bar others from producing or distributing the innovative product and to waive this entitlement in exchange for a licensing fee. The result of such market exclusivity is an artificially elevated sales price that, on average, enables innovators to recoup their R&D investment through selling products that, even at prices far above marginal cost, are in high demand.

In the case of patents, many are willing to overlook the standard objections to monopolies – that these are economically inefficient or are immoral restrictions of freedom – because they believe that the curtailment of individual freedom can be justified by the benefit, provided patents are carefully designed. One important design feature is that patents confer only temporary market exclusivity. Once the patent expires, competitors can freely enter the market with copies of the original innovation and consumers need thus no longer pay a large mark-up over the competitive market price. Temporal limits make sense because additional years of patent life barely strengthen innovation incentives. At a typical industry discount rate of 11 per cent per annum,[1] a ten-year effective patent life generates 68 per cent, and a fifteen-year effective patent life 82 per cent, of the profit (discounted to present value) that a permanent patent would generate.[2] It makes no sense to impose monopoly prices on all future generations for the sake of so slight a gain in innovation incentives.

During the life of the patent, everyone is legally barred from producing, selling and buying a patented medicine without permission from the patentee. This restraint hurts generic producers and it also hurts consumers by depriving them of the chance to buy such medicines at competitive market prices. But consumers also benefit from the impressive arsenal of useful medicines whose development is motivated by the prospect of patent-protected mark-ups.

It may seem obvious that this benefit outweighs the loss of freedom. But we must consider that not everyone is either affluent enough to buy advanced medicines at very high prices or fortunate enough to need them only after patent expiration. Many human beings are trapped in severe poverty. Most of them derive no benefit from patented medicines because they cannot get access to them. These people can object that the patent regime gives them nothing in return for the freedom it deprives them of. If the freedom to produce, sell and buy advanced medicines were not curtailed, then the affluent would need to find another (for them possibly less convenient) way of incentivizing pharmaceutical research. But advanced medicines would then be

[1] Joseph A. DiMasi, Ronald W. Hansen and Henry G. Grabowski, 'The Price of Innovation: New Estimates of Drug Development Costs' (2003) 22 *Journal of Health Economics* 151.

[2] Patent life is counted from the time the patent application is filed. Effective patent life is the time from receiving market clearance to the time the patent expires. My calculation in the text assumes constant nominal profit each year. In reality, annual profit may rise (due to increasing market penetration or population growth) or fall (through reduced incidence of the disease or through competition from 'me-too drugs' developed by competing firms). For most drugs, sales decline after they have been on the market for six years or so, and this strengthens the reasons for limiting patent life. My reasoning assumes that future health benefits are not to be discounted.

available at competitive market prices, and the poor would have a much better chance of gaining access to them through their own funds or with the help of national or international government agencies or non-governmental organizations. The loss of freedom patents inflict on the global poor – and they number in the billions – is a huge loss in terms of disease and premature death. There is no associated gain that could compensate those suffering these losses; and the gains that patents bring to the affluent cannot possibly justify these losses either.

This objection was less pertinent until the 1990s, when strict patent rules were mostly confined to the affluent states, which allowed the less-developed countries to have weaker patent protections or none at all. This exemption of poor countries had little effect on innovation incentives because, in these countries, those able to afford advanced medicines at patent-protected prices are few, relative to the one billion population of the high-income countries. But the exemption brought relief to many poor residents of poor countries: to all those who obtained at a competitive market price some new medicine they would not have been able to obtain if it had been under patent in their country.

The diversity of national regulations was destroyed in the 1990s when a powerful alliance of industries (software, entertainment, pharma and agribusiness) induced the Clinton Administration and other wealthy states to press strong, globally uniform intellectual property rules upon the world. Acceptance of this regime, enshrined in the Trade-Related Aspects of Intellectual Property Rights Agreement of 1994 ('TRIPS Agreement' or 'TRIPS'),[3] was made a condition of World Trade Organization ('WTO') membership, which, it was then promised, would allow poor countries to reap large benefits from trade liberalization. While the affluent states have been slow to lower their trade barriers and subsidies, they have worked hard towards instituting strong intellectual property rights in the less-developed countries – with devastating effects, for instance, on the evolution of the HIV/AIDS epidemic.

The world responds to the catastrophic health crisis among the global poor in a variety of ways: with the usual declarations, working papers, conferences, summits and working groups first and foremost, of course; but also with efforts to fund delivery of medicines to the poor through intergovernmental initiatives, governmental programmes,

[3] Marrakesh Agreement Establishing the World Trade Organization, opened for signature 15 April 1994, 1867 UNTS 3, annex 1C (Agreement on Trade-Related Aspects of Intellectual Property Rights) (entered into force 1 January 1995) ('TRIPS Agreement').

public–private partnerships, and through medicine donations from pharmaceutical companies; and with various efforts to foster the development of new medicines for the diseases of the poor, and various prizes as well as advance purchase commitments and advance market commitments.[4]

Such a busy diversity of initiatives looks good and creates the impression that a lot is being done to solve the problem. And most of these efforts are really doing good by improving the situation relative to what it would be otherwise. Still, these efforts are not nearly sufficient to protect the poor. It is unrealistic to hope that enough billions of dollars will be devoted to neutralizing the cost imposed on the world's poor by the globalization of twenty-year patents. And it is even more unrealistic to hope that such billions will reliably and efficiently be spent year after year. It makes sense then to look for a more systemic solution that addresses the global health crisis at its root. Involving institutional reform, such a systemic solution is politically more difficult to achieve. But, once achieved, it is also politically much easier to sustain. And it preempts most of the huge and collectively inefficient mobilizations currently required to sustain the many stop-gap measures, which can at best only mitigate the effects of structural problems they leave untouched.

The quest for such a systemic solution should start from an analysis of the main drawbacks of the newly globalized patent regime. These are:

- **High prices**. While a medicine is under patent, it will be sold near the profit-maximizing monopoly price, which is largely determined by the market demand of the affluent. When wealthy people really want a drug, then its price can be raised very high above the cost of production before increased gains from enlarging the mark-up are outweighed by losses from reduced sales volume. With patented medicines, mark-ups in excess of 1,000 per cent are not exceptional.[5] When such exorbitant mark-ups are charged, only a few of the poor can have access through the charity of others.
- **Neglect of diseases concentrated among the poor**. When innovators are rewarded with patent-protected mark-ups, diseases concentrated

[4] Details of these initiatives (and their drawbacks) are discussed in Aidan Hollis and Thomas Pogge, *The Health Impact Fund: Making New Medicines Accessible for All* (2008) ch. 9, www.yale.edu/macmillan/igh/hif_book.pdf at 16 February 2009.

[5] In Thailand, Sanofi-Aventis sold its cardiovascular disease medicine Plavix for 70 baht ($2.20) per pill, sixty times more than the price at which the Indian generic firm Emcure agreed to deliver the same medicine (clopidogrel). See Oxfam International, 'Investing for Life: Meeting Poor People's Needs for Access to Medicines through Responsible Business Practices' (Briefing Paper No 109, Oxfam, November 2007) 20.

among the poor – no matter how widespread and severe – are not attractive targets for pharmaceutical R&D. This is so because the demand for such a medicine drops off very steeply as the patentee enlarges the mark-up. There is no prospect, then, of achieving high sales volume *and* a large mark-up. Moreover, there is the further risk that a successful research effort will be greeted with loud demands to make the medicine available at marginal cost or even for free, which would force the innovator to write off its R&D investment as a loss. In view of such prospects, biotechnology and pharmaceutical companies predictably prefer even the trivial ailments of the affluent, such as hair loss and acne, over tuberculosis and sleeping sickness. This problem of neglected diseases has become known as the 10/90 problem, alluding to only 10 per cent of all pharmaceutical research being focused on diseases that account for 90 per cent of the GBD.[6]

- **Bias towards maintenance drugs**. Medicines can be sorted into three categories: curative medicines remove the disease from the patient's body; maintenance drugs improve wellbeing and functioning without removing the disease; and preventative medicines reduce the likelihood of contracting the disease in the first place. Under the existing patent regime, maintenance drugs are by far the most profitable, with the most desirable patients being ones who are not cured and do not die (until after patent expiration). Such patients buy the medicine week after week, year after year, delivering vastly more profit than would be the case if they derived the same health benefit from a cure or vaccine. Vaccines are least lucrative because they are typically bought by governments, which can command large volume discounts. This is highly regrettable because the health benefits of vaccines tend to be exceptionally great as vaccines protect from infection or contagion not merely each vaccinated person but also their contacts.[7] Once more, then, the present regime guides pharmaceutical research in the wrong direction – and here to the detriment of poor and affluent alike.
- **Wastefulness**. Under the present regime, innovators must bear the cost of filing for patents in dozens of national jurisdictions and then also the cost of monitoring these countries for possible infringements of their patents. Huge amounts are spent in many jurisdictions on costly litigation that pits generic companies, with strong incentives to

[6] See Global Forum for Health Research, *The 10/90 Report on Health Research 2003–2004* (2004), www.globalforumhealth.org at 16 February 2009.

[7] See Michael Selgelid, 'Ethics and Drug Resistance' (2007) 21 *Bioethics* 218.

challenge any patent on a profitable medicine, against patentees, whose earnings depend on their ability to defend, extend and prolong their patent-protected mark-ups. Even greater costs are due to the dead-weight loss 'on the order of US$200 bn' worldwide that arises from blocked sales to buyers who are willing and able to pay some price between marginal cost and the much higher monopoly price.[8]

- **Counterfeiting**. Large mark-ups also encourage the illegal manufacture of fake products that are diluted, adulterated, inert or even toxic. Such counterfeits often endanger patient health. They also contribute to the emergence of drug-specific resistance, when patients ingest too little of the active ingredient of a diluted drug to kill off the more resilient pathogenic agents. The emergence of highly drug-resistant disease strains – of tuberculosis, for instance – poses dangers to us all.
- **Excessive marketing**. When pharmaceutical companies maintain a very large mark-up, they find it rational to make extensive efforts to increase sales volume, often by scaring patients or by rewarding doctors. This produces pointless battles over market share among similar ('me-too') drugs as well as perks that induce doctors to prescribe medicines even when these are not indicated or when competing medicines are likely to do better. With a large mark-up it also pays to fund massive direct-to-consumer advertising that persuades people to take medicines they do not really need for diseases they do not really have (and sometimes for invented pseudo-diseases).[9]
- **The last-mile problem**. While the present regime provides strong incentives to sell even unneeded patented medicines to those who can pay or have insurance, it provides no incentives to ensure that poor people benefit from medicines they urgently need. Even in affluent countries, pharmaceutical companies have incentives only to sell products, not to ensure that these are actually used, properly, by patients whom they can benefit. This problem is compounded in poor countries, which often lack the infrastructure to distribute medicines as well as the medical personnel to prescribe them and to ensure

[8] Personal communication (13 November 2007) from Aidan Hollis, based on his rough calculation. For some discussion of alternative calculations see Aidan Hollis, 'An Efficient Reward System for Pharmaceutical Innovation' (Working Paper, University of Calgary, 2005) 8, where he quantifies the dead-weight loss in the region 'of $5 bn – 20 bn annually for the US. Globally the deadweight loss is certain to be many times this figure, because in many markets drug insurance is unavailable and so consumers are more price-sensitive.'

[9] See the special issue on disease mongering in the *Public Library of Science Medicine* (2006) 3, 425, collections.plos.org/plosmedicine/diseasemongering-2006.php at February 2009.

their proper use. In fact, the present regime even gives pharmaceutical companies incentives to disregard the medical needs of the poor. To profit under this regime, a company needs not merely a patent on a medicine that is effective in protecting paying patients from a disease or its detrimental symptoms. It also needs this target disease to thrive and spread because, as a disease waxes or wanes, so does market demand for the remedy. A pharmaceutical company helping poor patients to benefit from its patented medicine would be undermining its own profitability in three ways: by paying for the effort to make its drug competently available to them, by curtailing a disease on which its profits depend and by losing affluent customers who find ways of buying, on the cheap, medicines meant for the poor.

Contemplating these seven problems together, we see another reason to aim for a comprehensive and permanent solution in preference to the stop-gap measures that have been implemented and proposed: the practical value of efforts to mitigate one of the seven problems may be greatly reduced by one of the other problems that remains unaddressed; and efforts to mitigate one problem may aggravate another. For example, a drug donation for the benefit of the poor, intended to mitigate the problem of high prices, may actually do more harm than good because of the weak health infrastructure (last-mile problem) in the recipient countries. Lacking competent medical instruction and package inserts in their own language, poor patients may fail to take the medicine in the right doses, at the right times, or for the appropriate length of time. Such patients may not merely remain sick; they may also develop and spread drug-resistant strains of the disease, which (as in the case of multi-drug-resistant and extensively drug-resistant tuberculosis) can pose grave dangers to people everywhere.

Counter-productive effects can arise also from compulsory licences that some governments have issued or threatened to issue in order to gain for their populations cheaper access to patented medicines. Though specifically permitted by the TRIPS Agreement as reaffirmed in the Doha Declaration,[10] compulsory licences are energetically resented by pharmaceutical companies, and governments daring to issue such licences are routinely censured and penalized by these companies and by the rich-country governments doing their bidding. By issuing a

[10] See Ministerial Declaration on the TRIPS Agreement and Public Health: Adopted on 14 November 2001, WTO Doc WT/MIN(01)/DEC/1 (2001) [4]–[6]; TRIPS Agreement, above n. 3, articles 8(1), 27(2).

compulsory licence, a government authorizes the production and marketing of a cheaper generic version of a patented medicine on condition that the authorized generic firm pays a small licence fee to the patentee. Such a licence, and even the mere threat of one, will typically cause the price of the relevant medicine to fall substantially in the relevant country. But this welcome relief from the problem of high prices also aggravates the neglect of diseases concentrated among the poor. Pharmaceutical companies spend less on the quest for vital medicines – especially ones with a substantial share of their potential market in less-developed countries – when the uncertainties of development, testing and regulatory approval are compounded by the additional unpredictability of whether and to what extent successful innovators will be allowed to recoup their R&D investments through undisturbed use of their market exclusivity.

3. Reasoning

Counter-productive effects notwithstanding, the moral appeal of compulsory licensing is compelling. Consider a life-saving medicine whose patentee sells it at $100, of which $10 constitutes the long-run marginal cost of production and distribution. The high sales price effectively excludes poor patients many of whom, if the sales price were near cost, could gain access to the medicine, with the help of some international organization, perhaps, or on their own. What do we say to these patients who are suffering and dying even though they could obtain the medicine at the competitive market price? We tell them that, to merit access, they must pay not merely for the physical medicine but also for the intellectual property embodied in it: for the innovative idea or discovery or invention. But how can we impose such a huge mark-up for intellectual property on them, and thereby effectively exclude them from the medicine, when the cost to them of exclusion is sickness and death?

This question becomes even more pressing when we realize that including the poor adds nothing to the cost of innovation. It is a wonderful thing about the products of thought that their cost is independent of the number of beneficiaries. The intellectual labours of composing a novel are exactly the same, regardless of whether it has millions of readers or none at all. Likewise for discovering a new medically effective molecule. Millions can benefit from such intellectual efforts without adding at all to their cost. And this renders morally irresistible the conclusion that poor people, when their lives are at stake, must not be prevented from buying medicine from willing suppliers at competitive market prices. A compulsory licence secures this freedom for the poor.

But what about the innovator who has put in the effort and expense to achieve the innovation? Does not the innovation belong to him or her or it – to give or withhold or sell at will? Appealing to a Lockean natural right of appropriation, such an innovator might liken himself to someone who, by 'mixing his labour' with a formerly un-owned object while leaving 'enough and as good' for others, acquires this object and then denies others the freedom to use it. But this analogy is crucially defective. By asserting intellectual property rights, the medical researcher is denying others not merely the freedom to use what he has legitimately acquired, but also the freedom to use what they themselves have legitimately acquired. Through his invention, the rest of us supposedly lose our freedom to do what he did: to transform materials we legitimately own into a substance of the kind he first produced. Far from supporting monopoly rights in pharmaceuticals, the philosophical tradition friendliest to property rights thus refutes such intellectual property rights.[11]

The defender of intellectual property rights might reply that it is destructive of innovation to permit generic producers to copy an invention without having to buy the inventor's licence. Such permission would deprive us all of the powerful new medicines pharmaceutical innovators keep on producing.

This argument constitutes a change of venue, defending now patents not in the courtroom of natural rights but in the courtroom of mutual advantage. Does this defence succeed? It is indisputable that powerful new medicines whose development was motivated by the hope for profits have greatly benefited some patients: namely those affluent enough to buy them at monopoly prices or fortunate enough to need them after patent expiration. If all human beings were so affluent or fortunate, then patents might be defensible as in everyone's best interest: it would then be rational for all of us to accept the cost of laying down our rights to produce, sell and buy a new medicine invented by another in exchange for the much greater benefit of having available a broad and powerful arsenal of pharmaceuticals.

In fact, however, many human beings are trapped in severe poverty. Most of them derive little or no benefit from the marvellous arsenal of available medicines because they cannot, at prevailing prices, get access

[11] For a more extensive rejection of the Lockean claim (with specific discussion of Robert Nozick), see Hollis and Pogge, *The Health Impact Fund*, above n. 4, 62–8.

to them. For these people – and they number in the billions – it would be highly irrational to agree to lay down their freedom so that the affluent can more successfully use patents to stimulate pharmaceutical innovation. In the real world, the poor do not give such highly irrational consent. The often devastating cost is imposed on them by others who, for their own advantage, interpose the barrier of patents between poor people and the generic companies willing to supply the medicines they urgently need. This interposition is a grievous injustice that kills millions of poor people each year.

This injustice is manifest in national legislation: in India, for instance, where the poor have recently lost their legal freedom of access to medicines at competitive market prices. It is also manifest in international trading rules such as the TRIPS Agreement, which required India to implement these legislative changes as a condition of the limited access WTO membership affords Indian exporters to the markets of affluent countries. Perhaps the governments of India and other less-developed countries made a reasonable choice when they imposed unjust pharmaceutical access rules upon their poor for the sake of gaining a little more fairness in international trade. But the powerful affluent countries devising and imposing the present WTO regime have no such excuse. They are acting unjustly by pressing weaker countries to inflict this injustice on their poor. If rich countries and their citizens desire medical innovation, then they must find ways of funding it that either leave the freedom of the poor unreduced or else adequately compensate the poor for the loss of freedom imposed upon them.

Because it would be difficult, if not impossible, adequately to compensate poor people for disease and death, let us consider ways of funding pharmaceutical innovation that would not deprive the poor of their freedom of access to existing medicines at competitive market prices. The problem here is that, if the poor are left this freedom, it is difficult to collect from anyone the monopoly rents that stimulate pharmaceutical innovation. Though the affluent are often willing to buy advanced medicines at prices far above the marginal cost of production, many of them prefer to buy cheaper, even illegally. And clever brokers and smugglers, too, stand ready to exploit any substantial differential between the price charged to the rich and the competitive market price charged to the poor. Split markets with large price differentials thus generate unfairness as smugglers and the selfish affluent benefit at the expense of innovators and the honest affluent. More to the point, allowing the poor their freedom of access at competitive market prices substantially reduces the monopoly rents that can be extracted from affluent patients and thereby also the incentives of pharmaceutical companies to make large R&D investments in the first place.

To avoid all these problems with large price differentials, it is best then to level pharmaceutical prices in the opposite direction: instead of unjustly imposing monopoly prices also on the poor (which effectively excludes most of them from advanced medicines), we should grant open access at competitive market prices also to the affluent. In this way, we avoid the problem of high prices in an efficient way. We also eliminate high mark-ups entirely and thereby avoid the problems associated therewith: smuggling, wastefulness, counterfeiting, excessive marketing and the bias towards maintenance drugs.

Because pharmaceutical R&D is urgently needed, loss of funding from patents must be replaced somehow – with public funds – to ensure a reliable innovation flow for the long term. Such public funding can be designed to overcome the last two remaining problems of the present regime: the neglect of diseases concentrated among the poor and the last-mile problem.

Mechanisms of public financing are usually categorized under the labels of 'push' and 'pull'. A push programme selects and funds some particular innovator – a pharmaceutical company, perhaps, or a university or a national health agency – to undertake a specific research effort. The intent here is that, with adequate funding, the selected innovator will develop the desired innovation, which can then be made freely available for production by competing pharmaceutical manufacturers so as to ensure wide availability at competitive market prices.

A pull programme, by contrast, is addressed to many potential innovators, promising to reward whoever is first to achieve a valued innovation. Pull programmes have two interrelated advantages over push programmes: they avoid paying for failed research efforts and they generate strong financial incentives for innovators to work hard towards early success. The flip side of these advantages is that, in order to elicit such a serious research effort, the reward must be large enough to compensate for the risk of failure. This risk is twofold, as a research effort may fail either because the sought medicine proves elusive or because some competing innovator succeeds first. Potential innovators have incentives to try to develop a new medicine only if the reward for success, discounted by the probability of failure, is substantially greater than the expected cost of the R&D effort. In these respects, a pull programme is similar to the current patent regime.

Despite this extra cost, pull programmes can nevertheless be more effective than push programes, for three reasons: push programmes are more likely to fail because they get only one rather than several competing innovators to work on each problem; because the innovator is chosen on the basis of some outsider's confidence in it whereas in pull programmes each innovator's decision to try is based on *its own*, more competent and better motivated assessment of its capacities; and because the chosen innovator has much weaker incentives to work hard and cost-effectively towards early success. This higher probability of failure is compounded by the fact that such failures are paid for; in contrast to pull programmes, which pay nothing for failed efforts. Given this contrast, pull programmes are politically more easily sustainable.

Most prominent among pull programmes are prize competitions that promise a reward to the innovator who is first able to produce a medicine that meets certain specifications. This reward can be specified as some monetary amount or as an Advance Purchase Commitment ('APC') or Advance Market Commitment ('AMC'). Such rewards have been described with considerable ingenuity.[12] They clearly can be a valuable complement to existing patent rewards and have the potential of stimulating the development of medicines for currently neglected diseases.

Nonetheless, such ad hoc prize competitions have four drawbacks. First, politicians, bureaucrats or experts play a crucial role by deciding which diseases should be researched, how the sought remedy should be specified and how large a reward should be promised for a remedy meeting these specifications, inviting incompetence, corruption, gaming and lobbying by companies and patient groups. But the planners' own incentives to stimulate the most cost-effective innovations are weak. And their information about the cost of specific research efforts to innovators is likely to be of poor quality, as potential innovators have reason to exaggerate both the costs and the potential utility of their efforts.

Second, ad hoc rewards involve excessive specificity. Each reward must define a precise finish line, specifying at least what disease the medicine must attack, how bad the side effects of the medicine may be, and how effective and convenient it must minimally be. Such specificity is problematic because it presupposes the very knowledge whose acquisition is yet to be encouraged. Thus the sponsors' specification is likely to be seriously suboptimal even if they are single-mindedly devoted to the

[12] See especially Michael Kremer and Rachel Glennerster, *Strong Medicine: Creating Incentives for Pharmaceutical Research on Neglected Diseases* (2004).

goal of improving public health. Such suboptimality can take two forms. The specification may be overly demanding in at least one dimension, with the result that innovators give up the effort even though something close to the sought solution is within their reach. And the specification may be insufficiently demanding in some dimension(s), with the result that innovators, to save time and expense, deliver products that are just barely good enough to win the prize even when they could have done much better at little extra cost.[13]

The third disadvantage of ad hoc rewards is that the funding they depend on is likely to be haphazard and case-by-case. This is so because arbitrary factors and political contingencies will invariably enter into the choice of specific diseases and types of intervention around which prize competitions are organized. It is also likely that overall fund allocations will be erratic: when encountering budget problems, governments will tend to skip or to postpone planned reward competitions, and the conduct of other sponsors is also likely to be unduly influenced by extraneous factors (e.g., by their public relations needs or by how much money they must spend in the current year to retain their tax-deductible status).

A fourth serious defect of ad hoc rewards is that they fail to address the last-mile problem, which is especially severe in the context of currently neglected diseases that mostly affect the poor. The fact that a new vital medicine is available in large quantities, or can be produced very cheaply by generic producers, does not yet give poor populations real access to it. The reward pulls innovators to the invention of a new safe and effective medicine or even to its production in large quantities. But it does not pull this medicine the rest of the way to the patients who need it.

4. Solution

The exclusion of the poor by the existing patent regime requires reform. Given the foregoing discussion, a straightforward and moderate reform would create a supplementary mechanism that, by addressing the needs of the poor, would remedy the injustice now imposed upon them. This reform proposal comprises six elements. First, just as the patent regime provides a *general* innovation incentive, so its complement encourages pharmaceutical innovation through an incentive that is specified in

[13] For an excellent discussion, see Aidan Hollis, 'Incentive Mechanisms for Innovation' (Technical Paper No TP-07005, Institute for Advance Policy Research, University of Calgary, June 2007)15–16.

general terms: as a promise to reward *any* successful new medicine in proportion to its success. This kind of mechanism has been described as a *comprehensive* AMC.[14] Second, while the patent regime rewards medicines on the basis of the market demand each generates and then satisfies, thereby effectively excluding the poor, its complement gives equal standing to all by defining success simply in terms of human health. On this complementary track, the success of a medicine is assessed by the reduction in human morbidity and premature mortality it achieves – regardless of whether these harms are averted from rich or poor patients. Third, in order to help overcome the last-mile problem, the rewards available under the complementary mechanism should be tied not to what a medicine can do, but to what it *actually* achieves in the world. Fourth, when such a general mechanism provides large enough health impact rewards, it will attract sufficient innovation and sufficient efforts to ensure real access to new medicines worldwide. This avoids any need for compulsion. Innovators can be left free to choose between the two tracks, developing on the new track high-impact medicines needed also by many poor patients and on the conventional patent track low-impact medicines desired by the more affluent. Making the health-impact track optional is also crucial for the political success of the proposal. Fifth, in order to reinforce the incentive towards facilitating real access, health impact rewards should be conditional on the medicine being priced no higher than the lowest feasible cost of production and distribution.

Sixth, health impact rewards should be funded by governments as a public good. In order to minimize burdens and dead-weight losses due to taxes, the cost should be spread as widely as possible. This suggests that the complementary funding mechanism should be global (rather than national) in scope. The reasons that make the reform compelling in any one country or region make it compelling everywhere. Moreover, global scope avoids the problems associated with large price differentials. Global scope also brings huge efficiency gains by diluting the cost of the scheme without diluting its benefits: no matter how many beneficiaries we may add, the cost of achieving an innovation remains the same even while its aggregate benefit increases with the number of beneficiaries.[15] Finally, an international

[14] Aidan Hollis, 'The Health Impact Fund: A Useful Supplement to the Patent System?' (2008) 1 *Public Health Ethics* 124.

[15] In the case of medicines targeting communicable diseases, this benefit will increase super-proportionally: each user of such a medicine benefits from others using it as well, because wide use can decimate or even eradicate the target disease and thereby

agreement would also reinforce the commitment of individual countries to the scheme. Pharmaceutical innovation is therefore best encouraged by promising to reward any safe and effective new medicine in proportion to its *global* health impact. Such a promise constitutes an AMC that is *fully* comprehensive: by including not merely all diseases but also all patients.

The proposal is then for the creation of a new international agency that offers to reward any new medicine based on its health impact during its first decade or so.[16] This Health Impact Fund ('HIF') would provide ample rewards for the development of new high-impact medicines without excluding the poor from their use.

To provide stable incentives, member states must guarantee funding some fifteen years into the future to assure pharmaceutical innovators that, if they invest in expensive clinical trials now, they can claim a full decade of health-impact rewards upon marketing approval.[17] Such a solid guarantee is also in the interests of the funders who would not want the incentive power of their contributions to be diluted through sceptical discounting by potential innovators. States might guarantee fixed annual pools to be shared among registered medicines in proportion to their respective health impacts (subject to a reward rate ceiling) or they might promise a fixed monetary amount per unit of health impact.[18] These two design options differ in how they allocate the inevitable burden from uncertainty about how much health impact HIF-registered products will achieve in aggregate. The former solution makes the cost of the HIF predictable and is therefore more attractive to governments; but it imposes one more risk upon potential innovators by leaving them in the dark about the rate of reward per unit of health impact. The latter option removes this uncertainty from innovators, but then imposes on

reduce the probability that this disease will adapt and rebound with a drug-resistant strain: see Selgelid, 'Ethics and Drug Resistance', above n. 7.

16 This corresponds roughly to the effective patent life of twenty-year pharmaceutical patents, which are typically filed many years before marketing approval.

17 To allow for the registration of newly trialled traditional medicines and of new indications of existing medicines, the HIF should not require a patent as a precondition of registration. This issue is discussed by Katharine Liddell in this volume as well as by Talha Syed, 'Should a Prize System for Pharmaceuticals Require Patent Protection for Eligibility?', Discussion Paper Number 2, www.healthimpactfund.org .

18 Which for this discussion I assume is measured in quality-adjusted life years ('QALYs'). The QALY is a common measure of gains against the mortality and morbidity that constitute the GBD. It can be refined in various ways which I lack the space to discuss here. Basically, one QALY is an additional year of healthy life or a longer additional period of impaired life (e.g., 1.25 additional years with a 20 per cent impairment of age-specific functioning).

governments considerable uncertainty about what the HIF will cost each year.[19] There are also intermediate design options that split the burden of uncertainty between governments and pharmaceutical innovators.[20]

So constructed, the HIF is scalable, allowing governments to scale it up if it proves successful (downscaling is constrained by the fifteen-year guarantee). Any such scaling-up can be financed through an increased commitment by the member states and/or through the accession of new members.

The establishment and scaling-up of the HIF would be facilitated by a rule that divides the cost of the HIF in proportion to the member states' respective gross national incomes ('GNIs'). Thus, if one member state's GNI is 3.7 times that of another, then the contribution assigned to the former will be 3.7 times that assigned to the latter. Such rigidity has three main advantages. First, the contributions of the various partner countries are automatically adjusted in a way that tracks their varying fortunes – fast-growing countries automatically assume a larger share while countries in recession (declining GNI) find their burden alleviated. Second, it pre-empts protracted struggles over contribution proportions such as have marred the United Nations. Third, rigidity assures each country that any extra cost it agrees to bear by supporting an increase in the contribution schedule, say, is matched precisely by a corresponding increase in the contributions of all other member states.

If all countries of the world were to agree to join the effort, each would contribute less than 0.01 per cent of its gross national income for the first US$6 billion. As citizens, we would all pay an additional 0.01 per cent of our gross income in taxes (US$1 for every $10,000 in gross income). If countries representing only one third of global national incomes were willing to participate, their citizens would contribute 0.03 per cent of their gross incomes: still a trivial amount relative to its impact and mitigated, of course, by the much greater affordability of HIF-registered medicines.

Let us recapitulate how the HIF would provide a full systemic solution to the seven problems described earlier:

- **High prices** would not exist for HIF-registered medicines. Innovators would typically not even want a higher price as this would reduce their

[19] This may not be unacceptable. If more taxpayer money is spent because the HIF stimulates more successful innovation than expected, then health gains and consequent economic benefits for taxpayers will also be greater than expected.

[20] For further discussion of such design options, see Hollis and Pogge, *The Health Impact Fund*, above n. 4, ch. 2.

health impact rewards by impeding access to their product by most of the world's population. The HIF counts health benefits to the poorest of patients equally with health benefits to the richest.

- **Diseases concentrated among the poor**, insofar as they substantially aggravate the GBD, would no longer be neglected. In fact, the more destructive ones among them would come to present some of the most lucrative R&D opportunities for biotechnology and pharmaceutical companies. This would happen without undermining the profit opportunities such companies now enjoy by developing remedies for the ailments of the affluent.
- **Bias towards maintenance drugs** would be absent from HIF-encouraged R&D. The HIF assesses each registered medicine's health impact in terms of how its use reduces mortality and morbidity worldwide – without regard to whether it achieves this reduction through cure, symptom relief or prevention. This would guide firms to deliberate about potential research projects in a way that is also optimal for global public health: namely in terms of the expected global health impact of the new medicine relative to the cost of developing it. The profitability of research projects would be aligned with their cost-effectiveness in terms of global public health.
- **Wastefulness** would be dramatically lower for HIF-registered products. There would be no dead-weight losses from large mark-ups. There would be little costly litigation as generic competitors would lack incentives to compete and innovators would have no incentive to suppress generic products (because they enhance the innovator's health impact reward). Innovators might therefore often not even bother to obtain, police and defend patents in many national jurisdictions. To register a medicine with the HIF, innovators need show only once that they have an effective and innovative product.
- **Counterfeiting** of HIF-registered products would be unattractive. With the genuine item widely available near or even below the marginal cost of production, there is little to be gained from producing and selling fakes.
- **Excessive marketing** would also be much reduced for HIF-registered medicines. Because each innovator is rewarded for the health impact of its addition to the medical arsenal, incentives to develop 'me-too' drugs to compete with an existing HIF-registered medicine would be weak. (Getting a patient switched from a competitor's product to one's own equally good product is very profitable under the present system. But if the latter product is HIF-registered, then the switch is not

profitable because it brings no health improvement.) And innovators would have incentives to urge an HIF-registered drug upon doctors and patients only insofar as such marketing results in measurable therapeutic benefits for which the innovator would then be rewarded.

- **The last-mile problem** would be mitigated because each HIF-registered innovator would have strong incentives to ensure that patients are fully instructed and properly provisioned so that they make optimal use (dosage, compliance, etc.) of its medicines, which will then, through wide and effective deployment, have their optimal public-health impact. Rather than ignore poor countries as unprofitable markets, pharmaceutical companies would, moreover, have incentives to work with one another and with national health ministries, international agencies and NGOs towards improving the health systems of these countries in order to enhance the impact of their HIF-registered medicines there.

5. Conclusion

This essay describes and justifies a complement to the existing patent regime that would generate a flow of pharmaceutical innovation without depriving the poor of their freedom to buy new medicines at competitive market prices. In response one might ask why the HIF here described should be confined to new medicines. There are other means for reducing the GBD, such as access to safe drinking water, adequate nutrition, clean sanitation, protections (such as mosquito nets) against disease-carrying animals, off-patent medicines and many more. Why reward only new pharmaceutical remedies when there are alternative, perhaps more cost-effective ways of averting the same diseases?

A partial answer is that the efforts encouraged by HIF rewards would not be neatly confined to new medicines. Once a firm has registered a new drug, its reward will depend on how this drug affects the evolution of mortality and morbidity attributable to its target disease (the disease for which it is indicated). This impact will depend on many factors, some of which – for example, the quality of healthcare delivery in poor countries – the firm can affect. By helping to improve such healthcare delivery, an innovator can magnify its medicine's impact, which is strongly affected by the extent to which doctors and nurses are locally available, know about the medicine, have it on hand, prescribe it, ensure that patients have access to it in the best dosage and in sufficient quantity, and instruct patients in its proper use.

This answer does not fully overcome the objection. There are diseases – simple diarrhoea, for instance – against which new medicines would be of limited help, if any. Why should not efforts to reduce such diseases by securing access to off-patent medicines, to clean drinking water or to sanitation be funded insofar as they are no less cost-effective than the Health Impact Fund? I have no objection to such an extension of the reward scheme here sketched. We can think of this scheme as the central module of a larger health reform project. Once this central module is specified and implemented, it can certainly be extended to other social factors essential to human health. It makes sense, nonetheless, to begin with the central module that will provide a useful paradigm for possible extensions and an impetus for further reform.

But why start with *this* module, focused on new medicines? Would the money not do more to protect the health of poor populations if it were spent on a global programme of universal access to clean water or healthy nutrition? Perhaps it would. But let us not disregard the political realities. Bitter experience over many decades has shown that the world's governments are not prepared to spend billions of dollars on clean water or school lunch programmes. The provision of such basic goods is thought to deserve a few millions here and there, but certainly not billions. The idea of spending such sums on supporting domestic corporations, by contrast, is entirely familiar and commonplace – in fact, the affluent countries are spending *hundreds* of billions *each year* on export credits and subsidies, which aggravate severe poverty abroad, in the agricultural sector alone. A politically realistic way forward might then tie together the two objectives of protecting the poor and providing business opportunities to corporations. The HIF I have sketched is meant to fit this description. There may be more cost-effective schemes for protecting the poor. But such alternative schemes are useless nonetheless if they cannot attract the funds they plan to spend. Aligning with the powerful interests of the pharmaceutical and biotechnology industries, the HIF has better prospects for success.

I am aware that I have not had the space to discuss fully how the proposed HIF should best be designed. This is evidently a highly complex question. We have an interdisciplinary and international team – supported by the Australian Research Council, the BUPA Foundation and the European Commission – hard at work detailing workable solutions to the remaining challenges. Our work is documented, with some time lag, at www.HealthImpactFund.org. A book, describing the proposal in more detail, is available there.

6

The Health Impact Fund: a critique

KATHLEEN LIDDELL*

1. Introduction

Despite the remarkable ability of medical science to treat, cure and prevent human suffering, the reality is that relatively few people benefit from this knowledge. The principal reason is poverty, or more accurately the unequal distribution of wealth. While the rich have more than enough to afford complex new treatments for cancer, heart disease, diabetes and infertility (amongst many other disorders), the poor struggle to afford even the most basic healthcare services. And while the diseases of the rich present lucrative new markets for medical research, the diseases of the poor are largely invisible to profit-oriented scientists, so few drugs are available. These two problems have been dubbed the crises of access and innovation.[1]

The patent system, although significant for the economic sustainability of medical science, has exacerbated these problems. The strongest justification for the patent system is utilitarian. The argument is that in return for investing in the risky business of developing an invention and disclosing it to the public, the inventor is given up to twenty years of exclusivity during which they have the sole power within the jurisdiction of the patent to exploit the invention, or to license others to do so.[2] This is the foundation

* With special thanks to Laura Biron for her helpful and insightful comments on an earlier draft of this chapter. This chapter's discussion of the HIF idea is based mainly on Aidan Hollis and Thomas Pogge, *The Health Impact Fund: Making New Medicines Accessible for All* (2008), www.yale.edu/macmillan/igh/hif_book.pdf and therefore does not reflect later refinements that were stimulated in part by the critical attention the proposal received at and subsequent to the Australian National University's workshop on *Incentives for Global Public Health: Patent Law and Access to Essential Medicines* (Canberra, 26–28 May 2008).

[1] Maxwell Morgan, 'Medicines for the Developing World: Promoting Access and Innovation in the Post-TRIPS Environment' (2006) 64 *University of Toronto Law Review* 45, 48.

[2] This is the typical utilitarian justification offered for patent protection. Other theories exist. A familiar one is the argument that a patent is the natural right of an inventor who has invested intellectual labour, but amongst other problems, this struggles to explain why subsequent independent inventors who labour using entirely their own resources to

for a very flexible business model, wherein the patent owner can decide how they market their invention, whether and how they will invest in additional work needed to ready it for commercial use, whether they will keep the invention for their own sole use or allow other parties to use it and, if the latter, the price they will charge. Flexibility is important given the highly variable nature of inventions, but it also allows the patent owner to be aggressively entrepreneurial. In the context of the healthcare market this is problematic. Ruthless bargaining over an ordinary commodity is one thing, but over human pain and suffering it is quite another.[3]

Fortunately, the problems have caught the attention of policy-makers and academics, resulting in a wave of initiatives and proposals designed to improve the fairness of the patent system and, more generally, medical care in developing countries. In the main the proposals tackle *either* the high cost of drugs, *or* the lack of incentives for certain types of research.[4] Compulsory patent licensing and patent pools are examples of the former; research prizes and patent extensions are examples of the latter. Standing out from the crowd is a proposal recently published by Aidan Hollis and Thomas Pogge that unusually tries to address both problems (and several others as well) in a single policy package.[5] The Health Impact Fund ('HIF') is not a proposal for a timid policy-maker. It is extremely ambitious, requiring substantial donations of money from national governments, a special administrative body to analyse the clinical value of inventions and voluntary participation of patent owners. A crucial question is whether it is worth it?

A full appraisal of the HIF is impossible without expertise in a wide variety of disciplines: health economics, legal economics, public health surveillance and health technology assessment to name just a few. This chapter adopts a particular perspective, reflecting the author's own disciplinary background. It asks the question: from the perspective of intellectual property law, is the HIF proposal a sensible proposal?

produce the same knowledge are not similarly rewarded with protection but instead excluded from using their invention.

3 See generally, Edmund Pellegrino, 'The Commodification of Medical and Health Care: The Moral Consequences of a Paradigm Shift from a Professional to a Market Ethic' (1999) 24 *Journal of Medicine and Philosophy* 243. See also other articles in the symposium featured in this edition of the journal.

4 Very few have attempted to address the paucity of information on clinical utility.

5 Hollis and Pogge, *The Health Impact Fund*, above n. *. See also Thomas Pogge, 'The Health Impact Fund: Better Pharmaceutical Innovations at Much Lower Prices', in Thomas Pogge, Matthew Rimmer and Kim Rubenstein (eds.), *Incentives for Global Public Health: Patent Law and Access to Essential Medicines* (2010), 135.

Intellectual property specialists study the legal mechanisms that regulate the creation, use and exploitation of mental and creative labour. They are generally concerned with five questions:

(1) If the law grants a privilege or right that affects the liberty of third parties to use information, knowledge or ideas (e.g., by restricting access to knowledge that would otherwise be freely available), is it justified?
(2) Are the rules governing eligibility for the privilege appropriate? (Neither too demanding, nor too lax.)
(3) Does the scope of the privilege comport with the justification and the rules governing eligibility?
(4) Are the rules governing eligibility and scope practically enforceable?
(5) Is there an alternative constellation of laws that would better meet the alleged justification?

It will be argued that the HIF proposal is a fascinating but perplexing proposal. While it has no devastating flaw, such a large number of policy assumptions have been made that it is exceedingly difficult to assess, even roughly, whether it is sufficiently justified, appropriately curtailed and optimally designed. More specifically, several assumptions about the intersection of patent law and the HIF are rather cavalier.

While the chapter gives free rein to a contrarian impulse, the comments should not be misconstrued as a dismissal of Hollis and Pogge's proposal. Their work is a truly substantial and original contribution to innovation theory and could prove to be a sophisticated solution to several of the deficiencies of the patent system. It is also an excellent example of interdisciplinary scholarship and appeals, refreshingly, to a plurality of interests and moral values. The questions, quibbles and suggestions that this critique offers are intended to feed into its future refinement.

2. The HIF: a short description

The cornerstone of the HIF proposal is a Health Impact Fund which, if the proposal is accepted, would be comprised of several billion US dollars donated by national governments and administered by an international agency. This money would be used to finance a revenue stream for effective, cheaply priced drugs.

The general idea[6] is that the owner of a patented drug that has obtained market clearance in at least one country may elect to join the

[6] Hollis and Pogge, *The Health Impact Fund*, above n. *, 3–12.

HIF for a period of up to ten years, on condition that he or she does not sell the drug for more than the average cost of manufacture and distribution. In return, the patent proprietor is granted a share of the annual HIF moneys. The size of the share is determined by the clinical benefits achieved by the drug compared to the benefits achieved by other drugs registered with HIF. At the end of the ten-year HIF period, if the drug is still under patent, the patent owner must offer a royalty-free licence allowing any person to manufacture and sell the drug.[7]

Rather than replace the patent system or introduce a new intellectual property right (like the orphan drug scheme),[8] the HIF is an optional system for dealing with conventional patents. Patent owners can either deal with their patented product in the normal way (setting prices at a level that allows them to recoup costs and profit) *or* they can register with the HIF, sell at cost and boost their revenue with supplementary payments from the HIF. Either way they continue to own the original patent.

As described in the previous chapter, Hollis and Pogge argue that HIF has several distinctive features:

- It is committed to the sale of drugs at cost price. This reduces the number of people priced out of the market thus addressing the crisis of cost.
- The size of the reward is dependent on the extent to which a new drug reduces disease, rather than the wealth of the patient, which is expected to make research on neglected diseases a more attractive proposition and, more generally, to scale rewards according to an objective measure of value rather than a market-based measure.[9]
- The system is scalable. After piloting it with drugs useful in the treatment of neglected disease research, it might be extended to diagnostics, devices and mechanical inventions (e.g., water purifiers) and/or Western disease research.
- It provides an incentive not only for the creation and manufacture of new drugs, but also private investment in health-service infrastructure

[7] The royalty-free licence must apply to all patents in the patent owner's control that are necessary for the manufacture and sale of the product.

[8] Orphan drug schemes, strictly speaking, do not confer property rights, but rather a transferable privilege. The EU Database Directive is an example of a new intellectual property right: *Directive 96/9/EC of the European Parliament and of the Council of 11 March 1996 on the Legal Protection of Databases* [1996] OJ L 077.

[9] Although market-based measures put weight on scientific measurements of value, they are at the same time susceptible to bias from promotional advertising, gaps in evaluative information and consumers' wealth.

('the last mile'). Given that HIF payments are proportionate to clinical impact, companies have a reason to ensure the right drug reaches the right patient, in the right dose, at the right time.

- It does not require any substantial changes to the structure of intellectual property protection or licensing.
- It will allegedly lead to more co-operative, and therefore cost-efficient, relationships between patent owners and manufacturers of generics. Owners will be less likely to refuse reasonable licences and manufacturers of generics less likely to infringe patent owners' rights (i.e., manufacture without permission).
- Its normative underpinnings are both moral and prudential.[10]

Thus, at least in broad outline, the HIF is based on a plausible and appealing set of ideas: it promises more affordable medicines, less research bias on Western 'illnesses', co-operation between governments and pharmaceutical companies in the development of health services, co-operation between patent owners and generic producers of the drug, payment based on an evidence-based clinical value (rather than advertising hype about a drug's usefulness), and less wastage on litigation, and it has a compelling moral foundation. So why hesitate?

3. Concerns and criticisms

3.1 Justification of the HIF

3.1.1 Theoretical

The first question is whether the HIF proposal is sufficiently justified, or whether its very first premise – that companies need better economic incentives to solve the healthcare problems of the poor – is flawed.

Hollis and Pogge are sensibly critical of the current patent system, arguing that it is not a particularly effective way to 'incentivize' the creation and diffusion of new inventions in poor markets and not a particularly *cost*-effective method in wealthy markets. The HIF scheme is an idea that is intended to make the patent system a better incentive by tailoring it more closely to the end objective (clinically effective medicines) and making it less wasteful (e.g., by reducing the dead-weight loss and encouraging a less combative relationship between inventors and producers). In adopting this approach, the authors concede a very

[10] Hollis and Pogge, *The Health Impact Fund*, above n. *, 7–8, 51–70.

significant point, namely that companies *need economic incentives* before they will address the problems of the poor.

Undoubtedly companies will take an economic incentive if it is offered to them, but do they need one? Or more accurately, do they need an additional one when they already have access to copyright, patents, trademarks, trade secrecy and, in some jurisdictions, regulatory data exclusivity, orphan drug market exclusivity, database rights and unfair competition? Perhaps the same outcomes could be achieved without offering increased economic profits? Perhaps it would be better in the long term to encourage non-economic motivations for research? Perhaps we would lose something quite precious if we reinforce economic motivations yet again?

These questions are difficult to answer. Hollis and Pogge's argument is based on the view that companies respond best to mechanisms with profit-making potential and reasonable longevity (meaning long-term government buy-in). While sensible, perhaps they concede too much. The pharmaceutical industry is already one of the world's wealthiest industries. Do they really need more money? It is also arguable that non-economic incentives might out-perform economic incentives, if given a chance. A cultural shift, particularly amongst research financiers, could have far-reaching effects.[11] Along these lines, there is evidence to suggest that a number of organizations are conducting research into neglected diseases and, in some instances, patenting the results despite the fact that consumers are likely to have insufficient money to pay high prices. Chikosa Banda, a PhD student at the University of Cambridge, has undertaken empirical research to try to understand what motivates these organizations.[12] Interim results suggest that researchers in the field of neglected diseases are primarily motivated by enhanced scientific reputation (from technical breakthroughs), the kudos that can be gained from public-spirited research, the availability of research funding, and to some extent intellectual curiosity. The companies employing these researchers support such work, even in the absence of immediate profit margins, because developing countries represent emerging markets (where 'early positioning' can be useful) and in order to correct the negative image of patents and the pharmaceutical industry.

[11] Researchers are often amendable to the idea of conducting research for reasons unrelated to profit, but those who fund their work (e.g. corporate employers and investors) are generally profit-oriented.

[12] Communication with Chikosa Banda, PhD student, Faculty of Law, University of Cambridge.

In light of current successes, it is worth asking whether an economic incentive such as the HIF is necessary. In response, Hollis and Pogge might argue that, whether or not it is absolutely essential, an economic incentive such as the HIF would be a worthwhile supplement. In particular it might engage companies who to date have not participated in neglected disease research and encourage a greater investment from those currently involved. But this too requires further research. If the prospect of an economic incentive puts public-spirited motivations at risk, the HIF proposal might be a case of one step forward, two steps back. A different line of enquiry would be to consider how we could encourage a more socially responsible ethos in the field of pharmaceutical research.

Avoiding the expansionist tendency that accompanies a lot of intellectual property policy is particularly important. The idea that profit potential should be ratcheted up to make neglected disease research as attractive as research into Western diseases might address the present-day 'skew' (towards 'wealthy' disease research), but it would do so at too high a price if one believes that the pharmaceutical industry is already over-remunerated. The preferable approach would be 'to meet in the middle' with 'wealthy' disease rewards reduced and poor disease rewards increased.

3.1.2 Practical

The question uppermost in ordinary people's minds when they first hear about the HIF proposal is, how much would it cost? The authors suggest partner countries would need to make an initial commitment of US$6 billion per year guaranteed for twelve years, with funds being scaled up if the system is effective and popular.[13] They suggest the target could be reached equitably if partner countries contributed 0.03 per cent of their gross national incomes.[14] However, the authors are silent about the number of partners that must participate to make this a viable proposal. Presumably, contributions at this level will be insufficient if a few of the wealthier countries decline to participate. To support the suggested level of contributions, the authors note that the total global spending on pharmaceuticals in 2008 is expected to reach US$735 billion.[15] In light of this, US$6 billion seems a small sum. However, it

[13] Hollis and Pogge, *The Health Impact Fund*, above n. *, 4, 10.

[14] The authors state that 0.03 per cent of a gross national income in a country with an average income of US$40,000 equates to $12 per citizen per year: ibid., 10–11.

[15] Ibid., 47.

is equally telling that the total operating budget for the United Nations' enterprise is estimated at US$4.19 billion,[16] and even at this rate many countries are behind in their payments. Seen in this light the HIF proposal is a huge sum of money, and unlikely to be met by foreign aid budgets.[17]

3.2 *The appropriateness of the HIF's eligibility rules*

3.2.1 National patent criteria

Thus far, following Hollis and Pogge, I have referred to patent owners as if they were a single easily definable group. However, this conceals an important point that needs more extensive consideration in the HIF proposal. Patent systems are national systems which, albeit sharing many common characteristics, vary in significant ways. So for example, the US Government grants patents enforceable in its territories by US courts, and the UK Government grants patents conferring exclusivity in the UK which are enforced by UK courts. The nationalization of patents means that a patent valid in one country may not be valid in another, the claims may differ or the owner of the patent may differ. The question this raises is what type of patent, or set of patents, should authorize entry to the HIF.

Hollis and Pogge suggest that ownership of a single patent from a list of eligible countries should suffice. The list of countries is not specified, but implicit in this is the recognition that some countries have rudimentary patent examination procedures or low patent eligibility thresholds, hence it would be too indiscriminating to propose that any single patent is enough. On the other hand, they think requiring a patent in each of the HIF signatory countries would be too onerous. Accordingly, they propose a midway point, whereby the registrant must secure at least one patent from a restricted list of countries.[18]

This sounds like a pragmatic compromise, but the policy implications are more radical than they first appear. In effect the suggestion means that an inventor with protection in a listed country (e.g., the UK) will be eligible for a publicly funded payment that increases even when they sell

[16] United Nations Department of Public Information, News and Media Division, 'Fifth Committee Approves Assessment Scale for Regular, Peacekeeping Budgets, Texts on Common System, Pension Fund, as it Concludes Session' (Press Release, 22 December 2006).

[17] Whilst national departments of health could be approached it is rare for them to support initiatives that principally assist the health of foreigners.

[18] Hollis and Pogge, *The Health Impact Fund*, above n. *, 14, 24.

the drug in countries where they have no special rights (e.g., Australia, Nigeria, the US). Putting it bluntly, if the public could purchase the drug at competitive prices in these countries, why make them pay a premium for the privilege of having the HIF registrant sell at cost price? Reading between the lines, the authors' view is that if the UK patent owner had applied to patent the same drug in the other countries, he or she would probably have been successful and there is nothing to be gained by forcing the patent owner through the bureaucracy and fees of multiple patent systems. Furthermore, the authors might believe it is counter-productive for the HIF scheme to pressure inventors to claim exclusivity in a large number of countries, as this would simply increase the number of patent licences that need to be obtained. By setting the prerequisite at one patent from a recognized country, there will be fewer jurisdictions where the patentee can control production.

One question is whether other features of the HIF might flatten out the advantages Hollis and Pogge seem to assume will follow from the one-patent approach: namely fewer patents and less bureaucracy. For example, rates of patent filing might remain high if registrants saw an advantage in applying for more than one patent in order to prevent other companies from making the HIF-registered drug. One such advantage is that the administered cost is likely to be 'near cost' rather than 'at cost', which might mean patent exclusivity in several jurisdictions is an attractive proposition (see below). A second advantage is that the registrant's HIF revenue will be larger if they are the only one permitted to sell the drug (because HIF revenue depends on proof of drug sales). Without exclusivity, the HIF registrant may find themselves competing for sales with generic copycats some of whom may have manufacturing plants in cheaper countries. Another reason to patent inventions widely under the HIF is the role patents play in co-ordinating co-operation between research partners.[19]

A second issue concerns the soundness of the assumption that a drug patented in one country would probably be patentable in others. World Trade Organization ('WTO') members are obliged to grant patents to inventions that meet the minimum set of standards specified in the Agreement on Trade-Related Aspects of Intellectual Property Rights

[19] See, e.g., F. Scott Kieff, 'Coordination, Property, and Intellectual Property: An Unconventional Approach to Anticompetitive Effects and Downstream Access' (2006) 56 *Emory Law Journal* 327.

('TRIPS Agreement' or 'TRIPS').[20] This has a strong harmonizing effect on national patent systems, but there are still significant differences. For example, the US operates a 'first to invent' principle whereas other countries work on a 'first to file' system.[21] This means that the person eligible to own a patent in European countries might not be eligible to own the equivalent US patent. Another example concerns obviousness. As a result of article 27 of TRIPS, WTO members are obliged to make patents available for inventions that are 'new', 'involve an inventive step' and are 'capable of industrial application'. These phrases are not defined and national patent systems adopt slightly different definitions such that some drugs are patentable in one country but not another. Generally speaking, different conclusions are reached only in borderline cases. But since the public purse is at stake, the differences might be significant.

A third issue concerns the language in which the patent document is drafted. One of the cornerstones of the patent bargain is that the inventor must not only invent something, he or she must disclose it in a manner that is sufficiently clear and sufficiently complete for other skilled scientists to repeat it. This is called the 'doctrine of sufficient disclosure', the 'doctrine of enabling disclosure' or the 'doctrine of fair basis' (depending on the jurisdiction). When patent exclusivity expires, the invention is then straightforwardly available to the public without the need for reverse engineering. To complement the principle of disclosure, national patent systems also stipulate the permissible languages of the patent document. To ensure scientists within their own country are not disadvantaged or put to the expense of translations, this is commonly the official language of the country concerned. The costs of translation are then met by the patentee. Hollis and Pogge's suggestion that ownership of a single patent from a list of eligible countries should suffice threatens to undermine this. If the patent is published in one language only, HIF registrants reap the benefits of the scheme without clear and complete disclosure to scientists of all nationalities. A possible improvement would be to condition HIF entry upon submitting an English translation of the patent. This is not ideal for scientists for whom English is a second

20 Marrakesh Agreement Establishing the World Trade Organization, opened for signature 15 April 1994, 1867 UNTS 3, annex 1C (Agreement on Trade-Related Aspects of Intellectual Property Rights) (entered into force 1 January 1995) ('TRIPS Agreement').

21 In a first to file system, the person eligible to own a patent is any inventor (regardless of whether he or she was first to invent) who files a patent for an invention. Since the invention must also be new (the requirement of novelty), the earlier inventor(s) must not have made the invention available to the public.

language, but it is the obvious choice when most scientific journals use this language. That said, if debates about a European Community patent are any gauge, a suggestion of this kind could be seen as highly controversial.[22]

3.2.2 The merits of insisting on any form of patent protection

Putting to one side the question of *which* patent(s) should be a prerequisite, a more general question is whether *any* patent protection should be a prerequisite for joining HIF?

To stipulate that patent protection is a prerequisite for joining HIF essentially means that only those drugs that meet the conditions of patentability are eligible for a share of the HIF funds. This in turn means that research efforts will be skewed in the direction, broadly speaking, of drugs which are new, inventive, useful and sufficiently disclosed. The last two characteristics are fairly uncontroversial, but is it sensible to insist that the drug be new and inventive?

Novelty in patent law is generally an absolute and strict standard. For example in European Patent Convention countries, a drug is novel if it differs from the 'prior art'.[23] The prior art includes everything *made available to the public* (whether by writing, oral description, use or in any other way), in any country, and at any time before the date of filing, plus any art included in patent applications pending before the European Patent Office. This is very broad. For example, an invention lacks novelty even if it was only ever recorded in a book, written in Sanskrit and misshelved in the children's section of the library in Wagga Wagga, which has never been consulted. The rationale for such a strict approach is to avoid granting exclusive rights to those who merely 'reinvent the wheel'. However, under the HIF proposal it might be rational to encourage scientists to rescue wheels from obscurity. It is conceivable that there is a stock of drugs or techniques suitable for treating neglected diseases that although discovered has not been commercialized.[24]

[22] Robyn Jacob, 'Creating the Community Patent and its Court' in David Vaver and Lionel Bently (eds.), *Intellectual Property Law in the New Millennium: Essays in Honour of Willam R. Cornish* (2004) 79.

[23] Convention on the Grant of European Patents, opened for signature 5 October 1973 , 13 ILM 268, article 52 (entered into force 7 October 1977) ('European Patent Convention').

[24] It is not uncommon for companies to test the utility of a molecule in special patient groups and, if it shows weak performance, to drop it from the research programme rather than investigate it in other patient groups (for example people suffering from a different strain of the disease or living in environments with different confounding factors).

Inventive step is a more qualitative requirement than novelty. Typically national patent systems interpret it to mean that the inventive concept, when compared with the prior art, was *not obvious*.[25] Again in European Patent Convention countries, the prior art is defined as described above (although co-pending patent applications are not included). Roughly speaking the purpose of the inventive step requirement is to restrict the privileges of patent exclusivity to situations where there is 'clear water' between the invention and the prior art in order to avoid restricting competition unnecessarily. The question is how much clear water must be achieved? The conventional response in modern patent laws is that it must be a development that is not obvious, meaning the skilled, but unimaginative person familiar with the prior art would not have realized it at the date the patent was filed. The effect then is that imaginative developments qualify for patent protection, but unimaginative scientific developments are subject to market competition. Significantly, for the HIF, it is quite common for new chemical molecules (especially those predicted in the literature or similar to other molecules), new uses for known molecules and new dosage regimes to lack inventiveness. Under Hollis and Pogge's incentive scheme, it might be sensible to restrict HIF payments to inventions which are imaginative (not obvious) to avoid spending limited public funds on advances that even unimaginative scientists could come up with. But on the other hand, this condition might be too restrictive.

This is because the existence of a straightforward pathway to a beneficial medical invention does not mean it will be developed. There may be overriding concerns about profitability. For example, it might be obvious how to change a chemical formulation so that a drug remains stable at unrefrigerated sub-Saharan temperatures, but at the same time economically unattractive if the potential purchasers are poor. Another issue is that the 'straightforward pathway' might involve a lot of costly, albeit routine, steps (for example to confirm its safety and efficacy). A further example is that it might be obvious to screen a group of molecules to see which is the least toxic or how to go about modifying a known drug for another clinical use, but there is no guarantee of success, and even routine animal, tissue culture and human trials involve high costs. Another reason why obvious drugs are not produced is because the companies that recognize a pathway with a good chance of success

[25] See, e.g., European Patent Convention, above n. 23, article 56.

sometimes have 'bigger fish to fry', meaning more lucrative lines of enquiry.[26]

3.2.3 An alternative eligibility threshold

If participation in the HIF is limited to imaginative (non-obvious) drugs and uses of drugs, the HIF proposal will fail to encourage some important work. Furthermore, it will funnel HIF funds into the hands of more technically proficient Western companies. An alternative approach is for HIF registration to be conditional, not upon patent protection but simply upon *market authorization* in an eligible country. This would mean any company legitimately selling a drug at cost price could apply for a share of HIF moneys for a period of up to ten years.[27] An additional rule, to prevent perpetual registration of a drug by different companies, would see registration for all companies lapse ten years after the date the drug was first entered (by any company) into the HIF.

Theoretically, several companies might apply to the HIF to register the same drug during the ten-year period, but patent protection and regulatory data exclusivity (ten to twenty years) would limit this prospect, and in any event, HIF payments would be distributed according to proof of clinical impact.[28] If this is still considered slightly unfair, (perhaps because it costs more to get an inventive drug to market?), then a further refinement would involve giving patented registrants an uplift (e.g., by multiplying their quality-adjusted life years ('QALYs')[29] by a factor of 1.25). Alternatively, registration could be limited to market authorization of *new or clinically superior* drugs and drug indications, which would be similar to the threshold operated by orphan drug legislation.

In summary, it is arguable that the HIF should incentivize any kind of research that saves or improves lives. This is not simply an issue of extending the HIF beyond drugs to devices, diagnostics, food and

[26] For these reasons, the advantages offered under regulatory data exclusivity and orphan drug schemes are not limited to patented innovations.

[27] Or whatever duration is thought to be most appropriate. A different duration might apply for new uses of known drugs and new processes.

[28] Multiple registrations are likely to occur only for unpatented or partially patented drugs which are easy to take through clinical trials. The likelihood of multiple listings could be further limited by reducing the number of years of HIF payments to, say, five years (so that generic copycats would need to be very close behind in order to get any benefit from the HIF), or by awarding second entrants a shorter period of protection.

[29] For a brief discussion of the concept of QALYs see Pogge, 'The Health Impact Fund', above n. 5, fn 16.

engineering.[30] Legal rules setting thresholds of eligibility for HIF moneys are also of central concern, and the HIF should not blithely adopt those used in patent law. After all patent law has quite different policy objectives (i.e., encouraging *inventive* innovations). In particular the HIF's framers should consider the degree of originality that warrants a share of HIF moneys. Being inventive and the very first to disclose might be too restrictive. Some version of market authorization might suffice. This idea has its own problems – for example, how to enforce sufficient disclosure – but it illustrates the fact that alternatives exist.

3.3 *The appropriateness of the scope of the HIF privilege*

One of the key purposes of the HIF proposal is to offer patent owners an alternative way of dealing with their proprietary rights that gives them a more proportionate and tailored reward for their creative achievements. In a sense the authors are proposing to change the scope of the patent right with the agreement of the patent owner. Instead of taking their chances with consumers' payments for twenty years, during which time they can charge prices of their own choosing (the conventional way to deal with a patent), patent owners who join the HIF scheme would receive HIF payments for five or ten years during which time they can charge no more than 'cost price'. The HIF payments will be calculated with reference to the drug's clinical impact. After the payment period ends, the patent owner continues to own property in the patent for the remainder of the standard patent period, but must offer royalty-free licences, meaning anyone can use it for free.

From this summary, it is clear that there are four parameters crucial to the scope of the HIF privilege: (a) the duration of the HIF payments; (b) the calculation of a drug's permissible sale price; (c) the calculation of a drug's health impact; and (d) the patent owner's rights at the conclusion of the HIF period. These are very difficult assessments to get right (particularly in practice), but if the calculations are misjudged, the fairness of the HIF will be fundamentally compromised.

3.3.1 Duration

There is a good deal of mystery surrounding the length of intellectual property protection. For example, why does patent protection last for

[30] The HIF could be scaled up after piloting the programme with drugs.

twenty years from filing and not fifteen, thirty or fifty years? Why does an author's copyright last for the duration of his life plus seventy years whereas copyright in a sound recording and broadcast lasts fifty years from the year of production? There are different policy issues for the different types of rights, which explain some of the variation, but even so the precise number of years remains arbitrary.

The proposed duration of the HIF payments shares this problem. It is proposed that the registered owner of a new drug[31] can participate in the scheme for up to ten years, and the registered owner of a new use for a known drug can participate for up to five years.[32] There is little explanation for the particular choice of years (why not five or fifteen years for a new drug?), and no explanation as to why a new use qualifies for half as long (why not a tenth or two thirds?). That said, one can guess at the gist of the thinking. Presumably the scheme needs a figure that is roughly acceptable to the potential registrants, broadly acceptable to the public donors and dovetails appropriately with patent protection. The authors seem to think that ten years of HIF moneys meets these criteria. Ten years is long enough to soften the blow of an 'unlucky year' (e.g., where other registrants achieve high clinical impacts), and not too long for the public to wait for royalty-free licences. It is also likely to expire at roughly the same time as the patent (give or take a few years).[33] However, the authors also acknowledge that the choice is somewhat arbitrary. In fact, shorter periods might be equally acceptable to patent owners (since there will be fewer drugs registered each year), and in this case the royalty-free period might arrive sooner for the public.[34]

3.3.2 The calculation of the drug's permissible sale price

The proposal is that once signed up to the HIF scheme the drug's permissible price should be roughly equivalent to the cost of 'manufacture plus distribution'. The HIF Agency will be responsible for setting

[31] It is odd to exclude innovations such as new methods of treatment, diagnosis and manufacture. Clearly these could have a positive clinical impact, and even if this impact was less than that achieved by most drugs, the differences ought to be ironed out by the core proposition that HIF payments are proportional to clinical impact. It is even more peculiar to omit discussion of new dosage regimes (e.g., a single daily pill instead of several) and the period for which they should qualify. Possibly the intention is to address the inclusion of non-drug innovations at a later date.

[32] Hollis and Pogge, *The Health Impact Fund*, above n. *, 20.

[33] Assuming the patent owner does not delay entering the HIF for too long.

[34] Hollis and Pogge, *The Health Impact Fund*, above n. *, 20.

this price. One issue is how much allowance should be given to the patent owner's production preferences. For example, it might be considerably cheaper for the drug to be made in a country like India or China, but the patent owner might not be willing to manufacture the drug in those countries. It might prefer to use industrial plants in other countries (perhaps its own factories?) or have concerns about political stability, quality control or corporate culture in the cheapest countries. The style of packaging and money invested in trademarks and branding also affect the cost of the drug. Will the HIF Agency try to dictate this? Further complexity comes from the fact that distribution costs tend to vary markedly and the HIF Agency will be trying to predict the price range for an entire ten-year period.

The reality is that the HIF Agency will be limited to a rough and ready estimate. It will not arrive at the true cost price of production and distribution. At best it will be a 'near cost' price. Frank acknowledgement of this is important.

3.3.3 The calculation of a drug's health impact

The calculation of health impact is even more complicated. Having accepted the impossibility of producing a complete picture of the global burden of disease and then assessing a particular drug's contribution to its reduction, Hollis and Pogge suggest the HIF Agency will begin by finding a feasible baseline for comparison, for example, something like:

> the expected health level of consumers of the product being assessed, given the set of pharmaceuticals available, their approved indications, and their prices … excluding the new product and any others sold exclusively by the same registrant.[35]

The HIF Agency will then assess the change in health outcomes achieved by the drug in a given year. The authors hesitate to endorse a particular approach to this question. The most feasible option, they suggest, is to establish the number of drug units sold and, with the aid of clinical trials and field samples, the approximate effect one unit has on life years.[36] However they note several problems with this approach. Clinical trials (usually small and with a controlled patient group) do

[35] Ibid., 15. The reason for excluding other products sold by the registrant is to encourage the registrant to improve his products by removing the risk that he will 'cannibalize' his own HIF payments.

[36] This refers to the life years of the patient and, in the case of contagious diseases, other people he or she might infect.

not give accurate assessments of a drug's impact; the drug's impact may vary across different populations; the effect on life years may take life-times to assess; biomarkers (e.g., reduced cholesterol) often fail to give clear and certain information about clinical outcomes; and, most significantly, companies may develop tactics (e.g., fraud, aggressive marketing and advertising) to inflate sales figures and thereby exaggerate the apparent health impact.[37] Although this could be supplemented with field trials, the cost of such endeavours will constrain such efforts and their representativeness. These are very serious issues and cast doubt on the ability of the HIF fund to achieve the desired goal of a payment stream proportional to clinical benefit. These difficulties illustrate some of the reasons why the conventional patent system steered clear of evaluating an invention's utility, relying instead on market pricing to decide an inventor's 'reward'.

A further question is whether it is fair to consider the health impact in countries whose governments have approved the drug for market but have not donated to the HIF budget. For example, if the US does not support the proposal, would it be fair to assess the impact of a second generation antiretroviral with reference to its impact in Africa, Europe *and the US*, or should the HIF payment stream be analysed with reference to the drug's impact (i.e., sales) in Africa and Europe? Taking the former approach would mean US citizens obtain drugs at or near cost price without contributing to the cost of innovation. Taking the latter approach would make the proposal less attractive to industry and more cumbersome (and hence costly) to administer.

It should also be noted that linking measurements to the number of drug units sold (rather than clinical impact) undermines the 'last-mile' advantage that the authors hoped would be an additional benefit of the HIF scheme.[38] Patent owners will have little incentive to invest in health-service infrastructure, supply routes and patient compliance, if their annual results are principally audited by sales rather than field studies. In contrast they will have a very strong incentive to invest in advertising and promotional materials to shift as much stock as possible.

3.3.4 Residual rights at the conclusion of the HIF period

Hollis and Pogge propose that, at the end of the HIF period, the patent owner should be obliged to offer royalty-free licences to all would-be manufacturers and distributors of the drug.[39] This is a sensible TRIPS-compliant

[37] Hollis and Pogge, *The Health Impact Fund*, above n. *, 29–34. [38] Ibid., 76.
[39] Ibid., 14.

proposal to ensure that the drug continues to be available at competitive prices once the owner has had the benefit of HIF payments. But does it go far enough? More specifically, should it also be mandatory for HIF registrants to waive orphan drug market exclusivity and regulatory data exclusivity at the end of the HIF period?

Regulatory data exclusivity is a framework of (arguably TRIPS-Plus)[40] laws under which many countries limit the ability of drug approval agencies to use dossiers of clinical data submitted by one company in the analysis of the safety and efficacy of another drug.[41] Unless the drug approval agency has the company's permission, the dossier must be treated as confidential for five to eleven years (depending on the jurisdiction and other conditions). Since the agency's approval is essential for market entry, the effect is to force the competitor to invest money in their own clinical trials or wait until the period of data exclusivity expires. Accordingly, data exclusivity often gives de facto market exclusivity that is more valuable than patent protection.[42] Similarly, it is necessary to address rules that prevent the domestic registration of any generic version of a patented medicine without the patent holder's consent and that confer market exclusivity on orphan drugs.[43] Making royalty-free licences available at the end of the HIF registration will be of little public benefit if the patent owner is able to impose a formidable de facto barrier to market entry.

3.4 *Securing compliance with the objectives of HIF*

Scholars of regulation have been at pains to point out that legal rules, such as those proposed for the HIF scheme, are not self-executing.[44] They must be interpreted and, in the event of non-compliance, enforced.

[40] For a discussion of the meaning of the term TRIPS-Plus see Thomas Pogge, Matthew Rimmer and Kim Rubenstein, 'Introduction' in Thomas Pogge, Matthew Rimmer and Kim Rubenstein (eds.), *Incentives for Global Public Health: Patent Law and Access to Essential Medicines* (2010) 1.

[41] See, e.g., Directive 2004/27/EC of the European Parliament and of the Council of 31 March 2004 [2004] OJ L 136 amending Directive 2001/83/EC of the European Parliament and of the Council of 6 November 2001 on the Community Code Relating to Medicinal Products for Human Use [2001] OJ L 311.

[42] Trevor Cook, 'Regulatory Data Protection in Pharmaceuticals and Other Sectors' in Anatole Krattiger *et al.* (eds.), *Intellectual Property Management in Health and Agricultural Innovation: A Handbook of Best Practices* (2008) 437, 444–5.

[43] See, e.g., EU Regulation 141/2000 of the European Parliament and of the Council of 16 December 1999 on Orphan Medicinal Products [2000] OJ L 18.

[44] Bronwen Morgan and Karen Yeung, *An Introduction to Law and Regulation: Text and Materials* (2007) 153.

Hollis and Pogge have not entirely overlooked this point, but it is certainly under-represented in their description of the HIF. For example, what sort of legal system will be used to settle disputes? How will the HIF Agency police whether HIF-registered drugs are being sold at the administered price? What sort of punishments will be meted out if the HIF registrant fails to meet its obligations (e.g., to sell at cost price and to meet patient demand)? Will a less adversarial relationship between the patent owner and generic producers really be, as the authors assert, advantageous for compliance?

3.4.1 Dispute resolution

The discussion above about the complexities surrounding the calculations of permissible price and health impact indicate not only that there will be high administration costs, but that the HIF proposal is likely to generate a significant number of legal disputes. The disputes might centre on:

- the HIF Agency (e.g., its assessment of QALYs or the administered cost of production and distribution being too generous or not generous enough);
- registrants (e.g., those who sell at greater than the administered price or renege on the promise to offer royalty-free licences; those with patents of doubtful validity); or
- sovereign governments (e.g., those whose contributions are in arrears).

With US$6 billion and the health of thousands at stake, one could expect the disputes to be legalistic, politicized and drawn out. So it is likely that the HIF Agency will need a legal department with capacity to hear appeals and perhaps a more formal, independent mechanism to review whether due process has been followed (similar to judicial review) or the legal merits. Typically, international organizations include clauses in contracts to the effect that disputes that cannot be settled amicably will be settled by UNCITRAL arbitration.[45] Further consideration is necessary to establish whether this sort of approach would be suitable in the context of the HIF scheme, what sorts of remedies might be ordered (against governments and former HIF registrants), and how judgments might be enforced.

[45] Arbitration Rules of the United Nations Commission on International Trade Law, GA Res 31/98, UN GAOR, 31st sess, 99th plen mtg, UN Doc A/Res/31/98 (1976).

It is also necessary to consider how the HIF will police the marketplace. What sort of efforts will it make to check that HIF registrants are meeting their obligations to sell at cost price or to gain market approval in obscure countries? How will it administer and police the scheme of royalty-free licences that apply at the end of the HIF payment period?

3.4.2 Reduced litigiousness

The authors optimistically hope that the relationship between patent owners and generic producers will be less litigious under the HIF scheme.[46] Accordingly, they argue that their proposal will be more efficient than the conventional patent system. The crux of the argument is that a patent owner in the HIF scheme will care little about 'market exclusivity' and much more about 'clinical impact'. Thus, rather than attack manufacturers of generics who undercut his margin, the HIF-registered owner, who has no margin to be undercut (his drugs must be sold at cost price), will allow other companies to manufacture and sell his drug, increasing its clinical impact. The large sums of money saved from the pockets of lawyers could then be invested in medical research and cheaper prices.

But are such outcomes realistic? If clinical impact is assessed upon proof of the number of drug units sold (see above), then owners of HIF-registered drugs will not be advantaged by the sale of generic drugs because there will be no sales receipts to present to the HIF Agency (unless submission of receipts is a condition of licensing). Instead they will find that the infringer's sales simply take away from their own sales total.[47] All things considered, the HIF scheme might alter the cost-benefit equations for litigation and infringement (making both less advantageous), but it is unlikely to resolve the conflicts between the parties. The imitators will continue to circle, and patent owners will continue to object to their presence.

A further question is whether owners of HIF-registered drugs will be able to interest licensees in their patented products. Since HIF-registered drugs must be sold by the patent owner and its licensees at the administered price (i.e., near cost), the patent owner might actually need *to pay* licensees in order to interest them in a licence. This is quite a radical

[46] Hollis and Pogge, *The Health Impact Fund*, above n. *, 17.

[47] This problem may be minimal if the availability of cost-price drugs makes the prospect of infringing unappealing. However, infringers could develop marketing strategies to sell the drug with a small but sufficiently lucrative margin. Alternatively, they may decide that the 'near cost' set by HIF is more than enough for a comfortable existence.

reversal in roles, and it will take time for companies to adjust their negotiations. In effect, the patent owner will need to agree to share the HIF revenue with licensees, and he or she may need to be generous, or the value of the licence may be too little or too uncertain to interest any licensees. It is also significant that a generic producer could sell the drug above cost price if they do not take out a licence. The HIF Agency would have no power to prevent this. An HIF registrant might be able to bring patent infringement proceedings, but only if they had a valid patent for the particular territory at issue.

A more obscure issue, but something quite important if the HIF is scaled up, is whether a change in the relationship between patent owners and generic producers could affect the quality of patents granted. At present, a lot of 'bad' patents (by which I mean patents with invalid claims) are identified by competitors who initiate opposition or revocation proceedings (or re-examination in the US). Putting this another way, a degree of antagonism between the parties is healthy because it helps to supplement the patent office's examination of prior art and legal compliance. If the authors are right in thinking that HIF patent owners and their competitors will be on friendlier terms, the quality of patents in the HIF will be increasingly suspect. Generic producers might be happy to cut deals with the patent owner, thereby getting a share of the HIF revenues, rather than challenge the patent owner's eligibility for the revenue. Possibly existing HIF *registrants* will step into the role of challenging patent validity, because if they can remove an HIF drug from the register, their proportion of HIF revenues will increase. But since other registrants may not be expert in the same areas of medicine, it is doubtful whether they will fulfil this function as well as direct competitors. Another possibility is that generic producers might decide to challenge patent validity because if they succeed the drug will no longer be registered with the HIF (or subject to exclusivity), meaning the drug will no longer be available at cost price, creating a prospect of prices marginally above cost. All this is quite speculative, but it serves to demonstrate that there is much uncertainty about relationships between generics and patent owners under HIF and the impact the scheme could have on the validity of patents. The risk is that the HIF scheme will turn out to be a jolly good way to conceal weak patents at the public's expense.

3.4.3 Compulsory licences as a response to non-compliance

Given the likely difficulties negotiating voluntary licences, there is a real likelihood that patent owners will fail to meet patient demand in countries where the drug is legal and needed. This is made more likely by the fact that the patent owner's additional costs in treating hard-to-reach patients may not be matched by the proportional increase in the share of HIF revenues; so they simply might not bother to try to reach them. The authors' response is that if an HIF registrant fails to meet demand, the HIF Agency will have the power to issue compulsory licences.[48] Compulsory licences could also be used to penalize those who fail to sell the drug at cost price.

The power to compulsorily license would need to be a voluntary condition of joining the HIF as some countries have no compulsory licensing systems.[49] So it would actually be a 'voluntary compulsory licence'. It remains unclear whether it would be an effective penalty. As noted above, it will be difficult to find licensees willing to sell at cost, so presumably the HIF Agency will need to pay the potential licensee to take up the compulsory licence or find an alternative incentive. One incentive would be to make the holders of compulsory licences registrants in the HIF scheme. This would not disadvantage other registrants; the compulsory licensees' sales volume would simply be equal to the shortfall in the patent owner's production, leaving other registrants with their anticipated proportion of the HIF.

3.5 *Is there a better alternative to the HIF?*

The discussion above highlights a great many uncertainties about the effective operation of HIF, which makes one wonder whether it is in fact the best way forward. The importance of this question – the relative advantage of a proposed policy reform – was emphasized by Easterbrook J,[50] in an article sceptical about the need for new intellectual property rights to deal with new technology (e.g., software and genetic technology). He cautioned:

> All too many proposals commit the Nirvana Fallacy. They take the form: 'the existing legal regimen has the following costs and flaws; therefore my proposal is better. Patents raise price and discourage use; this is a flaw

[48] Hollis and Pogge, *The Health Impact Fund*, above n. *, 14.

[49] And because compulsory licences allowing drugs to be imported/exported to a country lacking sufficient domestic production capabilities are limited to public health emergencies: Declaration on the TRIPS Agreement and Public Health: Adopted on 14 November 2001, WTO Doc WT/MIN(01)/DEC/2 (2001) ('the Doha Declaration'); Implementation of Paragraph 6 of the Doha Declaration on the TRIPS Agreement and Public Health, WTO Doc WT/L/540 (2003) (WTO General Council Decision 30 August 2003); Amendment of the TRIPS Agreement, WTO Doc WT/L/641 (2005) (Decision of 6 December 2005 of the General Council) ('TRIPS Waiver').

[50] At the time of writing: Judge, United States Court of Appeals for the Seventh Circuit; Senior Lecturer, The Law School, University of Chicago.

> because some consumers who value the product at more than marginal cost can't afford it; therefore *my* proposal to [fill in the blank] should be adopted.' That's a non sequitur. Every way of handling intellectual property is costly and imperfect. All of these costs must be toted up and compared ...[51]

While Hollis and Pogge's HIF proposal could easily claim to be one of the most interesting proposals, it has very high establishment costs, considerable running costs, an uncertain magnitude of utility, and it needs to justify itself ahead of a long list of alternative options. These have been summarized by Morgan[52] and include policies to address access[53] (voluntary price discounts; Ramsey pricing; drug donation programmes; generic substitution; compulsory licensing; competition policy; voluntary licensing; patent waivers; bulk purchasing; price controls) and policies to address skewed innovation[54] (public and private charitable funding sources); public or private grants to researchers and their institutions; tax credits for R&D expenditures; international public–private partnerships; advance purchase commitments; a global pharmaceutical purchase fund; transferable patent extensions; prize-oriented research competitions; patent buyouts; orphan drug laws).[55]

Hollis and Pogge, familiar with the alternative policy options, argue they are less effective than the HIF.[56] For example, they argue in relation

[51] Frank Easterbrook J, 'Who Decides the Extent of Rights in Intellectual Property?', in Rochelle C. Dreyfuss, Diane Zimmerman and Harry First (eds.), *Expanding the Boundaries of Intellectual Property: Innovation Policy for the Knowledge Society* (2001) 405, 407.

[52] Maxwell Morgan, 'Medicines for the Developing World: Promoting Access and Innovation in the Post-TRIPS Environment' (2006) 64 *University of Toronto Law Review* 45, [56]–[109].

[53] These stimulate cheaper prices during the patent period and foster generic entry when the patent period ends. Morgan concludes that the best of these strategies include bulk purchasing, price control mechanisms (where there is sufficient regulatory capacity), capping local distributor mark-ups (a form of price control), differential pricing brought about through government assistance to promote vigorous generic competition in developing countries and a credible system of import/export compulsory licensing: ibid., [109]. Morgan also notes that care must be taken to avoid TRIPS-Plus provisions in bilateral and multilateral free trade agreements that jeopardize these approaches.

[54] Morgan argues that the most successful (or potentially most successful) of these policies to address innovation incentives include advance purchase commitments (perhaps supported by a global pharmaceutical purchase fund), public–private partnerships and orphan drug laws: ibid., [139].

[55] A drug or clinical indication directed at a condition that is rare in the US or Europe, but prevalent in other countries, can be registered for orphan drug market exclusivity.

[56] Hollis and Pogge, *The Health Impact Fund*, above n. *, 97–108.

to direct purchasing schemes that such schemes are subject to political influence, too fickle and result in high drug prices (when a patent owner anticipates its drug being the drug of choice).[57] In relation to differential pricing they point out that such schemes are unlikely to arise voluntarily and require government push. In relation to compulsory licensing, they note that the system is unpopular with the pharmaceutical industry and based on a bureaucratic case-by-case, country-by-country system.[58] In relation to advance purchasing commitments and prizes they argue that direct funding of research is unstable and inefficient when the funder has inadequate information to estimate the likely costs of research or the technical parameters that qualify for the money.[59]

However, Hollis and Pogge's counter-arguments are incomplete as they (1) address only some of the alternatives, usually as a singleton policy (rather than coupled with other proposals); and (2) do not discuss the relative cost-efficiency of the HIF compared with other proposals. Other proposals might lack some of the advantages of the HIF scheme, but the improvements that they *do* achieve could be considerably more cost-efficient as they do not require the setting-up of new agencies, international agreements, monitoring of market prices or in-depth measuring of clinical impact.

A crucial question for further consideration is whether a combination of ideas might cumulatively achieve most of what the HIF achieves, namely cheaper drugs and innovation directed at clinical needs, at a fraction of the cost. Such a combination is likely to include:

- more emphasis on value-based purchasing of drugs, particularly by government- and privately managed health services;
- larger donations by governments and pharmaceutical companies to organizations involved in the purchase of pharmaceuticals;
- more use of price controls and compulsory licensing; and
- more emphasis on civic and corporate social responsibility.

After all, the most significant problems with the conventional way of dealing with patents is not that it is inherently wrong but that (1) purchasers agree to deals that they should reject as being overpriced;[60] and (2) poor consumers lack the money to pay a reasonable price. The combination of policy proposals listed above would seem

[57] Ibid., 97–8. [58] Ibid., 99. [59] Ibid., 100–7.

[60] The suggestion is that purchasers should 'walk away' until the patent owner drops the price.

to address these issues without requiring a new international organization or treaty. They also have a much wider impact than twenty to thirty drugs per year, which is the HIF's projected target for a budget of US$6 billion.

4. Conclusion

This chapter has raised a number of issues and suggestions concerning the intellectual design of the HIF scheme. Drawing on a structure typical of intellectual property critiques (i.e., focusing on the rationales for a special incentive, the qualifying conditions, the scope of the privilege, systems for enforcement and policy comparisons), it questioned in particular: the wisdom of offering yet more profit-based incentives rather than nurturing corporate social responsibility; the likely cost-efficiency of the HIF; the rationale for requiring the registrant to own at least one patent and not necessarily more than one; the duration of the HIF payment stream; the systems for assessing cost price and clinical impact; the systems for enforcing the rules of the HIF; the likelihood of finding licensees for products that must be sold at cost price; the idea that the HIF will precipitate a less litigious and improved relationship between innovators and generic producers; and the suggestion that the HIF is preferable to other policy proposals.

Underneath these issues are three overriding concerns. First, there is a serious issue about the relationship between the HIF and the patent system. It is far from clear that it is necessary or desirable to piggyback the HIF system on patent protection: it introduces eligibility conditions of doubtful assistance and the territorial nature of patent protection raises many difficult policy questions for a scheme with global aspirations.

Second, there is an unsettling feeling that the proposal plays right into the hands of the pharmaceutical industry. It fuels their search for profits, offering them yet another optional method to increase their existing profit margins at the expense of the public purse, when they are already amongst the very wealthiest industries. The explanation seems to be that anything less than an attractive profit stands little chance of being supported by the politically powerful pharmaceutical industry (and therefore governments). In other words, unless the HIF scheme rivals what could be earned via instruments of exclusivity (e.g., patent protection, regulatory data protection, trade secrets, orphan drugs designation, database rights), it will simply be ignored. If this is true, the HIF will exacerbate the expansionist trend of intellectual property rights. If false, there is a serious risk that the HIF will short-change the public purse.[61]

The third issue is that there is insufficient empirical evidence to back key premises in the HIF proposal or to show that the benefits of the HIF justify such a major policy undertaking. This presents an awkward paradox: the HIF is a proposal that seeks to organize the cost and direction of scientific research on the basis of proven utility, yet the regulatory tools enlisted to achieve this lack an equivalent evidence base.

Fortunately, the architects of the HIF have exactly the sort of energy and expertise that might yet be able to resolve these concerns. They may yet deliver, not only the most interesting of innovation reforms, but also the most far-reaching.

[61] Hollis and Pogge's response is that industry concessions are acceptable if the end result betters the status quo and rivals other policy options. But, some concessions seem to have been granted without clear evidence of necessity, scoring points with the pharmaceutical industry but undermining the search for overlapping consensus.

7

A prize system as a partial solution to the health crisis in the developing world

WILLIAM W. FISHER AND TALHA SYED

1. Introduction

Each year, roughly nine million people in the developing world die from infectious diseases.[1] Millions more endure suffering caused by the same diseases. Many of those deaths and much of that pain could be avoided by modifying the combination of laws and government programmes that provide incentives for the development and distribution of drugs. In a recent paper, we argued that such modifications are morally imperative, despite the fact that they would increase the already substantial extent to which the cost of developing new drugs is borne by the residents of the developed world, either by raising their taxes or by increasing the prices they pay for patented pharmaceutical products.[2]

The difficult question, in our judgment, is not whether we should modify our laws and institutions to address this crisis, but which combination of reforms would alleviate the problem most fairly and efficiently. We are currently working on a book that examines and compares a wide variety of potential solutions.[3] In this chapter, we focus on one option: replacing or supplementing the patent system, as the main method by which we encourage the creation of new drugs, with a system of government prizes.[4]

Producing new pharmaceutical products – and then verifying their effectiveness and safety – is both expensive and risky. Substantial

[1] See World Health Organization, *World Health Report 2004 – Changing History* (2004).

[2] William W. Fisher and Talha Syed, 'Global Justice in Health Care: Developing Drugs for the Developing World' (2007) 40 *University of California Davis Law Review* 581.

[3] William W. Fisher and Talha Syed, *Drugs, Law, and the Health Crisis in the Developing World* (Stanford University Press, forthcoming).

[4] Which government, or consortium of governments, should implement such a system is itself a complex question, one taken up in the longer version of this chapter. Here, we adopt the simplifying assumption that it would be a single national government – namely, that of the US.

financial incentives are essential to induce firms to engage in this activity. The current patent system provides those incentives by empowering the firms that develop novel and non-obvious pharmaceutical products to prevent others from making, using, selling or importing those products. Armed with that authority, the firms are able to sell the products for prices much higher than the costs of manufacturing them. The resultant profits provide the carrots necessary to prompt the firms to engage in the inventive activity in the first instance.

A prize system would work quite differently. Instead of authorizing drug developers to exclude competitors, the government would pay successful developers. Other firms, including generic drug manufacturers, would be free to make and sell the drugs in question. The resultant competition would keep drug prices close to the modest costs of manufacturing them. The money necessary to run such a system would come, not from consumers (or their insurers), but from taxpayers.

Would a prize system of this general sort be better than the patent system? More to the point, would it be more effective in alleviating the health crisis in the developing world? A substantial body of literature addresses those questions. In this chapter, we marshal and critically evaluate that literature – and add to it a number of new arguments of our own.

The discussion is organized as follows. In section 2, we explore the major potential strengths and weaknesses of prize systems. In section 3, we consider how some key dimensions of a prize system focused on the production of drugs and vaccines aimed at communicable diseases might be shaped so as to capitalize on its strengths and mitigate its weaknesses.

2. Opportunities and hazards

A prize system of the sort sketched briefly above has four potential benefits. First, it would enable us to avoid the most serious of the drawbacks of the current patent system – namely, the social welfare losses caused by the monopoly pricing of patented products. The patent system, as we have seen, enables firms holding patents to charge consumers much more for the patented drugs than the cost of producing those drugs. Indeed, that's the point of the system. Unfortunately, pursuit of this strategy has the effect of placing the drugs out of the financial reach of some people. Economists commonly refer to the deaths or suffering of the people who are thus 'priced out of the market' as forms of 'deadweight loss'. In the developing world, this effect is especially grave, because so many people are both poor and uninsured and thus unable to afford the prices of patented products.

This drawback of a patent system can be mitigated in various ways – for example, through systems of price discrimination in the marketing of the drugs or through similarly discriminatory insurance systems. Such mitigation strategies are considered in other sections of our forthcoming book. Suffice it to say for present purposes that their capacity to solve the aspect of the problem that concerns us here – namely, welfare losses caused by the unavailability of affordable drugs in developing countries – is limited.

A prize system, by contrast, is capable of eliminating this problem altogether. As indicated above, competition among manufacturers of the drugs whose development is stimulated by the prizes would keep prices low for everyone. Access to the drugs would thus be radically increased.[5]

Second, a prize system can take advantage of the way in which knowledge concerning actual or potential pharmaceutical products is typically distributed.[6] Ordinarily, governments have (or can obtain) better information concerning the aggregate health benefits of drugs than private parties. Why? Because government agencies regularly collect and assess data concerning the incidence and impact of diseases and thus are well positioned to ascertain the welfare gains that could be reaped by developing and distributing vaccines or treatments for each ailment. By contrast, governments ordinarily have knowledge inferior to that of private firms concerning the relative merits of potential lines of innovation – which drugs aimed at particular diseases would work best, which of the possible ways of developing such drugs are most promising and the cost of each of those routes.

The inferiority of the government's information concerning the merits of potential lines of research gives both a prize system and a patent system a clear advantage over a system of government grants as a way of inducing innovation. In a grant system (sometimes called a 'push'

[5] See, e.g., Robert Guell and Marvin Fischbaum, 'Toward Allocative Efficiency in the Prescription Drug Industry' (1995) 73 *Milbank Quarterly* 213; Steven Shavell and Tanguy van Ypersele, 'Rewards versus Intellectual Property Rights' (2001) 44 *Journal of Law and Economics* 525; and Thomas Pogge, 'Human Rights and Global Health: A Research Program' (2005) 36 *Metaphilosophy* 182.

[6] See Michael Kremer, 'Creating Markets for New Vaccines, Part I: Rationale' (Working Paper No 7716, National Bureau of Economic Research, 2000) 53; and Brian D. Wright, 'The Economics of Invention Incentives: Patents, Prizes, and Research Contracts' (1983) 73 *American Economic Review* 691.

system), government officials must decide which projects are most likely to generate solutions to particular health problems. Too often, they make those decisions poorly.[7] By contrast, in both a patent system and a prize system, private firms compete to develop solutions to health problems. In doing so, they are able to rely upon their own information concerning the costs and probability of success of alternative routes – and to respond quickly to new information on those fronts.

The superiority of the government's information concerning the social benefits of particular innovations gives a prize system an equally clear advantage over a patent system, under which research and development ('R&D') investments are directed towards lines of innovation that private firms consider most potentially lucrative, not those that are most socially beneficial. Specifically, a government, relying on its superior knowledge, can construct and administer a prize system in ways that correct for all three of the biases that distort (from a social welfare standpoint) the output of new pharmaceutical products under the current patent-based system: the bias towards drugs aimed at ailments that disproportionately afflict the rich; the bias towards 'me-too' drugs (the term conventionally used to describe drugs that, when introduced into the market, offer little or no health benefits over extant drugs[8]); and the bias away from vaccines. Each of these distortions is well documented – and is discussed in detail in our forthcoming book – so we review them here only briefly.

The first bias finds its most significant manifestation in the fact that almost all of the diseases that primarily afflict residents of the developing world are so-called 'neglected diseases', meaning that the proportion of global pharmaceutical research devoted to their prevention or treatment is miniscule. This is a natural outgrowth of the fact that roughly 95 per cent of the revenue of American, European and Japanese pharmaceutical firms comes from developed countries, in which reside only 20 per cent of the world's population. It should not be surprising that the firms concentrate their resources on research projects likely to produce drugs that address diseases common in those countries. The second of the biases is harder to explain, but that it exists is now beyond dispute.

[7] See, e.g., Robert S. Desowitz, *The Malaria Capers: Tales of Parasites and People* (1991).

[8] An example: Prozac was the first commercially available antidepressant to rely upon the principle of suppressing the uptake of serotonin. Drugs that rely upon the same principle but were introduced into the market later – such as Paxil, Zoloft, and Celexa – are commonly considered 'me-too' drugs. They may work better for some populations, but their advantages over Prozac are modest. See Benedict Carey, 'Is Prozac Better? Is It Even Different?', *New York Times*, 21 September 2004.

One indication: in the US, 57 per cent of the new molecular entities licensed by the Food and Drug Administration between 1990 and 2004 constituted 'me-too' drugs – as evidenced by the fact that they were processed by the agency using its 'standard review' system, rather than its 'priority review' system.[9] The causes of the third bias are myriad: the inability of the sellers of vaccines to capture all of the positive externalities generated by their consumption; the heuristic that causes people to underestimate the likelihood that they will contract a serious disease; the greater stringency of the manufacturing regulations applicable to vaccines; the fact that the largest purchasers of vaccines are governments, which frequently use their bargaining power to drive prices down; and the continued threat to vaccine producers of product liability judgments, despite efforts by legislatures to shield them from this hazard. The aggregate effect of these pressures is striking: the number of vaccines currently on the market is tiny – roughly forty-seven in the US. All of these distortions could be reduced or eliminated by a prize system – most simply, by ensuring that the sizes of the prizes are adjusted to match the incremental health benefits of each innovation.

The third and final potential benefit of a prize system is that it could reduce socially wasteful expenditure by pharmaceutical firms. The largest potential source of savings consists of marketing costs. Estimates of the magnitude of those costs under the current regime vary, but most scholars suggest that they account for roughly one third of the firms' revenues.[10] For reasons explored in chapter 4 of our forthcoming book, only a portion of those expenditures redound to the benefit of society at large. In brief: to the extent that advertising better informs either patients or doctors concerning the merits of drugs and thus enables them to improve their own or their patients' health, it is plainly beneficial. However, to the extent that advertising functions to expand or stabilize

[9] See United States Food and Drug Administration, *CDER NDAs Approved in Calendar Years 1990–2004 by Therapeutic Potential and Chemical Type* (2008), www.fda.gov/cder/rdmt/pstable.htm at 19 February 2009. Other estimates of the percentage of drugs that consist of me-too drugs are even higher.

[10] See Marcia Angell, *The Truth about the Drug Companies: How They Deceive Us and What to Do about It* (2004); James Love and Tim Hubbard, 'The Big Idea: Prizes to Stimulate R&D for New Medicines' (2007) 82 *Chicago-Kent Law Review* 1519; Meredith Rosenthal *et al.*, *Demand Effects of Recent Changes in Prescription Drug Promotion* (2003); and Dean Baker and Noriko Chatani, 'Promoting Good Ideas on Drugs: Are Patents the Best Way? The Relative Efficiency of Patent and Public Support for Bio-Medical Research' (Briefing Paper, Center for Economic and Policy Research, 2002).

the market share of one of several substitute products – or leads to increases in drug consumption unjustified by health benefits – it is wasteful or pernicious. A prize system, if it were structured properly, might reduce these outlays. Most intriguing is the possibility that the mechanism for determining the magnitude of the awards might be designed so as to reduce firms' incentives to engage in pernicious forms of promotion, while preserving their incentives to engage in beneficial forms of promotion. Another potential source of savings involves litigation costs. The resources currently consumed by lawyers and the court system resolving disputes involving pharmaceutical patents are enormous.[11] A prize system would not be free of disputes, of course. But it might be designed to reduce the incidence of legal controversies and the costs of resolving them.

Unfortunately, the picture painted thus far is misleadingly rosy. Prize systems have major potential disadvantages as well. The first and perhaps most serious is that the increase in tax burdens necessary to finance a prize system can lead to an inefficient diminution in labour.[12] Knowing that they will earn less per hour, at least some of the residents of developed countries (upon whom the bulk of the taxes would be imposed) would likely work fewer hours. Predicting the magnitude of this effect is extremely difficult. One source of the difficulty is that some people are likely to react to an increase in their tax burdens in precisely the opposite way – by working harder or longer to offset their loss of income and thus maintain their standard of living. Most economists think that the diminution in labour of the former group will be larger than the increase in labour of the latter group, but economists disagree sharply concerning the magnitude of the net effect – and specifically concerning the magnitude of the welfare loss caused by this distortion. The majority think that it would be modest,[13] but not all agree.[14]

A second potential disadvantage of a prize system is that it could foster inefficient 'rent-seeking'. Pharmaceutical firms already spend substantial

[11] See Baker and Chatani, 'Promoting Good Ideas on Drugs', above n. 10, 11. For an extensive discussion of the rapidly rising costs of resolving patent disputes of all sorts, see James Bessen and Michael Meurer, *Patent Failure: How Judges, Bureaucrats, and Lawyers Put Innovators at Risk* (2008) 120–46.

[12] See Michael Abramowicz, 'Perfecting Patent Prizes' (2003) 56 *Vanderbilt Law Review* 115.

[13] See Arthur Snow and Ronald Warren, 'The Marginal Welfare Cost of Public Funds: Theory and Estimates' (1996) 61 *Journal of Public Economics* 289; Baker and Chatani, 'Promoting Good Ideas on Drugs', above n. 10, 7 fn 4.

[14] See Martin Feldstein, 'How Big Should Government Be?' (1997) 50 *National Tax Journal* 197.

sums on campaign contributions and lobbyists, seeking to persuade government officials to modify the patent system to their advantage.[15] From the standpoint of aggregate social welfare, such expenditures represent pure waste. Unfortunately, under a prize system, the amount spent on efforts to influence government – specifically, to affect the ways in which the prizes are calculated and allocated – could increase.

A third potential problem is that, in general, prize systems are clumsy in dealing with sequential innovation.[16] Suppose Firm A develops a breakthrough product. Firm B, building on A's research, develops a slightly improved version of the product. What should be the magnitude of the prize awarded to each? The answer is far from clear, and on that answer depends the capacity of the system to provide optimal incentives for innovation.

A fourth potential disadvantage of a prize system is that distrust of government may increase its costs. In the past, governments have sometimes failed to make good on their promises to award prizes to successful innovators. In the most famous of these episodes, the British government in the eighteenth century dithered inexcusably in awarding a prize to the developer of a device or technique that would enable mariners to determine longitude.[17] Such breaches of faith may make pharmaceutical firms hesitate to commit huge sums of money to new research ventures in reliance on a government's commitment to reward them if they are successful. To overcome that hesitation, the government may need to increase the magnitude of the promised prize. Bonuses of that sort would plainly increase the cost of the programme.[18]

The implications of the last of the differences between a prize system and the patent system are more ambiguous. The incentive of a patent system commonly leads multiple firms to pursue a particular research

[15] See Centre for Responsive Politics, *Pharmaceuticals/Health Products: Long-Term Contribution Trends*, www.opensecrets.org/industries/indus.php?ind=H04 at 19 February 2009; Centre for Responsive Politics, *Lobbying – Pharmaceuticals/Health Products: Industry Profile, 2008*, www.opensecrets.org/lobby/indusclient.php?lname=H04 &year=2008 at 19 February 2009.

[16] For discussion of the difficulty of designing a system that will deal effectively with situations in which innovation is cumulative, see Nancy Gallini and Suzanne Scotchmer, 'Intellectual Property: When Is It the Best Incentive System?' (Working Paper No E01–303, University of California, Berkeley, Department of Economics, 2001) 16–20.

[17] See Dava Sobel, *Longitude* (1995).

[18] See Stephen Maurer, *The Right Tool(s): Designing Cost-Effective Strategies for Neglected Disease Research* (Report to the World Health Organization Commission on Intellectual Property Rights, Innovation and Public Health, 2005).

goal simultaneously and to keep their work secret from one another. Whether such a 'patent race' is socially beneficial is unclear. On one hand, it can increase the likelihood that the goal will be achieved or the speed with which it is achieved, which both benefits the consumers of the patented innovation and may accelerate socially beneficial follow-on innovation.[19] On the other hand, it may lead to truly duplicative and thus plainly wasteful research, and it may engage minds and money that could be better applied to other projects.[20] Some level of overlapping activity is probably socially advantageous, but how much is uncertain.

Some scholars have tried to provide better guidance on this question with respect to pharmaceutical products. A recent study by Joseph DiMasi and Cherie Paquette confirms the prediction that multiple pharmaceutical firms often work independently on the same problem – as evidenced by the frequency with which breakthrough drugs are succeeded by other drugs in the same therapeutic categories more quickly than would be possible if the later entrants were building on the work of the pioneer.[21] F. M. Scherer has argued that this practice may be socially beneficial. When all possible projects that have the potential to generate a particular therapeutic outcome are risky, Scherer argues, a given firm will maximize its profits by pursuing in parallel several such projects – or, more subtly, by undertaking a series of groups of parallel projects. The lower the probability that any one path will succeed (and the more lucrative the goal) the greater the number of paths the firm will rationally pursue simultaneously. The same principle, Scherer suggests, may justify, from the standpoint of aggregate social welfare, the pursuit of parallel research paths by many firms within the pharmaceutical industry as a whole.[22]

Scherer's analysis neglects, however, some differences between the profit-maximizing behaviour of a single firm, and the pattern of behaviour induced by the patent system in the industry as a whole. First, an

[19] See Richard Nelson, 'Uncertainty, Learning, and the Economics of Parallel Research and Development' (1961) 43 *Review of Economics and Statistics* 351.

[20] See Steve Calandrillo, 'An Economic Analysis of Property Rights in Information: Justifications and Problems of Exclusive Rights, Incentives to Generate Information, and the Alternative of a Government-Run Reward System' (1998) 9 *Fordham Intellectual Property, Media & Entertainment Law Journal* 301, 329.

[21] Joseph DiMasi and Cherie Paquette, 'The Economics of Follow-On Drug Research and Innovation: Trends in Entry Rates and the Timing of Development' (2004) 22 *PharmacoEconomics* 1.

[22] See Frederic Scherer, 'Markets and Uncertainty in Pharmaceutical Development' (Working Paper No RWP07-039, John F. Kennedy School of Government, Harvard University, 2007) 10–16.

individual firm is unlikely to ask two or more teams to pursue two identical paths at the same time. Rather, it will (rationally) explore simultaneously several different possible routes to the same end – for example, several different molecules, each of which has a chance of achieving the desired outcome. By contrast, patent races may result in two or more firms pursuing identical projects. Moreover, an individual firm will likely encourage its various teams to share information in order to avoid reinventing wheels. Competitive firms, by contrast, do not share such information. The likelihood of waste at the industry level is thus significantly higher.

Another potentially important source of waste is obscured by Scherer's argument. Under the patent system, individual firms have an incentive to invest more resources in the development of 'me-too' drugs than would be justified by the profits attributable solely to the therapeutic advantages (by definition, modest in amount) of those drugs. The reason: they can appropriate some of the market for the drug from the pioneer. As a result, each firm may be less discouraged from entering a crowded field than it would be under a truly winner-takes-all regime by the fear of losing the patent race. It is not certain that this effect would occur. The prospect of earning substantial profits from a 'me-too' drug depends upon the ability of the pioneer and the follower(s) to engage in oligopolistic pricing, which might be difficult. And the prospect that one would have to share one's gains with a follower plainly reduces the incentives of the pioneer, which might diminish the number of firms willing even to start the race. However, from the other side, even when firms would prefer to steer clear of crowded lines of research, the secrecy with which other firms carry out their projects might disable them from doing so, and hence involve them in races they would sooner avoid. In short, many factors are at play here. And we may be able, through adjustment of other legal doctrines, such as antitrust law, to affect some of those factors. But the data offered by DiMasi and Paquette suggest that, under the present patent regime, the amount of research devoted to the development of what will become 'me-too' drugs is higher than optimal. Especially telling is the fact that many losers of patent races initiate clinical trials – the most expensive phase of the research – even after it is clear that they have been beaten to the punch and that the incremental health benefits of their own products are slight.[23]

[23] See DiMasi and Paquette, 'The Economics of Follow-On Drug Research and Innovation', above n. 21.

The complexity of the issue makes it very difficult to determine whether a prize system would be better or worse in this respect than the current patent system. The fact that the levels of duplication under the present regime appear to be too high creates at least the possibility that a well-designed prize system could achieve significant social gains. On the other hand, anecdotal evidence suggests that some prize systems are even worse than the patent regime in this regard.[24] In short, whether a prize system is more or less likely than the patent system to foster excessive levels of research redundancy seems to depend, in significant part, on how the prize system is designed. To such matters we now turn.

3. Optimal design

How might one construct and administer a prize system – and specifically, a prize system aimed at alleviating the health crisis in the developing world – in order to capitalize on the potential advantages and minimize the potential disadvantages just reviewed? A comprehensive answer to that question would require attention to a myriad issues, including: the types of innovation for which prizes would be available; whether the system should be optional or mandatory; how to attract the right number of contestants to each innovation 'race'; how to balance the incentives of pioneers and followers; how to deal with 'incrementally modified products'; and the appropriate geographic scope of the system. We deal with such matters elsewhere. In this chapter, we limit our attention to the dimension of the problem that is currently most controversial and, arguably, the most important: what should be the form and magnitude of the prize awarded to the developers of effective vaccines or cures?

3.1 Increased returns from other drugs

Potential answers to that question can be grouped into four clusters. In proposals of the first type, the prize would consist of enhanced patent

[24] See, e.g., Katie Hafner, 'And if You Liked the Movie, a Netflix Contest May Reward You Handsomely', *The New York Times*, 2 October 2006; and Tim Harford, 'Cash for Answers', *Financial Times Magazine*, 26 January 2008, describing a prize competition organized by Netflix, which (as of September 2008) had attracted more than 27,000 competitors, organized into more than 2,500 teams. For the argument that prize systems are generally worse on this score than the patent system, see Richard Newell and Nathan Wilson, 'Technology Prizes for Climate Change Mitigation' (Discussion Paper No 05–33, Resources for the Future, 2005).

protection for some other drug, presumably a lucrative drug that addresses a disease common in developed countries.[25] The enhancement might be achieved in various ways. The simplest, proposed by GlaxoSmithKline and by the late Jonathan Mann, would extend the life of the patent on the lucrative drug. Another variant would allow the applicant for a patent on a potentially lucrative drug to obtain 'priority review' by the US Food and Drug Administration ('FDA'), rather than 'standard review'.[26] The former procedure is ordinarily only available for drugs that offer 'significant improvement compared to marketed products in the treatment, diagnosis, or prevention of a disease', while the latter is employed in situations in which '[t]he drug appears to have therapeutic qualities similar to those of one or more already marketed drugs.'[27] Thus, the prize essentially would consist of the right to obtain expedited review of a 'me-too' drug.

In most proposals within this family, the enhanced rights would be transferable. Thus, if firm A succeeded in developing a malaria vaccine, it could sell to firm B the right to obtain priority review of a new drug for erectile dysfunction or high cholesterol.

Congress recently adopted a system of this sort. As part of the Food and Drug Administration Amendments Act 2007 (US), it authorized a firm that obtains FDA approval for a novel drug that addresses one of a set of specified tropical diseases to obtain a transferable 'priority review voucher' that can be employed to obtain accelerated review by the FDA of any other drug.[28] In a recent paper, Henry Grabowski, David Ridley and Jeffrey Moe argue persuasively that such vouchers could be highly valuable.[29] They point out that, in the past few years, priority review by the FDA has been roughly seven months faster than standard review. Even if the overall life of the patent on the drug for which the priority review was obtained remained the same, the ability to start collecting money seven months earlier could be worth a great deal. First-mover advantages – the ability to establish a reputation and a market before competitive drugs enter the field – would add to that benefit. Last but not

[25] See Hannah Kettler, *Narrowing the Gap between Provision and Need for Medicines in Developing Countries* (2000) 49–50.

[26] See David Ridley, Henry Grabowski and Jeffrey Moe, 'Developing Drugs for Developing Countries' (2006) 25 *Health Affairs* 313.

[27] See US Food and Drug Administration, above n. 9.

[28] 21 USC § 360(n).

[29] See Henry Grabowski, David Ridley and Jeffrey Moe, *Priority Review Vouchers to Encourage Innovation for Neglected Diseases* (2008), www.law.harvard.edu/programs/petrie-flom/workshops_conferences/2008_workshops/Grabowski.pdf.

least, Grabowski and his colleagues show that the interaction of the new system with the complex provisions of the Hatch-Waxman Act 1984 (US)[30] governing permissible extensions of the terms of pharmaceutical product patents will, under some circumstances, have the effect of accelerating the date on which the patentee may begin to collect money, without accelerating the termination date of the patent – thus effectively extending the patent life. The bottom line: in the right hands (and getting it into the right hands is, of course, made possible by its transferability), such a voucher is likely to be worth US$100 million and possibly much more.

A system of this sort has the obvious merit of channelling substantial resources into the development of new drugs that address neglected diseases. For that reason, Congress's action should surely be applauded. But such a system has four drawbacks, which, in combination, make it the least attractive of the design options. First, the new statute contains no requirement that the novel drug addressing tropical diseases be made available inexpensively in the countries in which those diseases are rampant. In other words, the new system is cumulative; it in no way alters the background rules of patent law. The upshot is that a firm might develop a new treatment for Buruli ulcer, rely upon that accomplishment to obtain priority review for its next anti-depression drug, and then sell both drugs at profit-maximizing prices, in developing countries as well as developed countries. The availability of this option means that the new system promises to address the 'incentive' problem – the fact that too few financial carrots currently exist for the creation of drugs focused on neglected diseases – but will do nothing to solve the 'access' problem – the fact that the drugs that do exist are often priced out of the reach of most developing country victims.

This first drawback, though very serious, could be redressed easily. The statute could be modified to require the patentee of the tropical disease drug to grant royalty-free licences to generic firms, permitting them to manufacture the drug and to distribute it on whatever terms they wish in developing countries. The result, of course, would be to drive the cost of the drug in those regions down close to the cost of production.

The other drawbacks of this approach, unfortunately, can not be remedied so easily. The most serious of the problems involves the pattern of incentives it creates. Suppose that a firm wishing to obtain a priority review voucher for an upcoming cholesterol drug might earn that right

[30] Drug Price Competition and Patent Term Restoration Act 1984 (US) 21 USC § 355 ('Hatch-Waxman Act').

by successfully completing one of three projects currently on its drawing boards: (1) the development of a palliative treatment for yaws, a serious but non-fatal disease currently afflicting roughly 500,000 people;[31] (2) the development of a vaccine for dengue fever, which causes roughly 19,000 deaths per year and a loss of 528,000 disability-adjusted life years ('DALYs');[32] and (3) the development of a vaccine for leishmaniasis, which causes roughly 51,000 deaths per year and a loss of 1,757,000 DALYs.[33] Assume, for simplicity, that the three projects would cost the same amount and (as is likely) would generate little or no profit for the firm because most of the beneficiaries are too poor to pay for them. Plainly the firm will choose the project with the greatest chance of success – i.e., the greatest chance of earning the firm a valuable voucher – and will ignore the radical differences in their potential health benefits. Conversely, if the projects have the same chance of success, the firm will choose the cheapest, even if its health benefits are modest. The bottom line: the system fails to direct research and development towards areas that will most efficiently improve public health.

The third drawback is that the new statute will increase the already excessive degree to which pharmaceutical firms are induced to concentrate R&D resources on 'me-too' drugs. All of the drugs upon which the vouchers will be used are 'me-toos'; otherwise they would already be entitled to priority review. By permitting firms to introduce those drugs into the market sooner, and then to protect them against competition longer, the statute will prompt firms to shift even more resources towards them – precisely the behaviour we don't want to induce.

Finally, the new statute may increase the safety risks of those drugs that receive expedited FDA review. This is a controversial issue; in their review of

[31] See Associated Press, 'WHO: Flesh-Eating Disease Making Comeback', *FoxNews.com* (online), 25 January 2007.

[32] The phrase, 'disability-adjusted life years', refers to an index, developed by the World Health Organization, designed to measure the losses caused by a particular disease both through premature deaths and through disabilities. One DALY 'can be thought of as one lost year of "healthy" life', and the burden of disease 'as a measurement of the gap between the current health of a population and an ideal situation in which everyone in the population lives into old age in full health': World Health Organization, above n. 1, 137. It is a highly controversial index. Elsewhere in our book, we examine its limitations and how they might be corrected. For the purposes of this chapter, however, we will assume that it represents a fair way of assessing the impact of a disease.

[33] See Pierre Cattand *et al.*, 'Tropical Diseases Lacking Adequate Control Measures: Dengue, Leishmaniasis, and African Trypanosomiasis', in Dean Jamison *et al.* (eds.), *Disease Control Priorities in Developing Countries* (2nd ed, 2006) 451, 454–5.

the somewhat conflicting evidence, Grabowski and his colleagues conclude that priority review is not correlated with any increase in the frequency of adverse events. We are not in a position to assess that claim here. We merely observe that, if they were correct, then the appropriate response would be to institute priority review for all drugs, not merely for those for which firms can obtain a voucher. In other words, the pace at which the FDA evaluates all applications should be increased, thereby enabling all people to gain access to all beneficial drugs more quickly, and we should look for other ways to provide incentives for the development of drugs focusing on neglected diseases.

3.2 *Mimicking the patent system*

The second family of proposals would tie the size of the prize to the value of the patent that the drug developer could obtain. This might be achieved in various ways. The simplest would be to require the drug developer to obtain a patent in the ordinary course, after which the government would acquire the patent, either by purchasing it for a mutually acceptable price, or by exercising its power of eminent domain. The government would then release the invention governed by the patent into the public domain, enabling generic manufacturers to make and sell the drug in question at close to the marginal cost of producing it.

The practical problem that besets all proposals of this type is how much money the government should pay. If it uses its power of eminent domain to compel the patentee to surrender the patent, then the government is obliged, both by the Constitution and by the arguably pertinent federal statute,[34] to pay the patentee the fair market value of the patent – i.e., the net present value of the profit that the firm could have earned through sales of the patented drugs during the duration of the patent.[35] To induce the patentee to sell the patent voluntarily, the government would have to offer at least that much. But how is that amount to be determined? Scholars have suggested various solutions. Robert Guell and Marvin Fischbaum propose that the drug be test marketed in a small geographic area, enabling the government to extrapolate the profits that

[34] See 28 USC § 1498(a).

[35] In proceedings brought under section 1498(a), the patentee is typically awarded a 'reasonable royalty'. For a persuasive argument that the award should also include lost profits, see Daniel R. Cahoy, 'Treating the Legal Side Effects of Cipro: A Reevaluation of Compensation Rules for Government Takings of Patent Rights' (2002) 40 *American Business Law Journal* 125.

the firm might earn globally. Michael Kremer has suggested a more complex and ingenious scheme, the heart of which is an auction. In brief: Firm A develops a drug and patents it. The government invites Firm A to submit the patent for valuation. If Firm A accepts, the government solicits bids from other firms (most of which are likely to be other pharmaceutical firms). In 10 per cent (selected at random) of the cases of this sort, the government offers to buy the patent for the price named by the highest bidder and then, if the patentee agrees to sell, resells the patent to the highest bidder for the same amount. In the other 90 per cent of the cases, the government offers to buy the patent for the price named by the highest bidder and then, if the patentee accepts, releases the technology into the public domain. The 10 per cent chance of actually obtaining the patent is what induces the other firms to participate in the auction.[36]

Each of these approaches has difficulties, most of which are thoroughly discussed in a recent paper by Michael Abramowicz.[37] For example, the technique suggested by Guell and Fischbaum would result in a significant delay while the test marketing occurred, and would require the drug developer to spend substantial sums on marketing, in order to stimulate demand for the drug and simulate a real market. Kremer's system would encounter other problems. To induce firms to invest the substantial resources necessary to prepare bids, the frequency with which the government resold the patent to the highest bidder would probably have to be well above 10 per cent, which would of course reduce the coverage (and thus the efficacy) of the system. In addition, Firm A would have an incentive to collude (explicitly or implicitly, through repeat behaviour) with one or more of the bidders, which would then result in misleadingly high auction prices. The system would result in an excessively low price if both of two substitute drugs were submitted (because of the high probability that one of them would end up in the public domain), and an excessively high price if both of two complementary drugs were submitted (again, because of the high probability that one would end up in the public domain, which in this context would enable the holder of the patent on the other to reap all of the monopoly profits on the cocktail). Last but not least, because the system requires many firms to expend substantial resources preparing bids (most of which have no

[36] See Michael Kremer, 'Patent Buyouts: A Mechanism for Encouraging Innovation' (1998) 113 *Quarterly Journal of Economics* 1137.

[37] See Abramowicz, 'Perfecting Patent Prizes', above n. 12, 128–36, 148–58.

chance of winning), the system would be economically wasteful. There are techniques – some proposed by Kremer, others by Abramowicz – for mitigating these problems, but none would be perfect.

The principal drawback of all members of this family of approaches is not, however, the difficulty associated with valuation; but rather that tying the size of the prize to the value of the patent that it would displace fails to generate a socially optimal pattern of incentives. It would do a decent (not perfect) job of getting the drugs that would be developed anyway into the bodies of people who desperately need them. But it would do nothing to redirect the research activities of the pharmaceutical firms towards neglected diseases.[38]

3.3 Fixed pot

The third and fourth families of proposals both seek to remedy this problem by tying the amounts of the prizes issued to drug developers to the social value of their products, measured by the DALYs they would save. The two families differ in one main respect: proposals of the third type would have the government allocate a fixed sum of money to be distributed in a given year to drug developers; that pot would then be divided among the participating firms in proportion to the relative social value of their inventions. Proposals of the fourth type, by contrast, would have the government pay each participating firm a specified amount of money for each DALY saved through the distribution of its products. Both approaches have important strengths; the choice between them is not easy. We will suggest that, on balance, the fourth approach is superior, but adoption of the third approach would not be irresponsible.

Assessment of their relative merits is complicated by the fact that, within each family, there are several variants, each of which has pros and cons. The simplest version of the fixed-pot approach would give each participating firm a share of the pot proportional to the number of DALYs saved as a result of the creation and administration of its drugs.[39] How would we ascertain those numbers? At first glance, the task seems relatively straightforward. The World Health Organization ('WHO') already gathers and publishes data concerning the disease burdens associated with particular diseases. As previously noted, many governments, including the US, already employ reasonably sophisticated

[38] See Aidan Hollis, 'An Optimal Reward System for Neglected Disease Drugs' (2005).
[39] Ibid.

pharmacoeconomic assessment systems to determine the efficacy of particular drugs in curing or preventing those diseases.[40] To determine the health benefits of a particular drug during a particular time period, we would thus need only the number of doses of that drug administered during that interval to patients suffering from particular diseases.

Unfortunately, several complications necessitate refinement of that methodology. The first relates to gathering the sales data. We would need to ascertain, not just how many doses were manufactured and distributed by the inventor, but also how many were manufactured and distributed by generic firms. Impediments to getting the necessary numbers would include the notorious reluctance of pharmaceutical firms to release information concerning their operations and the fact that many of the generic manufacturers do not operate in the US and thus would not be subject to American licensing requirements. Note, however, that the numbers we would need do not include prices, costs or profits. All we would need are retail sales data (which the generic firms would have no incentive to exaggerate). In the end, that could probably be obtained – if necessary, by paying the firms in question a fee.[41]

Second, as Aidan Hollis has pointed out, if we wished to award prizes solely for the intangible, innovative R&D activity underlying each drug product, we would have to subtract from the foregoing sales figures the per-unit costs of manufacturing and distributing the drug at issue.[42] Accommodation of this principle would, however, be difficult for two reasons: first it would require converting DALYs to dollars – a task we will take up shortly, but which is obviously fraught with controversy. Second, it would require obtaining data concerning manufacturing costs from the generic firms, which would likely be a good deal harder than obtaining sales data. Thus, ignoring Hollis's point is probably necessary as a practical matter. Because of the low costs of producing most drugs, it is probably tolerable as well.

Further, even (or especially) when the costs of producing and distributing the drugs are more substantial (as may be the case with 'biologics' or vaccines), there is a reason why we might reject Hollis's proposal: in some circumstances, we might want the prize system to go beyond

[40] See Michael Dickson *et al.*, *Survey of Pharmacoeconomic Assessment Activity in Eleven Countries*, Health Working Papers No 4 OECD (2003).

[41] Cf. Hollis, 'An Optimal Reward System for Neglected Disease Drugs', above n. 38 (suggesting that licensees could be required to submit sales data).

[42] Ibid.

rewarding the underlying R&D, so as also to subsidize a significant proportion of the manufacturing and distribution costs. This is where those afflicted with the disease are so poor that, while they would be willing to pay the marginal costs of producing and distributing the drug against a just background distribution of income/wealth, they cannot currently afford even that. In such circumstances, the case for subsidizing their purchases would be essentially the same as that motivating the substitution of DALYs for market prices as a measure of the social value of the drugs. Consequently, to subtract the entire marginal costs from the prize risks under-incentivizing either the invention itself (when, roughly, the ratio of average cost to DALY-price is high) or effective post-invention distribution (when the ratio of marginal cost to DALY-price is high).

The third, and most significant, set of complications results from drawbacks to relying, for the measure of the aggregate therapeutic impact of a drug, solely on sales volume multiplied by an FDA-type measure of safety and efficacy. As Aidan Hollis and Thomas Pogge have persuasively argued, the data concerning safety and efficacy derived from regulatory testing represent only a partial approximation of the real world therapeutic effects of a drug. The principal reasons for the limitations of such testing are: that the patients chosen to participate in clinical trials may be better suited to showcasing a drug's advantages than the general population of diagnosed patients, especially in countries with poor diagnostic systems; that the use of a drug over longer time periods, and in a larger patient population, may reveal greater variations in efficacy, dangers or side effects than are observed during testing; and that the administration of drugs in real world settings, especially in countries with poor drug delivery infrastructure, may be significantly less optimal than in trials with closely monitored patients.[43] Moreover, relying only on sales data leaves the system vulnerable to gaming by prize recipients who have an incentive to exaggerate the numbers, either through outright distortion or through product 'dumping'.[44] Although, as mentioned above, generic firms would not by themselves have the same incentive, the possibility of collusion remains.

To address these various deficits of 'naive aggregation of unit sales times estimated superiority as demonstrated in clinical trials', Hollis and Pogge persuasively advocate a more sophisticated approach to

[43] Aidan Hollis and Thomas Pogge, *The Health Impact Fund: Making New Medicines Accessible for All* (2008) 29–30.

[44] Ibid., 30.

measuring the health impact of drugs. Its key elements include: supplementing regulatory clinical-trial data with 'evidence from observational studies and pragmatic or practical trials which use data from normal clinical practice', evidence that will take some time to accumulate and hence lead to revised estimates over the life of the reward; audits to ascertain how many of the doses sold are ultimately dispensed; and, in some cases of widely sold products, population-level studies that measure overall disease burdens 'before' and 'after' the introduction of the innovation.[45] Although there is a significant increase in discretion and hence uncertainty and potential disputes – not to mention administrative costs – associated with this more complex approach, it seems to us to be, on balance, worth it.

The final complication relates to an important category of benefits from innovations in pharmaceuticals that are, strictly speaking, not the result of any added therapeutic value held out by a new drug product over existing treatments. Rather, these benefits stem from improvements in the suitability of pharmaceuticals to the drug delivery conditions of developing countries. Existing drugs, even if effective, are often hard to administer in poor tropical countries. For instance, Médecins Sans Frontières observes that the standard recommended therapy for tuberculosis – the Directly Observed Therapy, short course strategy ('DOTS') – is 'lengthy and difficult to apply', as it 'lasts 6–8 months and requires each patient to swallow the drugs in front of a health care worker every day for at least the first two months. It requires an effective health service, well-trained staff, and a regular supply of quality drugs.'[46] In such cases, a new pharmaceutical innovation might provide significant value in terms of added health impact without at all improving upon the strict therapeutic properties of the treatments already available. For instance, a more streamlined TB treatment might offer no improved safety or efficacy compared with DOTS, but provide massive health benefits by enabling greater penetration of and more effective administration to the patient population. Unfortunately, even the expansive Hollis and Pogge approach to measuring the overall health impact from innovations neglects benefits of this kind. To capture them, we offer the following friendly amendment to their methodology: at the

[45] Ibid., 30–1.

[46] See Médecins Sans Frontières, 'Campaign for Access to Essential Medicines – Target Diseases: Tuberculosis', accessible through The Internet Archive at web.archive.org/web/20071207071446/, www.accessmed-msf.org/campaign/tb01.shtm. The existing treatments for malaria and leishmaniasis suffer from similar limitations.

behest of the reward applicant, the prize authority may investigate and make estimates (subject to ongoing revision, like the other estimates) of the added value, in DALYs, of innovations of a non-strictly therapeutic sort, which improve a drug or vaccine's suitability for administration in developing country conditions.

Now let's return to the problem at hand: organizing a 'fixed-pot' approach to determining the form and size of the prizes awarded to innovators. Suppose that, using the foregoing method (refined in the ways we have suggested), we generated estimates of the aggregate health benefits of each participating firm's innovation. Then, under the simplest variant of the fixed-pot approach, we would give each innovator a share of the prize pot proportionate to its relative health benefits. The obvious advantage of this procedure is that it would draw R&D resources into fields where they would provide the greatest healthcare benefits. However, Jamie Love and Tim Hubbard argue, plausibly, that this variant has two related drawbacks: it ignores the fact that drug development costs are often unrelated to the number of people served by the drug at issue, and it fails to provide adequate incentives for the development of orphan drugs. In other words, this procedure will direct too much money to the developers of drugs that address common diseases and too little to the developers of drugs that address rare diseases.

To correct these biases, Love and Hubbard propose that the pot be divided on the basis of multiple factors. The Medical Innovation Prize Fund Act 2007 (US), a bill recently introduced by Senator Sanders, who in turn relied heavily on advice from Love and Hubbard, provides a good illustration of the method they prefer. It would create an annual fund equal in amount to 0.6 per cent of the gross domestic product of the US during the preceding year. In the 2008 financial year, that would come to roughly US$83 billion. The money would be divided among the firms that developed new 'drugs, biological processes, and manufacturing processes for drugs or biological processes' during the year in question or during any of the preceding ten years. The criteria for making the division would be set by a Board of Trustees, composed partly of government officials and partly of persons drawn from specified subsets of the private sector. In setting the criteria, the Board would be obliged to take into account (and weight) the following factors: the number of people who would benefit from each drug or process; the incremental therapeutic benefit of each drug or process; the degree to which each drug or process addressed priority healthcare needs, including global infectious diseases, rare severe illnesses and neglected diseases that primarily afflict the poor in developing countries; and finally the improved efficiency of each manufacturing process. In designing and administering the distribution system, the Board would be required to ensure that minimum amounts were applied to three areas of special need: 4 per cent for innovations addressing neglected diseases; 4 per cent for global infectious diseases and other public health priorities; and 10 per cent for orphan drugs. Finally, in a given year no one drug or process could earn its creator more than 5 per cent of the pot.[47]

Adoption of this bill would indeed address the two problems identified by Hubbard and Love. It would, however, have a major disadvantage: As Marlynn Wei observes (when commenting on a predecessor proposal), the ambiguity of the factors used to determine each firm's share, plus the discretion enjoyed by the administrative tribunal in balancing them, plus the large stakes of the game, would give rise to many disagreements among the potential claimants, the resolution of which would consume considerable resources.[48] In other words, this approach would likely give rise to especially severe forms of the rent-seeking and dispute resolution problems that section 3.1 suggested potentially afflict prize systems. To avoid this outcome, some way of making the distribution of the funds more mechanical and predictable seems imperative.

How might this be achieved without undercompensating the developers of orphan drugs? One technique, also suggested by Hubbard and Love, would be to divide the pot into two parts. The money in the first sector would be allocated to drug developers on the basis of the DALY benefits of their creations; the money in the second would be allocated to all 'successful new drugs'.[49] Unfortunately, this strategy fails to differentiate optimally among the developers of orphan drugs.

A better approach, we suggest, would be to maintain a focus on the DALYs saved through the distribution of each eligible drug, but to use a non-linear formula for taking them into account. For example, before multiplying the number of DALYs saved by a drug by the number of persons affected (to determine the most important component of the health benefits of the drug), we might square or cube or apply some

47 Medical Innovation Prize Act 2007 (United States) (s. 2210).

48 See Marlynn Wei, 'Should Prizes Replace Patents? A Critique of the Medical Innovation Prize Act of 2005' (2007) 13 *Boston University Journal of Science and Technology Law* 25.

49 See Love and Hubbard, 'The Big Idea', above n. 10, 17–19. A more elaborate version of the two-part approach can be found in James Love, *Modeling Prize Fund Rewards* (7 July 2006) Drug Development (With Access), www.cptech.org/blogs/drugdevelopment/2006/07/modeling-prize-fund-rewards.html at 20 February 2009.

other exponential function to the number of DALYs saved per person.[50] This adjustment would embody a judgment that, when making trade-offs across persons, serious afflictions suffered by a minority should be given due weight, and not swamped by the aggregate benefits of addressing a comparatively trivial affliction suffered by a large number of persons. More elaborate non-linear formulae can of course be imagined. Adoption of this proposal would have the effects of reducing the share of the pot awarded to the developers of 'blockbuster' drugs that treat comparatively mild conditions, enhancing the share awarded to the developers of orphan drugs that address comparatively more serious conditions, while still giving firms of all sorts incentives to direct their resources towards areas with greater potential aggregate health benefits. To be sure, the returns available to a firm considering pursuing a drug aimed at a disease that afflicted a truly tiny group of people might still be insufficient to justify the cost, but to us that seems morally acceptable.

To summarize, the variant of the fixed-pot approach that seems most attractive is one in which the pot is divided in proportion to some non-linear function of the number of DALYs saved by each eligible awardee. Now let's step back from these details and consider the strengths and weaknesses of this family of prize proposals as a whole. As Love and Hubbard point out, its great advantage is that it enables government officials to know, in advance, how much the programme will cost. US$83 billion is a lot of money, but at least it's a known quantity. Legislators considering adopting such a plan would know its cost, and the tax laws could be adjusted to raise the necessary revenue.

Love and Hubbard argue that the fixed-pot approach has another benefit as well: 'by fixing the size of the prize fund, the developers of products will have an incentive to lobby for fair and efficient methods of valuing inventions. If too much money is given to one inventor, prizes available for everyone else are smaller.'[51] This strikes us as overly optimistic. To be sure, each participating firm would have an incentive to challenge the data concerning the public health benefits of its competitors' drugs. But this is more likely to lead to assaults on the competitors' data than an effort to establish 'fair and efficient' valuation techniques. Thus, what Love and Hubbard see as a strength we see as a weakness: even variants of this approach that use mechanical distribution formulae

[50] We thank Roni Mann for helpful discussion of this issue.

[51] See Love and Hubbard, 'The Big Idea', above n. 10.

will be beset by the kind of rent-seeking and waste of resources highlighted by Wei.

An even more serious drawback of the fixed-pot approach is that it renders highly unpredictable the amount of money that a firm could earn by developing a drug aimed at a particular disease. The problem is especially severe with discretionary, multi-factored variants, like the proposed Medical Innovation Prize Fund Act 2007 (US). But it would be serious even if the distribution formula were mechanical and stable. The reason is that the amount of money that a firm could earn for a given drug depends upon what other drugs qualify for participation in the fund and the health benefits of each. Suppose, for example, a firm is considering investing in the development of a malaria vaccine. The amount that it stands to earn, if successful, would depend heavily upon whether, during the ten-year window in which the vaccine were eligible for prizes, another firm developed an effective HIV vaccine. Why? Because the health benefits of a malaria vaccine, large as they are, would pale in comparison to the health benefits of an HIV vaccine, and thus the latter would get the lion's share of the prize fund. This problem could be mitigated if, as in the Medical Innovation Prize Fund Act 2007 (US), the amount that any one drug could earn its maker were capped, but the imposition of such a cap would undermine the ability of the system as a whole to draw R&D resources into areas of greatest social need – such as HIV/AIDS. And, at most, caps could reduce, but not eliminate the problem.[52]

3.4 *Rewards for health benefits*

Approaches within the fourth family would avoid these problems – although, as we will see, they would have some difficulties of their own. The feature common to the members of this family is that the government would commit to paying the inventors of new drugs a certain amount of money for each DALY saved as a result of their inventions. Somewhat more specifically, under these systems the inventor would be paid a certain amount of money per DALY for the incremental health benefits of the new drug as compared to drugs already on the market at the time the new drug is introduced – estimated using the refined methodology outlined in the previous subsection.

[52] A less serious, but not trivial, related drawback: in a lean year for innovation, the government could end up paying a great deal for modest technological advances.

As already suggested, it would make most sense, not to try to predict the DALY benefits of a drug at the time it is first introduced, but rather to measure them over time. Each year, the government would collect sales, consumption and pharmacological efficacy data in the manner described above pertaining to each registered drug and derive from that data a total number of DALYs saved through administration of the drug. It would then multiply that number by the promised fee, and issue a prize to the inventor of the drug. To keep making such payments forever would be unwieldy and unnecessary; a limited term would suffice. Following Love and Hubbard, we might select, for simplicity, a term of ten years from the date the new drug is first introduced to the market.

The issue that most plagues and divides the proponents of this fourth approach is how much the government should pay per DALY. Plainly, the higher the amount, the more innovation we will stimulate and the more quickly we will alleviate the health crisis in the developing world. On the other hand, the higher the amount, the more expensive the programme and the greater the difficulty of securing its adoption.

The range of options is considerable. At one extreme, we could strive, as Professors Shavell and van Ypersele suggest, to select a number that will generate prizes equal in amount to the total social welfare benefits of each invention. That might, as they argue, generate optimal incentives for innovative activity – although the fact that we don't pay innovators in any other sector of the economy the full social value of their innovations casts doubt on that judgment.[53] But, in any event, it would be prohibitively costly. To illustrate, in the US, when assessing safety or pollution-control proposals, we commonly implicitly use cost-effectiveness thresholds of between $50,000 and $100,000 per DALY.[54] If we relied upon that number when selecting a prize for an effective, widely used vaccine for malaria, which currently has a global annual disease burden of 44,716,000 DALYs, we would have to pay the developer between two and four trillion dollars per year. Clearly, this is out of the question. Even if we could afford such a sum, the rent dissipation it would generate would likely be prohibitive.

[53] See William W. Fisher, *Promises to Keep: Technology, Law, and the Future of Entertainment* (2004) ch. 6.

[54] See Ernst R. Berndt *et al.*, 'Advance Market Commitments for Vaccines against Neglected Diseases: Estimating Costs and Effectiveness' (2007) 16 *Health Economics* 491; and Peter Neumann, Eileen Sandberg, Chaim Bell, Patricia Stone and Richard Chapman, 'Are Pharmaceuticals Cost-Effective? A Review of the Evidence' (2000) 19 *Health Affairs* 92.

Another possible approach: we might try to pick a number that, in practice, would provide the developer of a drug focused on a neglected disease a revenue stream comparable to the stream that it could earn from a drug aimed at a non-neglected disease – adjusted upward or downward depending upon whether we thought that the technical challenges associated with solving neglected diseases were either greater or lesser than the challenges associated with the typical commercial drug.

A variant of this approach is employed by Michael Kremer and his colleagues in calculating the magnitude of the 'advanced market commitments' ('AMCs') that would be necessary to induce the development of vaccines for malaria and similar diseases. Their conclusion: 'a commitment to pay $13–$15 per person immunized for the first 200 million people' would be necessary and sufficient.[55] If they are right, and if such a commitment led to the development of an effective malaria vaccine, we would reap health benefits of (coincidentally) roughly $15 per DALY. If similar commitments led to development of an HIV/AIDS vaccine and a tuberculosis vaccine, we would reap health benefits of $17 per DALY and $31 per DALY, respectively.[56] If, for reasons explored elsewhere in our book, we were sceptical of AMCs for specific diseases, and wished simply to offer drug developers prizes consisting of a certain amount of money per DALY saved as a result of the administration of their drugs, we could employ an average of the last set of numbers produced by Kremer and his colleagues: $21 per DALY.

There are reasons to be uneasy about this strategy, however. Most importantly, it takes as given the current costs of commercial drug development and seeks to offer the pharmaceutical firms similar returns for working on neglected diseases. To their credit, Kremer and his colleagues do not simply accept the profit levels that the firms themselves claim they achieve (or need), or the oft-criticized estimates of the costs of drug development generated by DiMasi and colleagues,[57] but seek to

55 The complex set of calculations that underlie this conclusion are set forth in Berndt *et al.*, 'Advance Market Commitments for Vaccines against Neglected Diseases', above n. 54, 492. See also Michael Kremer and Rachel Glennerster, *Strong Medicine: Creating Incentives for Pharmaceutical Research on Neglected Diseases* (2004) 86–90 for a similar methodology and result.

56 Berndt *et al.*, 'Advance Market Commitments for Vaccines against Neglected Diseases' above n. 54, 502.

57 Joseph DiMasi *et al.*, 'The Cost of Innovation in the Pharmaceutical Industry' (1991) 10 *Journal of Health Economics* 107; and Joseph DiMasi, Ronald Hansen and Henry Grabowski, 'The Price of Innovation: New Estimates of Drug Development Costs' (2003) 22 *Journal of Health Economics* 151.

derive more realistic numbers. They also make an effort to adjust the figures downward to take into account the savings in firms' marketing costs that implementation of their system would enable. But they still aspire to match 'the net present value of the revenues earned by a sample of recently launched commercial pharmaceutical products'.[58] Unless one believes that the R&D systems that have arisen under the extant patent-based regime are ideal,[59] that number is excessive.

A radically different approach would ask, not how much is necessary to stimulate innovation, but how much are 'we' (the residents of developed countries who would have to approve of and pay for such a programme) willing to pay to save a year of the life of a resident of a developing country. An answer might be obtained from a loosely democratic political procedure: we could set the figure at a low level in the first year of the programme – say, \$10 per DALY – and then gradually increase it in subsequent years. The overall cost of the programme would of course rise over time, not just because we would be paying more per DALY, but because more firms would be opting for prizes rather than patents, and because more and more projects aimed at neglected diseases would come to fruition. At the same time, the health benefits of the programme – the lives and pain saved in developing countries – would become increasingly concrete and visible. At some point, median public sentiment (reflected in the miscellaneous collection of polls, grass-roots campaigns, lobbying initiatives, etc., that – for better or worse – we rely upon for gauges of public attitudes) would deem us to have gone far enough to satisfy our moral obligations. Thereafter, we would hold the number steady – until such time as our collective altruism increased a notch.

One advantage of this approach is that it would catalyse public discussion of the underlying public-health problem and our responsibilities to address it. The global health crisis currently does not figure prominently in political conversations in developed countries. For example it did not surface in the recent presidential campaign in the United States.[60] One of the many reasons for our collective inattention is that the magnitude of the problem and the scale of our contributions to

[58] Berndt *et al.*, 'Advance Market Commitments for Vaccines against Neglected Diseases' above n. 54, 495.

[59] Reasons to doubt this assumption are explored in Chapter 4 of our forthcoming book.

[60] During the debate on 7 October 2008, both candidates insisted that the United States would never again sit by while a holocaust occurred – without acknowledging that we are in effect doing so now.

efforts to solve it are difficult to grasp. The procedure sketched above, by reducing the issue to a single question – how much are we willing to pay to save a year of the life of a person in a developing country? – should facilitate debate and foster more serious reflection on our duties.

A complication: but wouldn't such a procedure encourage firms to 'play the system'? Knowing that the reward per DALY will increase over time, wouldn't they hold off either beginning research projects or submitting successful drugs for prizes, hoping in later years to get a better price? Probably not, because such strategic delays would increase sharply the risk that they would be beaten out by competitors and thus would get nothing. If this proved to be a serious problem, it could be mitigated (although not eliminated) by applying each increased fee not merely to drugs first submitted during the year in which the increase occurred, but also to drugs that were first submitted during previous years but are still within the ten-year prize-distribution window.

A final complication: the variant of a dollars-for-DALYs approach outlined above is vulnerable to the same objection raised by Love and Hubbard in the context of a fixed-pot system that relied solely upon DALYs to determine the relative social value of innovations – namely, that it would overpay the developers of drugs that addressed mild common illnesses and underpay the developers of orphan drugs aimed at serious illnesses. To meet this objection, one could make an adjustment closely analogous to the adjustment discussed above: instead of paying a flat fee for each DALY saved by each drug, one could select a rate that would give greater weight to DALYs earned through alleviation of severe illnesses. The cleanest way to achieve this would be to square (or apply some other exponent to) the number of DALYs saved per person by the drug in question, multiply the resultant figure by the number of persons benefited, and then multiply the product by a flat rate.

Admittedly, this adjustment would reduce the simplicity and clarity of the system, which, in turn, would undermine somewhat the system's capacity to facilitate public conversation concerning 'our' moral obligations. But the adverse effect on public debate might not be as severe as it first appears. As we suggested earlier, ideally the exponential function used to make the key adjustment would be set through an iterative process of reflection and deliberation. Central to such a debate would be the shape and extent of the ethical claims of persons suffering from serious illnesses to receive larger shares of society's total healthcare resources than would be indicated by a purely utilitarian calculus. To be sure, raising that question runs the risk of distracting attention from the more fundamental moral issue of 'our' collective obligations to help those truly badly off. On the other hand, it might foster among the citizenry a heightened awareness of and interest in the significant normative issues that lurk behind otherwise opaque, seemingly 'hard' cost-benefit metrics such as wealth- or QALYs-maximization. Opening up such metrics to deliberative scrutiny may increase people's sensitivity to the need for social policy choices that make explicit distributive and other moral judgments, thereby perhaps even reinforcing the case for neglected-disease research, based as it is on a rejection of the equation of the social value of drugs with their market value. The outcry triggered by the proposed use in Oregon's state health plan of a QALYs-type cost-effectiveness metric in a reductive way – so as to provide, for instance, higher priority to dental caps than to potentially life-saving appendectomies[61] – is one indication of the potentially wide resonance of such concerns, and hence the potential that formally instantiating them in policy holds for catalysing further conversations.

In sum, a dollars-for-DALYs approach of the sort we have outlined would not be perfect. But, on balance, it seems the best of the four approaches.

[61] See Peter Neumann, 'Lessons from Oregon', in Peter Neumann (ed.), *Using Cost-Effective Analysis to Improve Health Care: Challenges and Opportunities* (2004) 58, 60.

8

Innovation and insufficient evidence: the case for a WTO–WHO Agreement on Health Technology Safety and Cost-Effectiveness Evaluation

THOMAS FAUNCE

1. Introduction

Health technology (particularly including pharmaceuticals and medical devices) constitutes an increasingly important item of international trade regulated by rules developed in large part by the World Trade Organization ('WTO'). Affordable access to such technologies long will remain a critical factor in national responses to infectious disease pandemics, as well as the prevention of morbidity and mortality associated with disease, war and natural disaster. For many people such equitable access will continue to be a basic precondition to health. All nations have developed regulatory processes for scientifically assessing the public health impacts of such health technologies – mostly in relation to safety issues, but often concerning their cost-effectiveness or health innovation (that is, their objectively demonstrated therapeutic significance to a community).

The causes and social impacts of the current global financial crisis have heightened concerns about both the safety and cost-effective pricing issues associated with the development of, and global trade in, new health technologies for profit by private multinational corporations. The WTO has already forged an agreement utilizing scientific assessment of evidence to protect the public interest in relation to international trade of one group of products (quarantine and phytosanitary regulatory measures concerned with agricultural trade). This is the Agreement on the Application of Sanitary and Phytosanitary Measures ('SPS Agreement'). The WTO has yet to seriously consider developing an Agreement on Health Technology Safety and Cost-Effectiveness Evaluation ('HSCE Agreement'). Nonetheless, it will be argued here that a case can be made for the WTO to begin negotiating such an agreement.

The obvious partner organization, it will be argued here, for such a development is the World Health Organization ('WHO'). The WHO Intergovermental Working Group on Public Health, Innovation and Intellectual Property ('IGWG'), for example, was granted a two-year mandate in 2006 to develop a global policy strategy and financing plan for identifying global health needs (including so-called 'neglected' diseases) as well as promoting the related discovery, development and delivery of necessary innovative medicines.[1] WHO Director-General Margaret Chan termed the committee's work 'a unique opportunity for public health' that could both spur innovation and make healthcare products more affordable, reducing gaps in health outcomes and making the benefits of advances in medicine and science more inclusive.[2] This impetus continued when, in 2007, the WHO celebrated the thirtieth anniversary of the concept of essential medicines and in May 2008 as it adopted a Global Strategy and Plan of Action on Public Health, Innovation and Intellectual Property ('the Global Strategy').[3] Many non-governmental organizations ('NGOs') and academics involved in the access to medicines debate similarly view such efforts by the WHO as an opportunity to devise global governance systems capable of better ensuring that communities achieved value for public expenditure in this area.[4] Recent academic proposals have specifically backed a convergence of WHO interests on major trade issues concerning medicine.[5]

Considerable debate has arisen and is likely to continue at the WHO about proposals to work with the WTO to achieve regulatory agreements to both prevent counterfeiting and anti-competitive practices in health technology trade and to ensure that future bilateral trade agreements do not endanger public health by excessively increasing intellectual property rights (IPRs) (or intellectual monopoly privileges (IMPs) as

[1] World Health Organization, *Public Health, Innovation and Intellectual Property* (2008), www.who.int/phi/en/ at 23 February 2009.

[2] 'Editorial' (2008) 12(16) *Bridges Weekly Trade News Digest* 7.

[3] Sisule Misungu, 'Opportunities for the Obama Administration and the G20 to Do Good for Global Health' (2009) 2(2) *Global Health Governance*, www.ghgj.org/Volume%20II%20Issue%202.htm at 22 June 2009.

[4] Devi Sridhar, Sanjeev Khagram and Tikki Pang, 'Are Existing Governance Structures Equipped to Deal with Today's Global Health Challenges? Towards Systematic Coherence in Scaling Up' (2009) 2(2) *Global Health Governance*, www.ghgj.org/Volume%20II%20Issue%202.htm at 22 June 2009.

[5] Jennifer Prah Ruger and Derek Yach, 'The Global Role of the World Health Organisation' (2009) 2(2) *Global Health Governance*, www.ghgj.org/Volume%20II%20Issue%202.htm at 22 June 2009.

the author prefers to term them).[6] If further progress is to be made in this direction the WHO will have to collaborate more closely with the WTO and the WTO will have to engage substantively with the development of hard international law norms related to the safety of, and equity of access to, health technologies.

This chapter suggests that such proposals for WHO–WTO collaboration are but manifestations of the contemporary debate about how to ensure that the public achieves value for its direct and indirect expenditure on new health technologies. A variety of long term academic reform proposals now exist for this area (some referring to the WHO) that do not directly involve the WTO.[7] This chapter, on the other hand, explores the potential role of WTO–WHO collaboration in progress towards a uniform global system of health technology safety and cost-effectiveness assessment. It argues that a WTO–WHO HSCE Agreement would provide an important vehicle for fulfilling the types of public-focused aims mentioned by the WHO Global Strategy; in effect it would seek to establish a transparent and impartial global regulatory appeal mechanism for domestic health technology safety and cost-effectiveness regulatory decisions.

To set the background for this argument, section 2 explains how the WTO has already developed an agreement (the SPS Agreement) predicated on expert scientific assessment of public health risks. Section 3 then sets out how the architecture of drug regulation initially supported a private-rights focused approach that did not support cost-effectiveness assessment and in fact often deprecated it as a 'non-tariff barrier to trade' (culminating in the WTO TRIPS Agreement and certain bilateral trade deals that sought to alter key mechanisms of domestic health technology cost-effectiveness systems). Section 4 discusses the conceptual background to states having a problematic interaction with cost-effectiveness regulation of pharmaceuticals. Section 5 discusses how the interest of states in regulating pharmaceutical cost-effectiveness regulation systems in bilateral trade agreements creates an important impetus for such negotiations to move to multilateral forums. Section 6 then describes

[6] Greg Martin, Corinna Sorenson and Thomas Faunce, 'Balancing Intellectual Monopoly Privileges and the Need for Essential Medicines' (2007) 3(4) *Globalization and Health*, www.globalizationandhealth.com/content/3/1/4 at 22 June 2009.

[7] Thomas Faunce and Hitoshi Nasu, 'Three Proposals for Rewarding Novel Health Technologies Benefitting People Living in Poverty: A Comparative Analysis of Prize Funds, Health Impact Funds and a Cost-Effectiveness/Competitive Tender Treaty' (2008) 1(2) *Public Health Ethics* 146.

evidence of increasing support in WTO and bilateral trade agreements for evidence-based methods of establishing health technology innovation in terms of cost-effectiveness. Section 7 analyses how these set the preconditions for a WTO–WHO HSCE Agreement. Section 8 discusses some of the obstacles that will need to be overcome to achieve such an agreement.

2. The WTO SPS Agreement and scientific assessment of evidence about public health impacts of trade

The WTO SPS Agreement provides a good example of a WTO agreement whose efficient functioning is predicated on expert assessment of scientific evidence about public impact. The SPS Agreement sets out the rights and obligations of WTO member states who seek to impose regulations on food, beverages and foodstuffs in order to prevent the spread of pests and diseases. It aims to reduce any so-called domestic market 'protectionist abuses' of the WTO permitted public health exception to 'free-trade' obligations. The SPS Agreement does this by requiring that quarantine regulations on food be based on scientific evidence.[8] This is the part of the SPS Agreement that is perhaps of most interest in terms of the present discussion. It also requires that such evidence-based regulations not be applied in a manner that would constitute a means of arbitrary or unjustifiable discrimination between members where the same conditions prevail or a disguised restriction on international trade.[9]

Article 5(7) of the SPS Agreement allows states to adopt provisional regulatory measures in situations of scientific 'insufficiency' of evidence about a disease threat. This is seen by many commentators as a WTO endorsement of the precautionary principle in certain justifiable situations.[10] Article 5(7) provides:

> In cases where relevant scientific evidence is insufficient, a Member may provisionally adopt sanitary or phytosanitary measures on the basis of available pertinent information, including that from the relevant international

[8] Marrakesh Agreement Establishing the World Trade Organization, opened for signature 15 April 1994, 1867 UNTS 3, annex 1A (Agreement on the Application of Sanitary and Phytosanitary Measures) articles 3(3), 5(1) (entered into force 1 January 1995) ('SPS Agreement').

[9] Ibid., preamble [1], article 2(3).

[10] Ilona Cheyne, 'Gateways to the Precautionary Principle in WTO Law' (2007) 19 *Journal of Environmental Law* 155; and Huei-Chih Niu, 'Can Article 5.7 of the WTO SPS Agreement Be a Model for the Precautionary Principle?' (2007) 4 *Script-ed* 367.

> organizations as well as from sanitary or phytosanitary measures applied by other Members. In such circumstances, Members shall seek to obtain the additional information necessary for a more objective assessment of risk and review the sanitary or phytosanitary measure accordingly within a reasonable period of time.

Article 3(2) of the WTO Dispute Settlement Understanding creates a dispute settlement system for clarifying obligations under WTO agreements and article 6(1) indicates that a finding by such a Panel or Appellate Body shall be adopted automatically unless all member states decide by negative consensus to reject it.

Of the over 250 disputes already formally raised under the WTO's dispute settlement system, twenty have alleged violation of the SPS Agreement, and in five cases, Panels have been established: two with regard to the EU ban on meat treated with growth-promoting hormones (WT/DS26 *US* v. *EU* and WT/DS48 *Canada* v. *EU*); two with regard to Australia's restrictions on imports of fresh, chilled or frozen salmon (WT/DS18 *Canada* v. *Australia* and WT/DS21 *US* v. *Australia*); and one to examine Japan's requirement that each variety of certain fruits be tested with regard to the efficacy of fumigation treatment (WT/DS76 *US* v. *Japan*). In other cases bilateral consultations have created mutually agreed solutions. Some cases are still pending such as WT/DS137 for Canada's complaint against EC restrictions due to pine wood nematodes; WT/DS/203, which was a US complaint against Mexico on measures affecting trade in live swine; WT/DS/205, which involved a Thai complaint against Egypt's GMO-related prohibition on imports of canned tuna with soybean oil, and WT/DS/237 concerning an Ecuadorian complaint against Turkey's import requirements for fresh fruit, especially bananas.

WT/DS135 involved a Panel hearing in Canada's complaint against EC (French) measures affecting asbestos, but this was primarily a WTO General Agreement on Tariff and Trade (GATT) article XX public health issue.[11] The WTO SPS Agreement cases of *Japan – Measures Affecting*

[11] Article XX of GATT provides: 'subject to the requirement that such measures are not applied in a manner which would constitute a means of arbitrary or unjustifiable discrimination between countries where the same conditions prevail, or a disguised restriction on international trade, nothing in this Agreement shall be construed to prevent the adoption or enforcement by any contracting party of measures: … (b) necessary to protect human, animal or plant life or health; … (d) necessary to secure compliance with laws or regulations which are not inconsistent with the provisions of this Agreement, including … (g) relating to the conservation of exhaustible natural resources if such measures are made effective in conjunction with restrictions on domestic production or consumption …'

Agricultural Products (hereafter referred to as '*Japan – Varietals*'),[12] *European Communities – Measures Concerning Meat and Products* (hereafter referred to as '*EC – Hormones*')[13] and *European Communities – Measures Affecting the Approval and Marketing of Biotech Products*[14] particularly focused on the concept of 'insufficient scientific evidence' or 'scientific uncertainty' under article 5(7).

Such WTO dispute settlement cases in relation to the SPS Agreement that have examined the precautionary principle provide interesting insights into how a similar agreement might operate in effect to provide a global regulatory appeal mechanism from domestic safety and cost-effectiveness expert assessment of scientific evidence about new health technologies.

3. Pharmaceutical patents as private rights not monopoly privileges: United States origins

At the beginning of pharmaceutical regulation in the US there was little to oppose the idea that cost-effectiveness assessment would play an important and routine role alongside patents. In the late 1960s Nordhaus influentially developed the concept that regulation should aim for an optimal duration of patent protection that balanced any resultant incentives for innovation against the social losses attendant upon monopoly exploitation.[15] Such social losses, including higher prices due to restricted competition, arguably were compounded in the health sector where heath professionals made purchase decisions rather than patients directly and often in situations where the opportunity cost in terms of morbidity and mortality was unacceptable. On such an analysis intellectual property laws, and patents in particular, granted balanced, legally enforceable rights to both the patent holder and to society. The former privilege (to receive royalties under a limited period of monopoly) could be enforced by civil actions by the patent

[12] *Japan – Measures Affecting Agricultural Products*, WTO Doc WT/DS76/AB/R, AB-1998–8 (1999) (Report of the Appellate Body); *Japan – Measures Affecting the Importation of Apples*, WTO Doc WT/DS245/R, WT/DS245/AB/R (2003) (Report of the Panel).

[13] *European Communities – Measures Concerning Meat and Products (Hormones)*, WTO Doc WT/DS26/R, WT/DS26/AB/R, WT/DS48/R, WT/DS48/AB/R (1998) (Reports of the Panel and Appellate Body).

[14] *European Communities – Measures Affecting the Approval and Marketing of Biotech Products*, WTO Doc WT/DS291/R, WT/DS292/R, WT/DS293/R (2006) (Reports of the Panel).

[15] William Nordhaus, *Invention, Growth and Welfare: A Theoretical Treatment of Technological Change* (1969).

holder. The latter social right (to have valuable knowledge and its benefits dispersed rapidly) could be enforced by anti-monopoly as well as cost-effectiveness regulators.

In 1959, the Kefauver committee found evidence of substantial abuse of monopoly power in the US pharmaceutical industry. As a result of its recommendations, the US Food and Drug Administration ('FDA') commenced a more rigorous evaluation of efficacy as well as bioequivalence of new pharmaceutical applications.[16] There was no obvious opposition at this stage should the decision have been made to establish a cost-effectiveness assessment authority to supplement the FDA's functions. The FDA argued that its increase in regulatory stringency had minimal effect on the number of new pharmaceutical products marketed and any statistical downturn was influenced by tranquillizers whose supply and demand were adversely affected by the thalidomide tragedy.[17] Further, the increased regulatory requirements appeared to have no dampening effect on pharmaceutical research and development ('R&D') spending, which continued to rise during this period.[18]

The US pharmaceutical industry, however, blamed recently enhanced government regulation for the decreased number of innovative molecular entities it was able to introduce in subsequent years.[19] They argued, ultimately successfully, that FDA burdens should be relaxed and patent terms extended to compensate for market time lost in regulatory review.[20]

Academic research subsequent to that of Nordhaus (increasingly initiated and supported financially by industry) attempted to show that optimal patent duration should be longer for cost-recovery reasons where enforcement is costly or incomplete.[21] Likewise, the case was made that the economic incentive of patent life should be shorter where competitors wasted resources with 'window dressing' inventions merely to improve market share.[22] The traditional Nordhaus model was

[16] William Comanor, 'The Political Economy of the Pharmaceutical Industry' (1986) 24 *Journal of Economic Literature* 1178.

[17] Peter Temin, *Taking your Medicine: Drug Regulation in the United States* (1980).

[18] Henry Grabowski and John Vernon, *The Regulation of Pharmaceuticals: Balancing the Benefits and Risks* (1983).

[19] Sam Peltzman, 'An Evaluation of Consumer Protection Legislation: The 1962 Drug Amendments' (1973) 81 *Journal of Political Economy* 1049.

[20] Steven Wiggins, 'The Impact of Regulation of Pharmaceutical Research Expenditures: A Dynamic Approach' (1983) 21 *Economic Inquiry* 115.

[21] Frederic Scherer, *Innovation and Growth: Schumpeterian Perspectives* (1984).

[22] Nancy Gallini, 'Patent Policy and Costly Imitation' (1992) 23 *Randal Journal of Economics* 52.

also contentiously modified to include the easier to satisfy standard of what is referred to as 'cumulative' or 'incremental' innovation.[23]

Some argued, prophetically given later globalization developments, that if such arguments were accepted, the patent monopoly privilege over pharmaceuticals would become a form of rent ruthlessly pursued by competing investors even at the cost of much relevant and anticipated social benefit being overstated, underachieved or dissipated through duplication.[24] One underemphasized line of analysis in this context, that also would have supported establishment of cost-effectiveness regulation, considered that much pharmaceutical innovation proceeds in public-funded institutions partly as a result of researchers' motivation to facilitate equitable dispersal of knowledge and promotion of public goods.[25] Of the twenty-one drugs with greatest therapeutic effect introduced between 1965 and 1992, for example, all but five were based on a discovery made in the public sector.[26]

The 1980 decision of the US Supreme Court in *Dawson Chemical Company* v. *Rohm & Haas*[27] overruled particular decisions where judges had deprecated patents as socially disadvantageous monopoly privileges with a tendency to erode competition and stifle innovation if continued too long. The Court now declared that 'the policy of free competition [for example facilitated by anti-trust regulation] runs deep in our law … but [that] of stimulating invention … underlies the entire patent system [and] runs no less deep'.[28] In *Haas* reward of technological 'innovation' though state grant of patents as private intellectual property rights (rather than monopoly privileges) began to be emphasized more than the counter-balancing public goods concepts such as strong anti-trust laws and cost-effectiveness assessment as critical to 'free market competition'.[29]

Likewise important in the debate of pharmaceutical regulation was the creation in 1982 of the Court of Appeals for the Federal Circuit

[23] Suzanne Scotchmer, 'Standing on the Shoulders of Giants: Cumulative Research and the Patent Law' (1991) 5 *Journal of Economic Perspectives* 29.

[24] Mark Grady and Jay Alexander, 'Patent Law and Rent Dissipation' (1992) 78 *Virginia Law Review* 305.

[25] Rebecca Eisenberg, 'Patents and the Progress of Science: Exclusive Rights and Experimental Use' (1989) 56 *University of Chicago Law Review* 1017

[26] Iain Cockburn and Rebecca Henderson, 'Public–Private Interaction and the Productivity of Pharmaceutical Research' (Working Paper No 6018, National Bureau of Economic Research, 1997).

[27] *Dawson Chemical Company* v. *Rohm & Haas*, 448 US 176 (1980).

[28] Ibid., 221.

[29] Lawrence Kastriner, 'The Revival of Confidence in the Patent System' (1991) 73 *Journal of Patent and Trademark Office Society* 5.

('CAFC'). This Court's ostensible purpose was to centralize patents, tariff and custom, technology transfer, trademarks, government contracts and labour disputes within one specialist jurisdiction. Fears expressed by critics that the new Court would be prone to isolation from broader normative systems appear to have been realized.[30] The CAFC has developed an extremely pro-patent jurisprudence rarely mentioning the word 'monopoly', readily granting large scale compensatory damages and permanent injunctions, whilst consistently upholding the interests, for example, of drug patent holders over generic suppliers or public interest regulation.[31]

Also important at this time was industry lobbying for a US federal economic policy positing level of output rather than amount of competition as the dominant regulatory end point. Government acceptance of this output-oriented policy allowed pharmaceutical companies in particular to promote high levels of market concentration as efficiencies rather than price-distorting monopolies and cartels. It also promoted the position that patents legitimately provided such corporations with a strategy to protect socially vital investments and increase revenue, if need be by excluding some competition from the market and at the expense of otherwise appropriate public interest regulation.[32] The CAFC decision in *Madey's* case, for example, to effectively restrict the research use exemption for university research,[33] was unsuccessfully appealed to the US Supreme Court by the Association of American Medical Colleges, the American Council on Education, various individual colleges, universities and medical schools, as highly likely to inhibit research into socially important but unprofitable diseases such as malaria, tuberculosis, diarrhoea and pneumonia.[34]

In 1983 the US Government passed the Drug Price Competition and Patent Restoration Act 1983 (US) (commonly known as the Hatch-Waxman Act). This legislation gave pharmaceutical patent holders an additional five years of patent life, allegedly to compensate for the period of pre-market testing and FDA safety, quality and efficacy evaluation. It allowed, as a response to the CAFC decision in *Roche Products, Inc.* v. *Bolar Pharmaceutical Co.*,[35] generic competitors to use original brand

[30] Jack Lever, 'The New Court of Appeals for the Federal Circuit' (1982) 64 *Journal of the Patent and Trademark Office Society* 178.

[31] Susan Sell, *Power and Ideas: The North–South Politics of Intellectual Property and Antitrust* (1998).

[32] Ibid. [33] *Madey* v. *Duke University*, 307 F 3d 1351 (Fed Cir, 2002).

[34] Petition for a Writ of Certiorari: Ibid. 1356.

[35] *Roche Products, Inc.* v. *Bolar Pharmaceutical Co.* 733 F 2d 858 (Fed Cir, 1984).

name data to prepare bioequivalence and other testing provided those activities were reasonably related to securing regulatory approval and 'springboarding' (generic drug companies using pre-existing safety data to market products rapidly) on expiry of the originator's patent. The statute accorded each such generic entrant 180 days of market exclusivity, but brand-name manufacturers were allowed to request a thirty-month injunction against marketing approval for any such generic drugs alleged to be infringing valid patents. This last provision established the practice, known as 'evergreening', by which the patent monopoly over large sales volume brand-name pharmaceuticals could be tactically extended.[36] The techniques of 'evergreening' developed here (as we'll see) were soon to be transported, by their incorporation into bilateral trade deals, into domestic health technology safety and cost-effectiveness regulatory systems around the world.

The most recent phase of this shift away from a policy of emphasizing drug patents as private rights that do not allow much counterbalancing regulation such as cost-effectiveness analysis involved the Medicare Prescription Drug Improvement and Modernization Act 2003 (US). Section 1013 of this statute created an inchoate federal system for cost-effectiveness assessment of pharmaceuticals. Section 1013(b)(1)(A), however, required that such developments 'not mandate national standards, of clinical practice or quality health care standards. Section 1013(d) required that data so produced for the Centers for Medicare & Medicaid Services not be used to withhold coverage of a prescription drug. These sections in effect prevented the creation of a robust US federal system for cost-effectiveness assessment of pharmaceuticals.

The legislation also directed the Secretary of Commerce, in consultation with the International Trade Commission, the Secretary of Health and Human Services and the United States Trade Representative, to conduct a study on drug cost-effectiveness and pricing practices of countries that are members of the Organisation for Economic Co-operation and Development ('OECD') and to report whether those practices utilize or comprise non-tariff barriers with respect to trade in pharmaceuticals. The study was required to estimate additional costs to US consumers because of such 'price controls' and the extent to which additional costs would be reduced for US consumers if such practices were reduced or eliminated. Pharmaceutical price controls in eleven OECD

[36] Thomas Faunce and Joel Lexchin, 'Linkage Pharmaceutical Evergreening in Canada and Australia' (2007) 4 *Australian and New Zealand Journal of Health Policy* 8.

countries were eventually studied.[37] The report set the benchmark for pharmaceutical prices as that in the US, because it allegedly represented a completely 'deregulated' market.

4. Pharmaceutical patents, market fundamentalism and the WTO

One factor restricting the capacity to introduce cost-effectiveness analysis into pharmaceutical regulation was the growing global influence of 'monetarism', an economic theory that required a small measure of state fiscal control over markets through central banks maintaining a steady money supply (achieved by controlling supply of their sound investment securities). At the same time it demanded (in an ideology known as economic rationalism or market fundamentalism) the down-scaling of bureaucracy, deregulation of industry and privatization of public assets. This, so the theory went, would allow private enterprise to achieve a natural balance between inflation, employment and production. Four broad categories of privatization were involved:

(1) putting state monopolies into competition with private or other public operators;
(2) outsourcing, where the state paid private actors to provide public goods and services;
(3) private financing in exchange for delegated management arrangements; and
(4) transfers to private control of publicly owned assets.

The resultant privatization policies were strategically promoted by corporate lobbyists and their acolyte politicians as an extension of Adam Smith's notion that interaction in a perfectly competitive market by a myriad of appropriately self-interested consumers and investors expressing free will to maximize relative utility would create an invisible sovereign hand that mechanistically placed an appropriate money value on all policy choices. It was a theory providing its adherents with a conceptual justification for disengagement from the wider social contract debate involving, in this context, responsibility for more efficiently reducing the global burden of scientifically proven disease.

[37] Medicare Prescription Drug Improvement and Modernization Act 2003 (US) 21 USC §108–73.

Monetarist ideology claimed that markets and prices were an expression of collective free will. It then followed, the theory's proponents argued, that many social problems (including poverty and lack of access to health services or essential medicines) could probably be traced to some unnecessary government interference in the market process. Clearly, to the zealous adherents of such an ideology, cost-effectiveness regulation systems could be regarded as just such an interference in the market.

Market fundamentalism was embraced by influential political leaders in the US (President Ronald Reagan) and the UK (Prime Minister Margaret Thatcher). In the 1990s, market fundamentalism was linked with trade 'liberalization' (which in this context generally meant non-discrimination against foreign corporations) and embraced in what was known as the Washington Consensus, by the IMF, the World Bank, the WTO and the US Treasury.

Concerns that the side effects of market fundamentalism were greater unemployment, income inequalities and dangers to public health strengthened when the doctrine began to underpin the lending policies of the World Bank and a series of WTO multilateral as well as bilateral agreements whose obligations were enforced by trade sanctions (appealable only to an unelected panel of trade lawyers). Such WTO agreements appeared to transfer decision-making power away from the world's people and towards the executives of multinational corporations, their expert advisers and politicians who (through, for example, campaign donations and promises of post-office employment) had become beholden to them.

The regulatory apotheosis of market fundamentalist ideology may be viewed as the failed OECD Multilateral Agreement on Investment ('MAI'), negotiated in secret between 1995 and 1998 without parliamentary oversight or consultation. The MAI would have allowed multinational corporations to sue domestic governments for implementing policies (such as environment protection, cost-effectiveness assessment and universal healthcare and access to medicines programmes) that would have the 'equivalent effect' of being an 'indirect appropriation' on investment and so restrain its 'enjoyment'.

By the late twentieth century evidence-based medicine, the conceptual core of health technology cost-effectiveness assessment, had become increasingly influenced by corporate investment in and thus control over the funding, co-ordination and publication of randomized control trials. The opinions of the most eminent and peer-revered doctors were frequently sought and influenced by corporate gifts – of biomaterials, discretionary funds, equipment, consultancy fees, honoraria for presentations, conference subsidies or hospitality, sponsorship of continuing medical education, advertising and lobbying.

It was at this time that the WTO Agreement on Trade-Related Aspects of Intellectual Property Rights ('TRIPS Agreement' or 'TRIPS') emerged as a powerful global influence on the regulation of trade in health technologies, particularly pharmaceuticals.[38] The WTO TRIPS Agreement was one of the twenty-eight agreements in the Final Act of the Uruguay Round of Multilateral Trade Negotiations leading to the WTO in 1994. TRIPS required all signature countries to adhere to minimum levels of intellectual property protection (including pharmaceutical patents). It was the first broadly subscribed to multilateral agreement to raise global intellectual property protections, being enforceable between governments and allowing them to resolve international intellectual property disputes more readily through the WTO dispute mechanism.

TRIPS, conceived by senior executives at twelve US corporations including, in particular, the pharmaceutical giant Pfizer, was primarily designed to enhance the profits available to private corporations of developed nations from two great emerging technologies, digital technology (through copyright, patents and protection for circuit layout designs) and biotechnology (through patents and trade secrets).

In the late 1980s at the time of the TRIPS negotiations, very little empirical or theoretical research existed concerning the economic, social or public health effects of increasing intellectual property rights in a country. Some evidence had emerged that stronger patent rights appeared to encourage incremental improvements by the originator, but also to create hindrance from prior inventors and freeze out future radical inventors.[39] Lerner, for example, studying 177 policy shifts in 60 countries over 150 years, found an 'inverted-U' relationship between patent strength and innovation. He suggested that strengthening patents had a positive effect on innovation when intellectual property protection was initially low, but a negative impact if patent protection was initially high.[40] The

[38] Marrakesh Agreement Establishing the World Trade Organization, opened for signature 15 April 1994, 1867 UNTS 3, annex 1C (Agreement on Trade-Related Aspects of Intellectual Property Rights) (entered into force 1 January 1995) ('TRIPS Agreement').

[39] Ted O'Donoghue, Suzanne Cotchmer and Jacques-François Thisse, 'Patent Breadth, Patent Life and the Pace of Technological Progress' (1998) 7 *Journal of Economics and Management* 1.

[40] Josh Lerner, '150 Years of Patent Protection' (Working Paper No 7478, National Bureau of Economic Research, 2001).

limited research that did support the trade–intellectual property linkage with pharmaceutical innovation appeared to have been generally written by drug company-funded institutes and academics.[41] The establishment of TRIPS in other words created an opportunity to include in this WTO agreement provisions relating to the acquisition of data about the societal impacts of the increased patents regime being proposed.

Although it became increasingly clear that TRIPS was likely to have a major adverse impact on public health in developing countries, neither the WHO nor any process for acquiring and evaluating scientific evidence about the societal impacts of patents was included in the TRIPS negotiations or final text. TRIPS article 30 conferred a general right of 'limited [public interest] exceptions to the exclusive rights conferred by a patent'. Article 7 recognized that the protection of intellectual property should contribute to the promotion of technological innovation and to the transfer and dissemination of technology, to the mutual advantage of its users and producers in a manner conducive to social and economic welfare and to a balance of rights and obligations. A clarification would be needed, however, to determine the extent to which this article allowed public health exceptions to pharmaceutical patent rights.

5. Bilateral trade agreements and their impact on pharmaceutical cost-effectiveness regulation

As well as the WTO TRIPS multilateral agreement, the US pharmaceutical industry has been working with the office of the United States Trade Representative ('USTR') to negotiate a series of bilateral trade agreements with provisions that impact on pharmaceutical safety regulatory processes, as well as scientifically objective ways of assessing the cost-effectiveness of therapeutic drugs and pricing them accordingly. This creates an important stimulus for the WTO to move such negotiations from the bilateral to the multilateral sphere.

A Conference Agreement on the Medicare Prescription Drug Improvement and Modernization Act 2003 (US) obliged the United States Trade Representative, the Secretary of Commerce and the Secretary of Health and Human Services, for example, to analyse whether bilateral or

[41] Justin Bekelman and Cary Gross, 'Scope and Impact of Financial Conflicts of Interest in Biomedical Research: A Systematic Review' (2003) 289 *Journal of the American Medical Association* 545.

multilateral trade or other negotiations presented an opportunity to address these price controls bearing in mind the negotiating objective set forth in the bipartisan Trade Promotion Authority Act 2002 (US) to achieve the elimination of government measures such as prescription drug price controls and reference pricing.[42] The Australia–United States Free Trade Agreement 2004 ('AUSFTA') was specifically mentioned in this context.[43]

Australia was deliberately targeted here because its Pharmaceutical Benefits Scheme ('PBS') had become an international benchmark of a cost-effectiveness system providing a scientifically objective means of making pharmaceutical prices in that nation more responsive to community benefits. Australia's safety and cost-effectiveness regulators (respectively the Therapeutic Goods Administration ('TGA') and Pharmaceutical Benefits Advisory Committee ('PBAC')) remain highly respected nationally and internationally as a successful articulation of a scientific approach to ensuring maximum public safety and benefit from new health technologies. Both regulatory systems operate under the four basic principles of the National Medicines Policy:

(1) timely access to the medicines that Australians need, at a cost individuals and the community can afford;
(2) medicines meeting appropriate standards of quality, safety and efficacy;
(3) quality use of medicines; and
(4) maintaining a responsible and viable medicines industry.

Before a new patented drug is listed in Australia, it must obtain safety, quality and efficacy marketing approval from the Australian TGA, which is that nation's equivalent of the FDA. Once this is done (in a step not present yet in the US) the supplier may apply to an independent statutory cost-effectiveness committee – the PBAC set up under the National Health Act 1953 (Cth). The PBAC is required to consider applications against certain cost-effectiveness criteria set out in the legislation. The PBAC cannot recommend a new drug for listing, for example, if it is 'substantially more costly than an alternative therapy' unless it 'provides

[42] Trade Act 2002 (United States) Pub.L. 107-210, 116 Stat. 933; 19 U.S.C. § 3803–3805, US Trade Promotion Authority Act 2002 (United States).

[43] Medicare Prescription Drug Improvement and Modernization Act 2003 (US) 21 USC Conference Agreement House Report 108–391 Title XI-Access to Pharmaceuticals, thomas.loc.gov/cgi-bin/cpquery/?&db_id=cp108&r_n=hr391.108&sel=TOC_2588886& at 28 February 2009; Trade Act 2002 (United States), 107–210 §2102(b)(8)(D).

a significant improvement in efficacy or reduction of toxicity over the alternative therapy or therapies'.[44]

Working through a hierarchy of evidence, the PBAC, its advisory subcommittee and contracted evaluators assess the cost-effectiveness of the submitted product against its best already marketed comparator. This is the core of the PBAC's evidence-based approach to assessing the community value of health technology innovation, a concept known as 'health innovation' and distinguished from lobbying and advertising or market-based approaches to establishing the innovation credentials of new health technologies. If the product is deemed not cost-effective, its price is referenced down to that of the comparitor in a cost-minimization exercise. Reference pricing, in its most fundamental sense under the PBS process, applies post-listing when new drug competitors (with lower prices) enter groups of medicines for specific conditions established for cost-effectiveness assessment purposes in relation to the Therapeutic Group Premium ('TGP') Policy.

If the PBAC recommends against listing a particular pharmaceutical, the manufacturer can still access the market and promote its product; however the patient will have to pay the full market price. The PBAC drug cost-effectiveness assessment process is thus not a non-tariff barrier to trade, or a process that interferes with the monopoly privileges accorded by pharmaceutical patents. It facilitates a more science-based approach to pharmaceutical pricing. The Pharmaceutical Benefits Pricing Authority (PBPA) uses the PBAC recommendation to negotiate a maximum amount the government will reimburse to pharmacists.

When it came into force in January 2005, annex 2C of the AUSFTA, which specifically focused on the PBS, led to changes including public summary documents of PBAC decisions, a new review mechanism (not an appeals process) for PBAC decisions and increased opportunities for industry submissions prior to evaluation.[45] Article 1 of annex 2C of the AUSFTA also emphasized the principle of valuing pharmaceutical 'innovation' through either the operation of 'competitive markets' (the US position) or by 'adopting or maintaining procedures that appropriately value the objectively demonstrated therapeutic significance of a pharmaceutical' (the Australian position). The potential importance to Australian and global medicines policy of this ambiguous definition of

[44] National Health Act 1953 (Cth) s. 101(3B)(a).

[45] Australia–United States Free Trade Agreement (AUSFTA) signed 18 May 2004 (entered into force 1 January 2005).

'innovation', has been highlighted by the author.[46] Annex 2C, however, established a Medicines Working Group ('MWG') comprising high level officials on medicines policy from both countries.[47] Documents obtained under a Freedom of Information application[48] reveal that the first AUSFTA MWG meeting discussed a newspaper article that included this statement: 'Truly innovative cures should be referenced against innovation in other classes, rather than against generics.'[49]

In the middle of 2007, the introduction of amendments to the National Health Act 1953 (Cth)[50] fractured the unitary PBS formulary into two. Two classes were introduced to divide pharmaceuticals: F1 for patented or allegedly 'innovative' medicines and F2 for generic medicines. Price cuts and disclosures are imposed *only* on F2 generic medicines.[51] Reference pricing will be limited to a few existing F1 therapeutic groups, or to where they have been established on the imprecise standard that comparitors are 'interchangeable on an individual patient basis' (proposed sections 84AG and 101(3)(BA)). The role of US trade agreement negotiators in promoting these changes through their role on the AUSFTA MWG is suspected, but unproven.[52]

6. Increased support in trade agreements for health technology cost-effectiveness systems

A major crisis in pharmaceutical regulation was needed before the WTO began to take seriously claims that the TRIPS Agreement was blind to important equity issues in public health. In 1997 the South African Government, as the result of the HIV/AIDS crisis affecting 50 per cent of its citizens in some districts and its inability to respond with cheap antiretroviral medications, passed its Medicines and Related Substances

[46] Thomas Faunce *et al.*, 'Assessing the Impact of the Australia–United States Free Trade Agreement on Australian and Global Medicines Policy' (2005) 1(15) *Globalisation and Health* 1.

[47] United States Department of Health and Human Services, *Australia–U.S. Medicines Working Group Holds First Meeting* (24 October 2007), www.globalhealth.gov/news/news/011406.html at 23 February 2009.

[48] Organized by Pat Ranald, Australian Fair Trade and Investment Network 2007.

[49] Andrew Laming, 'Let's Overhaul the Pharmaceutical Benefits Scheme', *The Australian* (Sydney) 10 January 2006, 10.

[50] See especially, National Health Act 1953 (Cth), sections 85AB, 85AC.

[51] Ibid., pt VII, div 3A.

[52] Thomas Faunce, 'Reference Pricing for Pharmaceuticals: Is the Australia–United States Free Trade Agreement Affecting Australia's Pharmaceutical Benefits Scheme?' (2007) 187 *Medical Journal of Australia* 240.

Control Amendment Act. Section 15C permitted the relevant Minister to 'prescribe conditions for the supply of more affordable medicines in certain circumstances so as to protect the health of the public'. It expanded the conditions for compulsory licences and parallel importation to facilitate the capacity of more poor South African citizens to gain access to cheap anti-HIV/AIDS pharmaceuticals.

The US threatened to bring the South African legislation before a WTO dispute settlement body. The US, and the Pharmaceutical Research and Manufacturers of America (PhRMA) interests it represented, claimed that the South African public health and equity interpretations of WTO TRIPS compulsory licensing and parallel importation articles were inconsistent with TRIPS. In 1998, as is now well known, forty-one pharmaceutical companies commenced litigation, partly based on TRIPS, against the South African Medicines and Related Substances Control Amendment Act. President Nelson Mandela was named as first defendant. In April 2001 the action was withdrawn, after a campaign by members of international civil society including Médecins Sans Frontières.

Partly in response to lobbying by such NGOs at the WTO Doha Ministerial Conference in November 2001, WTO Ministers issued a separate Declaration on the TRIPS Agreement and Public Health. Paragraph 6 of this equity clarification permitted WTO members with 'insufficient or no manufacturing capacities in the pharmaceutical sector' to issue compulsory licences for the production, or importation, of medicines without consent from the patent holder, where necessary to protect public health (such as to combat the HIV/AIDS crisis and promote 'access to medicines for all').[53] After a further WTO General Council Decision of 30 August 2003, members could unequivocally waive article 31(f) of TRIPS and respond to compulsory licences to export to markets other than domestic ones where that other country does not have the capacity to manufacture medicines itself. This ostensible extension of the international human right to health was not restricted to situations of national emergency. The Ministerial Declaration stressed the importance of 'implementing and interpreting' TRIPS 'in a manner supportive of public health, by promoting both access to existing medicines and research and development into new medicines'.[54]

[53] Ministerial Declaration: Adopted on 14 November 2001, WTO Doc WT/MIN(01)/DEC/1 (2001); and James Gathii, 'The Legal Status of the Doha Declaration on TRIPS and Public Health under the Vienna Convention on the Law of Treaties' (2002) 15 *Harvard Journal of Law and Technology* 291.

[54] Frederick Abbott, 'The WTO Medicines Decision: World Pharmaceutical Trade and the Protection of Public Health' (2005) 99 *The American Journal of International Law* 317.

The so-called 'paragraph 6' exemption has been little used and can even be viewed as an exercise in civil society distraction from the fundamental lack of involvement of WTO processes and texts in the great global public health crises that currently confront humanity.

The South Korean Government was so impressed by the socially and scientifically sound economic incentives offered by the Australian PBS evidence-based cost-effectiveness and reference pricing system, that it specifically requested the capacity to establish a similar process in its free trade negotiations with the United States subsequent to the AUSFTA.[55] Article 5(2) of the Republic of Korea–United States Free Trade Agreement 2007 (KORUSFTA) indicated that if South Korea did establish a reimbursement system for pharmaceuticals or medical devices where the amount paid was not based on 'competitive market-derived prices', then amongst other things it had to 'appropriately recognise the value of patented pharmaceutical products'.[56] 'Value' here appears to have been a constructive ambiguity, the US opting for 'valuing' through market forces and the Koreans through scientific evidence. Article 5(1)(c) mentioned, for example, PBAC-type 'sound economic incentives' as a method of facilitating access to patented medicines.

In the US calls have been made for a new generation of safety and cost-effectiveness regulation at the domestic level aimed at replacing existing industry-funded, impartiality-compromised organizations such as the US FDA where the Office of Drug Safety is part of the section responsible for evaluating and approving new drugs.[57]

7. Towards a WTO–WHO HSCE Agreement

As a result of the preceding analysis it should now be clear that the US domestic patent law, the WTO particularly through the TRIPS Agreement and specific US-initiated recent bilateral trade agreements, have played a major role in creating structures and processes designed to

[55] The Republic of Korea–United States Free Trade Agreement (KORUSFTA), signed 30 June 2007, ch. 5 (pending US Congress Approval).

[56] Ibid., article 5(2)(b)(i).

[57] In an internal survey conducted in 2002 of about 400 FDA scientists, two thirds said they lacked confidence that the FDA 'adequately monitors the safety of prescription drugs once they are on the market' and 18 per cent reported that they 'have been pressured to approve or recommend approval' for a drug 'despite reservations about the safety, efficacy, or quality': Phil Fontanarosa, Rennie Drummond and Catherine DeAngelis, 'Postmarketing Surveillance: Lack of Vigilance, Lack of Trust' (2002) 292 *Journal of the American Medical Association* 2647.

influence global safety and cost-effectiveness regulation of pharmaceuticals. At the same time the WHO has become increasingly interested (through, for example, its Global Strategy) in developing more equitable structures for regulation of the global pharmaceutical industry.

The recent global financial crisis precipitated by excessive financial sector deregulation has created an opportunity to formalize the already present informal professional relationships and sharing of data amongst networks of national assessors scrutinizing the safety and cost-effectiveness of new health technologies.[58]

What development of a WTO–WHO HSCE Agreement is likely to require is a combination of: (1) formalization in a multinational agreement of the basic principles by which new health technologies are assessed for safety and cost-effectiveness; and then (2) linkage through the same mechanism with domestic regulatory processes in which public funds are allocated to subsidize expenditure by citizens on new health technologies. The WTO–WHO HSCE Agreement could specify the ground rules that prevented such domestic safety and cost-effectiveness analysis becoming a non-tariff barrier to trade. It would create a mechanism whereby nations could appeal domestic safety and cost-effectiveness decisions, policies and legislation, much as takes place in the context of the SPS Agreement. Trade panels would assess such appeals on the basis of scientific evidence presented.

Working out a road map towards such a WTO–WHO HSCE Agreement would involve discussions about issues such as assessor reimbursement (for example possibly through a tax on global financial transactions distributed to nations in proportion to the need to establish the requisite domestic infrastructure). It would also involve the need for liability protection, co-ordination of a safety and cost-effectiveness clinical trials register with appropriate protections for participants, rationalization of commercial-in-confidence protections, standardization of post-marketing surveillance and performance indicators for conditional approvals and strategies to obtain information on marginal cost of production and price setting.

Once sufficient ratifications of such a WTO–WHO HSCE Agreement were achieved, the course of pharmaceutical R&D would be shaped as it would provide manufacturers and patent holders with potential access to

[58] Thomas Faunce, 'Toward a Treaty on Safety and Cost-Effectiveness of Pharmaceuticals and Medical Devices: Enhancing an Endangered Global Public Good' (2006) 2 *Globalization and Health* 5.

a level playing field of large and reliable sources of domestic funding once they have met the requisite evidence-based standards. The relationship between domestic safety and cost-effectiveness assessment of health technologies and international trade would no longer be regulated chiefly by bilateral trade agreements such as the AUSFTA and KORUSFTA. Such connection would be clarified and formalized and such regulation assessed through an evidence-based assessment of its benefit to public health ('health innovation'). Although the democratic deficit inherent in international law-making will not be perfectly rectified under this model, the involvement of experts in the regulatory process will assist the likelihood that the whole process will be more transparent and accountable to global health needs.

Working towards a WTO–WHO HSCE Agreement is going to be a difficult exercise. Drug industry lobbyists are likely to seek to block such a measure by raising the prospects of its tying innovation up in red tape, slowing down market access for new drugs and to some (as yet undefined) extent contravening TRIPS obligations.

The question of what constitutes worthwhile scientific information to assist a WTO dispute settlement process will need to be resolved for an HSCE Agreement, just as much as for the SPS Agreement.[59] One concern here would be that if the WTO did embrace an HSCE Agreement the WTO dispute settlement procedures and those who administer and arbitrate them would begin to become international scientific arbiters of safety, quality, efficacy and cost-effectiveness of health technologies despite such trade lawyers not necessarily having adequate scientific expertise to evaluate such issues.[60] This could result in corporate lobbying or influence upon such panellists to skew global regulatory standards. This would mean that to be effective an HSCE Agreement would have to allow disputes to be heard by panels which also comprised independent pharmaco-epidemiologists and toxicologists, as well as trade lawyers.

The adversarial nature of WTO dispute settlement proceedings may also not be the best place for resolution of complex issues surrounding regulatory assessment of health technologies. What would be the

[59] David Wirth, 'The Role of Science in the Uruguay Round and NAFTA Trade Disciplines' (1994) 27 *Cornell International Law Journal* 817.

[60] Vern Walker, 'Keeping the WTO from Becoming the "World Trans-science Organization": Scientific Uncertainty, Science Policy and Fact Finding in the Growth Hormones Dispute' (1981) 31 *Cornell International Law Journal* 251.

consequence if, for example, every time a new pharmaceutical was rejected from the Australian PBS or its Korean equivalent its manufacturer brought a dispute settlement action under the WTO–WHO HSCE Agreement?

8. Beyond the obstacles to a WTO–WHO HSCE Agreement

An approach to health technology regulation, which seeks (with the assistance of the WTO) to incorporate evidence-based cost-effectiveness assessment systems into WTO structures, carries the promise of helping the relevant domestic and international global regulatory institutions to broaden the normative range of their objects, principles and rules to include those associated with supporting global public goods. One such principle is 'sustainability' or intergenerational justice. Others are 'cosmopolitanism' (allegiance to global groupings of people committed to universally applicable principles) and 'solidarity' with endangered species and habitats, as well as with the degraded and 'diseased' Earth itself as a self-sustaining organism (the so-called 'Gaia hypothesis').[61] As naive and idealistic as these principles sound to some now, this will not be the case if the life-support biosystems of the Earth begin to collapse (as they will on current economic trends). Ensuring that new health technologies are not overpriced in relation to their impact on the global and domestic burden of disease is an important component of such public goods thinking.[62]

As the world emerges from an age which valorized unregulated corporate greed through the market state, the best hope for our long-term survival may be that communities will turn from the 'unfreedoms' that lie behind the ostensibly unlimited consumer choices permitted by multinational corporations towards the more genuine liberty implicit in adopting cosmopolitan identities, intermediate technologies and local sharing of resources and skills. The premise explored in this chapter is that WTO rules should be altered to allow societies to return to such universalist models without needing to compensate corporate actors; that such alternatives should be entitled to have their cost-effectiveness

[61] John Cairns Jr, 'Defining Goals and Conditions for a Sustainable World' (1997) 105 *Environmental Health Perspectives* 1164.

[62] Suerie Moon, 'Medicines as Global Public Goods: The Governance of Technological Innovation in the New Era of Global Health' (2009) 2(2) *Global Health Governance*, www.ghgj.org/Volume%20II%20Issue%202.htm at 22 June 2009.

assessed alongside that of new health technologies produced by the multinational corporate sector.

Safety and cost-effectiveness regulation of health technologies has been presented here as what may be termed a 'higher order global public good.' This refers to knowledge, material, infrastructure or measures that support, respect or fulfil the basic preconditions for human existence; provide benefits from which no individual should be excluded; span national, cultural and generational boundaries; and involve consumption theoretically not creating rivalry or diminishment by use.[63]

The WTO TRIPS system can be viewed as precisely defining the distinction between the public domain and the provision of public goods, as it constrains the former to secure higher-order, deliberately constructed non-rivalrous and non-excludable public goods.[64] The free dispersal of scientific knowledge, protection from fear and want, and the capacity for freedom of expression can usefully be viewed as global public goods regardless of whether they can also be characterized as encompassed by norms of international human rights law. The practical delivery of many such outcomes – whether higher level public goods, such as equity and efficiency in the distribution of pharmaceutical products, or more tangible public goods, such as the production of a new drug for a neglected disease – positively requires the effective operation of economic systems, typically a mix of both public expenditure and private incentive.[65]

This chapter has set out why global medicines policy has hitherto not embraced the idea of a WTO–WHO HSCE Agreement and then set out how such an agreement might operate in WTO dispute settlement settings in a similar manner to the WTO SPS Agreement. The conclusions are necessarily equivocal. Although some global co-ordination of health technology safety and cost-effectiveness regulation must take place, there is always the implicit danger of corporate capture and of the created institution ending up working against its primary aims.

[63] Keith Maskus and Jerome Reichman, 'The Globalisation of Private Knowledge Goods and the Privatisation of Global Public Goods', in Keith Maskus and Jerome Reichman (eds.), *International Public Goods and Transfer of Technology under a Globalised Intellectual Property Regime* (2005), 3.

[64] Antony Taubman, 'Saving the Village: Conserving Jurisprudential Diversity in the International Protection of Traditional Knowledge', in Keith Maskus and Jerome Reichman (eds.) *International Public Goods and Transfer of Technology under a Globalised Intellectual Property Regime* (2005) 521, 546–7.

[65] The theoretical basis for this normative view is expanded on in Thomas Faunce, *Who Owns our Health?: Medical Professionalism, Law and Leadership beyond the Age of the Market State* (2007).

Phrasing the fundamental ethical issues for WTO trade agreements in such a way is not as radical as it may initially sound. It is an extension of a process of reasoning encouraged by Amartya Sen's view of trade and the development it brings. Sen views trade and development as not merely precursors to the institution of public goods such as political freedom and fulfilment of the basic preconditions of the right to health, but necessarily requiring their simultaneous achievement.[66]

This chapter merely takes that analysis one step further and asks whether once trade has been reorganized to better facilitate the basic preconditions for health amongst all, including the chronically poor, what is then to be collectively encouraged as the goal of a well-lived human life? It is the type of question asked of foundational sustainability economists by E. F. Schumacher[67] and Kenneth Boulding[68] who argued it was more valuable to analyse the function of work (such as, in this case, the global provision of health technologies) as involving not just production for profit by individual persons (natural or artificial), but the conscious evolution of personal faculties by overcoming selfishness so that all may be given a reasonable chance to seek a deeper understanding of life's purpose.

66 Amartya Sen, *Development as Freedom* (1999).

67 E. F. Schumacher, *Buddhist Economics*, the E. F. Schumacher Society, www.schumacher-society.org/buddhist_economics/english.html at 26 February 2009.

68 Kenneth Boulding, 'Foreword', in Norman Myers (ed.), *The Gaia Atlas of Future Worlds: Challenge and Opportunity in an Age of Change* (1990), 5–7.

PART III

Intellectual property

9

Opening the dam: patent pools, innovation and access to essential medicines

DIANNE NICOL AND JANE NIELSEN

1. Introduction

It would be difficult to conceive of a world where the medicines necessary to treat the world's most prevalent diseases were not protected by patents. The patent system is so entrenched in the healthcare industry (particularly in the pharmaceutical sector) and the practice of applying for patents to protect the fruits of biomedical research so ingrained,[1] that anyone involved in the public health innovation cycle of discovery, development and delivery must find a way to traverse the increasingly complex patent landscape.[2] While some countries may be freed from patent fetters if they lack relevant patent legislation or if relevant patents have not been filed or granted, the number of countries in this category is ever decreasing and those that remain untouched by patent monopolies are likely to lack the capacity to undertake research or to manufacture medicines. Yet it has been explicitly stated in some of the highest international policy forums that intellectual property rights do not and should not prevent member states from taking measures to protect public health. The Intergovernmental

[1] The main justification for the patent system is that patents are necessary to induce innovation: see Mark Lemley, 'Ex Ante versus Ex Post Justifications for Intellectual Property' (2004) 71 *University of Chicago Law Review* 129. Empirical evidence on this issue is divided, but see, in particular, Richard Levin, Alvin Klevorick, Richard Nelson and Sidney Winter, 'Appropriating the Returns from Industrial Research and Development' (1987) 18 *Brookings Papers on Economic Activity* 783; and Wesley Cohen, Richard Nelson and John Walsh, 'Protecting their Intellectual Assets: Appropriability Conditions and Why U.S. Manufacturing Firms Patent (or Not)', (Working Paper No 7552, National Bureau of Economic Research, 2000). See also Edwin Mansfield, 'Patents and Innovation: An Empirical Study' (1986) 32 *Management Science* 173.

[2] Discovery, development and delivery are considered to be the three crucial components of the innovation cycle for drugs. See Commission on Intellectual Property Rights, Innovation and Public Health, *Public Health, Innovation and Intellectual Property Rights* (2006), 23.

Working Group on Public Health, Innovation and Intellectual Property ('IGWG') of the World Health Organization ('WHO') has stated as much in paragraph 20 of its draft Global Strategy on Public Health.[3] The question that needs to be addressed is how to achieve this end of protecting public health whilst at the same time maintaining the incentive to innovate.[4]

It is widely recognized in both policy and academic arenas that one of the ways in which access to essential medicines might be better facilitated is to place concrete limitations on the absoluteness of the patent monopoly.[5] In particular, collaborative management of relevant patents can be crucial. Patent pooling is recognized as one important collaborative mechanism that has the potential to facilitate access to medicines.[6] For example, the IGWG Global Strategy emphasizes the importance of developing new mechanisms to promote transfer of and access to key

[3] *Global Strategy and Plan of Action on Public Health, Innovation and Intellectual Property*, World Health Assembly 61st mtg, Res WHA61.21 (24 May 2008) ('*WHO Global Strategy*'), [20]. See also Marrakesh Agreement Establishing the World Trade Organization, opened for signature 15 April 1994, 1867 UNTS 3, annex 1C (Agreement on Trade-Related Aspects of Intellectual Property Rights) article 8 (entered into force 1 January 1995) ('TRIPS Agreement').

[4] The role of intellectual property rights in providing the necessary incentive to innovate has been debated extensively in the literature. It is difficult to do justice to the entirety of the debate in a chapter of this scope. Suffice it to say that '[i]ntellectual property rights have an important role to play in stimulating innovation in health-care products in countries where financial and technological capacities exist, and in relation to products for which profitable markets exist': Commission on Intellectual Property Rights, Innovation and Public Health, above n. 2, 22.

[5] The extent to which patent rights can be circumscribed in states that are members of the World Trade Organization ('WTO') is limited as a result of various provisions in TRIPS. In particular, article 31 defines the scope of uses of patents without the authorization of the patent holder. Article 30 is also relevant, in that it allows member countries to include a further category of uses without authorization for such matters as experimental use, prior use and regulatory approval of generic pharmaceuticals. Although TRIPS is littered with these and similar prescriptions, it must be recognized that there are also flexibilities inherent in this Agreement and that member states can tailor their laws to their own circumstances, provided that they meet the minimum standards. See ibid., 21.

[6] Other methods include clearing house mechanisms, aggregation of rights by one entity, cross licensing and Open Source licensing: see Dianne Nicol and Janet Hope, 'Cooperative Strategies for Facilitating Use of Patented Inventions in Biotechnology' (2006) 24 *Law in Context* 85; Geertrui Van Overwalle *et al*., 'Models for Facilitating Access to Patents on Genetic Inventions' (2006) 7 *Nature Reviews Genetics* 143; and Patrick Gaulé, 'Towards Patent Pools in Biotechnology?' (2006) 2 *Innovation Strategy Today* 123. Issues associated with Open Source licensing are canvassed in this collection by Krishna Ravi Srinivas, 'Open Source Drug Discovery: A Revolutionary Paradigm or a Utopian Model?', in Thomas Pogge, Matthew Rimmer and Kim Rubenstein (eds.), *Incentives for Global Public Health: Patent Law and Access to Essential Medicines* (2010), 263.

health-related technologies, including 'examination of the feasibility of voluntary patent pools of upstream and downstream technologies to promote innovation of and access to health products and medical devices'.[7]

A patent pool can be broadly defined as an agreement between two or more patent holders to aggregate or pool their respective technologies and license them as a single package, either by the group of owners or by a separate entity specifically created for that purpose.[8] Provided that a patent pool includes all relevant patents, it can create a platform for freedom to operate ('FTO') within the patent landscape. It gives pool members and licensees the opportunity to utilize the collection of technologies included in the pool, both to bring new products to market, thereby facilitating competition in the market-place and to carry out further research and development ('R&D'), thereby facilitating innovation. Without pooling, there is a risk that patents could reduce competition and deter innovation by increasing the transaction costs required to establish the FTO platform,[9] or by blocking competitors. But there is also a risk that patent pools could be both anti-competitive, particularly if they encourage collusion and shield weak patents, and anti-innovative (or innovation-neutral), particularly if they don't include all necessary patents or are poorly managed and inadequately resourced.

The aim of this chapter is to investigate the extent to which patent pooling could facilitate navigation through the patent landscape in the three phases of the public health innovation cycle: discovery, development and delivery. In the pharmaceutical sector, there can be little doubt that patents restrict the freedom to manufacture generic versions of patented drugs at the downstream delivery phase of the innovation cycle. Much of the debate about intellectual property and access to medicines centres around this issue. Patents relating to essential drugs provide their owners with powerful monopoly rights, which allow them to dictate terms of manufacture and supply, provided that they do so in compliance with regulatory requirements and that they do not

7 *WHO Global Strategy*, above n. 3, annex, article 4.3(a).

8 See, e.g., Anatole Krattiger and Stanley Kowalski, 'Facilitating Assembly of and Access to Intellectual Property: Focus on Patent Pools and a Review of Other Mechanisms', in Anatole Krattiger *et al.* (eds.), *Intellectual Property Management in Health and Agricultural Innovation: A Handbook of Best Practice* (2008) 131, 137.

9 UNITAID, 'UNITAID Moves towards a Patent Pool for Medicines' (2008), www.unitaid.eu/index.php/en/NEWS/UNITAID-moves-towards-a-patent-pool-for-medicines.html at 2 March 2009.

compromise the intellectual property of other rights holders. Patent pools are unlikely to be effective in the scenario where there is a single dominant patent that blocks manufacture of a particular drug without the permission of the rights holder. Clearing a platform for FTO by patent pooling is much more likely to be of relevance when there are multiple overlapping patents in the same space. For example, patent pooling may be useful in the manufacture and supply of cocktails of antiretroviral ('ARV') medication for the treatment of HIV/AIDS, or where holders of formulation or delivery method patents have the capacity to block off access to medicines in their most usable forms. Recent proposals for ARV patent pooling will be discussed later in this chapter.[10]

Patent pooling may also hold promise at the upstream discovery phase of the innovation cycle. Much of this research is carried out in universities and public and private research institutions. Over the past three decades or more, these institutions have increasingly turned to intellectual property as a means to protect and disseminate their knowledge.[11] Such strategies have led to inevitable increases in the quantum of patents at this end of the discovery–delivery continuum. Blurring of the distinctions between basic and applied research and between discoveries and inventions has added to the problem.[12] Indeed, there are increasing concerns that the research landscape is becoming so cluttered with thickets of patents that it is almost impossible to navigate, and as a consequence, it is inevitable that downstream innovation will be delayed or deterred.[13] Patent pools are being mooted as a means of overcoming some of the problems associated with patent thickets, particularly in some areas of biotechnology and stem cell technology.[14] But it is still

[10] Ibid.

[11] See, e.g., David Mowery *et al.*, 'The Growth of Patenting and Licensing by US Universities: An Assessment of the Effects of the Bayh-Dole Act of 1980' (2001) 30 *Research Policy* 99, 104, 110–16.

[12] See, e.g., Rebecca Eisenberg and Richard Nelson, 'Public vs. Proprietary Science: A Fruitful Tension?' (2002) 77 *Academic Medicine* 1392.

[13] Carl Shapiro, 'Navigating the Patent Thicket: Cross Licences, Patent Pools and Standard-Setting', in Adam Jaffe, Josh Lerner and Scott Stern (eds.), *Innovation Policy and the Economy*, Vol. 1 (2001); and Michael Heller and Rebecca Eisenberg, 'Can Patents Deter Innovation? The Anticommons in Biomedical Research' (1998) 280 *Science* 698.

[14] Jeanne Clark *et al.*, *Patent Pools: A Solution to the Problem of Access in Biotechnology Patents* (2000); Organisation for Economic Co-operation and Development, *Genetic Inventions, Intellectual Property Rights and Licensing Practices: Evidence and Policies* (2002); and Ted Ebersole, Marvin Guthrie and Jorge Goldstein, 'Patent Pools and Standard Setting in Diagnostic Genetics' (2005) 23 *Nature Biotechnology* 937.

unclear whether patent pooling is a feasible strategy for these particular areas, and we know even less about how it might or might not work more generally in the discovery phase of public health.

One of the challenges in public health is the long development phase between discovery and product delivery. The process of taking drug candidates through the development phase of the innovation cycle is particularly long and expensive, requiring pre-clinical and clinical trials and regulatory approval.[15] A key strategy for facilitating this phase of the innovation cycle for essential medicines is the development of public–private partnerships.[16] Rewards schemes, advanced purchase schemes and an R&D treaty have also been put forward as mechanisms for encouraging innovation at this level.[17] A role for patent pooling is much less clear, given that the FTO space will or should already have been cleared in the discovery phase. The issue here is not so much about FTO but about acquiring the necessary resources to take advantage of this FTO. For this reason this chapter will focus primarily on patent pooling in the discovery and delivery phases of the public health innovation cycle. This correlates with the IGWG recommendation on patent pooling in the Global Health Strategy, which calls for examination of upstream and downstream technologies.

However, it should also be recognized that the development phase of the innovation cycle is much less protracted in public health sectors other than pharmaceuticals, and as a consequence it is less important to make the distinction between upstream discovery, development and downstream delivery. For diagnostics, devices and vaccines the transition between discovery and delivery can be quite rapid and as a consequence it may be possible to establish patent pools that facilitate the entire innovation cycle in these sectors. However, even in these sectors, it is important to be clear about what patent pooling can and cannot achieve.[18] Traditional patent pools tend to be clustered around horizontal FTO platforms. Whether patent pools can be used to create vertical FTO

[15] See Commission on Intellectual Property Rights, Innovation and Public Health, *Public Health, Innovation and Intellectual Property Rights*, above n. 2, 65.

[16] See ibid., 70–8. [17] See ibid., 83–90.

[18] Krattiger and his collaborators, for example, argue that vaccine development for pandemic influenza is unlikely to accelerate R&D or leverage the investment needed for manufacture: Anatole Krattiger *et al.*, ‘Intellectual Property Management Strategies to Accelerate the Development and Access of Vaccines and Diagnostics: Case Studies on Pandemic Influenza, Malaria and SARS’ (2006) 2 *Innovation Strategy Today* 67, 68.

paths as well as more traditional horizontal platforms is a matter that needs due consideration.

A number of successful patent pools have been implemented across various industry sectors and some specific examples of humanitarian patent pooling are emerging in the discovery and product delivery phases. This chapter will use these examples to analyse the costs and benefits of patent pooling in relation to essential medicines, bearing in mind the unique issues for the pharmaceutical sector that arise, at least in part, from the prolonged development phase.

2. Patent pools and the global health crisis

2.1 The essential features of patent pools

Patent pooling involves the aggregation of patents held by a number of parties. They may be voluntary or mandated, and may take on a range of different configurations of participation and organization. Although simple arrangements involving as few as two parties may constitute patent pools, complex pooling arrangements can involve hundreds of patents and many parties. Members of patent pools agree to waive their enforcement rights and to share their patents and/or license them to third parties. Note, however, that despite the relatively loose terminology, 'patent pools' are narrowly defined in some regulatory instruments. For example, the European Commission's definition is as follows:[19]

> The notion of technology pools covers agreements whereby two or more parties agree to pool their respective technologies and license them as a package.

This definition would exclude a number of arrangements that may be included in a broader definition of a patent pool, including:[20]

- mandated patent pools, because the definition refers to 'agreements';
- cross-licensing agreements not involving licences to third parties; and
- patent clearing houses and similar mechanisms, the main purpose of which is to facilitate licensing arrangements by bringing together licensees and licensors but not licensing out patents as a single package.

[19] Commission Notice: Guidelines on the Application of Article 81 of the EC Treaty to Technology Transfer Agreements [2004] OJ C 101/02.

[20] See the discussion in Gaulé, 'Towards Patent Pools in Biotechnology?', above n. 6, 124.

In this chapter, we adopt a slightly broader view. Although we would not include patent clearing houses or simple cross-licensing arrangements in our definition, we do include non-voluntary patent pools in recognition of the fact that a number of proposals for patent pools for humanitarian use have involved options to mandate licensing to the pool.[21] Most of the industry patent pools that have developed to date have been voluntary in the sense that they have developed at the instigation of their members.[22] There have, however, been mandated patent pools where access to technologies was deemed necessary for reasons of public interest.[23]

An important component of patent pooling is the arrangements instituted in relation to pricing and royalty-sharing.[24] Methods of remunerating patent holders may vary, but are normally based on formulae that take into account the value of respective patents. Requests from potential licensees are often administered either through a management committee or through a separate company, particularly in the case of larger pools. The issue of remuneration is likely to be a major point of contention for humanitarian patent pooling. Working out a fair royalty for products created as a result of patent pooling at the delivery phase of the innovation cycle will always be challenging. But discovery phase patent pools are much more problematic because there are no products as such on which to levy royalties. The aim of patent pooling at this phase is to facilitate follow-on innovation rather than product development. Different methods of calibrating remuneration and valuation of contributions will need to be developed, particularly for drug discovery patent pools, given the long time lag between discovery and delivery.

Patent pools generally aggregate essential or complementary patents, thereby providing access to all of the essential components required to implement a particular technology or make a particular product.[25] Fundamentally, patent pools create FTO platforms in the patent landscape. The term 'assembly' has been used to describe this collation of disparate patent rights.[26] It is generally accepted that substitute or

[21] See, e.g., Essential Inventions Inc., *Essential Patent Pool for AIDS (EPPA): Background Information* (2005), www.essentialinventions.org/docs/eppa/ at 26 February 2009.

[22] Ibid. [23] Ibid.

[24] See Krattiger and Kowalski, 'Facilitating Assembly of and Access to Intellectual Property' above n. 8, 131.

[25] See Warren Kaplan, *Fostering R&D and Promoting Access to Medicines: Locating Common Ground: Operationalising Patent Pools for ARVs* (2007).

[26] Krattiger and Kowalski, 'Facilitating Assembly of and Access to Intellectual Property', above n. 8, 131.

competing patents should not be included because this may eliminate competition among licensors and thereby increase royalties, raising competition law concerns.[27] Rather, the driver is to include a core set of patents that parties wanting access must have.

It should be borne in mind that often 'the patent landscape in an industry falls far short of strict complementarity'.[28] Some have argued that this should not preclude the formation of pools if the benefits of forming an agreement outweigh the costs.[29] One question that needs to be answered by competition authorities is whether the requirements relating to essential patents should be applied to humanitarian patent pooling. Another concern is whether it is actually possible to identify essential and substitute patents for discovery phase patent pools, where there is a high level of uncertainty in the whole enterprise.

2.2 *Proposals for humanitarian patent pools for access to essential medicines*

The inclusion of patent pools on the IGWG agenda was largely at the instigation of Knowledge Ecology International ('KEI')[30] and Essential Inventions, Inc.[31] The efforts of these bodies in promoting collaborative patent-sharing strategies have demonstrated just how instrumental non-government organizations ('NGOs') can be in bringing matters to the attention of international organizations.[32] CPTech had earlier played an

[27] Krattiger *et al.*, 'Intellectual Property Management Strategies to Accelerate the Development and Access of Vaccines and Diagnostics', above n. 18, 68; and Richard J. Gilbert, 'Antitrust for Patent Pools: A Century of Policy Evolution' (2004) *Stanford Technology Law Review* 3.

[28] Robert Merges, 'Institutions for Intellectual Property Transactions: The Case of Patent Pools', in Rochelle C. Dreyfuss, Dianne Zimmerman and Harry First (eds.), *Expanding the Boundaries of Intellectual Property: Innovation Policy for the Knowledge Society* (2001), 164.

[29] Ibid., 163.

[30] See Judit Rius Sanjuam, 'Collective Management of Intellectual Property – Patent Pools to Expand Access to Essential Medical Technologies' (Research Note No 3(1), Knowledge Ecology International, 2007). Knowledge Ecology International ('KEI') is a corporate entity that was created in 2006 to support the Consumer Project on Technology ('CPTech'). See: www.keionline.org/index.php?option=com_frontpage&Itemid=1 at 2 March 2009.

[31] Essential Inventions, Inc. was also created by CPTech. See www.essentialinventions.org/ at 2 March 2009.

[32] See Noah Novogrodsky, 'Beyond TRIPS: The Role of Non-State Actors and Access to Essential Medicines', in Thomas Pogge, Matthew Rimmer and Kim Rubenstein (eds.), *Incentives for Global Public Health: Patent Law and Access to Essential Medicines* (2010), 343.

active role in urging the inclusion of patent pooling on the WHO agenda.[33] Collectively, these bodies have made various proposals for humanitarian patent pools in public health, going so far as to suggest that pooling could be mandated if patent holders expressed reluctance to voluntarily entering into such arrangements.[34]

The Commission on Intellectual Property Rights, Innovation and Public Health highlighted the role that patent pools might play in enhancing the discovery phase of the innovation cycle in its report to the WHO, stating that:

> [p]atent pools of upstream technologies may be useful in some circumstances to promote innovation relevant to developing countries. WHO and WIPO [the World Intellectual Property Organization] should consider playing a bigger role in promoting such arrangements, particularly to address diseases that disproportionately affect developing countries.[35]

The IGWG was established in 2006 by the World Health Assembly following receipt of the Report on Public Health, Innovation and Intellectual Property Rights from the Commission on Intellectual Property Rights, Innovation and Public Health[36] and recognition of the need to develop a global strategy and plan of action to support essential medical R&D.[37] From the outset, the IGWG recognized that the plan of action must address, *inter alia*, the development of capacities for the management of intellectual property and technologies in developing countries and the need for alternative incentive schemes for neglected infectious diseases.[38] The fact that the Commission's Report included consideration of a role for patent pooling necessarily meant that the IGWG also needed to consider the role that this strategy might take in supporting essential medical R&D. These intellectual property issues were recognized as being core components of the IGWG agenda even

[33] See, e.g., James Love, 'Proposal for an Essential Health Care Patent Pool' (Paper presented at the XIV International AIDS Conference, Barcelona, 8 July 2002).

[34] Ibid. See also Essential Inventions, Inc., *Essential Medical Inventions Licensing Agency Working Plan – June 2008* (rev. 17 July 2008), www.keionline.org/index.php?option=com_content&task=view&id=63&Itemid=1 at 2 March 2009.

[35] Commission on Intellectual Property Rights, Innovation and Public Health, *Public Health, Innovation and Intellectual Property Rights*, above n. 2, recommendation 2.8.

[36] Ibid.

[37] Public Health, Innovation, Essential Health Research and Intellectual Property Rights: Towards a Global Strategy and Plan of Action, 59th sess, WHA Res 59.24, article 2.

[38] World Health Organization, Regional Office for Europe, *Background Document for the Intergovernmental Working Group on Public Health, Innovation and Intellectual Property (IGWG) Process* (2007), 7–8.

though some delegations to the WHO doubted that intellectual property was within its remit.[39]

Ultimately the IGWG endorsed the view that the feasibility of voluntary patent pools warrants examination not just for upstream technologies, as recommended by the Commission, but also for downstream technologies. In parallel, KEI developed a proposal for an Essential Medical Inventions Licensing Agency ('EMILA'),[40] which includes model licensing-in and licensing-out agreements and authorizations with regard to health registration data. The EMILA's mission is 'to support the creation of one or more patent pools that facilitate the competitive manufacture and sale of medical products and vaccines'.[41] This mission suggests that the proposal focuses primarily on delivery phase pooling, although it is difficult to state with certainty that this is its intention.

3. The growth of patent pools as a method of intellectual property aggregation

Patent pools have been used in a variety of settings to facilitate innovation and clear patent bottlenecks.[42]

3.1 A potted history

Globally, patent pools have played a critical role in bringing new products to the market-place since the 1850s.[43]

3.1.1 Mandated pools

In some limited circumstances, patent pools have been mandated by government in order to facilitate the aggregation of key products, processes and technologies. In the early 1900s, for example, a patent pool was mandated in the US for aircraft manufacturing, resulting in the

[39] Ibid., 7.

[40] Essential Inventions, Inc., *Essential Medical Inventions Licensing Agency Working Plan*, above n. 34.

[41] Ibid., 4.

[42] The benefits that patent pools may offer are more fully explored below in section 4.1.

[43] Merges, 'Institutions for Intellectual Property Transactions', above n. 28, 133–153; Clark *et al.*, *Patent Pools*, above n. 14, 4; and David Serafino, 'Survey of Patent Pools Demonstrates Variety of Purposes and Management Structures' (Research Note No 6, Knowledge Ecology International, 2007).

creation of the Manufacturers Aircraft Association. The need for a mandatory patent pool arose at the onset of the First World War. Increased aircraft production was needed for the war effort, but manufacturers were being exposed to threats of infringement actions and high royalty charges by the relevant patent holders, the Wright brothers and Glenn Curtiss.[44] Jamie Love of KEI has likened this mandatory aircraft patent pool to assist with the war effort during the First World War to KEI's proposal for an essential medicines patent pool to facilitate the war on HIV/AIDS.[45] However, this example of a mandatory patent pool is most unusual.

3.1.2 Other 'delivery' phase pools

More often pools have been market-driven, developed privately at the instigation of industry members. For example, a patent pool was established in the sewing machine industry in 1856 in response to infringement litigation.[46] The pool created a benefit for consumers in that it allowed the design and manufacture for the first time of domestic sewing machines. However it also meant higher royalties could be charged.[47] A key feature of this and other patent pools is that they were created for the specific purpose of facilitating entry into the market of a new product that would otherwise be blocked because of strategic behaviour of certain patent holders and/or high transaction costs.[48] In each case, the permission of multiple patent holders was required for the manufacture of a single product. But frequent concerns have been raised that such pools have also encouraged anti-competitive conduct because they involved agreements between horizontal competitors.[49]

In contrast to these traditional patent pooling arrangements, proposals for discovery phase humanitarian patent pools focus on value adding for the purpose of facilitating downstream innovation rather than delivery of products to the market. Delivery phase patent pools in public health are more akin to the traditional pools. However, if such pools merely facilitate the delivery of new combinations of existing products (as is the case for the HIV/AIDS pool discussed below) then it would

[44] Ibid., 15. [45] Love, 'Proposal for an Essential Health Care Patent Pool', above n. 43.

[46] Serafino, 'Survey of Patent Pools Demonstrates Variety of Purposes and Management Structures', above n. 43, 3.

[47] Ibid.

[48] Richard Gold *et al.*, *Preliminary Legal Review of Proposed Medicines Patent Pool* (2007) 8–9.

[49] See, e.g., Gilbert, 'Antitrust for Patent Pools', above n. 27.

appear that their primary benefit is that they tend to reduce prices by encouraging competition rather than overcoming innovation problems associated with blocking and high transaction costs.[50]

3.1.3 Pools for standardization

Recently, there has been renewed interest in patent pooling internationally in a number of industries, particularly information technology software and hardware (examples include pools for MPEG and DVD technologies). The impetus for patent pooling in relation to such technologies is standardization. These industry sectors are characterized by multiple manufacturers and patents. Additionally, the products they produce are typically relatively inexpensive, and they are in areas where there is rapid consumer uptake of the technology. In such circumstances, the cost and time involved in inventing around patented technology or negotiating multiple licences and the public benefit to be gained from access to standardized technology have probably been the main drivers for pooling. In contrast, standardization is not a key feature of any of the proposed public health patent pools. Nor does it need to be: standardization is one basis on which patent pools may be entered into, but it is not an essential prerequisite as industry standards are not responsible for all transaction blockages.[51]

3.2 Patent pools for humanitarian purposes

The previous section has illustrated that the underlying rationale for humanitarian patent pooling may be quite different from that for traditional patent pooling. A number of patent pools are under consideration or in the process of being developed in areas where there is a perceived need for humanitarian intervention. These might provide more assistance in assessing the value of humanitarian patent pools more generally.

3.2.1 Delivery Phase – Golden Rice

A pool to collectively manage the patents relating to Golden Rice has been established to facilitate the provision of this technology to developing countries. The Golden Rice scenario is one of the few examples of a patent pool-like entity that is already established and operational in an

[50] On the latter point, see Gold *et al.*, *Preliminary Legal Review of Proposed Medicines Patent Pool*, above n. 48, 8–9.

[51] See Merges, 'Institutions for Intellectual Property Transactions', above n. 28, 163.

area of dire human need. The relevant technological development occurred in the 1980s, when Ingo Potrykus and Peter Beyer established a method for introducing genes into rice grains, which expressed b-carotene, a precursor to vitamin A.[52] By the time that the technology had been developed to the stage of commercial scale planting, around seventy relevant patents were in existence, held by multiple parties.[53]

The six key patent holders negotiated an agreement to license collectively and to distinguish between humanitarian use licences, which would be made available for free, and commercial licences, which were made available for a fee. A humanitarian board manages the licensing. Key aspects of the humanitarian use licences include, *inter alia*, that: the technology must be introduced into public seed varieties; no technology fee can be charged; sale and reuse of seed is authorized; improvements must be licensed for humanitarian use on the same terms.[54] Although there has been little or no use of the commercial licensing option to date, in many respects the Golden Rice patent pool resembles the traditional patent pool model established for aircraft,[55] sewing machines and the like. Effectively, the pool facilitates further development and delivery of a new product that might otherwise be delayed or prevented from market entry because of multiple potentially blocking patents.

The Golden Rice patent pool could provide a useful model for humanitarian patent pooling in public health. Certainly the willingness of commercial entities to accept management and licensing of their patents for humanitarian purposes is encouraging.[56] Indeed, the benefit to be gained from such altruistic acts in terms of positive publicity may be sufficient

[52] Ingo Potrykus, 'Golden Rice and Beyond' (2001) 125 *Plant Physiology* 1157. Vitamin A deficiency leads to a range of detrimental outcomes, including blindness and death, particularly affecting children.

[53] David Kryder, Stanley Kowalski and Anatole Krattiger, *The Intellectual and Technical Property Components of pro-Vitamin A Rice (GoldenRice^{TM}): A Preliminary Freedom-to-Operate Review* (2000).

[54] Anatole Krattiger and Ingo Potrykus, 'Golden Rice: A Product-Development Partnership in Agricultural Biotechnology and Humanitarian Licensing', in Anatole Krattiger *et al.* (eds.), *Executive Guide to Intellectual Property Management in Health and Agricultural Innovation: A Handbook of Best Practices* (2008) CS11.

[55] Although this patent pool differs in its mandatory nature.

[56] Other examples of co-operative non-commercial activities by commercial entities are also emerging. For example, the SNPs Consortium is a non-profit entity that was established to create a database of human single nucleotide polymorphisms to assist with mapping human genetic variation. It includes thirteen pharmaceutical and technology companies. See www.wellcome.ac.uk/Achievements-and-Impact/Initiatives/UK-biomedical-science/SNP-Consortium-and-International-HapMap/index.htm at 2 March 2009.

incentive of itself to encourage entry into such arrangements. However, these decisions are no doubt made easier by the fact that the discovery-to-delivery cycle is much shorter in agriculture than in healthcare. Once seeds have been genetically modified, they can be provided to multiple end users for planting without the need to expend significant development costs. By contrast, in public healthcare the huge financial and temporal investment required in the development phase must be taken into account because this is likely to be a significant deterrent for voluntary entry into pooling arrangements at both the discovery and delivery phase.

3.2.2 Delivery phase – HIV/AIDS

Various proposals have been put forward for patent pools in the area of access to essential medicines. One of the first such proposals – for an Essential Patent Pool for HIV/AIDS – was formally presented to the WHO, the Joint United Nations Programme on HIV/AIDS ('UNAIDS'), the Global Fund and the Secretariat to the Commission for Africa in January 2005 by Essential Inventions, Inc.[57] One key feature of the proposal is that owners would be asked to license voluntarily to the entity for use in low income countries, but if voluntary licensing were refused compulsory licences would be sought. While there is much promise in this proposal, the issue of compulsory licensing remains controversial.

More recently, the Board of UNITAID resolved to establish a patent pool for HIV/AIDS medications, focusing initially on paediatric ARVs and new combinations.[58] This resolution followed a submission by Médecins Sans Frontières to UNITAID proposing that a medicines patent pool should be established in this area, and a preliminary review of its legal feasibility conducted by The Innovation Partnership ('TIP') based at McGill University in Canada.[59] It was concluded by TIP that there was no legal reason to prevent the establishment of such a pool.[60] However, the group did express some reservations as to the legality of a pool based on non-voluntary licensing. As noted in the TIP report, the goals of a patent pool in this area are to:

[57] Documents relating to the proposal and model memoranda of understanding are available at: www.essentialinventions.org/docs/eppa/ at 2 March 2009.

[58] UNITAID identifies itself as an international drug purchase facility, established to provide long-term, sustainable and predictable funding to increase access and reduce prices of quality drugs and diagnostics for the treatment of HIV/AIDS, malaria and tuberculosis in developing countries. See www.unitaid.eu/ at 2 March 2009. See also UNITAID, 'UNITAID Moves towards a Patent Pool for Medicines', above n. 9.

[59] Gold *et al.*, *Preliminary Legal Review of Proposed Medicines Patent Pool*, above n. 48.

[60] Ibid., Executive Summary.

- put fixed-dose ARV combination medicines ('FDCs') and new formulations of existing medicines adapted to developing countries on the developing world market; and
- increase competition in the market for ARVs so as to lower prices through market forces.[61]

The situation with regard to the FDCs is quite unique when compared with other patent pools in that the products are already well established in the market-place. The drive here is to create new FDCs through a combination of existing products. These new FDCs will have the capacity to compete with existing FDCs and with other new FDCs, which is likely to increase competition but not necessarily encourage innovation.[62]

Medicines for diseases other than HIV/AIDS will not necessarily benefit from pooling if they are single products controlled by single dominant patents.[63] Patent pools will only come into play where multiple patents are essential to product manufacture and delivery. There may be scope for patent pooling in the delivery phase of public health innovation beyond the situation where new combinations of known medicines are required, for example, when particular formulations or delivery systems are essential to product delivery. In such scenarios, patent pooling could be both innovative and pro-competitive. More work needs to be done to map this part of the patent landscape to see if patent pooling is both necessary and feasible.

3.2.3 Discovery phase – SARS

Following the outbreak of severe acute respiratory syndrome ('SARS') in 2002 a number of laboratories were commissioned by the WHO to isolate and sequence the virus.[64] Following on from the successful sequencing effort, a number of patents were filed by the four main laboratories involved in the sequencing effort.[65] Before any patents were actually granted, the parties discussed the possibility of creating a patent pool. The WHO actively endorsed patent pooling to aggregate

[61] Ibid., 1. [62] See ibid., 8–9. [63] Ibid.

[64] For background see Matthew Rimmer, 'The Race to Patent the SARS Virus: The TRIPS Agreement and Access to Essential Medicines' (2004) 5 *Melbourne Journal of International Law* 335.

[65] These were the British Columbia Cancer Agency (patents were filed through Health Canada); Hong Kong University (through its technology transfer company, Versitech Ltd); Erasmus MC (through its spin out company CoroNovative BV); and the US Centers for Disease Control and Prevention. See James Simon *et al.*, 'Managing Severe Acute Respiratory Syndrome (SARS) Intellectual Property Rights: The Possible Role of Patent Pooling' (2005) 83 *Bulletin of the World Health Organization* 707.

patents over the SARS genome, recognizing that co-operation would promote the development of treatments and vaccines.[66]

The SARS scenario is different from the traditional model in a number of respects. First, the patent owners are mostly non-profit organizations. Other patent pools tend to be creatures of the commercial sector, or include at least some commercial partners.[67] Second, the technology is very much at the early discovery phase of the innovation cycle rather than the downstream delivery phase. Third, the patents have not yet been issued and so the scope of their claims is not yet known.[68] Finally, once issued, the patents may be competing rather than complementary, given that each of the participants was involved in sequencing the virus.[69]

While the SARS proposal might have provided a useful model for more broadly based discovery phase patent pooling, further development of the pool has been stalled given that there is no pressing need to develop a SARS vaccine at the present time. As a consequence, this model provides only limited assistance in our assessment of the potential role for humanitarian discovery phase patent pools in supporting essential medical R&D. Other discovery phase public health patent pools are likely to share many of the features of the proposed SARS pool, and may face many of the same hurdles.

3.2.4 Discovery through to delivery – vaccines for influenza, malaria and other pandemics

The proposed SARS pool focused very much on the most upstream discovery phase patents over viruses and gene sequences. There has been some discussion of a broader role for patent pooling in relation to other infectious diseases across the whole innovation cycle: of upstream virus identification and vaccine discovery, vaccine development including testing and regulatory approvals and vaccine delivery.[70] The scope of the problem and the urgent need to find solutions are illustrated by the preliminary FTO exercise carried out by Krattiger *et al.* to elucidate the

[66] Ibid. [67] This was the case with the Golden Rice pool.

[68] Krattiger *et al.*, 'Intellectual Property Management Strategies to Accelerate the Development and Access of Vaccines and Diagnostics', above n. 18, 69, also mention the impossibility of pooling 'tentative' intellectual property 'because no one knows how essential the IP [intellectual property] is, how valuable it is, or whether it confers market power'.

[69] On these points, see also Nicol and Hope, 'Cooperative Strategies for Facilitating Use of Patented Inventions in Biotechnology', above n. 6.

[70] See, e.g., Commission on Intellectual Property Rights, Innovation and Public Health, *Public Health, Innovation and Intellectual Property Rights*, above n. 2, 131.

likely number of relevant patents at each of the phases of the innovation cycle for pandemic influenza vaccines.[71] They estimated that there were a total of 118 relevant patents spanning the cycle and 10 major patent holders. In the delivery phase alone, they counted 17 patents controlled by 12 different parties.[72] Another group has estimated that 167 patent families are relevant in the malaria vaccine innovation cycle, filed by 75 different entities.[73]

Whether patent pooling would provide a solution to the problems created by these complex patent landscapes is a matter of debate. Broad pooling across the whole of the innovation cycle is fundamentally different from the traditional patent pool model. A difficulty with such proposed pools is that they aim to create an FTO path through the entire patent landscape rather than a horizontal FTO platform.[74] In such an environment, matters of essentiality, complementarity, patent validity, assembly and maintenance costs and remuneration could become intractable.

4. Benefits and costs of patent pooling

4.1 The benefits of patent pooling

Patent pools offer a number of benefits to patent holders and to third parties in the usual commercial context. First, they can overcome blocking patents that would be infringed in the course of practising another invention.[75] Second, patent pools reduce transaction costs by allowing potential licensees to negotiate with a single party.[76] They have the added benefit of reducing the considerable costs of patent mapping, not only because they reduce the need for patent searching and analysis, but also because they provide more certainty that the patents offered for licence are valid.[77] Third, they may circumvent problems associated with royalty

[71] Krattiger *et al.*, 'Intellectual Property Management Strategies to Accelerate the Development and Access of Vaccines and Diagnostics', above n. 18, 78.

[72] Ibid. [73] Ibid., 80. [74] Ibid.

[75] Steven C. Carlson, 'Patent Pools and the Antitrust Dilemma' (1999) 16 *Yale Journal on Regulation* 359; and Josh Lerner and Jean Tirole, 'Public Policy toward Patent Pools' (2007) *Innovation Policy and the Economy* 9.

[76] Merges, 'Institutions for Intellectual Property Transactions', above n. 28. Transaction costs include costs such as patent mapping and searching, and approaching and negotiating with licensees. These costs are exacerbated when negotiating with a multitude of patent holders.

[77] Gaulé, 'Towards Patent Pools in Biotechnology?', above n. 6, 126.

stacking. To this extent, pooling arrangements may remove the perceived burden that can arise from the 'tragedy of the anti-commons'.[78] Fourth, intellectual property other than patents may be included in the pool. This is particularly important because it may result in the disclosure of technical know-how related to patented inventions that would ordinarily be protected as a trade secret.[79] These benefits are all likely to have some relevance with regard to humanitarian patent pooling. Patent pools also present additional specific advantages for pool members. For discovery phase pools, the risks associated with R&D can be shared among pool members.[80] Combining the technical knowledge of a number of entities can lead to new and superior innovation.[81] Finally, patent pools eliminate the need for individual firms to manage their own patents, and where the control of litigation is centralized,[82] the burden of identifying infringers is passed on to the pool's administration.[83]

Where patent pools are being considered for humanitarian purposes, clearly they can provide significant social benefit. This should be taken into account in evaluating their worth. This social gain, along with other benefits such as the potential for reducing transaction costs, should be a significant factor in any evaluation as to the efficacy of a particular pooling arrangement. We do recognize that this social benefit may be more readily calculable for delivery phase pools, as opposed to more upstream discovery phase pools.

4.2 Costs of patent pools

There are also a number of potential costs associated with patent pooling, two of which are highlighted in this section.

[78] Heller and Eisenberg, 'Can Patents Deter Innovation?', above n. 13. A 'tragedy of the anti-commons' may arise where a complex patent landscape necessitates bargaining to gain access to a multitude of overlapping property rights over potential products or resources, or where the use of reach-through claims leads to licence stacking.

[79] Van Overwalle *et al.*, 'Models for Facilitating Access to Patents on Genetic Inventions', above n. 6, 144.

[80] Carlson, 'Patent Pools and the Antitrust Dilemma', above n. 75, 381–2.

[81] Clark *et al.*, *Patent Pools*, above n. 14, 8–10. This of course assumes that innovation is a component of the activities carried out by pool members, i.e., that the pool is a discovery phase pool.

[82] Josh Lerner, Jean Tirole and Marcin Strojwas, 'Cooperative Marketing Agreements between Competitors: Evidence From Patent Pools' (National Bureau of Economic Research Working Paper No 9680, 2003), 7–8, 22.

[83] Merges, 'Institutions for Intellectual Property Transactions', above n. 28.

4.2.1 Return on investment

Patent holders will have already made a significant investment in R&D in the process of creating patentable inventions or facilitating their creation, and will invariably be seeking to recover their costs. As a general rule, patent holders will need to be convinced that entry into a patent pool will secure return on investment better than working outside the pooling arrangement. One difficulty is that patent pools could actually lead to increased complexity and transaction costs.[84] They are expensive to establish and administer, and this tends to lessen the incentive to voluntarily enter into pooling arrangements.[85]

These factors have serious implications from the humanitarian perspective, because pools are far less likely to be viable where patent holders face the very real possibility that commercial returns will not be forthcoming. This raises particular concerns for discovery phase patent pools, where, even if the research has signs of being commercially promising, there can be no guarantee of any return on investment. The difficulty in accurately valuing intellectual property may also result in some pool members being inadequately remunerated, further deterring entry into pooling arrangements.[86] In the public health context, it would seem that patent pooling is only likely to be a viable strategy if, at the very least, the significant costs associated with establishment and administration are borne by a benefactor. Finding such a benefactor would be no easy task,[87] and even if one is found, patent holders may still prefer to work outside the pool because they remain unconvinced that entry into the pool is a better strategy for recovery of investment in R&D.

A major impediment to pool formation in public health also stems from the fact that the interests of pool members are frequently non-aligned.[88] This non-alignment issue is likely to be most pronounced for pools that attempt to span the whole innovation cycle. Holders of upstream research tool patents have very different motivations from holders of

84 Shapiro, 'Navigating the Patent Thicket: Cross Licences, Patent Pools and Standard-Setting', above n. 13.

85 Krattiger *et al.*, 'Intellectual Property Management Strategies to Accelerate the Development and Access of Vaccines and Diagnostics', above n. 18, 74. These authors estimate that around twenty-five parties would be required to establish a patent pool for vaccines, at a cost of around US$30 million over five years.

86 Van Overwalle *et al.*, 'Models for Facilitating Access to Patents on Genetic Inventions', above n. 6.

87 Krattiger *et al.*, 'Intellectual Property Management Strategies to Accelerate the Development and Access of Vaccines and Diagnostics', above n. 18, 68.

88 Ibid., 85.

downstream formulation patents, for example. Patents included in such pools are also likely to be owned by diverse parties, including research institutions, specialized research firms and pharmaceutical companies. Disparate rationales for entry into pooling agreements could result in bargaining failure between pool members.[89] Valuation issues are also likely to be intensified by this disparity. There is a further risk that not all relevant patents will be included in the pool.

It will often be difficult to determine essentiality, although this can be overcome by appointing an expert to determine the composition of the pool. A further deterrent to entering pools is the risk of freeriding by particular pool members where some patents are more 'essential' than others.[90] It is markedly easier to determine essentiality where patent pools arise from a necessity to co-ordinate industry standards.[91] Such pools directly benefit consumers by assisting in *establishing* industry standards. Biomedicine and public health lack such standards.[92] The Organisation for Economic Co-operation and Development has also highlighted the lack of any requirement for standards as being a major point of distinction between biomedicine and other industries.[93] Certainly it would make determining the issue of essentiality more difficult.[94] However, as we have pointed out, it should not be fatal to the formation of patent pools. The central issue for consideration remains the same: do the benefits of forming the pool outweigh the costs?[95]

4.2.2 Patent pools and competition law

Because they involve the horizontal aggregation of patent rights, patent pools may result in anti-competitive conduct. In recent years, regulators in a number of jurisdictions, most notably the US and the EU, have focused attention on developing guidelines to address emerging concerns

[89] Gaulé, 'Towards Patent Pools in Biotechnology?', above n. 6.

[90] Reiko Aoki and Sadao Nagaoka, 'The Consortium Standard and Patent Pools' (2004) 55 *The Economic Review* 345; and Krattiger *et al.*, 'Intellectual Property Management Strategies to Accelerate the Development and Access of Vaccines and Diagnostics', above n. 18.

[91] The primary examples are the MPEG-2 and DVD pools as well as the 3G platform. For further details on the parties to these pools see Gaulé, 'Towards Patent Pools in Biotechnology?', above n. 6, 124–5.

[92] See, e.g., Larry Horn, 'Alternative Approaches to IP Management: One-Stop Technology Platform Licensing' (2003) 9 *Journal of Commercial Biotechnology* 119.

[93] Organisation for Economic Co-operation and Development, *Genetic Inventions, Intellectual Property Rights and Licensing Practices*, above n. 14.

[94] Gaulé, 'Towards Patent Pools in Biotechnology?', above n. 6, 128.

[95] Merges, 'Institutions for Intellectual Property Transactions', above n. 28.

related to intellectual property management strategies, including the applicability of patent pooling in various industry sectors. The US anti-trust authorities have reviewed a considerable number of patent pools,[96] and the anti-competitive implications of pooling are well recognized.[97] At the same time, their pro-competitive potential has resulted in the approval by competition law authorities of a considerable number of patent pools.[98]

The US anti-trust authorities have established some parameters pertaining to the legality of patent pooling arrangements. Their *Antitrust Guidelines for the Licensing of Intellectual Property* acknowledge that patent pools can provide pro-competitive benefits by 'integrating complementary technologies, reducing transaction costs, clearing blocking positions, and avoiding costly infringement litigation'.[99] At the same time, they outline a number of possible anti-competitive consequences.[100] A number of complex questions raised in review letters issued by the Department of Justice[101] have now been condensed into the following two questions:

> (1) whether the proposed licensing program ... is likely to integrate complementary patent rights and if so;
> (2) whether the resulting competitive benefits are likely to be outweighed by competitive harm posed by other aspects of the program.[102]

[96] See, e.g., Serafino, 'Survey of Patent Pools Demonstrates Variety of Purposes and Management Structures', above n. 43.

[97] See, e.g., United States Department of Justice and the Federal Trade Commission, *Antitrust Enforcement and Intellectual Property Rights: Promoting Innovation and Competition* (2007) ch. 3, www.usdoj.gov/atr/public/hearings/ip/222655.pdf at 2 March 2009; Joel Klein, 'Cross Licensing and Antitrust Law' (Speech delivered at the San Antonio Marriott Rivercenter, Texas, 2 May 1997); and Clark *et al.*, *Patent Pools*, above n. 14, 10–11.

[98] For a detailed history see Serafino, 'Survey of Patent Pools Demonstrates Variety of Purposes and Management Structures', above n. 43; and United States Department of Justice and the Federal Trade Commission, *Antitrust Enforcement and Intellectual Property Rights: Promoting Innovation and Competition*, above n. 97, 68–74.

[99] United States Department of Justice and the Federal Trade Commission, *Antitrust Guidelines for the Licensing of Intellectual Property* (1995) § 5.5.

[100] Ibid. See further the discussion below.

[101] United States Department of Justice, 'Letter from Joel Klein to Gerrard Beeney' (26 June 1997) ('MPEG-LA Review Letter'); United States Department of Justice, 'Letter from Joel Klein to Gerrard Beeney' (16 December 1998) ('Sony Review Letter'); and United States Department of Justice, 'Letter from Joel Klein to Carey Ramos' (10 June 1999) ('Toshiba Review Letter'). These letters are available at www.usdoj.gov/atr/public/busreview/letters.htm at 2 March 2009 .

[102] Toshiba Review Letter, above n. 107.

The EU places similar emphasis on the nature of the pooled technologies in determining whether patent pools are likely to have a pro-competitive or anti-competitive effect.[103] The relevant guidelines presume that patent pools comprised of substitute technologies are likely to be anti-competitive, whilst pools made up of essential technologies are likely to be competitively beneficial.[104] The guidelines also provide guidance on licence terms commonly included in pooling agreements. For example, they specify that licences should be non-exclusive,[105] and that all relevant parties must be free to develop competing products and grant licences outside the pool.[106] The important point is that in the jurisdictions where these matters have been explored, determining essentiality is the key to ascertaining the competitive impact of a patent pool.

There are a number of competition law concerns relevant to the questions we explore in this chapter. In particular, patent pools could facilitate collusion and price-fixing because they may involve agreements between horizontal competitors and prevent other firms from competing.[107] As should be evident, patent pools are more likely to come to the attention of competition law authorities where substitute (rather than complementary) technologies are combined,[108] because complementary technologies would be less likely to compete in any case. Careful consideration of which patents are to be included in the pool would eliminate the risk of collusion and price fixing, although identifying whether patents are complementary (essential) or not is far from straightforward.[109] If patents were pooled for humanitarian purposes, collusion is less likely to be an issue because a careful evaluation of the patent landscape would be bound to have occurred prior to formation of the pool. If anything, such a pool would be subject to greater scrutiny than many other pooling arrangements due to the interest it would be likely to generate.

A related concern is that patent pools may inflate the cost of products produced by the pool, because patents that are legally blocking may be

[103] Commission Notice: Guidelines on the Application of Article 81 of the EC Treaty to Technology Transfer Agreements, above n. 19.

[104] Ibid., [219]–[221]. [105] Ibid., [226]. [106] Ibid., [227].

[107] Carlson, 'Patent Pools and the Antitrust Dilemma', above n. 75, 388–92.

[108] United States Department of Justice and the Federal Trade Commission, *Antitrust Enforcement and Intellectual Property Rights: Promoting Innovation and Competition*, above n. 97, 74–8.

[109] Ibid., 74. As pointed out in this report, different pools may employ different methods of essentiality: ibid., 74–75. See also Carlson, 'Patent Pools and the Antitrust Dilemma', above n. 75, 365–7.

factually competitive.[110] A patent pool would thus protect pool members and allow them to charge monopoly prices where they would ordinarily be prevented by competitors from doing so.[111] Again, careful evaluation of patents included in pooling arrangements is perhaps the best solution.[112]

Patent pools may also disadvantage licensees by requiring them to license all the patents in a package, even those that are not required by a particular licensee.[113] It is unlikely that a carefully tailored pool for the delivery of essential medicines would present such a difficulty, as potential licensees are likely to want access to all relevant patents. The proposed UNITAID patent pool provides a good example; current evaluations of the proposal include a careful compilation of the patents required to facilitate delivery of FDCs to licensees. For treatment to be effective, patients need access to the entire suite of patents. The situation is not so clear-cut where proposals for discovery phase patent pools are concerned.

Another issue is that patent pools may shield invalid patents.[114] However, the Federal Trade Commission has included processes to exclude invalid patents from pools it has approved, thereby alleviating this concern.[115] Patent pools developed for humanitarian purposes could similarly be protected in this way.

Finally, patent pooling agreements may include anti-competitive licence terms. For example, patent holders may be required to license exclusively to a pool,[116] while licensees may be forced to exclusively license to the pool any improvements made to the patented technology.[117] It would not be difficult for competition law authorities to scrutinize pool agreements to examine these terms. However, it is unlikely where patents are being sought to enable access to medicines by developing countries that there would be any real need to include these terms. Thus, this concern is likely to have little basis in reality. One matter that may be of concern is the royalties charged by the pool to outsiders in the event that the fees are higher than those proposed to be

[110] Ibid., 386. [111] Ibid. [112] Clark *et al.*, *Patent Pools*, above n. 14, 10.

[113] Carlson, 'Patent Pools and the Antitrust Dilemma', above n. 75, 388–90.

[114] Clark *et al.*, *Patent Pools*, above n. 14, 10–11.

[115] See, e.g., 'MPEG-LA Review Letter', above n. 101, 5.

[116] United States Department of Justice and the Federal Trade Commission, *Antitrust Enforcement and Intellectual Property Rights: Promoting Innovation and Competition*, above n. 97, 78–80.

[117] Known as a grant-back provision. For further discussion see ibid., 80–1.

charged to pool members.[118] Competition law authorities will generally not review royalties charged by patent pools, but will instead be concerned more with structure. Hence, licensees are more or less at the mercy of the pool and must accept the fee charged. It would be hoped that a pool established primarily for humanitarian purposes would offer licences at a reasonable royalty. This is, after all, a primary motivation for the establishment of a humanitarian pool.

To summarize, competition law concerns are unlikely to be especially problematic in relation to humanitarian patent pools that involve delivery of a specific drug or area of technology. It is difficult to imagine that a patent pool established for this purpose would be borne from a desire to act anti-competitively. Instead, the opposite is more likely to be true. At this stage of the innovation cycle, a comprehensive FTO analysis will have been completed. Essentiality will have been established and the downstream nature of the technology means that patents to be included in the pool will have been carefully considered. This will not be the case with more upstream research pools. Patent holders in such circumstances will need to be more mindful of competition law concerns, because the uncertain nature of the discovery process means that essentiality will be difficult to determine. Gaining the approval of competition law authorities may well be difficult.

TIP's review of the proposed UNITAID patent pool includes some limited consideration of the application of competition law.[119] The proposed patent pool would be established and administered in Switzerland, with most licensees from African and Asian countries. Competition laws of Switzerland would govern the formation and administration of the pool. The relevant legislation in Switzerland contains an exemption from competition laws for agreements that are necessary to safeguard a compelling public interest.[120] Although this provision may well be invoked to protect the UNITAID pool from strict compliance with competition law requirements, it would be less effective in the case of a general discovery phase pool. In such a case it would be difficult to tell whether the research being conducted is in the public interest because the research outcomes are unknown. Further, at this

[118] Where the pool comprises upstream patents this might have a corresponding effect on downstream competition: ibid., 82–3.

[119] See Gold *et al.*, *Preliminary Legal Review of Proposed Medicines Patent Pool*, above n. 48, 22–4.

[120] Federal Act on Cartels and Other Restraints on Competition of 6 October 1995 (Switzerland), article 8. Application to the Federal Council is required.

stage, the conduct of research is unlikely to be restricted to a single jurisdiction. The different competition laws of each jurisdiction would need to be considered, creating difficulties for pool members. In the case of delivery phase pools, the manufacture of drugs under licence would attract the competition laws in all relevant jurisdictions, and the competition laws of importing countries would also become applicable. This highlights the need to ensure the pool is not anti-competitive, because few jurisdictions have a 'public interest' exception in their competition legislation.

4.3 *Balancing the benefits and risks*

Clearly, patent pooling can offer significant benefits to pool participants, licensees and the community at large by facilitating innovation and encouraging competition. However, there are significant costs, particularly the financial risks for participants and the risks associated with anti-competitive conduct, both for competitors to pooling arrangements and for the broader community. Over time, structures have developed to ensure that the benefits of patent pooling are maximized and the costs minimized.

Aside from these general benefits and costs, humanitarian patent pooling raises new challenges. Its significant benefit is the facilitation of R&D in neglected areas for the benefit of the world's poor and sick and the actual delivery of healthcare products to those individuals. However, it is important to recognize that humanitarian patent pooling simply provides the FTO platform to achieve these ends. It is not an end in itself.[121] Even if on balance the benefits of patent pooling outweigh the costs, voluntary participation may still not be forthcoming due to complexity, time, expense, loss of exclusivity and inability to engage with all relevant parties. As such, enthusiasm for the adoption of voluntary patent pooling mechanisms by academics, policy-makers and NGOs does need to be tempered to some extent to reflect industry concerns. On the other hand, it may be that the industry is more willing to contribute to humanitarian pools than more commercially oriented pools because of the benefits associated with being seen to be 'doing the right thing'. But they will only do so if the pools are carefully structured so that they do not impinge on commercial markets or compromise intellectual property rights and do not require significant input of time or money.

[121] Krattiger *et al.*, 'Intellectual Property Management Strategies to Accelerate the Development and Access of Vaccines and Diagnostics', above n. 18.

5. Conclusion: are patent pools really a solution to the conundrum?

As we have outlined, there have been a number of proposals for patent pools to facilitate access to essential medicines, some of which have focused on the delivery of established medicines, and others that have been more expansive in their approach. A number of general observations may be made that go some way towards explaining why we aren't seeing a higher level of uptake of these proposals. To reiterate, our view is that delivery phase pools (such as the HIV/AIDS pool where a specific combination of patents is required to enable delivery of the required drugs) will often be more viable proposals than discovery phase ones. However, this is only likely to be the case where a clearly defined set of patents is required to tackle a particular disease. Where the patent landscape around a disease or drug is simpler, it is difficult to perceive a need for pooling arrangements.

Attempting to formulate a broader structure will be problematic. The EMILA proposal, for example, elucidates that its strategy is to facilitate the formation of pools that 'may be national, regional or multilateral, and they may (or may not) be limited to specific diseases or conditions, depending on the objectives of the partners'.[122] This ambitious attempt to form an overarching body to administer multiple patent pools aimed at facilitating access to essential medicines is unlikely to encourage their formation, because as we have stressed, pools are only likely to form under very specific circumstances. The huge administrative burden associated with pool formation means that critical mass is required before patent pools become viable.[123] As a general matter, due to the structure of the biomedical and pharmaceutical industries, there is significant non-alignment of interests. Research within the industry is intensely cumulative, and the diverse range of players compete with each other at various levels. Many universities and specialized research firms hold important patent portfolios, but exclusive licensing is frequently their preferred option for technology transfer. It may be difficult to persuade them out of this 'bunker mentality'.[124]

[122] Essential Inventions, Inc., *Essential Medical Inventions Licensing Agency Working Plan*, above n. 34, 5.

[123] See, e.g., Krattiger *et al.*, 'Intellectual Property Management Strategies to Accelerate the Development and Access of Vaccines and Diagnostics', above n. 18, 74–5.

[124] Horn, 'Alternative Approaches to IP Management', above n. 92, 123.

Discovery phase pools seeking to clear an FTO path will typically involve more uncertainty than delivery phase pools. This uncertainty stems from the fact that at an upstream stage of the research, there is no clear indication of what the patent landscape will look like and as a consequence it is difficult to predict whether a patent pool is needed. The difficulty in gauging essentiality also raises competition law concerns. At this stage, pooling is unlikely to be the most effective strategy for facilitating FTO and other forms of collaboration may well be more effective.

As an example, contrast the SARS virus with the SNP Consortium. For SARS, there is no reason to believe that patenting was the best strategy in the circumstances, or that the patent landscape would have been simplified through use of a patent pool, or even that effective collaboration could not have been achieved in other ways. The SNP Consortium provides a compelling example of the benefits of a low-cost collaborative structure outside the patent model.[125] In other circumstances, simple licensing agreements are likely to prove (and have to date proved) just as effective. The research exemption might also constitute a powerful tool to work around a crowded upstream research path.[126]

The Health Impact Fund proposed by Thomas Pogge is a further interesting alternative to pooling at the discovery phase.[127] On the assumption that the incentives it provides are an attractive enough inducement to discourage worldwide patenting, it constitutes a possible adjunct to the patent system that might just remove the impediments wrought by the patent system that appear to make discovery phase pooling such an attractive option.

In short, patent pools may be useful in a narrowly defined set of circumstances, but usually it will not be until medicines are ready for the delivery phase that the patent landscape will reveal whether or not patent pools can be usefully employed. One role for discovery phase patent pooling might be the creation of a pooled toolbox of generic research tools for all biomedical research, but the need for and feasibility of establishing such an entity remains to be determined.

[125] See Francis Collins, Mark Guyer and Aravinda Chakravarti, 'Variations on a Theme: Cataloguing Human DNA Sequence Variation' (1997) 278 *Science* 1580.

[126] See, e.g., Van Overwalle *et al.*, 'Models for Facilitating Access to Patents on Genetic Inventions', above n. 6, 143–4.

[127] Thomas Pogge, 'The Health Impact Fund: Better Pharmaceutical Innovations at Much Lower Prices', in Thomas Pogge, Matthew Rimmer and Kim Rubenstein (eds.), *Incentives for Global Public Health: Patent Law and Access to Essential Medicines* (2010), 135.

We have no doubt that patent pools may be useful for the delivery of drugs where the patent landscape is well established, and patents can be non-exclusively licensed into a pool for a defined field of use,[128] leaving patent holders free to license elsewhere. Although mandatory participation is a feature of some proposals,[129] we strongly support voluntary participation as the most viable option.[130] Incentives for joining patent pools could be considered. Just as prizes have been suggested as an incentive to encourage innovation,[131] they may be useful at a more downstream level, that is, to encourage licensing into a pool.[132] To this extent, they could form a supplement to the patent system.[133] The key here is to garner agreement between relevant patent holders, to ensure that access to all relevant patents is forthcoming.

While the focus of this chapter is on a particular mechanism that might achieve FTO within the existing patent regime, the varied mechanisms that are being canvassed by policy-makers, academics and NGOs should not in any way be seen as mutually incompatible. Rather, the aim of this collection of proposed mechanisms should be to provide a mutually supportive package of strategies for improving access to essential medicines overall. In order to achieve this end, it is necessary to properly assess and evaluate each option so that effort is directed towards implementing those strategies that are most likely to be of both immediate and long-term benefit.

[128] Horn, 'Alternative Approaches to IP Management', above n. 92.

[129] See, e.g., Essential Inventions, Inc., *Essential Patent Pool for AIDS (EPPA)*, above n. 21.

[130] See, e.g., Gold *et al.*, *Preliminary Legal Review of Proposed Medicines Patent Pool*, above n. 48, 38–41.

[131] Matthew Rimmer, 'The Lazarus Effect: The (RED) Campaign and Creative Capitalism', in Thomas Pogge, Matthew Rimmer and Kim Rubenstein (eds.), *Incentives for Global Public Health: Patent Law and Access to Essential Medicines* (2010), 313.

[132] James Love and Tim Hubbard, 'The Big Idea: Prizes to Stimulate R&D for New Medicines' (2007) 82 *Chicago-Kent Law Review* 1519, 1535–6. Essential Invention's *Working Plan* suggests that eligibility for innovation prizes could be tied with voluntary participation in patent pooling: Essential Inventions, Inc., *Essential Medical Inventions Licensing Agency Working Plan*, above n. 34, 9.

[133] See also Joseph Stiglitz, 'Scrooge and Intellectual Property Rights: A Medical Prize Fund Could Improve the Financing of Drug Innovations' (2006) 333 *British Medical Journal* 1279.

10

Open Source drug discovery: a revolutionary paradigm or a Utopian model?

KRISHNA RAVI SRINIVAS

1. Introduction

The success of Open Source software has attracted much attention and the applicability of Open Source models in non-software contexts has been proposed as an alternative innovation model and as a solution to some of the problems with the current intellectual property system.[1] In recent years the applicability of Open Source models for drug discovery and development has been discussed in academic literature.[2] Although there is much scepticism about the proposal to extend Open Source models/licences to non-software contexts, there is a growing interest in applying them in fields like biology and biotechnology, partly because of the success of non-proprietary initiatives like

[1] On Open Source software, see generally Steve Weber, *The Success of Open Source* (2004). On the applicability of Open Source strategies in non-software contexts, see Janet Hope, *BioBazaar: The Open Source Revolution and Biotechnology* (2008); Katherine Nolan-Stevaux, 'Open Source Biology' (2007) 23 *Santa Clara Computer & High Technology Law Journal* 271; Arti Rai, 'Proprietary Rights and Collective Action: The Case of Biotechnology Research with Low Commercial Value', in Keith Maskus and Jerome Reichman (eds.), *International Public Goods and Transfer of Technology* (2005) 288; and Krishna Ravi Srinivas, 'Intellectual Property Rights and Bio Commons: Open Source and Beyond' (2006) 58(188) *International Social Science Journal* 319.

[2] Stephen Maurer, 'Open Source Drug Discovery: Finding a Niche (Or Maybe Several)' (2007) 76 *University of Missouri at Kansas City Law Review* 405; Aled Edwards, 'Open Source Science to Enable Drug Discovery' (2008) 13 *Drug Discovery Today* 731; Maurice Schellekens, 'Open Source Biotechnology: A Drug for Developing Countries' Health Problems' (10 May 2007) *Social Sciences Research Network*, papers.ssrn.com/sol3/papers.cfm?abstract_id=1130798 at 3 March 2009; Stephen Maurer, Arti Rai and Andrej Sali, 'Finding Cures for Tropical Diseases: Is Open Source an Answer?' (2004) 1 *Public Library of Science, Medicine* 183; and Bernard Munos, 'Can Open Source R&D Reinvigorate Drug Research' (2006) 5 *Nature Reviews Drug Discovery* 723.

the SNP Consortium[3] and the HapMap project[4] and also because of initiatives like BIOS.[5] In this chapter it is suggested that Open Source drug discovery ('OSDD') is a workable idea that deserves support to enable it to be tested in the real world.[6] It is also contended that OSDD can be used with other initiatives to overcome the twin problems of access and affordability, although at this time one cannot assert that OSDD is always compatible with other proposals. Finally, OSDD is no panacea for all of the problems with pharmaceutical innovation, access and affordability. Its potential is untested but in the long run it may emerge as a workable model in drug discovery for neglected diseases and as a framework that is well suited for co-operation among developing countries in finding cures for diseases in those countries.[7] OSDD as a paradigm challenges the conventional wisdom on the role of intellectual property rights in drug discovery and development but this paradigm can coexist with the other frameworks in the larger innovation ecosystem.[8] As in the case of Open Source software, it might be possible to create hybrid models that 'mix' both proprietary and non-proprietary paradigms of ownership and use. It may be possible to use OSDD for some specific purposes, to create mechanisms and arrangements to fulfil objectives like creating a commons, and to use licences to ensure that mutual interests are not overridden by proprietary rights.

What exactly is Open Source is difficult to define as the phrase has been used in different contexts to denote different things including: a form of licensing; a mode of producing goods through collaboration; the development of software; production of knowledge including databases through collaboration; and software code that is not encumbered by

[3] Gudmundur Thorisson and Lincoln Stein, 'The SNP Consortium Website: Past, Present and Future' (2003) 31 *Nucleic Acids Research* 124–7.

[4] HapMap Project, www.hapmap.org/.

[5] BIOS, www.bios.net/daisy/bios/home.html.

[6] For reasons of space I am not discussing many issues in / aspects of OSDD and am avoiding detailed analysis of various types of licences or initiatives like BIOS. I hope to do an extensive analysis of these on another occasion.

[7] This does not mean that developing nations alone can solve the problem of finding cures for neglected diseases. While OSDD is a good model for South–South co-operation in drug discovery, it alone cannot solve all problems in finding cures for neglected/tropical diseases.

[8] If Open Source drug R&D takes hold, what will probably emerge is not replacement of one model by another, but an ecology in which big pharma, biotech and collaborative research compete and collaborate at the same time, feeding off each other synergistically while moving towards therapies along their own distinctive paths: Munos, 'Can Open Source R&D Reinvigorate Drug Research', above n. 2.

patent rights. Often 'open' and 'closed' are used to denote opposites like free for all and proprietary mechanism. Hence the note of caution expressed by Steve Weber is appropriate.[9]

Open Source biology or Open Source biotechnology need not be synonymous with what is known as Open Science. Although there are some parallels with the Mertonian paradigm of science, the Open Source mode of production is more complex in terms of organization and legal licences. The incentive system is also different from that of science.[10] Open Source is also considered as a mode of governance, bazaar governance.[11]

2. Intellectual property rights, innovation and access to drugs: issues and initiatives

There is already a large body of literature on the subject of intellectual property rights, innovation and access to pharmaceuticals.[12] While the report of the Commission on Intellectual Property Rights, Innovation and Public Health gives an excellent overview of the issues and solutions, for reasons of space I will not cover the report and subsequent developments at the World Health Organization ('WHO') or related developments in the World Intellectual Property Organization ('WIPO') and the World Trade Organization ('WTO').[13]

9 As Open Source technology has begun to attract broad public attention over the last few years, the term itself has been overused as a metaphor: generally Weber, *The Success of Open Source*, above n. 1, 267.

10 See generally Joseph Feller *et al.* (eds.), *Perspectives on Free and Open Source Software* (2005). See also Rai, 'Proprietary Rights and Collective Action', above n. 1.

11 Benoit Demil and Xavier Lecocq, 'Neither Market nor Hierarchy nor Network: The Emergence of Bazaar Governance' (2006) 27 *Organization Studies* 1447. For a comparison of Open Source and 'Open Technology' see Alessandro Nuvolari and Francesco Rullani, 'Curious Exceptions? Open Source Software and "Open" Technology', in Kirk St Amant and Brian Still (eds.), *Handbook of Research on Open Source Software: Technological, Economic and Social Perspectives* (2007) 227.

12 See, e.g., Draft Global Strategy and Plan of Action on Public Health, Innovation and Intellectual Property, WIPO Doc A/PHI/IGWG/2/INF.DOC./6 (31 August 2007) (Intergovernmental Working Group on Public Health, Innovation and Intellectual Property – Provisional Agenda Item 3); David Triggle, 'Treating Desires Not Diseases: A Pill for Every Ill and an Ill for Every Pill?' (2007) 12 *Drug Discovery Today* 161; Smita Srinivas, 'Intellectual Property Rights, Innovation and Healthcare: Unanswered Questions in Theory and Policy' (2008) 10(2) *Economica* (Rio de Janeiro) 106; and Carsten Fink, *Intellectual Property and Public Health: An Overview of the Debate with a Focus on US Policy* (2008).

13 See Jack Lerner, 'Intellectual Property and Development at WHO and WIPO' (2008) 34 *American Journal of Law and Medicine* 257.

Table 10.1 *Relationship between research funding and global disease burden (GDB); financial data for 2001*

Condition	GDB (in million DALYs)	% of total GDB	R&D funding (US$ million)	R&D funding per DALY (US$)
All	1,470	100	105,900	72
HIV/AIDS + TB + Malaria	167	11.4	1,400	8.4
CVD	148.19	9.9	9,402	63.45
Diabetes	16.19	1.1	1,653	102.07
Malaria	46.49	3.1	288	6.2
TB	34.74	2.3	378	10.88

Source: Andrés de Francisco and Stephen Matlin, *Monitoring Financial Flows for Health Research 2006: The Changing Landscape of Health Research for Development* (2006), 90.

According to the most recent estimate of financial flows for health research:

> Most (97%) spending on health R&D continues to be by high-income countries, with the remainder (3%) by low- and middle-income countries. Most of the US$ 155.2 billion spent by high-income countries goes towards generating products, processes and services tailored to their health-care markets.[14]

The mismatch between the global disease burden and R&D funding is captured in Table 10.1.

A similar disparity is evident in the case of drugs for neglected diseases: very few new drugs are developed for neglected/tropical diseases.[15] The growing interest shown by philanthropic foundations like

[14] Mary Anne Burke and Stephen Matlin, *Monitoring Financial Flows for Health Research: Prioritizing Research for Health Equity* (Geneva: Global Forum for Health Research, 2008), xvi.

[15] Ibid.; Oxfam International, 'Ending the R&D Crisis in Public Health: Promoting Pro-Poor Medical Innovation' (Briefing Paper No 122, Oxfam 2008); and Julian Reiss and Philip Kitcher, 'Neglected Diseases and Well-Ordered Science' (Technical Paper No 06/08, Centre for the Philosophy of Natural and Social Science Contingency and Dissent in Science, 2008).

the Bill & Melinda Gates Foundation in increasing investment in health R&D in low- and middle-income countries is a positive sign but this alone will not be sufficient to bridge the gap.[16] Pharmaceutical companies are not interested in investing in R&D for neglected diseases as the poor lack purchasing power and thus do not constitute viable markets. OSDD can help break the vicious cycle of low research and development in respect of diseases afflicting developing countries.

In the case of diseases like HIV/AIDS the issue is that of affordability rather than availability of drugs. Here too the market logic disfavours the poor in developing and least-developed countries, the countries that are worst affected by HIV/AIDS. The availability of low-cost generic drugs from countries like India and Brazil, the cuts in prices negotiated by foundations like the Clinton Foundation and use of compulsory licensing in some countries (e.g., Thailand) have mitigated to some extent the problem of affordability, but these solutions are not viable in the long term as they have limitations.[17] The Agreement on Trade-Related Aspects of Intellectual Property Rights ('TRIPS') has reduced the policy space available to countries, and the ill-effects of harmonization under TRIPS for production and provision of public goods, particularly drugs, is acknowledged now.[18] The TRIPS-Plus[19] provisions in various bilateral and regional free-trade agreements have restricted the

[16] Burke and Matlin, *Monitoring Financial Flows for Health Research*, above n. 14; and Oxfam International, 'Ending the R&D Crisis in Public Health', above n. 15.

[17] For an overview see Heinz Klug, 'Law, Politics, and Access to Essential Medicines in Developing Countries' (2008) 36 *Politics and Society* 207. See also Wolfgang Hein and Lars Kohlmorgen, 'Global Health Governance: Conflicts on Global Social Rights' (2008) 8 *Global Social Policy* 80.

[18] See generally Keith Maskus and Jerome Reichman (eds.), *International Public Goods and Transfer of Technology under a Globalized Intellectual Property Regime* (2005); Ken Shadlen, 'Policy Space for Development in the WTO and Beyond: The Case of Intellectual Property Rights' (Working Paper No 05/06, Global Development and Environment Institute, Tufts University, 2005); Christopher Arup, 'TRIPS as Competitive and Cooperative Interpretation', in Justin Malbon and Charles Lawson (eds.), *Interpreting and Implementing the TRIPS Agreement* (2008); Jerome Reichman, and Catherine Hasenzahl, '*Non-Voluntary Licensing of Patented Inventions*' (Issue Paper No 5, United Nations Conference on Trade and Development–International Centre for Trade and Sustainable Development, 2003), 11–12; Kevin Outterson, 'Should Access to Medicines and TRIPS Flexibilities Be Limited to Specific Diseases?' (2008) 34 *American Journal of Law and Medicine* 279.

[19] See Hitoshi Nasu, 'Public Law Challenges to the Regulation of Pharmaceutical Patents in the US Bilateral Free Trade Agreements', in Thomas Pogge, Matthew Rimmer and Kim Rubenstein (eds.), *Incentives for Global Public Health: Patent Law and Access to Essential Medicines* (2010), 77.

use of the flexibilities in TRIPS as well as the options available to governments to solve the problem of affordability.[20]

As a result of all these factors, humanity is witnessing a paradox today. That is, despite advances in science and technology, mortality from diseases that afflict the poor and from poverty-induced diseases is not declining. While higher investment in R&D and in policies that enhance access and address the issue of affordability can help solve these problems, the factors discussed above severely limit the reach and scope of such policies to be effective solutions. While R&D investment has increased as more countries have opted for patent protection in the post-TRIPS world, R&D investment in neglected diseases or diseases that mostly affect the poor has not increased alongside advances in patent protection.[21] Thus, the current drug discovery and development model may not be the appropriate solution to stimulate more R&D in neglected diseases.[22] Various proposals have been offered to rectify this deficit. These can be broadly classified as 'pull' approaches that focus on the expected pay-off from the innovation, and 'push' approaches that focus on contributing to the cost of R&D and providing funding for research.[23]

But the issue cannot simply be resolved by increasing R&D funding: despite an increase in pharmaceutical R&D in recent years, fewer drugs have been introduced in the market.[24] The decline in productivity

[20] See Carlos Correa, 'TRIPS and TRIPS-Plus Protection in Latin America', in Daniel Gervais (ed.), *Intellectual Property, Trade and Development* (2007), 221; and Ikechi Mgbeoji, 'TRIPS and TRIPS-Plus Impacts in Africa' in Daniel Gervais (ed.), *Intellectual Property, Trade and Development* (2007), 259.

[21] Margaret Kyle and Anita McGahan, 'Investments in Pharmaceuticals before and after TRIPS' (Working Paper, London Business School, 2008), 18, faculty.london.edu/mkyle/KM_TRIPS_081108.pdf at 2 March 2009.

[22] Ibid. Cf. Sudip Chaudhuri, 'Is Product Patent Protection Necessary in Developing Countries for Innovation' (Working Paper No 614, Indian Institute of Management Calcutta, 2007) 5: 'Where developing country markets matter – as in the case of neglected diseases – Indian companies are hardly involved in developing drugs. We find in Section III that, contrary to what was claimed during the TRIPS negotiations, the product patent regime has not prompted Indian companies to devote more resources to developing drugs for neglected diseases that exclusively or predominantly affect developing countries. NCE [New Chemical Entity] R&D is not yet a significant part of R&D activities of Indian companies.'

[23] For an analysis of these see Carl Nathan, 'Aligning Pharmaceutical Innovation with Medical Need' (2007) 13 *Nature Medicine* 304.

[24] The cost of developing a new drug is a controversial issue. For an analysis of the productivity in terms of new drugs and development costs see Congressional Budget

of pharmaceutical R&D is a major issue.[25] The industry has undergone a shift, from large vertically integrated firms that do almost all of the R&D related activities in-house to firms specializing in particular components of R&D and offering specialized services.[26] The application of the 'rational drug design' paradigm, the proliferation of biotech firms backed by venture capital, advances in the understanding of the human genome, the availability of patent protection for research tools and fragments of DNA, together with an increase in the number of patents for genetics and genome-related developments, and, finally, an increase in the patenting activity of non-profits like universities in the pharmaceutical field are the factors that have played an important role in the 'paradigm' shift.

According to Neil Niman and Brian Kench:

> [P]harmaceutical research has become less 'context specific' as the scientific knowledge embodied in pharmaceuticals has become more generic in nature. This has given rise to the development of a market for research ideas and development of networks of pharmaceutical companies where the research function has become modularized and decoupled from the manufacture, testing and marketing of new drugs.[27]

OSDD can take advantage of these developments and emerge as a new paradigm in pharmaceutical R&D.[28] The growth of Open Source bioinformatics and the use of Open Source software and tools in many scientific disciplines are factors that favour OSDD.[29] The other factors include the

Office, *Research and Development in the Pharmaceutical Industry* (2006); Michael Hu *et al.*, 'The Innovation Gap in Pharmaceutical Drug Discovery and New Models for R&D Success' (2007), www.kellogg.northwestern.edu/academic/biotech/faculty/articles/NewRDModel.pdf; and Margaret Kyle, *Innovation in the Pharmaceutical Industry* (2007).

25 Hu *et al.*, 'The Innovation Gap in Pharmaceutical Drug Discovery and New Models for R&D Success', above n. 24.

26 See Gary Pisano, *Science Business* (2006) chs. 4–5.

27 Iain Cockburn, 'The Changing Structure of the Pharmaceutical Industry', (2004) 23 *Health Affairs* 10; and Neil Niman and Brian Kench, *Open Source and Future of the Pharmaceutical Industry* (2005) (on file with the author) 8. Cf. Franco Malerba and Luigi Orsenig, 'Innovation and Market Structure in the Dynamics of the Pharmaceutical Industry and Biotechnology: Towards a History Friendly Model' (2002) 11 *Industrial and Corporate Change* 667.

28 For a sceptical view see Hu *et al.*, 'The Innovation Gap in Pharmaceutical Drug Discovery and New Models for R&D Success', above n. 24.

29 For reasons of space I will not discuss this in detail. See Maurer, 'Open Source Drug Discovery', above n. 2; Warren DeLano, 'The Case for Open Source Software in Drug Discovery' (2005) 10 *Drug Discovery Today* 213. See generally Glyn Moody, *Digital Code of Life: How Bioinformatics Is Revolutionizing Science, Medicine, and Business* (2004); Matthew Rimmer, 'Beyond Blue Gene: Intellectual Property and Bioinformatics' (2003)

emergence of contract research organizations ('CROs'),[30] public–private partnerships in drug discovery,[31] initiatives like the SNP Consortium and new models for sharing data and providing access without opting for patents.[32] The compatibility of OSDD with other initiatives for overcoming access and/or affordability issues is another factor in favour of OSDD.

Perhaps the most important factor that will make OSDD a viable option in developing countries is the increasing capability of developing countries to engage in drug discovery research. Specifically, generic producers and private sector firms with R&D capability have emerged to identify new molecules and develop them through to the final stage of approval. Moreover, universities and public sector entities have conducted vibrant research in basic and applied sciences supplemented by universities. Understanding the changes in the global innovation landscape is important.[33] In terms of funding, although developing countries are no match for the US or Europe, they are spending more on health R&D.[34] However, whether all this translates into workable Open Source models is a question for which there are no clear answers at this stage.

While these positive factors do enhance the credibility of OSDD as a model, how they will operate in the real world is difficult to predict. For instance, in a public–private partnership OSDD can be used for some stages of drug discovery and private sector partner(s) can be asked to take care of the clinical trials and commercialization in exchange for further

34 *International Review of Industrial Property and Copyright Law* 31; and Munos, 'Can Open Source R&D Reinvigorate Drug Research', above n. 2.

[30] Niman and Kench, *Open Source and Future of the Pharmaceutical Industry*, above n. 27, 11.

[31] For an overview see Stephen Matlin *et al.* (eds.), *Health Partnerships Review: Focusing Collaborative Efforts on Research and Innovation for the Health of the Poor* (2008); Dan Phair, 'Orphan Drug Programs, Public–Private Partnerships and Current Efforts to Develop Treatments for Diseases of Poverty' (2008) 4 *Journal of Health and Biomedical Law* 19.

[32] See generally Hope, *BioBazaar*, above n. 1; Maurer, 'Open Source Drug Discovery', above n. 2; and Rai, 'Proprietary Rights and Collective Action: The Case of Biotechnology Research with Low Commercial Value', above n. 1.

[33] See generally The World Bank, *Global Economic Prospects: Technology Diffusion in the Developing World* (2008), siteresources.worldbank.org/INTGEP2008/Resources/complete-report.pdf) at 5 February 2009; John Barton, 'New Trends in Technology Transfer' (Issue Paper No 18, International Centre for Trade and Sustainable Development, 2007). China is the leading producer of penicillin in the world. Four developing nations (India, Cuba, Brazil and Indonesia meet 60 per cent of the vaccine requirements of the UNICEF's Expanded Programme on Immunization. 67 per cent of India's drug exports and 74 per cent of Brazil's drug exports (in terms of dollars) are directed towards developing nations: Carlos Morel *et al.*, 'Health Innovation: The Neglected Capacity of Developing Countries to Address Neglected Diseases' (2005) 309 *Science* 401.

[34] Burke and Matlin, *Monitoring Financial Flows for Health Research*, above n. 14, xvi.

support to R&D. Similarly, the CROs themselves are mainly driven by profit considerations. So CROs in developing countries may not be interested in taking part in OSDD projects even if they have the relevant expertise.

3. Organizing OSDD

Although OSDD has been proposed as a strategy, currently there are not many ideas as to how to organize OSDD or what structure is best suited for it. Arti Rai has suggested 'virtual pharma' as a solution, has proposed a consortium, Tropical Diseases Initiative ('TDI'), and has suggested possible licensing options.[35] Aled Edwards has suggested that research-focused public-private partnerships can be a model for using Open Source science in drug discovery.[36] He has cited the SNP Consortium and the Structural Genomics Consortium as examples of successful public–private partnerships.

In designing a structure for OSDD, it is better to keep the objectives of the particular project in mind so that the structure and functions work towards fulfilling the objectives. Thus, it may not be possible to suggest a single structure or a network organization as the optimum structure. But fortunately there are already many examples of different types of arrangements, 'commons', consortia and initiatives that have distinct policies for data sharing, access, licensing and use of intellectual property to protect the mutual objectives. According to Robert Cook-Deegan:

> Genome projects spanned a full range of openness, from rapid open access under the Bermuda Rules, to subscription based access to genomic data and analytical tools at moderate cost (e.g., Celera) to highly proprietary gene-sequencing with public disclosure mainly limited to patents as they were granted and published.
>
> (Human Genome Science and Incyte)[37]

[35] In the 'virtual pharma' approach, governments and philanthropies fund teams to search out and subsidize the most promising private and academic research. Examples include the Institute for One World Health (www.iowh.org), a not-for-profit pharmaceutical company funded mainly through private sources and the Gates Foundation, and the Drugs for Neglected Diseases Initiative (www.dndi.org), a public sector not-for-profit organization designed to mobilize resources for R&D of new drugs for neglected diseases. Maurer, Rai and Sali, 'Finding Cures for Tropical Diseases: Is Open Source an Answer?', above n. 2.

[36] Edwards, 'Open Source Science to Enable Drug Discovery', above n. 2.

[37] Robert Cook-Deegan, 'The Science Commons in Health Research: Structure, Function, and Value' (2007) 32 *Journal of Technology Transfer* 133, 154; Cf. Maurice Cassier, 'Private Property, Collective Property, and Public Property in the Age of Genomics' (2002) 54(171) *International Social Sciences Journal* 83.

3.1 Scientific commons

However, what is important is the pivotal role played by scientific commons in the genome projects. In the absence of scientific commons some of the private sector initiatives would not have succeeded. In the case of OSDD, the need for such commons cannot be over-emphasized. There is also the possibility of OSDD resulting in compounds that can be used for downstream applications. Thus it is better to look at OSDD as an opportunity to create a commons as well as to develop new drugs. The commons and the structure that forms the basis of the OSDD project can be used for additional purposes once the OSDD project is completed. For example the libraries accumulated, the databases created, the compounds tested, classified and analysed, and the knowledge generated can be useful for other drug discovery projects, particularly OSDD projects. Currently the resources developed or generated in a commercial drug discovery project undertaken by pharmaceutical companies are not usually available to or accessible by others. Thus OSDD projects can result in developing new models of knowledge creation, sharing and utilization.

Analysing the Open Source initiatives in the human genome area, Allarakhia and Wensley point out that alliances have specific rules and arrangements for knowledge production, dissemination and appropriation. Many alliances were public–private partnerships and in only one alliance was knowledge dissemination enclosed within the private domain. In all other cases, knowledge dissemination was in the public domain irrespective of whether the knowledge was produced in the upstream discovery or downstream application stage.[38]

According to Allarakhia and Wensley:

> Open Source discovery initiatives are enabling companies to access disembodied knowledge-based resources critical to downstream drug development. The objective of these cooperative strategic alliances is to preserve the downstream technological opportunities for multiple firms. When upstream discovery research cannot yield commercial products and when the costs associated with excessive upstream competition are too high, companies jointly benefit from cooperative knowledge production and open knowledge dissemination.[39]

[38] Minna Allarakhia and Anthony Wensley, 'Systems Biology: A Disruptive Biopharmaceutical Research Paradigm' (2006) 74 *Technological Forecasting and Social Change* 1643.

[39] Ibid.

Co-operative knowledge production and open knowledge dissemination are key factors in the success of OSDD. In an OSDD project downstream opportunities may be preserved in many ways. A consortium can seek funding from government agencies and others by promising that downstream development will not be monopolized by a single firm and that the knowledge production and dissemination will be governed by rules that prevent knowledge enclosure through patenting. But even the private sector will be interested in such arrangements if knowledge production and dissemination will benefit all parties.

Public research communities can be effective in cases where such communities can be organized with common objectives and where access is not restricted by intellectual property rights. The worm (*C. elegans*) community is an interesting example where all research data is released into the public domain without restriction. In this project, funded by public money, the ko-mutation strains are deposited with the Caenorhabditis Genetics Center in St Paul, Minnesota where they are available to all researchers. This centre is also publicly funded. This policy has resulted in rapid dissemination of scientific information through publication in peer-reviewed journals. The number of papers published using the ko alleles from the consortium has increased from 21 in 2001 to 142 in 2006.

According to Professor Don Moreman:

> The worm is a model for public domain research and perhaps ironically, it is also a model for how an economy can grow and businesses can benefit. Products and drugs for 'apoptosis' and even more products for RNAi in various organisms abound. No IP [intellectual property] in the worm was given for either of these discoveries and yet several biotech companies, or at least divisions within companies, are based on these fundamental results.[40]

3.2 *Open access drug companies*

Carl Nathan suggests a model that deserves a closer look for its relevance to OSDD.[41] He suggests formation of open access drug companies. These companies would establish contract-based sites for

[40] Don Moerman, 'Is Public Domain Community Research Effective? The Nematode *Caenorhabditis elegans* as a Positive Case Study' (Paper presented at 'Genomics and Intellectual Property: Considering Alternatives to Traditional Patenting', Vancouver, 9 March 2007).

[41] Nathan, 'Aligning Pharmaceutical Innovation with Medical Need', above n. 23.

collaboration with academia and industry. The funders and not the contractors would control the use of intellectual property. Libraries that contain compounds (including those donated) would be set up. In return for open access users would pay a fee. Users could patent derivatives of the compounds, but not the Open Source compounds themselves.

There are many problems with this model. Users are not obliged to use Open Source licensing when they patent derivatives of compounds obtained from the library. This could block further research by others. Some users can use the system without making any contribution or by making a minimum contribution. Funders controlling intellectual property even when intellectual property is assigned to inventors is not a good solution because inventors and funders can have different opinions on the use of patents and intellectual property. Finally, an open access drug company as envisaged by Nathan may not work in practice as all participants and users need not be committed to the whole project and can disengage at any point. At what stage they will compete and at what stage collaborate is unclear. The interests of all stakeholders need not be compatible at all stages. For pharmaceutical companies this may provide access to knowledge and compounds without any obligation to the open access drug company except in the form of paying user fees.

In initiatives like the worm (*C. elegans*) community and the Alliance for Cell Signaling the objective of rapid knowledge generation and dissemination is met by making knowledge accessible to all researchers and by publication in journals. But in a drug discovery project the objective of knowledge generation and dissemination is part of a larger objective. In fact as drug discovery projects need the knowledge and expertise of researchers from different disciplines at different stages, the issue of co-ordinating relevant knowledge production, use and dissemination is a major issue, particularly when the knowledge accumulated over the years is not fully integrated in databases, libraries of compounds or depositories.

Niman and Kench suggest a model in which firms compete and co-operate at different stages of drug discovery.[42] This is represented in Table 10.2.

[42] Niman and Kench, *Open Source and Future of the Pharmaceutical Industry*, above n. 27, 9.

Table 10.2 *Competition and co-operation at different stages of drug development*

	Pre-Clinical	Clinical	Production
Co-operate	Shared Basic Science	Shared Knowledge	Shared Trials
Compete	New Discoveries	Regulatory Approval	Differentiated Products
Information Flows	Knowledge Base	Website	Market
Market-Places	Ideas	Trials	Products
Funding	Government Pharmaceutical Companies	Pharmaceutical Companies Financial Investors	Licences Pharmaceutical Companies

They acknowledge that co-ordination between the stages is needed and new co-ordination mechanisms are not considered.[43] They are of the view that when rights to basic research results are in the public domain, a new competitive market in the development of efficient co-ordination mechanisms may emerge. They also discuss the possibility of new options in funding for R&D including trials. They suggest the model of the HapMap project and the Open Source Development Laboratory ('OSDL') as institutional mechanisms. In my view their suggestions deserve further analysis. The weaknesses in their model stem from their assumptions about co-operation and competition at different stages of drug development. For companies, if the costs of co-operation are greater than the benefits, it is irrational to co-operate. If companies can obtain the advantages of co-operation through other means at a lesser cost they will prefer to compete than to co-operate. Niman and Kench's suggestion that users can be charged depending upon frequency of use or some other criteria ignores the fact that it is difficult to assess the value of information accessed.

[43] Janet Hope points out that a major difficulty in implementing the virtual pharmaceutical model is the problem of co-ordinating different contacts between many partners in various disciplines. She suggests that a bazaar model of governance backed by Open Source licences is an alternative to traditional partnership arrangements: Hope, *BioBazaar*, above n. 1.

Looking at their model further, the revenue from user fees may not be high enough for a university to act as a co-ordinator and disseminator. The licensing arrangement in their model is not clear. Moreover, the co-ordinating mechanism may not emerge unless all the participants feel the need for it. Some participants may enter at one stage and opt out at another. The OSDL is a working model but the interests of IBM and other companies in OSDL are different from those of pharmaceutical manufacturers. Supporting OSDL is beneficial for IBM as IBM has incorporated Linux into its products, and so continued improvement of the Linux platform suits the interests of IBM.[44] But, for pharmaceutical companies, the relevance of chemical compounds undergoing clinical trials or new chemical entities being developed is different from that of Linux for IBM, as Linux is a tested product.

3.3 *Open Source consortia*

However, some elements from their model can be used in OSDD projects. The co-ordinating mechanism can be established by government or by a consortium of funders. Securitization of part of the drug development and testing costs may be encouraged by providing tax incentives or similar concessions. Part of the tension between co-operation and competition can be resolved if there are incentives to co-operate. The model proposed by Niman and Kench is based on the understanding that the knowledge base necessary for pharmaceutical R&D is more 'divisible' now and that markets for research ideas and networks as well as modularization of the research function in networks are more widely available today. To what extent this is evident in practice needs to be examined.

It is obvious that innovation in the pharmaceutical sector occurs in different firms, of different sizes, specializing in different skills/services. Patents are more often used as bargaining chips or for strategic advantage than for use in the business. In other words, the motivations for

[44] 'IBM now reportedly contributes $100 million a year to the development of Linux and other Open Source software projects. IBM donated some components of its proprietary AIX software, the IBM flavor of Unix, to Linux to strengthen the latter's ability to provide enterprise-level capabilities and scalability. IBM also released the Eclipse software tools suite and framework on an Open Source basis and contributed resources to start an Open Source consortium to support and extend it': Pamela Samuelson, 'IBM's Pragmatic Embrace of Open Source' (2006) 49(10) *Communications of the Association for Computing Machinery* 21.

patenting and the use of patents for different purposes should be understood so that a network of players with different interests in patents can be formed. Can OSDD models be built using the different motivations to patent as a factor to bring in different stakeholders for a common purpose?

I think this is possible provided that the participants in networks are willing to use Open Source licensing for furthering common interests and use patents only when patenting is the best option or is done for defensive purposes. Such a network of non-profit institutions including publicly funded research institutes, universities and R&D centres can be developed as part of the larger OSDD project. Under the model I envisage these network partners would use patents not for the purpose of monopolizing but for defensive purposes. The partners would use Open Source licensing and material transfer agreements for sharing resources. They would pool patents and create commons consisting of such patents. There are examples of patent commons and eco-patent commons.[45] In both these cases, the companies have allowed patented inventions to be used by others (not necessarily members of the consortium that manages the commons) for specific purposes and subject to certain terms and conditions. Non-assertion of rights agreements that 'grant permission to third parties to practice a patent they would otherwise infringe'[46] for certain purposes and subject to certain conditions can be entered into. For example, a university can grant permission to use a patent for the development of a vaccine, provided it is not used for any other purpose. If the licensee uses it for any other purpose it would be considered an infringement and the permission to use it for the development of a vaccine would be withdrawn.

In the case of drug discovery, however, it is likely that the knowledge created, shared and owned by the non-profit organizations who have created the commons may be necessary but not sufficient for all stages of drug discovery and development. So the network needs access to, *inter alia*, patents, databases, libraries of components and research tools to

[45] For an analysis of eco-patent commons see Krishna Ravi Srinivas, 'Sink or Swim: Eco-Patent Commons and Transfer of Environmentally Sustainable Technologies' (2008) 2(2) *Bridges Trade BioRes* 17.

[46] Anatole Krattiger, 'The Use of Non-Assertion Covenants: A Tool to Facilitate Humanitarian Licensing, Manage Liability and Foster Global Access', in Anatole Krattiger *et al.* (eds.), *Intellectual Property Management in Health and Agricultural Innovation: A Handbook of Best Practices* (Oxford: Centre for the Management of Intellectual Property in Health Research and Development, 2008), 1739.

further the objective of drug discovery and development. It is also likely that pharmaceutical companies will need access to knowledge held by the network members. By creating a structure that facilitates exchange of knowledge and mutual access, many barriers can be overcome. For example, pharmaceutical companies may agree to provide access and licensing at the initial stages when use will not affect the companies' interests. They may impose conditions that the use should be for research purposes and, in the case of commercial applications, a licensing policy will be applicable. In the case of patents on research tools, they could be licensed for nominal amounts without restriction for research purposes. In the case of research for cures for neglected diseases, such arrangements will work as most pharmaceutical companies will not be doing research to find cures for those diseases. However, the real problems lie in identifying the relevant patents and in creating a structure that is capable of handling parties with different interests and stakes in the process. The public–private partnership model is a good model that can be adopted for the structure described above but public–private partnerships have not embraced the OSDD approach fully. Moreover, the public–private partnership model is yet to be proven as a successful model for all stages of drug discovery and development. Still, I am of the view that the experiences of the public–private partnerships will be relevant to OSDD projects, in particular in organizing for virtual pharma, bringing the private and public sectors together, performing relevant research for tropical/neglected diseases and managing research networks.

I am of the view that it is futile to think in terms of a single model or paradigm for organizing OSDD projects. It is possible that networks for OSDD, when formed, will evolve into stable arrangements and will create structures that are workable in a particular niche. It is also likely that some form of commons or collective will emerge for a specific purpose and once the purpose is served, another body or organization will take up the further work.[47] There are examples of networks like MalariaGEN (the Malaria Genomic Epidemiology Network) which are essentially research networks.[48] But their objective is different from that of a network dedicated to drug discovery and development. Inputs and data

[47] Cf. William Brody, 'The Uncensored Idea', in William Brody (ed.), *The Crossroads: Essays on Health Care in Modern America* (2008) 34.

[48] Dave Chokshi, Michael Parker and Dominic Kwiatkowski, 'Data Sharing and Intellectual Property in Genomic Epidemiology Network: Policies for Large-Scale Research Collaboration' (2006) 84 *Bulletin of the World Health Organization* 382.

from such networks will be useful for OSDD networks, which can also study the data-sharing, access and intellectual property policies of such networks for their relevance. As most of these networks are either publicly funded or funded by donors and as often the members are from the research/academic community, the same model and policies may not always be replicable in an OSDD network.

The OSDD network could function until the pre-clinical stage and, once the drug candidates are ready for clinical trials, the trials and the approval process would be handled by another organization or agency. In such cases, the network could entrust the management of intellectual property and related issues to a member or to a specialized agency and that member or agency would take up the issue of commercialization with specific mandates from the members. How such types of arrangements that involve two or more different structures will fit into the mode of bazaar governance of innovation is difficult to answer now. But just as the Open Source models themselves evolved over a period of time by mixing and matching proprietary and non-proprietary models through creative use of Open Source licensing, different modes of organization for OSDD may emerge in the future.

3.4 Product Development Partnerships

The Product Development Partnership ('PDP') for producing a low-cost version of existing malaria drugs is an interesting example of an Open Source model, although the number of parties is limited to three. In the PDP, the non-profit Institute for One World Health ('iOWH') funds the University of California, Berkeley for basic research and Amyris Biotechnologies Inc. for applied research and retains some funding itself for regulatory activities and product distribution. Under the three party agreement the University of California, Berkeley will grant licences to iOWH for drug distribution in the developing world and will license Amyris to produce and provide the drug to iOWH. Under this licence, Amyris can sell the patented compounds in the developed world for a royalty. The PDP is funded by the Bill & Melinda Gates Foundation.[49] In the case of OSDD projects the number of participants involved in basic and applied research will obviously be greater. However, the regulatory activities are better performed by a single organization/entity that should

[49] Carol Mimura, 'Technology Licensing for the Benefit of the Developing World' (2006) 18(2) *Journal of Association of University Technology Managers* 19.

act as the nodal agency for dealing with regulatory affairs and for co-ordinating clinical trials.

In drug R&D a significant portion of the costs involved relates to regulatory approval including clinical trials.[50] Although there is no guarantee that the trials will succeed and the drug will be approved, the process has to be undergone for commercialization and regulatory purposes. Companies are entitled to data protection for clinical trials data, although this protection is not available in all countries as TRIPS does not mandate this. If the costs of trials are underwritten fully or partly by the government or by other funders, there is no need to grant exclusive data protection to the pharmaceutical company. Putting the data in the public domain will benefit the generics industry and will also facilitate quicker regulatory approval for generics. It has been suggested that clinical trials should be treated as a public good.[51] This will act as an incentive for finding cures for neglected diseases as the cost of drug discovery and development is reduced. It will also create more options for philanthropic organizations to make essential medicines accessible as they can encourage the generics industry to make use of the data in the public domain for regulatory purposes.

Although the quantum of funding needed for this on a global scale is not known, this idea deserves a serious try. Governments can either subsidize the costs of trials in full or in part. If the government funds only 50 per cent of the costs then the companies should be entitled to data protection for half of the period to which they would be entitled had they fully funded the trials. The suggested model is based on the regulatory system in the US and replicating it elsewhere may not be fully feasible. Another issue is that many countries may not have the expertise or capacity to implement this suggestion fully. The suggestion that a broad category of products should be eligible for public funding raises issues of preferences and evaluations about eligibility. Whether a medical device or a diagnostic kit should be covered by government funding where funding is limited is an issue for which there are no easy answers. Finally, such public subsidies may be at the cost of resource allocation to more desirable health outcomes like

[50] For example Maurer states that 75 per cent of the cost of new drugs takes place after the beginning of clinical trials: Maurer, 'Open Source Drug Discovery', above n. 2.

[51] Tracy Lewis, Jerome Reichman and Anthony So, 'The Case for Public Funding and Public Oversight of Clinical Trials' (2007) 4(1) *The Economists' Voice* article 3, 1–4. See also *Working Document – Barbados and Bolivia: Proposal 6: Clinical Trials on Medicines as Global Public Goods* (2008), www.keionline.org/misc-docs/b_b_igwg/prop6_clinical_trials_as_as_global_public_goods.pdf at 4 March 2009.

vaccinations. Still this proposal is worth a try. Instead of the government funding trials, the sources of funding can be diverse. Suitable tax credits or other incentives can be given to companies for undertaking trials of neglected disease medicines. However, as the disease burden is not uniform across countries, countries will have to identify diseases for which finding a cure is a priority and support those.

When a consortium funds trials and bears a part of the development costs, it can license the potential drug to various firms for manufacturing in other markets or for the purpose of exporting to countries that lack manufacturing capacity. If the market for drugs is differentiated, that may induce companies to compete and co-operate at different stages. The consortium can examine this option to attract companies to take part in the drug development project. Ideally speaking, this arrangement will suit the OSDD process as a portion of the development costs are underwritten by the consortium. Issues relating to licensing can be resolved by choosing the appropriate licence for the purpose and the markets to be served. The suggestion by Maurer, that Open Source volunteers can collect and analyse data, may not be feasible because clinical trials involve hundreds, if not thousands, of pieces of data spread across different places. A good portion of these trials are now outsourced to and conducted in countries like China and India. Data collection and analysis cannot be efficiently done on a voluntary basis. Since the credibility and reliability of the data is important for regulators, it is better that data collection and analysis be done by pharmaceutical firms or firms specializing in the conduct of trials and the completion of other regulatory norms.

Thus organizing for OSDD will be a challenging task. Although there are some suggestions for prospective networks, until the ideas are put into practice it is difficult to say which one will work. Another issue is whether the virtual pharma model can be easily duplicated and what will be the linkage between the network/mechanism and the virtual pharma. In our view, it is premature to argue in favour of a single model at this stage. Only when some of them are tested will it be feasible to identify what works and what does not. Nevertheless, it is essential that ideas are developed further and the existing networks in drug discovery are studied. Perhaps a robust model will emerge from the experiences gained.

The Council for Scientific and Industrial Research ('CSIR') in India has launched its project to develop drugs for tuberculosis as an OSDD project.[52] The project is now funded by the Government of India and is likely to

[52] See Open Source Drug Discovery Net, www.osdd.net/.

secure funding from other sources also. The project is in its infancy. It is envisaged that students will be encouraged to participate in the project and will be assigned mentors to guide them. The data access policy is through a licence available on the project website. The project strives to put information in the public domain and provides access through a form of Open Source licensing. We anticipate that the network of laboratories and universities in India involved in this project will generate new ideas for drug discovery. The project aims to integrate knowledge held in 'silos' and make it accessible through a common source. It is too early to predict how the project will fare, but I am cautiously optimistic about the project as it is backed by an organization that has rich experience in applied research. On the downside, the funding from a single source may be inadequate and co-ordination of such a project is a big challenge even for an organization with as much experience as CSIR.

4. OSDD and other initiatives and proposals: synergies and problems

As indicated elsewhere many suggestions have been made for overcoming the problems of access and affordability. A range of these can be found in other chapters in this volume. For reasons of space I will not discuss them all here. To what extent OSDD is compatible with these suggestions is not clear for two reasons: first, OSDD is still at the conceptual level; and second, the full implications of some of the suggested options are not yet known, as ongoing debate persists on their finer aspects and they too are yet to be tested.

The Health Impact Fund ('HIF') proposed by Thomas Pogge in this volume[53] is compatible with OSDD because it supports the objective of making cures for neglected diseases available.[54] In the case of the HIF, the greater the health impact, the greater the financial reward which will accrue to patent holders. So for OSDD projects that result in cures which have a significant health impact, the HIF may be a potential research incentive. However, as the HIF does not fund the projects per se, in the crucial early stages of R&D the HIF is of little relevance to OSDD projects.

[53] Thomas Pogge, 'The Health Impact Fund: Better Pharmaceutical Innovations at Much Lower Prices', in Thomas Pogge, Matthew Rimmer and Kim Rubenstein (eds.), *Incentives for Global Public Health: Patent Law and Access to Essential Medicines* (2010), 135.

[54] Aidan Hollis and Thomas Pogge, *The Health Impact Fund: Making New Medicines Accessible for All* (2008), www.yale.edu/macmillan/igh/hif_book.pdf.

In the case of an R&D treaty, the objective is to enhance funding for R&D in diseases for which cures are not available. An R&D treaty model could be combined with OSDD and a portion of the funding could be earmarked for OSDD projects or OSDD projects could be given a preference for funding. Advance Market Commitments or Advance Purchase Commitments could be applied to OSDD projects. This will reduce the funding problems that OSDD projects may otherwise face. In my view, support in the form of Advance Purchase Commitments will enhance the credibility of OSDD projects. But it is also likely that OSDD projects may frequently be unable to compete with projects supported by the private sector. Since OSDD is not a proven model, it is necessary that some initial projects are funded by governments or international agencies so that the model is tested and refined further. For this purpose, it will be desirable to identify some feasible projects and try to implement them as OSDD projects. As pointed out earlier, the public–private partnership model can be chosen for this. Hughes comments: 'Some of the new, open-innovation initiatives like Sage and CollabRx and public–private partnerships like the Bio-Markers Consortium are some promising examples that are relevant for OSDD'.[55]

The compatibility of OSDD with various licences is an important issue. *Prima facie*, it appears that the OSDD project can be combined with such licences to enhance access and affordability. However, only a detailed analysis of each licence and its compatibility with OSDD will truly determine this.

5. Conclusion

Our brief analysis shows that OSDD is a paradigm in progress. It challenges the conventional wisdom but it may not be a substitute for the conventional framework in all cases. The changes in organizing and producing knowledge for drug discovery give it an edge over the conventional paradigm. But organizing for OSDD is a major challenge as it involves building structures and networks that are different from traditional pharmaceutical R&D. At the same time, this paradigm can complement the traditional model and thus be attractive to pharmaceutical companies in some contexts.

[55] Bethan Hughes, 'Harnessing Open Innovation' (2009) 8(5) *Nature Reviews Drug Discovery* 345.

11

Accessing and benefit sharing avian influenza viruses through the World Health Organization: a CBD and TRIPS compromise thanks to Indonesia's sovereignty claim?

CHARLES LAWSON AND BARBARA ANN HOCKING

1. Introduction

The potential of avian influenza to infect humans on a pandemic scale with high mortality has created a new challenge for the United Nations Convention on Biological Diversity ('CBD')[1] and the World Trade Organization's ('WTO') Agreement on Trade-Related Aspects of Intellectual Property Rights ('TRIPS' or 'TRIPS Agreement').[2] The challenge arises in the context of the legal arrangements for access and sharing of the influenza virus and the likely benefits resulting from that sharing. It is encapsulated in the following:

> A deal is being negotiated that could see Indonesia end its policy of withholding samples from human cases of avian flu. Until now, Indonesia has refused to share its samples with the World Health Organization (WHO), saying it is unfair that ownership of the samples passes to the WHO collaborating centres, and that it does not benefit from any resulting papers or patents.
>
> Indonesia says it will share samples under a material transfer agreement that allows research use, but gives Indonesia sovereign ownership of the samples. The country also wants access to vaccines developed using its samples. An international meeting [in November 2007] ended without

[1] Convention on Biological Diversity opened for signature 5 June 1992, [1993] ATS 32 (entered into force 29 December 1993) ('CBD').

[2] Marrakesh Agreement Establishing the World Trade Organization, opened for signature 15 April 1994, 1867 UNTS 3, annex 1C (Agreement on Trade-Related Aspects of Intellectual Property Rights) (entered into force 1 January 1995) ('TRIPS Agreement').

> agreement. But a statement, still being thrashed out by negotiators, is expected to open the way to concessions.[3]

There is a broadly accepted potential that vaccines can play a key role in limiting the impact of an avian influenza pandemic, although the most efficient and effective response requires access to the virus to make the appropriate vaccines.[4] As a consequence the existing legal frameworks, including the CBD and TRIPS, and the 'concession' made to Indonesia in making the H5N1 virus available to the World Health Organization's Global Influenza Surveillance Network ('GISN'), comprising the National Influenza Centres, WHO Collaborating Centres on Influenza and WHO H5 Reference Laboratories,[5] provides an unorthodox case study of the interaction between the CBD and TRIPS.

This chapter addresses the legal framework applying to the sharing of genetic resources (in this case the avian influenza virus) and the ability of this framework to function efficiently and effectively. In short, a case study of access and benefit sharing. It outlines the ongoing 'conflict' between the CBD and TRIPS, then provides an overview of the CBD's access and benefit sharing framework. It then addresses the WHO's arrangements in place for accessing viruses and the development of vaccines to respond to potential pandemics (and other lesser outbreaks), before setting out the compromise arrangement between Indonesia and the member states of the WHO so far. The chapter concludes with a discussion about the consequences of this compromise for the future implementation of the CBD and TRIPS arrangements, and the proposition that failure to negotiate a deal with Indonesia opens up the debate about the paramountcy of intellectual property and TRIPS, and the

[3] Nature News, 'Indonesia Edges Closer to Sharing Bird-Flu Samples' (2007) 450 *Nature* 598. See also Endang Sedyaningsih, Siti Isfandari, Triono Soendoro and Siti Fadilah Supari, 'Towards Mutual Trust, Transparency and Equity in Virus Sharing Mechanism: The Avian Influenza Case of Indonesia' (2008) 37 *Annals Academy of Medicine Singapore* 482.

[4] See, e.g., World Health Assembly, *Avian and Pandemic Influenza: Best Practice for Sharing Influenza Viruses and Sequence Data*, 60th World Health Assembly, WHO Doc A60/INF.DOC./1 (2007) (Report by the Secretariat); Scientific Advisory Group on Pandemic Influenza (UK), *Pre-Pandemic and Pandemic Influenza Vaccines: Scientific Evidence Base* (2008), www.dh.gov.uk at 6 March 2009; World Health Organization, *Global Pandemic Influenza Action Plan to Increase Vaccine Supply*, WHO Doc WHO/IVB/06.13, WHO/CDS/EPR/GIP/2006.1 (2006).

[5] See also World Health Organization, *A Summary of Tracking Avian Influenza A (H5N1) Specimens and Viruses Shared with WHO from 2003 to 2007* (2008), www.who.int/csr/disease/avian_influenza/TrackingHistoryH5N1_20080131.pdf at 6 March 2009.

potential for other policy imperatives to override respect for intellectual property and TRIPS.

2. Influenza as a CBD 'genetic resource'

The CBD was signed at the conclusion of the United Nations Conference on Environment and Development[6] with the objective of 'fair and equitable sharing of the benefits arising out of the utilization of genetic resources, including by appropriate access to genetic resources and by appropriate transfer of relevant technologies, taking into account all rights over those resources and to technologies, and by appropriate funding'.[7] This objective of benefit sharing the uses of genetic resources marked a fundamental shift in binding international measures to conserve biodiversity:[8] first, by recognizing that genetic resources are subject to a nation state's sovereign rights;[9] second, by linking access to those resources with the outcomes of scientific research and commercial uses, and access to technology on more favourable and non-commercial terms, including the products and technologies of the private sector derived from those genetic resources;[10] and third, by introducing intellectual property into the economic and policy debates about conserving genetic resources that might benefit future technological, economic and social development.[11]

The term 'genetic resources' was broadly defined in the CBD to mean 'genetic material of actual or potential value', where 'genetic material' means 'any material of plant, animal, microbial or other origin containing functional units of heredity'.[12] This broad definition was an attempt by the international community to establish principles for the uses of genetic resources from *all* sources, recognizing that 'biological materials

[6] See Michael Grubb *et al.* (eds.), *The Earth Summit Agreements: A Guide and Assessment* (1993).

[7] CBD, above n. 1, article 1.

[8] See, e.g., David Tilford, 'Saving the Blueprints: The International Legal Regime for Plant Resources' (1998) 30 *Case Western Reserve Journal of International Law* 373, 387–418; Keith Aoki, 'Weeds, Seeds and Deeds: Recent Skirmishes in the Seed Wars' (2003) 11 *Cardozo Journal of International and Comparative Law* 247, 305–13.

[9] CBD, above n. 1, article 15(1). [10] Ibid., articles 15, 16, 19.

[11] Ibid., preamble, articles 3, 10, 11, 15, 16, 19, 22. See also Organisation for Economic Co-operation and Development, *Harnessing Markets for Biodiversity: Towards Conservation and Sustainable Use* (2003) 18–19, 109; Commission on Intellectual Property Rights, *Integrating Intellectual Property Rights and Development Policy* (2002) 57–72 www.iprcommission.org/ at 5 February 2009.

[12] CBD, above n. 1, article 2.

containing genetic resources have significant value for applications such as pharmaceuticals, biotechnological processes, mining, fisheries and forestry'.[13] The term 'biological resources' includes 'genetic resources, organisms or parts thereof, populations, or any biotic component of ecosystems with actual or potential use or value to humanity'.[14]

The meaning of the term 'genetic resources' as defined in the CBD is not entirely clear, other than that the genetic resources over which access is being controlled are either from the state of origin of the resource or acquired by a party in accordance with the CBD.[15] While the meaning of this term is essential to developing effective measures to implement an access regime and to share the ensuing benefits fairly and equitably,[16] the parties to the CBD intended to cover a broader range of materials than the earlier United Nations Food and Agriculture Organization's International Undertaking on Plant Genetic Resources, and certainly included genetic materials from animals, plants and micro-organisms, whether terrestrial or marine.[17] The Conference of the Parties ('COP') noted that, in practice, the CBD definition had difficulties of under- and over-inclusion. Troublingly, the definition included human genetic materials,[18] left out biochemicals[19] and *ex situ* holdings acquired before 29 December 1993[20] and applied only to some marine resources:[21] '[t]he concern here was that, as these resources represent important and valuable manifestations of genetic diversity, leaving them outside the [CBD] would undermine the extent to which the [CBD] would be able to ensure the distribution of the full benefits of utilisation; a fundamental requirement of the equitable sharing of benefits'.[22]

Unfortunately neither the COP nor the CBD's Secretariat have provided a definitive explanation of what the term 'genetic resource' might mean, noting that in practice a number of contracting parties have

13 Conference of the Parties to the Convention on Biological Diversity, *Access to Genetic Resources and Benefit Sharing: Legislation, Administrative and Policy Information*, 2nd mtg, [4], UN Doc No UNEP/CBD/COP/2/13 (1995) (Report by the Secretariat).

14 CBD, above n. 1, article 2.

15 CBD, above n. 1, article 15(3).

16 See Conference of the Parties to the Convention on Biological Diversity, *Access to Genetic Resources*, 3rd mtg, [32], UN Doc UNEP/CBD/COP/3/20 (1996) (Note by the Executive Secretary).

17 Conference of the Parties to the Convention on Biological Diversity, *Access to Genetic Resources and Benefit Sharing*, above n. 13.

18 Ibid., [64]–[65]. 19 Ibid., [51]. 20 Ibid., [54]. 21 Ibid., [61]–[63].

22 Conference of the Parties to the Convention on Biological Diversity, *Access to Genetic Resources*, above n. 16.

adopted access regimes with broader scope than the CBD's definition, including 'genetic resources and derivatives'.[23] The ongoing elaboration and negotiation of an international regime on access and benefit sharing show the content of the CBD's term 'genetic resource' remains broad, flexible and contentious.[24]

The COP's discussions about avian influenza have focused on the potential impact on wildlife.[25] However, the WHO appears to conceive of avian influenza as something to which the CBD might apply, '[r]ecognizing the sovereign right of States over their biological resources',[26] and this also appears to be the position of Indonesia.[27] Thus, for avian influenza viruses found within the sovereign jurisdiction of Indonesia there appears to be a strong argument that they could be 'genetic resources' for the purposes of the CBD[28] – this is arguably strengthened by the broad interpretation of this term to include derivatives in putting the CBD into effect and accepted in the language of the WHO's ongoing discussions and negotiations about avian influenza virus sharing.[29]

23 Ibid., [34]; Conference of the Parties to the Convention on Biological Diversity, *Review of National, Regional and Sectoral Measures and Guidelines for Implementation of Article 15*, 4th mtg, [30]–[34], UN Doc UNEP/CBD/COP/4/23 (1998).

24 See Conference of the Parties to the Convention on Biological Diversity, *Report of the Conference of the Parties to the Convention on Biological Diversity on the Work of its Ninth Meeting*, 9th mtg, [194]–[195], UN Doc UNEP/CBD/COP/9/29 (2008).

25 See, e.g., Conference of the Parties to the Convention on Biological Diversity, *Report of the Eighth Meeting of the Parties to the Convention on Biological Diversity*, 8th mtg, [70]–[75], UNEP/CBD/COP/8/31 (2006).

26 Pandemic Influenza Preparedness: Sharing of Influenza Viruses and Access to Vaccines and Other Benefits, Res WHA60.28, World Health Assembly 60th mtg, preamble (2007).

27 See Indonesia, *Sharing of Influenza Viruses and Access to Vaccines and Other Benefits: Interdisciplinary Working Group on Pandemic Influenza Preparedness*, WHO Doc A/PIP/IGM/5 (2007), annex (Fundamental Principles and Elements for the Development of a New System for Virus Access and Fair and Equitable Benefit Sharing Arising from the Use of the Virus for the Pandemic Influenza Preparedness), [1] (Proposal by Indonesia).

28 Albeit some countries maintain viruses that are not natural resources covered by the CBD and object to the use of CBD language by the WHO: see Sangeeta Shashikant, 'Key Issues Unresolved at WHO Meeting on Influenza Virus Sharing' *Third World Network* (2008), www.twnside.org.sg/title2/health.info/2008/twnhealthinfo20081201.htm at 6 March 2009.

29 For example, the 'principles' addressed by the WHO in negotiating access and benefit sharing of viruses '[r]ecognize the sovereign right of States over their biological resources': World Health Organization, *Pandemic Influenza Preparedness: Sharing of Influenza Viruses and Access to Vaccines and Other Benefits, Open-Ended Working Group, Chair's Text – Draft – Pandemic Influenza Preparedness Framework for the Sharing of Influenza Viruses and Access to Vaccines and Other Benefits*, WHO Doc A/PIP/IGM/WG/6 (2008) [1.1].

3. The CBD and TRIPS context

At the time the CBD was being negotiated, there was almost universal consensus that the predominantly poor countries with the majority of the Earth's useful biological diversity (the South) should benefit from the exploitation of that diversity by the predominantly rich and technologically advanced countries (the North).[30] However, the content of the benefits to be shared from exploiting that accessed diversity and the issue of access to and transfer of technology to exploit those genetic resources remained contentious.[31] A central contention was the developed North's view that intellectual property should be maintained and respected,[32] while the South contended that its genetic resources had value and exploiting that value was an opportunity to address poverty alleviation and technological development requiring more favourable and non-commercial terms of access to useful technology.[33] The contentions over the CBD might be reduced to: '[t]he South wants the technology and the North wants the South to have it. But while the South sees itself as a potential partner, the North looks South and sees only paying customers.'[34]

The outcome of these contentions in the final text of the CBD was to postpone the resolution through agreeable diplomatic language effecting a compromise: 'that patents and other intellectual property rights may have an influence on the implementation of this [CBD]' with an obligation to 'cooperate in this regard subject to national legislation and international law in order to ensure that such rights are supportive of and do not run counter to its objectives'.[35] The diplomatic language allowed the technology-rich countries of the North (principally the United States,

[30] See, e.g., United Nations Development Programme, *Conserving Indigenous Knowledge: Integrating New Systems of Integration* (1994). The developed countries of the North, though, are not a homogeneous, cohesive or co-ordinated block: see Ranee Panjabi, *The Earth Summit at Rio: Politics, Economics and the Environment* (1997) 263–4.

[31] See Alexander Gillespie, 'Common Property, Private Property and Equity: Clash of Values and the Quest to Preserve Biodiversity' (1995) 12 *Environmental and Planning Law Journal* 388, 389–92 and accompanying footnotes.

[32] See generally, Panjabi, *The Earth Summit at Rio*, above n. 30.

[33] See, e.g., United Nations Environment Programme, *Report of the Ad Hoc Working Group on the Work of the Second Session in Preparation for a Legal Instrument on Biological Diversity*, 7, UN Doc UNEP/BioDiv2/3 (1990).

[34] Tilford, 'Saving the Blueprints', above n. 8, 419.

[35] CBD, above n. 1, article 16(5). See also Patricia Lucia and Cantuária Marin, *Providing Protection for Plant Genetic Resources: Patents, Sui Generis Systems, and Biopartnerships* (2002) 92.

European Union and Japan) to agree to preferential and concessional access to and transfer of technology using undefined terms that would not undermine the concern of the North to maintain their existing intellectual property arrangements.[36] The outcome was, at best, an in principle agreement to exchange genetic resources for benefits that might include access to and transfer of technology.[37]

This compromise also partly reflected the unresolved tensions between intellectual property negotiations in the areas of international trade and the environment being concurrently negotiated in different forums. The environmental CBD was negotiated under the auspices of the United Nations Environment Programme; the international trade TRIPS Agreement was being negotiated under the auspices of the General Agreement on Tariffs and Trade ('GATT').[38] The CBD attempted to set a balance by encouraging biodiversity-rich countries to maintain their resources so that they might be sustainably used by countries with highly developed technology, with the benefits accruing to both biodiversity-rich and -poor countries.[39] In contrast, TRIPS attempted to establish new rules and disciplines moving intellectual property into the realm of international trade laws so as to reduce distortions and impediments to international trade while encouraging new invention relying on the formula 'patents = free trade + investment = economic growth'.[40] According to the generalized South–North divide,[41] the CBD imposes obligations on the biodiversity-rich South to provide access to its genetic resources;[42] in return the technology-rich North facilitates access and transfer of technology, know-how, financial support and incentives[43] that

[36] See, e.g., Grubb *et al.*, *The Earth Summit Agreements*, above n. 6, 29.

[37] See, e.g., Secretariat of the Convention on Biological Diversity, *Handbook of the Convention on Biological Diversity* (2nd edition, 2003) 310.

[38] See, e.g., Secretariat of the World Trade Organization, *Trade and Environment at the WTO* (2004), www.wto.org/english/res_e/booksp_e/trade_env_e.pdf at 6 March 2009.

[39] See Organisation for Economic Co-operation and Development, *Harnessing Markets for Biodiversity*, above n. 11, 18–19, 109.

[40] Susan Sell and Aseem Prakash, 'Using Ideas Strategically: The Contest between Business and NGO Networks in Intellectual Property Rights' (2004) 48 *International Studies Quarterly* 143, 154. See also Peter Drahos, 'Global Property Rights in Information: The Story of TRIPS at the GATT' (1995) 13 *Prometheus* 6, 7.

[41] For a contemporaneous commentary, see Geoffrey Palmer, 'The Earth Summit: What Went Wrong at Rio?' (1992) 70 *Washington University Law Quarterly* 1005.

[42] CBD, above n. 1, articles 6–15. [43] Ibid., articles 16–21.

promote economic growth, directly addressing the development agenda to alleviate poverty.[44]

The expressed objection of the leading technology-rich North state, the United States, to the CBD's agreed text was that the treatment of finances, intellectual property, technology transfer and biotechnology were inadequate.[45] Of particular concern, the language dealing with intellectual property was 'a constraint to the transfer of technology rather than … a prerequisite'[46] reflecting the United States' biotechnology industry's perspective that the CBD opened the way for countries to reduce the level of intellectual property protection and introduce compulsory licensing arrangements.[47] However, the United States, following a change of administration, signed the CBD, subject to the following telling proviso:

> The United States declares its understanding that access to and transfer of technology subject to intellectual property rights under this [CBD] require the recognition of, and consistency with, the adequate and effective protection of intellectual property rights, and thus does not provide a basis for the use of compulsory licensing laws to compel private companies to transfer technology under this agreement … The United States declares its understanding of Art 16(2) that the phrase 'fair and favourable terms' means terms that are determined by a free market without trade restrictions and government coercion … *The United States declares its understanding that fair and equitable sharing of the benefits arising out of the utilisation of genetic resources requires members of this [CBD] to respect the rights of other member countries and of private parties to the technology that arise out of such utilisation of genetic resources* … For this reason the United States believes that the extension of adequate and effective intellectual property protection for the technology derived from the use of genetic resources is an essential prerequisite to the success of the [CBD].[48]

[44] See, e.g., Report of the United Nations Conference on the Environment and Development, annex 1 (Rio Declaration on Environment and Development), UN Doc A/CONF 151/26 (Vol I) (1992).

[45] Secretariat of the Convention on Biological Diversity, *Handbook of the Convention on Biological Diversity*, above n. 37, 311. See also United States, 'Declaration Made at the United Nations Environment Programme Conference for the Adoption of the Agreed Text of the Convention on Biological Diversity' (1992) 31 *International Legal Materials* 848.

[46] United States Department of State, 'Convention on Biological Diversity' (1992) 3 *US Department of State Dispatches* 423.

[47] United States Patent and Trademark Office, 'Biotech Group Explain Objection to Earth Summit's Biodiversity Treaty' (1992) 44 *Patent, Trademark and Copyright Journal* 120.

[48] Gillespie, 'Common Property, Private Property and Equity', above n. 31, 394 (emphasis added). See also Kal Raustiala, 'Domestic Institutions and International Regulatory Cooperation: Comparative Responses to the Convention on Biological Diversity' (1997) 49 *World Politics* 482, 492–4.

Following entry into force of the CBD on 29 December 1993, minimum intellectual property standards have been established and codified in TRIPS for WTO member states (from 1 January 1995). The interaction between the CBD and TRIPS remains contentious. The internationally contested inherent conflicts are that TRIPS requires genetic materials to be protected by patents or a *sui generis* plant variety that privately appropriates genetic resources over which a country has sovereign rights under the CBD. Further, these privileges do not also require the additional measures set out in the CBD, such as prior informed consent, mutually agreed terms and benefit sharing.[49]

4. CBD's framework for access and benefit sharing

Having articulated the general objective for the fair and equitable sharing of the benefits arising from using genetic resources, the CBD imposes a framework for its implementation. Thus, access to genetic resources is according to the authority of countries '[r]ecognising the sovereign rights of States over their natural resources'[50] with an obligation to facilitate access for 'environmentally sound uses' without imposing restrictions that are counter to the CBD's objectives.[51] Further, access must be from countries of origin or countries that have acquired the genetic resources according to the CBD,[52] on mutually agreed terms,[53] with prior informed consent,[54] and most importantly, taking:

> legislative, administrative or policy measures, as appropriate, and in accordance with arts 16 [access to and transfer of technology] and 19 [handling of biotechnology and distribution of its benefits] and where necessary through the financial mechanism established by arts 20 [financial resources] and 21 [financial mechanism] with the aim of sharing in a fair and equitable way the results of research and development and the benefits arising from the commercial and other utilisation of genetic resources with the Contracting Party providing such resources.[55]

[49] See Council for Trade-Related Aspects of Intellectual Property Rights, *The Relationship between the TRIPS Agreement and the Convention on Biological Diversity: Summary of Issues Raised and Points Made*, UN Doc IP/C/W/368/Rev.1/Corr.1 (2006) (Note by the Secretariat, Corrigendum); Conference of the Parties to the Convention on Biological Diversity, *The Relationship between the TRIPS Agreement and the Convention on Biological Diversity – Summary of Issues Raised and Points Made – Submission by the WTO Secretariat*, 8th mtg, UN Doc UNEP/CBD/COP/8/INF/37 (2006).

[50] CBD, above n. 1, article 15(1). See also article 3. [51] Ibid., article 15(2).

[52] Ibid., article 15(3). [53] Ibid., article 15(4). [54] Ibid., article 15(5).

[55] Ibid., article 15(7).

In dealing with the access to and transfer of technology, the CBD text provides:

> Each Contracting Party, recognising that technology includes biotechnology, and that both access to and transfer of technology among Contracting Parties are essential elements for the attainment of the objectives of this [CBD], undertakes subject to the provisions of this art [16] to provide and/or facilitate access for and transfer to other Contracting Parties of technologies that are relevant to the conservation and sustainable use of biological diversity or make use of genetic resources and do not cause significant damage to the environment.[56]

Where access to and transfer of technology is made and the technology is 'subject to patents and other intellectual property rights', then 'access and transfer shall be provided on terms which recognise and are consistent with the adequate and effective protection of intellectual property rights'.[57] Significantly, the CBD expressly provides that access to and transfer of technology to developing countries (and presumably this also includes the 'developing and least developed countries' as distinguished by TRIPS)[58] 'shall be provided and/or facilitated under fair and most favourable terms, including on concessional and preferential terms where mutually agreed, and where necessary in accordance with the financial mechanism'.[59] For all countries, the access to and transfer of technology 'protected by patents and other intellectual property rights' must be on 'mutually agreed terms' and 'in accordance with international law',[60] and:

> The Contracting Parties, recognising that patents and other intellectual property rights may have an influence on the implementation of this [CBD], shall cooperate in this regard subject to national legislation and international law in order to ensure that such rights are supportive of and do not run counter to its objectives.[61]

A key element in the access to and transfer of technology in exchange for access to genetic resources contemplated by the CBD text is that contracting states take 'legislative, administrative or policy measures' to require the private sector to facilitate 'access to, joint development and transfer of technology' for the benefit of 'both governmental institutions and the private sector of developing countries'.[62] In respect of biotechnology, measures include the 'effective participation in biotechnological

[56] Ibid., article 16(1). [57] Ibid., article 16(2).
[58] See TRIPS Agreement, above n. 2, article 66. [59] CBD, above n. 1, article 16(2).
[60] Ibid., article 16(3). [61] Ibid., article 16(5). [62] Ibid., article 16(4).

research activities'[63] and 'the results and benefits arising from biotechnologies based upon genetic resources'.[64] Other measures deal with the exchange of information[65] and technical and scientific co-operation.[66]

A further requirement is that, 'as far as possible and as appropriate', each contracting party should '[a]dopt measures relating to the use of biological resources to avoid or minimise adverse impacts on biological diversity'.[67] The CBD text also recognizes the special place of traditional and community knowledge, practices and innovations, requiring contracting parties, 'as far as possible and as appropriate', to:

> respect, preserve and maintain knowledge, innovations and practices of indigenous and local communities embodying traditional lifestyles relevant for the conservation and sustainable use of biological diversity and promote their wider application with the approval and involvement of the holders of such knowledge, innovations and practices and encourage the equitable sharing of the benefits arising from the utilisation of such knowledge, innovations and practices.[68]

Of particular significance to intellectual property, the CBD text also provides that contracting parties 'shall, as far as possible and as appropriate, adopt economically and socially sound measures that act as incentives for the conservation and sustainable use of components of biological diversity'.[69] The CBD is not intended to affect 'existing' rights and obligations of contracting parties 'except where the exercise of those rights and obligations would cause serious damage or a threat to biological diversity'.[70]

The voluntary Bonn Guidelines[71] proposed the establishment of a 'competent national authority',[72] identified the responsibilities of contracting parties that are the origin of genetic resources and the implementation of mutually agreed terms,[73] and set out the steps in the access and benefit sharing process.[74] While the Bonn Guidelines do not appear to favour a specific approach to intellectual property rights, they contemplate private contracts addressing intellectual property rights and

[63] Ibid., article 19(1). [64] Ibid., article 19(2). [65] Ibid., article 17. [66] Ibid., article 18.
[67] Ibid., article 10(b). [68] Ibid., article 8(j). [69] Ibid., article 11. [70] Ibid., article 22(1).
[71] See Conference of the Parties to the Convention on Biological Diversity, *Report of the Sixth Meeting of the Conference of the Parties to the Convention on Biological Diversity*, 6th mtg, annex 1 (Decisions Adopted by the Conference of the Parties to the Convention on Biological Diversity at its Sixth Meeting), VI/24(A) (Bonn Guidelines on Access to Genetic Resources and Fair and Equitable Sharing of the Benefits Arising out of their Utilization), UN Doc UNEP/CBD/COP/6/20 (2002) ('Bonn Guidelines').
[72] Ibid., [14]. [73] Ibid., [16]. [74] Ibid., [22]–[50].

other matters between the resource holder and the exploiter dealing with the access and benefit sharing arrangements.[75] However, the Bonn Guidelines do deal at some length with the various methods by which benefits might be shared, identifying those involved in the resource management, scientific and commercial process and the various kinds of monetary and non-monetary benefits.[76]

The development of an international regime is underway through the Ad Hoc Open-Ended Working Group on Access and Benefit-Sharing and distinct groups of technical and legal experts, which are presently establishing and negotiating the text of an agreement.[77] It seems unlikely at this stage that the proposed international regime will notably restrict or limit existing TRIPS obligations, although the potential remains.[78]

5. TRIPS framework's effect on access and benefit sharing

TRIPS was an annexure to the Final Act of the 1986–1994 Uruguay Round of Multilateral Trade Negotiations which created the WTO. TRIPS essentially establishes the minimum intellectual property standards that must be applied by all WTO member states.[79] In respect of access and benefit sharing the CBD's genetic resources patents are the major form of intellectual property that will apply.[80] TRIPS provides, in part, that 'patents shall be available for any inventions, whether products or processes, in all fields of technology, provided that they are new,

[75] Ibid., [45]–[50], annex, C. [76] Ibid., [45]–([50], appendix II.

[77] See Conference of the Parties to the Convention on Biological Diversity, *Report of the Seventh Meeting of the Conference of the Parties to the Convention on Biological Diversity*, 7th mtg, UNEP/CBD/COP/7/21 (2004) 298–313; Conference of the Parties to the Convention on Biological Diversity, *Report of the Eighth Meeting of the Parties to the Convention on Biological Diversity*, above n. 25, 128–38; Conference of the Parties to the Convention on Biological Diversity, *Report of the Conference of the Parties to the Convention on Biological Diversity on the Work of its Ninth Meeting*, above n. 24, 110–22.

[78] See Charles Lawson and Jay Sanderson, 'The Evolution of the CBD's Development Agenda that May Influence the Interpretation and Development of TRIPS', in Justin Malbon and Charles Lawson (eds.), *Interpreting and Implementing the WTO Trade Related Agreement on Intellectual Property Rights: Is TRIPS Fair?* (2008) 131, 150–1.

[79] TRIPS Agreement, above n. 2, article 1.

[80] See Life Sciences Program, World Intellectual Property Organization, *Patent Issues Related to Influenza Viruses and their Genes: An Overview* (2007), www.who.int/csr/disease/avian_influenza/WIPO_IP_%20paper19_10_2007.pdf at 8 March 2009; and World Health Organization, *Pandemic Influenza Preparedness: Sharing of Influenza Viruses and Access to Vaccine and Other Benefits, Patent Issues Related to Influenza Viruses and their Genes*, WHO Doc A/PIP/IGM/3 (2007) (Report by the Director-General).

involve an inventive step and are capable of industrial application … patents shall be available and patent rights enjoyable without discrimination as to the place of invention, the field of technology and whether products are imported or locally produced'.[81] The terms 'inventive step' and 'capable of industrial application' are synonymous with the concepts of 'non-obviousness' and 'usefulness', respectively. For patenting genetic materials these words have been interpreted in many countries, including Australia, in such a way that the composition of genetic materials (such as a virus isolated from a bodily fluid sample) can be claimed as an 'invention' once removed from 'nature' with an industrial 'use'.[82] The 'exclusive rights' of a patent owner are 'to prevent third parties not having the owner's consent from the acts of: making, using, offering for sale, selling, or importing for these purposes' the patented product, process and product of the process.[83] The only direct exceptions permitted from this general scheme are: (1) inventions 'necessary to protect *ordre public* or morality, including to protect human, animal or plant life or health or to avoid serious prejudice to the environment, provided that such exclusion is not made merely because the exploitation is prohibited by … law'; (2) 'diagnostic, therapeutic and surgical methods for the treatment of humans or animals'; and (3) 'plants and animals other than micro-organisms, and essentially biological processes for the production of plants or animals other than non-biological and microbiological processes'.[84] There is also a cumulative three-limbed indirect exception. Firstly, the exception must only be a 'limited exception'. Secondly, the exception must not 'unreasonably conflict with normal exploitation of the patent'. And finally, the exception must not 'unreasonably prejudice the legitimate interests of the patent owner, taking account of the legitimate interests of third parties',[85] and that a patent holder's exclusive rights may be diminished by an authorizing law after judicial or administrative processes have determined the patent to be anti-competitive, although each authorization must be considered on its individual merits.[86]

At least in theory, the property value established in the genetic resources by controlling access under the CBD can be distinguished

[81] TRIPS Agreement, above n. 2, article 27(1).

[82] See Charles Lawson and Catherine Pickering, 'Patenting Genetic Materials – Failing to Reflect the Value of Variation in DNA, RNA and Amino Acids' (2000) 11 *Australian Intellectual Property Journal* 69, 71–9.

[83] TRIPS Agreement, above n. 2, article 28. [84] Ibid., article 27(2)–(3).

[85] Ibid., article 30. [86] Ibid., article 31.

from the value of the potential intellectual property from using that genetic resource, so that some of the value of the intellectual property can contribute to the compensation and incentive for biological diversity conservation.[87] At its most simple, the property rights over the accessed genetic resources under the CBD deal *only* with the tangible 'genetic resources'. TRIPS patents, meanwhile, relate *only* to the intangible innovation and creativity in products and processes that result from using the biological resource. Thus a patent deals with an 'invention' that is novel, non-obvious and industrially useful, is described in a way that can be followed by others, and establishes property (or 'exclusive rights') to certain dealings with the 'invention'. These are different economic commodities, one the tangible genetic resource and the other the intangible application of that genetic resource for an innovative or creative and useful purpose.[88] This distinction may not, however, be so elegant in practice as a patent confounds the right to deal with the genetic resource as it is embodied in a tangible form (such as a purified and isolated virus sequence, or a composition per se) with the right to prevent others from using the genetic resource in other embodiments (such as the virus sequence in a diagnostic device or the preparation of a vaccine).[89] In short, the uncertainty arises because past claims (and disclosures in the public domain) to compositions per se may limit the value of future uses of the same or similar compositions, even where those uses are entirely different, because the patent's 'exclusive rights' are attached to the composition per se (according to its definition and description) rather than its many and varied useful applications. As a consequence, the problem posed by patents is the potential to undermine the value of the

[87] For an overview of the issues see, e.g., Timothy Swanson and Timo Goeschl, 'Property Rights Issues Involving Plant Genetic Resources: Implications of Ownership for Economic Efficiency' (2000) 32 *Ecological Economics* 75, 79–85.

[88] See Life Sciences Program, World Intellectual Property Organization, *Patent Issues Related to Influenza Viruses and their Genes*, above n. 80, 14–16. See also World Health Organization, *Patent Issues Related to Influenza Viruses and their Genes*, above n. 80; Initiative for Vaccine Research, World Health Organization, *Mapping of Intellectual Property Related to the Production of Pandemic Influenza Vaccines* (2007).

[89] See, e.g., Lawson and Pickering, 'Patenting Genetic Materials', above n. 82; Charles Lawson, 'Patenting Genetic Diversity – Old Rules May Be Restricting the Exploitation of a New Technology' (1999) 6 *Journal of Law and Medicine* 373. See also Life Sciences Program, World Intellectual Property Organization, *Patent Issues Related to Influenza Viruses and their Genes*, above n. 80, 27–33; European Community, *Global Status and Trends in Intellectual Property Claims: Genomics, Proteomics and Biotechnology*, Ad Hoc Open-Ended Working Group on Access and Benefit-Sharing, 3rd mtg, 32–52, UN Doc UNEP/CBD/WG-ABS/3/INF/4 (2005) (Submission by the European Community).

accessed genetic resource and other *in situ* genetic resources by creating uncertain proprietary and use rights in the tangible accessed materials, and the uses of that material in innovative or creative and useful embodiments.[90] In the context of avian influenza the consequence is potentially even starker: existing patents claiming a virus, or part of a virus composition per se, or a step in the development of a vaccine using a virus, or part of a virus composition per se, may prevent the use of that composition or require consent of the patent holder to exercise the patented product, process or product of the process. The real potential for these kinds of results is readily apparent from an analysis of the existing avian influenza and vaccine patents[91] and goes to the core of Indonesia's concern that an Indonesian provided H5N1 virus sample provided to the WHO's Global Influenza Surveillance Network ('GISN') was given to an Australian vaccine manufacturer that intended to patent (in some respect) the vaccine that Indonesia would then need to purchase.[92]

Notably, TRIPS was embroiled in contentions between its members about 'the gravity of the public health problems afflicting many developing and least-developed countries, especially those resulting from HIV/AIDS, tuberculosis, malaria and other epidemics'[93] and the potential of patents to exacerbate those public health crises.[94] This arose in the context of whether TRIPS might be ameliorated by taking advantage of one of its 'principles': 'Members may … adopt measures necessary to protect public health and nutrition, and to promote the public interest in sectors of vital importance to their socioeconomic and technological

90 For overly broad patent claims to biological materials see Lawson and Pickering, 'Patenting Genetic Materials', above n. 82. For uncertain definitions and descriptions see Charles Lawson, 'Depositing Seeds to Comply with the Patents Act 1990 (Cth) – The Adequacy of Definition and Description?' (2004) 23 *University of Tasmania Law Review* 68. See also Life Sciences Program, World Intellectual Property Organization, *Patent Issues Related to Influenza Viruses and their Genes*, above n. 80.

91 See World Health Organization, *Patent Issues Related to Influenza Viruses and their Genes*, above n. 80; Life Sciences Program, World Intellectual Property Organization, *Patent Issues Related to Influenza Viruses and their Genes*, above n. 80; Initiative for Vaccine Research, World Health Organization, *Mapping of Intellectual Property Related to the Production of Pandemic Influenza Vaccines*, above n. 88.

92 See Sedyaningsih *et al.*, 'Towards Mutual Trust, Transparency and Equity in Virus Sharing Mechanism', above n. 3, 486.

93 Declaration on the TRIPS Agreement and Public Health: Adopted on 14 November 2001, WTO Doc WT/MIN(01)/DEC/2 (2001) ('the Doha Declaration'), [1].

94 See, e.g., Jane Nielsen and Dianne Nicol, 'Pharmaceutical Patents and Developing Countries: The Conundrum of Access and Incentive' (2002) 13 *Australian Intellectual Property Journal* 21, 21–4.

development'.[95] These issues were first formally identified in the Doha Declaration,[96] and then in the Declaration on the TRIPS Agreement and Public Health that provided, in part: 'we affirm that the Agreement can and should be interpreted and implemented in a manner supportive of WTO members' right to protect public health and, in particular, to promote access to medicines for all'.[97]

Subsequent work by the TRIPS Council and General Council extended the pharmaceutical product patent obligations until 2016 (para. 7),[98] and formulated a resolution for importing pharmaceuticals under compulsory licence to members without the necessary manufacturing capability to produce their own essential medicines.[99] By the time of the Hong Kong Ministerial Conference the issue had further advanced,[100] so that through the amendment of TRIPS (specifically, the addition of article 31*bis*) there may be a solution to making patented pharmaceuticals available in public health programmes.[101] The significance of these developments has been to confirm that 'TRIPS does not and should not prevent members from taking measures to protect public health',[102] and that a solution exists for the making of vaccines through compulsory licensing where 'WTO members with insufficient or no manufacturing

95 TRIPS Agreement, above n. 2, article 8(1).

96 Ministerial Declaration: Adopted on 14 November 2001, WTO Doc WT/MIN(01)/DEC/1 (2001) [17].

97 The Doha Declaration, above n. 93, [4]–[7].

98 See Extension of the Transition Period under Article 66.1 of the TRIPS Agreement for Least-Developed Country Members for Certain Obligations with Respect to Pharmaceutical Products, WTO Doc IP/C/25 (2005) (Decision by the Council for TRIPS of 27 June 2002); Council for Trade-Related Aspects of Intellectual Property Rights, Extension of the Transition Period under Article 66(1) of the TRIPS Agreement for Least-Developed Country Members for Certain Obligations with Respect to Pharmaceutical Products, IP/C/25 (2002); Least-Developed Country Members – Obligations under Article 70.9 of the TRIPS Agreement with Respect to Pharmaceutical Products, WTO Doc WT/L/478 (2002) (Decision of the General Council of 8 July 2002).

99 See Implementation of Paragraph 6 of the Doha Declaration on the TRIPS Agreement and Public Health, WTO Doc WT/L/540 (2003) (WTO General Council Decision of 30 August 2003).

100 Doha Work Programme, Ministerial Conference 6th sess, WTO Doc WT/MIN(05)/DEC (2005) [40] (Ministerial Declaration).

101 See World Trade Organization, *Protocol Amending the TRIPS Agreement – Status of Acceptances*, WTO Doc IP/C/W/490/Rev.1 (2007) (Note from the Secretariat – Revision).

102 The Doha Declaration, above n. 93, [4]. See also Interdisciplinary Working Group, *Sharing of Influenza Viruses and Access to Vaccines and Other Benefits: Interdisciplinary Working Group on Pandemic Influenza Preparedness*, above n. 27, annex.

capacities in the pharmaceutical sector could face difficulties in making effective use of compulsory licensing under the TRIPS'.[103]

Despite all these developments, the threshold TRIPS obligations to respect patent rights remain subject only to the limited exceptions allowed by the 'flexibility' in TRIPS, and the possibility of compulsory licensing in the absence of necessary manufacturing capability. In addressing avian influenza and the likely resultant pandemic the response will require both improvements to domestic production capacity and efficacy of pandemic influenza vaccines targeted to the specific influenza variants.[104] The concern for countries of the South is that existing patents claiming a virus, or part of a virus composition per se, or a step in the development of a vaccine using a virus, or part of a virus composition per se, may prevent the use of that composition or require agreement with the patent holder to exercise the patented product, process or product of the process.[105] And while some of these patents may not be applicable in the particular jurisdiction, the technology necessary to develop efficient and effective vaccines needs to be accessed from patent holders in the countries of the North together with the related know-how and regulatory submissions data.[106] In short, intellectual property is a central concern in developing effective responses to avian influenza and the likely resultant pandemic.

6. WHO and avian influenza

The WHO's International Health Regulations (2005) established a framework (effective from 15 June 2007) for preventing, controlling and responding to the international spread of diseases such as avian influenza.[107] As part of the general obligation on states 'to prevent, protect

[103] The Doha Declaration, above n. 93, [6]. See also Interdisciplinary Working Group, *Sharing of Influenza Viruses and Access to Vaccines and Other Benefits: Interdisciplinary Working Group on Pandemic Influenza Preparedness*, above n. 27.

[104] See Kelley Lee and David Fidler, 'Avian and Pandemic Influenza: Progress and Problems with Global Health Governance' (2007) 2 *Global Public Health* 215, 218–24. See also World Health Organization, *Global Pandemic Influenza Action Plan to Increase Vaccine Supply*, above n. 4.

[105] See World Health Organization, *Patent Issues Related to Influenza Viruses and their Genes*, above n. 80; Life Sciences Program, World Intellectual Property Organization, *Patent Issues Related to Influenza Viruses and their Genes*, above n. 80; and Initiative for Vaccine Research, World Health Organization, *Mapping of Intellectual Property Related to the Production of Pandemic Influenza Vaccines*, above n. 88.

[106] See, e.g., ibid., 1–2.

[107] Revision of the International Health Regulations, World Health Assembly 58th mtg (2005), Res WHA58.3 ('International Health Regulations (2005)'); See also Application of the

against, control and provide a public health response to the international spread of disease',[108] there is a more specific obligation to deal with 'biological substances':

> States Parties shall, subject to national law and taking into account relevant international guidelines, facilitate the transport, entry, exit, processing and disposal of biological substances and diagnostic specimens, reagents and other diagnostic materials for verification and public health response purposes under these Regulations.[109]

In implementing the International Health Regulations (2005), however, members were 'urged' to 'disseminate to WHO collaborating centres information and relevant biological materials related to highly pathogenic avian influenza and other novel influenza strains in a timely and consistent manner'.[110] In addition to these measures, and expressly in response to the H5N1 avian influenza, the WHO convened a consultation with national immunization programmes, national regulatory authorities, vaccine manufacturers and the research community to draw up the Global Pandemic Influenza Action Plan to Increase Vaccine Supply to identify and prioritize practical solutions for reducing the anticipated gaps in vaccine supply.[111] Subsequently, and after considering the developments, responses and follow-ups to avian and pandemic influenza,[112] members reaffirmed their obligations under the International Health Regulations (2005), recognizing 'the sovereign right of States over their biological resources', and recognizing that 'intellectual property rights do not and should not prevent Member States from taking measures to protect public health'.[113] Members also requested the Director-General of the WHO to undertake work directed at resolving the apparent conflicts between access to and benefit sharing

International Health Regulations (2005), World Health Assembly 59th mtg, Res WHA59.2 (2006); Strengthening Pandemic-Influenza Preparedness and Response, World Health Assembly 58th mtg, Res WHA58.5 (2005).

108 International Health Regulations (2005), above n. 107, article 2.

109 Ibid., article 46.

110 Application of the International Health Regulations (2005), Res WHA59.2, World Health Assembly 59th mtg (2006), [4(4)].

111 See World Health Organization, *Global Pandemic Influenza Action Plan to Increase Vaccine Supply*, above n. 4. See also ibid.; Strengthening Pandemic-Influenza Preparedness and Response, above n. 107.

112 See World Health Organization, *Global Pandemic Influenza Action Plan to Increase Vaccine Supply*, above n. 4.

113 Pandemic Influenza Preparedness: Sharing of Influenza Viruses and Access to Vaccines and Other Benefits, World Health Assembly 60th mtg, Res WHA60.28, preamble (2007).

of the virus.[114] Importantly, the request specifically addressed the access to and benefit sharing of viruses from which vaccines could be made to deal with avian and other pandemic influenzas.[115] This request involved both an interdisciplinary working group[116] and an intergovernmental meeting.[117]

In response, the Director-General convened an interdisciplinary working group[118] that addressed access and benefit sharing, in part, in the context of 'sharing of viruses and information, and subsequent benefits' and 'development of standard terms and conditions and terms of reference for the transfer of influenza viruses'.[119] While failing to provide a comprehensive consensus view, the interdisciplinary working group reported that the 'overriding concern expressed by most members … was that neither intellectual property rights nor prior informed-consent requirements, if any, should stand in the way of developing and producing a pandemic influenza vaccine'.[120] The interdisciplinary working group also reported on the content of the proposed terms and conditions. The group considered that no party receiving, handling or using virus specimens should claim ownership,[121] intellectual property claims needed to disclose the specimen's country of origin, and any 'financial gain' from intellectual property should require an equivalent financial contribution to the WHO.[122] This latter agreement set out a range of benefit sharing options including: cash, access to technology, transfer of technology and know-how, and provision of vaccines and their developmental components.[123] The outcomes of the interdisciplinary working group then contributed to the subsequent intergovernmental meeting.[124]

[114] Ibid., [2]. [115] Ibid., [2(5)]. [116] Ibid., [2(5)]. [117] Ibid., [2(7)].

[118] Interdisciplinary Working Group, *Sharing of Influenza Viruses and Access to Vaccines and Other Benefits: Interdisciplinary Working Group on Pandemic Influenza Preparedness*, WHO Doc A/PIP/IGM/4 (2007), annex [1] (Report by the Director-General).

[119] Ibid., annex [4]. [120] Ibid., annex [11].

[121] Ibid., annex, appendix 3 (Standard Terms and Conditions for the Transfer and Use of Influenza Biological Materials) [30].

[122] Ibid., annex, appendix 3 (Standard Terms and Conditions for the Transfer and Use of Influenza Biological Materials) [31]–[32].

[123] Ibid., annex, appendix 3 (Standard Terms and Conditions for the Transfer and Use of Influenza Biological Materials) (Contribution Agreement to WHO's Coordinated International Sharing of Influenza Viruses & Benefits By and between WHO and [Company Name]).

[124] See ibid.

The Director-General also convened an intergovernmental meeting 'to identify and propose, in close consultation with Member States, frameworks and mechanisms that aimed to ensure fair and equitable sharing of benefits'.[125] The outcome of this intergovernmental meeting was to identify and reaffirm the relevant 'guiding principles' for 'the sharing of, and access to, benefits that result from the sharing of influenza viruses'.[126] There was also an 'interim statement' from the intergovernmental meeting that appeared to accept that the existing domestic and international legal frameworks were not appropriate.[127]

The outcome of this intergovernmental meeting was to 'establish a technical and feasible system as soon as possible within WHO to track all shared H5N1 and other potentially pandemic human viruses and the parts thereof' (a traceability mechanism) and to 'establish an advisory mechanism to monitor, provide guidance to strengthen the functioning of the system and undertake necessary assessment of the trust-based system needed to protect public health' (an advisory mechanism).[128] In the interim however, 'viruses and samples are to be shared within the WHO system, consistent with national laws and regulations, while the detailed framework for virus sharing and benefit sharing continues to be developed'.[129] The interim traceability measures required that 'each A

[125] World Health Organization, *Reports by the Director-General: Summary Progress Reports*, WHO Doc A/PIP/IGM/2 Rev.1 (2007) [1].

[126] Ibid., [2]. See also Pandemic Influenza Preparedness: Sharing of Influenza Viruses and Access to Vaccines and Other Benefits, above n. 26, [2(5)]; World Health Organization, *Avian and Pandemic Influenza: Developments, Response and Follow-Up, and Application of the International Health Regulations (2005): Best Practice for Sharing Influenza Viruses and Sequence Data*, Executive Board 120th sess, WHO Doc EB120/INF.DOC./3 (2007) [7] (Report by the Secretariat).

[127] World Health Organization, *Pandemic Influenza Preparedness: Sharing of Influenza Viruses and Access to Vaccines and Other Benefits – Intergovernmental Meeting: Report of Progress to Date*, Executive Board 122nd sess, WHO Doc EB122/5 (2008) annex 5 (Interim Statement of the Intergovernmental Meeting on Pandemic Influenza Preparedness: Sharing of Influenza Viruses and Access to Vaccine and Other Benefits) preamble ('*Pandemic Influenza – Annex 5 – Interim Statement*'). See also World Health Organization, *Pandemic Influenza Preparedness: Sharing of Influenza Viruses and Access to Vaccines and Other Benefits – Intergovernmental Meeting: Report of Progress to Date*, Executive Board 122nd sess, WHO Doc EB122/5 (2008) annex 6 (Consolidated Outcome Text: Index) [2]–[2.5] ('*Pandemic Influenza – Annex 6 – Consolidated Outcome Text: Index*').

[128] *Pandemic Influenza – Annex 5 – Interim Statement*, above n. 127, [1]–[2]. See also *Pandemic Influenza – Annex 6 – Consolidated Outcome Text: Index*, above n. 127.

[129] *Pandemic Influenza – Annex 5 – Interim Statement*, above n. 127, [3]. See also *Pandemic Influenza – Annex 6 – Consolidated Outcome Text: Index*, above n. 127.

(H5N1) virus so submitted [be] assigned a unique identifier and data on it [be] stored in an electronic database'. The data to be stored in this was to 'include the location of each virus, information on analyses that have been done on the virus, further use of the virus in the development of H5N1 vaccine viruses, and recipients of the vaccine viruses and other viruses'.[130] The meeting also agreed to convene an open-ended working group to further advance the work of developing a traceability mechanism and an advisory mechanism[131] before suspending proceedings.[132] While there remained considerable work to be done before reaching a comprehensive agreement about the sharing of viruses, it was apparent at this stage that the core requirements of the CBD for sovereign rights over biological resources, prior informed consent and access and benefit sharing according to agreement would form part of the resolution.[133] What essentially remained to be resolved was the text of the access and benefit sharing 'arrangements', some contention remaining about whether these were the definition and scope for the sharing of viruses or a 'standard Material Transfer Agreement'.[134] Notably, Indonesia preferred the latter.[135] The significance of the terminology reflected the likely sources of influence on the 'arrangements' with the phrase 'standard Material Transfer Agreement' having resonance for the CBD and other similar genetic resource sharing legal frameworks, such as the Food and Agriculture Organization of the United Nations' International Treaty on Plant Genetic Resources for Food and Agriculture.[136]

Following this intergovernmental meeting the open-ended working group convened and decided 'to further the work on sharing influenza viruses and access to vaccines and other benefits by discussing, in an issue-based manner, aspects on which it was likely for the meeting to

[130] World Health Assembly, *Pandemic Influenza Preparedness: Sharing of Influenza Viruses and Access to Vaccines and Other Benefits*, World Health Assembly 61st mtg, WHO Doc, A61/4 (2008) [4] (Report by the Secretariat).

[131] *Pandemic Influenza – Annex 5 – Interim Statement*, above n. 127, [4]. See also *Pandemic Influenza – Annex 6 – Consolidated Outcome Text: Index*, above n. 127.

[132] World Health Assembly, *Pandemic Influenza Preparedness: Sharing of Influenza Viruses and Access to Vaccines and Other Benefits*, above n. 130, [3].

[133] See *Pandemic Influenza – Annex 5 – Interim Statement*, above n. 127, [6]. See also *Pandemic Influenza – Annex 6 – Consolidated Outcome Text: Index*, above n. 127.

[134] *Pandemic Influenza – Annex 6 – Consolidated Outcome Text: Index*, above n. 127.

[135] Ibid.

[136] See Charles Lawson, 'Patents and the CGIAR System of International Agricultural Research Centres' Germplasm Collections under the *International Treaty on Plant Genetic Resources for Food and Agriculture*' (2004) 55 *Australian Journal of Agricultural Research* 307.

reach consensus'.[137] A 'Chair's text' was to be prepared for a future meeting and 'benefit sharing' was identified as 'crucial', with the minutes recording that 'the issue will be discussed' at that future meeting.[138] The 'Chair's text' was subsequently prepared and considered by the resumed open-ended working group and then an intergovernmental meeting.[139] The intergovernmental meeting considered a traceability mechanism,[140] an advisory mechanism,[141] and updated virus sample sharing negotiations.[142] The outcome was to entrench the bipolarity of views between South and North: the South, being the predominant providers of viruses, wanted to avoid development-stage intellectual property restrictions through benefit sharing arrangements; the North, hosting the laboratories and manufacturing capacity to produce vaccines and other medical products, wanted to allow intellectual property claims and avoid detailed (and potentially restrictive) benefit sharing arrangements.[143] The meeting was eventually suspended with disagreement remaining about the form and content of the benefit sharing arrangements and obligations.[144]

7. WHO compromise arrangement

An early outcome of the WHO's action on avian influenza was an agreement to negotiate the terms of an instrument addressing issues relating to the sharing of viruses, including: sovereign rights, benefit sharing, capacity building, intellectual property, oversight mechanisms, technology transfer and transparency and accountability.[145] The content

137 Open-Ended Working Group, *Report on Progress to Date*, WHO Doc A/PIP/IGM/WG/5 (2008) [9].

138 Ibid., [10]; World Health Organization, *Pandemic Influenza Preparedness: Sharing of Influenza Viruses and Access to Vaccines and Other Benefits*, Executive Board 124th sess, WHO Doc EB124/4 (2008) [3] (Report by the Secretariat).

139 See World Health Organization, *Chair's Text – Draft – Pandemic Influenza Preparedness Framework for the Sharing of Influenza Viruses and Access to Vaccines and Other Benefits*, above n. 29.

140 See World Health Organization, *Reports by the Director-General: Summary Progress Reports – WHO Influenza Virus Traceability Mechanism*, WHO Doc A/PIP/IGM/9 (2008).

141 See World Health Organization, *Reports of the Director-General: Establishment of the Advisory Mechanism*, WHO Doc A/PIP/IGM/8 (2008).

142 See World Health Organization, *Chair's Text – Draft – Pandemic Influenza Preparedness Framework for the Sharing of Influenza Viruses and Access to Vaccines and Other Benefits*, above n. 29.

143 See Shashikant, *Key Issues Unresolved at WHO Meeting on Influenza Virus Sharing*, above n. 28.

144 See ibid.

145 *Pandemic Influenza – Annex 6 – Consolidated Outcome Text: Index*, above n. 127.

of the negotiating text falls within the obligations imposed by both the CBD and TRIPS and highlights the conflict between these obligations.[146]

Significantly, at the same time that these debates were taking place about avian influenza and virus sharing, the WHO was also considering a policy formulated by the Commission on Intellectual Property Rights, Innovation and Public Health and an intergovernmental working group directed to 'an analysis of intellectual property rights, innovation, and public health, including the question of appropriate funding and incentive mechanisms for the creation of new medicines and other products against diseases that disproportionately affect developing countries'.[147] The outcome was the adoption of a 'global strategy and the agreed parts of the plan of action on public health, innovation and intellectual property' for the period 2008–15.[148]

The 'global strategy' and the 'agreed parts of the plan of action' do not displace the existing internationally contested provisions of the CBD or TRIPS. Essentially, the WHO's 'global strategy' position maintains the status quo for the CBD and TRIPS. This is important, as the negotiation of the 'global strategy' and the 'agreed parts of the plan of action' expressly excluded propositions that might have limited the application of the CBD or TRIPS.[149] So, for example, the statement that '[t]he right to health takes precedence over commercial interests'[150] was removed and the phrase 'promote transfer of technology and production of health products in developing countries through investment and capacity building, including by providing guidance on appropriate technologies' was reduced to 'promote transfer of technology and production of health products in developing countries through investment and capacity building'.[151] Similarly, the phrase 'avoid the incorporation of

[146] See, e.g., ibid., articles 5.2–5.3, 7.1–7.2.

[147] Intellectual Property Rights, Innovation and Public Health, World Health Assembly 56th mtg, Res WHA56.27 (2003) [2(2)]; Application of the International Health Regulations (2005), World Health Assembly 59th mtg, Res WHA59.2 (2006) [3(1)].

[148] Global Strategy and Plan of Action on Public Health, Innovation and Intellectual Property, World Health Assembly 61st mtg, Res WHA61.21 (2008) [1], annex (Global Strategy on Public Health, Innovation and Intellectual Property) [13].

[149] Compare the final text: ibid., annex (Global Strategy on Public Health, Innovation and Intellectual Property) with the negotiating text: World Health Assembly, *Report of the Intergovernmental Working Group on Public Health, Innovation and Intellectual Property*, 61st mtg, WHO Doc A61/9 (2008) annex 1.

[150] World Health Assembly, *Report of the Intergovernmental Working Group on Public Health, Innovation and Intellectual Property*, above n. 149, [18].

[151] Ibid., [34].

TRIPS-Plus measures in any trade agreements and in national legislation that may have negative impact on access to health products or treatments in developing countries' was removed.[152] Notably, provisions were also included that expressly maintained the effect of existing international agreements, such as the phrase 'frame and implement policies to improve access to safe and effective health products, especially essential medicines, at affordable prices, *consistent with international agreements*',[153] and so on.

The 'Chair's text' considered by the open-ended working group and the intergovernmental meeting[154] reflected these tensions about intellectual property although there was acceptance by all parties that a resolution was necessary for global preparedness to deal with avian influenza and the likely resultant pandemic.[155] Thus, for example, the 'Chair's text' set out principles apparent in both the CBD and TRIPS: the sovereign right of states over their biological resources, the role of intellectual property as an incentive, the development of new healthcare products and the taking of measures to protect public health.[156]

The 'Chair's text' envisions a 'standard Materials Transfer Agreement' that 'will be standardized, universal and globally applicable to all transfers of PIP biological materials and not subject to further negotiation'.[157] The 'ownership' of transferred materials remains contested with the possibility that ownership is either not transferred or not asserted.[158] Further, the proposed intellectual property provision again reflects tensions apparent in both the CBD and TRIPS.[159]

The outcome of the intergovernmental meeting in December 2008 failed to reach agreement and will resume during the May 2009 World Health Assembly.[160] The role and place of intellectual property and

[152] Ibid., [36].

[153] Global Strategy and Plan of Action on Public Health, Innovation and Intellectual Property, above n. 148, [39] (emphasis added).

[154] See World Health Organization, *Chair's Text – Draft – Pandemic Influenza Preparedness Framework for the Sharing of Influenza Viruses and Access to Vaccines and Other Benefits*, above n. 29.

[155] See, e.g., Ministers of Foreign Affairs of Brazil, France, Indonesia, Norway, Senegal, South Africa and Thailand, 'Oslo Ministerial Declaration – Global Health: A Pressing Foreign Policy Issue of our Time' (2007) 369 *The Lancet* 1373.

[156] World Health Organization, *Chair's Text – Draft – Pandemic Influenza Preparedness Framework for the Sharing of Influenza Viruses and Access to Vaccines and Other Benefits*, above n. 29, [1.1] (PP7–PP10).

[157] Ibid., [5.3.2]. [158] Ibid., annex 1 [11]. [159] Ibid., annex 1 [12].

[160] See Shashikant, *Key Issues Unresolved at WHO Meeting on Influenza Virus Sharing*, above n. 28.

benefit sharing remain contentious with there being a polarizing of interests between the South and North countries: essentially, the South countries asserting the significance of linkages between access and benefit sharing and the North countries asserting the contrary.[161]

8. Discussion

Generally, 'genetic resources' are understood to have value. However, it is frequently the case that a particularly valuable resource will be found together with large quantities of presently valueless materials with the potential of significant upfront expenditure to distinguish between the valuable and other useless materials.[162] In those circumstances the negotiating power generally lies with those wanting to access the genetic resources (the bio-prospectors) and as a consequence the value of 'genetic resources' has generally been valued at a low level – the value does not reflect the costs that would be reasonable, adequate and sufficient as an incentive for biological diversity conservation.[163] However, in the case of Indonesia's H5N1 viruses, Indonesia as the 'genetic resource' holder has the negotiating power and is in a position to dictate terms of use. The significance of the 'concession' made to Indonesia in making the H5N1 virus available to elements of the WHO's GISN is that it is one of the first instances where the provider of 'genetic resources' is in a position where they have a clearly identifiable material that others (bio-prospectors) want, and also have a driving imperative to obtain so as to mitigate their public health responses to pandemic influenza. Further, Indonesia is a country of the South (with the interests of the predominantly poor countries with the majority of the Earth's useful biological diversity), hoping to benefit from the exploitation of its genetic diversity by the predominantly rich and technologically advanced countries of the North. In this context, Indonesia's H5N1 viruses provide an unorthodox case study of the interaction between the CBD and TRIPS.

While the final details of the agreement for accessing Indonesia's H5N1 viruses has been generalized by the WHO processes to accessing all viruses, the development towards agreement has followed the contours of the CBD (and TRIPS) obligations.[164] That is, Indonesia has been

[161] See ibid.

[162] See John Voumard, *Access to Biological Resources in Commonwealth Areas* (2000), 93–103.

[163] See Charles Lawson, 'Regulating Access to Biological Resources: The Market Failure for Biodiversity Conservation' (2006) 24 *Law in Context* 137, 146–51.

[164] See also Ministers of Foreign Affairs of Brazil, France, Indonesia, Norway, Senegal, South Africa and Thailand, above n. 155.

specific in pressing its concerns about benefit sharing and tied these closely with the obligations established by the CBD. So, for example, the Indonesian proposal suggested the following 'fundamental elements' should be taken into account when developing any new system addressing access and benefit sharing:

> The originating country providing access to virus: (1) retains sovereign rights over the virus and any virus material contained or incorporated in any substances or products created; (2) has the right to get immediately the results of the risk assessment; (3) has the right to timely receive seed virus and isolated virus at no cost; (4) has the right to participate in the execution of research and participate actively in publications; and (5) has the right to be adequately acknowledged.[165]

Within these 'fundamental elements' is embedded the 'sovereign rights' of Indonesia to regulate access to all viruses within its sovereign jurisdiction. As a party to the CBD this also coincides with the obligation that access must be from countries of origin or countries that have acquired the genetic resources according to the CBD,[166] on mutually agreed terms,[167] with prior informed consent[168] and the equitable sharing of benefits.[169]

Perhaps Indonesia's recourse to these obligations is to be expected, as a direct result of the GISN apparent breach of trust.[170] The publication of laboratory analyses based on Indonesian H5N1 viruses provided to GISN without timely involvement of Indonesian collaborators; the limited release of Indonesian H5N1 virus sequence data by GISN; and the use by private pharmaceutical companies of Indonesian H5N1 viruses (supplied by GISN) to manufacture vaccines without Indonesia's participation resulted in Indonesia's drastic action to withhold Indonesian H5N1 viruses from the WHO's GISN.[171] Before these events Indonesia's H5N1 viruses were collected and supplied without charge or obligation to elements of the GISN.[172] However, in a broader context the

[165] Interdisciplinary Working Group, *Sharing of Influenza Viruses and Access to Vaccines and Other Benefits: Interdisciplinary Working Group on Pandemic Influenza Preparedness*, above n. 27, annex [6].

[166] CBD, above n. 1, article 15(3). [167] Ibid., article 15(4). [168] Ibid., article 15(5).

[169] Ibid., article 15(7).

[170] See *Pandemic Influenza – Annex 5 – Interim Statement*, above n. 127, preamble. See also *Pandemic Influenza – Annex 6 – Consolidated Outcome Text: Index*, above n. 127.

[171] See Sedyaningsih *et al.*, 'Towards Mutual Trust, Transparency and Equity in Virus Sharing Mechanism', above n. 3, 485–6.

[172] See ibid., 485; World Health Organization, *A Summary of Tracking Avian Influenza A (H5N1) Specimens and Viruses Shared with the WTO from 2003 to 2007*, above n. 5.

international legal obligations established by the CBD and TRIPS have direct application.

The sting for the WHO's GISN accessing Indonesian H5N1 viruses, however, is that compliance with the CBD's obligations entails a contract-based access and benefit sharing arrangement, whereas North country rhetoric demands compliance with intellectual property: namely, that the terms and conditions of intellectual property must be determined as a part of the access and benefit sharing contract, and that the existing intellectual property standards must be respected. Framing Indonesia's position within the context of the CBD and TRIPS obligations suggests Indonesia's response is entirely reasonable (albeit eliciting moral outrage from some).[173] However, Indonesia's response also poses a specific dilemma for the North countries and their past actions in asserting the paramountcy of intellectual property in the debates about access to medicines that were eventually addressed, at least in part, in the Declaration on the TRIPS Agreement and Public Health.[174] Further, the North countries have consistently failed to negotiate a resolution to the South countries' concerns about intellectual property claims over genetic resources (or 'bio-piracy') in the CBD's forums,[175] and those concerns have spilled over into the TRIPS forum (and other WTO forums) with the countries of the North maintaining the necessity for intellectual property over other policy objectives.[176] The result is that Indonesia's proposition that the WHO negotiate a contractual arrangement to access viruses found within Indonesia's sovereign territory and that the terms and conditions of access reflect the agreement between the parties is, in effect, adopting exactly what has been agreed at the CBD.

[173] See, e.g., Staff Writer, 'International Health Regulations: The Challenges Ahead' (2007) 369 *The Lancet* 1763; European Centre for Disease Prevention and Control, *Interim ECDC Scientific and Public Health Briefing: Sharing Influenza Virus Samples* (2008) 1–2, ecdc.europa.eu/pdf/ECDC_influenza_briefing.pdf at 9 March 2009. See also Laurie Garrett and David Fidler, 'Sharing H5N1 Viruses to Stop a Global Influenza Pandemic' (2007) 4(11) *Public Library of Science Medicine* 1712, doi:10.1371/journal.pmed.0040330 at 9 March 2009.

[174] See the Doha Declaration, above n. 93, [4]–[7]. See also Pedro Roffe, Christoph Spennemann and Johanna von Braun, 'From Paris to Doha: The WTO Doha Declaration on the TRIPS Agreement and Public Health', in Pedro Roffe, Geoff Tansey and David Vivas-Eugui (eds.), *Negotiating Health Intellectual Property and Access to Medicines* (2006), 9.

[175] These developing contentions are detailed in Lawson and Sanderson, 'The Evolution of the CBD's Development Agenda', above n. 78, 135–43.

[176] See, e.g., ibid., 143–6.

The concern for countries of the South is that existing patents may prevent the use of a patented product, process or product of the process thereby tying up the technology necessary to develop efficient and effective vaccines.[177] Enhancing the production capacity and efficacy of pandemic influenza vaccines almost certainly depends on technology accessed from patent holders in countries of the North together with the related know-how and regulatory submissions data.[178] These concerns are specifically reflected in Indonesia's 'fundamental elements' that should be taken into account when developing any new system addressing access and benefit sharing:

> [A] framework of benefit sharing is to be developed through agreed terms and conditions to ensure global stockpile of pre-pandemic and pandemic vaccines, accessibility of vaccine at an affordable price, access to and transfer of technology and know-how for production of vaccines, and empowerment and capacity building of vaccine manufacturing in developing countries.[179]

The challenge for the North which wants access to the Indonesian H5N1 viruses is that compliance with the CBD (and TRIPS) obligations is critical to mitigating their public health responses to pandemic influenza. This will require negotiation of a deal with Indonesia where Indonesia has the negotiating power and is in a position to dictate terms, including limiting the ownership of intellectual property, requiring the transfer of technology and know-how (probably establishing vaccine research and manufacturing facilities in Indonesia) and assistance in regulatory submissions data so that the vaccines are both safe and efficacious. The alternative will be to undermine the careful position which the countries of the North have engineered in establishing the paramountcy of TRIPS over the CBD and other policy objectives, and open the floodgates to the South's desire to limit the effect of TRIPS on the CBD and of TRIPS itself.

[177] See World Health Organization, *Patent Issues Related to Influenza Viruses and their Genes*, above n. 80; Life Sciences Program, World Intellectual Property Organization, *Patent Issues Related to Influenza Viruses and their Genes*, above n. 80; Initiative for Vaccine Research, World Health Organization, *Mapping of Intellectual Property Related to the Production of Pandemic Influenza Vaccines*, above n. 88.

[178] See, e.g., ibid., 1–2, 19.

[179] Interdisciplinary Working Group, *Sharing of Influenza Viruses and Access to Vaccines and Other Benefits: Interdisciplinary Working Group on Pandemic Influenza Preparedness*, above n. 27, annex (Fundamental Principles and Elements for the Development of a New System for Virus Access and Fair and Equitable Benefit Sharing Arising from the Use of the Virus for the Pandemic Influenza Preparedness), [9].

In short, failure to negotiate a deal with Indonesia according to the terms and conditions agreeable to Indonesia opens up the debate about the paramountcy of intellectual property rights and TRIPS, and introduces the potential for other policy imperatives to override respect for intellectual property rights – in other words, if the North does not comply with its CBD and TRIPS rhetoric and commitments, why should the South?

12

The Lazarus Effect: the (RED) Campaign and creative capitalism

MATTHEW RIMMER*

1. Introduction

> 4,400 people die every day of AIDS in sub-Saharan Africa. Treatment exists. In about 60 days, a patient can go from here to here. We call this transformation the Lazarus Effect. It is the result of two pills a day taken by a HIV/AIDS patient for about 60 days. Learn more about how you can help give people the chance of life and joinred.com.
>
> The Lazarus Effect video, the (RED) Campaign[1]

In the recent literature, there has been much critical discussion about the role of patent law in promoting research and development in respect of neglected diseases. There has also been much exploration of alternative mechanisms – such as prizes,[2] the Health Impact Fund,[3] patent pools,[4]

* The author is grateful for the advice and feedback from Professor Thomas Pogge, Professor Rochelle Cooper Dreyfuss and Jennifer Bowles.

1 The (RED) Campaign, *The Lazarus Effect* (2007) YouTube, www.youtube.com/watch?v=W82SoRp9Au4 at 10 March 2009.

2 Joseph Stiglitz, 'Scrooge and Intellectual Property Rights: A Medical Prize Fund Could Improve the Financing of Drug Innovations' (2006), 333 *British Medical Journal* 1279; James Love and Tim Hubbard, 'The Big Idea: Prizes to Stimulate R&D for New Medicines' (2007), 82 *Chicago-Kent Law Review* 1519; Knowledge Ecology International, 'Selected Innovation Prizes and Reward Programs' (Research Note 1, Knowledge Ecology International, 7 March 2008), www.keionline.org/misc-docs/research_notes/kei_rn_2008_1.pdf at 10 March 2009.

3 Aidan Hollis and Thomas Pogge, *The Health Impact Fund: Making New Medicines Available for All* (2008), www.yale.edu.macmillan/igh/hif.book.pdf.

4 UNITAID, 'Eighth Board Meeting: Unitaid Moves towards a Patent Pool for Medicines' (Geneva, 2–3 July 2008), www.unitaid.eu/en/Eighth-Board-Meeting-Geneva-2-3-July-2008.html at 10 March 2009; UNITAID, *UNITAID Moves toward a Patent Pool for Medicines*, www.unitaid.eu/en/NEWS/UNITAID-moves-towards-a-patent-pool-for-medicines.html at 10 March 2009; Knowledge Ecology International, *Cost Benefit Analysis of UNITAID Patent Pool* (20 June 2008), www.keionline.org/misc-docs/1/_benefit_UNITAID_patent_pool.pdf at 10 March 2009.

Open Source drug discovery[5] and priority review mechanisms[6] – to encourage innovation in respect of essential medicines.

A number of non-government organizations, charities and philanthropists have promoted 'grants' as a means of stimulating investment in research and development into neglected diseases. The (RED) Campaign has been designed to boost private funding for the Global Fund to Fight AIDS, Tuberculosis and Malaria ('The Global Fund').[7] The Bill & Melinda Gates Foundation ('Gates Foundation'),[8] and the William J. Clinton Foundation ('Clinton Foundation')[9] have played an important role in funding research and development in respect of infectious diseases. It is worthwhile analysing the ways in which such charities, foundations and philanthropists have sought to deploy trade-marks, celebrity endorsements and corporate social responsibility to promote access to medicines.

First, non-government organizations, charities and philanthropists have relied upon trademarks to perform a number of functions in their marketing campaigns in respect of access to essential medicines. Trademarks have long been used to encourage corporate social responsibility and promote consumer awareness. In her classic article, 'Expressive Genericity', Rochelle C. Dreyfuss comments upon the evolution of trademarks: 'In a sense, trademarks are the emerging lingua franca: with a sufficient command of these terms, one can make oneself understood the world over, and in the process, enjoy the comforts of

[5] Yochai Benkler, *The Wealth of Networks* (2006), 344–6; Amy Kapczynski, Samantha Chaifetz, Zachary Katz and Yochai Benkler, 'Addressing Global Health Inequities: An Open Licensing Approach for University Innovations' (2005) 20 *Berkeley Technology Law Journal* 1031; Stephen Maurer, Arti Rai and Andrej Sali, 'Finding Cures for Tropical Diseases: Is Open Source an Answer?' (2004) 1 *Public Library of Science, Medicine* 183; Stephen Maurer, 'Open Source Drug Discovery: Finding a Niche (or Maybe Several)' (2007) 76 *University of Missouri at Kansas City Law Review* 405; Don Tapscott and Anthony Williams, *Wikinomics: How Mass Collaboration Changes Everything* (2006); and Janet Hope, *BioBazaar: Biotechnology and the Open Source Revolution* (2008).

[6] David Ridley, Henry Grabowski and Jeffrey Moe, 'Developing Drugs for Developing Countries' (2006) 25 *Health Affairs* 313; Duke University, 'Duke Faculty Propose Incentives for Developing Drugs for Neglected Diseases', Duke University, 7 March 2006; section 1102 of the Food and Drug Administration Amendments Act 2007 (United States) 21 USC §301 (2007).

[7] The (RED) Campaign, www.joinred.com/ at 10 March 2009; The Global Fund to Fight AIDS, Tuberculosis and Malaria, www.theglobalfund.org/EN/ at 10 March 2009.

[8] The Bill & Melinda Gates Foundation, www.gatesfoundation.org/Pages/home.aspx.

[9] The William J. Clinton Foundation, clintonfoundation.org/.

home'.[10] A number of social movements – such as the Fairtrade,[11] and Make Poverty History[12] campaigns – have relied upon trademarks to promote progressive causes. In much the same vein, the (RED) Campaign has exploited trademarks to raise awareness and money for the Global Fund.[13]

Second, non-government organizations, charities and philanthropists have relied upon a variety of celebrities to promote causes in respect of access to medicines. Rosemary Coombe has noted the power and significance of the celebrity name and image: 'In societies characterized by mass production, consumer capitalism, and mass-media communications, the celebrity image holds both seductive power and significant economic and cultural value'.[14] It is notable that the (RED) Campaign, the Gates Foundation and the Clinton Foundation are all based around a 'cult of personality' – with a leading celebrity acting as the figurehead of each organization. The (RED) Campaign was established by Bono. He has enlisted a galaxy of popular celebrities to the (RED) Campaign – including Oprah Winfrey, Elle Macpherson, Christy Turlington, Penelope Cruz, Kanye West and Scarlett Johansson. With the Gates Foundation, Bill Gates has sought to convert his considerable economic capital into symbolic capital, to use the terms of Pierre Bourdieu.[15] Similarly, Bill Clinton has converted his political capital into a cultural, symbolic influence.[16]

[10] Rochelle C. Dreyfuss, 'Expressive Genericity: Trademarks as Language in the Pepsi Generation' (1989–1990) 65 *Notre Dame Law Review* 397. See also Rochelle C. Dreyfuss, 'Reconciling Trademark Rights and Expressive Values: How to Stop Worrying and Learn to Love Ambiguity', in Graeme Dinwoodie and Mark Janis (eds.), *Trademark Law and Theory: A Handbook of Contemporary Research* (2008), 261.

[11] Fairtrade Labelling Organizations International, www.fairtrade.net/. See also Ron Layton, 'Enhancing Intellectual Property Exports through Fair Trade', in J. Michael Finger and Philip Schuler (eds.), *Poor People's Knowledge: Promoting Intellectual Property in Developing Countries* (2004) 75; Sasha Courville, 'Use of Indicators to Compare Supply Chains in the Coffee Industry' (2004) 43 *Greener Management International* 93.

[12] Make Poverty History, www.makepovertyhistory.org/.

[13] The (RED) Campaign: www.joinred.com/ and the Global Fund to Fight AIDS, Tuberculosis and Malaria: www.theglobalfund.org/EN/.

[14] Rosemary Coombe, *The Cultural Life of Intellectual Properties: Authorship, Appropriation, and the Law* (Duke University Press, 1998), 89.

[15] Pierre Bourdieu, *Outline of a Theory of Practice* (1977).

[16] On the politics of celebrity, see McKenzie Wark, *Celebrities, Culture and Cyberspace: The Light on the Hill in a Postmodern World* (1999).

Third, there has been a focus by such organizations upon encouraging companies to participate in access to medicines programmes, as part of their corporate social responsibilities.[17] In setting its Access to Medicine Index, the Access to Medicine Foundation notes: 'While all of us share a common responsibility to improve global access to drugs, diagnostics, vaccines and other healthcare technologies, it is also clear that pharmaceutical companies, as the owners of unique knowledge, technology and infrastructure, have to be an integral part of such efforts'.[18] The Foundation charts the variety of contributions that can be made by corporations: 'For example, they can invest in research and development geared towards treatments for poverty-related and neglected diseases; they can increase efforts to out-license patented products to generics producers in developing countries; they can apply equitable pricing mechanisms for brand product; they can help build sustainable research, manufacturing and distributing capacity in low-income countries; or they can limit their drug donation programs to situations where better options are not available.'[19] The co-founder of Microsoft and budding philanthropist, Bill Gates, would call such developments 'creative capitalism'.

This chapter explores how a number of non-government organizations, charities and philanthropists have promoted 'grants' as a means of stimulating investment in research and development into neglected diseases. Each section considers the nature of the campaign; the use of intellectual property rights, such as trademarks; and the criticisms made of such endeavours. Section 2 looks at the (RED) Campaign, which is designed to boost corporate funding and consumer support for the Global Fund. Section 3 examines the role of the Gates Foundation in funding research and development in respect of infectious diseases. It explores the championing by Bill Gates of 'creative capitalism'. Section 4 considers the part of the Clinton Foundation in the debate over access to essential medicines. The chapter concludes that, despite their qualities,

[17] Jean-François Rischard, *High Noon: 20 Global Problems, 20 Years to Solve Them* (2002). The first stage is 'charity' where the company's key motivation is philanthropic. The second stage is 'defensive corporate social responsibility', where the key motivation is reputation protection. The third stage is 'offensive corporate social responsibility' where the aim is to be recognized as a world-class company. The fourth stage is 'development agent' where the motivation is to help out where governments fail. The fifth stage is 'global problem-solver' which involves collaborative insurgent global problem solving.

[18] Veronique Menou, Allison Hornstein and Elizabeth Lipton-McCombie, *Access to Medicine Index: Ranking Access to Medicine Practices* (June 2008), 10.

[19] Ibid.

such marketing initiatives fail to address the underlying inequalities and injustices of international patent law.

2. The (RED) Campaign

In 2006, Bono – lead singer of the Irish rock band, U2 – and Bobby Shriver – chairman of DATA (Debt, AIDS, Trade, Africa) – developed the (RED) Campaign to raise awareness and money for the Global Fund.[20] The social activists explained that the campaign was branded '(Product) RED' because 'red is the colour of emergencies, and that is the only way to describe the AIDS pandemic'.[21] Bono has explained the impulse behind the creation of the Campaign:

> If you buy a (RED) product from GAP, Motorola, Armani, Converse or Apple, they will give up to 50% of their profit to buy AIDS drugs for mothers and children in Africa. (RED) is the consumer battalion gathering in the shopping malls. You buy the jeans, phones, iPods, shoes, sunglasses, and someone – somebody's mother, father, daughter or son – will live instead of dying in the poorest part of the world. It's a different kind of fashion statement. You might think (RED) sounds too simple. But AIDS is no longer a death sentence. Just two pills a day will bring someone who is at death's door back to full health, back to a full life. Doctors call it 'the Lazarus effect'.[22]

Bill Gates lauded the (RED) Campaign as a triumphant instance of 'creative capitalism': 'It's a great thing: the companies make a difference while adding to their bottom line, consumers get to show their support for a good cause, and – most important – lives are saved.'[23]

The (RED) initiative was welcomed by the Global Fund. The executive director, Richard Feachem, commented: 'By making socially responsible consumption appealing to consumers and profitable for companies, (RED) is pioneering a sustainable model for the involvement of the private sector in the fight against disease and poverty.'[24] He noted: 'Companies expand their customer base and bottom-line by combining their products with a brand that is both culturally significant and compassionate,

[20] The (RED) Campaign, www.joinred.com/.

[21] Bono, 'Message 2U: Editorial', *Vanity Fair*, July 2007.

[22] Bono, 'Product (RED)', 12 October 2006. [23] Ibid.

[24] Richard Feachem, 'The Global Fund Welcomes RED' (Press Release, 26 January 2006), www.joinred.com/news/press-release.asp?145141242006; The Global Fund to Fight AIDS, Tuberculosis and Malaria: www.theglobalfund.org/EN/.

while the Global Fund and its recipients gain not only critical financial resources but also publicity for their work.'[25]

Bobby Shriver, Chief Executive Officer of Product (RED) said, '(RED) partners expect that they will broaden their own customer base and increase loyalty in a manner that delivers a sustainable revenue stream to both the company and the Global Fund.'[26] Sheila Roche, the Director of Communications, observed:

> It's a win-win-win situation. The companies get a lot of benefits – they still get to make their profits. Consumers get these great products that do this incredibly powerful thing and they don't have to pay the premium for it. And the ultimate winner is somebody in Africa who gets to have their life 'borrowed' for them, by access to anti-retroviral drugs.[27]

Tamsin Smith, the president of Product (RED), explained that the project was an instance of 'punk rock capitalism': '(RED) provides a very immediate empowering mechanism for someone to do something quite revolutionary, to cause a big corporation to break off a portion of its profit and put it towards a huge social challenge.'[28]

2.1 The marketing of the (RED) Campaign

The (RED) Campaign relies upon trademark protection in order to garner support from both technology developers and consumers. The Chief Executive Officer, Susan Smith Ellis, hopes to build the (RED) Brand, create value for its current partners and form new partnerships: 'Given the team we have and will assemble, given the support we have received from the (RED) community, given the power of the message, I am certain we will make (RED) a part of everyday life.'[29]

A search of the United States Patent and Trade Mark Office registry reveals that a family of trademarks have been registered in respect of the (RED) Campaign. Such trademarks relate to the word marks – 'Do the

[25] Ibid.

[26] The RED Campaign, 'Bono and Bobby Shriver Launch Product RED to Harness Power of the World's Iconic Brands to Fight AIDS in Africa' (Press Release, 26 January 2006), www.joinred.com/news/press-release.asp?1048491252006.

[27] Jess Worth, 'Punk Rock Capitalism', *New Internationalist*, 11 January 2006, www.encyclopedia.com/doc/IG1155174516.html at 10 March 2009.

[28] Ibid.

[29] The (RED) Campaign, '(RED) Names Susan Smith Ellis as CEO' (Press Release, 28 June 2007), joinred.com/news/press-release.asp?06282007.

(RED) Thing',[30] '(Product) RED',[31] '(RED)',[32] and 'The RED Campaign'.[33] The trademark '(Product) RED'[34] has been registered in respect of a wide range of goods and services – including paints and varnishes; personal care products; pharmaceutical drugs; tableware; condoms and surgical clothing; lighting; jewellery; music instruments and accessories; household furnishings and furniture; household accessories; hair accessories; and carpets and other coverings. Most importantly, the trademark relates to 'charitable services, retail services, and selling services', 'promoting the goods and services of others through the use of advertising and marketing campaigns and distributing advertising materials' and 'promoting public awareness of AIDS in Africa and other humanitarian relief efforts'. Although it is possible to obtain trademarks upon distinctive colours, the (RED) Campaign has made no such effort to claim protection in respect of the colour red in its trademarks.[35] The ownership of the trademarks resides with a public relations entity known as The Persuaders LLC. Another company called Signal Rock Communications deals with media relations and communications requests.

The (RED) Campaign was deliberately designed to engage major corporations. Bono explained: 'We believed that to ignore the neon and creative force afforded by corporate America would be to ignore the truth about where most Americans live and work.'[36] The social activists received advice from Robert Rubin – the former United States Treasury Secretary – about how best to establish the endeavour.[37] J. J. Asongu has argued that the resulting marketing campaign is an exemplar of corporate social responsibility: 'The significance of the RED campaign is that it places the concern of society vis-à-vis the

[30] US Trade Mark Numbers: 78765008 and 77393917.

[31] US Trade Mark Numbers: 78666830 and 77393913.

[32] US Trade Mark Number: 78666768.

[33] US Trade Mark Number: 78693606.

[34] US Trade Mark Numbers: 78666830 and 77393913.

[35] On behalf of the Supreme Court of the United States, Breyer J held: 'We cannot find in the basic objectives of trademark law any obvious theoretical objection to the use of color alone as a trademark, where that color has attained "secondary meaning" and therefore identifies and distinguishes a particular brand (and thus indicates its "source")': *Qualitex Co.* v. *Jacobson Products Co., Inc.*, 514 US 159 (1995); *Woolworths Limited* v. *BP*, [2006] FCAFC 132; *Cadbury Limited*, [2002] ATMO 56 (28 June 2002); *Darrell Lea Chocolate Shops Pty Ltd* v. *Cadbury Limited*, [2008] ATMO 6 (15 January 2008); *Cadbury Schweppes Pty Ltd* v. *Darrell Lea Chocolate Shops Pty Ltd (No 4)*, [2006] FCA 446; *Cadbury Schweppes Pty Ltd* v. *Darrell Lea Chocolate Shops Pty Ltd (No 8)*, [2008] FCA 470.

[36] Bono, 'Message 2U: Editorial', above n. 21. [37] Ibid.

epidemic at the center of its strategy, designing a whole line of products exclusively to raise funds to solve a societal problem.'[38]

The (RED) Campaign involves collaboration with the world's most iconic brands to produce (RED) branded products – including American Express, Apple Inc., Converse, Motorola, GAP, Emporio Armani, Hallmark, Microsoft and Dell. A portion of profits from each product sold goes directly to the fund to invest in African AIDS programmes, with a focus on women and children. The (RED) Campaign also has media partnerships with the web 2.0 site, MySpace, and AIM. Betsy Spethmann has sought to analyse the contractual obligations of partners of the (RED) Campaign:

> Brand marketers like GAP sign a five-year licensing deal, and get category exclusivity. They also commit to developing a line of high-quality items that are central to their portfolio. In addition, licensees must specify that their RED goods are the same or better quality as their flagship products. And they can't be priced at a premium. Donations vary by licensing contract. GAP donates 50% of its profits after marketing costs ... Armani contributes 40% of its gross profit from RED sales in its Emporio Armani stores; the price tags range from $58 to $228. Motorola chips in 8% to 10% of the price of its $165 RED MotoRazr phone and its $60-to-$70 Bluetooth H500 headset. And Converse is forking out over 10% of net wholesale sales of its RED shoes, priced from $47 to $140. And, as a special contribution, it is kicking in 15% from each purchase of its $60 version, Make Mine RED, for which online shoppers can choose their own colors and detailing.[39]

The (RED) Campaign website lacks a comprehensive catalogue of the contracts entered into with the various companies. There is nothing as substantive as an annual report. As a result of this lack of transparency and accountability, it is difficult to properly assess the licensing arrangements that have been entered into between the parties.

The (RED) Campaign has also enlisted a range of celebrities to support its endeavour. Most notably, the opinion-leader, Oprah Winfrey, lent her considerable influence and fame to the (RED) Campaign, declaring: 'I want the whole world to go (RED)!'[40] Amy Elizabeth Martin recounts the spectacular launch of the venture in the United States:

[38] J. J. Asongu, 'Generating Sustainable Funds through Branding: RED Campaign Introduces New Business Model for CSR' (2007), 1(1) *Journal of Business and Public Policy* 1.

[39] Betsy Spethmann, 'The RED Brigade', *Promo Magazine*, 1 January 2007.

[40] The Oprah Winfrey Show, 'Oprah and Bono Paint the Town Red', *The Oprah Winfrey Show*, 13 October 2006, www.oprah.com/slideshow/world/globalissues/oprahshow3_ss_20061013 at 10 March 2009.

> On October 13, 2006, Chicago's Magnificent Mile was decorated in a new color: red. Pedestrians looked quizzically at some of the famous shops now toting this new color and logo. Consumers saw the '(RED)' logo plastered on the main windows of the two-story Gap® store, along with pictures of famous celebrities donning the newest fashion with those recognizable features. Shoppers finally realized what was happening when Bono and Oprah Winfrey stepped out of their red convertible with bright red shopping bags and multiple cameramen. Their entrance into the Gap® signified the Product (RED) Campaign launch in the United States.[41]

On the Oprah Winfrey show, Bono employed a variety of 'emergency' rhetoric, comparing the crisis in respect of access to essential medicines to both natural disasters and terrorist attacks: 'Two Twin Towers a day. A tsunami a month. One hundred and fifty thousand Africans die of a preventable, treatable disease every month.'[42]

The (RED) Campaign has used an array of media to publicize its cause. The organization has used traditional television advertisements – for instance, Motorola had spots featuring Chris Rock saying 'Use RED, Nobody's Dead'. The lifestyle magazine *Vanity Fair* featured a special issue, edited by Bono.[43] The photographer Annie Leibovitz helped put together twenty different covers for the special edition – featuring Presidential nominee Barack Obama, Muhammad Ali, Condolezza Rice and others. The (RED) Campaign maintains an active website, a blog and a Facebook group. The campaign has released YouTube videos promoting the 'Lazarus effect' of antiretrovirals.[44] The (RED) Campaign is also planning to establish a digital music service, which enables record companies to contribute a share of profits on certain products to the Global Fund.[45] The venture will release new songs from the likes of U2, Bob Dylan, Elvis Costello, Elton John, Emmylou Harris, and Death Cab for Cutie.[46] Bono and British artist Damien Hirst hosted an art auction for the (RED) Campaign, which featured work donated by 100 leading international

[41] Amy Elizabeth Martin, *Seeing (RED): A Qualitative Analysis of the Product (RED) Campaign and Integration of Public Relations and Marketing Theory* (Master of Mass Communication Thesis, Louisana State University, 2008) 1.

[42] The Oprah Winfrey Show, 'Oprah and Bono Paint the Town RED', above n. 40.

[43] See *Vanity Fair*, www.vanityfair.com/politics/africa.

[44] The (RED) Campaign, 'The Lazarus Effect', www.youtube.com/watch?v=W82SoRp9Au4.

[45] Robert Levine, 'Online Tunes, in Service to Africa', *The New York Times*, 30 June 2008.

[46] Ibid.

artists.[47] The website for the (RED) Campaign features testimonials from various luminaries – such as Ziggy Marley, Elle MacPherson, Natasha Bedingfield, Scarlett Johansson and Joss Stone.

2.2 *A critique of the (RED) Campaign*

Four substantive criticisms have been made of the (RED) Campaign.

First, there has been much critical debate as to whether the (RED) Campaign has been an effective vehicle to promote consumer awareness about HIV/AIDS, tuberculosis and malaria. The (RED) product marketing campaign has its detractors. Esther Lim is more sceptical of the use of the brand: 'Until it becomes more proactive in communicating the issues as well, [the (RED) campaign] will remain just another marketing scheme that does more good for the profile and sales of the corporations involved than for the fight against AIDS.'[48] Will Horwitz, an HIV/AIDS activist, has been similarly unconvinced: 'With its grandiose claims and complete lack of a political message, I can't see how Product (RED) can be a positive force.'[49]

Second, there has been scrutiny of the model of corporate social responsibility promoted by the (RED) Campaign. Mark Rosenman is critical of the cause-related marketing of Product (RED): 'In reality, it's just one more example of the corporate world aligning its operations with its central purpose of increasing shareholder profit, except this time it is being cloaked in the patina of philanthropy.'[50] He makes a number of objections to 'corporate generosity':

> First, it is self-serving, further diminishing true altruism in the corporate world. We live in a society where values are threatened, and avarice and greed need to be better balanced by a sense of the greater good – the commonweal. If values erode further in the market, nonprofits and the rest of us are all in deeper trouble. Second, all of us need to understand that, in the words of Buy(Less), shopping is not a solution. We cannot consume our way to charity and to a better world. Doing good sometimes requires sacrifice, and we ought not allow ourselves to be convinced that we've done our part because of the color of what we use. Third, we

[47] Ted Winner, 'Bono and Hirst Paint the Town Red: Rock Star Bono and Artist Damien Hirst Teamed Up and Raised $42.5M For Africa', *ABC News*, 15 February 2008.

[48] Ibid. [49] Ibid.

[50] Mark Rosenman, 'The Patina of Philanthropy', *Stanford Social Innovation Review* (11 April 2007), www.ssireview.org/opinion/entry/the_patina_of_philanthropy/ at 10 March 2009.

> generally don't know how much goes to the cause and how much goes to profit for each sale or in the aggregate; there is no true transparency or accountability … Fourth and last, we need to remember that there really is a profound difference between doing well and doing good.[51]

Rosenman suggests that cause-related marketing is pernicious: 'It ties consumers' desires to see a social good with the corporations' desires to see higher profits.'[52] He observes that 'corporations spent more than $100 million advertising their association with (RED) while raising under $18 million for charity'.[53] Rosenman concludes: 'Corporate altruism has shrunk as corporate avarice has grown.'[54]

Third, sceptics have questioned whether the (RED) Campaign has been an effective fundraiser for the Global Fund. In the *Advertising Age*, Mya Frazier contended that there was a backlash against the (RED) Campaign and the brands involved: 'The disproportionate ratio between the marketing outlay and the money raised is drawing concern among nonprofit watchdogs, cause-marketing experts and even executives in the ad business.'[55] Such sharp criticism has provoked outrage and fury from the operators and the supporters of the (RED) Campaign. Jack Valenti, president of Friends of the Global Fight against AIDS, Tuberculosis and Malaria, responded that the accusations were a 'hollow charge'.[56] He observed that 'the money raised by (RED) is hardly an anemic sum'; indeed, 'It is substantially more than what the Global Fund has received from corporations since its inception.'[57] Valenti maintained that 'anything that contributes more resources to wage war on the AIDS pandemic, one that kills 5,500 people in sub-Saharan Africa alone every day, with too many children counted among the dead, must not be treated casually'.[58]

Fourth, there have been larger questions about the transparency, accountability and corporate governance of the (RED) Campaign. Amy Elizabeth Martin has undertaken a comprehensive analysis of the public relations and marketing models adopted by the (RED) Campaign.[59] She concluded that the (RED) Campaign would benefit from greater transparency and accountability: 'While campaign organizers did mention

[51] Ibid. [52] Ibid. [53] Ibid. [54] Ibid.

[55] Mya Frazier, 'Costly RED Campaign Reaps Meager $18 Million: Bono & Co. Spend Up to $100 Million on Marketing, Incur Watchdogs' Wrath', *Advertising Age* (New York), 5 March 2007.

[56] Jack Valenti, 'Letter to the Editor', *Advertising Age* (New York), 2007, wwwwww.joinred.com/archive/adage/valenti.asp+red+campaign+valenti (internet archive).

[57] Ibid. [58] Ibid. [59] Martin, *Seeing (RED)*, above n. 41.

themes of transparency and building consumer-brand connections with credibility and transparency, those strategies were not as present in communications as the researcher hoped.'[60] She contended that 'if detailed specifics of the Global Fund distributions and tangible results were presented, Product (RED) organizers might see a renewed interest in the products because consumers are more apt to consider the products knowing distinct facts about the non-profit organization'.[61] Martin was doubtful whether the (RED) Campaign was a good model for other corporate social responsibility endeavours.[62]

3. The Gates Foundation and 'creative capitalism'

> Philanthropy is commendable, but it must not cause the philanthropist to overlook the circumstances of economic injustice which make philanthropy necessary.
>
> Martin Luther King, Jr[63]

There has been a long-standing historical debate in the United States about capitalists and corporations becoming involved in charity and philanthropy. There has been much debate about the role of such as Andrew Carnegie,[64] John D. Rockefeller[65] and David Guggenheim. Stanley Katz comments upon this phenomenon: 'If charity was the giving of alms – that is, the alleviation of individual cases of distress – philanthropy was a strategy for doing good works in gross.'[66] Some suggest that such entrepreneurs were robber barons intent upon converting their economic capital into symbolic capital.[67] Others argue that such capitalists should be considered more kindly for bringing order and stability to society.[68] Stanley Katz observes: 'The founding era of philanthropists created a novel legal and organizational structure, the private foundation, as the vehicle to realize their goals.'[69]

[60] Ibid., 62–3. [61] Ibid., 62–3. [62] Ibid., 66.

[63] National Philanthropic Trust, *Philanthropy Quotes*, www.nptrust.org/philanthropy/philanthropy_quotes.asp at 10 March 2009.

[64] David Nasaw, *Andrew Carnegie* (2007).

[65] Allan Nevins, *John D. Rockefeller: The Heroic Age of American Enterprise* (1940).

[66] Stanley Katz, 'Philanthropy's New Math' (2007), 53(22) *The Chronicle of Higher Education* B2.

[67] Matthew Josephson, *The Robber Barons: The Great American Capitalists, 1861–1901* (1934).

[68] Nevins, *John D. Rockefeller*, above n. 65.

[69] Katz, 'Philanthropy's New Math', above n. 66.

Bill Gates explained the origin of the Gates Foundation: 'Melinda and I started our foundation because we want to be part of a different movement – this time, to help create a world where no one has to live on a dollar a day or die from a disease we know how to prevent.'[70] In a speech to the World Health Assembly in 2005, he explained that the Foundation would aim to address inequities in access to healthcare:

> The world is failing billions of people. Rich governments are not fighting some of the world's most deadly diseases because rich countries don't have them. The private sector is not developing vaccines and medicines for these diseases, because developing countries can't buy them. And many developing countries are not doing nearly enough to improve the health of their own people … All these factors together have created a tragic inequity between the health of the people in the developed world and the health of those in the rest of the world.[71]

Gates emphasized that there were four priorities in addressing world healthcare issues. First, in his view 'governments in both developed and developing countries must dramatically increase their efforts to fight disease'.[72] Second, he noted that: 'The world needs to direct more scientific research to health issues that can save the greatest number of lives – which means diseases that disproportionately affect the developing world.'[73] Third, Gates emphasized that 'the world has to devote more thinking and funding to delivering interventions – not just discovering them'.[74] Finally, the entrepreneur concluded that 'to find new discoveries and deliver them, we need to make political and market forces work better for the world's poorest people'.[75]

As co-founder of Microsoft, Bill Gates has established a significant reputation as a Promethean entrepreneur in the field of information technology. A commentator, Kathy Bowrey, has analysed his celebrity status: 'Gates speaks not just for his own interests but as a Captain of the Information Industry, with Microsoft's success, failings and future explained in terms of the significance of the global economy and its potential.'[76] The phrase 'the Bill & Melinda Gates Foundation' has been registered as a service mark in respect of 'philanthropic and charitable monetary services relating to making grants in the fields of health

[70] Ibid.

[71] Bill Gates, 'Remarks at the World Health Assembly' (Speech delivered at the 58th World Health Assembly, Geneva, Switzerland, 16 May 2005), www.who.int/mediacentre/events/2005/wha58/gates/en/index.html at 10 March 2009.

[72] Ibid. [73] Ibid. [74] Ibid. [75] Ibid.

[76] Kathy Bowrey, *Law and Internet Cultures* (2005) 105, 106.

and learning'.[77] The trademark disclaims any exclusive rights in respect of the term 'foundation' and notes that Bill and Melinda Gates are living persons. There does not seem to be any registration of the term 'creative capitalism' at present.

The Gates Foundation is informed by a particular credos, 'Guided by the belief that every life has equal value, the Bill & Melinda Gates Foundation works to reduce inequities and improve lives around the world.'[78] The 2007 annual report explains the two-tiered structure of the philanthropy. The Gates Foundation distributes money to grantees.[79] The Gates Foundation Trust manages the endowment and makes contributions to fund the Gates Foundation's grant-making operations. The combined entities have US$38.7 billion as endowment assets available for charitable activities. The Gates Foundation has benefited particularly from the gift of shares worth approximately US$30.7 billion from the American businessman and philanthropist Warren Buffett.[80] There is a US$4.4 billion liability for future year payments on already approved grants. On a cash basis, the combined entities paid approximately US$2.0 billion in grants.

The Gates Foundation has played an important role in respect of generating funds to deal with access to medicines. Indeed, it has contributed US$450 million and pledged another US$200 million to the Global Fund in addition to its other activities.[81] The Gates Foundation seeks to promote research to develop health solutions that are effective, affordable and practical, and 'access to existing vaccines, drugs, and other tools to fight diseases common in developing countries'.[82] Harold Varmus explained that the venture assumed 'that, with greater encouragement and funding, contemporary science and technology could remove some of the obstacles to more rapid progress against diseases that disproportionately affect the developing world'.[83] Jon Cohen of the *Science Magazine* observed: 'The foundation has rearranged the public health universe so speedily that many have yet to comprehend the change.'[84]

[77] Bill & Melinda Gates Foundation Trust, 'Bill & Melinda Gates Foundation', United States Trade Mark Registration Number: 2638659.

[78] The Gates Foundation, www.gatesfoundation.org/AboutUs/. [79] Ibid.

[80] Roger Lowenstein, *Buffett: The Making of an American Capitalist* (2008).

[81] The Global Fund to Fight AIDS, Tuberculosis, and Malaria, *Pledges and Donations*, www.theglobalfund.org/en/funds_raised/pledges/ at 10 March 2009.

[82] The Gates Foundation, www.gatesfoundation.org/GlobalHealth/.

[83] Harold Varmus *et al.*, 'Grand Challenges in Global Health' (2003) 302 *Science* 398.

[84] Jon Cohen, 'Gates Foundation Rearranges Public Health Universe' (2002) 295 *Science* 2000.

3.1 *The credos of 'creative capitalism'*

In an interview with *Time Magazine*, Bill Gates promoted 'creative capitalism'.[85] He argued that there is a significant role to be played by corporations in addressing questions of development – including access to medicines:

> Capitalism has improved the lives of billions of people – something that's easy to forget at a time of great economic uncertainty. But it has left out billions more. They have great needs, but they can't express those needs in ways that matter to markets. So they are stuck in poverty, suffer from preventable diseases and never have a chance to make the most of their lives. Governments and nonprofit groups have an irreplaceable role in helping them, but it will take too long if they try to do it alone. It is mainly corporations that have the skills to make technological innovations work for the poor. To make the most of those skills, we need a more creative capitalism: an attempt to stretch the reach of market forces so that more companies can benefit from doing work that makes more people better off. We need new ways to bring far more people into the system – capitalism – that has done so much good in the world.[86]

Gates suggests that companies should be rewarded by some kind of return for their participation in development projects: 'It's not just about doing more corporate philanthropy or asking companies to be more virtuous.'[87] In his view, 'It's about giving them a real incentive to apply their expertise in new ways, making it possible to earn a return while serving the people who have been left out.'[88]

In a conversation with Warren Buffett, Bill Gates observes that the reputation of brand-name pharmaceutical drugs has been tarnished by the ongoing controversy over patent law and access to medicines.[89] He remarked on the value of 'symbolic capital' for companies: 'When I talk to executives from pharmaceutical companies, they tell me that they want to do more for neglected diseases – but they at least need to get credit for it.'[90] He noted: 'Publicity is very valuable, but sometimes it's still not enough to persuade companies to get involved.'[91] Gates reflected:

[85] Bill Gates, 'Making Capitalism More Creative', *Time Magazine*, 31 July 2008.

[86] Ibid. [87] Ibid. [88] Ibid.

[89] Michael Kinsley, *Bill Gates and Warren Buffett Discuss 'Creative Capitalism'* (Interview Transcript) (2008) Creative Capitalism – A Conversation, creativecapitalism.typepad.com/creative_capitalism/2008/06/bill-gates-and.html#more at 10 March 2009. See also Michael Kinsley (ed.), *Creative Capitalism: A Conversation with Bill Gates, Warren Buffett and Other Economic Leaders* (2009).

[90] Bill Gates, 'Making Capitalism More Creative', *Time Magazine*, 31 July 2008.

[91] Ibid.

'Even the best [public relations] may not pay the bill for 10 years of research into a new drug.'[92] He argued that the Access to Medicine Index initiative needed to be expanded upon: 'We can expand the report-card idea beyond the pharmaceutical industry and make sure the rankings get publicity so companies get credit for doing good work.'[93] Emphasizing that 'consumers can reward companies that do their part by buying their products' and 'employees can ask how their employers are contributing', Gates observed: 'If more companies follow the lead of the most creative organizations in their industry, they will make a huge impact on some of the world's worst problems.'[94]

Strikingly, Gates has been supportive of further financial incentives for patent owners, such as the Priority Review Voucher.[95] He exclaimed: 'It's a fantastic way for governments to go beyond the aid they already give and channel market forces so they improve even more lives.'[96] Gates has remained an unapologetic supporter of the strong protection of intellectual property rights. He noted somewhat simplistically:

> If a drug company ever invents a treatment for something like malaria, it'd be immediately beset by calls to give the drug away. So they choose never to work in those areas. The current incentive system isn't doing it. I think if you invent drugs, you should be able to charge for them. That may seem radical.[97]

His position in respect of patent protection of pharmaceutical drugs is similar to his support of strong intellectual property protection in respect of information technology. The dominance of Microsoft was built around a combination of strong protection of trade secrets, copyright and patents in respect of key computer software.[98] Bill Gates has also been a great critic of open-access communities – such as the Free

[92] Ibid. [93] Ibid. [94] Ibid.

[95] Ibid. On the priority review voucher, see: Ridley, Grabowski and Moe, 'Developing Drugs for Developing Countries', above n. 6; section 1102 of the Food and Drug Administration Amendments Act 2007, above n. 6.

[96] Bill Gates, 'Making Capitalism More Creative', above n. 85.

[97] Thomas Goetz, 'Bill Gates on Pharmaceuticals: The System Isn't Working', *Wired Science* (22 April 2008), blog.wired.com/wiredscience/2008/04/bill-gates-what.html at 10 March 2009.

[98] On trade secrets litigation, see, e.g.: *Google, Inc.* v. *Microsoft Corp*, 415 F Supp 2d 1018 ND Cal 2005; on patent disputes, see: *Z4 Technologies, Inc.* v. *Microsoft Corp.* 507 F 3d 1340 CA Fed (Tex) 2007; on copyright litigation, see, e.g.: *Microsoft Corporation* v. *PC Club Australia Pty Ltd* [2005] FCA 1522; and on designs litigation, see: *Microsoft Corporation* [2007] ADO 1 (14 February 2007).

Software Foundation, the Open Source Movement and the Creative Commons.

3.2 A critique of 'creative capitalism'

An editorial in the scientific magazine *Nature* welcomed the contribution of philanthropists, private foundations and non-profit organizations to the field of biomedical research: 'The current increase in scientific funding from individual philanthropists, private foundations and non-profit organizations, particularly in biomedical science is a welcome development in a field that is largely dominated by governments.'[99] However, the Gates Foundation and its advocacy of 'creative capitalism' have received a number of substantive criticisms.

First, there have been ethical and philosophical objections to the notion of 'creative capitalism'. The idiosyncratic law and economics academic and judge Richard Posner has been highly sceptical of the notion of 'creative capitalism': 'The embrace of massive corporate charity, the criticism of capitalism by its greatest beneficiaries, and the frequent resort by the advocates of "creative capitalism" to platitudes ... along with the vagueness of the term itself, leave me with an uncomfortable feeling.'[100] Posner observes that corporations have long used charity as a means of public relations: 'Corporations have long made charitable donations, quite properly from a profit-maximizing standpoint, in order to curry favor with politicians and interest groups, advertise the corporation to potential consumers (as by underwriting cultural events), create diffuse goodwill, disguise greed, and ward off criticisms.'[101] He suggests that 'A corporation that makes charitable donations that are not profit maximizing is not only breaking faith with its shareholders (unless they unanimously support the diversion of corporate profits to the managers' preferred charities), but also weakening itself in competition with profit-maximizing firms.'[102] This position reflects a long tradition of thought that corporations should not be involved in charity.[103]

[99] Editorial, 'Health Cheques' (2007) 447 *Nature* 231.

[100] Richard Posner, 'Against Creative Capitalism', *Creative Capitalism – A Conversation* (26 June 2008), www.creativecapitalismblog.com/creative_capitalism/2008/06/against-creativ.html at 10 March 2009.

[101] Ibid. [102] Ibid.

[103] See, e.g., Nic Francis, *The End of Charity: Time for Social Enterprise* (2008).

Second, there has been some doubt as to the health outcomes of the Gates Foundation's projects. Dr Peter Piot, the outgoing director of the Joint United Nations Programme on HIV/AIDS, or UNAIDS, observes: 'I really think they should be funding solutions to the delivery problem, not so much the science.'[104] In an incisive piece, Stephen Maurer is critical of the failure of the Gates Foundation and other philanthropists to be circumspect in their funding of research projects: 'In the private sector, CEOs routinely demand to know evidence, options and tradeoffs. Leaders of large sponsors like the Gates and Rockefeller Foundations should do the same.'[105]

He concluded: 'Neglected disease R&D – which receives vast funds from The Gates Foundation – should be run just as carefully as Microsoft itself.'[106] James Love of Knowledge Ecology International is also suspicious of such an approach: 'The Advanced Purchase Commitment ('APC') and Advance Marketing Commitment ('AMC') models backed by various Gates Foundation funded groups and by certain European governments, include strong monopoly supply provisions.'[107]

Third, there have been concerns raised about the transparency, accountability, and governance of the Gates Foundation. Professor Joel Fleishman of Duke University has studied the growth and changing nature of philanthropy in his book, *The Foundation*.[108] He contends: 'I think it's fair to say the Gates Foundation is not yet very transparent or accountable.'[109] Meredith Wadman observes: 'These new givers – the gigaphilanthropists – are perceived to be making an impact on the research landscape that is much greater than the sum of their dollars.'[110] She notes that '[p]rivate foundations have a flexibility and agility with their spending that industry and government agencies do not'.[111] Indeed,

104 Tom Paulson, 'Gates Foundation Follows New Paths: Giving Away $3 Billion a Year Is Not Easy as It Seems', *Seattle Post-Intelligencer*, 24 June 2008.

105 Stephen Maurer, 'Choosing the Right Incentive Strategy for Research and Development in Neglected Diseases' (2006) 84 (5) *Bulletin of the World Health Organization* 376.

106 Ibid.

107 James Love, 'Open Licensing vs Monopoly Controlled Supply', Knowledge Ecology International (27 April 2008), www.keionline.org/component/option,com_jd-wp/Itemid,/p,112/ at 10 March 2009.

108 Joel Fleishman, *The Foundation: A Great American Secret; How Private Money Is Changing the World* (2007).

109 Paulson, 'Gates Foundation Follows New Paths', above n. 104.

110 Meredith Wadman, 'Biomedical Philanthropy: State of the Donation' (2007) 447 *Nature* 248.

111 Ibid.

'[t]hey are not answerable to shareholders or venture capitalists; nor do they labour under the political and public scrutiny experienced by the National Institutes of Health and other spenders of public money'.[112] Wadman worries 'that too many important decisions with an impact on biomedicine will be made in the boardrooms of foundations with little scientific expertise – and no public input or accountability'.[113]

Fourth, there has been concern that the Gates Foundation could restrain different views among scientists and have implications for WHO's policy-making duties. A related concern has been that the Gates Foundation has diverted and drained crucial health resources away from other, better uses. The chief of malaria for the WHO, Dr Ararata Kochi, complained that the Gates Foundation's money could have 'far-reaching, largely unintended consequences'.[114] He complained that many of the leading malaria scientists were 'locked up in a "cartel" with their own research funding being linked to those of others within the group'.[115] He expressed concern that the Gates Foundation's research preferences 'could have implicitly dangerous consequences on the policy-making process in world health'.[116] There has been particular controversy over the Gates Foundation funding private entities to perform a confidential project proposal by a public researcher on an innovative stem cell treatment for heart damage caused by Chagas.[117]

In a reflective piece in the *New York Times Magazine*, philosopher Peter Singer has defended the motivations of Bill Gates and Warren Buffett.[118] He noted that the motives of such entrepreneurs deserved close ethical and philosophical attention: 'Should we praise them for giving so much or criticize them for not giving still more?'[119] Singer contended: 'Giving away large sums, rather than spending the money on corporate advertising or developing new products, is not a sensible strategy for increasing personal wealth.'[120] He observed: 'When we read that someone has given away a lot of their money, or time, to help

[112] Ibid. [113] Ibid.

[114] Donald McNeil, 'Gates Foundation's Influence Criticized', *The New York Times*, 16 February 2008.

[115] Ibid. [116] Ibid.

[117] Lilian Joensen, 'Gates Philanthropy in Stem Cell Transplant for Damaged Heart', *The Institute of Science in Society* (Press Release, 1 August 2007), www.i-sis.org.uk/GatesPhilanthropyStemCells.php at 10 March 2009.

[118] Peter Singer, 'What a Billionaire Should Give – and What Should You?', *New York Times Magazine*, 17 December 2006.

[119] Ibid. [120] Ibid.

others, it challenges us to think about our own behavior.'[121] Singer was positive about Gates's philanthropy. He contended 'that, if judged by the proportion of his wealth that he has given away, Gates compares very well with most of the other people on the Forbes 400 list'.[122]

One wonders whether the Gates Foundation will have the longevity and sustainability of other well-established charities, such as the Rockefeller Foundation.

4. The Clinton Foundation and the philosophy of 'giving'

In his book, *Giving: How Each of Us Can Change the World*, former US president, Bill Clinton, discusses the 'explosion of private citizens doing public good'.[123] He observes that there is a need for individuals, non-profit organizations, business and governments to address pressing questions of development, including access to medicines: 'The fact that one in four people who die this year will succumb to AIDS, tuberculosis, malaria, or infections related to dirty water casts a pall over all our children's future.'[124] Clinton emphasizes that 'in many areas, regardless of the quality of government, a critical difference is being made by citizens working as individuals, in businesses, and through non-governmental non-profit organizations'.[125] In his view, 'An NGO is any group of private citizens who join together to advance the public good.'[126]

Clinton explains his motivations in setting up the Clinton Foundation at the end of his term as United States president: 'When I left the White House in 2001, I hoped that through my foundation I could make such a difference and keep working to move our nation and the world away from poverty, disease, conflict, and climate change.'[127] The Clinton Foundation established an 'HIV/AIDS initiative' in order 'to expand access to life-saving medicines and help developing countries systematize their approach to HIV/AIDS treatment'.[128] The organization entered into agreements with generic drug manufacturers that would significantly reduce the price of second-line antiretroviral drugs and make available child-friendly formulations. Clinton says of the

[121] Ibid. [122] Ibid.

[123] William Clinton, *Giving: How Each of Us Can Change the World* (2007).

[124] Ibid., 3. [125] Ibid., 4. [126] Ibid., 5. [127] Ibid.

[128] The Clinton Foundation, *Treating HIV/AIDS & Malaria: Clinton HIV/AIDS Initiative – Our Approach*, www.clintonfoundation.org at 10 March 2009.

achievements of the Clinton Foundation: 'Our program now works in twenty-five countries to diagnose, test, and care for people with HIV/AIDS, and forty-four more nations are able to buy low-cost drugs and testing materials under our contract.'[129] He observes: 'As of mid-2007, about 750,000 more people are receiving treatment purchased under the [Clinton Foundation HIV/AIDS initiative] agreements, representing about a third of all those in the developing world receiving treatment today.'[130]

The Clinton Foundation applies a 'unique business-oriented approach to changing the market for medicines and diagnostics and supporting developing countries to scale up HIV/AIDS care and treatment programs.'[131] Its access programmes 'work with generic pharmaceutical companies and other suppliers to reduce the cost of lifesaving antiretroviral medicines, testing and diagnostic equipment, malaria treatment, and nutrition'.[132] Its 'major programs specialize in specific areas of need, including paediatric treatment, increasing access to care and treatment in rural areas, strengthening countries' human resource capacity for health, and preventing the transmission of HIV/AIDS from mother to child'.[133] The Clinton Foundation's 'In-Country Programs' assist 'national governments and their ministries of health to develop sound health care policies around HIV/AIDS, strengthen management capacity, and implement cost-effective and comprehensive national responses to this epidemic'.[134]

4.1 *The charity of the Clinton Foundation*

The Clinton Foundation has registered two standard character marks at the United States Patent and Trademark Office in respect of 'charitable fund raising services', 'library and museum services' and 'educational services, namely, conducting seminars and educational research programs in the fields of health security, economic empowerment, leadership development, citizen service and racial, ethnic and religious reconciliation'.[135] The trademark register notes that William J. Clinton

[129] William Clinton, *Giving*, above n. 123, 5. [130] Ibid.

[131] The Clinton Foundation, *Treating HIV/AIDS & Malaria*, above n. 128.

[132] Ibid. [133] Ibid. [134] Ibid.

[135] The William J. Clinton Foundation, United States Trademark Registration No: 3109025 and Trademark Registration No: 3003762.

provided consent for the use of his name, portraits and signatures shown in the marks, as is required by United States trademark law.[136]

Bill Clinton has certainly used his political and celebrity status to persuade both governments and corporations. Seth Berkley, the president and founder of the International AIDS Vaccine Initiative, praised Clinton for using his 'charisma' to work on treatment strategies and drive drug prices down.[137] Stephen Lewis, a former United Nations envoy, was also grateful for his intervention:

> Clinton and his people move with tremendous urgency – call it a sense of emergency – that is qualitatively different from everyone in the field. It's the sheer force of his personality and the tremendous access he has. The way they work is so focused and with such energy that I know of no parallel as I wander around Southern Africa.[138]

In his book, *The Gridlock Economy*, Michael Heller further articulates his notion of the 'tragedy of the anti-commons', in which research and development in respect of pharmaceutical drugs is frustrated by fragmented rights, blocking patents, patents thickets, exclusive/expensive licensing and high transaction costs.[139] He suggests that charismatic individuals can help overcome the 'tragedy of the anti-commons', particularly in the field of patent law: 'Inspired leadership makes a difference, and shame can be a potent tool for forging agreement.'[140] He notes: 'Reputation matters: firms like to advertise their involvement in successful humanitarian ventures.'[141]

[136] §2(c) of the Trademark Act 1946 (US) ('Lanham Act'), 15 USC § 1052 provides that 'no trademark by which the goods of the applicant may be distinguished from the goods of others shall be refused registration on the principal register on account of its nature unless it .... consists of or comprises a name, portrait, or signature identifying a particular living individual except by his written consent, or the name, signature, or portrait of a deceased president of the United States during the life of his widow, if any, except by the written consent of the widow'. *In re Masucci*, 179 USPQ 829 (TTAB 1973), the United States Trademark Trial and Appeal Board refused registration of the name 'Eisenhower', a portrait of President Dwight D. Eisenhower and the words 'President Eisenhower Registered Platinum Medallion', for greeting cards, on the ground that the mark comprises the name, signature or portrait of a deceased United States president without the written consent of his widow. See also § 1206.02 of United States Patent and Trademark Office, *Trademark Manual of Examining Procedure: Fifth Edition* (2007).

[137] David Remnick, 'The Wanderer: Bill Clinton's Quest to Save the World, Reclaim his Legacy and Elect his Wife', *The New Yorker*, 18 September 2006.

[138] Ibid.

[139] Michael Heller, *The Gridlock Economy: How Too Much Ownership Wrecks Markets, Stops Innovation and Costs Lives* (2008).

[140] Ibid., 56. [141] Ibid.

Anne-Christine D'Adesky notes that 'The Clinton model promotes a public–private multisector response in which private groups and NGOs work closely together to boost the public and private infrastructure for health-care delivery.'[142]

Bill Clinton explains in his book *Giving: How Each of Us Can Change the World* about how the Clinton Foundation sought to negotiate reductions in prices for antiretroviral pharmaceutical drugs. He notes that his associate, Ira Magaziner, sought to negotiate price reductions from pharmaceutical companies and to improve the productivity and efficiency of the supply chain: 'The manufacturers and suppliers of essential ingredients – Cipla, Ranbaxy, Aspen PharmaCare, Hetero, and Matrix – agreed to shift from a low-volume, high-margin, uncertain payment business to a high-volume, low-margin, certain payment one.'[143] Bill Clinton also emphasizes the role played by donors and philanthropists from around the world in supporting the HIV/AIDS programme.[144] The former president proudly boasts 'almost 750,000 people are receiving treatment with drugs purchased under our contract terms, about a third of all those receiving treatment in the developing world today'.[145] He concludes that 'the lower prices our partners set and the big sales increases they sparked had a ripple effect on the market, accelerating considerable price decreases for other purchasers of AIDS generics'.[146]

Bill Clinton has also sought to use the Clinton Global Initiative as a catalyst for achieving development goals: 'Heads of state, corporate and non-profit executives, academics, media representatives, religious leaders, university students, and global citizens join within the CGI [Clinton Global Initiative] community to develop unique solutions to some of the world's most pressing challenges.'[147] The final event to the 2008 conference featured a conversation between Bill Clinton and Bill Gates on the theme of 'giving'. Clinton observed:

> When you look at AIDS, and, to a lesser extent, some of these other serious diseases, the price of the medicine and the availability of the funds to buy them is no longer the primary barrier to dealing with the problem.

142 Anne-Christine D'Adesky, *Moving Mountains: The Race to Treat Global AIDS* (2004) 295.

143 William Clinton, *Giving*, above n. 123, 180.

144 Ibid., 181. 145 Ibid. 146 Ibid., 182.

147 The Clinton Global Initiative, *Our Model*, www.clintonglobalinitiative.org/NETCOMMUNITY/Page.aspx?pid=2370&srcid=2358 at 10 March 2008.

> It is, in my opinion – and I know you have spent a lot of money on this – it is the absence of functioning healthcare systems.[148]

In response, Gates noted that 'the treatment story is amazing and the Clinton Foundation not only has gotten the drug price down, they are also looking at what are the best practices in terms of how you train people, how you keep the costs of all the non-drug things very low so that we can continue this scale-up'.[149] He feared, though, that the rate of infection remained high: 'Over 2.5 million people a year are still acquiring the disease and there are some of the things where we were looking at microbocides or different vaccines, the scientific results have not panned out'.[150]

4.2 A critique of 'giving'

Notwithstanding its good works, there has been some veiled criticism of the Clinton Foundation, and its philosophy of 'giving'. David Remnick has noted: 'Many of the leading activists and scientists in the HIV/AIDS field are so grateful for the Clinton Foundation's current activities and so loath to alienate Clinton that they only reluctantly criticize his record as President.'[151]

First, there has been criticism that Bill Clinton did not achieve more on access to medicines during his terms as president. A former official from the Clinton Administration told the *New Yorker*:

> His failure as President on AIDS is incredible. He knew all about the issue, but he let people push him away from it … The great question is why he didn't do more in Africa, where he is a rock star, and it goes to the negative side of the balance sheet of the Clinton Presidency.[152]

Remnick notes: 'When the South African government fought drug patents in order to get cheaper drugs, the Clinton Administration backed the American pharmaceutical companies.'[153] Indeed, the Clinton Administration initially lent its support to pharmaceutical drug manufacturers in their dispute with the Government of South Africa

[148] William Clinton and Bill Gates, 'Giving: A Conversation between President Clinton and Bill Gates', The Clinton Global Initiative (2008 Annual Meeting Transcript) (24 September 2008), www.clintonglobalinitiative.org/NETCOMMUNITY/Page.aspx?pid=2947&srcid=2827 at 10 March 2009.

[149] Ibid. [150] Ibid. [151] Remnick, 'The Wanderer', above n. 137. [152] Ibid.

[153] Ibid.

over its parallel importation and compulsory licensing provisions.[154] The Clinton administration only moderated its position after the presidential aspirant, Al Gore, was picketed by ACT UP ('AIDS Coalition to Unleash Power') protestors.[155] In a notable omission, there is no mention of the role of the Clinton Administration in expanding the protection afforded to pharmaceutical drug patents in *Giving: How Each of Us Can Change the World*. D'Adesky notes that 'AIDS activists were initially wary of Clinton's foray into global AIDS work because of his failure to confront AIDS when president, including his role in publishing globalization, structural reform, and trade deals like NAFTA (the North American Free Trade Agreement 1994) and the Global Agreement on Tariffs and Trade.'[156]

Second, there has been some discussion as to the health outcomes achieved by the Clinton Foundation. Seth Berkley, the president and founder of the International AIDS Vaccine Initiative, observed that there was a need to develop sustainable plans to deal with the public health epidemic: 'my wish is that Clinton would put ending the epidemic back at the top of his AIDS advocacy, and match his current work on AIDS treatment with renewed leadership to create a vaccine'.[157] In rejoinder, Clinton observed: 'most of that has to be done either by governments or, frankly, by the Gates Foundation, because they've got the bread, the money'.[158] He concluded: 'I think I'm doing what is best for me to do, and what will save the largest number of lives.'[159]

Third, much like with the Gates Foundation, there has been concern about the transparency, accountability and sustainability of the Clinton Foundation. There has been much criticism that the Clinton Foundation did not disclose the identity of its donors and contributors, during the 2007–8 Democratic Presidential Nomination Race.[160] With the nomination of Hilary Clinton as Secretary of State, William Clinton has agreed

[154] *Pharmaceutical Manufacturers' Association of South Africa* v. *Government of South Africa*, Case No: 4183/98 (High Court of South Africa, Transvaal Provincial Division, 2001); Ruth Mayne, 'The Global Campaign on Patents and Access to Medicines: An Oxfam Perspective', in Peter Drahos and Ruth Mayne (eds.), *Global Intellectual Property Rights: Knowledge, Access and Development* (2002) 249; Susan Sell, *Private Power, Public Law: The Globalization of Intellectual Property Rights* (2003) 152.

[155] Charles Babcock and Ceci Connolly, 'AIDS Activists Badger Gore Again', *The Washington Post*, 18 June 1999.

[156] D'Adesky, *Moving Mountains*, above n. 142, 296.

[157] Remnick, 'The Wanderer', above n. 137. [158] Ibid. [159] Ibid.

[160] Matthew Yglesias, 'Who's Giving Money to Bill Clinton?', *Los Angeles Times*, 4 October 2007.

to disclose the names of every contributor to the Clinton Foundation and to refuse donations from foreign governments. The former president observed: 'If she is going to be secretary of state and I operate globally and I have people who contribute to these efforts globally, I think that it's important to make it totally transparent.'[161] Bill Clinton also agreed to the separate incorporation of the Clinton Global Initiative from the Clinton Foundation. The former president agreed to the conditions, reportedly to avoid the appearance of a conflict of interests and the potential for foreign influence of United States international policy – even though he thought that the measures were 'over and above what the law requires'.[162] The Clinton Foundation website released a comprehensive list of donors in December 2008.[163]

Given its close identification with its charismatic founder, one wonders whether the Clinton Foundation will be sustainable after Bill Clinton ceases to play an instrumental role in the organization.

5. Redwashing: conclusion

This chapter has considered the role of charities, foundations and philanthropists in the debate over access to essential medicines. It has sought to analyse the strategies and tactics of the (RED) Campaign, the Gates Foundation, and the Clinton Foundation. This chapter has considered how such organizations have deployed trademarks and celebrity endorsements in public relations and marketing efforts in the field of access to medicines. The (RED) Campaign, the Gates Foundation and the Clinton Foundation rely upon a combination of trademarks, personality rights, celebrity endorsements and corporate social responsibility. The case studies suggest that such marketing devices have potential for leveraging consumer and corporate support for public

[161] DPA, 'Hilary Shocked at Obama's Choice', *The Sydney Morning Herald*, 4 December 2008.

[162] Ibid.

[163] The Clinton Foundation, 'William J. Clinton Foundation Publishes Names of All Contributors on Foundation Website' (Press Release, 18 December 2008); The Clinton Foundation, *Contributor Information*, www.clintonfoundation.org/contributors/index.html at 10 March 2009. Notably, The Children's Investment Fund Foundation and UNITAID contributed more than US$25,000,000. AUSAID, The Bill & Melinda Gates Foundation, Stephen L. Bing, COPRESIDA-Secretariado Tecnico, Fred Eychaner, The Radcliffe Foundation, Tom Golisano, The Hunter Foundation, Kingdom of Saudi Arabia, The ELMA Foundation and Theodore W. Waitt contributed between $10,000,001 and $25,000,000.

good initiatives. This chapter has highlighted the strengths of such models in respect of promoting consumer awareness, corporate social responsibility and fundraising. It has also emphasized the limitations of these efforts – in terms of transparency, accountability and sustainability, and in addressing underlying problems associated with justice and equity. There are also concerns that such initiatives marginalize national governments; offer weak consumer protection; and do not provide adequate consultation for recipients of grants and aid.

Furthermore, there is a concern that non-government organizations, charities and philanthropic foundations have not transcended the problems associated with research and development. Critically, the (RED) Campaign, the Gates Foundation and the Clinton Foundation have avoided dealing with the larger questions in respect of procedural and substantive patent law reform. This is problematic. Bono, Bill Gates and Bill Clinton have all subscribed to a belief in strong protection of intellectual property rights. Such figures have been oblivious to the pressing problems associated with the quality of patents granted in respect of pharmaceutical drugs.[164] There could be a concern that the charities engage in 'redwashing' of strong intellectual property rights protection.[165] There has been a great debate over the need for procedural harmonization of patent regimes. Developed countries, developing countries and least-developed countries have been grappling with reforms to domestic patent regimes to facilitate the import and export of essential medicines.[166] There has been a collective push in a number of international forums for substantive law reform in respect of patent law and access to essential medicines: specifically, in respect of patent thresholds; exceptions to patent infringement; and remedies for patent holders.[167]

[164] The Patent Reform Act 2007 (US) (H.R. 1908, S. 1145); The Committee on the Judiciary, US Congress, *The Patent Reform Act of 2007: Report Together with Additional and Minority Views (to Accompany S. 1145)*, Report No 110–259 (2008); Adam Jaffe and Josh Lerner, *Innovation and its Discontents: How our Broken Patent System is Endangering Innovation and Progress, and What to Do about It* (2004); James Bessen and Michael Meurer, *Patent Failure: How Judges, Bureaucrats, and Lawyers Put Innovators at Risk* (2008).

[165] Arnica Rowan, '(REDWASHING): Will Thousands of Red iPods, T-Shirts, and Cellphones Really Make the World a Better Place?', *Unlimited Magazine*, 30 October 2007.

[166] Matthew Rimmer, 'Race against Time: The Export of Essential Medicines to Rwanda' (2008) 1(2) *Public Health Ethics* 89.

[167] Peter Yu, 'Access to Medicines, BRICS Alliances and Collective Action' (2008) 34 *American Journal of Law and Medicine* 345.

Furthermore, the (RED) Campaign, the Gates Foundation, and the Clinton Foundation have not embraced such initiatives as prizes, the Health Impact Fund, patent pools and open drug discovery. As a result, the dominant models of such charities and foundations could divert both funds and public attention away from some of the promising alternative models of research and development promoted at the World Health Organization.

Sadly, at present, creative capitalists have been singularly unimaginative on the question of the reform of intellectual property laws to enhance access to essential medicines.

PART IV

Healthcare

13

Beyond TRIPS: the role of non-state actors and access to essential medicines

NOAH BENJAMIN NOVOGRODSKY

1. Introduction

With ever greater frequency, non-state and supra-state actors are defining the struggle for claims to health, specifically access to medicines that permit individuals to live longer, higher quality lives. Non-governmental organizations ('NGOs'), including the Treatment Action Campaign, Knowledge Ecology International, ACT UP and Médecins Sans Frontières ('MSF' or 'Doctors Without Borders') have revolutionized advocacy on the national and international stage, most dramatically with respect to antiretroviral drugs used to combat HIV/AIDS. Equally important, brand and generic pharmaceutical manufacturers have come to play an increased role in the development of global rules and incentives for production. Large philanthropic foundations, specifically the Bill & Melinda Gates Foundation[1] and the William J. Clinton Foundation,[2] have promoted bulk purchasing, preferential pricing and the rollout of antiretrovirals to developing countries and communities in need.[3] Many large research universities, themselves the recipients of public funding, are engaged in multi-faceted licensing agreements. The Global Fund for AIDS, Malaria and Tuberculosis ('the Global Fund'), for its part, operates as a public–private partnership. In turn, the Global

[1] The Bill & Melinda Gates Foundation, which declares that it is driven by the view that 'all lives – no matter where they are being led – have equal value' has given or pledged nearly US$8 billion to global health initiatives, including at least US$650 million to the Global Fund, www.gatesfoundation.org/ at 2 March 2009.

[2] The Clinton Foundation Programs: HIV/AIDS Initiative, www.clintonfoundation.org/cf-pgm-hs-ai-home.htm at 2 March 2009. The Foundation has been instrumental in negotiating price reductions and bulk procurement opportunities from pharmaceutical companies.

[3] Although the Gates Foundation dwarfs the budget of many developing states, it is not formally accountable to any entity save its own charitable status.

Fund is championed by Jeffrey Sachs, Bono and other celebrity supporters of the (RED) Campaign, advisers and advocates perhaps, but otherwise quintessentially non-governmental actors.

This chapter examines the role of certain non-state actors in the struggle to increase access to essential medicines.[4] As an illustration of that effort, I rely on the global campaign (usually spearheaded by national or sub-national NGOs) to ensure that people living with HIV/AIDS ('PLWHA') obtain antiretrovirals.[5] The pathogenic threat posed by AIDS exceeds the interest or capacity of any single state and thus serves as a fertile example of the power contained in trans-state organizations, corporations, networks and funding mechanisms.[6]

Section 2 of this chapter explores the traditional role of NGOs in combating AIDS, identifies some of the costs associated with the outsider roles claimed or assigned to non-state actors in the creation of

[4] To be sure, non-state actors are a polyglot group and even among international NGOs, there is a great variety of organizations. As used here, the term NGO refers to organizations that are in no way connected to governments or international institutions. In recent years, several distinct NGOs referred to in this piece – MSF, KEI, Health Gap and Health Action International among them – have formed a coalition that frequently acts in concert on access to medicine issues and which seeks to shape and reflect an emerging social movement.

[5] The demand for treatment is often, but not always, represented as a right provided by national law and reinforced by international human rights instruments. See e.g., Alicia Yamin, 'Not Just a Tragedy: Access to Medications as a Right under International Law' (2003) 21 *Boston University International Law Journal* 325, 344; Zita Lazzarini, 'Access to HIV Drugs: Are We Changing the Two-World Paradigm?' (2002) 17 *Connecticut Journal of International Law* 281, 288. The right to treatment of antiretrovirals is plainly a part of access but the claim is narrower than a demand for access to knowledge or to essential medicines, all of which raise definitional questions that include the concepts 'affordability' and 'sustainability'. See the World Health Organization's policy perspectives on medicines, *Equitable Access to Essential Medicines: A Framework for Collective Action* (2004), whqlibdoc.who.int/hq/2004/WHO_EDM_2004.4.pdf at 2 March 2009. Importantly, the struggle for access is not limited to the developing world. In *Abigail Alliance for Better Access to Developmental Drugs* v. *C. Von Eschenbach*, 495 F.3d 695 (D.C. Cir. 2007), petition for writ of certiorari denied, 128 S.Ct. 1069 (2008 WL 114305), the US Court of Appeals for the District of Columbia held that the Constitution does not provide terminally ill patients with a due process right of access to experimental drugs that have passed limited safety trials but have not yet been proven safe and effective.

[6] See Laurie Garrett, *The Coming Plague* (1994); David Fidler, 'Fighting the Axis of Illness: HIV/AIDS, Human Rights and US Foreign Policy' (2004) 17 *Harvard Human Rights Journal* 99; Jem Spectar, 'The Olde Order Crumbleth: HIV-Pestilence as a Security Issue and New Thinking about Core Concepts in International Affairs' (2003) 13 *Indiana International and Comparative Law Review* 481; Noah Benjamin Novogrodsky, 'The HIV/AIDS Pandemic and Human Security' (2006) 100 *American Society of International Law Proceedings* 345, 349.

intellectual property rights and contrasts that status with the insider position of many corporate interests at WTO negotiations. Section 3 of the chapter examines the relationship between non-state actors and state delegations (particularly from the global South) at the Agreement on Trade-Related Aspects of Intellectual Property Rights ('TRIPS' or 'TRIPS Agreement')[7] deliberations. The final section – section 4 – probes some of the alternative roles available to NGOs and casts non-state actors as a central force in the fight to bring life-saving medicines to people in need.

2. Absent at the inception

In the beginning, most NGOs were conspicuously absent from the debates surrounding the creation of global intellectual property mechanisms. Indeed, although individual academics[8] and representatives of some developing nations[9] raised alarm at the TRIPS talks, negotiators from states of the global North – generally knowledge-based industry exporters – succeeded in narrowing the gaps in domestic systems and ensuring that minimum levels of intellectual property protection existed in the domestic laws of all WTO member states.[10] Before TRIPS, approximately fifty states excluded pharmaceutical products from patent protection. Despite the concern that the extension of patent protection

[7] Marrakesh Agreement Establishing the World Trade Organization, opened for signature 15 April 1994, 1867 UNTS 3, annex 1C (Agreement on Trade-Related Aspects of Intellectual Property Rights) (entered into force 1 January 1995) ('TRIPS Agreement').

[8] See, e.g., Marco C. E. J. Bronckers, 'The Impact of TRIPS: Intellectual Property Protection in Developing Countries' (1994) 31 *Common Market Law Review* 1245.

[9] This draft contrasts developing countries with developed countries. In the WTO framework, 'developing countries' self-identify themselves as such, subject to challenges from other countries. See World Trade Organization, 'Who Are the Developing Countries in the WTO?', www.wto.org/english/tratop_e/devel_e/d1who_e.htm at 2 March 2009. Generally, however, this term refers to poor nations, using criteria based almost exclusively on per capita income. The countries in this group include states which are variously labelled as developing countries, underdeveloped countries, low-income countries, Majority World, the South or the Third World. These nations generally have low levels of technology, basic living standards and little in the way of an industrial base. Their economies are mainly agricultural and are characterized by cheap, unskilled labour and a scarcity of investment capital. Per capita incomes are below US$5,000 and often less than US$1,500. Around 70 per cent of the world's population live in developing countries, almost all of which are in Africa, Asia, Oceania and Latin America. Andy Crump, *The A-Z of World Development* (1998) 78–9. Within the WTO, 'developing countries' are contrasted to 'least-developed countries'.

[10] Margaret Chon, 'Intellectual Property and the Development Divide' (2006) 27 *Cardozo Law Review* 2813.

would lead to higher pharmaceutical prices (particularly in states that historically had not patented medicines), virtually all developing states accepted TRIPS as part of the package of Uruguay Round agreements, including WTO provisions that promised greater access to developed state markets in textiles and agricultural goods.[11] The incorporation of uniform intellectual property protections into the fabric of the global trading system continued through a series of bilateral free-trade agreements. These include many that incorporate additional ('TRIPS-Plus') provisions, enabling patent holders to extend or evergreen their monopoly rights beyond the twenty years dictated by TRIPS, or which impede competition through data exclusivity provisions or restrictions on the use of compulsory licences.

TRIPS is an agreement by and of sovereign states and serves to globalize intellectual property rights that were historically granted under domestic law for the territory of a particular state. And while those rights are not absolute, the few mechanisms recognized by the TRIPS Agreement for evading the force of patent protection – compulsory licensing and parallel importing among them – generally require state action. Similarly, the World Health Organization is populated by member states, and the recently convened Intergovernmental Working Group ('IGWG') meetings on Public Health, Innovation and Intellectual Property represent another instantiation of sovereign country debates regarding global health and access to medicines.[12]

States, however, are only part of the story. Well-financed corporations played a prominent role in the development of TRIPS.[13] In the period before and during the Uruguay Round, industry groups created a trade committee to forge a common agenda that united Hollywood producers, the chemical and pharmaceutical industries, publishing interests and the software sector. As Amy Kapczynski explains:

[11] Why developing states would make such concessions is a matter of some debate. Many accounts point to the lack of personnel in attendance at the Uruguay Round of talks as well as the failure of trained trade lawyers working on behalf of states in the global South. Several NGOs have since emerged in an attempt to remedy the gulf between developed and developing country delegations, including ILEAP (International Lawyers and Economists against Poverty), which provides support to developing country delegations in WTO negotiations, www.ileap-jeicp.org/index.html at 2 March 2009.

[12] In this respect, the IGWG continues the intergovernmental tradition represented by the '3 x 5' initiative, the WHO-led effort to put 3 million people on antiretroviral treatment by the end of 2005.

[13] See Peter Drahos, 'Global Property Rights in Information: The Story of TRIPS at the GATT' (1995) 13 *Prometheus*, 1, 12–13.

> Part of how they united and gained the support of policymakers was by forging a common identity as 'intellectual property' industries, by articulating their collective centrality to the US economy, and by framing the use of their products without permission as 'theft'.[14]

No company was more influential in lobbying US trade negotiators than Pfizer and no CEO more committed to linking trade and intellectual property rights than Pfizer's CEO, Edmund Pratt. Employing his network of established business contacts, Pratt used industry gatherings and high-level meetings to communicate the importance to his firm of linking trade and patent protections.[15] Pratt also headed the Advisory Committee on Trade Negotiations, through which private sector representatives gained direct access to the United States Trade Representative.

In short, transnational corporations – non-state actors with a unique pedigree – leveraged their relationship with state officials to shape trade law and influence the robust expansion of intellectual property rights into previously unreached markets. At a pivotal moment of accelerated globalization, the lobbying of a single pharmaceutical company with substantial investments in the developing world generated an outsized effect.

Where were civil society groups in this period? In the world of AIDS, they were – as Douglas Webb details – busy becoming service providers for treatment, education and prevention services.[16] In Haiti, for example, the NGO Partners in Health revolutionized AIDS service delivery by training community health workers called 'accompagnateurs' to distribute antiretrovirals, supervise home-based therapy and ensure adequate feeding.[17] Following the creation of the US President's Emergency Plan for AIDS Relief (PEPFAR) in 2003, church groups and other religious

[14] Amy Kapczynski, 'The Access to Knowledge Mobilization and the New Politics of Intellectual Property' (2008) 117 *Yale Law Journal* 804, 848.

[15] See Peter Drahos, 'Expanding Intellectual Property's Empire: The Role of FTAs' (2003) *International Centre for Trade and Sustainable Development*, ictsd.net/i/ip/24737/ at 2 March 2009.

[16] See Douglas Webb, 'Legitimate Actors? The Future Roles for NGOs against HIV/AIDS in Sub-Saharan Africa', in Nana Puku and Alan Whiteside (eds.) *The Political Economy of AIDS in Africa* (2004) 19, 20. Webb argues that there are at least three reasons for the outsized role of NGOs as AIDS service providers in Africa. 'Firstly, the rise of NGOs has been in direct response to the inaction or neglect of the state where a clear mandate to act has been dismissed. Secondly, NGO proliferation has been in response to the absence or limited nature of government credibility with its own constituency, leaving a vacuum of representation at local levels. Finally, and more rarely, governments have encouraged NGO activities in HIV/AIDS.'

[17] Paul Farmer, 'From "Marvelous Momentum" to Health Care for All' (2007) 86 *Foreign Affairs* 155, 156.

organizations joined established international NGOs in a scramble to extend AIDS programming.[18] In many countries, civil society organizations trained their attention on national leaders and the enormous challenge of persuading sometimes recalcitrant leaders to adopt laws, policies and practices to assist PLWHA.[19] What civil society groups were not doing was shaping the legal, economic and political environment that now links access to medicines and the fulfilment of some human rights to the international trade regime.

3. Advocacy through proxies

It is no exaggeration to say that civil society groups examining TRIPS after 1994 found a fully formed, institutionalized, multilateral and comprehensive mechanism for addressing intellectual property-related issues and disputes embedded within a framework of international trade. Compared to pre-existing instruments, the TRIPS Agreement contains a complete provision on enforcement and imposes detailed obligations on states. TRIPS also 'establishes a strong monitoring and supervisory scheme through the machinery of the TRIPS Council, a marked departure from the norm of previous conventions'.[20] Within TRIPS, compliance and enforcement questions are addressed through the WTO dispute resolution system, a scheme that ensures a permanent, quasi-judicial state-centric dispute resolution mechanism. Generic manufacturers, NGOs and foundations prepared to promote enhanced access to essential medicines are marginalized, even erased, within the arrangement. Instead, a global compact by and among sovereign states serves to 'freeze the comparative advantages'[21] that ensure Northern technological supremacy and counter Northern countries' declining competitive position in the global market (particularly vis-à-vis labour costs).

In view of the statist composition of the new international intellectual property regime, it is unsurprising that many prominent NGOs sought to partner with sympathetic state parties to the WTO in order to enhance access to medicines. Brazilian and South African advocates,

[18] Helen Epstein, *The Invisible Cure: Africa, the West, and the Fight against AIDS* (2007).

[19] Raymond A. Smith and Patricia D. Siplon, *Drugs into Bodies: Global AIDS Treatment Activism* (2006).

[20] Uche Ewelukwa, 'Patent Wars in the Valley of the Shadow of Death: The Pharmaceutical Industry, Ethics and Global Trade' (2005) 59 *University of Miami Law Review* 203, 213.

[21] Carlos M. Correa, *Intellectual Property Rights, the WTO and Developing Countries: The TRIPS Agreement and Policy Options* (2000).

collaborating with international human rights organizations, urged their respective governments to use TRIPS flexibilities, particularly permissible compulsory licensing provisions, to increase the flow of antiretrovirals to combat HIV/AIDS.[22] The issuance (or threatened issuance) of compulsory licences in each of these cases engendered intense criticism from patent-holding pharmaceutical companies and their political allies.[23] In South Africa, thirty-nine multinational pharmaceutical companies challenged the country's Medicines and Related Substances Control Amendment Act[24] (legislation that would have allowed parallel importing and compulsory licensing while encouraging generic competition); it took a sustained civil society campaign led by the Treatment Action Campaign to persuade the firms to withdraw the action.[25]

By 1999, public health and development NGOs began actively pursuing an international agenda to support developing countries in their efforts to negotiate solutions to the problems arising from higher prices for patented medicines. The activities of NGOs raised the profile of the access to medicines debate and provided important succour to developing countries on the eve of the fourth WTO Ministerial Conference held in Doha in 2001. MSF,[26] for example, initiated a highly publicized campaign to track drug prices, to advocate for increased generic production of antiretrovirals, and to expose the ways that the TRIPS Agreement contributes to the neglect of diseases afflicting the poor.[27]

[22] See João Biehl, *Will to Live: AIDS Therapies and the Politics of Survival* (2007), which argues that Brazil's AIDS policy is emblematic of novel forms of state action on and towards public health.

[23] See, e.g., *AIDS Access Foundation et al.* v. *Bristol-Myers Squibb Company and Department of Intellectual Property*, Central Intellectual Property and International Trade Court, Black Case No Tor Por 34/2544, Red Case No 92/2545 (Thailand 2002); and Lisa Forman, 'Incentivizing Justice: Linking Human Rights, Trade and Access to Medicines' (2005–6) *MCIS Briefings, Comparative Program on Health and Society Lupina Foundation Working Papers Series* (cataloguing the pressure applied to Thailand, Mexico, Chile, Brazil, Indonesia, Bolivia, Colombia, Ecuador, Peru, Venezuela, South Korea and South Africa as they considered compulsory licensing).

[24] The Medicines and Related Substances Control Amendment Act, No 90 1997, South Africa.

[25] *Pharmaceutical Manufacturers' Association and 41 Others* v. *President of South Africa and 9 Others*, High Court of South Africa, Transvaal Provincial Division, Case No 4183/98 (2001).

[26] MSF treats more than 72,000 people with antiretrovirals in nineteen different countries.

[27] See Ellen F. M. 't Hoen, 'TRIPS, Pharmaceutical Patents and Access to Essential Medicines: Seattle, Doha and Beyond' (2002) 3 *Chicago Journal of International Law* 27.

Some NGOs, particularly MSF, the Consumer Project on Technology (now Knowledge Ecology International) and Health Action International, played a significant role in the processes leading up to the adoption by WTO members of a declaration on TRIPS and Public Health at the Doha Conference on 14 November 2001.[28] While affirming that 'the TRIPS Agreement should be interpreted and implemented in a manner supportive of WTO members' right to protect public health and, in particular, to promote access to medicines', and reaffirming 'the right of WTO Members to use, to the full, the provisions in the TRIPS Agreement, which provide flexibility for this purpose', nonetheless rely entirely on the metric of state parties. Several NGOs, working with independent journalists, effectively silenced predictable US opposition to expanded compulsory licensing by publicizing the apparent hypocrisy of the US threat to issue a compulsory licence to increase the availability of Ciprofloxacin to treat anthrax, under the authority of 28 USC § 1498,[29] while opposing the use of TRIPS flexibilities to scale up antiretroviral therapy in developing countries.

NGOs grouped as a campaign for access to medicines also played a crucial role in the subsequent two-year period of negotiations on the implementation of the Doha Declaration that led to the WTO General Council Decision of 30 August 2003 on the Implementation of Paragraph 6 of the Declaration.[30] In this period, NGOs worked closely with select countries of the global South (particularly Brazil, India and Thailand) to develop positions related to the Doha talks, to train and educate delegation members, and to ensure cohesion amongst the bloc of developing states.

NGOs have also laboured to take advantage of the 30 August 2003 Decision. The example of Canada's Access to Medicines Regime ('CAMR') provides a poignant illustration. Drafted after the 2003 round of World Trade Organization talks in Doha, CAMR amended Canada's Patent Act to promote the export of generic versions of essential medicines, including antiretrovirals, through compulsory licensing.

[28] Declaration on the TRIPS Agreement and Public Health: Adopted on 14 November 2001, WT/MIN(01)/DEC/2 (2001) ('Doha Declaration').

[29] Senator Chuck Schumer, 'New Cipro Source Could Dramatically Increase Supply', (October 16 2001) Press Release, www.senate.gov/~schumer/SchumerWebsite/pressroom/press_releases/PR00728.html at 2 March 2009.

[30] Implementation of Paragraph 6 of the Doha Declaration on the TRIPS Agreement and Public Health, WTO Doc WT/L/540 (2003) (WTO General Council Decision of 30 August 2003). The decision sets out the mechanism to allow countries with insufficient or no pharmaceutical manufacturing capacities to import generic versions of essential medicines from a foreign generic producer.

MSF, and a generic pharmaceutical company, quickly applied for a compulsory export licence to produce a triple fixed dose combination therapy for HIV and AIDS. In order to issue the licence, however, Canadian officials require a reciprocal import licence from a least-developed country demonstrating a need for the drug and affirming the state's inability to produce the product itself. MSF is barred from applying for the import licence. To complete the application process, it appears as if each country that wants MSF to distribute the drug will need to make the appropriate notification to the WTO or the Government of Canada; the NGO may not make the notification on the country's behalf.

The CAMR suffers from a number of additional shortcomings. As the Canadian HIV/AIDS Legal Network has observed, the existing Canadian law requires Health Canada regulatory approval, as opposed to WHO or other qualified certification, it extends any export licence for only two years, limits the products subject to compulsory licensing and permits patent holders to sue generic competitors for perceived infringement in the licensing process.[31] In this environment, well-meaning non-state actors have been stymied in their effort to increase access to medicines using the Canadian compulsory licensing regime. The University of Toronto and its NGO partners engaged in a multi-year effort with Ghanaian officials to promote compulsory licensing and the use of CAMR as well as GATT article 24 flexibilities or regional-level licences. After more than two years of work, Ghana issued a compulsory licence for a single antiretroviral but filled the order from an Indian firm with a product that was readily available at a price that Canadian firms were unlikely to match.

A second effort was marginally more successful. MSF, the Canadian HIV/AIDS Legal Network and the generic producer Apotex persuaded Rwanda to issue a compulsory licence for a single triple combination AIDS drug. Almost five years after CAMR was announced, Apotex filled the order, a process that is unlikely to be repeated.[32] To date, Rwanda is the only state to have met the Canadian requirements for parallel compulsory licences.

[31] Richard Elliott, 'TRIPS from Doha to Cancún … to Ottawa: Global Developments in Access to Treatment and Canada's Bill C-56' (2003) 8(3) *Canadian HIV/AIDS Policy and Law Review* 1; Richard Elliott, 'Steps Forward, Backward, and Sideways: Canada's Bill on Exporting Generic Pharmaceuticals' (2004) 9(3) *Canadian HIV/AIDS Policy and Law Review* 1.

[32] Apotex recently indicated that the legislation is so cumbersome that it does not intend to seek additional export licences under CAMR.

At the recently concluded Intergovernmental Working Group meetings of the WHO in Geneva – the group moniker clearly identifies who has a seat at the table – NGOs again embraced the role of advisers to sympathetic states. Although the ranks of civil society groups have swelled and their means of disseminating information have expanded,[33] non-state actors continue to work on the margins of multilateral forums such as the IGWG.[34] In this capacity, NGOs have named and shamed (including identifying the Colombian delegate by name and detailing his stalling tactics), offered briefing reports, authored op-eds and provided real-time accounts of country positions. Several large NGOs have also provided delegates from developing countries (particularly those from smaller states) with technical assistance, prepared substantive policy inputs and co-ordinated information-gathering among civil society groups.[35] Knowledge Ecology International, for example, has worked with delegations from Barbados and Bolivia to propose a global prize system to stimulate innovation.[36] In that dynamic, US, Canadian, Australian and European NGO staffers find themselves criticizing their country of origin in the name of developing states. As a strategy of reform from within an institution, this technique ensures that the NGO perspective is actively debated. It nonetheless remains a proxy battle and one that is weighted against the inclusion of non-state actors.

4. Imagining alternatives

Should NGOs continue to work through states to reform TRIPS or to expand flexibilities under the agreement? The absence of civil society representation or developing country perspectives in the original drafting of the agreement (put differently, the capture of the TRIPS agenda by industry interests in alliance with Northern states) and the modest success of the Doha Round talks suggests that NGOs have a role to

33 Bloggers and posters to the IP-Health list provided hourly accounts of activities at the IGWG negotiations, lists.essential.org/mailman/listinfo/ip-health at 2 March 2009.

34 For some NGOs at international conferences, being relegated to the hallway is literally unbearable; at the Rome Conference that created the International Criminal Court, Richard Dicker of Human Rights Watch took Somalia's country placard (knowing that Somalia had sent no one to the conference) and used it to gain entry to the direct negotiations.

35 Duncan Matthews, 'The Role of International NGOs in the Intellectual Property Policy-Making and Norm-Setting Activities of Multilateral Institutions' (2007) 82 *Chicago-Kent Law Review* 1369.

36 See www.keionline.org at 2 March 2009.

play in bolstering the trade delegations of the global South. Likewise, the attempt to exploit TRIPS flexibilities while brokering generic competition has allowed groups like the Canadian HIV/AIDS Legal Network to test TRIPS-influenced domestic legislation and to monitor and evaluate pragmatic efforts to expand access to medicines. By participating in the supporting roles assigned to NGOs under CAMR and similar legislative schemes, civil society groups demonstrate their willingness to serve as change agents, however limited the scope of their involvement.

While such work has produced tangible results, NGOs can do more than advise developing country delegations at multilateral trade and intellectual property negotiations. By embracing their identity as citizen-representatives with standing to submit valuable alternative notions, NGOs can challenge authority and shape the discourse through at least four modalities.

First, non-state actors, including academics, are the source and disseminators of desperately needed ideas. Prize funds,[37] patent pools and alternative registration schemes are powerful ideas that challenge the orthodoxy of institutionalized patent monopolies as the only acceptable model. Viewed in this light the Health Impact Fund,[38] describing a complement to the existing patent regime that would generate a flow of pharmaceutical innovation without depriving the poor of their freedom to buy new medicines at competitive market prices, is a crucial counter-narrative to TRIPS-centric incentives. Academics and access to medicine campaigners have identified existing practices and flexibilities (such as parallel importing, the expansion of compulsory licensing, non-exclusive uses and process rather than product patents) while imagining workable alternatives. These ideas and their cross fertilization in a variety of forums are potentially as important as the medical innovations protected by the TRIPS Agreement.

Second, NGOs must redouble efforts to influence *developed* countries and their negotiating posture. While TRIPS is likely to frame intellectual property rights for the foreseeable future, vertical advocacy and lobbying have produced tangible results, from President Clinton's overdue announcement at Seattle in 1999, to the Lawyers' Collective's campaign

[37] James Love and Tim Hubbard, 'The Big Idea: Prizes to Stimulate R&D for New Medicines' (2007) 82(3) *Chicago-Kent Law Review* 1519–54.

[38] See Thomas Pogge, 'The Health Impact Fund: Better Pharmaceutical Innovations at Much Lower Prices', in Thomas Pogge, Matthew Rimmer and Kim Rubenstein (eds.), *Incentives for Global Public Health: Patent Law and Access to Essential Medicines* (2010), 135.

to shape India's 2005 Patent Act, to the Canadian HIV/AIDS Legal Network's consistent opposition to unnecessary obstacles embedded in CAMR.[39] Advocacy of this nature is rooted in the work of ACT UP and the Gay Men's Health Crisis and adapted by Health Gap, all of which have sought to break the silence around AIDS by loudly and effectively championing the needs of infected people.[40] By staging die-ins and appearing in public bound and gagged or demonstrating at political events, activists have created performances that embarrass politicians and decision-makers while demonstrating the link between patents and the need of PLWHA. Of course, the access to medicine movement has also forged political alliances (including unlikely bedfellows Bono and Michael Gerson, Bill Clinton – as citizen, not as president – and Jesse Helms) and employed a wide array of methods to expose the costs of a patent regime that permits no exceptions. The desacralization of intellectual property rights owes as much to the advocacy of Stephen Lewis, Jamie Love, Zackie Achmat, Jeffrey Sachs and others as it does to formal amendments to TRIPS.

NGOs concerned with public health cannot cede domestic influence to the US-based Pharmaceutical Research and Manufacturers Association ('PhRMA') and its allies around the globe. PhRMA's political supporters routinely deride access to medicine campaigners as politically unaccountable. Charges of this sort require consistent and principled opposition, particularly where the democratic process has broken down (as in South Africa) and where TAC has assumed the additional burden of countering government denialism.[41]

Third, NGOs are only beginning to tap the potential of horizontal advocacy. *Hazel Tau et al.* v. *GlaxoSmithKline, Boehringer Ingelheim et al.*[42] demonstrates the efficacy of direct action by one non-state actor against another in the context of an anti-trust suit before South Africa's National Competition Commission. There, the complainants, working with the Treatment Action Campaign, alleged that the firms had breached article 8(a) of the Competition Act 1998 (South Africa) by charging

[39] See Richard Elliott, 'Delivery Past Due: Global Precedent Set under Canada's Access to Medicines Regime' (2008) 13 (1) *HIV/AIDS Policy and Law Review* 1.

[40] See J. G. Twomey Jr, 'AIDS Activism' (1990) 20 *Hastings Centre Report* 39.

[41] See William Forbath, 'The "Transformative Constitution": Treatment Action Campaign and the Politics of Social Rights in South Africa' (8 October 2008), ssrn.com/abstract=1292879 at 2 March 2009 (working paper).

[42] *Hazel Tau & Others* v. *GlaxoSmithKline and Boehringer Ingelheim*, Competition Commission of South Africa (2003).

excessive prices for antiretroviral medicines to the detriment of consumers. The complainants charged that 'The excessive pricing of antiretrovirals is directly responsible for premature, predictable and avoidable deaths of people living with HIV/AIDS, including both children and adults.'[43] The Competition Commission found for the complainants, although it allowed the defendants to amortize development costs.[44]

Claims against corporations under domestic law and the use of national patent flexibilities (such as India's opportunity for pre-grant opposition to patent applications or Canada's CAMR export licence procedures) offer tested avenues for increasing access to medicines. In this vein, the challenge to patents (or defence of infringement actions) waged by generic firms or competitors is essential, if not paradigm-shifting, work. Universities Allied for Essential Medicine ('UAEM') offers another example of institutional accountability. UAEM is an activist organization at forty universities across the US and Canada that works to increase access to drugs developed at universities.[45] The goal of UAEM is to change the licensing practices of universities so that when they license a university-discovered drug to a pharmaceutical corporation or biotech company they include provisions that ensure that the drug will be made generically available in the developing world to increase research in those diseases that affect the developing world, and to change the metrics by which universities measure the success of a drug. Similarly, the dynamic of Health Gap and ACT UP organizing boycotts of Abbott for the pricing of the antiretroviral Kaletra, or Ira Magaziner's effort on behalf of the Clinton Foundation to persuade pharmaceutical companies to provide voluntary licences to generic

[43] Ibid.

[44] The Commission's decision promoted a settlement between the parties under which GlaxoSmithKline and Boehringer Ingelheim agreed to grant voluntary licences on their patented medicines to generic firms in exchange for a royalty. The AIDS Law Project, acting on behalf of the Treatment Action Campaign, recently filed another complaint with the South African Competition Commission to investigate the refusal by Merck and its South African subsidiary to allow sufficient competition to lower the price of Efavirenz.

[45] The movement started in 2001 at Yale when students realized that the drug, d4t, essential for treating AIDS/HIV was discovered at Yale by Dr Prusoff but was licensed out to BMS and was being sold for US$1600 per patient year – a price no patient in Africa could afford. Students mobilized and asked the university to leverage its power to lower the price, but the university resisted. Students continued to pressure the university and BMS and after a front page story in the *New York Times* by Dr Prusoff, BMS agreed to sell at cost price in Africa. A few months later, BMS agreed to allow generic competition which led to a price of US$55 per patient year.

companies making antiretrovirals, suggests both that horizontal advocacy has exploded in new and important ways and that state parties no longer enjoy a monopoly in the ordering of international trade terms and intellectual property governance.

Fourth, NGOs operating in this space are part of a broad movement that has served to politicize the previously arcane field of intellectual property law. Under the rubric of access to knowledge, 'NGOs and activist coalitions that emerged independently of one another to contest the contours of intellectual property rights in seeds, medicines, software, genetic material, and cultural goods, are beginning to build links to one another.'[46] The connections among these groups take the form of a network that has allowed its members to create a set of shared principles, arguments and identities that has introduced a development agenda to the World Intellectual Property Organization ('WIPO'). Access to medicine campaigners have much in common with Open Source advocates and creative licence proponents. Solidarity with other advocates pursuing the broad dissemination of knowledge and opportunity will ensure that the access to medicines movement is neither isolated nor exceptional. Just as corporate actors did in the run-up to TRIPS, it is in the interest of NGOs concerned with public health to strengthen the network of relationships and positions formed by other knowledge-based sectors.

5. Conclusion

NGOs at the forefront of the struggle for affordable and accessible medicines stand poised to force a reconception of allegiances, values and state–citizen relationships. In the post-TRIPS era, the alliance with developing countries has allowed access to medicines advocates to participate in multilateral talks by proxy and to introduce alternative perspectives, but NGOs still do not have a seat at the table. This simple fact should persuade advocates that the future of the access to medicines movement will be defined by direct action and the nurturing of new ideas rather than the quality of advice provided to country delegations. In this space, NGOs and foundations, like corporations before them, are becoming essential units of analysis in the world of international trade, human rights and access to medicines.

[46] Kapczynski, 'The Access to Knowledge Mobilization and the New Politics of Intellectual Property', above n. 14, 835.

14

Securing health through rights

KATHARINE G. YOUNG*

1. Introduction

While 'rights-talk' is an important emancipatory discourse of our time, it is a form of discourse that is easier to conceptualize than institutionalize. In the language of rights, fundamental interests in food, shelter, education or housing, whose fulfilment is doubtless central to an emancipated life, become notoriously difficult to secure in appropriately institutional terms. These difficulties are perhaps nowhere more evident than with respect to the right to health. As a material interest so heavily influenced by economic and social determinants, by the availability and constraints of scientific and cultural knowledge, and by background protections of property and contract rights, the right to health presents momentous legal challenges. Its claims raise seemingly endless chains of causation and duties (and obfuscations from the role of genetics and luck) that defy our legal–institutional, as well as moral, categories.

Yet despite all this, the right to health remains a popular discursive strategy for social movements advocating for medicines, healthcare or public health protections. More than just a galvanizer, the right to health may in fact prefigure and produce actual legal–institutional outcomes. Indeed, if we investigate political strategies around the right to health and the use by health rights movements of litigation, legislation and constitutional rights, we may observe a less fixed and certain, but possibly far-reaching, way in which health is secured through rights. This chapter examines two such cases, involving access to affordable medicines in South Africa and access to healthcare in Ghana.

The right to health is recognized as both a human and a constitutional right. The Universal Declaration of Human Rights of 1948 declares that

* My thanks to Frank Michelman, Vlad Perju and Lucie White for helpful comments on a prior draft.

'[e]veryone has the right to a standard of living adequate for [their] health and well-being ... including food, clothing, housing and medical care and necessary social services'.[1] The International Covenant on Economic, Social and Cultural Rights of 1966 recognizes 'the right of everyone to the enjoyment of the highest attainable standard of physical and mental health'.[2] Many modern constitutions have guaranteed the right to health or healthcare, alongside traditional public health protections.[3] The South African Constitution of 1996 guarantees the right of everyone to have access to healthcare subject to available resources, as well as the right to emergency medical treatment and a right to an environment that is not harmful to health.[4] The Ghanaian Constitution of 1992 protects the 'right to good health care'[5] as a constitutionally entrenched directive principle of state policy. Many constitutions in Latin America, such as those of Colombia and Brazil, recognize the right to healthcare and offer highly developed models of enforcement.[6] For some constitutions, such as India's Constitution, the

[1] Universal Declaration of Human Rights, GA Res. 217A (III), UN Doc A/810 (1948), article 25.

[2] International Covenant on Economic, Social and Cultural Rights, opened for signature 16 December 1966, 993 UNTS 3 (entered into force 3 January 1976), article 12(1). The steps to be taken in the progressive realization of the right include (in article 12(2)): '(a) The provision for the reduction of the stillbirth-rate and of infant mortality and for the healthy development of the child; (b) The improvement of all aspects of environmental and industrial hygiene; (c) The prevention, treatment and control of epidemic, endemic, occupational and other diseases; (d) The creation of conditions which would assure to all medical service and medical attention in the event of sickness.' A right to healthcare is also found in the Convention on the Elimination of Discrimination against Women (article 12), the Convention on the Rights of the Child (article 24), and the African Charter on Human and Peoples' Rights (article 16). For a full list, see United Nations Economic and Social Council, Committee on Economic, Social and Cultural Rights, *General Comment No. 14: The Right to the Highest Attainable Standard of Health (Article 12 of the International Covenant on Economic, Social and Cultural Rights)* ¶ 33, UN Doc E/C.12/2004 (11 August 2000).

[3] Eleanor D. Kinney and Brian Alexander Clark, 'Provisions for Health and Health Care in the Constitutions of the Countries of the World' (2004) 37 *Cornell International Law Journal* 285 (presenting data that suggests that two thirds of all constitutions contain provisions protective of health or healthcare, and noting that more recent constitutions are more likely to reflect statements of duty and entitlement). In the case studies presented in this chapter, the lawyers and social movements used the 'right to health' as a more general frame, but focused specifically on the 'right to healthcare' available in local laws. This chapter uses the two in the same sense.

[4] South African Constitution 1996, § 27; see also § 24.

[5] Constitution of the Republic of Ghana 1992, s. 34.

[6] The textual protections of such rights in Colombia, Brazil and India, and the developing judicial responses, are documented in two recent books: see Varun Gauri and Daniel

right to health has been indirectly recognized by the judiciary, by interpreting the fundamental right to life as one which includes the provision of emergency healthcare.[7] For others, such as Thailand, the right to health has been defended by the executive on the basis of public health protections combined with ratification of certain international human rights instruments.[8] This chapter examines the ways in which the legal instruments recognizing the right to health are relied upon by lawyers and social movements to secure particular health outcomes. This effect is described and assessed by attention to 'praxis'.[9]

A focus on praxis departs from a positivist attempt to define the meaning of a right to health; or a normative attempt to provide it with a settled justificatory theory. Instead, the examination of praxis accepts that both legal and philosophical theories of a right to health are likely to remain unsettled and incomplete.[10] This is because a right to health raises boundary problems as to its object, conceptual problems as to its correlative duties, and reasonable disagreement on the priority of values that make it worthy of protection. Instead, attention to a theoretically informed practical action, captured by the concept of praxis, can clarify

M. Brinks (eds.), *Courting Social Justice: Judicial Enforcement of Social and Economic Rights in the Developing World* (2008); and Roberto Gargarella, Pilar Domingo and Theunis Roux (eds.), *Courts and Social Transformation in New Democracies: An Institutional Voice for the Poor* (2006).

7 The Indian Constitution 1950 , article 21, article 47; see further *Samity* v. *State of W.B.*, (1996) 4 S.C.C. 37 (Sup. Ct. India). For a similar approach to interpreting health through the right to life (article 6 of the International Covenant on Civil and Political Rights) see Compilation of General Comments and General Recommendations Adopted by Human Rights Treaty Bodies, 127, UN Doc HRI/GEN/1/Rev.6 (2003).

8 See, e.g., Statement by H.E. Ambassador Sihasak Phuangketkeow, Permanent Representative of Thailand to the United Nations, *On the Report of the Special Rapporteur on the Right of Everyone to the Enjoyment of the Highest Attainable Standard of Physical and Mental Health*, Mr Paul Hunt, (A/HRC/7/11 dated 31 January 2008) (7th Session of the HRC, 12 March 2008).

9 'Praxis' suggests action through experience. For an attempt to connect the philosophical movements of Marxism, pragmatism and analytical philosophy, see Richard J. Bernstein, *Praxis and Action* (1971, new edn, 1991) (presenting praxis as crystallized forms of human activity which can bridge theory and practice). This theme resembles a dual focus on the 'law-on-the-books' and the 'law-in-action'.

10 For an examination of how a right to health may be seen as incompletely theorized, but reliant on notions of human capability, see Jennifer Prah Ruger, 'Toward a Theory of a Right to Health: Capability and Incompletely Theorized Agreements' (2006) 18 *Yale Journal of Law and Humanities* 273, 306–11; and Norman Daniels, *Just Health: Meeting Health Needs Fairly* (2007) (presenting a justification for health based on equality of opportunity and accepting the rhetorical value of a 'right' to health).

the institutional potentials of a right to health, even as it accepts its inevitable limitations.

This chapter therefore describes a model of legal–political practice around health rights in grounded, qualitative terms. In the first part, it sets out how a model of praxis departs from the positivist view of legal rights. In the second part, it describes two cases – from South Africa and from Ghana – to suggest the potential of a right to health to effect legal change in the direction of enhanced health outcomes. The first involves a defence of the regulation of medicine prices in South Africa and an innovative political and legal use of the constitutional right to access healthcare and the international right to health. The second involves a more contained instance of rights advocacy in Ghana that took the governing structures of health financing (and user fees health delivery) as its target, making use of statute-based, constitutional and international law, and legal and community fora. Finally, I suggest that both cases provide lessons for health rights movements elsewhere, by focusing attention on the aspects of praxis that force an encounter between 'aspirational' legal rights and the background healthcare financing regimes. I conclude the chapter by examining the ways in which the speculative nature of the assessment of the two cases equates with the orientation of praxis itself.

2. Health rights praxis: the points of departure

Within a traditional conception of legal rights, practical action is conceived in a model that has been developed in the context of private claims against others, or public claims against the state. This model, which I term the 'private law model', has three main features, which conspire to displace the legal relevance of the right to health.

First, economic and social rights are conceived as positive rights, and positive rights are conceived as non-justiciable. Rights which require action by government, rather than non-interference, are unsuited to litigation, but belong in the more 'democratic' branches of government, where they may be open to contestation.[11]

Second, legal rights are conceived as coterminous with remedies. Relief will flow according to the harm caused by the breach of a duty, from duty holder to rights holder. A successful enforcement of a right is

[11] E.g., Frank Cross, 'The Error of Positive Rights' (2001) 48 *University of California Los Angeles Law Review* 857.

measured by the form of relief to the claimant. Where multiple – or possibly countless – duty holders exist, an appropriate remedy remains elusive.[12]

Third, health may be conceived as a private good, consumed (as healthcare) through a market-based or other allocative mechanism, and further defended (as bodily integrity) by tort and criminal law. Where health is accessed collectively, as a public good, it is protected by discrete environmental, occupational and public health laws. Outside these regimes, it is realized practically, but voluntarily, by the countless (and often merely risk-allocative) choices made by individuals and institutions, among them clinics and hospitals (both public and private), pharmaceutical companies, insurance companies, international financial institutions, bureaucracies, legislatures, agencies, schools and families.[13] A 'right' to health is incompatible with this complexity.

A fourth feature applies the above orientation to the role of the human right to health in international law. According to the private law model, international human rights are only as strong as their enforcement machinery. Trade rights have stronger enforcement machinery than human rights (especially economic, social and cultural rights): the Panel and Appellate Body reports of the World Trade Organization ('WTO') are enforceable; the country reports and general comments of the Committee on Economic, Social and Cultural Rights are not.[14] International human rights to health may exist in moral, 'soft' terms, but they are separate from 'hard' law.

These features of the private law model identify, albeit in a somewhat overstated fashion, a main source of scepticism around the right to

[12] For a classic exposition, see Lon L. Fuller, 'The Forms and Limits of Adjudication' (1978) 92 *Harvard Law Review* 353, 394–8, referring to a polycentric (or 'many centreed') problem as one unsuited to resolution by adjudication; and Aryeh Neier, 'Social and Economic Rights: A Critique' (2006) 13(2) *Human Rights Brief* 1 (former Executive Director of Human Rights Watch suggesting that 'rights only have meaning if it is possible to enforce them'.)

[13] For a demonstration of this complexity, see Theodore W. Ruger, 'Health Law's Coherence Anxiety' (2008) 96 *Georgetown Law Journal* 625 (describing the inevitable incoherence of health law).

[14] Michael J. Dennis and David P. Stewart, 'Justiciability of Economic, Social, and Cultural Rights: Should There Be an International Complaints Mechanism to Adjudicate the Rights to Food, Water, Housing, and Health?' (2004) 98 *American Journal of International Law* 462 (suggesting that a justiciability mechanism is inappropriate for the ICESCR); see recently Kenneth Roth, 'Defending Economic, Social and Cultural Rights: Practical Considerations Faced by an International Human Rights Organization' (2004) 26 *Human Rights Quarterly* 63.

health. Within this picture, a right to health is hortatory at best and a dangerously naive distraction at worst. The components of this picture contribute to the suspicion that the constitutional trend of entrenching a right to health, and codifying it in international and regional human rights instruments, makes little actual difference to health outcomes.

Yet the influence of the private law model is displaced by a second model, which is informed by public rather than private law.[15] This model, which I term a 'praxis' model because of its links with practical action and pragmatism, accepts an ongoing contestation and contingency around economic and social rights, including the right to health. Where the private law model seeks institutional certainty, the praxis model recognizes a programmatic open-endedness in securing the object of the right. Where the private law model privileges court-led reforms, the praxis model includes legislative and popular sites of action. Where the private law model seeks jurisdictional certainty, the praxis model operates at local, national and international levels, and sometimes at all three.

I suggest that this model of health rights praxis allows us to observe how the meaning of a legal right to health is created, challenged and changed within particular cases and contexts. We may summarize these developments, in opposition to the three main features of the prior model, as follows.

First, economic and social rights entail both positive and negative obligations, similar to all fundamental rights: the description of 'positive rights' is a misnomer. While positive obligations raise greater challenges for enforcement than negative obligations, differently calibrated forms of judicial review and remedy may help to resolve them.[16]

Second, legal rights can operate as 'objective principles' or 'institutional guarantees', as well as subjective claim rights. A successful judicial enforcement of an objective principle can effect institutional change, even as it fails to provide individualized relief. Remedies may be unhinged from individualized compensatory or restitution-based forms of relief, to follow a spectrum of judicial response, such as declarations, construing or severing legislation, promoting negotiated remedies

[15] For a classic exposition, see Abram Chayes, 'The Role of the Judge in Public Law Litigation' (1976) 89 *Harvard Law Review* 1281.

[16] For a study of the relations between the political branches employed by enforcement of social welfare rights, see Mark Tushnet, *Weak Courts, Strong Rights: Judicial Review and Social Welfare Rights in Comparative Constitutional Law* (2008).

between public agencies, or suggesting further social movement participation in the delivery of the object of the right.[17]

Third, praxis around the right to health does not purport to resolve the complexity of healthcare delivery or other programmes that are necessary for securing particular health outcomes. A constitutional or human right to health can exist alongside numerous regimes and institutions, such as the regulation of preventive health services, pharmaceutical and medical insurance companies, and hospitals and clinics. What the right to health may achieve is to allow advocates to exert pressure on the public and private actors who provide health services. This pressure resembles legal pressure, irrespective of whether a judicial response is available.[18]

The model of praxis allows us to observe legal obligations operating in various contexts. In this way, the right to heath works less as a basis for judicial enforcement than as framing the pressure on law-makers to take 'their best effort to devise, adopt and execute policies and measures that will result in the desired social-outcome targets'.[19] Rights work to mobilize, galvanize, educate and inform. The recognition of rights may be assisted by litigation, but litigation does not form the centre of the strategy. The two case studies set out below suggest this effect in the context of essential medicines in particular and commodified healthcare in general.

3. Health rights praxis: two examples

In the following two case studies from South Africa and Ghana, lawyers and social movements work together to secure health through rights. While the lawyers primarily follow litigation strategies, they also engage in mobilizing and organizing. The social movements working with them rely on the litigation as a performative tool, and also utilize the press, sit-ins, petitions and other actions. The claim-making process focuses on individual stories of health treatment, and targets both public and private institutions. The complex facts underlying medical or financing scenarios are made accessible through court-related processes, as well as the

[17] Charles F. Sabel and William H. Simon, 'Destabilization Rights: How Public Law Litigation Succeeds' (2004) 117 *Harvard Law Review* 1016.

[18] Lawrence Sager, *Justice in Plainclothes: A Theory of American Constitutional Practice* (2004) (presenting a theory of 'underenforced norms' which may include economic and social rights).

[19] Frank Michelman, 'Socioeconomic Rights in Constitutional Law: Explaining America Away' (2008) *International Journal of Constitutional Law* 1, 6.

didactic strategies not uncommon in human rights advocacy. Each case study suggests a more fluid role for advocacy, which bridges both national and international domains, and both courts and political branches. Each case study also suggests a more nuanced balancing of different forms of legal rights within healthcare settings.

3.1 *South Africa: the Pharmaceutical Manufacturers' Association litigation*

South Africa is the site of the first case study involving litigation and accompanying action around the right to health. This three-year campaign began as a defensive strategy by the Treatment Action Campaign ('TAC') in support of the South African Government's amendments to its medicines regime. The litigation was itself initiated by the Pharmaceutical Manufacturers' Association ('PMA'), which together with thirty-nine pharmaceutical companies challenged the amendments to the Medicines and Related Substances Control Amendment Act 1997 (South Africa).[20] The litigation and the campaign raised various constitutional protections, including section 27 of the South African Constitution, which recognizes a right to access healthcare. In the cases decided before and after the PMA litigation, the Constitutional Court has determined that the constitutional right to access healthcare requires 'reasonable' policies on healthcare rationing or restrictions, to which a court may apply critical assessment.[21] Despite being a key case for securing health for South Africans, the PMA litigation does not leave any formal precedent on the developing scope of section 27. This is so for two reasons. First, the case was primarily argued by the PMA as implicating the Constitution's property rights rather than the right to health. Second, and more importantly, the case was withdrawn by the applicants before the High Court of South Africa (Transvaal Provincial Division) delivered judgment.

[20] The Medicines and Related Substances Control Amendment Act, No 90 of 1997 (South Africa) ('Medicines Amendment Act') was passed by the National Assembly on 31 October 1997 and signed by then-President Mandela on 25 November 1997.

[21] *Soobramoney* v. *Minister of Health, Kwazulu-Natal* 1998 (1) SA 765 ('*Soobramoney*') (Constitutional Court rejecting an individual's claim for dialysis treatment because it did not constitute an emergency and the rationing policy was reasonable); and *Minister of Health* v. *Treatment Action Campaign* 2002 (5) SA 721 (Constitutional Court finding a government policy to restrict the roll-out of antiretrovirals to expectant mothers, where they would prevent mother to child transmission of HIV, was unreasonable).

Notwithstanding the withdrawal of the case before a judgment was reached, the PMA litigation reveals the important paths of institutional protection for the right to health that are established by legal recognition and practical action within and outside courts. From this viewpoint, I suggest that three consequences flowed particularly from the availability of a constitutional 'right to have access to health care services'.[22] First, the presence of the right contributed to the standing of the TAC, which requested to join the litigation as *amicus curiae* (friend of the court) in 2001, changing the pace and arguably the course of the litigation. Second, the right to health became an orienting value between the international and national movements that mobilized together in defence of the legislation. Third, and more speculatively, the presence of the constitutional right to health made available a different assessment of the merits of the PMA's arguments about property rights. If the High Court had decided the case, it might have been required to explicitly balance health rights against property rights.

The Medicines Amendment Act had introduced compulsory licensing, generic substitution of off-patent medicines and parallel importation, and a pricing committee.[23] The PMA sought and were awarded an injunction against the Medicines Amendment Act in the High Court, claiming an infringement of both constitutional and international law.[24] First, the PMA claimed that certain provisions of the Medicines Amendment Act constituted an arbitrary deprivation of their constitutional property rights or were alternatively expropriations without compensation, contrary to section 25 of the Constitution.[25] Second, they claimed that the same provisions of the Medicines Amendment Act were contrary to South Africa's obligations

[22] Section 27 of the South African Constitution 1996 provides that: '(1) Everyone has the right to have access to – (a) health care services, including reproductive health care; … (2) The state must take reasonable legislative and other measures, within its available resources, to achieve the progressive realisation of each of these rights. (3) No one may be refused emergency medical treatment.'

[23] Medicines Amendment Act, above n. 20, sections 15C, 22F and 22G. Compulsory licensing occurs when a government allows another party to produce the patented medicine product or process without the consent of the patent owner. Parallel importation occurs when a government imports a medicine under patent from a country where the patentee sells it at a lower price than in the local market.

[24] The *Pharmaceutical Manufacturers' Association of South Africa* v. *Government of South Africa*, Notice of Motion, Case Number 4183/98, in the High Court of South Africa (Transvaal Provincial Division) .

[25] South African Constitution, section 25 states, *inter alia*, that '(1) No one may be deprived of property except in terms of law of general application, and no law may permit arbitrary deprivation of property. (2) Property may be expropriated only in terms of law of general application – (a) for a public purpose or in the public interest; and

under the Trade-Related Aspects of Intellectual Property ('TRIPS') Agreement.[26] Because of a lack of capacity to respond, the Ministry of Health postponed its defence of the legislation, to which the PMA readily agreed, since its injunction continued to delay the implementation of the Medicines Amendment Act.

The tempo and substance of the defence changed after the TAC joined as *amicus* in January 2001. The TAC is a prominent social movement in South Africa, and has, since 1998, mobilized to 'ensure access to affordable and quality treatment for people with HIV/AIDS', to 'prevent and eliminate new HIV infections', and to 'improve the affordability and quality of health-care access for all'.[27] The admission of the *amicus* to litigation is not automatic: a prospective *amicus* must show that it can provide additional and relevant insights for the court.[28] In this case, the TAC pointed to the effect of the Medicines Amendment Act on lowering the price of medicines for HIV/AIDS patients, which it submitted was part of the constitutional duty of the government to realize progressively the right to access healthcare.[29] The effect of this duty on medicines regulation was based on the causal claim that the price of medicines was a major barrier to access and required regulation.[30] The TAC also pointed

(b) subject to compensation'. The PMA's arguments would appear to be weakened by the proportionality analysis that is included within this section, even without a constitutionally entrenched right to access healthcare. A study of the property clause is not the purpose of the current chapter, but has been clarified considerably by *First National Bank of SA Ltd t/a Wesbank* v. *Commissioner, South African Revenue Service* 2002 (4) SA 768 (CC); see further A. J. van der Walt, *Constitutional Property Law* (2005).

26 This argument was very similar to that submitted by Novartis in the *Glivec* case: Rajshree Chandra, 'The Role of National Laws in Reconciling Constitutional Right to Health with TRIPS Obligations: An Examination of the *Glivec* Patent Case in India', in Thomas Pogge, Matthew Rimmer and Kim Rubenstein (eds.), *Incentives for Global Public Health: Patent Law and Access to Essential Medicines*, (2010), 381.

27 See the mission statement of the Treatment Action Campaign, available at www.tac.org.za, at 2 March 2009.

28 *Rules of the Constitutional Court of South Africa* 2003 r. 10(6)(c). For example, in *Hoffmann* v. *South African Airways* 2001 (1) SA 1 (CC, South Africa), the *amicus* was able to furnish expert medical opinions about the progression, treatment and transmission of Human Immunodeficiency Virus (HIV) which 'altered the course of the appeal', at [10] (Constitutional Court finding unconstitutional the South African Airways' practice of refusing to employ as cabin attendants people who are living with HIV).

29 E.g. Founding Affidavit, 'Application to be admitted as an *amicus curiae*', *The Pharmaceutical Manufacturers' Association of South Africa* v. *Government of South Africa*, Case Number 4183/98, in the High Court of South Africa (Transvaal Provincial Division), paras. 58–71.

30 Obviously several factors outside patent law are responsible for drug prices, such as transport and storage costs, import tariffs and taxes, and dispensing fees. The Medicines and Related Substances Act No 101 of 1965 (South Africa) was attempting to regulate all

to a range of international human rights conventions that would make its participation relevant.

As one participant observed, the inclusion of the TAC transformed the case from a 'dry legal contest into a matter about human lives'.[31] The arguments that were made by the TAC in Court, as well as the practical action that took place outside the courtroom, formed an innovative praxis around the South African Constitution's guarantee of a right to access to healthcare services. The arguments focused on both TRIPS and the constitutional protection of property rights.

First, the PMA litigation required the PMA, the government, and the TAC to present arguments about the compatibility of the Medicines Amendment Act with the TRIPS regime. The protection of patents in TRIPS is based on the normative claim that knowledge-producers are morally entitled to reward for their knowledge, as well as the positive (and equally contentious) claim that extensive patents are necessary for research and development cost recovery and for incentives to innovate. It is not the purpose of this chapter to address these claims apart from indicating the potential scrutiny under which they are put in a court action involving medicines regulation and claims of a right to healthcare.[32] For instance, the PMA asserted that research and development would be jeopardized by the lesser protections of patents, thus implying a net loss to health. The TAC relied on expert evidence as to the joint public–private funding of research, as well as the profitability of such research. The PMA also asserted that the TAC's interest in the drugs was not substantive, because it had offered price discounts on medicines to the South African Government. The TAC, while benefiting from the access to information about price discounts that this defence engendered, responded that corporate benevolence could not remove the need for regulation. Finally, the PMA argued that the Medicines Amendment Act would make South Africa a pariah state, referring to the 150 countries that were co-signatories to TRIPS. The TAC addressed

of these areas. Moreover, affordable pricing is only one determinant of access to medicines: the rational use of medicines, adequate infrastructures and sustainable financing also play an important role: see Lisa Forman, 'Trade Rules, Intellectual Property, and the Right to Health' (2007) 21 *Ethics and International Affairs* 337.

31 Mark Heywood, 'Debunking "Conglomo-Talk": A Case Study of the Amicus Curiae as an Instrument for Advocacy, Investigation and Mobilisation' (2001) 5 *Law, Democracy and Development* 133.

32 For an investigation, see Edwin Cameron and Jonathan Berger, 'Patents and Public Health: Principle, Politics and Paradox' (2005) 131 *Proceedings of the British Academy* 331, 340.

this assertion with evidence of the practice of generic substitution and price controls in many other countries, including the US.

The PMA's opposition to the health rights dimensions of the TAC's submissions reveals the unsettled nature of the right to health. In opposing the interpretation of the right to access healthcare asserted by the TAC, the PMA suggested an interpretation that focused on healthcare entitlements. It suggested that the constitutional obligation to provide access to healthcare services would require the government to distribute free medicines to the poor, with the cost met by general taxation. In this way, it attempted to compel the state to deliver the medicines, by emphasizing the government's duty to protect constitutional rights and respect other rights (such as property rights) in the process.[33] This interpretation of the right to healthcare would give rise to a centralized, command-and-control mechanism. The 'entitlement' model would take a compensatory form, would be targeted to those in the greatest need and would be paid for by general taxation. Within this interpretation of the right to healthcare, the pharmaceutical industry would be regulated separately, as an entirely different sector. It would be subject to its own state-conferred benefits, in the form of, for example, the guarantees of market exclusivity conferred by patents.

In its turn, the TAC's arguments were based on a criticism of the compensatory entitlement model of health rights and relied instead on a connection between the pharmaceutical sector and the general regime of healthcare financing. This defence suggests that an entitlements-based interpretation of the right to healthcare, which depends upon a tax-and-transfer model of social provision, is not the only, and is perhaps in some cases not even a tenable, model for rights protection. This model tends to create its own inefficiencies even as it avoids others, and places particular burdens on the state. For example, for economies with large class-based and regional inequalities like South Africa, adequate entitlement programmes may not be realistically funded through the transfer of funds from taxing productive capital without threatening the capacity of that sector.

The TAC's submission in the PMA litigation invoked a very different form of economic and social rights protection. Rather than the compensatory entitlement form, its arguments defended an approach to securing

[33] There are interesting parallels between this argument and those employed by the Constitutional Court in a later case, involving the state's duty to provide alternative housing for unlawful occupiers of private land: see *President of the Republic of South Africa* v. *Modderklip Boerdery (Pty) Ltd* 2005 (5) SA 3 (CC).

health through the regulation of medicines prices. This approach addresses the negative efficiency aspects of tax-and-transfer by regulating private actors.[34] It contends that public and private healthcare systems are interdependent rather than autonomous. In regulating both, and in making private healthcare more affordable, public healthcare also becomes more accessible.[35] The private law model of health rights described above has no application to the PMA litigation. Instead, the right to healthcare retains a more open structure as an objective principle which guides the interpretation of other rights. The constitutional property right retains a subjective character, but is itself balanced by competing interests.

This conceptualization of health rights suggests the possible doctrinal arguments that might have influenced the High Court had it been required to deliver judgment. Because the PMA withdrew the case, we can only speculate on the impact of such arguments. We can, however, examine the effect of the right to health on the activities that took place outside the Court. These activities occurred in South Africa and abroad.

For example, the right to health and the PMA litigation proved to be a significant focal point for organizing support for the South African legislation internationally. Again, this was a defensive strategy against challenges brought by the pharmaceutical industry. In 1998, for example, South Africa was placed on the United States Trade Representatives' ('USTR') 301 Watch List, which may give rise to trade sanctions and other measures. This occurred as a result of the pharmaceutical industry's complaint against the Medicines Amendment Act. AIDS advocates, primarily in the US, succeeded in having South Africa removed from this list. By May 2000 President Bill Clinton signed Executive Order 13155, which recognized the rights of African countries to pass legislation to promote access to HIV/AIDS medicines without interference from the US, as long as the statutes were TRIPS compliant.[36]

Within South Africa, the XIII International AIDS Conference held in Durban in June 2000 focused international opposition against the PMA

[34] For a similar suggestion along more general lines, see Cass Sunstein, *The Second Bill of Rights: FDR's Unfinished Revolution and Why We Need It More than Ever* (2004) 197.

[35] Mark Heywood, 'Debunking "Conglomo-Talk"', above n. 31 (describing the inherited healthcare system of 1994 as composed of a private health sector, serving 20 per cent of the mostly white population but accounting for 80 per cent of the national expenditure on health).

[36] Executive Order 13155 of 10 May 2000 , 'Access to HIV/AIDS Pharmaceuticals and Medical Technologies', www.archives.gov/federal-register/executive-orders/2000.html.

litigation. The TAC also engaged in acts of disobedience in favour of changing the laws governing access to medicines. For example, Zackie Achmat, its chairperson, returned from Thailand in October 2000 with 5,000 generic tablets of an AIDS medication, in defiance of South African patent laws.

The relationship between the domestic contestation around the PMA litigation and international advocacy has been described as catalytic.[37] The court hearing was preceded by a vigil outside the High Court, with members of the TAC and the South African trade union COSATU present. On the day of the hearing (5 March 2001), 5,000 people marched past the High Court and on to the US Embassy. This march was paralleled by demonstrations in thirty cities worldwide, including mobilizations in Brazil, the Philippines, the US, Britain, Kenya, Thailand, France, Italy, Denmark, Australia and Germany. A petition against the legal action was signed by over 250 organizations in thirty-five countries, which was published as a full page advertisement in *Business Day* on 8 March 2001. The humanitarian group Doctors Without Borders/ Médecins Sans Frontières ('MSF') also played a crucial part in persuading the European Union and Dutch Government to pass resolutions calling for the case to be withdrawn. After this vigorous pressure from different advocacy groups, the PMA withdrew its case on 19 April 2001, leaving the South African Government free to implement the Medicines Amendment Act.

In fact, the mobilization generated by the litigation set in motion new alliances between AIDS advocates and health and human rights groups, with far-reaching effect. These were later to play a crucial part in the negotiations around TRIPS which took place at the World Trade Organization's Ministerial Conference in Doha in November 2001: effectively lending diffuse international pressure to efforts to allow states to adopt measures necessary for protecting public health as a flexible aspect of TRIPS. The Declaration by Ministers confirmed the rights of WTO members to determine what constitutes a national emergency, including in respect of public health crises involving HIV/AIDS,

[37] Heinz Klug, 'Campaigning for Life: Building a New Transnational Solidarity in the Face of HIV/AIDS and TRIPS', in Boaventura de Sous Santos and César Rodríguez-Garavito (eds.) *Law and Globalization from Below: Towards a Cosmopolitan Legality* (2005), 118 (describing the expansion from the South African movement to the forum of the World Trade Organization).

tuberculosis, malaria and other epidemics, and how these may justify a flexible interpretation of TRIPS.[38]

Although it is difficult to single out the role played by the 'right to health' in the international and domestic politics around the South African Medicines Amendment Act, it is clear that it opened up significant legal arguments and institutional alliances for the actors agitating for health. For example, social movements defending access to essential medicines,[39] and those defending access to treatment for HIV/AIDS,[40] were bridged by movements drawing on the human right to health. In South Africa, the right to health was significant in helping the TAC to press the government to observe its constitutional obligations towards health. It enabled the TAC to join the litigation process and offer a competing interpretation of how the government should protect the right to health. This strengthened the movement to litigate additional cases supportive of the right to health.[41] In turn, the domestic success of the arguments assisted the movement internationally.[42]

[38] Declaration on the TRIPS Agreement and Public Health Adopted on 14 November 2001, WT/MIN(01)/DEC/2 (2001) ('the Doha Declaration'). See, e.g., para. 5, which confirms that 'each Member has the right to grant compulsory licenses and the freedom to determine the grounds upon which such licenses are granted', and that 'Each member has the right to determine what constitutes a national emergency or other circumstances of extreme urgency, it being understood that public health crises, including those relating to HIV/AIDS, tuberculosis, malaria and other epidemics, can represent a national emergency or other circumstances of extreme urgency.' An amendment to article 31 of TRIPS, to the benefit of least-developed countries, was later formalized in August 2003. See Implementation of Paragraph 6 of the Doha Declaration on the TRIPS Agreement and Public Health, WTO Doc WT/L/540 (2003) (WTO General Council Decision of 30 August 2003). For the problems inherent in the reforms, see Noah Benjamin Novogrodsky, 'Beyond TRIPS: The Role of Non-State Actors and Access to Essential Medicines', in Thomas Pogge, Matthew Rimmer and Kim Rubenstein (eds.), *Incentives for Global Public Health: Patent Law and Access to Essential Medicines* (2010), 343.

[39] Amy Kapczynski, 'The Access to Knowledge Mobilization and the New Politics of Intellectual Property' (2008) 117 *Yale Law Journal* 804 (describing social movements from the entertainment industry, software development and farming, who teamed up with medicines protesters).

[40] For one participant's account of how this came to pass, which canvasses the actions in Brazil as well as South Africa, and the self-interest of the US in light of the anthrax crisis, see Ellen 't Hoen, 'TRIPS, Pharmaceutical Patents, and Access to Essential Medicines: A Long Way from Seattle to Doha' (2002) 3 *Chicago Journal of International Law* 27, 42–3.

[41] The TAC went on to litigate the important case of *Minister of Health* v. *Treatment Action Campaign*, above n. 21.

[42] This is akin to a reverse-'boomerang' effect: see, e.g., Margaret E. Keck and Kathryn Sikkink, *Activists beyond Borders* (1998) (describing the success of transnational rights advocacy networks who bypass the home country to find success abroad, before returning to the domestic sphere).

3.2 Ghana: the case against user fees

A case study of litigation around health rights in Ghana provides an important contrast to the PMA litigation in South Africa. Like the PMA litigation, the Ghanaian case described in this chapter involves a challenge to the distributive implications of commodified healthcare within a poor country.[43] As the first country in colonial Africa to achieve independence (in 1957), Ghana inherited the British common law legal system and the formal structures of democracy with an independent executive, parliament and courts. The health system of Ghana has been particularly shaped in international forums, in this context by the structural adjustment reforms of the World Bank and the International Monetary Fund ('IMF'). Like the PMA litigation, the Ghanaian case incorporates a combination of careful legal arguments and concerted political action, but it is more contained, in both temporal and participant terms. The case study is therefore described below in more detail.

While Ghana has managed to avoid the HIV/AIDS pandemic that has racked South Africa and many other countries in sub-Saharan Africa, the ongoing experience of needless suffering from treatable ill health is common. Many basic health needs are unmet; many clinics (especially in the rural areas) stand empty, malaria is rife, and malnutrition, inadequate access to potable water and the inadequate provision of prenatal and maternal care are all central causes of disability and death.

The Constitution of Ghana protects 'the right to good health care' as part of the directive principles of state policy that guide the application and interpretation of the Constitution, by citizens, courts and legislatures.[44] While these directive principles are expressed in the language of 'rights', they are not directly enforceable. However, as the operation of the directive principles of India's Constitution suggests, such principles

[43] For an indication of the extent of poverty, see, e.g., United Nations, *Report 03 Human and Income Poverty: Developing Countries, Population Living Below $2 a Day (%)* (2007–8), hdrstats.undp.org/indicators/24.html at 2 March 2009. Ghana has 78.5 per cent of its population living below $2 per day, and South Africa has 34.1 per cent.

[44] Constitution of the Republic of Ghana 1992, s. 34: '(1) The Directive Principles of State Policy … shall guide all citizens, Parliament, the President, the Judiciary, the Council of State, the Cabinet, political parties and other bodies and persons in applying or interpreting this Constitution or any other law and in taking and implementing any policy decisions, for the establishment of a just and free society. (2) The President shall report to Parliament at least once a year all the steps taken to ensure the realization of the policy objectives … in particular, the realization of basic human rights, a healthy economy, the right to work, the right to good health care and the right to education.'

may guide the interpretation of other constitutional rights, legislation or the common law.[45] Ghana is a party to the International Convention on Economic, Social and Cultural Rights,[46] and is therefore under a formal obligation to progressively realize the right to health laid out in that instrument. This obligation has not, however, been incorporated into domestic legislation.

In January 2003, the right to healthcare was relied on as part of a mobilization against the 'user fee' model of health financing employed in Ghana at that time. User fees for public health services rely on a quintessential market mechanism, in order to reduce inefficiency, raise revenue and improve public facilities. In fact, since the late 1980s, this system has been a widespread method of organizing and meeting the costs of healthcare in Africa.[47] The World Bank and the IMF have recommended user fee mechanisms for delivering social services, like health and education, and have conditioned loans to many countries on the basis of their implementation.[48] Ghana's original decision to adopt user fees had been reinforced by such conditions.[49] As well as improving efficiency, user fees for health were understood to foster equity by including exemptions for poor patients, especially for essential interventions that will have the biggest impact on their (and others') health, such as immunizations. In the case of Ghana, for example, the Hospital Fees

[45] These directive principles are expressed in the language of duties. See Indian Constitution 1950, Part III Fundamental Rights, article 21 ('protection of life and personal liberty'), see also Part IV Directive Principles of State Policy, article 47 ('Duty of the State to raise the level of nutrition and the standard of living and to improve public health'). See further Rajshree Chandra, 'The Role of National Laws in Reconciling Constitutional Right to Health with TRIPS Obligations: An Examination of the *Glivec* Patent Case in India', in Thomas Pogge, Matthew Rimmer and Kim Rubenstein (eds.), *Incentives for Global Public Health: Patent Law and Access to Essential Medicines*, (2010), 381.

[46] Ghana acceded to the International Convention on Economic, Social and Cultural Rights in September 2000.

[47] The Bamako Initiative, co-ordinated between African Health Ministers and launched in 1987, was implemented by almost every country in sub-Saharan Africa. See World Health Organization, *Guidelines for Implementing the Bamako Initiative* (1988).

[48] See, e.g., World Bank, *Financing Health Services in Developing Countries: An Agenda for Reform* (1987). In 1998, for example, 75 per cent of ongoing World Bank projects in sub-Saharan Africa included the establishment or expansion of user fees: see Guy Hutton, 'Charting the Path to the World Bank's "No Blanket Policy on User Fees"' (2004), DFID Health Systems Resource Centre, 2.5.

[49] Lynne Brydon and Karen Legge, *Adjusting Society: The World Bank, the IMF and Ghanaians* (1996) (describing Ghana 'as an exemplary member of the club of poorer nations' in complying with IMF and World Bank conditions).

Act 1971 (Ghana) exempted children, the elderly and those 'unable to pay ... fees on the ground of poverty' from the payment of fees.[50]

The user fees system therefore offered a compensatory entitlement (in the form of an exemption) for poor users. Despite this formal exemption, however, the poor were unable to access healthcare without payment, because the exemptions were rarely, if ever, enforced. In large part, this was due to a lack of revenue within the system. Payments by users were insufficient to raise funds for subsidizing those unable to pay; and there was a lack of general budgeting for poor users. There were no regulations as to who should be defined as 'unable to pay' under the legislation. Without the exemptions, the poor engaged in inappropriate or incomplete treatment, or did not seek treatment at all.[51]

These features were at the centre of a right to health campaign. The user fee system was challenged by the Legal Resources Centre ('LRC'), a ten-year-old non-governmental organization which had experimented with litigation, organizing and political advocacy to press the interests of the community of Nima, in Accra, in which it is based. The LRC combines legal advocacy with organizing work with members of the Nima community, including local mothers and youth groups who meet at their premises. It is also host to a rotating group of academics and student interns from American law schools.[52]

The similarities between the advocacy strategies of the LRC in Ghana and those described in the PMA litigation are not accidental. One of the founders of the Ghanaian LRC had interned at the original Legal Resources Centre of South Africa, a public interest law organization that has worked on many of South Africa's economic and social rights cases, including the health rights case that the TAC pursued after the withdrawal of the PMA suit.[53] As well as understanding the potential doctrinal arguments informing the defence of economic and social rights in South Africa, the lawyers of the LRC were therefore wholly informed by the public interest law strategies practised there.

This connection meant that litigation was not the first strategy of the LRC's 'right to health' campaign. The lawyers of the LRC had earlier

50 Hospital Fees Act 1971 (Ghana), ss. 2(a), 4(2).

51 See, e.g., Lucy Gilson, 'The Lessons of User Fee Experience in Africa' (1997) 12 *Health Policy and Planning* 273.

52 Many of the tactical intricacies of this campaign have been spearheaded by Professor Lucie White, of Harvard Law School, in collaboration with the founders of the LRC, Raymond Ataguba and Mahama Ayariga.

53 *Minister of Health* v. *Treatment Action Campaign*, above n. 21.

embarked on an education campaign, installing posters in clinics and holding regular information sessions to inform the community of their rights to exemption from user fees. At these meetings, they learned of the priorities of the members of the community with respect to their health-care. At the same time, the LRC gathered affidavits of the experiences of many people who had been turned away at a health clinic or hospital because of their inability to pay. These affidavits were assembled not only for later use in litigation, but as a strategy to organize the community and provide a platform for expressing their grievance.[54] Yet this campaign had stalled. Because the clinics themselves could not afford to grant exemptions (since they would not be reimbursed if they did so), the demands by patients of their legal rights were ineffective. Thus, although nurses, doctors and clinics were a critical part of awarding exemptions, they were themselves constrained by the lack of funds. In order to solve the problem of user fees and its failure to adequately provide for the health needs of the poor, the system of financing had to be addressed.

The action that focused contestation around user fees occurred in January 2002, when the LRC learned of the detention in a local public hospital of a patient who had not paid for his treatment. This patient, a subsistence farmer from northern Ghana, had been brought by relatives to Accra for emergency hernia surgery. After his recovery, he was discharged and handed a bill that included the costs of his dressing, injections, laboratory, theatre, sanitation and accommodation. This bill was equivalent to US$240. Unable to pay an amount which represented more than three times his annual wage, Mr Zakari was informed by the social welfare officer at the hospital that he would not be released until he assembled the funds. For the next six weeks, he was detained within the boundaries of the hospital, without food or bed.

The right to be free from arbitrary detention is a fundamental human right, perceived in quintessentially 'negative' terms. Mr Zakari's detention highlights the ways in which all human rights are weakened when rights involving fundamental material interests are not respected.[55] In fact, this form of detention is part of the foreseeable range of

[54] The details of this decade-long, community-based campaign and the political moment of the Zakari case are described in Jeremy Perelman and Katharine Young, 'Freeing Mohammed Zakari: Footprints toward Hope', in Jeremy Perelman and Lucie White (eds.), *Stones of Hope: How African Activists Reclaim Human Rights to Challenge Global Poverty* (2010, forthcoming).

[55] Paul Farmer, *Pathologies of Power: Health, Human Rights, and the New War on the Poor* (2005), 16–17 (observing how 'political rights are intertwined with social and economic

consequences when a user fee system operates without an exemption scheme.[56] Yet unlike the other burdens experienced by the poor with this system of healthcare, this aspect of the user fee system was actionable in the courts. The LRC responded to Mr Zakari's detention by assembling a habeas corpus action, based on the long-standing constitutional protection of personal liberty from arbitrary incarceration at the hands of the state. This action would require the state to show due cause for Mr Zakari's detention, and, if none were forthcoming, to literally release the body.

In seeking relief, the LRC therefore asked the court for Mr Zakari's release, the habeas remedy which correlates with the right. However, the LRC sought further remedies flowing from the state's additional infringement of Mr Zakari's right to health. These arguments were based on the statutory entitlements to exemptions, as well as the constitutional principle that had set out the importance of the right to good healthcare. The lawyers at the LRC argued that the hospital acted illegally and unconstitutionally, not only by detaining Mr Zakari, but by failing to provide him an exemption from his hospital fees, given his indigent status. And in recognition that this failure extended far beyond the hospital's own discretion, the lawyers added the Ministry of Health and the Ministry of Finance to their claim, challenging the state's failure to make regulations as to the criteria and procedures for defining at the time of initial registration whether a prospective patient would be 'unable to pay … fees on the ground of poverty'.[57] It also challenged the failure to allocate funds in the state budget towards making this exemption scheme operable.

Significantly, the LRC asked the Court to order a consultative process between Ghanaian Members of Parliament, the Ministry of Health, the Ministry of Finance, health system and finance experts, healthcare providers and low income health consumer groups, in order to negotiate an appropriate, rights-protective response to user fees. This would include the establishment of new regulations for the Hospital Fees Act, which would specify criteria for who would be eligible for exemption on the

rights, or, rather, how the absence of social and economic power empties political rights of their substance'); Amartya Sen, *Development as Freedom* (1999).

[56] There is evidence that hospitals elsewhere in Africa have engaged in a similar practice: See, e.g., Juliane Kippenberg, Jean Baptiste Sahokwasama and Joseph Amon, 'Detention of Insolvent Patients in Burundian Hospitals' (2008) *Health Policy and Planning* 14 (documenting a widespread practice of detention, and the contracts of the security guards who maintain surveillance on hospitals).

[57] Hospital Fees Act 1971 (Ghana), ss. 2(a), 4(2).

basis of poverty. Moreover, the LRC requested that these regulations earmark appropriate funds in order to be implemented.

At the same time, the LRC circulated a petition in Nima demanding Mr Zakari's release from hospital. The petition also demanded the recognition of the community's entitlements to emergency healthcare, to the statutory exemptions and to the right to healthcare. A public march on Parliament and a press conference were planned to coincide with the filing of the suit.

The plans for the lawsuit and the press conference were altered when Mr Zakari was secretly released from hospital, prior to the filing of the suit. An anonymous benefactor – possibly a public official responding to the political pressure – settled his bill and informed his relatives that he was free. The habeas claim was no longer actionable. Yet not to be deflected from their challenge to the administration of the user fee system, the lawyers changed their cause of action from habeas corpus to wrongful imprisonment, and retained the additional requests for relief directed to the reform of the user fee system. Plans for the press conference were only slightly altered – Mohammed Zakari himself was asked to speak.

The campaign on the right to health seemed to have met with success. As a performative exercise, the lawsuit and press conference helped to focus political pressure on the user fee model of healthcare financing and its deficiencies. A few days later, the government promised to put aside 3 billion cedis (US$350,000) into the healthcare system to pay for the exemptions scheme, so that hospitals would not detain people who genuinely could not pay.[58] And Mr Zakari walked free.

Ultimately, the action around the lawsuit, like that occurring during the PMA litigation, produced political rather than legal results for advocates of the right to health. After meetings with the government, the LRC withdrew the suit, on the condition that it would be included as a participant in attempts to negotiate the parameters of financing the health system through a national insurance scheme. Such a scheme had been proposed as an alternative to user fees and is now in effect in Ghana. The campaign therefore helped to put political pressure on the government to consider a different programme for securing health, rather than using law and legal pressure to force the government to deliver healthcare

[58] Staff Writer, '3 Billion Cedis Voted for Medical Bills', *Daily Graphic* (Ghana), 29 January 2003.

in the form of entitlements. This protection led to a more open-ended result than what is conventionally understood to be the role of litigation.

The framing of the case as one involving a right to health (rather than merely habeas corpus) was important for both legal and institutional reasons. Like the PMA litigation, the litigation seeking Mr Zakari's release followed a different course because of the availability of the constitutional right to healthcare and the movement's choice to rely on that right. The presence of this right meant that new parties could be joined to the litigation. Moreover, the availability of the right to health meant that actors sought different remedies than they would otherwise have done. For example, a successful habeas corpus claim, without an accompanying claim involving the right to healthcare, might simply have resulted in Mr Zakari's release from hospital. It might also have put an end to the practice of detaining impecunious patients in hospitals. Yet it also might have created a more pernicious precedent. If hospitals were left without the option of detaining patients until payment of their medical bill, they might also have ceased to provide any treatment to indigents. By including the right to healthcare and the statutory entitlement to exemption within the lawsuit, and by seeking negotiation by different public agencies, the LRC sought instead to effect change at the level of how healthcare was financed.

Second, the action dovetailed with an international action against user fees in Africa. For example, in 2001, advocates prompted Congress and the Clinton Administration to oppose any World Bank or International Monetary Fund loan that required user fees for access to primary education or healthcare.[59] The arguments around a right to health brought different social movements together, arguing at the level of both constitutional rights and human rights. In focusing action at the national level, the suit also brought critical local pressure to a growing turn against user fees that had influenced economists and policy-makers at the international level, but had not yet translated to domestic action.[60]

4. Conclusions: lessons from praxis

The examination of practical action around the right to health in South Africa and Ghana demonstrates how the right to health is made

[59] David P. Forsythe and Eric A. Heinze, 'On the Margins of the Human Rights Discourse', in Rhoda E. Howard-Hassman and Claude E. Welch, Jr (eds.) *Economic Rights in Canada and the United States* (2006), 55, 69.

[60] Hutton, 'Charting the Path to the World Bank's "No Blanket Policy on User Fees"', above n. 48.

meaningful through legal and political strategies that seek neither to define a fixed legal entitlement nor a settled normative claim. Put simply, the inquiry into praxis is an approach that connects rights theory and political lawyering practice around health. Such an approach benefits from the insights of socio-legal studies that have identified successful civil rights, community organizing, or cause lawyering approaches in different country settings.[61]

These two instances of health rights praxis challenge the assumptions against the effectiveness of the legal right to health catalogued by the private law model of health rights presented in the first part of this chapter. In South Africa, litigation against compulsory licensing legislation was withdrawn because of the efforts of the TAC and co-ordinated social movements, in a striking combination of national and international agitation around access to medicines, HIV/AIDS and human and constitutional rights. While South Africa's constitutional right to healthcare only became part of the litigation at a later stage, its presence allowed an important social movement to join as *amicus* to the litigation. It also raised the possibility that the High Court would engage in a different assessment of the PMA's property rights arguments, although this issue was ultimately left undecided by the Court. In Ghana, a campaign for the release of a detained patient, unable to pay for treatment in a user fee system, exposed the punitive features of the healthcare services market to a potential judicial assessment. A long-running campaign on the right to health and the inequities flowing from user fees for healthcare culminated in a legal action against the state for detaining an impecunious individual in a public hospital. The availability of the right to health helped to connect the structural features of the health system to the constitutional prohibition against arbitrary detention. Again, although the case involved litigation that was withdrawn before judgment, we can observe certain practical effects of the right to health on the course of the dispute.

The two cases do not suggest that litigation is a necessary or sufficient strategy for health rights praxis: in the first case, litigation was instigated by companies defending their property rights, and was pursued defensively by health rights advocates in the courts alongside political action in

[61] For an approach which asserts a similar attitude towards critical race theory, see Eric K. Yamamoto, 'Critical Race Praxis: Race Theory and Political Lawyering Practice in Post-Civil Rights America' (1997) 95 *Michigan Law Review* 821. See further, e.g., Austin Sarat and Stuart A. Scheingold (eds.) *Cause Lawyers and Social Movements* (2006).

both national and international forums. In the second, it came after a lengthy education strategy and was carried out concurrently with other political actions, including petitions, marches and press conferences. In both South Africa and Ghana, the social movements helped to make the litigation more accessible to poor groups, for whom the expense of litigation is often prohibitive.

What the two cases do best is dislodge the private law model of health rights that obscures the potential, in some contexts, for a right to health to secure particular outcomes. These assumptions include the view that health rights belong in the category of 'positive' rights and thus do not belong in courts, that legal rights are coterminous with remedies and that health is an incoherent object in legal terms. Instead, what we find in the two cases are the possibilities of health rights operating in courts as a balancing exercise against other legal rights, and as a framework for political strategies. The withdrawal of each case serves to support, rather than detract, from this model.

In sum, the cases discussed here refocus our attention on the relationship between law, politics and rights. They suggest new models for practical action and legal understanding of health rights. Just as they reveal how health rights movements can resist the choice of either politics or courts (frequently engaging a mixture), they reveal the mix of targets – in both international and domestic, and public and private domains, in a responsive and flexible rights praxis.

15

The role of national laws in reconciling constitutional right to health with TRIPS obligations: an examination of the *Glivec* patent case in India

RAJSHREE CHANDRA

1. Introduction

Together with the notion that people should have access rights over external resources, and that people have rights over their own persons and powers, another notion has gained ground – the idea that people should have access, as a matter of moral right, to certain welfare conditions. A moral right, as Henry Shue states, provides the rational basis for a justified demand, that the actual enjoyment of a substance be socially guaranteed against standard threats.[1] This notion in fact became the very grounds on which group rights and human rights were claimed, as moral minimums or 'basic rights'[2] – basic because they precondition the enjoyment of all other rights. The right to health is one such right, premised on the fact that ill health leaves a person incapable of engaging in autonomous activity and therefore enjoying any rights that protect such activity. The classification of health as a basic right is useful in order to qualify this right as vital to a minimally adequate existence and, in so doing, justify the priority of this right over rights that are based on wants or desires. From the perspective of this chapter it is important to draw this distinction so as to assert the primacy of the right to health vis-à-vis innovators' rights protected by the Trade-Related Aspects of Intellectual Property

[1] Henry Shue, *Basic Rights: Subsistence, Affluence and U.S. Foreign Policy* (2nd edn, 1996), 23.

[2] A term used by Henry Shue to qualify these rights as entitlements to basic needs, i.e. food, shelter, clothing, clean water, healthcare and minimal standards of education. Ibid.

Rights[3] ('TRIPS' or 'TRIPS Agreement') regime, which are more in the nature of economic rewards stimulating innovation and not, generally, preconditioning survival. The legal terms of adjudication between these two oft competing rights ought to be based on a cognisance of this distinction.

In legal terms, fundamental human rights treaties recognize the right to the 'enjoyment of the highest attainable standard of physical and mental health'.[4] Health is now beginning to be seen in the context of human rights protection in response to debilitating, life-threatening and life-altering diseases like HIV/AIDS, cancer, tuberculosis, malaria and a whole host of infectious diseases that are seriously neglected in terms of international attention and research. There are today huge gaps between the health needs that confront people and the means that are available to satisfy them, especially in poorer nations.[5]

Addressing health needs is increasingly seen as critical for poverty alleviation and human development. The sheer scale of the problem and its endemic link with poverty have been a prime stimulus in the linking of health needs of peoples with the human rights discourse as well as with the discourse on global justice.

In recent times the expanding TRIPS regime has allowed the exclusive rights and remedies of patent holders to trump the health rights of communities. An important aspect of a rights claim is its compossibility with different conceptions and forms of welfare and human rights which have acquired centrality in the rights discourse. The effects that intellectual property rights generate for rights – like health – are significant as the latter is linked to issues of survival and a dignified, disability free existence. How they relate to each other, the way these rights are given content and are upheld juridically, are always a subject of examination and concern. When confronted by intellectual property rights, the right to health has remained stuck at the first level of articulation; it exists more in statements of intent, or remains relegated to the purpose and objective

[3] Marrakesh Agreement Establishing the World Trade Organization, opened for signature 15 April 1994, 1867 UNTS 3, annex 1C (Agreement on Trade-Related Aspects of Intellectual Property Rights) (entered into force 1 January 1995) ('TRIPS Agreement' or 'TRIPS').

[4] See article 12 of the International Covenant on Economic, Social and Cultural Rights, opened for signature 16 December 1966, 993 UNTS 3 (entered into force 3 January 1976) ('ICESCR').

[5] The 10/90 gap is instructive in this regard. For details see Louis Currat, Andres de Francisco, Sameera Al-Tuwaijri, Abdul Ghaffar and Susan Jupp, *Global Forum Health 10/90 Report* (2004).

sections of documents. The right to health is not yet as justiciable as intellectual property rights. It is for this reason that Katharine Young's chapter in this volume[6] argues that the rights discourse has been underinclusive, as it has been unable to lend a conceptual and institutional content to claims for food, shelter, education or health, interests central to an emancipated life.

These are slow beginnings however – attempts are being made both at the national and international levels to institutionalize the right to health and lend it more legal teeth. Superior court judgments in India,[7] Venezuela,[8] Bangladesh,[9] South Africa[10] and Ecuador,[11] for instance, convey a broad interpretation of the right to health as a right to life. Health as a right to life approach heralds a paradigm shift in the understanding of health dynamics. The journey of understanding health as it

[6] Katharine Young, 'Securing Health through Rights', in Thomas Pogge, Matthew Rimmer and Kim Rubenstein (eds.), *Incentives for Global Public Health: Patent Law and Access to Essential Medicines* (2010), 357.

[7] The Supreme Court has held in a number of cases that the right to life, enshrined in article 21 under the Constitution does not stand for animal existence but the right to life with human dignity. Right to health is now recognized as a fundamental right in India. In *Bandhua Mukti Morcha* v. *Union of India* (AIR 1984 SC 802) the Supreme Court held that article 21 closely linked Directive Principles of State Policy, particularly clause (e) and (f) of article 39, article 41 and article 42. 'It must include protection of the health and strength of workers, men and women, and tender age children against abuse, opportunities and facilities for children to develop in a healthy manner and in conditions of freedom and dignity, educational facilities, just and human conditions of work and maternity relief.' These are minimum requirements which must exist in order to enable a person live with dignity. In the case of *State of Punjab* v. *Mahindrasingh Chawla* (AIR 1997 SC 1225) the Supreme Court of India held that right to life includes the right to health: 'It is now settled that the right to health is integral to the right to life'. Similarly, in *Paschim Banga Khet Mazdoor Society* v. *State of West Bengal* (AIR 1996 SC 2426) the Supreme Court held that timely medical treatment in a government hospital is a fundamental right.

[8] For instance, *Cruz Bermude, et al.* v. *Ministerio de Sanidad y Asistencia Social* (Case No 15.789, Decision No 916, 15 July 1999). The court ruled that the rights to health, to life and to have access to scientific and technological advances are closely related.

[9] In *Farooque* v. *Bangladesh & Ors* (Writ Petition No 92 of 1996), the Supreme Court of Bangladesh granted an injunction to prevent radiation affected milk being released into the open market, because it was a violation of the constitutional right to life.

[10] For instance, *Minister of Health* v. *Treatment Action Campaign*, 2002 (5) SA 721 (CC) (South Africa). For further exploration of this case see Katharine Young, 'Securing Health through Rights', in Thomas Pogge, Matthew Rimmer and Kim Rubenstein (eds.), *Incentives for Global Public Health: Patent Law and Access to Essential Medicines* (2010), 357.

[11] *Mendoza and Ors* v. *Minister of Public Health and the Director of the National AIDS-HIV-STI Programme* (Resolucion No 0749–2003-RA, 28 January 2004).

relates to illness and medicine, to one where health is viewed as a human right, begins with the premise that health cannot be explained in isolation. The health outcomes of a population in any geographical space depend on a range of factors, from medical ones such as the spread of virus or the response of a drug to a disease, to underlying factors thrown up by larger socio-cultural and economic realities or global dynamics. New levels of articulation of health rights are also beginning to prefigure in the ways in which intellectual property laws, pertaining to the rights of pharmaceutical innovators, are being conceptualized and interpreted at national levels. National laws, particularly of developing countries like India, Thailand and Brazil, reflect the dilemmas of both limitation and resistance when developing countries struggle between protection of public health and protection of intellectual property.

Questions of 'rights' invariably raise issues of entitlements and obligations. Health rights raise obligations on varied entities. Morally, of course, these are global obligations to be borne by the international community and their respective governments. The moral obligation of the international community arises out of the fact, as Thomas Pogge argues,[12] that there are global institutional and structural factors, upheld and supported by the global community, which result in the creation of certain adverse medical conditions. Therefore this global community is 'materially involved in the causation of such medical conditions'.[13] As such there exists an obligation on this community to mitigate these conditions. These obligations relate to the fact that the existence of chronic health problems constitutes a failure to uphold health rights, while also recognizing the duty-bearer's causal responsibility for such adverse medical conditions. The progressive realization of health outcomes, therefore, without doubt requires global strategies for mitigation of adverse health conditions. Not only is there a global causative chain that can be traced but there is also the nature of health impacts that have trans-border and global impacts. Globalization has ensured that these

[12] Thomas Pogge, 'Relational Conceptions of Justice: Responsibilities for Health Outcome', in Sudhir Anand, Fabienne Peter and Amartya Sen (eds.), *Public Health, Ethics and Equity* (2005) 135–41.

[13] Pogge makes a compelling argument where he asserts that national institutions have an equal moral obligation towards health rights of compatriots as well as foreigners. Rights emerging out of conditions of deprivation and poverty have strong domestic or local contributing factors. However, they are also a factor of material conditions created by global political and economic institutions, which places a moral obligation on governments to go beyond upholding citizenship rights. Ibid.

problems are no longer viewed as mere local health concerns. Both the plight of the affected people and the global and epidemic nature of these diseases have ensured demand for health rights to be conceptualized and institutionalized beyond the rights of the citizen; as 'morally universalistic rights' or 'cosmopolitan rights', linked to issues of global justice.[14]

However, while the global community may be the moral constituency for addressing health issues, there is often a lack of agency and ownership of these rights when conceived in non-citizenship terms. There is need for an institutional context in which these rights are formally grounded. Health outcomes are necessarily dependent on global dynamics, but there is also a role for the state, which cannot be compromised, for the state is the only entity upon whom accountability and obligation can be fixed. The state provides the institutional context within which rights are formulated and recognized and is the agency through which a commitment to rights may become tangible.

This chapter seeks to adopt a dialectic approach that tries to justify a universal foundation of human rights whilst considering the demands for their promotion at the national level. The notion of universal moral rights might generate only a weak duty of charity or assistance which would leave unchallenged the patterns of social inequality, leaving the right's claim without content. Thus, although the universal human rights claim to health has been recognized by international treaties and covenants, they find articulation as enforceable rights via the domestic laws of sovereign states. Universal moral rights, including the right to health, are universal and moral in a strong sense but are *rights* – enforceable and justiciable – only in a weak sense. They are enforceable in a stronger sense only as rights of citizens in sovereign domains of particular states.

This chapter envisages a role for national laws in securing the health needs of its peoples in the context of TRIPS-defined rights of innovators. While the dynamics of TRIPS and the material conditions that it creates for health rights are global in nature, and the claim for the protection of health rights vis-à-vis rights of innovators in the pharmaceutical sector are universal, this chapter argues that national laws have the potential to translate these moral claims into institutionalized rights of citizens, and may play an irreplaceable role in adding content to health rights claims. However these rights, developed in nationalized contexts, conceived in citizenship terms may have, as Miller states, a

[14] Thomas Pogge, 'Cosmopolitanism and Sovereignty' (1992) 103(1) *Ethics* 48.

'universalist perspective'.[15] The *Novartis/Glivec* case outlined in this paper reflects this perspective.[16]

An Indian case – the Novartis battle for patent rights on its anti-cancer drug Glivec – highlights the potential role that a national legislature can play in not only securing the rights of its citizens but also in addressing global concerns. The *Glivec* case presents an instance of a health safeguard being grounded, ironically, not in justiciable health rights but in a section of Indian patent law.[17] It is significant to note that, unlike in the case of South Africa,[18] the right to health in India is a non-justiciable right. It is part of Chapter IV of the Constitution, 'Directive Principles of State Policy', which as the title suggests, functions as 'directive' and is not justiciable, except when there are legislative amendments to the Constitution based on these directives.[19] However, as mentioned earlier, there have been attempts by the Supreme Court of India to interpret the right to health as a derivative of the right to life. This approach does have limitations, however, for the content of the right and the nature of the claim remain unspecified, and therefore nebulous.

The *Novartis-Glivec* case, to begin with, did not rest on the provisions of the Indian Constitution. The case hinged on a provision of section 3(d) of the Patents Act 1970 (India) as amended by the Patents (Amendment) Act 2005 (India) which had been included as a health safeguard. The case became the global face of a battle to allow the supply of generic drugs and to protect the sovereign right of a nation to legislate on intellectual property rights in health related products. A brief look at the evolution of patent law in India is helpful in understanding the reasoning behind an influential provision.

[15] David Miller, 'The Ethical Significance of Nationality' (1988) 98 *Ethics* 647–62.

[16] *Novartis AG and another* v. *Union of India and others* (6 August 2007, High Court of Judicature at Madras for W.P. Nos. 24759 and 24760 of 2006), judis.nic.in/chennai/qrydisp.asp?tfnm=11121.

[17] Section 3(d) of the Patents Act 1970 (India) as amended by the Patents (Amendment) Act 2005 (India).

[18] For further consideration of the South African context, see Katharine Young, 'Securing Health through Rights', in Thomas Pogge, Matthew Rimmer and Kim Rubenstein (eds.), *Incentives for Global Public Health: Patent Law and Access to Essential Medicines* (2010), 357.

[19] The obligation of the state to ensure the creation and the sustaining of conditions congenial to good health is cast by the Constitutional directives contained in articles 39(e) and (f), 42 and 47 in part IV of the Indian Constitution 1950.

2. Patent laws in India

Initially a number of developing countries like India viewed patent law quite differently, deliberately deciding to deny patent protection to pharmaceutical products and to grant protection only to processes for producing pharmaceuticals.[20] In the context of patent claims for food or medicine it stated – 'no patent shall be granted in respect of claim for the substances themselves, but claims for the methods or processes of manufacture shall be patentable'.[21] The Patents Act 1970 (India) specifically indicated that patents are granted to encourage innovation and not merely to enable patentees to enjoy a monopoly for the importation of the patented articles.[22] This law was one of the reasons that the Indian generic drug industry was able to evolve to make and market copies of drugs still on patent in wealthier countries. India became a major international supplier of drugs to countries where these products can be marketed legally because they have not been patented locally. Thus India began to be known as the 'pharmacy to the developing world'. This situation was poised for a change in 2005 when India was due to become fully TRIPS compliant.

In March 2005 India enacted the Patents (Amendment) Act 2005 (India), which amended the Patents Act 1970 (India). The amendment to the Patents Act 1970 (India) provided for patent protection for pharmaceutical inventions, instating the concept of 'product patents' in this category, for the first time since 1970. International criteria of patentability (novelty, non-obviousness, utility and adequate disclosure) were retained, but the Act instituted some additional requirements as well. The new Act's section 3(d) limits patents only to chemical entities that employ at least one new reactant. Additional criteria of demonstrating enhanced efficiency were also prescribed. In the context of the pharmaceutical and biotechnology sectors, the amendments to the Patents Act included restrictions as to what would be regarded as patentable inventions.[23]

Section 3(d) was introduced to clarify that a patentable invention does not include:

> the mere discovery of a new form of a known substance which does not result in the *enhancement of the known efficacy of that substance* or the

[20] Section 5, Patents Act 1970 (India). [21] Ibid.

[22] Section 83, Patents Act 1970 (India).

[23] A move that can be argued to be in consonance with article 30 of TRIPS which allows for limited exceptions to exclusive rights.

> mere discovery of any new property or new use for a known substance or of the mere use of a known process, machine or apparatus unless such known process results in a new product or employs at least one new reactant.

The enhancement in efficacy was further qualified in the subsection's explanation:

> For the purposes of this clause, salts, esters, ethers, polymorphs, metabolites, pure form, particle size, isomers, mixtures of isomers, complexes, combinations and other derivatives of known substance shall be considered to be the same substance, unless they differ significantly in properties with regard to efficacy.

The enhanced efficacy must exhibit significant differences in properties. Thus the requirement for an eligible subject matter to be considered for grant of a patent is *efficacy*. Efficacy is an important criterion for there exists a class of patents, known as 'selection patents' (derived from patent law jurisprudence in UK courts), where the novelty is derived from the use not the product. A selection patent will be tested for novelty and inventive step in the normal way but these may be found in its use.[24]

It is in this context that section 3(d) assumes significance. It is an endeavour to ensure 'novelty of use' in the absence of novelty of form. Being efficacious is a feature which may emphasize the use as an inventive step. Section 3(d) therefore makes it clear that a number of technical creations are not inventions, unless they present a significant increase in efficacy. Indian patent law is therefore relying on utility to transform non-patentable inventions into patentable inventions. It is important to note that section 3(d) draws a distinction between 'evergreening' and incremental innovation. As Basheer adds, by making derivates with added efficacy patentable, section 3(d) encourages sequential developments of existing products or technologies that help bring improved products to the market, capable of addressing unmet public health needs.[25]

[24] In *Apotex Inc.* v. *Sanofi-Synthelabo Canada Inc.*, [2008] 3 S.C.R. 265, Rothstein J of the Supreme Court of Canada held that 'selection patents' were justified, notwithstanding policy concerns about 'evergreening'. His Honour held that 'selection patents encourage improvements by selection'. The judge observed: 'the inventor selects only a bit of the subject matter of the original genus patent because that bit does something better than and different from what was claimed in the genus patent'.

[25] Shamnad Basheer, 'The "*Glivec*" Patent Saga: A 3-D Perspective on Indian Patent Policy and TRIPS Compliance', ATRIP, 2007, www.atrip.org/upload/files/essays/Shamnad%20Basheer%20Glivec%20Patent%20Saga.doc at 11 August 2008.

Section 3(d) of the Patents Act constitutes an important public health safeguard which prevents 'evergreening' and tweaking of old medicines to make or extend patent claims. These exceptions are significant for they seek to make patent claims for new drugs conditional on the *novelty and the efficacy* of the new innovation, thereby ensuring that patents for drugs are not claimed for mere incremental improvements over existing drugs.

The 3(d) safeguard was introduced keeping in mind India's pharmaceutical export potential and public health concerns. To this extent there was perhaps a conflation of interests between those of consumers and those of the domestic drug industry. Drastic levels of poverty and problems of drug access related to drug pricing warranted a reduction in the scope of patent grants. On the other hand, India's industrial and innovation imperatives warrant that domestic majors such as Ranbaxy, Dr Reddy's and Cipla's generic production capacities and export potential were protected.[26] The dual concerns are based on the fact that over a period of time Indian drug companies would lose the opportunity to develop processes for patent protected drugs in the country and therefore would cease to be a supplier of affordable generic drugs to millions across the world.[27] It is in the context of these changes and amendments to Indian patent law that the Novartis patent claim for Glivec needs to be evaluated. This case brings two issues into focus: first, the right of a sovereign country to build in safeguards in its patent laws in order to protect the public interest; and second, the issue of drug access, so vital for the realization of health as a human right.

[26] Basheer's article seems to suggest that consumer groups' interests became the rallying point 'because they tallied with the views of indigenous pharmaceutical producers' and that the latter's interests would be better protected if India did not adopt an excessively restrictive efficacy standard. Consumers' interests, access to medicines, issues of drug access and 'the ex post effects of a patent in the form of high prices etc can be addressed via measures such as price control, compulsory licensing etc', he adds. These conclusions derive from innovators' rights and therefore restrict themselves to issues of innovators' interests. A different set of conclusions would be derived if the issue were approached from the perspective of health rights. See also Shamnad Basheer, 'India's New Patent Regime: Aiding Access or Abetting Genericide', (2007) 9(2) *International Journal of Biotechnology* 122.

[27] The parliamentary debates on the eve of India becoming fully TRIPS compliant in February 2005 do reveal health and related concerns of the legislators, see Lok Sabha Debates, 'Part II Proceedings Title: Combined discussion on the Statutory Resolution regarding disapproval of Patents (Amendment) Ordinance, 2004 (No 7 of 2004) (India) and the Patents (Amendment) Bill, 2005 (India)' 22 March 2005, 164.100.24.230/Webdata/datalshom001/dailydeb/22032005.htm at 12 September 2008.

3. The Glivec battle in India: a case study

Glivec (imatinib mesylate) is a cancer drug crucial in prolonging the life of patients suffering from chronic myeloid leukaemia. Since imatinib mesylate controls the cellular action that allows the cancer to grow but does not cure the disease, patients must take it for the rest of their lives, unless another type of treatment or cure is available. Glivec is produced and marketed internationally by the Swiss pharmaceutical company Novartis and various Indian generic producers like Cipla, Ranbaxy, Natco and Hetero. Generic versions of the drug in the Indian market are priced at about US$2,100 per patient per year.[28] Novartis is charging high prices for Glivec worldwide: from about US$25,000 to more than US$50,000 per patient per year. Glivec is an important drug for Novartis, grossing US$2.17 billion in global sales for the company in 2005.[29]

3.1 Patent claim by Novartis

In 1998 Novartis filed an application in the Chennai Patent Office for a patent on Glivec. Based on the patent application and section 92A of the Indian Patents Act, in November 2003 Novartis obtained exclusive marketing rights ('EMR') until patent was granted – if the patent were rejected the EMR would be cancelled. EMR operated like a patent monopoly preventing Indian pharmaceutical companies from producing affordable generic versions of the drug imatinib mesylate. Indian generic companies had to withdraw the production and sale of the generic versions of the drug for the domestic market and export to other developing countries. The cancer patients' access to generic Glivec was affected. With an over tenfold increase in the price of the drug, the Cancer Patients Aid Association and some of the NGOs who provided the more affordable generic versions to patients for their treatment had to withdraw their medical support to cancer patients. Patients of other developing countries who were importing generic versions of the drug were also seriously affected by the unavailability of the affordable versions.

Novartis's patent application on Glivec came up for examination in 2005. Armed with the 3(d) provision, pre-grant opposition was filed by

[28] Julien Reinhard, 'Novartis Files Case in India Challenging Patent Controller's Order and Patent Law', *Berne Declaration* (9 October 2006), www.evb.ch/en/p25011414.html#note1#note1 at 20 April 2009.

[29] Ibid.

Natco Pharmaceuticals, Alternative Law Forum ('ALF'), and Lawyers Collective on behalf of the Cancer Patients Aid Association[30] in September 2005, against the Novartis patent application for Glivec, claiming that, first, this application only concerned a modification of an already existing drug that did not improve its efficacy, as required by section 3(d) of the Patents Act, and second, that the non-availability and non-affordability of any form of imatinib mesylate to chronic myeloid leukaemia patients would violate their constitutional rights under article 14 (right to equality before law) and article 21 (right to life and personal liberty) of the Constitution.[31]

There were two points in the Novartis patent claim to which attention needs to be drawn for they are instructive in how the criteria of novelty and non-obviousness are manipulated. Novartis preferred to file an application in India for the beta crystalline form of imatinib mesylate (Glivec) in 1998. Imatinib as a 'free base' molecule was invented by Novartis in 1992 and patented in the US and other countries in 1993. The 1993 US patent of imatinib, disclosed the salt as 'Pyrimidine Derivatives' (imatinib mesylate).[32] In 1998, Novartis came up with an application for a beta crystalline form of imatinib mesylate which was claimed to be a new form of a known substance. Multiple tests performed by the Indian Institute of Chemical Technology, Hyderabad and Indian Institute of Technology, Delhi confirmed that this 'new' salt was a beta-isomer of the already disclosed imatinib mesylate and isomers were considered to be the same substance, unless they differed significantly in properties with regard to efficacy.[33]

There was a second issue to the patent claim. Even if the newness of form was demonstrated by Novartis it had to cross the hurdle of 3(d).

[30] As did Cipla, Natco Pharma, Sun Pharmaceuticals and Ranbaxy in their own right. Natco Pharma, which launched a generic version of Glivec under the brand 'Veenat', had also challenged the grant of EMRs to Novartis.

[31] Text of the Writ Petition No 24759 of 2006 in the High Court of Judicature at Madras. Clause 16.

[32] Jurg Zimmerman, 'Pyrimidine Derivatives and Processes for the Preparation Thereof', US Patent No 5,521,184 (filed 28 April 1994; issued 28 May 1996). See also corresponding European Patent No 0564409. The patent term extension certificate granted by US Patent Office for the 1993 patent explicitly mentions imatinib mesylate (Gleevec) as the product. For details see *Novartis* v. *the Union of India* (6 August 2007), Order of High Court of Judicature at Madras for W.P. Nos. 24759 and 24760 of 2006, (section 9.3 and 9.4 of the affidavit filed by Petitioner Novartis), www.cptech.org/ip/health/c/india/novartis-v-india.doc at 23 September 2007.

[33] See 'Explanation', section 3(d) of the Patents Act 1970 (India) as amended by the Patents (Amendment) Act 2005 (India).

The new form of a known substance, as per 3(d), would meet the requirements for patentability if it resulted in the enhancement of the known efficacy of that substance. In full knowledge of this requirement of the Indian law, Novartis tried to demonstrate before the Controller how there was an enhancement of efficacy, and submitted that there was an enhanced bioavailability of 30 per cent in studies conducted on rats. Novartis's case suffered as they had produced a bioavailability study conducted on rats while the drug was admittedly in the market for many years and was consumed by humans. Then again, it was not shown how the 30 per cent increase was critical in the performance of the drug and how the increase in enhancement of efficacy made a difference when compared to known efficacy.[34]

Following these grounds of pre-grant oppositions, the Assistant Controller of Patents and Designs, Mr V. Rengasamy, in his ruling said he was not convinced by the contentions of Novartis that a new substance was present: 'It is found that this patent application claims only a new form of a known substance without having any significant improvement in efficacy.' Further, stating that Novartis failed to prove enhanced efficacy of the beta-isomer over the known substance, the Assistant Controller concluded that, 'the subject matter of this (patent) application (filed by Novartis) is not patentable under Section 3(d) of [the Patents Act 1970 (India) as amended by the Patents (Amendment) Act 2005 (India)]'.

3.2 The Novartis challenge

On 17 May 2006, aggrieved by the order of the Controller, Novartis filed two cases challenging the rejection of the Glivec patent application and Indian patent law itself. Not only did Novartis appeal the patent office decision, but in a rather controversial move, it challenged the TRIPS compatibility and constitutionality of section 3(d). Novartis approached the High Court of Judicature at Madras with two batches of writ petitions:

(1) challenging the constitutional validity of section 3(d) of the Patents Act 1970 (India) as amended by the Patents (Amendment) Act 2005 (India); and

[34] Serious technical challenges were submitted to the Controller about the enhanced efficacy of the new compound by Natco Pharma Ltd. See C. R. Sukumar, 'Novartis Loses Patent Claim on Cancer Drug – Patents Controller Upholds Natco Contention', *The Hindu Business Line*, 26 January 2006.

(2) challenging the patent order of the Chennai Patent Office rejecting the Glivec patent application filed by Novartis.

In the Writ Petition No 24759 of 2006 in the High Court of Judicature at Madras, sections S and T, the petitioner, Novartis, alleged the following:

(1) that section 3(d) of the Patents Act is unconstitutional on the ground that it violates Article 14 of the Constitution of India, the Right to Equality, as it discriminates against the pharmaceutical sector vis-à-vis other technology sectors;
(2) the 'new Section 3(d) is in violation of India's obligation as a signatory to the TRIPS' under article 1(1) and article 27;
(3) that section 3(d) was vague and arbitrary, that a discovery becomes an invention if the substance in question results in enhancement of known efficacy is a very 'ingenious concept' and 'defies logic'. [35]

On 23 February 2007, the High Court of Judicature at Madras, in accordance with the Patents Act 1970 (India), converted one part of its case – the challenge to the patent office's decision to not grant a patent for Glivec – from a writ petition to an appeal and transferred it to the Intellectual Property Appellate Board ('IPAB').

The case, at this stage, was divided into three parts: (1) the patentability of Glivec; (2) the compliance of the Patents (Amendment) Act 2005 (India) with TRIPS; and (3) the constitutional validity of section 3(d) of the Patents Act 1970 (India) as amended by the Patents (Amendment) Act 2005 (India)

The first part of the case still rests with IPAB. It is believed likely that the patent rejection by the Chennai Patent Office will be upheld. To win, Novartis must convince the IPAB that (1) in relation to 3(d) the 30 per cent increase in bioavailability is an enhanced efficacy and so the beta crystalline form is patentable, and (2) the beta crystalline form of the mesylate salt is not an obvious form of the free base form.

For the second part, the court considered the Dispute Settlement Board, instituted as part of the TRIPS framework, a more appropriate forum and stated that it was outside the purview of the court to adjudicate in this matter. Consequently the matter in the court hinged on the constitutionality of section 3(d) of the Patents Act 1970 (India) as amended by the Patents (Amendment) Act 2005 (India).

[35] See *Novartis AG and another* v. *Union of India and others*, above n. 16, judis.nic.in/chennai/qrydisp.asp?tfnm=11121.

The High Court of Judicature at Madras on 6 August 2007 upheld the validity of section 3(d) of the Patents Act 1970 (India). It said that 'India, being a welfare and a developing country, which is predominantly occupied by people below poverty line, it has a constitutional duty to provide good health care to its citizens by giving them easy access to life saving drugs. In so doing, the Union of India would be right, it is argued, to take into account the various factual aspects prevailing in this big country and prevent "ever-greening" by allowing generic medicine to be available in the market.'[36]

It ruled that 'there is no ambiguity or vagueness in the expressions under attack as found incorporated in the amended section and the explanation attached to it'.[37] Also section 3(d) sets an 'obviousness' standard and member states are free to define the standard in a manner consistent with their national policy. Further it added that one of the fears of the petitioner was that the amended section 3(d) could lead to arbitrary interpretations and misuse. The conclusions of the court ruling were that 'no law can be declared illegal because there is a possibility of its misuse' and 'the Legislature has a duty to safeguard the economic interest of the country'.[38]

The court held that the amended section was not in violation of article 14 of the Constitution of India. Section 3(d) of the Patents Act 1970 (India) as amended by the Patents (Amendment) Act 2005 (India) does not 'discriminate' against the pharmaceutical sector but only makes a 'justified' differentiation, given the specificity of salt forms in the pharmaceutical sector: other technology sectors such as mechanicals and electronics do not face issues arising from 'different salt forms'.

4. The *Glivec* case from a larger perspective

It is important to underscore why the *Glivec* case is so significant in understanding the manner in which intellectual property rights in medicinal drugs are infringing upon health rights. Novartis claims that this battle is for protection of its intellectual property on grounds of principle.[39] It states that Glivec, through the Glivec International Patient

[36] *Novartis AG and another* v. *Union of India and others* (6 August 2007, High Court of Judicature at Madras for W.P. Nos. 24759 and 24760 of 2006) (The Novartis petition challenging the rejection of Glivec patent claim), www.scribd.com/doc/456550/High-Court-order-Novartis-Union-of-India.

[37] Ibid. [38] Ibid.

[39] Novartis, 'Novartis Concerned that Indian Court Ruling Will Discourage Investments in Innovation Needed to Bring Better Medicines to Patients' (Press Release, 6 August 2007), www.novartis.com/newsroom/news/index.shtml at 20 April 2009.

Assistance Program, is being distributed widely and successfully among the needy and poor:

> In 2006, our access-to-medicines program reached 33.6 million patients. Novartis spent US$ 755 million last year alone ... The [Glivec International Patient Assistance Program] is one of the most far-reaching patient assistance programs ever implemented on a global scale. In India, 99% of patients who receive Glivec receive it free from Novartis [6,600 people].[40]

The patent right for Glivec, it was therefore claimed, would not conflict with health interests because Novartis was distributing Glivec free of charge to around 7,000 patients in India. Novartis alleged that there was virtually no commercial market for Glivec in India. Its official website quotes that the price of Glivec is almost irrelevant in India as 99 per cent of the patients who need the medicine receive it free from Novartis through the Glivec International Patient Assistance Program.[41] The pharmaceutical giant claims that the lawsuit was in order to align Indian IP laws with TRIPS and their 'concern is with the non-recognition of intellectual property rights'.[42]

The claims made are debatable. Novartis claims to benefit 7,000 patients in India so far. However, the Cancer Patients Aid Association claim that there are at least 27,000 new cases of chronic myeloid leukaemia every year.[43] Almost ten patients die every day from chronic myeloid leukaemia and the demand for this drug is nearly 30 lakh capsules per month.[44] Such demand cannot be met by giving the patenting right to a single entity.

Novartis's Glivec International Patient Assistance Program is fraught with inequities and irregularities as has been demonstrated by cases in Brazil,[45]

[40] Quoted in Brook Baker, 'A Deconstruction of Novartis's Defense of its Challenge to the India Patent Regime', *Consumer Project on Technology*, 7 February 2007, www.cptech.org/ip/health/c/india/hgap02072007.html at 27 March 2009.

[41] Novartis, 'Glivec Patent Case in India: Fact vs. Fiction' (Press Release, not dated), www.novartis.com/downloads/about-novartis/facts-vs-fiction-india-glivec-patent-case.pdf at 27 March 2009.

[42] Ibid.

[43] Manu Joseph, 'The Future of the Medical Bill', *The Times of India* (Mumbai), 5 April 2007, www.cpaaindia.org/aboutus/PublicEyeAwards.htm at 6 September 2007.

[44] Ibid.

[45] Joana Ramos, 'New Definition of "Patient Assistance Program" in Brazil' (2005) 23(1) *Healthy Skepticism International News*, www.healthyskepticism.org/news/issue.php?id=7 at 11 July 2007.

Argentina[46] and Korea.[47] In the much publicized case of South Korea, Novartis refused to comply with the official Glivec price and threatened to pull Glivec out of the South Korean market; chronic myeloid leukaemia patients could not obtain Glivec because of supply instability.[48] In India too the Glivec International Patient Assistance Program has not been without contention. Novartis began its donations of Glivec with a warning that it would halt the programme if the government let local companies eat into its profits by selling generic versions of the drug. After India cleared generic versions of Glivec, like Veenat (marketed by Natco Pharmaceuticals) for sale, Novartis discontinued its free Glivec programme. The *New York Times* described the Glivec donations as both the promise and the perils of corporate philanthropy.[49] This drug donation programme was resumed only after the EMR was granted in November 2003 which removed, as mentioned earlier, the generic versions from the market. The Cancer Patients Aid Association in the High Court of Judicature at Madras brought evidence of denial of access to Glivec to many genuine patients in India including the workers who have insurance coverage under the Employees State Insurance Scheme or the Central Health Insurance Scheme, but are not reimbursed the cost of treatment of diseases like chronic myeloid leukaemia.[50]

Philanthropy has often been used as a pressure tactic to increase intellectual property protection in developing countries. It has also been used to lobby or pressure a country not to use TRIPS safeguards or introduce their own safeguards to protect public health, as was the case with section 3(d) of the Patents Acts 1970 (India). While patenting has become a logical corollary to cover the cost of R&D and innovation, for diseases in poor countries, donated or discounted drugs offered under the banner of corporate social responsibility have become the

[46] Joana Ramos, 'Novartis Glitch with Glivec in Argentina?', *Essential Drugs.org*, 15 May 2006, www.essentialdrugs.org/edrug/archive/200608/msg00070.php at February 2007.

[47] For a brief synopsis of the issues in the Korean GIPAP programme, see HeeSeob Nam and SungHo Park, 'Request for a Compulsory License from KIPO on Behalf of People's Health Coalition for Equitable Society, Association of Physicians for Humanism, and Korean Pharmacists for Democratic Society', glivec.jinbo.net/Request_for_CL_Final_version.htm at 5 September 2007.

[48] Ibid.

[49] Stephanie Storm and Matt Fleischer-Black, 'Drug Maker's Vow to Donate Cancer Medicine Falls Short', *The New York Times* (New York), 5 June 2003.

[50] *Novartis* v. *the Union of India* (6 August 2007), Order of High Court of Judicature at Madras for W.P. Nos. 24759 and 24760 of 2006 (Affidavit in Reply filed by the Respondent), 28, 29.

legitimizing principle for forcing patents and discouraging the production of generic life-saving drugs.

The core issue being debated is not the success or the failure of Novartis's Glivec International Patient Assistance Program or even the merits and flaws of corporate philanthropy and social responsibility (CSR).[51] The point being argued here is that donations or forms of corporate philanthropy ought not to add weight to a patent claim. Donations cannot become a counter-argument to an infringement of public interest. Further it cannot become a proxy for rights. There are many life-saving drugs like Glivec that need to be taken all life long. Few drug donation programmes can sustain this demand. However corporate donations are not a sustainable solution as they are: (1) frequently hard to access; (2) revocable; (3) not offered across the broad spectrum of patented medicines that poor people need; and (4) designed primarily to forestall generic competition by removing market incentives. The assumption that the issue of public health and access to drugs can be addressed through donations, philanthropy and corporate social responsibility is fundamentally flawed as it does not even begin to see health as a human right or a right to life.

For health to be seen as a right, the issue of access to drugs becomes fundamental to the claim. It is in this context that the *Glivec* case assumes importance and it is for this reason that it became the face of the global campaign to save generic production of drugs in India. India has been a very large player in the production and export of generic medicines the world over. The following figures compiled by Médecins Sans Frontières ('MSF') highlight the importance of India as a crucial player in access to affordable medicines:

(1) 67 per cent of medicines produced in India are exported to developing countries.
(2) 75–80 per cent of all medicines distributed by the International Dispensary Association (IDA) to developing countries are manufactured in India.
(3) In Zimbabwe, 75 per cent of tenders for medicines for all public sector health facilities come from Indian manufacturers. 90 per cent of the antiretrovirals (ARV) used in Zimbabwe's national treatment programme for AIDS come from India.
(4) The state procurement agency in Lesotho, NDSO, states it buys nearly 95 per cent of all ARVs from India.

[51] For the successes of the Glivec International Patient Assistance Program see Roger Bate, 'India and the Drug Patent Wars', *Health Policy Outlook*, 7 February 2007, www.aei.org/outlook/25566.

(5) India ranks second on the list of countries from which UNICEF purchases medical supplies. Belgium only ranks first because of vaccines (e.g. combination vaccines are not yet being produced in India).
(6) 80 per cent of ARVs used by MSF are purchased in India and distributed in treatment projects in over thirty countries.
(7) Over 90 per cent of all patients using AZT/3TC in MSF projects are on generic versions of the drug.
(8) Globally, 70 per cent of the treatment for patients in eighty-seven developing countries, purchased by UNICEF, IDA, the Global Fund (GFATM) and the Clinton Foundation since July 2005, has come from Indian suppliers.
(9) PEPFAR, the US President's AIDS initiative, also purchases ARVs from India for distribution in developing countries, thus resulting in cost-savings of up to 90 per cent. 89 per cent of the generic ARVs approved by the US Food and Drug Administration for PEPFAR are from India.[52]

In recent times, the most striking success of Indian pharmaceutical companies has been their ability to provide access to HIV/AIDS drugs at an affordable price. In fact the issue of access to drugs and the need to make cheaper drugs available arose primarily in the context of HIV/AIDS. India is the world's primary source of affordable antiretrovirals as it is one of the few countries with the capacity to produce these newer medicines as generics. The average cost of the AIDS cocktail in the West is $10,000 to $15,000 per patient per year. Yusuf Hamied, Cipla Chairman, stated in the aftermath of the South African crisis that the high drug prices are 'not because the drugs are prohibitively expensive to produce; they're not. It is the drug pricing structure imposed by multinational manufacturers which makes the drugs prohibitively expensive. Secondly, the international patent and trade regime at present seeks to choke off any large-scale attempt to produce and market the drugs at affordable levels.'[53]

Most AIDS programmes today use India as their main source of products. A three-in-one cocktail pill introduced by generic manufacturers

[52] The Office of the United States Global AIDS Coordinator, *Bringing Hope: Supplying ARVs for HIV/AIDS Treatment: The United States President's Emergency Plan for AIDS Relief* (2006), www.state.gov/documents/organization/66513.pdf at 23 August 2008.

[53] Kavaljit Singh, 'Patents v. Patients: AIDS, TNCs and Drug Price Wars', *Third World Network* (2001), www.twnside.org.sg/title/twr131c.htm at 11 July 2007.

Table 15.1 *Price comparisons (in US$) of three ARV drugs for year 2001*[54]

ARV Drug	Price of Patented Drug (Company)	Price of Generic Drug (Company)
Lamuvudine	$3,271 (Glaxo)	$190 (Cipla); $98 (Hetero)
Stavudine	$3,589 (Bristol-Myers Squibb)	$70 (Cipla); $47 (Hetero)
Nevirapine	$3,508 (Boehringer Ingelheim)	$340 (Cipla); $202.1 (Hetero)

substituted two pills for six pills per day. Thus the FDCs (Fixed Dose Combinations – AZT/3TC) increased the accessibility as well as availability of antiretroviral drugs. The introduction of FDCs became possible only because of the absence of product patent protection in India. National HIV treatment programmes in India, Burkina Faso, Mongolia, Central African Republic, Malawi, Peru, the Republic of Kyrgyzstan, Cambodia, Ukraine and Swaziland rely heavily on generic AZT/3TC. The availability of affordable quality generic versions of Combivir (AZT/3TC) and other antiretroviral medicines has allowed developing countries to put more people on treatment and thus extend their lives.

The price comparisons between the patented and generic drugs are substantial enough to merit the panic that the *Glivec* case created. A comparison of prices for HIV/AIDS medicines (see Table 15.1) illustrates the fact that pharmaceutical companies sell their patented medicines at much higher prices than those charged by generic producers.

An observational study of brand and generic supply based on a dataset of 2,162 orders of AIDS drugs for sub-Saharan Africa reported to the Global Price Reporting Mechanism at the WHO from January 2004 to March 2006 was performed. Generic companies supplied 63 per cent of the drugs studied, at prices that were on average about a third of the prices charged by brand companies. 96 per cent of the procurement was of first-line drugs, which were provided mostly by generic firms, while the remaining 4 per cent, of second-line drugs, was sourced primarily from brand companies. 85 per cent of the generic drugs in the sample were manufactured in India, where the majority of the drugs procured were ineligible for patent protection.[55] A President's Emergency Plan for

[54] Adapted from Singh, 'Patents v. Patients', above n. 53.

[55] World Health Organization, 'AIDS Medicine and Diagnostic Services' (3 by 5 Technical Brief, 3 by 5 Initiative, 2003), www.who.int/3by5/publications/briefs/amds/en/index.html at 16 August 2006.

AIDS Relief report acknowledges this when it states that 'in every case generic prices present an opportunity for cost savings; in some cases, the branded price per pack of a drug is up to 11 times the cost of the approved generic version'.[56]

The affordability of generic drugs is not limited to HIV/AIDS drugs. It extends to virtually every sector that has generic alternatives to patented drugs. The importance and affordability of generic drugs cannot be overemphasized. For example, in March 2001, an Indian company, Cipla, announced that it would offer the combination of anti-AIDS drugs at a cost of US$600 per patient per year (to MSF), and later announced that they could bring down their costs to US$350. The offer by Cipla created ripples in the international drug industry because the prices of these drugs in the US and other developed countries were between $10,000 and $15,000 per patient per year. Cipla's offer was matched within weeks by two other generic drug producing companies, Hetero Drugs and Ranbaxy. These offers are, to date, by far the cheapest made anywhere in the world.[57]

Price differentials also have a downward cascading effect which results in a general lowering of market prices of related drugs. The Cipla offer resulted in almost every transnational drug corporation announcing substantial reductions in their drug prices. MSF has witnessed the impact of patents on the prices and availability of medicines, in particular newer medicines, and has documented patent practice in the countries where it works.[58] Thus the lower price of generic versions has also triggered a price war, bringing about a significant reduction in the cost of patented drugs, making them more affordable and consequently more accessible.

Price, though not the only factor, constitutes a very important dimension of drug access. The availability of generic drugs not only provides the option of medicines at cheaper rates but also has an impact on price cuts of patented drugs.[59] Generic drugs, thus, have become a vital cog in

[56] The Office of the United States Global AIDS Coordinator, *Bringing Hope*, above n. 52.

[57] For details on price wars, see Singh 'Patents v. Patients', above n. 53.

[58] Médecins Sans Frontières, *Drug Patents under the Spotlight: Sharing Practical Knowledge about Pharmaceutical Patents* (2003), www.who.int/3by5/en/patents_2003.pdf.

[59] For a discussion, see Médecins Sans Frontières, 'A Guide to the Post 2005 World: TRIPS, R&D and Access to Medicines', 18 January 2005, www.msf.org/msfinternational/invoke.cfm?objectid=88694E5B-0FED-434A-A21EDA1006002653&component=toolkit.article&method=full_html.

the wheel upholding the access rights of people. While drug access has multiple contributing factors, patents constitute a vital connection.

As a signatory to the TRIPS Agreement there is often little room for manoeuverability. The flexibilities provided by TRIPS are outlined in articles 27.2, 30 and 31(c). In a rising incidence, compelled by domestic health imperatives, countries have used the TRIPS health safeguards of compulsory licensing implied in article 31(c).[60] The potential role of compulsory licensing in promoting access to medicines, however, is replete with compelling issues. The issue of compulsory licences is also mired in the politics of bilateral relations[61] and has proven a contentious way to address critical public health concerns. In the absence of national patent legislation protecting public health concerns, compulsory licensing may not be the best strategy.[62]

There is a need, therefore, to secure a domain for health safeguards outside global politics and within the realms of national law where it can receive sovereign protection. It is in this context that the *Glivec* judgment acquires salience. The judgment is significant for three reasons. First, it ensures the availability of cheaper versions of Glivec to chronic myeloid leukaemia patients. Indian companies can now make available generic medicines for leukemia at roughly one tenth the price Novartis charges for Glivec.

Second, it sets a precedent for future conflicts between generic and patented versions of drugs that have been incrementally improved, and whose 'enhanced efficacy' is not clearly demonstrable. The *Novartis* case threatens drugs that are not truly innovative.[63] A recent example is the patent filing by Abbott Laboratories Inc. for Aluvia, an anti-HIV drug.

60 Some instances of compulsory licensing being used to address health emergencies are: Thailand for ARV Efavirenz in November 2006 and Kaletra in February 2007; Indonesia for manufacture of generic Lamivudine and Nevirapine in October 2004; Malaysia for import from India for antiretrovirals dd1, AZT and Combivir in February 2003; Taiwan in November 2005 for manufacture of Tamiflu.

61 Mogha Kamal Smith of Oxfam said that the space given to developing countries by the August 2003 agreement is being taken away by bilateral and regional FTAs with developed countries, especially the United States. For details see Martin Khor, 'Patents, Compulsory License and Access to Medicines: Some Recent Experiences', *Policy Innovations* (February 2007), www.policyinnovations.org/ideas/policy_library/data/patents_compulsory_license; and Sangeeta Shashikant, 'More Countries Use Compulsory License, but New Problems Emerge', *Third World Network* (19 May 2005), www.twnside.org.sg/title2/health.info/twninfohealth004.htm.

62 For an exposition of this position see Khor, 'Patents, Compulsory License and Access to Medicines: Some Recent Experiences', above n. 60.

63 For a view that the majority of research conducted by industry is for higher-priced and similar versions of existing medicines ('me-too' medicines with little added therapeutic

Pre-grant oppositions have been filed in the US and in India on grounds that the drug is a combination of Lopinavir and Ritonavir drugs. Aluvia is similar to its original version Kaletra, but is an updated version – it has the same drug combination as Kaletra, but is in the form of a heat-resistant tablet (eliminating costly refrigeration) instead of the soft gel capsule form of Kaletra. A legal action was brought by the Initiative for Medicines, Access & Knowledge (I-MAK), and patient groups, such as the Network of Positive People and the Indian Network for People Living With HIV/AIDS.[64] The group filed a pre-grant opposition in the Indian Patent Office in Mumbai, claiming that section 3(d) of the Indian patent law bars patents on derivatives of older drugs without there being a substantial rise in efficacy.[65]

Lawyers Collective, a group of advocates engaged in public health and drug access issues in India, have challenged the grant of patents to several HIV drugs such as Merck's Efavirenz, Gilead Sciences' Tenofovir and Amprenavir, and also Roche's hepatitis drug Pegasys, contesting the incremental innovation claimed by the applicants. According to Anand Grover, project director of the HIV/AIDS unit at the Lawyers Collective, the group has filed a series of pre-grant oppositions against patent applications.[66] There are 150 pre-grant oppositions likely to be affected by the *Glivec* ruling. Prominent among these 150 'pre-grant' oppositions are AstraZeneca's lung cancer drug and a cholesterol-lowering medicine; a Pfizer treatment for fungal infections; Roche's Tamiflu bird flu medicine; and Eli Lilly's erectile

benefit), or monopoly extensions for new uses of old medicines, see Henry Mintzberg, 'Patent Nonsense: Evidence Tells of an Industry Out of Social Control' (2006) 175(4) *Canadian Medical Association Journal* 374, www.cmaj.ca/cgi/content/full/175/4/374 at 20 April 2009. These medicines are rarely innovative: only 15 per cent of the new drug applications approved by the US Food and Drug Administration (FDA) from 1989 to 2000 were identified as clinical improvements over products already on the market, see National Institute for Health Care Management, *Changing Patterns of Pharmaceutical Innovation*, May 2000, www.nihcm.org/~nihcmor/pdf/innovations.pdf at 20 April 2009.

64 For the text of their pre-grant opposition see the *Network of Positive People, and the Indian Network for People Living With HIV/AIDS* v. *Abbott Laboratories*, Indian Application No IN/PCT/2001/01312/MUM, 4 August 2006, www.i-mak.org/storage/PgOppKaletraSoftGel.pdf.

65 For the I-MAK pre-grant opposition see *The Initiative for Medicines, Access & Knowledge (I-MAK)* v. *Abbott Laboratories*, Indian Patent Application No 339/MUM/2006 filed on 23 August 2004, 16 August 2007, www.i-mak.org/storage/I-MAK%20Pregrant%20Opp%20339%20MUM%202006%20.pdf.

66 See Lawyers Collective, 'Patent Opposition', Lawyers Collective Affordable Medicines and Treatment Campaign, www.lawyerscollective.org/amtc/patent-opposition at 24 June 2009.

dysfunction drug.[67] The 3(d) provision and the adverse verdict in the *Glivec* case have no doubt had a bearing on these cases.

There is a third and larger issue under consideration here, namely the relationship between intellectual property, the proprietary system that it advances, and the right to health. The existing TRIPS rules that incentivize pharmaceutical research are deeply problematic. The utility of intellectual property protection (in itself questionable),[68] even if that were to be its most powerful defence, cannot be judged in terms of the innovation generated. Innovation is a means to an end: the end utility being the wellbeing of the people. If a third of the world's population does not have access to basic drugs, then clearly innovation is not meeting its desired objectives.[69] Access to drugs is a component of the human right to health and one that is closely linked to patenting of drugs. Denial of access is denial of the right to health. Lack of access to basic health necessities can, at best, preclude a minimally decent and autonomous life or, at worst, prove to be fatal for its victims. From the health victim's perspective, the object of this right is more important than that of many other traditional libertarian rights.

5. Conclusion

The ramifications of this case are wide: they extend beyond India, beyond the drug Glivec, bringing the ethics of patenting medical drugs into focus and questioning the fundamental basis of intellectual property rights in the medical field. It also highlights the need to adopt a system of priority in adjudicating claims between competing rights, such as the right to health and life, and the right to intellectual property. Adjudication of these claims calls for clear, justiciable articulation of laws that protect and prioritize 'basic' or 'prior' rights like health before innovators' rights. Significantly, it also brings into focus the right of a sovereign country to grant, uphold or delimit rights in consonance with its socioeconomic conditions. Rights

[67] Ed Silverman, 'India's Gleevec Ruling Is Bad News for Other Drugmakers Too', *Pharmalot*, 7 August 2007, www.pharmalot.com/2007/08/indias-gleevec-ruling-is-bad-news-for-other-drugmakers-too/ at 4 October 2007.

[68] See Adam B. Jaffe and Josh Lerner, *Innovation and its Discontents: How our Broken Patent System is Endangering Innovation and Progress, and What to Do about It* (2004); Michele Boldrin and David K. Levine, 'The Case against Intellectual Property' (2002) 92 *American Economic Review* 209; and Sunil Kanwar and Robert Evenson, 'Does Intellectual Property Protection Spur Technological Change?' (2001) Center Discussion Paper No 83, Economic Growth Center, Yale University.

[69] See United Nations Development Programme, *Human Development Report 2003* (2003).

impose duties and obligations on states and, where these duties and obligations are absent, the claim to a right to health remains weakly articulated and lacking in content. Arising out of these obligations are institutional provisions and legal recourse for health claims that empower the right. Rights themselves can never be empowering and will always remain under-inclusive if they are not empowered by institutional and juridical mechanisms that provide and support them.

In the absence of health as a fundamental, justiciable right in the Indian Constitution, section 3(d) of the Patents Act 1970 (India) as amended by the Patents (Amendment) Act 2005 (India) emerges as both an unlikely, and somewhat ironic, hero in the battle for health rights. The provision is not an outcome of a long history of public policy debates on health rights or safeguards. The 3(d) provision was more a reactive policy measure to placate the domestic outrage that ensued in the face of the prospect of full TRIPS compliance and its implications for health security and health rights.[70] Under pressure from the US and the World Trade Organization (WTO) to meet the 2005 deadline, India hastily signed the TRIPS Agreement, and even more hastily inserted this safeguard, which, in effect, was to function as a health safeguard. That perhaps explains the international concern about the efficacy clause which is not clearly enunciated and therefore would be open to competing or arbitrary interpretations. What constitutes enhanced efficacy of a drug, and the implications of this for future patent applications, is still ambiguous. Section 3(d) does not settle the debate on what constitutes invention and what is useful. If anything it adds complexity to the debate over the definition of 'novel'. However, what 3(d) does, and what the *Glivec* judgment based on this section does, is bring about a shift in the interpretative framework of the TRIPS Agreement.

Section 3(d) of the Patents Act 1970 (India) as amended by the Patents (Amendment) Act 2005 (India) interrogates hierarchies at two levels: first at the level shifting the interpretative onus away from the quarters of the WTO. There has been amplification and an enunciation of what comprises 'novelty' outside the juridical premises of the WTO. There may be future attempts to refine and add sophistication to 3(d) and similar provisions across the globe,[71] but there is no doubt that this

[70] Along with health rights, farmers' rights and food security were other areas of concern voiced vociferously by political parties and non-government organizations.

[71] Sections 22 and 26 of the Intellectual Property Code 1997 (The Philippines) [Republic Act No 8293] and sections 5 and 9 of the Patent Act 1979 (Thailand) B.E. 2522 (as

provision has initiated a dialogue which may have significant bearings on the manner in which the novelty/non-obviousness clause is executed in future. Second, by enunciating what it thinks novelty ought to be, 3(d) effectively devises the terms of adjudication between health rights and intellectual property rights.[72] Further, in construing what constitutes a 'novel' drug, it has undermined the capacity of TRIPS in de-prioritizing health-based considerations, at least in India and at least for the time being.

There is no doubt that this piece of legislation is limited in its scope for it seeks to provide a safety net for access rights only vis-à-vis incrementally changed drugs. Beyond its jurisdiction is an entire range of drugs that have viable patent claims but may impinge upon health rights of people. Rectifying the exclusion or marginalization of particular groups or rights requires analysis of the overall institutional framework of TRIPS. This means examining patterns of exclusion and dysfunction that cut across different countries and issues. By finding areas of common concern, broadening the constituencies and pushing for change, nations can expose problems and create pressure for institutional re-evaluation of pharmaceutical drug patents.

amended by The Patent Act (No 2) B.E 2535) expand on what does and does not constitute an inventive step.

72 The Madras High Court judges stated, 'We have borne in mind the object which the Amending Act wanted to achieve, namely ... to provide easy access to the citizens of this country to life-saving drugs and to discharge the constitutional obligation of providing good health care to its citizens.'

16

Tipping point: Thai compulsory licences redefine essential medicines debate

JONATHAN BURTON-MACLEOD

1. Introduction

In November 2006 Thailand's Ministry of Public Health issued a compulsory licence for the Merck-patented AIDS drug Efavirenz. This announcement was followed by two other compulsory licences issued in January of 2007, for the AIDS drug Kaletra and the cardiac drug Plavix. Compulsory licensing is an oft-used mechanism under article 31 of the Agreement on Trade-Related Aspects of Intellectual Property Rights ('TRIPS Agreement' or 'TRIPS')[1] but Thailand's action was notable as it represented the first use of a compulsory licence for a second-line antiretroviral – at once more lucrative and more effective than the first-line AIDS drugs that had preceded it. In the context of the access to essential medicines debate, this was the confrontation that drug companies, civil society and their derivative allies had been anticipating.

1.1 The dispute

Dispute over the proper use of compulsory licences erupted as Thailand ordered the generic equivalents from India.[2] Abbott Laboratories, patent holder for Kaletra, withdrew its patent applications from the Thai market for a period.[3] After initial mixed messages, the United States Trade

[1] Marrakesh Agreement Establishing the World Trade Organization, opened for signature 15 April 1994, 1867 UNTS 3, annex 1C (Agreement on Trade-Related Aspects of Intellectual Property Rights) (entered into force 1 January 1995) ('TRIPS Agreement' or 'TRIPS')

[2] Nopporn Wong-Anan, 'Thailand Issues More Compulsory Drug Licenses', *Reuters* (25 January 2007), lists.essential.org/pipermail/ip-health/2007-January/010433.html at 20 March 2009.

[3] Kaiser News Network, 'Abbott to Stop Launching New Drugs in Thailand in Response to Country's Compulsory License for Antiretroviral Kaletra', *Kaiser News Network* (16 March 2007), www.medicalnewstoday.com/articles/65274.php at 20 March 2009.

Representative ('USTR') placed Thailand on the punitive 301 list, citing in part Thailand's diminishing regard for intellectual property rights.[4] For its part Thailand, under a new military junta, pushed ahead with its generic supply purchases, refusing to rule out further usage of additional compulsory licences.

The legal–political import of Thailand's licensing use flowed in large part from the fact that this was the first time that the flexibilities under TRIPS article 31(b) had been applied to second-line antiretroviral drugs targeting HIV/AIDS. In fact, five previous uses of compulsory licensing by developing world nations had passed without incident since 2004.[5]

The traditional argument that patents ensure remuneration for investments made in research and development reincarnates itself forcefully in relation to second-line antiretrovirals, representing, as they do, a significant research advance on first-line antiretrovirals. The Thai Government countered with a fundamental argument of its own: developing world patients possess an inalienable right to health and don't deserve second-rate medicines.

1.2 Essential medicines background

Since 2001, the Doha Round of TRIPS negotiations had focused attention squarely on the relationship between patent rights and the health needs of the developing world. The resultant Doha Declaration on the TRIPS Agreement and Public Health ('Doha Declaration')[6] had sought to establish flexibilities within the TRIPS Agreement that would enable access to medicines initiatives. Notably, article 5(b) of the Doha Declaration highlighted the role of compulsory licensing under article 31(b) of TRIPS,[7] emphasizing the autonomy of member nations to 'determine the grounds upon which such licenses are granted'.

With the focus on compulsory licensing, however, came concern about the viability of the mechanism for least-developed countries ('LDCs'), member nations with little or no manufacturing capacity.

[4] United States Trade Representative, *Special 301 Report* (30 April 2007), www.ustr.gov/Document_Library/Press_Releases/2007/April/SPECIAL_301_Report.html at 20 March 2009.

[5] Cecilia Oh, 'Compulsory Licenses: Recent Experiences in Developing Countries' (2006) 1 *International Journal of Intellectual Property Management* 25; World Health Organization, *Report of the WHO Mission to Thailand* (2008).

[6] Declaration on the TRIPS Agreement and Public Health: Adopted on 14 November 2001, WT/MIN(01)/DEC/2 (2001) ('the Doha Declaration')

[7] For content and analysis of article 31(b) see below section 2.1.

Article 31(f), after all, limits the use of compulsory licences for 'predominantly domestic purposes'. This became known as the 'Paragraph 6 Problem'. A response initiated by the TRIPS Council as the result of protracted negotiations ('WTO General Council Decision of 30 August 2003') was later formalized as a permanent amendment and entrenched in article 31*bis*.[8]

The compulsory licensing employed by Thailand under article 31(b) does not overlap with the article 31*bis* mechanism as a partial 'solution' to the essential medicines problem, as the two avenues largely cater for differing groups of TRIPS member nations. The article 31*bis* mechanism is aimed at LDCs, with a utility for middle-income nations limited to those who can demonstrate insufficient domestic pharmaceutical manufacturing capacity for the patent in question.[9] However, with article 31*bis* hitherto the focus for access to essential medicines efforts, the political overlap as well as the legal analogy with article 31(b) compulsory licensing needs to be examined. This chapter concludes that the political and legal effects will be significant, particularly as customary international law meets the global administrative law of the TRIPS Agreement.

1.3 *Framework for analysis*

This chapter aims to describe and assess the impact of the Thai compulsory licences in the current context of the access to medicines debate. First, this chapter analyses the Thai use of compulsory licences as a form of precedent in interpreting the parameters for subsequent uses of compulsory licensing under article 31 of TRIPS. Sections 2 and 3 focus on interpretation of key terms in article 31(b) in the conversation between the Thai Government and intellectual property interests. The analysis highlights that the normative boundaries that are the focus of discussion represent a complex commingling of the requirements in article 31(b) as established by the Doha Declaration.

[8] Implementation of Paragraph 6 of the Doha Declaration on the TRIPS Agreement and Public Health, WTO Doc WT/L/540 (2003) (WTO General Council Decision of 30 August 2003). See WTO 'Members OK Amendment to Make Health Flexibility Permanent' (Press Release, 6 December 2005), www.wto.org/english/news_e/pres05_e/pr426_e.htm.

[9] The Doha Declaration, above n. 6, [1(b)], 'insufficient manufacturing capacity' defined in annex part (i) and (ii).

The properly reoriented question is one of legal methodology: whether Thailand's interpretation of article 31(b) represents a necessarily embellished application of minimum requirements under TRIPS, or whether it establishes TRIPS-Plus like requirements as an inaccurate legal precedent for subsequent applications of article 31(b). Section 4 considers the pragmatic effect of Thailand's compulsory licensing on the charged political environment surrounding both article 31(b) and 31*bis* approaches to the intellectual property essential medicines debate.

2. The Thai dispute: constructing the conversation

In July 2007 in the aftermath of Thailand's compulsory licences, European Union Commissioner for External Trade, Peter Mandelson, penned an intimidating letter to the Thai Minister of Commerce.[10] Thailand's action, warned Mandelson, 'could lead to the isolation of Thailand from the global biotechnology investment community'. He continued:

> Other means should be explored to increase the access to essential medicines among the Thai people before resorting to such exceptional measures. *Neither the TRIPS Agreement nor the Doha Declaration appear to justify a systematic policy of applying compulsory licenses wherever medicines exceed certain prices.* (emphasis added)

In April 2007, the USTR disciplined Thailand by placing it on its 'Special 301' Priority Watch List, reserved for countries that do not provide adequate intellectual property rights protection. 'The lack of transparency and due process exhibited in Thailand [during the issuance of compulsory licences] represents a serious concern', according to the report.[11] Placement on the list can correlate with more skittish investment and tags the offending country for intensified bilateral negotiations (read pressure) with the USTR.[12]

Abbott's legal representatives, the global law firm Baker & McKenzie, delivered the most detailed criticism of Thailand's compulsory licences in an open letter to the *Bangkok Post*, published 23 April 2007. The editorial contended that the Ministry of Public Health had failed to

[10] Peter Mandelson, 'Compulsory Licensing of Pharmaceutical Patents in Thailand', *Knowledge Ecology International*, 10 July 2007, www.keionline.org/misc-docs/thai/070710-PM-MoC.pdf at 20 March 2009.

[11] United States Trade Representative, *Special 301 Report*, above n. 4.

[12] Ibid.

comply with TRIPS in a number of important respects including: lack of prior consultations with patent holders (article 31(b)), inadequate royalty rates (article 31(h)) and failure to consider the case on 'its individual merits' or lack of due process (article 31(a)).[13]

Dr Mongkol Na Songkhla, Thailand's then Minister of Public Health responded to Commissioner Mandelson's letter, outlining the case for issuing the compulsory licences under TRIPS, as well as against other intellectual property and public health norms.[14] Dr Na Songkhla emphasized that the generic medicines produced under the compulsory licence would be used only by public patients under Thailand's universal access antiretroviral programme for HIV/AIDS patients:[15] not so for patients under the private healthcare system who would continue to pay full price for patented drugs. The letter further asserted that the actions of the Ministry were consonant with TRIPS guidelines for compulsory licensing under article 31. Dr Na Songkhla stressed that though article 31(b) contained no requirement for prior negotiation with the patent holders, ongoing efforts had been made to engage the patent holders in negotiations, a contention seemingly borne out by news reports of the process.[16]

Dr Na Songkhla's response to the expressed intellectual property concerns is drawn from, and expanded by a Thai Government White Paper policy statement issued in February of 2007.[17] An attempt to preempt the criticism that would surely come, the White Paper is the most thorough representation of the Thai Government's position. The White Paper starts from the premise that, contrary to the assertions of Baker & McKenzie, the three compulsory licences are legal under the TRIPS provisions.

[13] Peerapan Tungsuwan and William McKay, 'Compulsory Drug Licenses Violate World Trade Treaty', *Bangkok Post*, Op-Ed, 23 April 2007.

[14] Mongkol Na Songkhla, Minister for Public Health, Thailand, 'Letter to His Excellency Friedrich Hamburger', 18 July 2007, www.actupparis.org/IMG/pdf/Answer_Thai.pdf at 20 March 2009.

[15] Launched 1 October 2003, see text of the government use compulsory licence for Efavirenz, www.cptech.org/ip/health/c/thailand/thaicl4efavirenz.html at 20 March 2009.

[16] See, e.g., Reuters, 'Thailand Talking with Drug Firms – U.S. Chamber', *Reuters*, 20 March 2007, lists.essential.org/pipermail/ip-health/2007-March/010800.html at 20 March 2009.

[17] Ministry of Public Health and National Health Security Office, Thailand, *Facts and Evidences on the 10 Burning Issues Related to the Government Use of Patents on Three Patented Essential Drugs in Thailand* (16 February 2007), www.moph.go.th/hot/White%20Paper%20CL-EN.pdf at 31 March 2009 ('Thai White Paper').

2.1 Legal requirements under TRIPS

What, then, constitute the basic legal requirements outlined in article 31(b)? Article 31 of TRIPS contemplates 'other use' of a patent without authorization from the patent holder, implicitly supporting the ability of member nations to engage in compulsory licensing subject to the several restrictions contained in the article. The restrictions are as a whole not burdensome, with the pertinent provisions including enabling domestic legislation with the right to appeal the licensing decision,[18] payment of adequate remuneration to the patent holder,[19] and limits on usage of the licence to 'the purpose for which it is authorised'.[20]

Perhaps most importantly in Thailand's context, paragraph (b) outlines the level of interaction necessary between the licence user and the patent holder. In other words, it describes the level of 'due process' required before issuance of a compulsory licence. According to paragraph (b), use may be permitted only in the presence of prior effort to obtain authorization from the right holder 'on reasonable commercial terms' for a 'reasonable period of time'. This requirement may be waived, however, in the case of 'a national emergency or other circumstances of extreme urgency or in cases of public non-commercial use', with only a notification requirement to the right holder.

At the instigation of a coalition of developing world member nations, the Doha Declaration confirmed the validity of compulsory licensing under article 31 as a mechanism for accessing essential medicines, and further interpreted article 31(b) as conferring freedom for member nations to determine 'appropriate' grounds for the grant of a compulsory licence.[21] As a matter of treaty interpretation, the Doha Declaration has significant influence on the interpretation of the TRIPS text. James Gathii argues that the Doha Declaration 'mandates reading the TRIPS Agreement in light of its objectives and principles, thereby giving countries a legal basis in the Agreement itself to argue in favor of public policies' under article 31(3)(a) of the Vienna Convention on the Law of Treaties.[22]

[18] Article 31(i), (j) of the TRIPS Agreement. [19] Article 31(h) of the TRIPS Agreement.

[20] Article 31(c) of the TRIPS Agreement. Compulsory licensing under article 31 is also subject to termination when the circumstances that led to its authorization cease to occur (article 31(g)), and to consideration of the 'individual merits' of each compulsory licence (article 31(a)).

[21] The Doha Declaration, above n. 6.

[22] Vienna Convention on the Law of Treaties, opened for signature 22 May 1969, 1155 UNTS 331 (entered into force 27 January 1980). See James Thou Gathii, 'The Legal Status of the Doha Declaration on TRIPS and Public Health under the Vienna

2.2 *Justifying the 'legal': TRIPS-Minimums or TRIPS-Plus?*

The legality of the compulsory licences under article 31 of TRIPS read in light of the Doha Declaration may be, contrary to the claims of Baker & McKenzie, the most easily supportable assertion made by the Thai Government. USTR Ambassador Susan Schwab acknowledged as much in a letter to US law-makers concerned about the retributive appearance of Thailand's placement on the Priority Watch List: 'We have not suggested that Thailand has failed to comply with particular national or international rules.'[23] A chorus of academic and civil society evaluators likewise contend that, as far as article 31 is concerned, Thailand has met its international legal obligations.[24]

However, the White Paper, along with Dr Na Songkhla's response, exhibits the perceived need to go beyond legal justification on the basis of article 31(b). The question for this paper is what, if anything is required beyond the minimum legal requirements in TRIPS? And, second, what might such extended 'legal' obligations represent? Is Thailand's expanded justification a necessary application of the minimum requirements of TRIPS to the complex and controversial area of essential medicines? Or does it create a precedent for TRIPS-Plus-like requirements, akin to the additional obligations that result from bilateral free trade negotiations initiated by the US and the EU[25] that do not reflect textual legal obligations, particularly in light of Doha?

Whether the expanded parameters of the conversation create TRIPS-Plus requirements or represent the application of TRIPS minimum standards, the Thai dispute represents a seminal application of article

Convention on the Law of Treaties' (2002) 15 *Harvard Journal of Law and Technology* 291, 305.

23 Susan Schwab, 'Letter to Congressman Thomas Allen', 17 January 2008.

24 'There is little doubt that Thailand would win a dispute settlement action based on the TRIPS-compliance of its government issue licensing': Frederick Abbott and Jerome Reichman, 'The Doha Round's Public Health Legacy: Strategies for the Protection and Diffusion of Patented Medicines under the Amended TRIPS Provisions' (2007) 10(4) *Journal of International Economic Law* 921, 950, 956; Ellen 't Hoen, 'Undermining TRIPS: Protectionism at its Worst' (2007) 369(9555) *The Lancet* 2; Brook Baker, Sean Flynn and Judit Rius Sanjuan, 'Premiere Law Firm's Specious Arguments on Thailand's Compulsory Licenses', *IP Health*, 25 April 2007; 'The fact that the license will be used to support a public interest program may be sufficient grounds for justification': World Health Organization, *Report of the WHO Mission to Thailand*, above n. 5.

25 For a description of TRIPS-Plus bilateral negotiations, see Hitoshi Nasu, 'Public Law Challenges to the Regulation of Pharmaceutical Patents in the US Bilateral Free Trade Agreements', in Thomas Pogge, Matthew Rimmer and Kim Rubenstein (eds.), *Incentives for Global Public Health: Patent Law and Access to Essential Medicines* (2010), 77.

31(b) compulsory licensing flexibilities.[26] As such, the assertions made and justifications offered in the political–legal spheres have the potential to set normative precedents for subsequent licensing in the access to essential medicines context.

3. New normative boundaries for access to essential medicines disputes

3.1 *Identifying new normative boundaries*

The justifications offered and the discussion spawned by the decision of the Thai Government to issue the three compulsory licences function to extend the political–legal conversation well beyond the requirements outlined in TRIPS. This section analyses the conversation, identifying three major normative focuses that have precedent-setting value. Thailand's experience raises the possibility that, seemingly contrary to the Doha Declaration, member countries who use the compulsory licensing mechanism may have diminished 'freedom to determine the grounds upon which such licenses are granted'.[27] The following sections examine the new normative boundaries.

3.1.1 Brackish water: 'national emergency' and 'public non-commercial' requirements co-mingle

Article 31(b) allows patent use without the permission of the patent holder in the case of 'national emergency', 'other cases of extreme urgency' or in cases of 'public non-commercial use'. Article 5(c) of the Doha Declaration explains that 'public health crises, including those relating to HIV/AIDS, tuberculosis, malaria and other epidemics, can represent a national emergency or other circumstances of extreme urgency'.

The definition of 'public non-commercial use' is considerably more nuanced. Multiple criteria exist for defining public non-commercial use, but basic requirements for the essential medicines context would likely include that the medicines be used for public benefit and that the nature of the transaction be either 'not-for-profit' or for the supply of public institutions.[28] There is some debate as to the role that a private

[26] Section 3 discusses how Brazil followed Thailand's example, issuing a compulsory licence in April 2007.

[27] Article 5(b), the Doha Declaration, above n. 6.

[28] United Nations Conference on Trade and Development and International Centre for Trade and Sustainable Development, *Resource Book on TRIPS and Development* (2005), 471.

commercial entity could ever play in such a transaction. A World Bank interpretation restricts appropriate entities to 'a government procurement authority purchasing medications for distribution through public clinics without seeking to make any commercial profit from such distribution'.[29] However, other definitions are considerably more expansive, claiming that 'the language of the TRIPS Agreement is focused on the 'use' made of the licensed product, not who the manufacturer or distributor is'.[30] According to the WHO Mission to Thailand in January of 2007, 'the fact that the license will be used to support a public interest program may be sufficient grounds for justification'.[31]

The language of article 31(b) presents 'national emergency' and 'public non-commercial use' as either/or threshold requirements. The Doha Declaration would suggest that, particularly for the compulsory licensing of the second-line HIV/AIDS drugs, Thailand's action could be easily described as responding to a national emergency. However, the discussion between the Thai Government and those with intellectual property interests seems to indicate a more compounded requirement.

In the Thai White Paper and in Dr Songkhla's response to the European Trade Commissioner, additional justifications relating to the public non-commercial use of the patent were offered. Dr Songkhla emphasized that the generic medicines produced under the compulsory licence would be used only by public patients under Thailand's universal access antiretroviral programme for HIV/AIDS patients. The White Paper expands on the three national public health insurance schemes that cover 98 per cent of the population with a commitment to universal access for essential medicines.[32]

In all, the discussion surrounding the Thai licences suggests a loose but tangible 'above and beyond' precedent that generates several possible normative expansions for article 31(b) requirements in the essential medicines context: (1) justification on the basis of a public health

[29] The World Bank, *Battling HIV/AIDS: A Decision Maker's Guide to the Procurement of Medicines and Related Supplies* (2004), 121.

[30] Baker, Flynn and Sanjuan, 'Premiere Law Firm's Specious Arguments on Thailand's Compulsory Licenses', above n. 24. Likewise, 'even a private entity charged with exploiting a patented invention for the benefit of the public' could come within the scope of 'public non-commercial use'. See Oh, 'Compulsory Licenses', above n. 5.

[31] World Health Organization, *Report of the WHO Mission to Thailand*, above n. 5. Although ironically the WHO would later discourage Thailand from seeking a compulsory licence on Kalitra, see discussion in section 3.

[32] Thai White Paper, above n. 17, 1–2.

emergency may be insufficient; (2) public non-commercial use must co-exist with a public health emergency, and vice versa; and (3) heightened and recalibrated requirements for public non-commercial use apply.

The first normative expansion is evidenced in the exchange between the Thai Government and Commissioner Mandelson, and expanded upon in the White Paper. The second is an extrapolation of the first, and highlights the potential compounding of threshold requirements if the more complex 'public non-commercial use' requirements outlined above are added to that of a 'national emergency'.

The third normative expansion may vest in the specific facts of the Thai case. Thailand's justification for public non-commercial use was based on (1) the presence of a national universal access programme; and (2) the distinction between public and private health markets. A universal access programme, coincidentally implemented in both Thailand and Brazil, the first users of article 31(b) flexibilities, may represent an emerging gold standard for public non-commercial purpose, and may become a tacit requirement for government use compulsory licensing.

Second, where elements of the healthcare market are mixed, as is the case in Thailand,[33] in justifying 'public non-commercial use' focus may be put on the necessary extent of a 'watertight' distinction between public and private markets.[34] Where watertight-ness may be a matter for concern, as is arguably the case in Thailand where only 62 per cent of patients under the universal access programme are restricted to the public healthcare system, a heightening of the meaning of (public health) 'national emergency' may re-emerge in the spiralling justification equation.[35]

3.1.2 'Due process' in a public health emergency? Separating the demands of pragmatism and rhetoric

Article 31(b) waives negotiation requirements with the patent holder on either 'national emergency' or 'public non-commercial use' grounds.

[33] Ibid., 1–4 (Issue No 1).

[34] A third normative expansion may revisit focus on the 'agent' versus 'use' elements of the 'public non-commercial use' definition. Abbott's lawyers focused on the identity of the Thai Government Procurement Organization ('GPO'), arguing that because the GPO was not statutorily mandated as a not-for-profit agency, its function as an agent did not fit into the public non-commercial use requirement.

[35] Normative expansion on the meaning of 'national emergency' is discussed further at p. 420 below.

However the USTR, in taking disciplinary action against Thailand, identified a 'lack of transparency' in the decision to issue the compulsory licences. Abbott's lawyers also slammed the lack of prior consultations with the patent holders, required by article 31(b), suggesting that negotiations were a standing requirement, regardless of emergency or non-commercial use justifications.[36] While these protests hint more at political pragmatism than legal requirement, they are not without precedent-setting value.

The Thai Government did, according to news sources[37] and the White Paper,[38] attempt to negotiate a price reduction with the patent holder prior to implementing government use licences. The extent of good faith of these negotiations may be a matter for contention. However, the potential precedent exists that if negotiations are pursued, the possibility arises of an emerging distinction between forms of public health emergencies, only the worst of which do not require some form of negotiations with the patent holder for uses under article 31(b), lending in turn an epidemic-level threshold to the 'public health emergency' wording in the Doha Declaration where post facto notification of the patent holder would be considered acceptable.[39]

3.1.3. Defining 'essential medicines': both sides push the limits

The types of eligible public health issues, and therefore patents, that might meet the requirements for compulsory licensing of essential medicines has long been a matter for debate. Indeed, prior to the Doha Round, the US negotiating stance held that only HIV/AIDS would meet the definition of public health emergency and engage the discussed flexibilities;[40] an interpretation ultimately rejected in Doha. The scope of diseases and situations covered has consequently been the

[36] Tungsuwan and McKay, 'Compulsory Drug Licenses Violate World Trade Treaty', above n. 13.

[37] Reuters, 'Thailand Talking with Drug Firms – U.S. Chamber', *Reuters*, 20 March 2007, lists.essential.org/pipermail/ip-health/2007-March/010800.html at 20 March 2009.

[38] Thai White Paper, above n. 17, 5–10 (Issue Nos 2–3)

[39] The requirement for enabling domestic legislation automatically incorporates aspects of due process, particularly as suggested in article 31(a), that each use be considered on its own merits. In Thailand's case, s. 51 of the Patents Act 1979 (Thailand) B.E. 2522 establishes a subcommittee (to implement the government use of patented drugs) that identifies candidate essential medicine patents for government use licences according to internal criteria: see Thai White Paper, 18–19 (Issue No 7).

[40] Gathii, 'The Legal Status of the Doha Declaration on TRIPS and Public Health under the Vienna Convention on the Law of Treaties', above n. 22, 307.

frontline in interpreting flexibilities for essential medicines under TRIPS.

Already discussed in the Thai context is the suggestion that due process requirements may differ depending on the nature of the public health threat, evidence that defining parameters for government use and essential medicines often circles back to arguments about public health.

However the Thai Government itself pushes the boundaries of conventional public health interpretations of TRIPS by issuing a licence for the cardiac drug Plavix[41] in addition to two second-line AIDS drugs. At first glance Plavix is an unlikely candidate for government use under the terms of article 31(b). Plavix, unlike the other drugs subject to government use, is not on the WHO list of essential medicines. Plavix plays a similar physiological role to aspirin but is significantly more expensive.[42] On the other hand, Plavix is the second-best-selling drug in the world,[43] suggesting a significant public health advantage.

The question of whether chronic diseases constitute public health emergencies for the purposes of article 31(b) overlaps with whether a public non-commercial use is sufficient in the essential medicines context. Chronic disease is not a national emergency that is particularly unique to the developing world context, unlike HIV/AIDS, for example. However, according to the Thai Minister of Health, Plavix constitutes a significant budgetary portion of cardiac care requirements.[44] Arguably, if a particular drug has a disproportionate effect on a universal access budget, that could be grounds for definition as a public health emergency. The Thai compulsory licence text itself seems to justify government use of Plavix on the grounds that it is for public non-commercial use, and to justify it simply by the high impact of cardiovascular disease on public health.[45]

[41] Clopidogrel, patented by Bristol-Myers Squibb and Sanofi-Aventis.

[42] Malcolm Cook, 'The Bangkok Challenge: From Conflict to Cooperation and Beyond – Outcomes Report', *The Lowy Institute for International Policy* (2007) 2–5, www.lowyinstitute.org/Publication.asp?pid=612 at 20 March 2009.

[43] With sales totalling US$7.3 billion in 2007. See Matthew Perrone and Marley Seaman, 'Study: Concerns on Mixing Plavix, Heartburn Drugs', *Associated Press*, 11 November 2008, naturalhealthnews.blogspot.com/2008/11/plavix-and-nexium-combo-nixed.html at 15 April 2009.

[44] Ministry of Public Health, Thailand, 'Announcement Regarding Exploitation of Patents on Drugs and Medical Supplies for Clopidogrel' (Press Release, 25 January 2007), www.cptech.org/ip/health/c/thailand/thai-cl-clopidogrel_fn.pdf at 20 March 2009.

[45] Ibid.

3.1.4 Normative precedents as subsequent state practice affecting treaty interpretation

In many ways, the discussion ends where it began – at an interpretation of limits to the flexibilities for member countries to define public health emergency as per the Doha Declaration's 'national emergency' in article 31(b). What this chapter seeks to emphasize, however, is that the negotiations innate in this first major application of article 31(b) will shape that process for successive uses. As such the definition of these key legal interpretations forms the contested area for advocates on both sides of the debate.

In the scheme of international law-making, these normative precedents arguably represent customary interpretation of treaty obligations under TRIPS. Authority for the role of subsequent state practice in treaty interpretation is well established in article 31(3)(b) of the Vienna Convention on the Law of Treaties, and confirmed in the more recent International Court of Justice case concerning *Kasikili/Sedudu Island.*[46] Whether the normative precedents amount to customary modification of treaty obligations is a matter for debate, and forms the subject matter for the concluding discussion in section 3.3, below.

*3.2 Reflections from/on article 31*bis

This section considers the extent to which interpretation of the article 31*bis* mechanism[47] provides legal analogy for the interpretation of article 31(b) representing, as they both do, an application of TRIPS to the essential medicines context.[48] Specifically, the text of article 31*bis* seems to provide commentary on the meaning of public health emergency in appropriating flexibilities under TRIPS, within the limits of the analogy.

The analogy is limited because article 31*bis*[49] provides a particular form of flexibility that represents a managed attempt to circumvent one

[46] *Kasikili/Sedudu Island (Botswana* v. *Namibia) (Judgment)* [1999] ICJ Rep 1045, 1075–6 [47]–[49]. State action that constitutes customary interpretation is, of course, always a fluid consideration. However, with the basis for the conversation communications between the USTR, the EU Trade Commissioner and the Thai Government – all government proxies – the conversation falls within the range of communications that evidence custom.

[47] The Doha Declaration, above n. 6.

[48] Part III considers the effect – largely political – of Thailand's government use compulsory licences on the interpretation and utilization of article 31*bis*

[49] WTO General Council Decision of 30 August 2003, above n. 8.

of the safeguards in article 31 – that compulsory licensing should be predominantly for domestic use – article 31(f). The WTO General Council Decision of 30 August 2003 that led to first the waiver and then the amendment also represents a consensus of the TRIPS Council; quite apart from the aim of the Doha Declaration, which was to reassert the right for developing world nations to define for themselves the terms of a public health emergency, the starting point for article 31(b).

Caveats aside, issues of the applicable public health scope of the waiver featured prominently in the WTO General Council Decision of 30 August 2003 and its legislative interpretations. Consonant with the Doha Declaration, this decision places no restriction on the definition of pharmaceutical products, either in the form of a list of pharmaceutical products or a list of diseases for which generic drugs may be issued under a compulsory licence. In fact, this issue of eligible pharmaceutical products featured large in delaying a final consensus leading to the WTO General Council Decision of 30 August 2003 itself.[50] Whatever the process, its unrestricted language suggests reinforcement of the flexibilities in the Doha Declaration. This would seem to lend further support to the ability of Thailand to identify the shape of a public health emergency. However the idea of gradations to public health emergencies is never far from conversation. The Doha Declaration itself highlights epidemics as particularly exemplifying the need for flexibilities in article 31.[51]

Similarly, legislative interpretations of the WTO General Council Decision of 30 August 2003 guidelines have not been so permissive. One of the earliest pieces of legislation enacted in response to the Decision was Canada's Jean Chrétien Pledge to Africa Act (2004).[52] The Canadian legislation, in contrast to the Decision, lists the pharmaceutical products eligible for export under any granted compulsory licence, with a focus on epidemic-related medicines.[53]

[50] Richard Elliott, 'Steps Forward, Backward, and Sideways: Canada's Bill on Exporting Generic Pharmaceuticals' (2004) 9(3) *Canadian HIV/AIDS Law & Policy Review* 17.

[51] Article 5(c), The Doha Declaration, above n. 6.

[52] An Act to Amend the Patent Act and the Food and Drugs Act, SC 2004, c. 23 ('The Jean Chrétien Pledge to Africa Act') (Canada).

[53] Section 21.03(1)(a) Bill C-9. Sch. 1 of Bill C-9 set out a list of fifty-six pharmaceutical products considered eligible for generic production and export. The list is primarily derived from the World Health Organization's model list of Essential Medicines, but also includes all antiretrovirals currently approved for treatment of HIV/AIDS in Canada. According to the legislation, the list is not static, and the Minister can, upon recommendation of an

This discussion brings full circle the question of whether the flexibilities under TRIPS – whether in article 31(b) or, specifically, exceptions in article 31*bis* – apply simply to sub-Saharan Africa's levels of epidemics or whether the legal consensus permits member countries to define, per the Doha Declaration, the context-specific nature of a public health emergency. This unclarified answer may partner with requirements, described above, relating to 'public non-commercial use' to set heightened normative parameters for compulsory licensing under article 31(b).

3.3 TRIPS-Minimum or TRIPS-Plus reconsidered

Whether there is a level that constitutes a 'misuse' of the flexibilities may be as much a political as a legal threshold, although the WTO Dispute Panel has yet to voice an opinion on the issue. Until or unless it does, focus remains on the developing standards of acceptable practice as elicited by this first major interpretation of the article 31(b) flexibilities. Put simply, the normative precedents developed in this exchange will set expectations for further use.

Theoretically, the apparent merging of the threshold and due process requirements attached to the terms 'national emergency' and 'public non-commercial use' can be divergently (and perhaps simultaneously) characterized as TRIPS-Minimum or TRIPS-Plus requirements.

Under the TRIPS-Minimum model, the TRIPS Agreement sets out minimum standards for intellectual property.[54] The application of TRIPS provisions to a particular context, then, is the application of minimum standards to a specific situation, resulting in a context-specific set of parameters. Under this model, the merging of public non-commercial and national emergency definitions and requirements, as pushed for by intellectual property interests, is necessitated by the application of article 31(b) to novel practice in the essential medicines context.

Under the TRIPS-Plus interpretation, however, elements of the intellectual property discussion that result in heightened threshold and due process requirements, in the Thai context, represent unnecessary limits on the acceptable legal application of article 31(b). It is instead a matter

advisory committee, add or remove pharmaceutical products from the list. Section 21.03(1)(a); section 21.18.

[54] See, e.g., TRIPS Agreement, article 1.

of power imbalance that results in a justification phenomenon, setting the potential for normative precedent that is unreflective of legal requirements.

So which is it? Section 3.1.4, above, considered the formal nature of the normative precedents emerging from the Thai dispute, concluding that Thai practice could represent the beginnings of either mere interpretation or outright modification of treaty obligations through subsequent state practice. If the normative precedents represent merely an interpretation of TRIPS, the appropriate paradigm would be a TRIPS-Minimum model. On the other hand, normative precedents that appear to modify treaty obligations through subsequent practice would describe a TRIPS-Plus scenario.

Return must be made to the normative precedents themselves, outlined in sections 3.1.1 to 3.1.3, above. The two strongest normative precedents arising from the Thai dispute are, first, that article 31(b) requiring compulsory licences to be issued *either* in the context of a national emergency *or* for public non-commercial use has arguably become a requirement for both criteria, and second, that a national emergency has arguably become an objective definition rather than a self-definition, as clarified by the Doha Declaration.

Any requirement for the dual preconditions of national emergency and public non-commercial use would seem at odds with the ordinary meaning of article 31(b). Further, for a definition of national emergency to take on universally recognized parameters seems at odds with the Doha Declaration. As such, it would appear as a tentative conclusion that the normative precedents in question represent potential modification of treaty obligations through subsequent practice, rather than mere interpretation, and are best described as TRIPS-Plus-like requirements.[55]

Legal taxonomy aside, however, the establishment of normative precedents for usage of article 31(b) depends on the trajectory of the larger access to essential medicines context, where notions of a right to health are pitted against necessary protections for research and development.

[55] This is not to take away from the possibility that these precedents could be established through subsequent practice including and following from the Thai dispute. Even in cases where the Doha Declaration as subsequent agreement and subsequent state practice are at odds, it is the latter in time which may form binding international law authority.

4. Beyond TRIPS: the politics of access to essential medicines disputes

This section considers recent political trends in access to essential medicines disputes, and attempts to place article 31(b) usage in a broader context.

4.1 Political will as currency

Legally, Thailand's usage of article 31(b) does not mean much for the article 31*bis* mechanism for accessing essential medicines, beyond shared interpretations of TRIPS terminology. Article 31*bis* has its own discrete set of guidelines governing compulsory licensing of generic drugs on behalf of member nations without manufacturing capacity.

Thailand's invocation of article 31(b) (followed by Brazil soon after) has, however, unsettled the political context surrounding the access to essential medicines debate, and may well change the political environment in which the article 31*bis* mechanism was intended to operate.

Politically the compulsory licensing uses by both Thailand and Brazil came after years of blustering from both sides. Brazil and Thailand have led the way in negotiating lower prices from patent holders by threatening use of compulsory licensing under article 31.[56]

Quickly following Thailand's example, the Brazilian Ministry of Health issued a compulsory licence for Merck's ARV Efavirenz on 25 April 2007.[57] Together with recent permissive Indian High Court decisions[58] that seem to balk at unquestioning implementation of the 2005 TRIPS deadlines, the context begins to take on the characteristics of a middle-class revolt in the area of essential medicines.

The political fallout of Thailand's actions is uncertain. Leading public health advocates have called for more of the same, suggesting that such unilateral national action will loosen the constriction of TRIPS

[56] See timelines associated with the Thailand and Brazil compulsory licensing disputes: www.cptech.org/ip/health/ at 20 March 2009.

[57] Tove Gerhardsen, 'Brazil Takes Steps to Import Cheaper AIDS Drug under Trade Law' *Intellectual Property Watch*, 7 May 2007, www.ip-watch.org/weblog/index.php?p=614 at 20 March 2009.

[58] Tatum Anderson, 'India Cancer Patients Seek to Use Courts for Access to Patented Drugs', *Intellectual Property Watch*, 3 April 2003, www.ip-watch.org/ at 11 February 2009. For analysis, see Radhika Bhattacharya, 'Are Developing Countries Going Too Far on TRIPS? A Closer Look at the New Laws in India' (2008) 34 *American Journal of Law and Medicine* 413.

requirements in the essential medicines context.[59] On the other hand, the resultant USTR penalties along with Abbott's punitive reaction to Thailand's compulsory licences suggest that the result could be to tighten, rather than restrict, the intellectual property environment. It will likely take several iterations of case studies such as Thailand's to understand the legal and political parameters that will evolve around use of article 31(b). Pragmatically, these parameters may often be context specific, varying with the political and economic clout of the particular country, together with variables related to other trade interests negotiated in parallel.[60]

The most important ongoing variable may be the political will associated with an essential medicines solution. To date this political will has been tied together by civil society. Despite the discrete aims of articles 31(b) and 31*bis*, civil society's support for Thailand's unilateral approach may be in part fuelled by the stagnation of article 31*bis* as a collective access to essential medicines solution.[61] However, in Thailand's case, ongoing political will may be affected by the shape of continued uses of compulsory licensing under article 31(b). In March of 2008, after initial vacillation, a new Thai Health Minister bowed to public pressure and declared implementation of compulsory licences for three new cancer drugs.[62] A microcosm of the conflicted political response to Thailand's unilateral initiatives is illustrated by the EU's response.

4.2 'The EU divide': consternation and compatibility

The executive (EU Commission) and legislative (EU Parliament) branches of the EU are publicly at odds in their approach to Thailand's compulsory

[59] See, e.g., James Love quoted in Keith Alcorn, 'Brazil Issues Compulsory License on Efavirenz', *Aidsmap*, 7 May 2007, www.aidsmap.com/news at 20 March 2009: 'James Love of Knowledge Ecology International, an organisation which is promoting alternative approaches to intellectual property and public health, predicted that "with Brazil and Thailand expanding the market for generic versions of Efavirenz, greater economies of scale should push prices down further, eventually to less than $0.24 per day".'

[60] Article 31(b) of the TRIPS Agreement dealing with compulsory licensing could become a bargaining chip for both sides in ongoing Free Trade Agreements. For information on the stalled Thailand–United States Free Trade Agreement, see www.cptech.org/ip/health/c/thailand/us-thai-fta.html at 20 March 2009.

[61] For a description of the limited successes of article 31*bis*, see Matthew Rimmer, 'Race against Time: The Export of Essential Medicines to Rwanda' (2008) 1 *Public Health Ethics* 89.

[62] Reuters, 'Thailand Will Override Cancer Drug Patents', *Reuters* (10 March 2008), www.reuters.com/article/healthNews/idUSBKK14764720080310 at 20 March 2009.

licensing initiatives.[63] Trade Commissioner Mandelson's communication with Thailand drew a reprimand from the Parliament.[64] In addition to formalizing legislation enacting the Permanent Amendment, the EU Parliament passed a resolution 'endorsing full implementation of the flexibilities in the TRIPS agreement as recognized in the Doha Declaration'.[65] Simultaneously, the EU Commission continued to apply pressure to Thailand's new Minister of Health to reverse the compulsory licensing practices of the previous regime.[66]

5. Conclusion

Until or unless the WTO Dispute Panel is recruited, interpretation of article 31(b) will remain a fluid process, heavily shaped by the early examples set by Thailand and Brazil. The justifications adopted by Thailand surrounding article 31(b) compulsory licence use create normative precedents that could result in significant legal effects on further use. Legal rigidification of precedent through further state practice has always been tethered to political will, but perhaps in this area uniquely relies upon the advocacy of civil society that disproportionately informs state practice.[67] Ellen 't Hoen, Director of Médecins sans Frontières, describes the Thai compulsory licensing dispute as 'taking international law into uncharted territory'.[68] The ways in which the normative precedents evident in the Thai dispute are given legal meaning could represent a tipping point for any further direction in the area of intellectual property and essential medicines, giving urgency for thoughtful engagement to essential medicines advocates as well as middle-income states.

63 David Cronin, 'EU Split over Thai Effort to Obtain Cheaper Patented Drugs', *Intellectual Property Watch*, 5 September 2007, www.ip-watch.org/weblog/index.php?p=732&res=1024_ff&print=0 at 15 April 2009.

64 David Cronin, 'European Parliament Set to Reprimand Mandelson for Pressuring Thailand', *IP Watch*, 9 May 2008, www.ip-watch.org/weblog/index.php?p=1032 at 20 March 2009.

65 EU Parliament Resolution of 12 July 2007 on TRIPS Agreement and Access to Medicines, P6_TA(2007) 0353, [I], www.europarl.europa.eu/ at 20 March 2009.

66 David Cronin, 'EU Decries Thailand for Using Licensing to Get Medicine', *IP Health*, 2 March 2008.

67 For further commentary on the role of civil society, see Noah Benjamin Novogrodsky, 'Beyond TRIPS: The Role of Non-State Actors and Access to Essential Medicines', in Thomas Pogge, Matthew Rimmer and Kim Rubenstein (eds.), *Incentives for Global Public Health: Patent Law and Access to Essential Medicines*, (2010), 343.

68 Ellen 't Hoen, 'Undermining TRIPS', above n. 24.

BIBLIOGRAPHY

Books/Monographs/Journal Articles

Abbott, Frederick, 'Intellectual Property Provisions of Bilateral and Regional Trade Agreements in Light of U.S. Federal Law' (2006) *United Nations Conference on Trade and Development – International Centre for Trade and Sustainable Development Issue Paper No 12*, www.ictsd.org/pubs/index.htm at 27 January 2009.

'Intellectual Property Rights in a Global Trade Framework: IP Trends in Developing Countries' (2004) 98 *American Society of International Law and Procedure* 95.

'Managing the Hydra: The Herculean Task of Ensuring Access to Essential Medicines' in Keith Maskus and Jerome Reichman (eds.), *International Public Goods and Transfer of Technology under a Globalized Intellectual Property Regime* (Cambridge University Press, 2005), 393–424.

'The Doha Declaration on the TRIPS Agreement and Public Health and the Contradictory Trend in Bilateral and Regional Free Trade Agreements' (Quaker United Nations Office Occasional Paper No 14, 2004) www.quno.org at 28 January 2009.

'The Doha Declaration on the TRIPS Agreement and Public Health: Lighting a Dark Corner at the WTO' (2002) 5 *Journal of International Economic Law* 469.

'The WTO Medicines Decision: World Pharmaceutical Trade and the Protection of Public Health' (2005) 99 *The American Journal of International Law* 317.

'Toward a New Era of Objective Assessment in the Field of TRIPS and Variable Geometry for the Preservation of Multilateralism' (2005) 8 *Journal of International Economic Law* 77.

Abbott, Frederick and Graham Dukes, *Global Pharmaceutical Policy: Ensuring Medicines for Tomorrow's World* (Cheltenham and Northampton, MA: Edward Elgar, 2009).

Abbott, Frederick and Jerome Reichman, 'The Doha Round's Public Health Legacy: Strategies for the Protection and Diffusion of Patented Medicines under the Amended TRIPS Provisions' (2007) 10(4) *Journal of International Economic Law* 921.

Abramowicz, Michael, 'Perfecting Patent Prizes' (2003) 56 *Vanderbilt Law Review* 115.

AIDS-Free World, www.aids-freeworld.org/.

Alcorn, Keith, 'Brazil Issues Compulsory License on Efavirenz', *Aidsmap* (7 May 2007) www.aidsmap.com/news at 20 March 2009.

Allarakhia, Minna and Anthony Wensley, 'Systems Biology: A Disruptive Biopharmaceutical Research Paradigm' (2006) 74 *Technological Forecasting and Social Change* 1643.

Anand, Sudhir, Fabienne Peter and Amartya Sen, *Public Health, Ethics and Equity* (Oxford University Press, 2005).

Anderson, Tatum, 'India Cancer Patients Seek to Use Courts for Access to Patented Drugs', *Intellectual Property Watch*, 3 April 2003, www.ip-watch.org/weblog/2008/04/03/india-cancer-patients-seek-to-use-courts-for-access-to-patented-drugs/ at 11 February 2009.

Anderson, Tatum, 'Rejected Novartis Cases Leave India's TRIPS Compliance Unchallenged', (7 August 2007) *Intellectual Property Watch*, www.ip-watch.org/weblog/index.php?p=712 at 20 March 2009.

Angell, Marcia, *The Truth about the Drug Companies: How They Deceive Us and What to Do about It* (New York: Random House, 2004).

Anonymous, 'Discretion and Legitimacy in International Regulation' (1993–4) 107 *Harvard Law Review* 1099.

Antras, Pol, Mihir Desai and Fritz Foley, 'Multinational Firms, FDI Flows and Imperfect Capital Markets' (Working Paper No W12855, National Bureau of Economic Research, 2007).

Aoki, Keith, 'Weeds, Seeds and Deeds: Recent Skirmishes in the Seed Wars' (2003) 11 *Cardozo Journal of International and Comparative Law* 247.

Aoki, Reiko and Sadao Nagaoka, 'The Consortium Standard and Patent Pools' (2004) 55 *The Economic Review* 345.

Arup, Christopher, 'TRIPS as Competitive and Cooperative Interpretation' in Justin Malbon and Charles Lawson (eds.), *Interpreting and Implementing the TRIPS Agreement* (Cheltenham and Northampton, MA: Edward Elgar, 2008)

Asongu, J. J., 'Generating Sustainable Funds through Branding: RED Campaign Introduces New Business Model for CSR' (2007) 1(1) *Journal of Business and Public Policy* 1.

Associated Press, 'WHO: Flesh-Eating Disease Making Comeback', FoxNews.com (online), 25 January 2007.

Aymé, Ségolène, Gert Matthijs and Sirpa Sioni, 'Patenting and Licensing in Genetic Testing' (2008) 16 *European Journal of Human Genetics* 53.

Babcock, Charles and Ceci Connolly, 'AIDS Activists Badger Gore Again', *The Washington Post*, 18 June 1999.

Baker, Brook, 'A Deconstruction of Novartis's Defense of its Challenge to the India Patent Regime', *Consumer Project on Technology*, 7 February 2007, www.cptech.org/ip/health/c/india/hgap02072007.html at 27 March 2009.

'Arthritic Flexibilities for Accessing Medicines: Analysis of WTO Action Regarding Paragraph 6 of the Doha Declaration on the TRIPS Agreement and Public Health' (2004) 14 *Indiana International and Comparative Law Review* 613.

'GSK Access to Medicines: The Good, the Bad, and the Illusory', *Intellectual Property Health List*, 15 February 2009.

Baker, Brook, Sean Flynn and Judit Rius Sanjuan, 'Premiere Law Firm's Specious Arguments on Thailand's Compulsory Licenses', *IP Health*, 25 April 2007.

Baker, Dean and Noriko Chatani, 'Promoting Good Ideas on Drugs: Are Patents the Best Way? The Relative Efficiency of Patent and Public Support for Bio-Medical Research' (Briefing Paper, Center for Economic and Policy Research, 2002).

Bale, Harvey, 'The Pharmaceutical Industry and Corporate Social Responsibility', 2003, *International Federation of Pharmaceutical Manufacturers Associations*, www.responsiblepractice.com/english/insight/ifpma/ at 18 May 2009.

Banda, Chikosa, 'The Transactional Role of Patents: The Case of Product Development Partnerships' (Paper presented at the Global Governance of HIV/AIDS: Intellectual Property and Access to Essential Medicines Conference, University of Liverpool, 8 October 2008).

Bank, Helene, 'Differential Pricing and Politics of Health Development', 25 April 2001, *Third World Network*, www.twnside.org.sg/title/politics.htm at 6 February 2009.

Barder, Owen, Michael Kremer and Heidi Williams, 'Advance Market Commitments: A Policy to Stimulate Investment in Vaccines for Neglected Diseases' (2006) *Economists' Voice*, www.bepress.com/ev at 10 February 2009.

Barfield, Claude, *Free Trade, Sovereignty, Democracy: The Future of the World Trade Organization* (Washington, DC: American Enterprise Institute Press, 2001).

Barré-Sinoussi, Françoise, 'Isolation of a T-lymphotropic Retrovirus from a Patient at Risk for Acquired Immune Deficiency Syndrome (AIDS)' (1983) 220 *Science* 868–71.

Barry, Christian and Matt Peterson, 'Shallow Cuts: GSK's Voluntary Price Reductions and Patent Pooling Are Not Enough' (4 March 2009) *Policy Innovations*, www.policyinnovations.org/ideas/commentary/data/000113.

Bartels, Lorand and Federico Ortino (eds.), *Regional Trade Agreements and the WTO Legal System* (Oxford University Press, 2006).

Barton, John, 'New Trends in Technology Transfer' (Issue Paper No 18, International Centre for Trade and Sustainable Development, 2007).

Basheer, Shamnad, 'India's New Patent Regime: Aiding Access or Abetting Genericide' (2007) 9(2) *International Journal of Biotechnology* 122.

Basheer, Shamnad, 'The "Glivec" Patent Saga: A 3-D Perspective on Indian Patent Policy and Trips Compliance' (2007) ATRIP, www.atrip.org/upload/files/essays/Shamnad%20Basheer%20Glivec%20Patent%20Saga.doc at 11 August 2008.

Basheer, Shamnad and Prashant Reddy, 'The "Efficacy" of Indian Patent Law: Ironing Out the Creases in Section 3(d)' (2008) 5 *Script-ed* 232, www.law.ed.ac.uk/ahrc/script-ed/vol5–2/basheer.asp at 15 January 2009.

Bate, Roger, 'India and the Drug Patent Wars', *Health Policy Outlook* (7 February 2007), www.aei.org/outlook/25566.

Bekelman, Justin and Cary Gross, 'Scope and Impact of Financial Conflicts of Interest in Biomedical Research: A Systematic Review' (2003) 289 *Journal of the American Medical Association* 545.

Benkler, Yochai, *The Wealth of Networks: How Social Production Transforms Markets and Freedom* (New Haven, CT and London: Yale University Press, 2006).

Bennett, Belinda and George Tomossy (eds.), *Globalisation and Health: Challenges for Bioethics and Health Law* (Dordrecht: Springer, 2006).

Benvenisti, Eyal and George Downs, 'The Empire's New Clothes: Political Economy and the Fragmentation of International Law' (2007) 60 *Stanford Law Review* 595.

Berndt, Ernst, Rachel Glennerster, Michael Kremer, Jean Lee, Ruth Levine, Georg Weizsäcker and Heidi Williams, 'Advance Market Commitments for Vaccines against Neglected Diseases: Estimating Costs and Effectiveness' (2007) 16 *Health Economics* 491.

Bernstein, Richard J., *Praxis and Action* (Philadelphia, PA: University of Pennsylvania Press, 1971, new edn, 1991).

Bessen, James and Michael Meurer, *Patent Failure: How Judges, Bureaucrats and Lawyers Put Innovators at Risk* (Princeton University Press, 2008).

Bhattacharya, Radhika, 'Are Developing Countries Going Too Far on TRIPS? A Closer Look at the New Laws in India' (2008) 34 *American Journal of Law and Medicine* 413.

Biehl, João, *Will to Live: AIDS Therapies and the Politics of Survival* (Princeton University Press, 2007).

Boldrin, Michele and David Levine, 'The Case against Intellectual Property' (2002) 92 *American Economic Review* 209.

Bombach, Kara, 'Can South Africa Fight AIDS? Reconciling the South African Medicines and Related Substances Act with the TRIPS Agreement' (2001) 19(2) *Boston University International Law Journal* 273.

Bono, 'Message 2U: Editorial', *Vanity Fair*, July 2007.

'Product (RED)', 12 October 2006; reprinted at action.one.org/blog/?p=195.

Boulding, Kenneth, 'Foreword', in Norman Myers (ed.), *The Gaia Atlas of Future Worlds: Challenge and Opportunity in an Age of Change* (New York: Anchor Books/Doubleday, 1990).

Bourdieu, Pierre, *Outline of a Theory of Practice* (Cambridge University Press, 1977).

Bowrey, Kathy, *Law and Internet Cultures* (Cambridge University Press, 2005).

Boyle, James, 'A Manifesto on WIPO and the Future of Intellectual Property' (2004) 9 *Duke Law and Technology Review* 1–12, www.law.duke.edu/journals/dltr/articles/pdf/2004DLTR0009.pdf.

The Public Domain: Enclosing the Commons of the Mind (New Haven, CT and London: Yale University Press, 2008).

Braga, Carlos Alberto Primo, Carsten Fink and Claudia Paz Sepulveda, *Intellectual Property Rights and Economic Development* (Washington, DC: World Bank, 2000).

Brody, William, 'The Uncensored Idea', in William Brody (ed.), *The Crossroads: Essays on Health Care in Modern America* (Baltimore, MD: Johns Hopkins University, 2008).

(ed.), *The Crossroads: Essays on Health Care in Modern America* (Baltimore, MD: Johns Hopkins University, 2008).

Bronckers, Marco, 'The Impact of TRIPS: Intellectual Property Protection in Developing Countries' (1994) 31 *Common Market Law Review* 1245.

Broude, Tomer, *International Governance in the WTO: Judicial Boundaries and Political Capitulation* (London: Cameron, 2004).

Broude, Tomer and Yuval Shany (eds.), *The Shifting Allocation of Authority in International Law* (Oxford and Portland, ME: Hart Publishing, 2008).

Brydon, Lynne and Karen Legge, *Adjusting Society: The World Bank, the IMF and Ghanaians* (London: I. B. Tauris, 1996).

Burk, Dan and Mark Lemley, *The Patent Crisis and How Courts Can Solve It*, (University of Chicago Press, 2009).

Burke, Mary Anne and Stephen Matlin, *Monitoring Financial Flows for Health Research: Prioritizing Research for Health Equity* (Geneva: Global Forum for Health Research, 2008).

Cahoy, Daniel, 'Treating the Legal Side Effects of Cipro: A Reevaluation of Compensation Rules for Government Takings of Patent Rights' (2002) 40 *American Business Law Journal* 125.

Cairns, John, Jr, 'Defining Goals and Conditions for a Sustainable World' (1997) 105 *Environmental Health Perspectives* 1164.

Calandrillo, Steve, 'An Economic Analysis of Property Rights in Information: Justifications and Problems of Exclusive Rights, Incentives to Generate Information, and the Alternative of a Government-Run Reward System' (1998) 9 *Fordham Intellectual Property, Media & Entertainment Law Journal* 301.

Cameron, Edwin and Jonathan Berger, 'Patents and Public Health: Principle, Politics and Paradox' (2005) 131 *Proceedings of the British Academy* 331.

Carey, Benedict, 'Is Prozac Better? Is It Even Different?', *The New York Times*, 21 September 2004.

Carlsen, Laura, *Timely Demise for Free Trade Area of the Americas* (23 November 2005) Americas Program, Center for International Policy, americas.irc-online.org/am/2954 at 2 February 2009.

Carlson, Steven, 'Patent Pools and the Antitrust Dilemma' (1999) 16 *Yale Journal on Regulation* 359.

Cass, Deborah, *The Constitutionalization of the World Trade Organization: Legitimacy, Democracy, and Community in the International Trading System* (Oxford University Press, 2005).

Cassier, Maurice, 'Private Property, Collective Property, and Public Property in the Age of Genomics' (2002) 54(171) *International Social Sciences Journal* 83.

Castellano, Richard, 'Patent Law for New Medical Uses of Known Compounds and Pfizer's Viagra Patent' (2006) 46 *IDEA* 283.

Cattand, Pierre, Phillippe Desjeux, M. G. Guzmãn, Jean Jannin, A. Kroeger, André Medici, Philip Musgrove, Mike B. Nathan, Aleandra Shaw and C. J. Schofield, 'Tropical Diseases Lacking Adequate Control Measures: Dengue, Leishmaniasis, and African Trypanosomiasis', in Dean Jamison, Jeol G. Breman, Anthony R. Measam, George Alleyne, Mariam Claeson, David B. Evans, Prabhat Ja, Anne Mills and Philip Musgrove (eds.), *Disease Control Priorities in Developing Countries* (2nd edn, Oxford University Press, 2006) 451.

Centre for Responsive Politics, 'Lobbying – Pharmaceuticals/Health Products: Industry Profile', (2008) www.opensecrets.org/lobby/indusclient.php?lname=H04&year=2008 at 19 February 2009.

'Pharmaceuticals/Health Products: Long-Term Contribution Trends', www.opensecrets.org/industries/indus.php?ind=H04 at 19 February 2009.

Champ, Paul and Amir Attaran, 'Patent Rights and Local Working under the WTO TRIPS Agreement: An Analysis of the U.S.–Brazil Patent Dispute' (2002) 27(2) *The Yale Journal of International Law* 365–93.

Chaudhuri, Sudip, 'Is Product Patent Protection Necessary in Developing Countries for Innovation' (Working Paper No 614, Indian Institute of Management, Calcutta, 2007).

Chayes, Abram, 'The Role of the Judge in Public Law Litigation' (1976) 89 *Harvard Law Review* 1281.

Chayes, Abram and Antonia Chayes, *The New Sovereignty: Compliance with International Regulatory Agreements* (Cambridge, MA: Harvard University Press, 1995).

Cheyne, Ilona, 'Gateways to the Precautionary Principle in WTO Law' (2007) 19 *Journal of Environmental Law* 155.

Chirac, Pierre and Els Toreele, 'Global Framework on Essential Health R&D' (2006) 367 *The Lancet* 1560.

Chokshi, Dave, Michael Parker and Dominic Kwiatkowski, 'Data Sharing and Intellectual Property in Genomic Epidemiology Network: Policies for

Large-Scale Research Collaboration' (2006) 84 *Bulletin of the World Health Organization* 382.

Chon, Margaret, 'Intellectual Property and the Development Divide' (2006) 27 *Cardozo Law Review* 2821.

Clark, Jeanne, Joe Piccolo, Brian Stanton and Karin Tyson, *Patent Pools: A Solution to the Problem of Access in Biotechnology Patents* (Washington, DC: United States Patent and Trademark Office, 2000).

Clemens, Michael and Gunilla Pettersson, 'New Data on African Health Professionals Abroad' (2008) 6(1) *Human Resources for Health*, www.human-resources-health.com/content/6/1/1.

The Clinton Foundation, *Contributor Information*, www.clintonfoundation.org/contributors/index.html at 10 March 2009.

Treating HIV/AIDS & Malaria: Clinton HIV/AIDS Initiative – Our Approach, www.clintonfoundation.org/cf-pgm-hs-ai-home.htm at 10 March 2009.

'William J. Clinton Foundation Publishes Names of All Contributors on Foundation Website' (Press Release, 18 December 2008).

The Clinton Global Initiative, *Our Model*, www.clintonglobalinitiative.org/ at 10 March 2008.

Clinton, William, *Giving: How Each of Us Can Change the World* (London: Hutchinson, 2007).

Clinton, William and Bill Gates, 'Giving: A Conversation between President Clinton and Bill Gates', The Clinton Global Initiative (2008 Annual Meeting Transcript) (24 September 2008), www.clintonglobalinitiative.org/ at 10 March 2009.

Cockburn, Iain, 'The Changing Structure of the Pharmaceutical Industry' (2004) 23 *Health Affairs* 10.

Cockburn, Iain and Rebecca Henderson, 'Public–Private Interaction and the Productivity of Pharmaceutical Research' (Working Paper No 6018, National Bureau of Economic Research, 1997).

Cohen, Jon, 'Gates Foundation Rearranges Public Health Universe' (2002) 295 *Science* 2000.

Cohen, Wesley, Richard Nelson and John Walsh, 'Protecting their Intellectual Assets: Appropriability Conditions and Why U.S. Manufacturing Firms Patent (or Not)' (Working Paper No 7552, National Bureau of Economic Research, 2000).

Cohen-Kohler, Jillian, Lisa Forman and Nathaniel Lipkus, 'Addressing Legal and Political Barriers to Global Pharmaceutical Access: Options for Remedying the Impact of the Agreement on Trade-Related Aspects of Intellectual Property Rights (TRIPS) and the Imposition of TRIPS-Plus Standards' (2008) 3 *Health Economics, Policy and Law* 229.

Collins, Francis, Mark Guyer and Aravinda Chakravarti, 'Variations on a Theme: Cataloguing Human DNA Sequence Variation' (1997) 278 *Science* 1580.

Comanor, William, 'The Political Economy of the Pharmaceutical Industry' (1986) 24 *Journal of Economic Literature* 1178.

Consumer Project on Technology, 'Statement of Information to the Competition Commission of South Africa on Complaint against GlaxoSmithKline and Boehringer Ingelheim' (3 February 2003) www.cptech.org/ip/healthcl/cl-cases/rsa-tac/cptech-statement.doc.

Cook, Malcolm, 'The Bangkok Challenge: From Conflict to Cooperation and Beyond – Outcomes Report' (2007) *The Lowy Institute for International Policy*, 2–5, www.lowyinstitute.org/Publication.asp?pid=612 at 20 March 2009.

Cook, Trevor, 'Regulatory Data Protection in Pharmaceuticals and Other Sectors', in Anatole Krattiger, Richard T. Mahoney, Lita Nelsen, Jennifer A. Thomson, Alan B. Bennett, Kanikaram Satyanarayana, Gregory D. Graff, Carlos Fernandez and Stanley Kowalski (eds.), *Intellectual Property Management in Health and Agricultural Innovation: A Handbook of Best Practices* (Oxford: Centre for the Management of Intellectual Property in Health Research and Development, 2008), 437.

Cook-Deegan, Robert, 'The Science Commons in Health Research: Structure, Function, and Value' (2007) 32 *Journal of Technology Transfer* 133.

Coombe, Rosemary, *The Cultural Life of Intellectual Properties: Authorship, Appropriation, and the Law* (Durham, NC and London: Duke University Press, 1998).

Coote, Anna, *The Welfare of Citizens: Developing New Social Rights* (London: Institute of Public Policy Research, 1992).

Correa, Carlos, 'Implications of Bilateral Free Trade Agreements on Access to Medicines' (2006) 84 *Bulletin of the World Health Organization* 399.

Intellectual Property Rights, the WTO and Developing Countries: The TRIPS Agreement and Policy Options (New York: Zed Books, Third World Network, 2000).

Trade Related Aspects of Intellectual Property Rights: A Commentary on the TRIPS Agreement (Oxford University Press, 2007).

'TRIPS and TRIPS Plus Protection in Latin America' in Daniel Gervais (ed.), *Intellectual Property, Trade and Development* (Oxford University Press, 2007), 221.

Correa, Carlos and Sisule Musungu, 'The WIPO Patent Agenda: The Risks for Developing Countries' (Working Paper No 12, Trade-Related Agenda, Development and Equity, South Centre, 2002).

Courville, Sasha, 'Use of Indicators to Compare Supply Chains in the Coffee Industry' (2004) 43 *Greener Management International* 93.

Cronin, David, 'EU Decries Thailand for Using Licensing to Get Medicine', *Interpress Service*, 2 March 2008.

'EU Split over Thai Effort to Obtain Cheaper Patented Drugs', *Intellectual Property Watch*, 5 September 2007, www.ip-watch.org/weblog/index.php?p=732&res=1024_ff&print=0 at 15 April 2009.

'European Parliament Set to Reprimand Mandelson for Pressuring Thailand', *IP Watch*, 9 May 2008, www.ip-watch.org/weblog/index.php?p=1032 at 20 March 2009.

Cross, Frank, 'The Error of Positive Rights' (2001) 48 *University of California Los Angeles Law Review* 857.

Crump, Andy, *The A-Z of World Development* (Oxford: New Internationalist, 1998).

Currat, Louis, Andrés de Francisco, Sameera Al-Tuwaijri, Abdul Ghaffar and Susan Jupp, *Global Forum Health 10/90 Report 2003–2004* (Geneva: Global Forum for Health Research, 2004).

D'Adesky, Anne-Christine, *Moving Mountains: The Race to Treat Global AIDS* (London and New York: Verso, 2004).

Daniels, Norman, *Just Health: Meeting Health Needs Fairly* (Cambridge University Press, 2007).

Danzon, Patricia and Adrian Towse, 'Theory and Implementation of Differential Pricing for Pharmaceuticals', in Keith Maskus and Jerome Reichman (eds.), *International Public Goods and Transfer of Technology under a Globalized Intellectual Property Regime* (Cambridge University Press, 2005), 425–56.

de Beer, Jeremy (ed.), *Implementing the World Intellectual Property Organization's Development Agenda* (Ottawa: Wilfred Laurier University Press, 2009).

de Carvalho, Nuno Pires, *The TRIPS Regime of Patent Rights* (Alphen aan den Rijn: Kluwer Law International, 2003).

de Francisco, Andrés and Stephen Matlin, *Monitoring Financial Flows for Health Research 2006: The Changing Landscape of Health Research for Development* (Geneva: Global Forum for Health Research, 2006).

DeLano, Warren, 'The Case for Open-Source Software in Drug Discovery' (2005) 10 *Drug Discovery Today* 213.

Demil, Benoit and Xavier Lecocq, 'Neither Market nor Hierarchy nor Network: The Emergence of Bazaar Governance' (2006) 27 *Organization Studies* 1447.

Dennis, Michael J. and David P. Stewart, 'Justiciability of Economic, Social, and Cultural Rights: Should There Be an International Complaints Mechanism to Adjudicate the Rights to Food, Water, Housing, and Health?' (2004) 98 *American Journal of International Law* 462.

Desowitz, Robert, *The Malaria Capers: Tales of Parasites and People* (New York: W.W. Norton, 1991).

Dickson, Michael, Jeremy Hurst and Stephane Jacobzone, *Survey of Pharmacoeconomic Assessment Activity in Eleven Countries* (Health Working Paper No 4, OECD, 2003).

DiMasi, Joseph, Ronald Hansen and Henry Grabowski, 'The Price of Innovation: New Estimates of Drug Development Costs' (2003) 22 *Journal of Health Economics* 151.

DiMasi, Joseph, Ronald Hansen, Henry Grabowski and Louis Lasagna, 'The Cost of Innovation in the Pharmaceutical Industry' (1991) 10 *Journal of Health Economics* 107.

DiMasi, Joseph and Cherie Paquette, 'The Economics of Follow-On Drug Research and Innovation: Trends in Entry Rates and the Timing of Development' (2004) 22 *Pharmacoeconomics* 1.

Dinwoodie, Graeme, 'The International Intellectual Property Law System: New Actors, New Institutions, New Sources' (2004) 8 *Proceedings of the 98th Annual Meeting of the American Society of International Law* 213.

Dinwoodie, Graeme and Rochelle C. Dreyfuss, 'Diversifying without Discriminating: Complying with the Mandates of the TRIPS Agreement' (2007) 13 *Michigan Telecommunication and Technology Law Review* 445.

'Intellectual Property Law and the Public Domain of Science' (2004) 7 *Journal of International Economic Law* 431.

'TRIPS and the Dynamics of International Property Lawmaking' (2004) 36 *Case Western Reserve Journal of International Law* 95.

Dinwoodie, Graeme and Mark Janis (eds.) *Trademark Law and Theory: A Handbook of Contemporary Research* (Cheltenham and Northampton, MA: Edward Elgar, 2008).

DPA, 'Hilary Shocked at Obama's Choice', *The Sydney Morning Herald*, 4 December 2008.

Drahos, Peter, 'An Alternative Framework for the Global Regulation of Intellectual Property Rights' (2005) 21(4) *Journal Für Entwicklungspolitik* 44.

'BITS and BIPS: Bilateralism in Intellectual Property' (2001) 4 *Journal of World Intellectual Property* 791–808.

'Expanding Intellectual Property's Empire: The Role of FTAs' (2003) *International Centre for Trade and Sustainable Development*, ictsd.net/i/ip/24737/ at 2 March 2009.

'Global Property Rights in Information: The Story of TRIPS at the GATT' (1995) 13 *Prometheus* 1.

'Negotiating Intellectual Property Rights: Between Coercion and Dialogue', in Peter Drahos and Ruth Mayne (eds.), *Global Intellectual Property Rights: Knowledge, Access and Development* (New York: Palgrave Macmillan, 2002), 161.

'The Regulation of Public Goods' (2004) 7 *Journal of International Economic Law* 321.

'Weaving Webs of Influence: The United States, Free Trade Agreements and Dispute Resolution' (2007) 41(1) *Journal of World Trade* 191–210.

Drahos, Peter and John Braithwaite, *Information Feudalism: Who Owns the Knowledge Economy?* (London: Earthscan, 2002).

Drahos, Peter and Ruth Mayne (eds.), *Global Intellectual Property Rights: Knowledge, Access and Development* (New York: Palgrave Macmillan, 2002).

Dreyfuss, Rochelle C. 'Expressive Genericity: Trademarks as Language in the Pepsi Generation' (1989–90) 65 *Notre Dame Law Review* 397.

'Reconciling Trademark Rights and Expressive Values: How to Stop Worrying and Learn to Love Ambiguity', in Graeme Dinwoodie and Mark Janis (eds.) *Trademark Law and Theory: A Handbook of Contemporary Research* (Cheltenham, UK and Northampton, MA: Edward Elgar, 2008), 261.

'Regulating Dynamic Innovation in a Complex Political Economy: Administering Intellectual Property on the International Stage' (Paper presented at the CPR and NYU Workshop on Global Regulatory Governance: India, the South and the Shaping of Global Administrative Law, The Ambassador Hotel, New Delhi, 5–6 January 2008).

'TRIPS – Round II: Should Users Strike Back?' (2004) 71 *University of Chicago Law Review* 21.

Dreyfuss, Rochelle C. and Andreas Lowenfeld, 'Two Achievements of the Uruguay Round: Putting TRIPS and Dispute Settlement Together' (1997) 37 *Virginia Journal of International Law* 275.

Dreyfuss, Rochelle C., Diane Zimmerman and Harry First (eds.), *Expanding the Boundaries of Intellectual Property: Innovation Policy for the Knowledge Society* (Oxford University Press, 2001).

Drugs for Neglected Diseases Working Group, *Fatal Imbalance: The Crisis in Research and Development for Drugs for Neglected Diseases* (Geneva: Médecins Sans Frontières and Drugs for Neglected Diseases Working Group, 2001) (also at www.msf.org/source/access/2001/fatal/fatal.pdf).

Duke University, 'Duke Faculty Propose Incentives for Developing Drugs for Neglected Diseases', Duke University, 7 March 2006.

Easterbrook, Frank, 'Who Decides the Extent of Rights in Intellectual Property?', in Rochelle C. Dreyfuss, Diane Zimmerman and Harry First (eds.), *Expanding the Boundaries of Intellectual Property: Innovation Policy for the Knowledge Society* (Oxford University Press 2001), 405.

Ebersole, Ted, Marvin Guthrie and Jorge Goldstein, 'Patent Pools and Standard Setting in Diagnostic Genetics' (2005) 23 *Nature Biotechnology* 937.

Editorial, 'Editorial' (2008) 12(16) *Bridges Weekly Trade News Digest* 7.

Editorial, 'Health Cheques' (2007) 447 *Nature* 231.

Editorial, 'India's Choice', *The New York Times*, 18 January 2005.

Edwards, Aled, 'Open-Source Science to Enable Drug Discovery' (2008) 13 *Drug Discovery Today* 731.

Ehin, Piret, 'Competing Models of EU Legitimacy: The Test of Popular Expectations' (2008) 46 *Journal of Common Market Studies* 619.

Ehlerman, Claus-Dieter and Lothar Ehring, 'Decision-Making in the World Trade Organization' (2005) 8 *Journal of International Economic Law* 51.

'The Authoritative Interpretation under Article IX:2 of the Agreement Establishing the World Trade Organization: Current Law, Practice and

Possible Improvements' (2005) 8 *Journal of International Economic Law* 803.

Eisenberg, Rebecca, 'Patents and the Progress of Science: Exclusive Rights and Experimental Use' (1989) 56 *University of Chicago Law Review* 1017.

Eisenberg, Rebecca and Richard Nelson, 'Public vs. Proprietary Science: A Fruitful Tension?' (2002) 77 *Academic Medicine* 1392.

Elliott, Richard, 'Delivery Past Due: Global Precedent Set under Canada's Access to Medicines Regime' (2008) 13(1) *Canadian HIV/AIDS Policy and Law Review* 1.

'Steps Forward, Backward, and Sideways: Canada's Bill on Exporting Generic Pharmaceuticals' (2004) 9(3) *Canadian HIV/AIDS Policy and Law Review* 1.

'TRIPS from Doha to Cancún ... to Ottawa: Global Developments in Access to Treatment and Canada's Bill C-56' (2003) 8(3) *Canadian HIV/AIDS Policy and Law Review* 1.

Endeshaw, Assafa, 'Free Trade Agreements as Surrogates for TRIPs-Plus' (2006) 28 *European Intellectual Property Review* 374.

Epstein, Helen, *The Invisible Cure: Africa, the West, and the Fight against AIDS* (New York: Farrar, Straus and Giroux, 2007).

Essential Inventions, Inc., *Essential Medical Inventions Licensing Agency Working Plan – June 2008* (rev. 17 July 2008), www.keionline.org/index.php?option=com_content&task=view&id=63&Itemid=1 at 2 March 2009.

Essential Patent Pool for AIDS (EPPA): Background Information (2005), www.essentialinventions.org/docs/eppa/ at 26 February 2009.

Esty, Daniel, 'Good Governance at the Supranational Scale: Globalizing Administrative Law' (2006) 115 *Yale Law Journal* 1490.

European Centre for Disease Prevention and Control, *Interim ECDC Scientific and Public Health Briefing: Sharing Influenza Virus Samples* (2008), ecdc.europa.eu/pdf/ECDC_influenza_briefing.pdf at 9 March 2009.

Evans, Gail, 'Strategic Patent Licensing for Public Research Organizations: Deploying Restriction and Reservation Clauses to Promote Medical R&D in Developing Countries' (2008) 34(2–3) *American Journal of Law and Medicine* 175–223.

Ewelukwa, Uche, 'Patent Wars in the Valley of the Shadow of Death: The Pharmaceutical Industry, Ethics and Global Trade' (2005) 59 *University of Miami Law Review* 203.

Farmer, Paul, 'From "Marvelous Momentum" to Health Care for All' (2007) 86 *Foreign Affairs* 155.

Pathologies of Power: Health, Human Rights, and the New War on the Poor (Berkeley, CA and London: University of California Press, 2005).

Faunce, Thomas, 'Global Intellectual Property Protection for Innovative Pharmaceuticals: Challenges for Bioethics and Health Law', in Belinda

Bennett and George Tomossy (eds.), *Globalisation and Health: Challenges for Bioethics and Health Law* (Dordrecht: Springer, 2006), 87.

'Reference Pricing for Pharmaceuticals: Is the Australia–United States Free Trade Agreement Affecting Australia's Pharmaceutical Benefits Scheme?' (2007) 187 *Medical Journal of Australia* 240.

'Toward a Treaty on Safety and Cost-Effectiveness of Pharmaceuticals and Medical Devices: Enhancing an Endangered Global Public Good' (2006) 2 *Globalization and Health* 5.

Who Owns our Health?: Medical Professionalism, Law and Leadership beyond the Age of the Market State (Sydney: University of New South Wales Press, 2007).

Faunce, Thomas, Evan Doran, David Henry, Peter Drahos, Andrew Searles, Brita Pekarsky and Warwick Neville, 'Assessing the Impact of the Australia–United States Free Trade Agreement on Australian and Global Medicines Policy' (2005) 1(15) *Globalisation and Health* 1.

Faunce, Thomas and Joel Lexchin, 'Linkage Pharmaceutical Evergreening in Canada and Australia' (2007) 4 *Australian and New Zealand Journal of Health Policy* 8.

Faunce, Thomas and Hitoshi Nasu, 'Three Proposals for Rewarding Novel Health Technologies Benefitting People Living in Poverty: A Comparative Analysis of Prize Funds, Health Impact Funds and a Cost-Effectiveness/Competitive Tender Treaty' (2008) 1(2) *Public Health Ethics* 146.

Feachem, Richard, 'The Global Fund Welcomes RED' (Press Release, 26 January 2006), www.joinred.com/news/press-release.asp?145141242006 at 10 March 2009.

Feinberg, Richard, 'The Political Economy of United States' Free Trade Arrangements' (2003) 26 *World Economy* 1019.

Feldstein, Martin, 'How Big Should Government Be?' (1997) 50 *National Tax Journal* 197.

Feller, Joseph, Brian Fitzgerald, Scott Hissam and Karim Lakhani (eds.), *Perspectives on Free and Open Source Software* (Cambridge, MA: MIT Press, 2005).

Fidler, David, 'Fighting the Axis of Illness: HIV/AIDS, Human Rights and US Foreign Policy' (2004) 17 *Harvard Human Rights Journal* 99.

Finger, J. Michael and Philip Schuler (eds.), *Poor People's Knowledge: Promoting Intellectual Property in Developing Countries* (Washington, DC: The World Bank, 2004), 75.

Fink, Carsten, *Intellectual Property and Public Health: An Overview of the Debate with a Focus on US Policy* (Washington, DC: Center for Global Development, 2008).

'Intellectual Property Rights and US and German International Transactions in Manufacturing Industries' (Manuscript, The World Bank, 1997).

Fink, Carsten and Keith Maskus (eds.), *Intellectual Property and Development: Lessons from Recent Economic Research* (Washington, DC: The World Bank, 2005).

Fink, Carsten and Patrick Reichenmiller, 'Tightening TRIPS: The Intellectual Property Provisions of Recent US Free Trade Agreements' (2005) 20 *The World Bank Trade Note*, siteresources.worldbank.org/INTRANETTRADE/Resources/Pubs/TradeNote20.pdf at 23 January 2009.

Fischer-Lescano, Andreas and Gunther Teubner (Michelle Everson, trans.), 'Regime-Collisions: The Vain Search for Legal Unity in the Fragmentation of Global Law' (2004) 25 *Michigan Journal of International Law* 999.

Fisher, William W., *Promises to Keep: Technology, Law, and the Future of Entertainment* (Stanford University Press, 2004).

Fisher, William W. and Talha Syed, *Drugs, Law, and the Health Crisis in the Developing World* (Stanford: Stanford University Press, 2010, forthcoming).

'Global Justice in Health Care: Developing Drugs for the Developing World' (2007) 40 *University of California Davis Law Review* 581.

Fleishman, Joel, *The Foundation: A Great American Secret; How Private Money Is Changing the World* (New York: Public Affairs, 2007).

Flynn, Sean, Aidan Hollis and Mike Palmedo, 'An Economic Justification for Open Access to Essential Medicine Patents in Developing Countries' (2009) 37 *Journal of Law, Medicine & Ethics* 184.

Fontanarosa, Phil, Rennie Drummond and Catherine DeAngelis, 'Postmarketing Surveillance: Lack of Vigilance, Lack of Trust' (2002) 292 *Journal of the American Medical Association* 2647.

Forbath, William, 'The "Transformative Constitution": Treatment Action Campaign and the Politics of Social Rights in South Africa' (Working Paper, 8 October 2008), ssrn.com/abstract=1292879 at 2 March 2009.

Forman, Lisa, 'Incentivizing Justice: Linking Human Rights, Trade and Access to Medicines' (MCIS Briefings, Comparative Program on Health and Society Lupina Foundation Working Papers Series, 2005–6).

'Trade Rules, Intellectual Property, and the Right to Health' (2007) 21 *Ethics and International Affairs* 337.

Forsythe, David P. and Eric A. Heinze, 'On the Margins of the Human Rights Discourse', in Rhoda E. Howard-Hassman and Claude E. Welch Jr (eds.), *Economic Rights in Canada and the United States* (Philadelphia, PA: University of Pennsylvania Press, 2006), 55, 69.

Francis, Nic, *The End of Charity: Time for Social Enterprise* (Sydney: Allen & Unwin, 2008).

Franck, Thomas, 'Can the United States Delegate Aspects of Sovereignty to International Regimes?', in Thomas Franck (ed.), *Delegating State Powers: The Effect of Treaty Regimes on Democracy and Sovereignty* (New York: Transnational Publishers, 2000).

(ed.), *Delegating State Powers: The Effect of Treaty Regimes on Democracy and Sovereignty* (New York: Transnational Publishers, 2000).

The Power of Legitimacy among Nations (New York: Oxford University Press, 1990).

Frankel, Susy, 'A Patentable Invention: Will Current Proposed Law Reform Clarify Patentable Subject Matter?' (2005) *New Zealand Business Law Quarterly* 350.

Frazier, Mya, 'Costly RED Campaign Reaps Meager $18 Million: Bono & Co. Spend Up to $100 Million on Marketing, Incur Watchdogs' Wrath', *Advertising Age* (New York), 5 March 2007.

Freckleton, Ian and Hugh Selby (eds.) *Appealing to the Future: Michael Kirby and his Legacy* (Sydney: Law Book Co., 2009).

Frost & Sullivan Asia Pacific, *The Asian Generic Pharmaceutical Market* (2002), pharmalicensing.com at 5 February 2009.

The Generic Invasion – An Inside Scoop to the Pot of Gold (2003), pharmalicensing.com at 5 February 2009.

Fuller, Lon L. 'The Forms and Limits of Adjudication' (1978) 92 *Harvard Law Review* 353.

Gallini, Nancy, 'Patent Policy and Costly Imitation' (1992) 23 *Randal Journal of Economics* 52.

Gallini, Nancy and Suzanne Scotchmer, 'Intellectual Property: When Is It the Best Incentive System?' (Working Paper No E01–303, University of California, Berkeley, Department of Economics, 2001).

Gallo, Robert, 'Statement', *New Scientist*, 7 October 2008, www.newscientist.com/commenting/thread?id=dn14881–4.

Gallo, Robert and Luc Montagnier, 'Prospects for the Future' (2002) 298 *Science* 1730–1.

Gallo, Robert, S. Z. Salahuddin, M. Papovic *et al.*, 'Frequent Detection and Isolation of Cytopathic Retroviruses (HTLV-III) from Patients with AIDS and at Risk for AIDS' (1984) 224 *Science* 500–3.

Gargarella, Robert, Pilar Domingo and Theunis Roux (eds.), *Courts and Social Transformation in New Democracies: An Institutional Voice for the Poor* (Aldershot and Burlington, CA: Ashgate, 2006).

Garrett, Laurie, *The Coming Plague* (New York: Farrar, Straus and Giroux, 1994).

Garrett, Laurie and David Fidler, 'Sharing H5N1 Viruses to Stop a Global Influenza Pandemic' (2007) 4(11) *Public Library of Science Medicine* 1712, doi:10.1371/journal.pmed.0040330 at 9 March 2009.

Gates, Bill, 'Making Capitalism More Creative', *Time Magazine*, 31 July 2008.

'Remarks at the World Health Assembly' (Speech delivered at the 58th World Health Assembly, Geneva, Switzerland, 16 May 2005), www.who.int/mediacentre/events/2005/wha58/gates/en/index.html at 10 March 2009.

Gathii, James Thou, 'The Legal Status of the Doha Declaration on TRIPS and Public Health under the Vienna Convention on the Law of Treaties' (2002) 15 *Harvard Journal of Law and Technology* 291.

Gaulé, Patrick, 'Towards Patent Pools in Biotechnology?' (2006) 2 *Innovation Strategy Today* 123.

Gauri, Varun and Daniel M. Brinks (eds.), *Courting Social Justice: Judicial Enforcement of Social and Economic Rights in the Developing World* (Cambridge University Press, 2008).

Geiger, Christophe, Jonathan Griffiths and Reto Hilty, 'Towards a Balanced Interpretation of the "Three-Step Test" in Copyright Law' (2008) 30(12) *European Intellectual Property Review* 489.

Gerhardsen, Tove, 'Brazil Takes Steps to Import Cheaper AIDS Drug under Trade Law', *Intellectual Property Watch* (7 May 2007), www.ip-watch.org/weblog/index.php?p=614 at 20 March 2009.

Gervais, Daniel (ed.), *Intellectual Property, Trade and Development: Strategies to Optimize Economic Development in a TRIPS-Plus Era* (Oxford University Press, 2007).

The TRIPS Agreement: Drafting History and Analysis (2nd edn, London: Sweet & Maxwell, 2003).

Gilbert, Richard, 'Antitrust for Patent Pools: A Century of Policy Evolution' (2004) *Stanford Technology Law Review* 3.

Gillespie, Alexander, 'Common Property, Private Property and Equity: Clash of Values and the Quest to Preserve Biodiversity' (1995) 12 *Environmental and Planning Law Journal* 388.

Gilson, Lucy, 'The Lessons of User Fee Experience in Africa' (1997) 12 *Health Policy and Planning* 273.

Global Ethics Monitor, 'Corporate Responsibility News', www.globalethicsmonitor.com at 9 February 2009.

Global Forum for Health Research, *The 10/90 Report on Health Research 2003–2004* (Geneva: Global Forum for Health Research, 2004), www.globalforumhealth.org at 16 February 2009.

The Global Fund to Fight AIDS, Tuberculosis, and Malaria, *Pledges and Donations*, www.theglobalfund.org/en/funds_raised/pledges/ at 10 March 2009.

Goetz, Thomas, 'Bill Gates on Pharmaceuticals: The System Isn't Working', *Wired Science* (22 April 2008), blog.wired.com/wiredscience/2008/04/bill-gates-what.html at 10 March 2009.

Gold, Richard, Tina Piper, Jean-Frédéric Morin, L. Karen Durell, Julie Carbone and Elisa Henry, *Preliminary Legal Review of Proposed Medicines Patent Pool* (Montreal: The Innovation Partnership, 2007).

Goldsmith, Jack and Eric Posner, *The Limits of International Law* (Oxford University Press, 2005).

Gostin, Lawrence, *The AIDS Pandemic: Complacency, Injustice, and Unfulfilled Expectations* (Chapel Hill, NC: The University of North Carolina Press, 2006).

Grabowski, Henry, David Ridley and Jeffrey Moe, *Priority Review Vouchers to Encourage Innovation for Neglected Diseases* (Harvard Law School, 2008), www.law.harvard.edu/programs/petrie-flom/workshops_conferences/2008_workshops/Grabowski.pdf.

Grabowski, Henry and John Vernon, *The Regulation of Pharmaceuticals: Balancing the Benefits and Risks* (Washington, DC: American Enterprise Institute, 1983).

Grady, Mark and Jay Alexander, 'Patent Law and Rent Dissipation' (1992) 78 *Virginia Law Review* 305.

Greig, Donald, *Invalidity and the Law of Treaties* (London: British Institute of International and Comparative Law, 2006).

Grubb, Michael, Matthias Koch, Abby Munson, Francis Sullivan and Koy Thomson (eds.), *The Earth Summit Agreements: A Guide and Assessment* (Washington DC: Brookings Institution Press, 1993).

Guell, Robert and Marvin Fischbaum, 'Toward Allocative Efficiency in the Prescription Drug Industry' (1995) 73 *Milbank Quarterly* 213.

Gurry, Francis, *WIPO's New Director General Outlines Challenges and Priorities* (Geneva: World Intellectual Property Organization, 22 September 2008), www.wipo.int/about-wipo/en/dgo/dg_gurry_acceptance_speech_2008.html.

Hafner, Katie, 'And if You Liked the Movie, a Netflix Contest May Reward You Handsomely', *The New York Times*, 2 October 2006.

Halbert, Debora, 'The World Intellectual Property Organization: Past, Present and Future' (2007) 54 *Journal of the Copyright Society of the USA* 253.

Hancher, Leigh and Michael Moran (eds.), *Capitalism, Culture, and Economic Regulation* (Oxford: Clarendon Press, 1989).

Hancher, Leigh and Michael Moran, 'Organizing Regulatory Space', in Leigh Hancher and Michael Moran (eds.), *Capitalism, Culture, and Economic Regulation* (Oxford: Clarendon Press, 1989), 271.

Harford, Tim, 'Cash for Answers', *Financial Times Magazine*, 26 January 2008.

Heathcote, Sarah, 'Les biens publics mondiaux et le droit international: quelques réflexions à propos de la gestion de l'intérêt commun' (2002) 13 *L'Observateur des Nations Unies* 137.

Hein, Wolfgang and Lars Kohlmorgan, 'Global Health Governance: Conflicts on Global Social Rights' (2008) 8 *Global Health Policy* 80.

Helfer, Laurence, 'Regime Shifting: The TRIPS Agreement and New Dynamics of International Intellectual Property Lawmaking' (2004) 29 *Yale Journal of International Law* 1.

'Toward a Human Rights Framework for Intellectual Property' (2007) 40 *University of California Davis Law Review* 971.

Heller, Michael, *The Gridlock Economy: How Too Much Ownership Wrecks Markets, Stops Innovation and Costs Lives* (New York: Basic Books, 2008).

Heller, Michael and Rebecca Eisenberg, 'Can Patents Deter Innovation? The Anticommons in Biomedical Research' (1998) 280 *Science* 698.

Hellman, Hal, *Great Feuds in Medicine: Ten of the Liveliest Disputes Ever* (New York: John Wiley & Sons, 2001).

Henkin, Louis, *Constitutionalism, Democracy and Foreign Affairs* (New York: Columbia University Press, 1990).

Hestermeyer, Holger, *Human Rights and the WTO: The Case of Patents and Access to Medicines* (Oxford University Press, 2007).

Heywood, Mark, 'Debunking "Conglomo-Talk": A Case Study of the Amicus Curiae as an Instrument for Advocacy, Investigation and Mobilisation' (2001) 5 *Law, Democracy and Development* 133.

Hilts, Philip, 'Federal Inquiry Finds Misconduct by a Discoverer of the AIDS Virus', *The New York Times*, 31 December 1992.

'Key Patent on AIDS to Favor the French', *The New York Times*, 12 July 1994.

Hoekman, Bernard, Keith Maskus and Kamal Saggi, 'Transfer of Technology to Developing Countries: Unilateral and Multilateral Policy Options' (2005) 33 *World Development* 1587.

Hogerzeil, Hans, 'Essential Medicines and Human Rights: What Can They Learn from Each Other?' (2006) 84 *Bulletin of the World Health Organization* 371.

Hollis, Aidan, 'An Efficient Reward System for Pharmaceutical Innovation' (Working Paper, University of Calgary, 2005).

'An Optimal Reward System for Neglected Disease Drugs' (Unpublished, Department of Economics, University of Calgary, 2005).

'Incentive Mechanisms for Innovation' (Technical Paper No TP-07005, Institute for Advance Policy Research, University of Calgary, June 2007).

Prize, Advanced Market Commitments and Pharmaceuticals for Developing Countries (2007), www.iprsonline.org/ictsd/Dialogues/2007-10-22/7%20ThinkPiece_Hollis.pdf at 10 February 2009.

'The Health Impact Fund: A Useful Supplement to the Patent System?' (2008) 1 *Public Health Ethics* 124–33.

Hollis, Aidan and Thomas Pogge, *The Health Impact Fund: Making New Medicines Accessible for All* (New Haven, CT: Incentives for Global Health, 2008), www.yale.edu/macmillan/igh/hif_book.pdf.

Hope, Janet, *BioBazaar: Biotechnology and the Open Source Revolution* (Cambridge, MA: Harvard University Press 2008).

Horn, Larry, 'Alternative Approaches to IP Management: One-Stop Technology Platform Licensing' (2003) 9 *Journal of Commercial Biotechnology* 119.

Howard-Hassman, Rhoda E. and Claude E. Welch Jr (ed.) *Economic Rights in Canada and the United States* (Philadelphia, PA: University of Pennsylvania Press, 2006).

Hu, Michael, Karl Schultz, Jack Sheu and Daniel Tschopp, 'The Innovation Gap in Pharmaceutical Drug Discovery and New Models for R&D Success' (2007), www.kellogg.northwestern.edu/academic/biotech/faculty/articles/NewRDModel.pdf.

Hugenholtz, Bernt and Ruth Okediji, *Conceiving an International Instrument on Limitations and Exceptions to Copyright: Final Report* (Open Society Institute, 2008), www.ivir.nl/publications/hugenholtz/limitations_exceptions_copyright.pdf at 16 January 2009.

Hughes, Bethan, 'Harnessing Open Innovation' (2009) 8(5) *Nature Reviews Drug Discovery* 345.

Hutton, Guy, 'Charting the Path to the World Bank's "No Blanket Policy on User Fees"' (DFID Health Systems Resource Centre, 2004), 2.5.

International Intellectual Property Alliance, 'Initial Survey of the Contribution of the Copyright Industries to Economic Development' (April 2005), www.iipa.com/pdf/2005_Apr27_Economic_Development_Survey.pdf at 23 April 2009.

International Intellectual Property Institute, *Patent Protection and Access to HIV/AIDS Pharmaceuticals in Sub-Saharan Africa* (2000), www.iipi.org/reports/HIV_AIDS_Report.pdf at 5 February 2009.

Jacob, Robyn, 'Creating the Community Patent and its Court', in David Vaver and Lionel Bently (eds.), *Intellectual Property Law in the New Millennium: Essays in Honour of William R. Cornish* (Cambridge University Press, 2004).

Jaffe, Adam and Josh Lerner, *Innovation and its Discontents: How our Broken Patent System Is Endangering Innovation and Progress, and What to Do about It* (Princeton University Press, 2004).

Jaffe, Adam, Josh Lerner and Scott Stern (eds.), *Innovation Policy and the Economy*, Vol. 1 (Cambridge, MA: MIT Press, 2001).

Jamison, Dean, J. Breman, A. R. Measham *et al.* (eds.), *Disease Control Priorities in Developing Countries* (2nd edn, Oxford University Press, 2006).

Javorcik, Beata, 'Does Foreign Direct Investment Increase the Productivity of Domestic Firms? In Search of Spillovers through Backward Linkages' (2004) 94 *American Economic Review* 605.

Joensen, Lilian, 'Gates Philanthropy in Stem Cell Transplant for Damaged Heart', The Institute of Science in Society, Press Release, 1 August 2007, www.i-sis.org.uk/GatesPhilanthropyStemCells.php at 10 March 2009.

Jorge, Maria Fabiana, 'Trade Agreements and Public Health: Are US Trade Negotiators Building an Intellectual Property Platform against the Generic Industry? Are They Raising the Standards to Go beyond the US Law?' (2007) 4 *Journal of Generic Medicines* 169.

Joseph, Manu, 'The Future of the Medical Bill', *The Times of India* (Mumbai), 5 April 2007, www.cpaaindia.org/aboutus/PublicEyeAwards.htm at 6 September 2007.

Josephson, Matthew, *The Robber Barons: The Great American Capitalists, 1861–1901* (New York: Harcourt, Brace and Company, 1934).

Kaiser News Network, 'Abbott to Stop Launching New Drugs in Thailand in Response to Country's Compulsory License for Antiretroviral Kaletra', *Kaiser News Network*, 16 March 2007, www.medicalnewstoday.com/articles/65274.php at 20 March 2009.

Kanwar, Sunil and Robert Evenson, 'Does Intellectual Property Protection Spur Technological Change?' (2001) Center Discussion Paper No 83, Economic Growth Center, Yale University.

Kapczynski, Amy, 'The Access to Knowledge Mobilization and the New Politics of Intellectual Property' (2008) 117 *Yale Law Journal* 804.

Kapczynski, Amy, Samantha Chaifetz, Zachary Katz and Yochai Benkler, 'Addressing Global Health Inequities: An Open Licensing Approach for University Innovations' (2005) 20 *Berkeley Technology Law Journal* 1031.

Kaplan, Warren, *Fostering R&D and Promoting Access to Medicines: Locating Common Ground: Operationalising Patent Pools for ARVs* (International Centre for Trade and Sustainable Development, 2007).

Kastriner, Lawrence, 'The Revival of Confidence in the Patent System' (1991) 73 *Journal of Patent and Trademark Office Society* 5.

Katz, Stanley, 'Philanthropy's New Math' (2007) 53(22) *The Chronicle of Higher Education* B2.

Kaul, Inge, Isabelle Grunberg and Marc A. Stern (eds.), *Global Public Goods: International Cooperation in the 21st Century* (New York: Oxford University Press, 1999).

Keck, Margaret E. and Kathryn Sikkink, *Activists beyond Borders* (Ithaca, NY: Cornell University Press, 1998).

Kettler, Hannah, *Narrowing the Gap between Provision and Need for Medicines in Developing Countries* (London: Office of Health Economics, 2000).

Khor, Martin, 'Patents, Compulsory License and Access to Medicines: Some Recent Experiences', *Policy Innovations*, February 2007, www.policyinnovations.org/ideas/policy_library/data/patents_compulsory_license.

'Patents System Facing Legitimacy Crisis', *Third World Network*, 26 March 2001, www.twnside.org.sg/title/et0110.htm at 5 February 2009.

Kieff, F. Scott, 'Coordination, Property, and Intellectual Property: An Unconventional Approach to Anticompetitive Effects and Downstream Access' (2006) 56 *Emory Law Journal* 327.

Kingsbury, Benedict, Nico Krisch and Richard Stewart, 'The Emergence of Global Administrative Law' (2005) 68 *Law and Contemporary Problems* 15.

Kinney, Eleanor and Brian Alexander Clark, 'Provisions for Health and Health Care in the Constitutions of the Countries of the World' (2004) 37 *Cornell International Law Journal* 285.

Kinsley, Michael, 'Bill Gates and Warren Buffett Discuss "Creative Capitalism"', *Creative Capitalism* (Interview Transcript, 2008), creativecapitalism.typepad.com/creative_capitalism/2008/06/bill-gates-and.html#more at 10 March 2009.

(ed.), *Creative Capitalism: A Conversation with Bill Gates, Warren Buffett and Other Economic Leaders* (New York: Simon & Schuster, 2008).

Kippenberg, Juliane, Jean Baptiste Sahokwasama and Joseph Amon, 'Detention of Insolvent Patients in Burundian Hospitals' (2008) *Health Policy and Planning* 14.

Kirby, Michael, 'Foreword', in Matthew Rimmer (ed.), *Intellectual Property and Biotechnology: Biological Inventions* (Cheltenham and Northampton, MA: Edward Elgar, 2008).

Kirk, Michael, 'Competing Demands on Public Policy' (Paper presented at the WIPO Conference on the International Patent System, Geneva, 25–27 March 2002).

Kitch, Edmund, 'The Patent System: A Design for All Seasons?' (Paper presented at the WIPO Conference on the International Patent System, Geneva, 25–27 March 2002)

Klein, Joel, 'Cross Licensing and Antitrust Law' (Speech delivered at the San Antonio Marriott Rivercenter, Texas, 2 May 1997).

Klug, Heinz, 'Access to Essential Medicines – Promoting Human Rights over Free Trade and Intellectual Property Claims', in Keith Maskus and Jerome Reichman (eds.), *International Public Goods and Transfer of Technology under a Globalized Intellectual Property Regime* (Cambridge University Press, 2005), 481–92.

'Campaigning for Life: Building a New Transnational Solidarity in the Face of HIV/AIDS and TRIPS', in Boaventura de Sous Santos and César Rodríguez-Garavito (eds.), *Law and Globalization from Below: Towards a Cosmopolitan Legality* (Cambridge University Press, 2005).

'Law, Politics, and Access to Essential Medicines in Developing Countries' (2008) 36 *Politics and Society* 207.

Knowledge Ecology International, 'Cost Benefit Analysis of UNITAID Patent Pool' (20 June 2008), http://www.keionline.org/misc-docs/1/cost_benefit_UNITAID_patent_pool.pdf at 10 March 2009.

'KEI Statement to Resumed IGWG II Bis', 1 May 2008.

'Prizes to Stimulate Innovation', www.keionline.org.

'Selected Innovation Prizes and Reward Programs' (Research Note 1, Knowledge Ecology International, 7 March 2008), www.keionline.org/misc-docs/research_notes/kei_rn_2008_1.pdf at 10 March 2009.

'Statement of James Love, Director of Knowledge Ecology International on End of IGWG II Bis' 3 May 2008, www.keionline.org/index.php?option=com_content&task=view&id=177&Itemid=1.

Kogan, Lawrence A., 'Brazil's IP Opportunism Threatens U.S. Private Property Rights' (2007) 38 *University of Miami Inter-American Law Review* 1.

Kolata, Gina, 'Co-Payments Go Way Up for Drugs with High Prices', *The New York Times*, 14 April 2008.

Krattiger, Anatole, 'The Use of Non-Assertion Covenants: A Tool to Facilitate Humanitarian Licensing, Manage Liability and Foster Global Access', in Anatole Krattiger, Richard T. Mahoney, Lita Nelsen, Jennifer A. Thomson, Alan B. Bennett, Kanikaram Satyanarayana, Gregory D. Graff, Carlos Fernandez and Stanley Kowalski (eds.), *Intellectual Property Management in Health and Agricultural Innovation: A Handbook of Best Practices* (Oxford: Centre for the Management of Intellectual Property in Health Research and Development, 2008), 1739.

Krattiger, Anatole, Richard T. Mahoney, Lita Nelsen, Jennifer A. Thomson, Alan B. Bennett, Kanikaram Satyanarayana, Gregory D. Graff, Carlos Fernandez and Stanley Kowalski (eds.), *Intellectual Property Management in Health and Agricultural Innovation: A Handbook of Best Practices* (Oxford: Centre for the Management of Intellectual Property in Health Research and Development, 2008).

Krattiger, Anatole and Stanley Kowalski, 'Facilitating Assembly of and Access to Intellectual Property: Focus on Patent Pools and a Review of Other Mechanisms', in Anatole Krattiger, Richard T. Mahoney, Lita Nelsen, Jennifer A. Thomson, Alan B. Bennett, Kanikaram Satyanarayana, Gregory D. Graff, Carlos Fernandez and Stanley Kowalski (eds.), *Intellectual Property Management in Health and Agricultural Innovation: A Handbook of Best Practices* (Oxford: Centre for the Management of Intellectual Property in Health Research and Development, 2008), 131.

Krattiger, Anatole, Stanley Kowalski, Robert Eiss and Anthony Taubman, 'Intellectual Property Management Strategies to Accelerate the Development and Access of Vaccines and Diagnostics: Case Studies on Pandemic Influenza, Malaria and SARS' (2006) 2 *Innovation Strategy Today* 67.

Krattiger, Anatole and Ingo Potrykus, 'Golden Rice: A Product-Development Partnership in Agricultural Biotechnology and Humanitarian Licensing', in Anatole Krattiger, Richard T. Mahoney, Lita Nelsen, Jennifer A. Thomson, Alan B. Bennett, Kanikaram Satyanarayana, Gregory D. Graff, Carlos Fernandez and Stanley Kowalski (eds.), Executive Guide to *Intellectual Property Management in Health and Agricultural Innovation: A Handbook of Best Practices* (Oxford: Centre for the Management of Intellectual Property in Health Research and Development, 2008), CS11.

Kremer, Michael, 'Creating Markets for New Vaccines, Part I: Rationale' (Working Paper No 7716, National Bureau of Economic Research, 2000).

'Patent Buyouts: A Mechanism for Encouraging Innovation' (1998) 113 *Quarterly Journal of Economics* 1137.

Kremer, Michael and Rachel Glennerster, *Strong Medicine: Creating Incentives for Pharmaceutical Research on Neglected Diseases* (Princeton University Press, 2004).

Kryder, David, Stanley Kowalski and Anatole Krattiger, *The Intellectual and Technical Property Components of pro-Vitamin A Rice (GoldenRice^{TM}): A*

Preliminary Freedom-to-Operate Review (International Service for the Acquisition of Agri-biotech Applications, 2000).

Kyle, Margaret, *Innovation in the Pharmaceutical Industry* (London Business School, 2007).

Kyle, Margaret and Anita McGahan, 'Investments in Pharmaceuticals before and after TRIPS' (Working Paper, London Business School, 2008) 18, faculty.london.edu/mkyle/KM_TRIPS_081108.pdf at 2 March 2009.

Lall, Sanjaya and Manuel Albaladejo, 'Indicators of the Relative Importance of IPRs in Developing Countries' (Working Paper No 85, Queen Elizabeth House Working Paper Series, QEHWPS85, 2002).

Laming, Andrew, 'Let's Overhaul the Pharmaceutical Benefits Scheme', *The Australian*, 10 January 2006, 10.

Lamy, Pascal, 'Access to Medicines Has Been Improved' (Geneva: The World Trade Organization), 9 December 2008, www.wto.org/english/news_e/sppl_e/sppl111_e.htm.

Lanjouw, Jean, 'A New Global Patent Regime for Diseases: U.S. and International Legal Issues' (2002) 16 *Harvard Journal of Law and Technology* 85.

Lawson, Charles, 'Depositing Seeds to Comply with the Patents Act 1990 (Cth) – The Adequacy of Definition and Description?' (2004) 23 *University of Tasmania Law Review* 68.

'Patenting Genetic Diversity – Old Rules May Be Restricting the Exploitation of a New Technology' (1999) 6 *Journal of Law and Medicine* 373.

'Patents and the CGIAR System of International Agricultural Research Centres' Germplasm Collections under the International Treaty on Plant Genetic Resources for Food and Agriculture' (2004) 55 *Australian Journal of Agricultural Research* 307.

'Regulating Access to Biological Resources: The Market Failure for Biodiversity Conservation' (2006) 24 *Law in Context* 137.

Lawson, Charles and Catherine Pickering, 'Patenting Genetic Materials – Failing to Reflect the Value of Variation in DNA, RNA and Amino Acids' (2000) 11 *Australian Intellectual Property Journal* 69.

Lawson, Charles and Jay Sanderson, 'The Evolution of the CBD's Development Agenda that May Influence the Interpretation and Development of TRIPS', in Justin Malbon and Charles Lawson (eds.), *Interpreting and Implementing the WTO Trade Related Agreement on Intellectual Property Rights: Is TRIPS Fair?* (Cheltenham and Northampton, MA: Edward Elgar, 2008), 131.

Lawyers Collective, 'Patent Opposition', Lawyers Collective Affordable Medicines and Treatment Campaign, www.lawyerscollective.org/amtc/patent-opposition at 24 June 2009.

Layton, Ron, 'Enhancing Intellectual Property Exports through Fair Trade', in J. Michael Finger and Philip Schuler (eds.), *Poor People's Knowledge:*

Promoting Intellectual Property in Developing Countries (Washington, DC: The World Bank, 2004), 75.

Lazzarini, Zita, 'Access to HIV Drugs: Are We Changing the Two-World Paradigm?' (2002) 17 *Connecticut Journal of International Law* 281.

Lee, Jeong-Yeon and Edwin Mansfield, 'Intellectual Property Protection and U.S. Foreign Direct Investment' (1996) 78 *The Review of Economics and Statistics* 181.

Lee, Kelley and David Fidler, 'Avian and Pandemic Influenza: Progress and Problems with Global Health Governance' (2007) 2 *Global Public Health* 215.

Lemley, Mark, 'Ex Ante versus Ex Post Justifications for Intellectual Property' (2004) 71 *University of Chicago Law Review* 129.

Lerner, Jack, 'Intellectual Property and Development at WHO and WIPO' (2008) 34 *American Journal of Law and Medicine* 257.

Lerner, Josh, '150 Years of Patent Protection' (Working Paper No 7478, National Bureau of Economic Research, 2001).

Lerner, Josh and Jean Tirole, 'Public Policy toward Patent Pools' (2007) *Innovation Policy and the Economy* 9.

Lerner, Josh, Jean Tirole and Marcin Strojwas, 'Cooperative Marketing Agreements between Competitors: Evidence from Patent Pools' (Working Paper No 9680, National Bureau of Economic Research, 2003).

Lever, Jack, 'The New Court of Appeals for the Federal Circuit' (1982) 64 *Journal of the Patent and Trademark Office Society* 178.

Levin, Marianne and Annette Kur, *Towards More Balanced, User-Friendly Paradigms in IP Law: A Project Reform of TRIPS* (Special Session at the Annual Meeting of the International Association for the Advancement of Teaching and Research in Intellectual Property, 5 September 2006).

Levin, Richard, Alvin Klevorick, Richard Nelson and Sidney Winter, 'Appropriating the Returns from Industrial Research and Development' (1987) 18 *Brookings Papers on Economic Activity* 783.

Levine, Michael and Jennifer Forrence, 'Regulatory Capture, Public Interest and Public Agenda: Toward a Synthesis' (1990) 6 *Journal of Law, Economics and Organization* 167.

Levine, Robert, 'Online Tunes, in Service to Africa', *The New York Times*, 30 June 2008.

Lewis, Stephen, *Race against Time* (Toronto: House of Anansi Press, 2005).

Lewis, Tracy, Jerome Reichman and Anthony So, 'The Case for Public Funding and Public Oversight of Clinical Trials' (2007) 4(1) *The Economists' Voice* article 3, 1.

Lockhart, Nicolas and Andrew Mitchell, 'Regional Trade Agreements under GATT 1994: An Exception and its Limits', in Andrew Mitchell (ed.), *Challenges and Prospects for the WTO* (London: Cameron May, 2005), 217.

Lok Sabha Debates, 'Part II Proceedings Title: Combined discussion on the Statutory Resolution regarding disapproval of Patents (Amendment)

Ordinance, 2004 (No 7 of 2004) (India) and the Patents (Amendment) Bill, 2005 (India)', 22 March 2005, 164.100.24.230/Webdata/datalshom001/dailydeb/22032005.htm at 12 September 2008.

Love, James, 'Measures to Enhance Access to Medical Technologies, and New Methods of Stimulating Medical R&D' (2007) 40 *University of California, Davis Law Review* 679.

'Modeling Prize Fund Rewards', Drug Development (With Access), 7 July 2006, www.cptech.org/blogs/drugdevelopment/2006/07/modeling-prize-fund-rewards.html at 20 February 2009.

'Open Licensing vs Monopoly Controlled Supply', *Knowledge Ecology International* (27 April 2008), www.keionline.org/component/option,com_jd-wp/Itemid,/p,112/ at 10 March 2009.

'Proposal for an Essential Health Care Patent Pool' (Paper presented at the XIV International AIDS Conference, Barcelona, 8 July 2002).

Love, James and Tim Hubbard, 'The Big Idea: Prizes to Stimulate R&D for New Medicines' (2007) 82 *Chicago-Kent Law Review* 1519.

Lowenfeld, Andreas, *International Economic Law* (2nd edn, Oxford University Press, 2008).

Lowenstein, Roger, *Buffett: The Making of an American Capitalist* (New York: Random House, 2008).

Lu, John and William Comanor, 'Strategic Pricing of New Pharmaceuticals' (1998) 80 *Review of Economics and Statistics* 108.

Lucia, Patricia and Cantuária Marin, *Providing Protection for Plant Genetic Resources: Patents, Sui Generis Systems, and Biopartnerships* (The Hague: Kluwer Law International, 2002).

Lucyk, Scott, 'Patents, Politics and Public Health: Access to Essential Medicines under the TRIPS Agreement' (2006–7) 38 *Ottawa Law Review* 191.

Mackay, Donald R., 'Challenges Confronting the Free Trade Area of the Americas' (Canadian Foundation for the Americas Policy Paper, June 2002), www.focal.ca at 2 February 2009.

Majone, Giandomenico, 'The Rise of the Regulatory State in Europe' (1994) 17 *West European Politics* 77.

Makkai, Toni and John Braithwaite, 'In and Out of the Revolving Door: Making Sense of Regulatory Capture' (1992) 12 *Journal of Public Policy* 61.

Malbon, Justin and Charles Lawson (eds.), *Interpreting and Implementing the WTO Trade Related Agreement on Intellectual Property Rights: Is TRIPS Fair?* (Cheltenham and Northampton, MA: Edward Elgar, 2008).

Malerba, Franco and Luigi Orsenig, 'Innovation and Market Structure in the Dynamics of the Pharmaceutical Industry and Biotechnology: Towards a History Friendly Model' (2002) 11 *Industrial and Corporate Change* 667.

Mandelson, Peter, 'Compulsory Licensing of Pharmaceutical Patents in Thailand', *Knowledge Ecology International* (10 July 2007), www.keionline.org/misc-docs/thai/070710-PM-MoC.pdf at 20 March 2009.

Mansfield, Edwin, 'Intellectual Property Protection, Foreign Direct Investment and Technology Transfer' (Working Paper No 19, The World Bank, 1994).

'Patents and Innovation: An Empirical Study' (1986) 32 *Management Science* 173.

Mara, Kaitlin and William New, 'WHO IP and Health Group Concludes with Progress; Tough Issues Remain for Assembly', *Intellectual Property Watch* (6 May 2008), www.ip-watch.org/ at 10 February 2009.

'WHO Members Inch toward Consensus on IP, Innovation and Public Health' *Intellectual Property Watch* (2 May 2008), www.ip-watch.org/weblog/index.php?p=1024 at 10 February 2009.

Martin, Amy Elizabeth, *Seeing (RED): A Qualitative Analysis of the Product (RED) Campaign and Integration of Public Relations and Marketing Theory* (Master of Mass Communication Thesis, Louisana State University, 2008).

Martin, Greg, Corinna Sorenson and Thomas Faunce, 'Balancing Intellectual Monopoly Privileges and the Need for Essential Medicines' (2007) 3(4) *Globalization and Health*, www.globalizationandhealth.com/content/3/1/4 at 22 June 2009.

Maskus, Keith, 'Intellectual Property Rights and Foreign Direct Investment' (Policy Discussion Paper No 22, Centre for International Economic Studies, University of Adelaide, 2000).

Intellectual Property Rights in the Global Economy (Washington DC: Peterson Institute for International Economics, 2000).

Parallel Imports in Pharmaceuticals: Implications for Competition and Prices in Developing Countries (Geneva: World Intellectual Property Organization, 2001).

'Regulatory Standards in the WTO' (Working Paper No WP00–1, Peterson Institute for International Economics, 2000).

'The International Regulation of Intellectual Property' (1998) 134 *Review of World Economics* 186.

Maskus, Keith and Jerome Reichman, 'The Globalisation of Private Knowledge Goods and the Privatisation of Global Public Goods', in Keith Maskus and Jerome Reichman (eds.), *International Public Goods and Transfer of Technology under a Globalised Intellectual Property Regime* (Cambridge University Press, 2005), 3.

Maskus, Keith and Jerome Reichman (eds.), *International Public Goods and Transfer of Technology under a Globalized Intellectual Property Regime* (Cambridge University Press, 2005).

Mathis, James, *Regional Trade Agreements in the GATT/WTO: Article XXIV and the Internal Trade Requirement* (The Hague: TMC Asser Press, 2002).

Matlin, Stephen, A. de Francisco and L. Sundaram (eds.), *Health Partnerships Review: Focusing Collaborative Efforts on Research and Innovation for the Health of the Poor* (Geneva: Global Forum for Health Research, 2008).

Matthews, Duncan, 'From the August 30, 2003 WTO Decision to the December 6, 2005 Agreement on an Amendment to TRIPS: Improving Access to Medicines in Developing Countries' (2006) 2 *Intellectual Property Quarterly* 91.

'The Role of International NGOs in the Intellectual Property Policy-Making and Norm-Setting Activities of Multilateral Institutions' (2007) 82 *Chicago-Kent Law Review* 1369.

'WTO Decision on Implementation of Paragraph 6 of the Doha Declaration on the TRIPS Agreement and Public Health: A Solution to the Access to Essential Medicines Problem?' (2004) 7 *Journal of International Economic Law* 73.

Maurer, Stephen, 'Choosing the Right Incentive Strategy for Research and Development in Neglected Diseases' (2006) 84 *Bulletin of the World Health Organization* 376.

'Open Source Drug Discovery: Finding a Niche (Or Maybe Several)' (2007) 76 *University of Missouri at Kansas City Law Review* 405.

The Right Tool(s): Designing Cost-Effective Strategies for Neglected Disease Research (Report to the World Health Organization Commission on Intellectual Property Rights, Innovation and Public Health, 2005).

Maurer, Stephen, Arti Rai and Andrej Sali, 'Finding Cures for Tropical Diseases: Is Open Source an Answer?' (2004) 1 *Public Library of Science, Medicine* 183.

May, Christopher, *The World Intellectual Property Organization: Resurgence and the Development Agenda* (New York and Oxford: Routledge, 2007).

Mayne, Ruth, 'The Global Campaign on Patents and Access to Medicines: An Oxfam Perspective', in Peter Drahos and Ruth Mayne (eds.), *Global Intellectual Property Rights: Knowledge, Access and Development* (Basingstoke: Palgrave Macmillan, 2002), 249.

McNair, Lord, *The Law of Treaties* (Oxford: Clarendon Press, 1961).

McNeil, Donald, 'Gates Foundation's Influence Criticized', *The New York Times*, 16 February 2008.

Médecins Sans Frontières, 'Access to Essential Medicines: Can the World Health Organization Do More?', 15 May 2001.

'A Guide to the Post 2005 World: TRIPS, R&D and Access to Medicines', 18 January 2005, www.msf.org/msfinternational/invoke.cfm?objectid=88694E5B-0FED-434A-A21EDA1006002653&component=toolkit.article&method=full_html.

'Campaign for Access to Essential Medicines – Target Diseases: Tuberculosis', accessible through the Internet Archive at web.archive.org/web/20071207071446, www.accessed-msf.org/campaign/tb01.shtm.

Drug Patents under the Spotlight – Sharing Practical Knowledge about Pharmaceutical Patents (June 2004), www.who.int/3by5/en/patents_2003. pdf.

'Generics and Access to Influenza Treatment' (7 May 2009), www.msfaccess.org/main/access-patents/generics-and-access-to-influenza-treatment/.

Neither Expeditious, nor a Solution: The WTO August 30th Decision Is Unworkable (August 2006), www.accessmed-msf.org/fileadmin/user_upload/medinnov_accesspatents/WTOaugustreport.pdf at 23 January 2009.

Menou, Veronique, Allison Hornstein and Elizabeth Lipton-McCombie, *Access to Medicine Index: Ranking Access to Medicine Practices* (Haarlem: Access to Medicine Foundation, June 2008).

Mercurio, Bryan, 'Resolving the Public Health Crisis in the Developing World: Problems and Barriers of Access to Essential Medicines' (2007) 5 *Northwestern University Journal of International Human Rights* 1.

'TRIPS-Plus Provisions in FTAs; Recent Trends', in Lorand Bartels and Federico Ortino (eds.), *Regional Trade Agreements and the WTO Legal System* (Oxford: Oxford University Press, 2006), 215.

Merges, Robert, 'Institutions for Intellectual Property Transactions: The Case of Patent Pools', in Rochelle C. Dreyfuss, Dianne Zimmerman and Harry First (eds.), *Expanding the Boundaries of Intellectual Property: Innovation Policy for the Knowledge Society* (Oxford University Press, 2001), 123.

Mgbeoji, Ikechi, 'TRIPS and TRIPS-Plus Impacts in Africa', in Daniel Gervais (ed.), *Intellectual Property, Trade and Development* (Oxford University Press, 2007), 259.

Michelman, Frank, 'Socioeconomic Rights in Constitutional Law: Explaining America Away' (2008) *International Journal of Constitutional Law* 1.

Miller, David, 'The Ethical Significance of Nationality' (1988) 98 *Ethics* 647.

Mimura, Carol, 'Technology Licensing for the Benefit of the Developing World' (2006) 18(2) *Journal of Association of University Technology Managers* 19.

Mintzberg, Henry, 'Patent Nonsense: Evidence Tells of an Industry Out of Social Control' (2006) 175(4) *Canadian Medical Association Journal* 374, www.cmaj.ca/cgi/content/full/175/4/374 at 20 April 2009.

Misungu, Sisule, 'Opportunities for the Obama Administration and the G20 to Do Good for Global Health' (2009) 2(2) *Global Health Governance*, www.ghgj.org/Volume%20II%20Issue%202.htm at 22 June 2009.

Mitchell, Andrew (ed.), *Challenges and Prospects for the WTO* (London: Cameron May, 2005).

Mitchell, Andrew and Tania Voon, 'Patents and Public Health in the WTO, FTAs and Beyond: Tension and Conflict in International Law' (2009) 43(3) *Journal of World Trade* 571.

Moerman, Don, 'Is Public Domain Community Research Effective? The Nematode *Caenorhabditis elegans* as a Positive Case Study' (Paper presented at Genomics and Intellectual Property: Considering Alternatives to Traditional Patenting, Vancouver, 9 March 2007).

Montagnier, Luc, *Virus: The Co-Discoverer of the Virus Tracks its Rampage and Charts its Future* (New York: W. W. Norton and Co., 1999).

Montagnier, Luc, Jean-Claude Chermann, Françoisé Barre-Sinoussi *et al.*, 'Human Immunodeficiency Viruses Associated with Acquired Immune Deficiency Syndrome (AIDS), a Diagnostic Method for AIDS and pre-AIDS, and a Kit Therefor', United States Patent No: 4,708,818.

Moody, Glyn, *Digital Code of Life: How Bioinformatics Is Revolutionizing Science, Medicine, and Business* (Hoboken, NJ: John Wiley and Sons, 2004).

Moon, Suerie, 'Medicines as Global Public Goods: The Governance of Technological Innovation in the New Era of Global Health' (2009) 2(2) *Global Health Governance*, www.ghgj.org/Volume%20II%20Issue%202.htm at 22 June 2009.

Morel, Carlos, Tara Acharya, Denis Broun, Ajit Dangi, Christopher Elias, N. K. Ganguly, Charles A. Gardner, R. K. Gupta, Jane Haycock, Anthony D. Heher, Gerald T. Keusch, Peter J. Hotez, Anatole F. Krattiger, Fernando T. Kreutz, Sanjaya Lall, Keun Lee, Richard Mahoney, Adolfo Martinez-Palomo, R. A. Mashelkar, Stephen Matlin, Hong-Ki Min, Mandi Mzimba, Joachim Oehler, William Pick, Rob G. Ridley, Pramilla Senanayake, Peter Singer and Mikyung Yun, 'Health Innovation: The Neglected Capacity of Developing Countries to Address Neglected Diseases' (2005) 309 *Science* 401.

Morgan, Bronwen and Karen Yeung, *An Introduction to Law and Regulation: Text and Materials* (Cambridge University Press, 2007).

Morgan, Maxwell, 'Medicines for the Developing World: Promoting Access and Innovation in the Post-TRIPS Environment' (2006) 64 *University of Toronto Law Review* 45.

Mowery, David, Richard Nelson, Bhaven Sampat and Arvids Ziedonis, 'The Growth of Patenting and Licensing by US Universities: An Assessment of the Effects of the Bayh-Dole Act of 1980' (2001) 30 *Research Policy* 99.

Munos, Bernard, 'Can Open-Source R&D Reinvigorate Drug Research' (2006) 5 *Nature Reviews Drug Discovery* 723.

Musungu, Sisule, Susan Villanueva and Roxana Blasetti, *Utilizing TRIPS Flexibilities for Public Health Protection through South–South Regional Frameworks* (Geneva: South Centre, 2004).

Myers, Norman (ed.), *The Gaia Atlas of Future Worlds: Challenge and Opportunity in an Age of Change* (New York: Anchor Books/Doubleday, 1990).

Na Songkhla, Mongkol, Minister for Public Health, Thailand, 'Letter to His Excellency Friedrich Hamburger', 18 July 2007, www.actupparis.org/IMG/pdf/Answer_Thai.pdf at 20 March 2009.

Nam, HeeSeob and SungHo Park, 'Request for a Compulsory License from KIPO on Behalf of People's Health Coalition for Equitable Society, Association of Physicians for Humanism, and Korean Pharmacists for Democratic Society', glivec.jinbo.net/Request_for_CL_Final_version.htm at 5 September 2007.

Nasaw, David, *Andrew Carnegie* (New York: Penguin Books, 2007).

Nathan, Carl, 'Aligning Pharmaceutical Innovation with Medical Need' (2007) 13 *Nature Medicine* 304.

National Institute for Health Care Management, *Changing Patterns of Pharmaceutical Innovation*, May 2000, www.nihcm.org/~nihcmor/pdf/innovations.pdf at 20 April 2009.

National Philanthropic Trust, *Philanthropy Quotes*, www.nptrust.org/philanthropy/philanthropy_quotes.asp at 10 March 2009.

Nature News, 'Indonesia Edges Closer to Sharing Bird-Flu Samples' (2007) 450 *Nature* 598.

Neier, Aryeh, 'Social and Economic Rights: A Critique' (2006) 13(2) *Human Rights Brief* 1.

Nelson, Richard, 'Uncertainty, Learning, and the Economics of Parallel Research and Development' (1961) 43 *Review of Economics and Statistics* 351.

Netanel, Neil Weinstock (ed.), *The Development Agenda: Global Intellectual Property and Developing Countries* (Oxford University Press, 2008).

Neumann, Peter, 'Lessons from Oregon', in Peter Neumann (ed.), *Using Cost-Effective Analysis to Improve Health Care: Challenges and Opportunities* (New York: Oxford University Press, 2004), 58–70.

Neumann, Peter (ed.), *Using Cost-Effective Analysis to Improve Health Care: Challenges and Opportunities* (New York: Oxford University Press, 2004).

Neumann, Peter, Eileen Sandberg, Chaim Bell, Patricia Stone and Richard Chapman, 'Are Pharmaceuticals Cost-Effective? A Review of the Evidence' (2000) 19 *Health Affairs* 92.

Nevins, Allan, *John D. Rockefeller: The Heroic Age of American Enterprise* (New York: C. Scribner & Sons, 1940).

Newell, Richard and Nathan Wilson, 'Technology Prizes for Climate Change Mitigation' (Discussion Paper No 05–33, Resources for the Future, 2005).

Nicol, Dianne and Janet Hope, 'Cooperative Strategies for Facilitating Use of Patented Inventions in Biotechnology' (2006) 24 *Law in Context* 85.

Nielsen, Jane and Dianne Nicol, 'Pharmaceutical Patents and Developing Countries: The Conundrum of Access and Incentive' (2002) 13 *Australian Intellectual Property Journal* 21.

Niman, Neil and Brian Kench, *Open Source and Future of the Pharmaceutical Industry* (2005) (on file with the author).

Niu, Huei-Chih, 'Can Article 5.7 of the WTO SPS Agreement Be a Model for the Precautionary Principle?' (2007) 4 *Script-ed* 367.

The Nobel Assembly at Karolinska Institute, 'The Nobel Prize in Physiology or Medicine in 2008', 6 October 2008, nobelprize.org/nobel_prizes/medicine/laureates/2008/press.html.

Nolan-Stevaux, Katherine, 'Open Source Biology' (2007) 23 *Santa Clara Computer and High Technology Law Journal* 271.

Nordhaus, William, *Invention, Growth and Welfare: A Theoretical Treatment of Technological Change* (Cambridge, MA: MIT Press, 1969).

Novartis, 'Glivec Patent Case in India: Fact vs. Fiction' (Press Release, not dated), www.novartis.com/downloads/about-novartis/facts-vs-fiction-india-glivec-patent-case.pdf at 27 March 2009.

'Novartis Concerned that Indian Court Ruling Will Discourage Investments in Innovation Needed to Bring Better Medicines to Patients' (Press Release, 6 August 2007), www.novartis.com/newsroom/news/index.shtml at 20 April 2009.

Novogrodsky, Noah Benjamin, 'The HIV/AIDS Pandemic and Human Security' (2006) 100 *American Society of International Law Proceedings* 345.

Nuffield Council on Bioethics, *The Ethics of Patenting DNA: A Discussion Paper* (2002).

Nuvolari, Alessandro and Francesco Rullani, 'Curious Exceptions? Open Source Software and "Open" Technology', in Kirk St Amant and Brian Still (eds.), *Handbook of Research on Open Source Software: Technological, Economic and Social Perspectives* (New York: Information Science Reference, 2007), 227.

Odell, John (ed.), *Negotiating Trade: Developing Countries in the WTO and NAFTA* (Cambridge University Press, 2006).

Odell, John and Susan Sell, 'Reframing the Issue: The WTO Coalition on Intellectual Property and Public Health, 2001', in John Odell (ed.), *Negotiating Trade: Developing Countries in the WTO and NAFTA* (Cambridge University Press, 2006).

O'Donoghue, Ted, Suzanne Cotchmer and Jacques-François Thisse, 'Patent Breadth, Patent Life and the Pace of Technological Progress' (1998) 7 *Journal of Economics and Management* 1.

Oh, Cecilia, 'Compulsory Licenses: Recent Experiences in Developing Countries' (2006) 1 *International Journal of Intellectual Property Management* 25.

Okediji, Ruth, 'The International Relations of Intellectual Property: Narratives of Developing Country Participation in the Global Intellectual Property System' (2003) 7 *Singapore Journal of International and Comparative Law* 315.

Ollier, Peter, 'Philippines Plans to Follow India in Limiting Patentability', *Managing Intellectual Property Weekly News* (Hong Kong), 6 May 2008.

Ong'wen, Odour, 'Crocodile Tears: How "TRIPS" Serves West's Monopoly', *The East African* (Nairobi), 12 March 2001.

Opderbeck, David, 'Patents, Essential Medicines, and the Innovation Game' (2005) 58 *Vanderbilt Law Review* 501.

The Oprah Winfrey Show, 'Oprah and Bono Paint the Town Red', *The Oprah Winfrey Show*, 13 October 2006, www.oprah.com/slideshow/world/global issues/oprahshow3_ss_20061013 at 10 March 2009.

Outterson, Kevin, 'Should Access to Medicines and TRIPS Flexibilities Be Limited to Specific Diseases?' (2008) 34 *American Journal of Law and Medicine* 279.

Oxfam International, 'Ending the R&D Crisis in Public Health: Promoting Pro-Poor Medical Innovation' (Briefing Paper No 122, Oxfam 2008).

'Investing for Life: Meeting Poor People's Needs for Access to Medicines through Responsible Business Practices' (Briefing Paper No 109, Oxfam, November 2007).

Palmer, Geoffrey, 'The Earth Summit: What Went Wrong at Rio?' (1992) 70 *Washington University Law Quarterly* 1005.

Panjabi, Ranee, *The Earth Summit at Rio: Politics, Economics and the Environment* (Boston, MA: Northeastern University Press, 1997).

Paulson, Tom, 'Gates Foundation Follows New Paths: Giving Away $3 Billion a Year Is Not Easy as It Seems', *Seattle Post-Intelligencer*, 24 June 2008.

Paulus, Andreas L., 'Subsidiarity, Fragmentation and Democracy: Towards the Demise of General International Law?', in Tomer Broude and Yuval Shany, (eds.) *The Shifting Allocation of Authority in International Law* (Oxford and Portland, ME: Hart Publishing, 2008) 193.

Pellegrino, Edmund, 'The Commodification of Medical and Health Care: The Moral Consequences of a Paradigm Shift from a Professional to a Market Ethic' (1999) 24 *Journal of Medicine and Philosophy* 243.

Peltzman, Sam, 'An Evaluation of Consumer Protection Legislation: The 1962 Drug Amendments' (1973) 81 *Journal of Political Economy* 1049.

Perelman, Jeremy and Lucie White (eds.), *Stones of Hope: How African Activists Reclaim Human Rights to Challenge Global Poverty* (Palo Alto, CA: Stanford University Press, 2009).

Perelman, Jeremy and Katharine Young, 'Freeing Mohammed Zakari: Footprints toward Hope', in Jeremy Perelman and Lucie White (eds.), *Stones of Hope: How African Activists Reclaim Human Rights to Challenge Global Poverty* (Palo Alto, CA: Stanford University Press, 2009).

Perkins, Sarah and Melanie de Wit, 'The African Private Sector Steps in to Fill the Drug Gap' (2007) 370 *The Lancet* 722.

Perrone, Matthew and Marley Seaman, 'Study: Concerns on Mixing Plavix, Heartburn Drugs', *Associated Press*, 11 November 2008, naturalhealthnews.blogspot.com/2008/11/plavix-and-nexium-combo-nixed.html at 15 April 2009.

Petersmann, Ernst-Ulrich, 'Challenges to the Legitimacy and Efficiency of the World Trading System: Democratic Govenance and Competition Culture in the WTO' (2004) 7 *Journal of International Economic Law* 585.

Phair, Dan, 'Orphan Drug Programs, Public–Private Partnerships and Current Efforts to Develop Treatments for Diseases of Poverty' (2008) 4 *Journal of Health and Biomedical Law* 19.

Pharmaceutical Shareholders Group (PSG), *Investor Statement and Framework on Pharmaceutical Companies and the Public Health Crisis in Emerging Markets* (March 2003), 2.

Pisano, Gary, *Science Business* (Boston, MA: Harvard Business School Press, 2006).

Pogge, Thomas, 'Cosmopolitanism and Sovereignty' (1992) 103(1) *Ethics* 48.

'Human Rights and Global Health: A Research Program' (2005) 36 *Metaphilosophy* 182.

'Relational Conceptions of Justice: Responsibilities for Health Outcomes', in Sudhir Anand, Fabienne Peter and Amartya Sen (eds.), *Public Health, Ethics and Equity* (Oxford: Oxford University Press, 2005).

Posner, Richard, 'Against Creative Capitalism', *Creative Capitalism – A Conversation*, 26 June 2008, www.creativecapitalismblog.com/creative_capitalism/2008/06/against-creativ.html at 10 March 2009.

Potrykus, Ingo, 'Golden Rice and Beyond' (2001) 125 *Plant Physiology* 1157.

Prosser, Tony, 'Theorising Utility Regulation' (1999) 62 *Modern Law Review* 196.

Public Library of Science Medicine, 'Disease Mongering Collection' (2006) 3(4) *Public Library of Science Medicine* 191, colletions.plos.org/plosmedicine/diseasemongering-2006.php at February 2009.

Puku, Nana and Alan Whiteside (eds.), *The Political Economy of AIDS in Africa* (Farnham: Ashgate Publishing, 2004) 19.

Rai, Arti, 'Proprietary Rights and Collective Action: The Case of Biotechnology Research with Low Commercial Value', in Keith Maskus and Jerome Reichman (eds.), *International Public Goods and Transfer of Technology* (Cambridge University Press, 2005) 288.

Ramos, Joana, 'New Definition of "Patient Assistance Program" in Brazil' (2005) 23(1) *Healthy Skepticism International News*, www.healthyskepticism.org/news/issue.php?id=7 at 11 July 2007.

'Novartis Glitch with Glivec in Argentina?', *Essential Drugs.org*, 15 May 2006 www.essentialdrugs.org/edrug/archive/200608/msg00070.php at February 2007.

Raustiala, Kal, 'Compliance and Effectiveness in International Regulatory Cooperation' (2000) 32 *Case Western Reserve Journal of International Law* 387.

'Domestic Institutions and International Regulatory Cooperation: Comparative Responses to the Convention on Biological Diversity' (1997) 49 *World Politics* 482.

The (RED) Campaign, 'Bono and Bobby Shriver Launch Product RED to Harness Power of the World's Iconic Brands to Fight AIDS in Africa' (Press Release, 26 January 2006).

'(RED) names Susan Smith Ellis as CEO' (Press Release, 28 June 2007), joinred.com/news/pressrelease.asp?06282007.

The Lazarus Effect (2007) YouTube www.youtube.com/watch?v=W82SoRp9Au4 at 10 March 2009.

Reichman, Jerome, 'From Free Riders to Fair Followers: Global Competition under the TRIPS Agreement' (1997) 29 *New York University Journal of International Law and Politics* 11.

'Nurturing a Transnational System of Innovation' (2007) 16 *Journal of Transnational Law and Policy* 143.

Reichman, Jerome and Rochelle C. Dreyfuss, 'Harmonization without Consensus: Critical Reflections on Drafting a Substantive Patent Law Treaty' (2007) 57 *Duke Law Journal* 85.

Reichman, Jerome and Catherine Hasenzahl, 'Non-Voluntary Licensing of Patented Inventions' (Issue Paper No 5, United Nations Conference on Trade and Development – International Centre for Trade and Sustainable Development, 2003).

Reichman, Jerome and Pamela Samuelson, 'Intellectual Property Rights in Data' (1997) 50 *Vanderbilt Law Review* 51.

Reinhard, Julien, 'Novartis Files Case in India Challenging Patent Controller's Order and Patent Law', Berne Declaration, 9 October 2006, www.evb.ch/en/p25011414.html#note1#note1 at 20 April 2009.

Reiss, Julian and Philip Kitcher, 'Neglected Diseases and Well-Ordered Science' (Technical Paper No 06/08, Centre for the Philosophy of Natural and Social Science Contingency and Dissent in Science, 2008).

Remnick, David, 'The Wanderer: Bill Clinton's Quest to Save the World, Reclaim his Legacy and Elect his Wife', *The New Yorker*, 18 September 2006.

Resnik, David and Kenneth De Ville (2002) 'Bioterrorism and Patent Rights: "Compulsory Licensure" and the case of Cipro' (2002) 2(3) *The American Journal of Bioethics* 29–39.

Reuters, 'Thailand Talking with Drug Firms – U.S. Chamber', *Reuters*, 20 March 2007, lists.essential.org/pipermail/ip-health/2007-March/010800.html at 20 March 2009.

'Thailand Will Override Cancer Drug Patents', *Reuters*, 10 March 2008, www.reuters.com/article/healthNews/idUSBKK14764720080310 at 20 March 2009.

Ridley, David, Henry Grabowski and Jeffrey Moe, 'Developing Drugs for Developing Countries' (2006) 25(2) *Health Affairs* 313–24.

Rimmer, Matthew, 'A Submission to the Joint Standing Committee on Treaties: The Hong Kong Amendment to the TRIPs Agreement' (Submission 2, 9 May 2007), works.bepress.com/matthew_rimmer/58/.

'Beyond Blue Gene: Intellectual Property and Bioinformatics' (2003) 34 *International Review of Industrial Property and Copyright Law* 31.

Intellectual Property and Biotechnology: Biological Inventions (Cheltenham and Northampton, MA: Edward Elgar, 2008).

'Race against Time: The Export of Essential Medicines to Rwanda' (2008) 1 *Public Health Ethics* 89.

'The Jean Chrétien Pledge to Africa Act: Patent Law and Humanitarian Aid' (2005) 15 *Expert Opinion on Therapeutic Patents* 889.

'The Race to Patent the SARS Virus: The TRIPS Agreement and Access to Essential Medicines' (2004) 5 *Melbourne Journal of International Law* 335.

Rischard, Jean-François, *High Noon: 20 Global Problems, 20 Years to Solve Them* (New York: Basic Books, 2002).

Roffe, Pedro, Christoph Spennemann and Johanna von Braun, 'From Paris to Doha: The WTO Doha Declaration on the TRIPS Agreement and Public Health', in Pedro Roffe, Geoff Tansey and David Vivas-Eugui (eds.), *Negotiating Health Intellectual Property and Access to Medicines* (London: Earthscan Publications Ltd, 2006) 9.

Roffe, Pedro, Geoff Tansey and David Vivas-Eugui (eds.), *Negotiating Health Intellectual Property and Access to Medicines* (London: Earthscan Publications Ltd, 2006).

Rosenman, Mark, 'The Patina of Philanthropy', *Stanford Social Innovation Review*, 11 April 2007, www.ssireview.org/opinion/entry/the_patina_of_philanthropy/ at 10 March 2009.

Rosenthal, Meredith, Ernst Berndt, Julie Donohue, Arnold Epstein and Richard Frank, *Demand Effects of Recent Changes in Prescription Drug Promotion* (Kaiser Family Foundation, 2003).

Roth, Kenneth, 'Defending Economic, Social and Cultural Rights: Practical Considerations Faced by an International Human Rights Organization' (2004) 26 *Human Rights Quarterly* 63.

Rowan, Arnica, '(REDWASHING): Will Thousands of Red iPods, T-Shirts, and Cellphones Really Make the World a Better Place?', *Unlimited Magazine*, 30 October 2007.

Ruger, Jennifer Prah, 'Toward a Theory of a Right to Health: Capability and Incompletely Theorized Agreements' (2006) 18 *Yale Journal of Law and Humanities* 273.

Ruger, Jennifer Prah and Derek Yach, 'The Global Role of the World Health Organisation' (2009) 2(2) *Global Health Governance*, www.ghgj.org/Volume%20II%20Issue%202.htm at 22 June 2009.

Ruger, Theodore W., 'Health Law's Coherence Anxiety' (2008) 96 *Georgetown Law Journal* 625.

Sabel, Charles F. and William H. Simon, 'Destabilization Rights: How Public Law Litigation Succeeds' (2004) 117 *Harvard Law Review* 1016.

Sadurski, Wojciech, 'Law's Legitimacy and "Democracy-Plus"' (2006) 26 *Oxford Journal of Legal Studies* 377.

Sager, Lawrence, *Justice in Plainclothes: A Theory of American Constitutional Practice* (New Haven, CT: Yale University Press, 2004).

Samuelson, Pamela, 'IBM's Pragmatic Embrace of Open Source' (2006) 49(10) *Communications of the Association for Computing Machinery* 21.

Sanchez, Gimena and Vicki Gass, 'WOLA's Human Rights Arguments against the Colombia FTA' (Washington Office on Latin America, 7 April 2008), www.wola.org/ at 27 January 2009.

Sanjuan, Judit Rius, 'Collective Management of Intellectual Property – Patent Pools to Expand Access to Essential Medical Technologies' (Research Note No 3(1), Knowledge Ecology International, 2007).

Santa Cruz, Maximiliano, 'Intellectual Property Provisions in European Union Trade Agreements: Implications for Developing Countries' (2007) *United Nations Conference on Trade and Development – International Centre for Trade and Sustainable Development Issue Paper No 20*, www.ictsd.org/pubs/index.htm at 27 January 2009.

Santos, Boaventura de Sous and César Rodríguez-Garavito (eds.), *Law and Globalization from Below: Towards a Cosmopolitan Legality* (Cambridge University Press, 2005).

Sarat, Austin and Stuart Scheingold (eds.) *Cause Lawyers and Social Movements* (Palo Alto, CA: Stanford University Press, 2006).

Sarngadharan, Mangalasseril G., Mikulas Popovic, Lilian Bruch, Jörg Schupback and Röbert Gallo, 'Antibodies Reactive with Human T-lymphotropic Retroviruses (HTLV-III) in the Serum of Patients with AIDS' (1984) 224 *Science* 506–8.

Scharpf, Fritz, *Governing in Europe: Effective and Democratic?* (Oxford University Press, 1999).

Schellekens, Maurice, 'Open Source Biotechnology: A Drug for Developing Countries' Health Problems' (10 May 2007) *Social Sciences Research Network*, papers.ssrn.com/sol3/papers.cfm?abstract_id=1130798 at 3 March 2009.

Scherer, Frederic, *Innovation and Growth: Schumpeterian Perspectives* (Cambridge, MA: MIT Press, 1984).

'Markets and Uncertainty in Pharmaceutical Development' (Working Paper No RWP07–039, John F. Kennedy School of Government, Harvard University, 2007).

Scherer, Frederic and Jayashree Watal, 'Post-TRIPS Options for Access to Patented Medicines in Developing Nations' (2002) 5 *Journal of International Economic Law* 913.

Schumacher, E. F., *Buddhist Economics*, The E.F. Schumacher Society, www.schumachersociety.org/buddhist_economics/english.html at 26 February 2009.

Schumer, Chuck, 'New Cipro Source Could Dramatically Increase Supply' (Press Release, 16 October 2001), www.senate.gov/~schumer/SchumerWebsite/pressroom/press_releases/PR00728.html at 2 March 2009.

Schupbach, Jörg, Mikulas Popovic, Raymond Gilden, Matthew Gonda, Mangalasseril Sarngadharan and Robert Gallo, 'Serological Analysis of a Subgroup of Human T-lymphotropic Retroviruses (HTLV-III) Associated with AIDS' (1984) 224 *Science* 503–5.

Schwab, Susan, 'Letter to Congressman Thomas Allen', 17 January 2008.

Scotchmer, Suzanne, 'Standing on the Shoulders of Giants: Cumulative Research and the Patent Law' (1991) 5 *Journal of Economic Perspectives* 29.

Scott, Colin, 'Analysing Regulatory Space: Fragmented Resources and Institutional Design' (2001) *Public Law* 329.

Sedyaningsih, Endang, Siti Isfandari, Triono Soendoro and Siti Fadilah Supari, 'Towards Mutual Trust, Transparency and Equity in Virus Sharing Mechanism: The Avian Influenza Case of Indonesia' (2008) 37 *Annals Academy of Medicine Singapore* 482.

Selgelid, Michael, 'Ethics and Drug Resistance' (2007) 21 *Bioethics* 218.

Sell, Susan, 'Industry Strategies for Intellectual Property and Trade: The Quest for TRIPS, and Post-TRIPS Strategies' (2002) 10 *Cardozo Journal of International and Comparative Law* 79.

'Intellectual Property Protection and Antitrust in the Developing World: Crisis, Coercion, and Choice' (1995) 49 *International Organization* 315.

Power and Ideas: The North–South Politics of Intellectual Property and Antitrust (Albany, NY: State University of New York Press, 1998).

Private Power, Public Law: The Globalization of Intellectual Property Rights (Cambridge University Press, 2003).

Sell, Susan and Aseem Prakash, 'Using Ideas Strategically: The Contest between Business and NGO Networks in Intellectual Property Rights' (2004) 48 *International Studies Quarterly* 143.

Sen, Amartya, *Development as Freedom* (Oxford: Oxford University Press, 1999).

Serafino, David, 'Survey of Patent Pools Demonstrates Variety of Purposes and Management Structures' (Research Note No 6, Knowledge Ecology International, 2007).

Shadlen, Ken, 'Policy Space for Development in the WTO and Beyond: The Case of Intellectual Property Rights' (Working Paper No 05/06, Global Development and Environment Institute, Tufts University, 2005).

Shaffer, Ellen, Howard Waitzkin, Joseph Brenner and Rebeca Jasso-Aguilar, 'Global Trade and Public Health' (2005) 95 *American Journal of Public Health* 23.

Shaffer, Gregory, *Defending Interests: Public Private Partnerships in W.T.O. Litigation* (Washington, DC: Brookings Institution Press, 2003).

Shapiro, Carl, 'Navigating the Patent Thicket: Cross Licences, Patent Pools and Standard-Setting', in Adam Jaffe, Josh Lerner, and Scott Stern (eds.), *Innovation Policy and the Economy*, Vol. 1 (Cambridge, MA: MIT Press, 2001).

Shapiro, Martin, *Who Guards the Guardians?: Judicial Control of Administration* (Athens, GA: University of Georgia Press, 1988).

Shashikant, Sangeeta, 'Key Issues Unresolved at WHO Meeting on Influenza Virus Sharing', *Third World Network* (2008), www.twnside.org.sg/title2/health.info/2008/twnhealthinfo20081201.htm at 6 March 2009.

'More Countries Use Compulsory License, but New Problems Emerge', *Third World Network* (19 May 2005), www.twnside.org.sg/title2/health.info/twninfohealth004.htm.

Shavell, Steven and Tanguy van Ypersele, 'Rewards versus Intellectual Property Rights' (2001) 44 *Journal of Law and Economics* 525.

Shue, Henry, *Basic Rights: Subsistence, Affluence and U.S. Foreign Policy* (2nd edn, Princeton University Press, 1996).

Silverman, Ed, 'India's Gleevec Ruling Is Bad News for Other Drugmakers Too' *Pharmalot*, 7 August 2007, www.pharmalot.com/2007/08/indias-gleevec-ruling-is-bad-news-for-other-drugmakers-too/ at 4 October 2007.

Simon, James, Eric Claassen, Carmen Correa and Albert D. M. E. Osterhause, 'Managing Severe Acute Respiratory Syndrome (SARS) Intellectual Property Rights: The Possible Role of Patent Pooling' (2005) 83 *Bulletin of the World Health Organization* 707.

Sinclair, Ian, *The Vienna Convention on the Law of Treaties* (2nd edn, Manchester University Press, 1984).

Singer, Peter, 'What a Billionaire Should Give – and What Should You?', *New York Times Magazine*, 17 December 2006.

Singh, Kavaljit, 'Patents v. Patients: AIDS, TNCs and Drug Price Wars', *Third World Network* (2001), www.twnside.org.sg/title/twr131c.htm at 11 July 2007.

Smith, Pamela, 'How Do Foreign Patent Rights Affect U.S. Exports, Affiliate Sales, and Licenses?' (2001) 55 *Journal of International Economics* 411.

Smith, Raymond and Patricia Siplon, *Drugs into Bodies: Global AIDS Treatment Activism* (Westport: Praeger, 2006).

Snow, Arthur and Ronald Warren, 'The Marginal Welfare Cost of Public Funds: Theory and Estimates' (1996) 61 *Journal of Public Economics* 289.

Sobel, Dava, *Longitude* (New York: Walker & Company, 1995).

Spectar, Jem, 'The Olde Order Crumbleth: HIV-Pestilence as a Security Issue and New Thinking about Core Concepts in International Affairs' (2003) 13 *Indiana International and Comparative Law Review* 481.

Spethmann, Betsy, 'The RED Brigade', *Promo Magazine*, 1 January 2007.

Sridhar, Devi, 'Improving Access to Essential Medicines: How Health Concerns can be Prioritised in the Global Governance System' (2008) 1 *Public Health Ethics* 83.

Sridhar, Devi, Sanjeev Khagram and Tikki Pang, 'Are Existing Governance Structures Equipped to Deal with Today's Global Health Challenges? Towards Systematic Coherence in Scaling Up' (2009) 2(2) *Global Health Governance*, www.ghgj.org/Volume%20II%20Issue%202.htm at 22 June 2009.

Srinivas, Krishna Ravi, 'Intellectual Property Rights and Bio Commons: Open Source and Beyond' (2006) 58(188) *International Social Science Journal* 319.

'Sink or Swim: Eco-Patent Commons and Transfer of Environmentally Sustainable Technologies' (2008) 2(2) *Bridges Trade BioRes* 17.

Srinivas, Smita, 'Intellectual Property Rights, Innovation and Healthcare: Unanswered Questions in Theory and Policy' (2008) 10(2) *Economica* (Rio de Janeiro) 106.

St Amant, Kirk and Brian Still (eds.), *Handbook of Research on Open Source Software: Technological, Economic and Social Perspectives* (New York: Information Science Reference, 2007).

Staff Writer, '3 Billion Cedis Voted for Medical Bills', *Daily Graphic* (Ghana), 29 January 2003.

Staff Writer, 'First Generic Drugs En Route to Africa under 5-Year-Old WTO Deal' (2008) 12(31) *Bridges Weekly Trade News Digest* 5.

Staff Writer, 'International Health Regulations: The Challenges Ahead' (2007) 369 *Lancet* 1763.

Steger, Debra, 'The Culture of the WTO: Why it Needs to Change' (2007) 10 *Journal of International Economic Law* 483.

Steinberg, Richard, 'Judicial Lawmaking at the WTO: Discursive Constitutional and Political Constraints' (2004) 98 *American Journal of International Law* 247.

Stiglitz, Joseph, 'Knowledge as a Global Public Good', in Inge Kaul, Isabelle Grunberg and Marc A. Stern (eds.), *Global Public Goods: International Cooperation in the 21st Century* (New York: Oxford University Press, 1999), 306.

'Scrooge and Intellectual Property Rights: A Medical Prize Fund Could Improve the Financing of Drug Innovations' (2006) 333 *British Medical Journal* 1279.

Storm, Stephanie and Matt Fleischer-Black, 'Drug Maker's Vow to Donate Cancer Medicine Falls Short', *The New York Times*, 5 June 2003.

Strange, Susan, 'The Erosion of the State' (1997) 11 *Current History* 365.

Subramanian, Arvind, 'The AIDS Crisis, Differential Pricing of Drugs, and the TRIPS Agreement' (2001) 4 *Journal of World Intellectual Property* 323.

Sukumar, C. R., 'Novartis Loses Patent Claim on Cancer Drug – Patents Controller Upholds Natco Contention', *The Hindu Business Line*, 26 January 2006.

Sunstein, Cass, *The Second Bill of Rights: FDR's Unfinished Revolution and Why We Need It More than Ever* (New York: Basic Books, 2004).

Swanson, Timothy and Timo Goeschl, 'Property Rights Issues Involving Plant Genetic Resources: Implications of Ownership for Economic Efficiency' (2000) 32 *Ecological Economics* 75.

Syed, Talha, 'Should a Prize System for Pharmaceuticals Require Patent Protection for Eligibility?', Discussion Paper Number 2, www. healthimpactfund.org.

Sykes, Sir Richard, 'Presentation at the Royal Institute of International Affairs', London, 14 March 2002).

't Hoen, Ellen, 'Report of the Commission on Intellectual Property Rights, Innovation and Public Health: A Call to Governments' (2006) 84 *Bulletin of the World Health Organization* 421.

The Global Politics of Pharmaceutical Monopoly Power: Drug Patents, Access, Innovation and the Application of the WTO Doha Declaration on TRIPS and Public Health (Diemen: AMB Publishers, 2009).

'TRIPS, Pharmaceutical Patents and Access to Essential Medicines: A Long Way from Seattle to Doha' (2002) 3 *Chicago Journal of International Law* 27.

'Undermining TRIPS: Protectionism at its Worst' (2007) 369 *The Lancet* 2.

Tapscott, Don and Anthony Williams, *Wikinomics: How Mass Collaboration Changes Everything* (New York: Portfolio, Penguin Books, 2006).

Taubman, Antony, 'Rethinking TRIPS: "Adequate Remuneration" for Non-Voluntary Patent Licensing' (2008) 11(4) *Journal of International Economic Law* 927–70.

'Saving the Village: Conserving Jurisprudential Diversity in the International Protection of Traditional Knowledge', in Keith Maskus and Jerome Reichman (eds.) *International Public Goods and Transfer of Technology under a Globalised Intellectual Property Regime* (Cambridge University Press, 2005), 521.

Temin, Peter, *Taking your Medicine: Drug Regulation in the United States* (Cambridge, MA: Harvard University Press, 1980).

Thomas, Patricia, *Big Shot: Passion, Politics and the Struggle for an AIDS Vaccine* (New York: Public Affairs, 2001).

Thorisson, Gudmundur and Lincoln Stein, 'The SNP Consortium Website: Past, Present and Future' (2003) 31 *Nucleic Acids Research* 124–7.

Tilford, David, 'Saving the Blueprints: The International Legal Regime for Plant Resources' (1998) 30 *Case Western Reserve Journal of International Law* 373.

Trachtman, Joel, 'International Trade: Regionalism', in Andrew Guzman and Alan Sykes (eds.), *Research Handbook in International Economic Law* (Cheltenham: Edward Elgar, 2007), 151.

'Regulatory Jurisdiction and the WTO' (2007) 10 *Journal of International Economic Law* 631.

'The Constitutions of the WTO' (2006) 17 *European Journal of International Law* 623.

Triggle, David, 'Treating Desires Not Diseases: A Pill for Every Ill and an Ill for Every Pill?' (2007) 12 *Drug Discovery Today* 161.

Trouiller, Patrice, Piero Olliaro, Els Torreele, James Orbinski, Richard Laing and Nathan Ford, 'Drug Development for Neglected Diseases: A Deficient Market and a Public-Health Policy Failure' (2002) 359 *The Lancet* 2188.

Tucker, Todd and Lori Wallach, *The Rise and Fall of Fast Track Trade Authority*, (Washington, DC: Public Citizen's Global Trade Watch, 2008), www.citizen.org/documents/riseandfall.pdf at 27 January 2009.

Tungsuwan, Peerapan and William McKay, 'Compulsory Drug Licenses Violate World Trade Treaty', *Bangkok Post*, 23 April 2007.

Tunsarawuth, Sinfah, 'Thailand: 20 More Drugs in Pipeline for Possible Compulsory Licences', *Intellectual Property Watch*, 2 November 2007, www.ip-watch.org/ at 11 February 2009.

Tushnet, Mark, *Weak Courts, Strong Rights: Judicial Review and Social Welfare Rights in Comparative Constitutional Law* (Princeton University Press, 2008).

Twomey, J. G. Jr, 'AIDS Activism' (1990) 20 *Hastings Centre Report* 39.

Valenti, Jack, 'Letter to the Editor', *Advertising Age* (New York), 2007

van der Walt, A. J., *Constitutional Property Law* (Cape Town: Juta Law Publishers, 2005).

van Gelder, Alec and Franklin Cudjoe, 'Patent-Busting: Punishing the Poor', *The Straits Times* (Singapore), 2 May 2008.

Van Overwalle, Geertrui, 'Reconciling Patent Policies and University Mission' (2006) 13 *Ethical Perspectives* 234.

Van Overwalle, Geertrui, Esther van Zimmeren, Birgit Verbeure and Gert Matthijs, 'Models for Facilitating Access to Patents on Genetic Inventions' (2006) 7 *Nature Reviews Genetics* 143.

Varmus, Harold, Richard Klausner, Elias Zerhouni, Tara Acharya, Abdallah Daar and Peter Singer, 'Grand Challenges in Global Health' (2003) 302 *Science* 398.

Vaughan, Martin, 'US–Peru Trade Deal: The First Test of Renegotiated IP Provisions', *Intellectual Property Watch*, 5 November 2007, www.ip-watch.org at 23 January 2009.

Vaver, David and Lionel Bently (eds.), *Intellectual Property Law in the New Millennium* (Cambridge University Press, 2004).

von Schoen-Angerer, Tido, 'MSF Intervention at IGWG 2.2', 2008, www.accessmed-msf.org/msf-intervention-at-igwg-22/.

Voumard, John, *Access to Biological Resources in Commonwealth Areas* (Canberra: The Commonwealth, 2000).

Wadman, Meredith, 'Biomedical Philanthropy: State of the Donation' (2007) 447 *Nature* 248.

Walker, Vern, 'Keeping the WTO from Becoming the "World Trans-science Organization": Scientific Uncertainty, Science Policy and Fact Finding in the Growth Hormones Dispute' (1981) 31 *Cornell International Law Journal* 251.

Wallach, Lori M., 'Our Statements: Majority of House Democrats Stand Up for Constituents', *Public Citizens*, 8 November 2007, citizen.typepad.com/eyesontrade/2007/11/our-statement-m.html at 3 February 2009.

Wark, McKenzie, *Celebrities, Culture and Cyberspace: The Light on the Hill in a Postmodern World* (Sydney: Pluto Press, 1999).

Watchirs, Helen, *Measuring Legal Implementation of International Human Rights Norms in the Context of HIV/AIDS* (Canberra: ANU College of Law, 2001).

Webb, Douglas, 'Legitimate Actors? The Future Roles for NGOs against HIV/AIDS in Sub-Saharan Africa', in Nana Puku and Alan Whiteside (eds.), *The Political Economy of AIDS in Africa* (Farnham: Ashgate Publishing, 2004) 19.

Weber, Steve, *The Success of Open Source* (Cambridge, MA: Harvard University Press, 2004).

Wei, Marlynn, 'Should Prizes Replace Patents? A Critique of the Medical Innovation Prize Act of 2005' (2007) 13 *Boston University Journal of Science and Technology Law* 25.

Weissbrodt, David and Kell Schoff, 'A Human Rights Approach to Intellectual Property Protection: The Genesis and Application of Sub-Commission Resolution 2000/7' (2003) 5 *Minnesota Intellectual Property Review* 1.

Westerhaus, Michael and Arachu Castro, 'How Do Intellectual Property Law and International Trade Agreements Affect Access to Antiretroviral Therapy' (2006) 3(8) *The Public Library of Science Medicine* 1230–6.

Wiggins, Steven, 'The Impact of Regulation of Pharmaceutical Research Expenditures: A Dynamic Approach' (1983) 21 *Economic Inquiry* 115.

Wilder, Richard, 'Market Segmentation: Techniques, Actors and Incentives – The Use of Intellectual Property Rights' (Paper presented at the Workshop on Differential Pricing and Financing of Essential Drugs, WHO and WTO Secretariats, Norway, 8–11 April 2001).

Winner, Ted, 'Bono and Hirst Paint the Town Red: Rock Star Bono and Artist Damien Hirst Teamed Up and Raised $42.5M for Africa', *ABC News*, 15 February 2008.

Wirth, David, 'The Role of Science in the Uruguay Round and NAFTA Trade Disciplines' (1994) 27 *Cornell International Law Journal* 817.

Witty, Andrew, 'Big Pharma as a Catalyst for Change', Harvard Medical School, 13 February 2009, www.gsk.com/media/Witty-Harvard-Speech-Summary.pdf.

Wolfe, Robert, 'Decision-Making and Transparency in the 'Medieval' WTO: Does the Sutherland Report Have the Right Prescription?' (2005) 8 *Journal of International Economic Law* 631.

Wong-Anan, Nopporn, 'Thailand Issues More Compulsory Drug Licenses', *Reuters* (25 January 2007), lists.essential.org/pipermail/ip-health/2007-January/010433.html at 20 March 2009.

World Business Council for Sustainable Development, *Corporate Social Responsibility: Making Good Business Sense* (Geneva and Washington, DC: World Business Council for Sustainable Development, 2000).

Worth, Jess, 'Punk Rock Capitalism', *New Internationalist*, 11 January 2006, www. encyclopedia.com/doc/1G1-155174516.html at 10 March 2009.

Wright, Brian, 'The Economics of Invention Incentives: Patents, Prizes, and Research Contracts' (1983) 73 *American Economic Review* 691.

Yamamoto, Eric K. 'Critical Race Praxis: Race Theory and Political Lawyering Practice in Post-Civil Rights America' (1997) 95 *Michigan Law Review* 821.

Yamin, Alicia, 'Not Just a Tragedy: Access to Medications as a Right under International Law' (2003) 21 *Boston University International Law Journal* 325.

Yglesias, Matthew, 'Who's Giving Money to Bill Clinton?', *Los Angeles Times*, 4 October 2007.

Yu, Peter, 'Access to Medicines, BRICS Alliances and Collective Action' (2008) 34 *American Journal of Law and Medicine* 345.

Zimmerman, Jurg, 'Pyrimidine Derivatives and Processes for the Preparation Thereof', U.S. Patent No 5,521,184 (filed 28 April 1994; issued 28 May 1996).

Judicial Decisions

Abigail Alliance for Better Access to Developmental Drugs v. *C. Von Eschenbach*, 495 F 3d 695 (DC Cir. 2007).

Actavis UK Ltd v. *Merck & Co. Inc.*, [2008] EWCA Civ 444.

AIDS Access Foundation et al. v. *Bristol-Myers Squibb Company and Department of Intellectual Property, Central Intellectual Property & International Trade Court*, Black Case No Tor Por 34/2544, Red Case No 92/2545 (Thailand 2002).

Anheuser-Busch Inc. v. *Portugal*, (10 October 2005) App No 73049/01 Eur Court HR.

Apotex Inc. v. *Sanofi-Synthelabo Canada Inc.*, [2008] 3 S.C.R. 265.

Apotex Inc. v. *Wellcome Foundation Ltd*, [2002] 4 S.C.R. 153.

Bandhua Mukti Morcha v. *Union of India*, (AIR 1984 SC 802).

Cadbury Limited, [2002] ATMO 56 (28 June 2002).

Cadbury Schweppes Pty Ltd v. *Darrell Lea Chocolate Shops Pty Ltd (No 4)*, [2006] FCA 446.

Cadbury Schweppes Pty Ltd v. *Darrell Lea Chocolate Shops Pty Ltd (No 8)*, [2008] FCA 470.

Consumer Project on Technology, 'Statement of Information to the Competition Commission of South Afria on Complaint against GlaxoSmithKline and Boehringer Ingelheim' (3 February 2003), www.cptech.org/ip/health/cl/cl-cases/rsa-tac/cptech-statement.doc.

Cruz Bermude, et al. v. *Ministerio de Sanidad y Asistencia Social*, (Case No 15.789, Decision No 916, 15 July 1999).

Darrell Lea Chocolate Shops Pty Ltd v. *Cadbury Limited*, [2008] ATMO 6 (15 January 2008).

Dawson Chemical Company v. *Rohm & Haas*, 448 US 176 (1980).

Farooque v. *Bangladesh & Ors*, (Writ Petition No 92 of 1996).

First National Bank of SA Ltd t/a Wesbank v. *Commissioner, South African Revenue Service*, 2002 (4) SA 768 (CC).

Google, Inc. v. *Microsoft Corp.*, 415 F Supp 2d 1018 ND Cal 2005.

Hazel Tau & Others v. *GlaxoSmithKline and Boehringer Ingelheim*, Competition Commission of South Africa (2003).

Hoffmann v. *South African Airways*, 2001 (1) SA 1 (CC, South Africa).

In re Masucci, 179 USPQ 829 (TTAB 1973).

The Initiative for Medicines, Access & Knowledge (I-MAK) v. *Abbott Laboratories, Indian Patent Application No 339/MUM/2006 filed on 23 August 2004*, 16 August 2007.

Kasikili/Sedudu Island (Botswana v. *Namibia) (Judgment)*, [1999] ICJ Rep 1045, 1075–6.

Madey v. *Duke University*, 307 F 3d 1351 (Fed Cir, 2002).

Mendoza and Ors v. *Minister of Public Health and the Director of the National AIDS-HIV-STI Programme*, (Resolucion No 0749–2003-RA, 28 January 2004).

Merck KGAA v. *Integra Lifesciences I, Inc.*, 545 U.S. 193 (2005).

Microsoft Corporation, [2007] ADO 1 (14 February 2007).

Microsoft Corporation v. *PC Club Australia Pty Ltd*, [2005] FCA 1522.

Minister of Health v. *Treatment Action Campaign*, 2002 (5) SA 721.

Network of Positive People, and the Indian Network for People Living With HIV/AIDS v. *Abbott Laboratories*, Indian Application No IN/PCT/2001/01312/MUM, 4 August 2006, www.i-mak.org/storage/PgOppKaletraSoftGel.pdf.

Novartis AG and another v. *Union of India and others*, (6 August 2007, High Court of Judicature at Madras for W.P. Nos. 24759 and 24760 of 2006), judis.nic.in/chennai/qrydisp.asp?tfnm=11121.

Novartis v. *Union of India* (6 August 2007), Order of High Court of Judicature at Madras for W.P. Nos. 24759 and 24760 of 2006), (Affidavit filed by Petitioner Novartis), www.cptech.org/ip/health/c/india/novartis-v-india.doc at 23 September 2007.

Novartis v. *Union of India* (6 August 2007), Order of High Court of Judicature at Madras for W.P. Nos. 24759 and 24760 of 2006), (Affidavit in Reply filed by the Respondent).

Novartis v. *Union of India* (6 August 2007), Order of High Court of Judicature at Madras for W.P. Nos. 24759 and 24760 of 2006), (The Novartis petition challenging the rejection of Glivec patent claim), www.scribd.com/doc/456550/High-Court-order-Novartis-Union-of-India.

Paschim Banga Khet Mazdoor Society v. *State of West Bengal* (AIR 1996 SC 2426).

The Pharmaceutical Manufacturers' Association of South Africa v. *Government of South Africa*, Notice of Motion, Case Number 4183/98, in the High Court of South Africa (Transvaal Provincial Division).

The Pharmaceutical Manufacturers' Association of South Africa v. *Government of South Africa*, Case Number 4183/98, in the High Court of South Africa (Transvaal Provincial Division), paras. 58–71 Founding Affidavit, 'Application to be admitted as an *amicus curiae*'.

President of the Republic of South Africa v. *Modderklip Boerdery (Pty) Ltd*, 2005 (5) SA 3 (CC).
Qualitex Co. v. *Jacobson Products Co., Inc.*, 514 US 159 (1995).
Roche Products, Inc. v. *Bolar Pharmaceutical Co.*, 733 F 2d 858 (Fed Cir, 1984).
Samity v. *State of W.B.*, (1996) 4 S.C.C. 37 (Sup. Ct. India).
Soobramoney v. *Minister of Health, Kwazulu-Natal*, 1998 (1) SA 765 ('*Soobramoney*').
State of Punjab v. *Mahindrasingh Chawla*, (AIR 1997 SC 1225).
Woolworths Limited v. *BP* [2006] FCAFC 132.
Z4 Technologies, Inc. v. *Microsoft Corp.*, 507 F 3d 1340 CA Fed (Tex) (2007).

Legislation

An Act to Amend the Patent Act and the Food and Drugs Act (Canada), SC 2004, c. 23 ('The Jean Chrétien Pledge to Africa Act').
An Act to amend the Public Health Service Act to provide protections and countermeasures against chemical, radiological, or nuclear agents that may be used in a terrorist attack against the United States by giving the National Institutes of Health contracting flexibility, infrastructure improvements, and expediting the scientific peer review process, and streamlining the Food and Drug Administration approval process of countermeasures (Project Bioshield Act) 2004 (United States) Pub L No 108-276 (2004), codified in 42 USC § 2001.
Constitution of the Republic of Ghana 1992.
Constitution of the Republic of India 1950.
Constitution of the Republic of South Africa 1996.
Constitution of the United States of America 1787.
Drug Price Competition and Patent Term Restoration Act 1984 (United States), Pub L No 98-417, 98 Stat. 1585 (1984), codified in 21 USC § 355, 360 (2000), 35 USC § 156, 271, 282 (2000) ('the Hatch-Waxman Act').
Executive Order 13155 of 10 May 2000 (United States), 'Access to HIV/AIDS Pharmaceuticals and Medical Technologies', www.archives.gov/federal-register/executive-orders/2000.html.
Federal Act on Cartels and Other Restraints on Competition of 6 October 1995 (Switzerland).
Federal Food, Drug, and Cosmetic Act 2008 (United States) 21 USC § 355.
Food and Drug Administration Amendments Act 2007 (United States) 21 USC § 301 (2007).
Hospital Fees Act 1971 (Ghana).
Intellectual Property Code 1997 (The Philippines) [Republic Act No 8293].
Medical Innovation Prize Fund Act 2007 (United States) (S. 2210).
Medicare Prescription Drug Improvement and Modernization Act 2003 (United States) Pub L No 108-173, 117 Stat. 2066 (2003).

Medicines and Related Substances Act 101 of 1965 (South Africa).
Medicines and Related Substances Control Amendment Act 1997 (South Africa).
National Health Act 1953 (Cth).
Patent Act 1952 (United States) 35 USC § 1.
Patent Act 1979 (Thailand) B.E. 2522.
The Patent Reform Act 2007 (United States) (H.R. 1908, S. 1145).
Patents Act 1970 (India).
Patents Act 1990 (Cth).
Patents Amendment Act 2002 (India).
Patents (Amendment) Act 2005 (India).
Patents (Amendment) Ordinance 2004 (No 7 of 2004) (India).
Rules of the Constitutional Court of South Africa 2003 (South Africa).
Trade Act 1974 (United States) 19 USC § 2102 (1974).
Trade Act 2002 (United States) 19 USC § 3801 (2002).
Trade Promotion Authority Act 2002 (United States), title XXI of Pub L No 107-210 (2002), div. B, Aug. 6, 2002, 116 Stat. 993, codified in 19 USC § 3805.
Trademark Act 1946 (United States) ('Lanham Act'), 15 USC § 1052 (1946).
Universally Accessible Cheaper and Quality Medicines Act 2008 (the Philippines).
University and Small Business Patent Procedures Act 1980 (United States) (the 'Bayh-Dole Act') 35 USC § 200–12 (1980).

Official Publications

Commission on Intellectual Property Rights, *Integrating Intellectual Property Rights and Development Policy* (2002), www.iprcommission.org/ at 5 February 2009.
Joint Standing Committee on Treaties. *Protocol Amending the TRIPS Agreement*, (Canberra: Australian Parliament, August 2007), www.aph.gov.au/house/committee/jsct/9may2007/report/chapter9.pdf.
Ministers of Foreign Affairs of Brazil, France, Indonesia, Norway, Senegal, South Africa and Thailand, 'Oslo Ministerial Declaration – Global Health: A Pressing Foreign Policy Issue of our Time' (2007) 369 *The Lancet* 1373.
Ministry of Public Health, Thailand, 'Announcement Regarding Exploitation of Patents on Drugs and Medical Supplies for Clopidogrel' (Press Release, 25 January 2007), www.cptech.org/ip/health/c/thailand/thai-cl-clopidogrel_en.pdf at 20 March 2009.
Ministry of Public Health and National Health Security Office, Thailand, *Facts and Evidences on the 10 Burning Issues Related to the Government Use of Patents on Three Patented Essential Drugs in Thailand* (16 February 2007) www.moph.go.th/hot/White%20Paper%20CL-EN.pdf at 31 March 2009 ('Thai White Paper').
The Office of the United States Global AIDS Coordinator, *Bringing Hope: Supplying ARVs for HIV/AIDS Treatment: The United States President's Emergency Plan for AIDS Relief* (Washington DC: United States

Department of State, May 2006), www.state.gov/documents/organization/66513.pdf at 23 August 2008.

The Royal Society of the United Kingdom, *Keeping Science Open: The Effects of Intellectual Property Policy on the Conduct of Science* (London: The Royal Society of the United Kingdom, 2003).

United Kingdom Department for International Development ('DFID'), *Increasing People's Access to Essential Medicine in Developing Countries: A Framework for Good Practice in the Pharmaceutical Industry* (March 2005), www.dfid.gov.uk/Pubs/files/pharm-framework.pdf at 18 May 2009.

United States, 'Declaration Made at the United Nations Environment Programme Conference for the Adoption of the Agreed Text of the Convention on Biological Diversity' (1992) 31 *International Legal Materials* 848.

United States Department of Health and Human Services, *Australia–U.S. Medicines Working Group Holds First Meeting* (24 October 2007), www.globalhealth.gov/news/news/011406.html at 23 February 2009.

United States Department of Justice, 'Letter from Joel Klein to Carey Ramos' (10 June 1999) ('Toshiba Review Letter').

'Letter from Joel Klein to Gerrard Beeney' (26 June 1997) ('MPEG-LA Review Letter').

'Letter from Joel Klein to Gerrard Beeney' (16 December 1998) ('Sony Review Letter').

United States Department of Justice and Federal Trade Commission, *Antitrust Enforcement and Intellectual Property Rights: Promoting Innovation and Competition* (2007), www.usdoj.gov/atr/public/hearings/ip/222655.pdf at 2 March 2009.

Antitrust Guidelines for the Licensing of Intellectual Property (1995).

United States Department of State, 'Convention on Biological Diversity' (1992) 3 *US Department of State Dispatches* 423.

United States Food and Drug Administration, *CDER NDAs Approved in Calendar Years 1990–2004 by Therapeutic Potential and Chemical Type* (2008), www.fda.gov/cder/rdmt/pstable.htm at 19 February 2009.

United States Government Accountability Office, *International Trade – An Analysis of Free Trade Agreements and Congressional and Private Sector Consultations under Trade Promotion Authority* (November 2007), www.gao.gov/new.items/d0859.pdf at 27 January 2009.

United States House of Representatives Committee on Government Reform – Minority Staff Special Investigations Division, *Trade Agreements and Access to Medications under the Bush Administration* (June 2005), www.reform.house.gov/ at 27 January 2009.

United States Patent and Trademark Office, 'Biotech Group Explain Objection to Earth Summit's Biodiversity Treaty' (1992) 44 *Patent, Trademark and Copyright Journal* 120.

Trademark Manual of Examining Procedure: Fifth Edition (Alexandria, VA: United States Patent and Trade Mark Office, 2007).

United States Trade Representative, *Special 301 Report* (30 April 2007) www.ustr.gov/Document_Library/Press_Releases/2007/April/SPECIAL_301_Report.html at 20 March 2009.

'United States Files WTO Cases against China over Deficiencies in China's Intellectual Property Rights Laws and Market Access Barriers to Copyright-Based Industries' (Press Release, 9 April 2007).

International Materials

Africa – The African Proposal for the establishment of a Development Agenda for WIPO (Inter-Sessional Intergovernmental Meeting on a Development Agenda for WIPO, 3rd sess, 20–22 July 2005) (IMM/3/2 Rev), www.wipo.int/edocs/mdocs/mdocs/en/iim_3/iim_3_2_rev.doc at 19 May 2009.

African, Caribbean and Pacific Group of States, *Paragraph 6 of the Doha Declaration on the TRIPS Agreement and Public Health*, WTO Doc IP/C/W/401 (2003) (Communication from the African, Caribbean and Pacific Group of States).

African Charter on Human and Peoples' Rights, OAU Doc. CAB/LEG/67/3 rev. 5; 1520 UNTS 217; 21 ILM 58 (1982).

Agreement between the World Intellectual Property Organization and the World Trade Organization, WIPO Doc WO030 (22 December 1995), www.wipo.int/treaties/en/agreement/pdf/trtdocs_wo030.pdf at 16 January 2009.

Amendment of the TRIPS Agreement, WTO Doc WT/L/641 (2005) (Decision of 6 December 2005 of the General Council) ('TRIPS Waiver').

Amendment of the TRIPS Agreement – Extension of the Period for the Acceptance by Members of the Protocol Amending the TRIPS Agreement, WTO Doc WT/L/711 (2007) (Decision of the General Council of 18 December 2007).

Amendment of the TRIPS Agreement: Proposal for a Decision on an Extension of the Period for the Acceptance by Members of the Protocol Amending the TRIPS Agreement, WTO Doc IP/C/45 (2007).

Application of the International Health Regulations (2005), World Health Assembly 59th mtg Res WHA59.2 (2006).

Arbitration Rules of the United Nations Commission on International Trade Law, GA Res 31/98, UN GAOR, 31st sess, 99th plen mtg, UN Doc A/Res/31/98 (1976).

Argentina and Brazil, *Proposal by Argentina and Brazil for the Establishment of a Development Agenda for WIPO*, 31st (15th extraordinary) sess, WIPO Doc WO/GA/31/11 Add (27 August 2004).

Australia–United States Free Trade Agreement (AUSFTA), signed 18 May 2004 (entered into force 1 January 2005).

Bahrain–United States Free Trade Agreement, signed 14 September 2004 (entered into force 4 August 2006).

Berne Convention for the Protection of Literary and Artistic Works, opened for signature 9 September 1886, 1161 UNTS 3 (entered into force 29 January 1970).

Brazil – Measures Affecting Patent Protection, WT/DS199/4, G/L/454, IP/D/23/Add.1, 19 July 2001, (01–3506).

Canada – Notification under Paragraph 2(C) of the Decision of 30 August 2003 on the Implementation of Paragraph 6 of the Doha Declaration on the TRIPS Agreement and Public Health, WTO Doc IP/N/10/CAN/1 (2007).

Canada – Patent Protection of Pharmaceutical Products: Arbitration under Article 21.3(c) of the Understanding on Rules and Procedures Governing the Settlement of Disputes, WTO Doc WT/DS114/R (2000) (Award of the Arbitrator James Bacchus) ('*Canada – Pharmaceuticals*').

Canada – Patent Protection of Pharmaceutical Products, WTO Doc WT/DS114/R (2000) (Report of the Panel) ('*Canada – Pharmaceutical Patents*').

Canada – Term of Patent Protection, WTO Doc WT/DS170/AB/R, AB-2000–7 (2000) (Report of the Appellate Body).

Central American Free Trade Agreement–Dominican Republic Free Trade Agreement, signed 5 August 2004 (entered into force between the United States and El Salvador on 1 March 2006, followed by Honduras and Nicaragua on 1 April 2006, Guatemala on 1 July 2006, and the Dominican Republic on 1 March 2007. The remaining partner country, Costa Rica, approved the agreement in a national public referendum on 7 October 2007, although entry into force is pending passage of necessary implementation legislation by the Costa Rican legislature).

Chan, Margaret, 'Opening Remarks at the Intergovernmental Working Group on Public Health, Innovation and Intellectual Property', (Geneva: World Health Organization, 28 April 2008).

Chile – IPEG Survey on Copyright Limitations and Exceptions: Preliminary Report on Copyright Limitations and Exceptions, APEC Doc 2008/SOM1/IPEG/007 (2008).

Chile – Provisional Committee on proposals related to a WIPO Development Agenda (1st sess, 20–24 February, 2006): Proposal by Chile (PCDA/1/2), www.wipo.int/edocs/mdocs/mdocs/en/pcda_1_2.doc at 19 May 2009.

Chile–United States Free Trade Agreement, signed 6 June 2003 (entered into force 1 January 2004).

China – Measures Affecting the Protection and Enforcement of Intellectual Property Rights, WTO Doc WT/DS362/R (2008) (Report of the Panel).

China – Measures Affecting the Protection and Enforcement of Intellectual Property Rights, WT/DS362/R (26 January 2009).

China – Measures Affecting Trading Rights and Distribution Services for Certain Publications and Audiovisual Entertainment Products, WTO Doc WT/DS363 (2008).

Colombia – Provisional Committee on proposals related to a WIPO Development Agenda (1st sess, 20–24 February 2006): Proposal by Colombia (PCDA/1/3), www.wipo.int/edocs/mdocs/mdocs/en/pcda_1/pcda_1_3.doc at 19 May 2009.

Colombia–United States Free Trade Agreement, signed 22 November 2006 (pending US Congress approval).

Commission Notice: Guidelines on the Application of Article 81 of the EC Treaty to Technology Transfer Agreements [2004] OJ C 101/2.

Commission on Intellectual Property Rights, Innovation and Public Health, *Public Health, Innovation and Intellectual Property Rights* (Geneva: World Health Organization, 2006).

Committee on Development and Intellectual Property, *Revised Draft Report*, 2nd sess, WIPO Doc CDIP/2/4 Prov. 2 (2008).

The Committee on the Judiciary, United States Congress, *The Patent Reform Act of 2007: Report Together with Additional and Minority Views (to Accompany S. 1145)*, Report No 110–259 (2008).

Compilation of General Comments and General Recommendations Adopted by Human Rights Treaty Bodies, 127, UN Doc HRI/GEN/1/Rev.6 (2003).

Conference of the Parties to the Convention on Biological Diversity, *Access to Genetic Resources and Benefit Sharing: Legislation, Administrative and Policy Information*, 2nd mtg, UN Doc No UNEP/CBD/COP/2/13 (1995) (Report by the Secretariat).

Access to Genetic Resources, 3rd mtg, UN Doc UNEP/CBD/COP/3/20 (1996) (Note by the Executive Secretary).

The Relationship between the TRIPS Agreement and the Convention on Biological Diversity – Summary of Issues Raised and Points Made – Submission by the WTO Secretariat, 8th mtg, UN Doc UNEP/CBD/COP/8/INF/37 (2006).

Report of the Conference of the Parties to the CBD on the Work of its Ninth Meeting, 9th mtg, UN Doc UNEP/CBD/COP/9/29 (2008).

Report of the Eighth Meeting of the Parties to the Convention on Biological Diversity, 8th mtg, UNEP/CBD/COP/8/31 (2006).

Report of the Seventh Meeting of the Conference of the Parties to the Convention on Biological Diversity, 7th mtg, UNEP/CBD/COP/7/21 (2004).

Report of the Sixth Meeting of the Conference of the Parties to the Convention on Biological Diversity, 6th mtg, annex 1 (Decisions Adopted by the Conference of the Parties to the Convention on Biological Diversity at its

Sixth Meeting), VI/24(A) (Bonn Guidelines on Access to Genetic Resources and Fair and Equitable Sharing of the Benefits Arising out of their Utilization) UN Doc UNEP/CBD/COP/6/20 (2002) ('Bonn Guidelines').

Review of National, Regional and Sectoral Measures and Guidelines for Implementation of Article 15, 4th mtg, UN Doc UNEP/CBD/COP/4/23 (1998).

Congressional Budget Office, *Research and Development in the Pharmaceutical Industry* (Washington, DC: Congressional Budget Office, 2006).

Convention on Biological Diversity, opened for signature 5 June 1992, [1993] ATS 32 (entered into force 29 December 1993).

Convention Establishing the World Intellectual Property Organization, opened for signature 14 July 1967, 848 UNTS 3 (entered into force 26 April 1970) ('WIPO Convention').

Convention on the Elimination of Discrimination against Women, GA Res 34/180, 34 UN GAOR Supp (No 46) at 193, UN Doc A/34/46, entered into force 3 September 1981.

Convention on the Grant of European Patents, opened for signature 5 October 1973, 13 ILM 268 (entered into force 7 October 1977) ('European Patent Convention').

Convention on the Rights of the Child, GA Res 44/25, annex, 44 UN GAOR Supp (No 49) at 167, UN Doc A/44/49 (1989), entered into force 2 September 1990.

Council of the European Union, Instrument of Acceptance, SGS7/16652 (Brussels, 19 November 2007), www.wto.org/english/tratop_e/trips_e/popup_amendment_ec_e.htm.

Council for Trade Related Aspects of Intellectual Property Rights, *The Relationship between the TRIPS Agreement and the Convention on Biological Diversity: Summary of Issues Raised and Points Made*, UN Doc IP/C/W/368/Rev.1/Corr.1 (2006) (Note by the Secretariat, Corrigendum).

Decision on Differential and More Favourable Treatment, Reciprocity, and Fuller Participation of Developing Countries, GATT BISD 26S/203, GATT Doc L/4903 (28 November 1979) ('Enabling Clause').

Declaration on the TRIPS Agreement and Public Health: Adopted on 14 November 2001, WTO Doc WT/MIN(01)/DEC/2 (2001) ('the Doha Declaration').

Directive 96/9/EC of the European Parliament and of the Council of 11 March 1996 on the Legal Protection of Databases [1996] OJ L 077.

Directive 2001/83/EC of the European Parliament and of the Council of 6 November 2001 on the Community Code Relating to Medicinal Products for Human Use [2001] OJ L 311.

Directive 2004/27/EC of the European Parliament and of the Council of 31 March 2004 [2004] OJ L 136.

Doha Work Programme, Ministerial Conference 6th sess, WTO Doc WT/MIN (05)/DEC (2005) [40] (Ministerial Declaration).

Draft Global Strategy and Plan of Action on Public Health, Innovation and Intellectual Property, WIPO Doc A/PHI/IGWG/2/INF.DOC./6 (31 August 2007) (Intergovernmental Working Group on Public Health, Innovation and Intellectual Property – Provisional Agenda Item 3).

Economic Community of West African States, *ECOWAS Member States*, www.ecowas.int/ at 23 April 2009.

Revised Treaty, WTO Doc WT/COMTD/N/21 (2005) (Notification from the Parties to the Agreement).

EU Parliament Resolution of 12 July 2007 on TRIPS Agreement and access to medicines, P6_TA(2007) 0353, [I], www.europarl.europa.eu/ at 20 March 2009.

EU Regulation 141/2000 of the European Parliament and of the Council of 16 December 1999 on Orphan Medicinal Products, [2000] OJ L 18.

European Communities – Measures Affecting the Approval and Marketing of Biotech Products, WTO Doc WT/DS291/R, WT/DS292/R, WT/DS293/R (2006) (Reports of the Panel).

European Communities – Measures Concerning Meat and Products (Hormones), WTO Doc WT/DS26/R, WT/DS26/AB/R, WT/DS48/R, WT/DS48/AB/R (1998) (Reports of the Panel and Appellate Body).

European Communities – Protection of Trademarks and Geographic Indications for Agricultural Products and Foodstuffs, WTO Doc WT/DS174/R (2005) (Report of the Panel) ('*EC – GI*').

European Communities – Trade Description of Sardines, WTO Doc WT/DS231/AB/R, AB-2002–3 (2002) (Report of the Appellate Body).

European Community, *Global Status and Trends in Intellectual Property Claims: Genomics, Proteomics and Biotechnology*, Ad Hoc Open-Ended Working Group on Access and Benefit-Sharing 3rd mtg, 32–52, UN Doc UNEP/CBD/WG-ABS/3/INF/4 (2005) (Submission by the European Community).

Extension of the Transition Period under Article 66.1 for Least-Developed Country Members, WTO Doc IP/C/40 (2005) (Decision of the Council for TRIPS of 29 November 2005).

Extension of the Transition Period under Article 66.1 of the TRIPS Agreement for Least-Developed Country Members for Certain Obligations with Respect to Pharmaceutical Products, WTO Doc IP/C/25 (2005) (Decision by the Council for TRIPS of 27 June 2002).

The Friends of Development, 'Proposal to Establish a Development Agenda for WIPO: An Elaboration of Issues Raised in Document WO/GA/31/11', Inter-Sessional Intergovernmental Meeting on a Development Agenda for WIPO, IIM/1/4 (6 April 2005).

General Agreement on Tariffs and Trade 1994, www.wto.org/english/res_e/booksp_e/analytic_index_e/gatt1994_e.htm.

Geneva Declaration on the Future of the World Intellectual Property Organization 2004, www.cptech.org/ip/wipo/futureofwipodeclaration.pdf at 5 February 2009.

Global Strategy and Plan of Action on Public Health, Innovation and Intellectual Property, World Health Assembly 61st mtg, Res WHA61.21 (2008) ('WHO Global Strategy').

The Implementation of the Doha Declaration on the TRIPS Agreement and Public Health, WTO Doc IP/C/W/402 (2003) (Communications by the European Communities and their Member States).

Implementation of Paragraph 6 of the Doha Declaration on the TRIPS Agreement and Public Health, WTO Doc WT/L/540 (2003) (WTO General Council Decision of 30 August 2003).

India – Patent Protection for Pharmaceutical and Agricultural Chemical Products, WTO Doc WT/DS50/AB/R, AB-1997–5 (1997) (Report of the Appellate Body) ('*India – Pharmaceuticals*').

Indonesia, *Sharing of Influenza Viruses and Access to Vaccines and Other Benefits: Interdisciplinary Working Group on Pandemic Influenza Preparedness*, WHO Doc A/PIP/IGM/5 (2007), annex (Fundamental Principles and Elements for the Development of a New System for Virus Access and Fair and Equitable Benefit Sharing Arising from the Use of the Virus for the Pandemic Influenza Preparedness) (Proposal by Indonesia).

Initiative for Vaccine Research, World Health Organization, *Mapping of Intellectual Property Related to the Production of Pandemic Influenza Vaccines* (Geneva: World Health Organization, 2007).

Intellectual Property Rights, Innovation and Public Health, World Health Assembly 56th mtg, Res WHA56.27 (2003).

Interdisciplinary Working Group, *Sharing of Influenza Viruses and Access to Vaccines and Other Benefits: Interdisciplinary Working Group on Pandemic Influenza Preparedness*, WHO Doc A/PIP/IGM/4 (2007) (Report by the Director-General).

International Covenant on Civil and Political Rights, GA Res 2200A (XXI), 21 UN GAOR Supp (No 16) at 52, UN Doc A/6316 (1966), 999 UNTS 171, entered into force 23 March 1976.

International Covenant on Economic, Social and Cultural Rights, opened for signature 16 December 1966, 993 UNTS 3 (entered into force 3 January 1976).

Israel–United States Free Trade Agreement, signed 22 April 1985 (entered into force 1 September 1985).

Japan – Measures Affecting Agricultural Products, WTO Doc WT/DS76/AB/R, AB-1998–8 (1999) (Report of the Appellate Body).

Japan – Measures Affecting the Importation of Apples, WTO Doc WT/DS245/R, WT/DS245/AB/R, (2003) (Report of the Panel).

Jordan–United States Free Trade Agreement, signed 24 October 2000 (entered into force 17 December 2001).

Least-Developed Country Members – Obligations under Article 70.9 of the TRIPS Agreement with Respect to Pharmaceutical Products, WTO Doc WT/L/478 (2002) (Decision of the General Council of 8 July 2002).

Life Sciences Program, World Intellectual Property Organization, *Patent Issues Related to Influenza Viruses and their Genes: An Overview* (2007), www.who.int/csr/disease/avian_influenza/WIPO_IP_%20paper19_10_2007.pdf at 8 March 2009.

Marks, Stephen, *Report of the High-Level Task Force on the Implementation of the Right to Development on its Second Meeting*, UN Doc E/CN.4/2005/WG.18/TF/3 (2005).

Marrakesh Agreement Establishing the World Trade Organization, opened for signature 15 April 1994, 1867 UNTS 3 (entered into force 1 January 1995) ('Marrakesh Agreement').

Marrakesh Agreement Establishing the World Trade Organization, opened for signature 15 April 1994, 1867 UNTS 3 (entered into force 1 January 1995), annex 1A (Agreement on Technical Barriers to Trade) ('TBT').

Marrakesh Agreement Establishing the World Trade Organization, opened for signature 15 April 1994, 1867 UNTS 3, annex 1A (Agreement on the Application of Sanitary and Phytosanitary Measures) (entered into force 1 January 1995) ('SPS Agreement').

Marrakesh Agreement Establishing the World Trade Organization, opened for signature 15 April 1994, 1867 UNTS 3, annex 1C (Agreement on Trade-Related Aspects of Intellectual Property Rights) (entered into force 1 January 1995) ('TRIPS Agreement').

Marrakesh Agreement Establishing the World Trade Organization, opened for signature 15 April 1994, 1867 UNTS 3, annex 2 (Understanding on Rules and Procedures Governing the Settlement of Disputes) (entered into force 1 January 1995) ('DSU').

Ministerial Declaration: Adopted on 14 November 2001, WTO Doc WT/MIN (01)/DEC/1 (2001).

Morocco–United States Free Trade Agreement, signed 15 June 2004 (entered into force 1 January 2006).

Motoc, Julia-Antoanella, *Specific Human Rights Issues – Human Rights and the Human Genome: Interim Report Submitted by the Special Rapporteur*, UN Doc E/CN.4/Sub.2/2005/38 (2005).

Negotiating Group on Trade-Related Aspects of Intellectual Property Rights, Including Trade in Counterfeit Goods, *Status of Work in the Negotiating Group: Chairman's Report to the GNG*, GATT Doc MTN.GNG/NG11/W/76 (23 July 1990).

Negotiations on Improvements and Clarifications of the Dispute Settlement Understanding: Further Contribution of the United States on Improving

Flexibility and Member Control in WTO Dispute Settlement, WTO Doc TN/DS/W/82/Add.1 (2005) (Communication from the United States).

Ng, Elizabeth Siew-Kuan, *The Impact of the International Patent System on Developing Countries*, WIPO Doc A/39/13 Add.3 (2003) (Report presented to the WIPO under terms of a Special Service Agreement).

North American Free Trade Agreement, signed 17 December 1992 (entered into force 1 January 1994).

Oman–United States Free Trade Agreement, signed 19 January 2006 (entered into force 1 January 2009).

Open-Ended Working Group, *Report on Progress to Date*, WHO Doc A/PIP/IGM/WG/5 (2008).

Organisation for Economic Co-operation and Development, *Genetic Inventions, Intellectual Property Rights and Licensing Practices: Evidence and Policies* (Berlin: Organisation for Economic Co-operation and Development, 2002).

Harnessing Markets for Biodiversity: Towards Conservation and Sustainable Use (Berlin: Organisation for Economic Co-operation and Development, 2003).

'Short Summary Report of the Workshop on Genetic Inventions, Intellectual Property Rights and Licensing Practices' (Berlin, 24–25 January 2002), www.oecd.org/ at 9 February 2009.

Panama–US Trade Promotion Agreement, signed 28 June 2007 (pending US Congress approval).

Pandemic Influenza Preparedness: Sharing of Influenza Viruses and Access to Vaccines and Other Benefits, World Health Assembly 60th mtg, Res WHA60.28 (2007).

Paris Convention for the Protection of Industrial Property, opened for signature 20 March 1883, 21 UST 1583 (entered into force 26 April 1970) ('Paris Convention').

Peru–United States Trade Promotion Agreement, signed 14 December 2007 (entered into force 1 February 2009).

Phuangketkeow, Sihasak, Permanent Representative of Thailand to the United Nations, *On the Report of the Special Rapporteur on the Right of Everyone to the Enjoyment of the Highest Attainable Standard of Physical and Mental Health*, Mr Paul Hunt, (A/HRC/7/11 dated 31 January 2008) (7th Session of the HRC, 12 March 2008).

Proposed Thailand–United States Free Trade Agreement, www.cptech.org/ip/health/c/thailand/us-thai-fta.html at 20 March 2009.

Protocol on Trade in the Southern African Development Community, WTO Doc WT/REG176/N/1/Rev.1 (2004) (Notification by Tanzania – Revision).

Public Health, Innovation, Essential Health Research and Intellectual Property Rights: Towards a Global Strategy and Plan of Action, 59th sess, WHA Res 59.24, apps.who.int/gb/ebwha/pdf_files/WHA59/A59_R24-en.pdf.

Report of the United Nations Conference on the Environment and Development, annex 1 (Rio Declaration on Environment and Development), UN Doc A/CONF 151/26 (Vol I) (1992).

The Republic of Korea–United States Free Trade Agreement (KORUSFTA), signed 30 June 2007 (pending US Congress approval).

Request for a Compulsory License from KIPO to Grant a Compulsory License for Registered Patent No 261366 (Glivec patent) in Accordance with Article 107 (1)(iii) of the Korean Patent Law (30 January 2002), glivec.jinbo.net/Request_for_CL_Final_version.htm at 20 April 2009.

Revision of the International Health Regulations, World Health Assembly 58th mtg, Res WHA58.3 (2005).

Rwanda – Notification under Paragraph 2(A) of the Decision of 30 August 2003 on the Implementation of Paragraph 6 of the Doha Declaration on the TRIPS Agreement and Public Health, WTO Doc IP/N/9/RWA/1 (2007).

Scientific Advisory Group on Pandemic Influenza (UK), *Pre-Pandemic and Pandemic Influenza Vaccines: Scientific Evidence Base* (Department of Health, UK, 2008), www.dh.gov.uk at 6 March 2009.

Secretariat of the Convention on Biological Diversity, *Handbook of the Convention on Biological Diversity* (2nd edn, Montreal: Secretariat of the Convention on Biological Diversity, 2003).

Secretariat of the World Trade Organization, *Trade and Environment at the WTO* (Geneva: World Trade Organization, 2004), www.wto.org/english/res_e/trade-env_e.pdf at 6 March 2009.

Singapore–United States Free Trade Agreement, signed 6 May 2003 (entered into force 1 January 2004).

South African Development Community, *Background to the Free Trade Area*, www.sadc.int/fta/index/browse/page/57 at 23 April 2009.

Standing Committee on the Law of Patents, *Report on the International Patent System*, 12th sess, WIPO Doc SCP/12/3 (2008) www.wipo.int/edocs/mdocs/scp/en/scp_12/scp_12_3.pdf at 19 January 2008.

Strengthening Pandemic-Influenza Preparedness and Response, World Health Assembly 58th mtg, Res WHA58.5 (2005).

UNDP, UNDP Millennium Development Goals: Goal 8, www.undp.org/mdg/goal8.shtml at 19 May 2009.

UNITAID, 'Eighth Board Meeting: UNITAID Moves toward a Patent Pool for Medicines' (Geneva, 2–3 July 2008), www.unitaid.eu/en/Eighth-Board-Meeting-Geneva-2–3-July-2008.html at 10 March 2009.

'UNITAID Moves toward a Patent Pool for Medicines', www.unitaid.eu/en/NEWS/UNITAID-moves-towards-a-patent-pool-for-medicines.html at 10 March 2009.

United Nations, *Fragmentation of International Law: Difficulties Arising from the Diversification and Expansion of International Law*, UN Doc A/CN.4/L.682 (13 April 2006) ('Koskenniemi Report').

Report 03 Human and Income Poverty: Developing Countries, Population Living Below $2 a Day (%) (2007–8), hdrstats.undp.org/indicators/24.html at 2 March 2009.

Report of the High Commissioner – The Impact of the Agreement on Trade-Related Aspects of Intellectual Property Rights on Human Rights, UN Doc E/CN.4/Sub.2/2001/13 (2001).

United Nations Conference on Trade and Development and International Centre for Trade and Sustainable Development, *Resource Book on TRIPS and Development* (Cambridge University Press, 2005).

United Nations Department of Public Information, News and Media Division, 'Fifth Committee Approves Assessment Scale for Regular, Peacekeeping Budgets, Text on Common System, Pension Fund, as it Concludes Session' (Press Release, 22 December 2006).

United Nations Development Programme, *Conserving Indigenous Knowledge: Integrating New Systems of Integration* (United Nations Development Programme, 1994).

Human Development Report 2007/2008 (Basingstoke: Palgrave Macmillan, 2007).

United Nations Economic and Social Council, Committee on Economic, Social and Cultural Rights, *General Comment No 14: The Right to the Highest Attainable Standard of Health (Article 12 of the International Covenant on Economic, Social and Cultural Rights)* ¶ 33, UN Doc E/C.12/2004 (11 August 2000).

United Nations Environment Programme, *Report of the Ad Hoc Working Group on the Work of the Second Session in Preparation for a Legal Instrument on Biological* Diversity, 7, UN Doc UNEP/BioDiv2/3 (1990).

United States – Omnibus Appropriations Act of 1998, WTO Doc WT/DS176/AB/R, AB-2001–7 (2001) (Report of the Appellate Body).

United States – Section 110(5) of US Copyright Act: Request for the Establishment of a Panel by the European Communities and their Member States, WTO Doc WT/DS160/R, 70 (2000) ('*US – 110(5)*').

United States – Standards for Reformulated and Conventional Gasoline, WTO Doc WT/DS2/AB/R, AB-1996–1 (20 May 1996) (Report of the Appellate Body).

Universal Declaration of Human Rights, GA Res. 217A (III), UN Doc A/810 (1948).

Vienna Convention on the Law of Treaties, opened for signature 22 May 1969, 1155 UNTS 331 (entered into force 27 January 1980).

Working Document – Barbados and Bolivia: Proposal 6: Clinical Trials on Medicines as Global Public Goods (2008), www.keionline.org/misc-docs/b_b_igwg/prop6_clinical_trials_as_as_global_public_goods.pdf at 4 March 2009.

The World Bank, *Battling HIV/AIDS: A Decision Maker's Guide to the Procurement of Medicines and Related Supplies* (Washington, DC: The World Bank, 2004).

Financing Health Services in Developing Countries: An Agenda for Reform (Washington, DC: The World Bank, 1987).

Global Economic Prospects and the Developing Countries (Washington, DC: The World Bank, 2001), siteresources.worldbank.org/INTGEP2002/Resources/gep2002complete.pdf at 6 February 2009.

Global Economic Prospects: Technology Diffusion in the Developing World (Washington, DC: The World Bank, 2008), siteresources.worldbank.org/INTGEP2008/Resources/complete-report.pdf at 5 February 2009.

Intellectual Property: Balancing Incentives with Competitive Access (2001), 128, siteresources.worldbank.org/INTGEP2002/Resources/gep2002complete.pdf at 23 April 2009.

World Health Assembly, *Avian and Pandemic Influenza: Best Practice for Sharing Influenza Viruses and Sequence Data*, 60th World Health Assembly, WHO Doc A60/INF.DOC./1 (2007) (Report by the Secretariat).

Pandemic Influenza Preparedness: Sharing of Influenza Viruses and Access to Vaccines and Other Benefits, 61st mtg, WHO Doc A61/4 (2008) (Report by the Secretariat).

Report of the Intergovernmental Working Group on Public Health, Innovation and Intellectual Property, 61st mtg, WHO Doc A61/9 (2008).

World Health Organization, *A Summary of Tracking Avian Influenza A (H5N1) Specimens and Viruses Shared with WHO from 2003 to 2007* (Geneva: World Health Organization, 2008).

'AIDS Medicine and Diagnostic Services' (2003), www.who.int/3by5/publications/briefs/amds/en/index.html at 16 August 2006.

Avian and Pandemic Influenza: Developments, Response and Follow-Up, and Application of the International Health Regulations (2005): Best Practice for Sharing Influenza Viruses and Sequence Data, Executive Board 120th sess, WHO Doc EB120/INF.DOC./3 (2007) (Report by the Secretariat).

Chair's Text – Draft – Pandemic Influenza Preparedness Framework for the Sharing of Influenza Viruses and Access to Vaccines and Other Benefits, WHO Doc A/PIP/IGM/WG/6 (2008).

Draft Global Strategy and Plan of Action on Public Health, Innovation and Intellectual Property, Intergovernmental Working Group on Public Health, Innovation, and Intellectual Property (3 May 2008) www.who.int/phi/documents/IGWG_Outcome_document03Maypm.pdf ('Draft Global Strategy').

Equitable Access to Essential Medicines: A Framework for Collective Action (2004), whqlibdoc.who.int/hq/2004/WHO_EM_2004.4.pdf.

Essential Medicines Model List (Revised April 2002), www.who.int/medicines/organization/par/edl/eml.shtml at 23 July 2003.

Essential Medicines Model List (15th list, March 2007), www.who.int/medicines/publications/08_ENGLISH_indexFINAL_EML15.pdf at 29 April 2009.

Global Pandemic Influenza Action Plan to Increase Vaccine Supply, WHO Doc WHO/IVB/06.13, WHO/CDS/EPR/GIP/2006.1 (2006).

Globalization, TRIPS and Access to Pharmaceuticals: WHO Policy Perspectives on Medicines, No 3, WHO Doc WHO/EDM/2001.2 (March 2001).

Guidelines for Implementing the Bamako Initiative (Geneva: World Health Organization, 1988).

'Influenza A (H1N1)', www.who. int/csr/disease/swineflu/en/index.html at 18 June 2009.

'Member States' Comments and Inputs to the IGWG 2 Conference Paper', A/PHI/IGWG/2/Conf.Paper1/Rev.1 (Geneva: World Health Organization, January 2008), www.who.int/phi/submissions/submissions_confpaper/en/index.html.

Pandemic Influenza Preparedness: Sharing of Influenza Viruses and Access to Vaccines and Other Benefits, Executive Board 124th sess, WHO Doc EB124/4 (2008) (Report by the Secretariat).

Pandemic Influenza Preparedness: Sharing of Influenza Viruses and Access to Vaccines and Other Benefits – Intergovernmental Meeting: Report of Progress to Date, Executive Board 122nd sess, WHO Doc EB122/5 (2008) annex 5 (Interim Statement of the Intergovernmental Meeting on Pandemic Influenza Preparedness: Sharing of Influenza Viruses and Access to Vaccine and Other Benefits).

Pandemic Influenza Preparedness: Sharing of Influenza Viruses and Access to Vaccines and Other Benefits – Intergovernmental Meeting: Report of Progress to Date, Executive Board 122nd sess, WHO Doc EB122/5 (2008) annex 6 (Consolidated Outcome Text: Index).

Pandemic Influenza Preparedness: Sharing of Influenza Viruses and Access to Vaccines and Other Benefits, Open Ended Working Group, Chair's Text Draft – Pandemic Influenza Preparedness Framework for the Sharing of Influenza Viruses and Access to Vaccines and Other Benefits, WHO Doc A/PIP/IGM/WG/6 (2008).

Pandemic Influenza Preparedness: Sharing of Influenza Viruses and Access to Vaccines and Other Benefits, Patent Issues Related to Influenza Viruses and their Genes, WHO Doc A/PIP/IGM/3 (2007) (Report by the Director-General).

Public Health, Innovation and Intellectual Property (Geneva: World Health Organization, 2008), www.who.int/phi/en/ at 23 February 2009.

Report of the WHO Mission to Thailand (Geneva: World Health Organization, 2008).

Report on Developments Since the First Session of the Intergovernmental Working Group on Public Health, Innovation and Intellectual Property, Summary of the Second Hearing, A/PHI/IGWG/2/INF.DOC./4, (Geneva: World Health Organization, 2 November 2007), www.who.int/gb/phi/pdf/igwg2/PHI_IGWG2_ID4-en.pdf.

Reports by the Director-General: Summary Progress Reports, WHO Doc A/PIP/IGM/2 Rev.1 (2007).

Reports by the Director-General: Summary Progress Reports – WHO Influenza Virus Traceability Mechanism, WHO Doc A/PIP/IGM/9 (2008).

Reports of the Director-General: Establishment of the Advisory Mechanism, WHO Doc A/PIP/IGM/8 (2008).

The Global Burden of Disease: 2004 Update (Geneva: World Health Organization, 2004), www.who.int/healthinfo/global_burden_disease/2004_report_update/en/index.html.

'World Health Assembly Closes: Agreement Reached on Influenza Virus Sharing, Intellectual Property' (Geneva: World Health Organization, 23 May 2007).

World Health Report 2004 – Changing History (Geneva: World Health Organization, 2004), www.who.int/csr/disease/avian_influenza/TrackingHistoryH5N1_20080131.pdf at 6 March 2009.

World Health Organization, Regional Office for Europe, *Background Document for the Intergovernmental Working Group on Public Health, Innovation and Intellectual Property (IGWG) Process* (Geneva: World Health Organization, 2007).

World Health Organization Commission on Macroeconomics and Health, *Macroeconomics and Health: Investing in Health for Economic Development* (Geneva: World Health Organization, 2001).

Scaling Up the Response to Infectious Diseases – A Way Out of Poverty (Geneva: World Health Organization, 2002).

World Health Organization Constitution 1946.

World Intellectual Property Organization, *Advice on Flexibilities under the TRIPS Agreement*, www.wipo.int/ip-development/en/legislative_assistance/advice_trips.html at 16 January 2009.

Agenda for Development of the International Patent System, WIPO Doc A/36/14 (6 August 2001).

Development Agenda, www.wipo.int/ip-development/en/agenda/.

Draft Agenda, Provisional Committee on Proposals Related to a WIPO Development Agenda, 4th sess, WIPO Doc PCDA/4/1 Prov. (2007) ('PCDA').

Patent Agenda: Options for Development of the International Patent System, WIPO Doc A/37/6 (19 August 2002).

Patent Agenda: Options for Development of the International Patent System, WIPO Doc A/37/6 (2002), annex I (Memorandum of the Director-General).

Striking a Balance: Patents and Access to Drugs and Health Care (Geneva, World Intellectual Property Organization), www.wipo.int/export/sites/www/freepublications/en/patents/491/wipo_pub_491.pdf at 5 February 2009.

World Trade Organization, *Accessions: Republic of Liberia*, www.wto.org/english/thewto_e/acc_e/a1_liberia_e.htm at 23 April 2009.

Annual Report (2006) of the Council for TRIPS, WTO Doc IP/C/44 (2006).

Annual Review of the Decision on the Implementation of Paragraph 6 of the Doha Declaration on the TRIPS Agreement and Public Health, WTO Doc IP/C/33 (2004) (Report to the General Council).

Annual Review of the Decision on the Implementation of Paragraph 6 of the Doha Declaration on the TRIPS Agreement and Public Health, WTO Doc IP/C/37 (2005) (Report to the General Council).

Annual Review of the Decision on the Implementation of Paragraph 6 of the Doha Declaration on the TRIPS Agreement and Public Health, WTO Doc IP/C/42 (2006) (Report to the General Council).

Annual Review of the Decision on the Implementation of Paragraph 6 of the Doha Declaration on the TRIPS Agreement and Public Health, WTO Doc IP/C/46 (2007) (Report to the General Council).

Factual Presentation – Protocol on Trade in the Southern African Development Community (SADC): Report by the Secretariat, WTO Doc WT/REG176/4 (2007) (Report by the Secretariat).

Members Accepting Amendment of the TRIPS Agreement, www.wto.org/english/tratop_e/trips_e/amendment_e.htm at 23 April 2009.

Members and Observers, www.wto.org/english/thewto_e/whatis_e/tif_e/org6_e.htm at 23 April 2009.

'Members OK Amendment to Make Health Flexibility Permanent', (Press Release, 6 December 2005), www.wto.org/english/news_e/pres05_e/pr426_e.htm.

Minutes of Meeting Held in the Centre William Rappard on 25, 26 and 30 August 2003, WTO Doc WT/GC/M/82 (13 November 2003).

Minutes of Meeting Held in the Centre William Rappard on 28 August 2003, WTO Doc IP/C/M/41 (7 November 2003) (Council for TRIPS).

Notifications by Exporting WTO Members, www.wto.org/english/tratop_e/trips_e/public_health_notif_export_e.htm at 23 April 2009.

Notifications by Importing WTO Members, www.wto.org/english/tratop_e/trips_e/public_health_notif_import_e.htm at 23 April 2009.

Protocol Amending the TRIPS Agreement – Status of Acceptances, WTO Doc IP/C/W/490/Rev.1 (2007) (Note from the Secretariat – Revision).

Regional Trade Agreements Notified to the GATT/WTO and in Force: A–Z Table, www.wto.org/english/tratop_e/region_e/a_z_e.xls at 23 April 2009.

INDEX